Algebra

UNDER THE EDITORSHIP OF Carl B. Allendoerfer

Algebra

by Jacob K. Goldhaber *and* Gertrude Ehrlich

UNIVERSITY OF MARYLAND

The Macmillan Company

Collier-Macmillan Limited, London

Second Printing, 1971

Library of Congress catalog card number: 77-84437

THE MACMILLAN COMPANY
COLLIER-MACMILLAN CANADA, LTD., TORONTO, ONTARIO

Printed in the United States of America

Preface

This book is intended as a text for a one-year course in algebra at the beginning graduate level. It includes enough material to allow for some variability in the selection of topics. The entire book can be covered in a leisurely three-semester course.

In our presentation of fundamental results in commutative and non-commutative algebra, we have attempted to convey some of the flavor of the mathematics of our time. The emphasis throughout is on maps as the basic stuff of algebra. We deal but briefly with category theory per se, but make frequent use of universal mapping properties in defining algebraic entities.

Our treatment of modules, fields, and rings with minimum condition owes a large debt to Bourbaki. In particular, in our discussion of separability, we follow Bourbaki in treating algebraic and transcendental extensions together; this may raise the level of difficulty somewhat, but we believe that it makes the essence of the theory more apparent.

We have attempted to guide our reader from the classical to the modern. There will be those who feel that our book does not provide precisely the right number of arrows; may they refrain from using their bows.

J. K. G.
G. E.

College Park, Maryland

Contents

Chapter 0 / Background

Chapter 1 / Groups

Chapter 2 / Rings; integral domains

Chapter 3 / Modules

Chapter 4 / Finite-dimensional vector spaces

Chapter 5 / Field Theory

Chapter 8 / The structure of rings

Glossary of Symbols

$\in$	is an element of
$\{x \in A \mid P(x)\}$	set of all $x \in A$ satisfying condition $P(x)$
$\{X_i\}_{i \in J}$	family indexed on set J
$\bigcup_{i \in J} X_i$	union of $\{X_i\}_{i \in J}$
$\bigcap_{i \in J} X_i$	intersection of $\{X_i\}_{i \in J}$
$X \times Y$	Cartesian product of X and Y
$\varnothing$	empty set
$\subset$	is a subset of
$\Rightarrow$	implies
$\Leftrightarrow$	if and only if
$\alpha: X \to Y$	α is a map of X into Y
$\alpha(x)$ or αx	image of $x \in X$ under $\alpha: X \to Y$
$\alpha: x \mapsto y$	$y = \alpha x$, where $\alpha: X \to Y$, $x \in X$, $y \in Y$
$\operatorname{Im} \alpha$ or αX	$\{y \in Y \mid y = \alpha x$ for some $x \in X\}$

$\begin{array}{ccc} A & \xrightarrow{\alpha} & B \\ & \gamma \searrow \quad \swarrow \beta & \\ & C & \end{array}$	Commutative diagram if $\alpha: A \to B$ $\beta: B \to C$ $\gamma: A \to C$ are maps such that $\beta\alpha = \gamma$
$\mathbf{Z}$	set of all integers
$\mathbf{Q}$	set of all rational numbers
$\mathbf{R}$	set of all real numbers
$\mathbf{C}$	set of all complex numbers
$\mathbf{N}'$	set of all positive integers
$\mathbf{N}$	set of all nonnegative integers
$\|X\|$ or card X	cardinality of set X
$\aleph_0$	cardinality of $\mathbf{N}$
Ker α	kernel of homomorphism α
$\triangleleft$	is a normal subgroup of
$\triangleleft\!\cdot$	is a maximal normal subgroup of
G/H	factor group (residue class ring) of G modulo H
$[S]$	subgroup (subring, submodule) generated by S
$\|G\|$	order of group G
$\prod_{i \in J} X_i$	product of $\{X_i\}_{i \in J}$
$\coprod_{i \in J} X_i$	coproduct of $\{X_i\}_{i \in J}$
$\coprod'_{i \in J} X_i$	direct sum of $\{X_i\}_{i \in J}$
$\bigoplus_{i \in J} X_i$	internal direct sum of $\{X_i\}_{i \in J}$
$[G: H]$	index of subgroup H in group G
$N_K(S)$	normalizer of S in K
$CK(S)$	centralizer of S in K
$C(G)$	center of G
$\cong$	is isomorphic to
(S)	ideal generated by S
$A[x]$	polynomial domain over A in one indeterminate x
$A[x_1, \ldots, x_n]$	polynomial domain over A in n indeterminates, $x_1, \ldots, x_n$
AS^{-1}	quotient ring of A relative to a multiplicative system S

$A_{\mathfrak{p}}$	local ring of integral domain A at prime ideal $\mathfrak{p}$
$\sum_{i \in J} X_i$	submodule generated by $\{X_i\}_{i \in J}$
$\mathrm{Hom}_A(X, Y)$	set of all A-homomorphism of X into Y
$\mathrm{Hom}_A(-,-)$	Hom functor
$X \otimes_A Y$	tensor product over A of X and Y
$- \otimes_A -$	tensor product functor
$\mathrm{End}_A(X)$	ring of all A-endomorphisms of A-module X
A_l	ring A considered as a left A-module
A_r	ring A considered as a right A-module
$\mathrm{Det}\ \tau$	determinant of the linear transformation τ (on a finite-dimensional space)
$\mathrm{tr}\ \tau$	trace of the linear transformation τ (on a finite-dimensional space)
X^*	dual module of the A-module X
$\langle E/F, \varepsilon \rangle$	a field extension E of a field F, with ε the monomorphism of F into E
$m_{\alpha/F}$	minimum polynomial of α over F
$\mathrm{tr.d.}E/F$	transcendence degree of E over F
$\varphi_{(\alpha_1,\alpha_2,\ldots,\alpha_n)/F}$	map which sends a polynomial $f(x_1,x_2,\ldots,x_n)$ to $f(\alpha_1,\alpha_2,\ldots,\alpha_n)$
$F[\alpha]$	$\mathrm{Im}\ \varphi_{\alpha/F}$
$F(\alpha)$	subfield generated by F and α
$F[S]$	subring generated by F and S
$F(S)$	subfield generated by F and S
$\mathrm{Mon}_F(E,K)$	set of F-monomorphisms of E into K
$\mathcal{G}(E/F)$	Galois group of E over F
$\mathfrak{f}(H)$	fixed field of group H
$\mathfrak{g}(K)$	fixing group of field K
$N_{E/F}$	norm from E to F
$\mathrm{tr}_{E/F}$	trace from E to F

$F_{\mathfrak{P}}$	completion of F at prime spot
$\tilde{F}_{\mathfrak{P}}$	algebraic closure of $F_{\mathfrak{p}}$
$\mathcal{O}_F(\mathfrak{p})$	ring of local integers of F at $\mathfrak{p}$
$\mathcal{M}_F(\mathfrak{p})$	maximal ideal of F at $\mathfrak{p}$
$\mathscr{V}(F,\| \|)$	value group of F under the valuation $\| \|$
$n(\mathfrak{P}\|\mathfrak{p})$	local degree of E over F at $\mathfrak{P}$
$e(\mathfrak{P}\|\mathfrak{p})$	ramification index of $\mathfrak{P}$ over $\mathfrak{p}$
$f(\mathfrak{P}\|\mathfrak{p})$	residue class field degree of $\mathfrak{P}$ over $\mathfrak{p}$
$\sqrt{\mathfrak{a}}$	radical of the ideal $\mathfrak{a}$
$V_{E^{(n)}/F}(\mathfrak{a})$	algebraic set in $E^{(n)}$ associated with the ideal $\mathfrak{a}$
$\mathscr{I}_F(V_{E^{(n)}/F}(\mathfrak{a}))$	ideal belonging to $V_{E^{(n)}/F}(\mathfrak{a})$
l_a	endomorphism of left A-module X which sends $x \in X$ to ax
r_a	endomorphism of right A-module X which sends $x \in X$ to xa
$\mathscr{L}_{A,X}$	$\{l_a \| a \in A\}$
$\mathscr{R}_{A,X}$	$\{r_a \| a \in A\}$
$\mathscr{L}_A$	$\mathscr{L}_{A,A_l}$
$\mathscr{R}_A$	$\mathscr{R}_{A,A_l}$
$\mathscr{R}(A)$	radical of ring A
▮	end of proof
☐	end of statement of theorem (corollary, etc.) not proved in text
///	end of definition

Chapter 0 / Background

0. Introduction

In this chapter, we collect some of the background material which is used throughout the book. We assume that the reader has acquired a rudimentary set-theoretic vocabulary. In Sections 1 and 2 we discuss informally some of the properties of binary relations, mappings and binary operations, and introduce the concepts and terminology associated with structure-preserving mappings (homomorphisms), using the example of monoids.

In Section 3 we give postulates for the integers and state, without proof, some of the important theorems of arithmetic. (We assume that the reader has been exposed to a formal treatment of the integers, and refer him to the literature for further detail.)

In Sections 4 and 5 we state the Axiom of Choice and several equivalent versions of Zorn's Lemma, and discuss properties of finite and infinite sets.

Our treatment, in Section 6, of cardinal and ordinal numbers is intended to provide minimal background for the applications of transfinite arithmetic which occur in the book. The treatment is informal, to facilitate a quick, intuitive grasp of some of the fundamental notions of transfinite arithmetic. For details and a more formal treatment, we refer the reader to the literature.

The Spanning Lemma (Theorem 6.5) embodies the common set-theoretic character of two algebraic theorems: one concerning the existence of a basis and the invariance of dimension in vector spaces (Chapter 4, Theorem 1.1), and the other concerning the existence of a transcendence base and the invariance of transcendence degree for transcendental field extensions (Chapter 5, Theorem 1.8). From part b, case 1, of the Spanning Lemma, we infer the invariance of dimension in arbitrary modules having an infinite basis (Chapter 3, Theorem 1.8). These matters need not be considered until they become relevant in their algebraic settings.

1. Sets; Relations; Maps

Throughout this book we use the standard vocabulary of basic set theory regarding classes, sets, elements of sets, subsets, unions, and intersections. For discussions of these concepts, in an informal, or in an axiomatic framework, we refer the reader to the reference works listed at the end of this chapter.

If A, B are sets, then the set $A \times B$ whose elements are the ordered pairs (a,b), $a \in A$, $b \in B$, is the Cartesian product of A and B. We shall refer to any subset of the Cartesian product $A \times B$ as a *binary relation from A to B*.

Certain kinds of binary relations are of particular interest to us. For any set A, any subset of the Cartesian product $A \times A$ is called a *binary relation in A*. If R is a binary relation in A (i.e., $R \subset A \times A$), we write aRb to indicate that $(a,b) \in R$. If R is a binary relation from A to B, $C \subset A$, then the restriction, $R|_C$, of R to C is the set $\{(a,b)|(a,b) \in R, a \in C\}$.

Definition 1.1. Let R be a binary relation in a set A. Then R is:

a. *Reflexive* if aRa holds for each $a \in A$.

b. *Symmetric* if aRb implies bRa $(a,b \in A)$.

c. *Transitive* if aRb and bRc implies aRc $(a,b,c \in A)$.

d. *Trichotomous* if, for each $a,b \in A$, exactly one of the following holds: aRb, $a = b$, bRa.

e. *Antisymmetric* if aRb and bRa implies $a = b$.

A binary relation R in a set A is

a. A *partial order* if it is reflexive, antisymmetric, and transitive.

b. A *total order* if it is transitive and trichotomous.

c. An *equivalence relation* if it is reflexive, symmetric, and transitive.

If R is a partial (total) order in A, then the ordered pair $\langle A,R\rangle$ is a *partially* (*totally*) *ordered set*.

If R is a partial, or total, order relation in a set X, $Y \subset X$ and $t \in X$, then

a. t is an *R-upper bound* for Y if yRt for each $y \in Y$.

b. t is a *least R-upper bound* for Y if yRt for each $y \in Y$, and tRu for each R-upper bound u.

c. t is an *R-maximal element* for Y if $t \in Y$ and $t \not R y$ for each $y \in Y$.

(Corresponding definitions of *R-lower bound, greatest R-lower bound,* and *R-minimal element* are left to the reader.)

If $Y \subset X$ is totally ordered by R, then Y is an *R-chain.* ///

REMARKS: If $\mathscr{P}(S)$ is the set of all subsets (power set) of a given set S, then $\subset$ and $\supset$ are partial order relations in $\mathscr{P}(S)$. We omit the designation "R-" when referring to upper bounds, etc., with respect to $\subset$. A $\subset$-chain in $\mathscr{P}(S)$ is called an *ascending* chain, and a $\supset$-chain is called a *descending* chain.

We say that a subset Q of the power set of a given set satisfies the *ascending (descending) chain condition* if every ascending (descending) chain in Q is a finite set (see Definition 5.1). It is customary in algebra to use the term ascending (descending) chain in the sense of ascending (descending) *sequence* (see p. 6). The ascending (descending) chain condition, as stated above, is equivalent to the condition that every ascending (descending) sequence contain but finitely many distinct terms.

We turn now to equivalence relations.

Definition 1.2. Let R be an equivalence relation defined in a set A. Then, for each $a \in A$, the set $\bar{a} = \{x | xRa \, (x \in A)\}$ is the *equivalence class* of a, with respect to R. The set of all equivalence classes with respect to R is the *factor set of A with respect to R.* ///

Definition 1.3. If A is a set, P a set of subsets of A such that

a. $A = \bigcup_{X \in P} X$,

b. $X \cap Y = \varnothing$ if $X \neq Y \, (X, Y \in P)$,

then P is a *partition* of A (or P *partitions* A).

If P is a partition of A, S a subset of A such that, for each $X \in P$, $S \cap X$ consists of exactly one element then S is a *complete set of representatives* of P. ///

Theorem 1.1. (Fundamental Partition Theorem.) *Let A be a set, and let R be an equivalence relation in A. Then,*

a. $xRy \Leftrightarrow \bar{x} = \bar{y} \, (x, y \in A)$,

b. *The equivalence classes with respect to R form a partition of A.*

If P is a partition of A consisting of nonempty subsets of A, then the set $R = \{(a,b) | a,b \in X \text{ for some } X \in P\}$ *is an equivalence relation in A, with factor set P.*

PROOF.

a. Suppose xRy $(x,y \in A)$. If $z \in \bar{x}$, then zRx; hence zRy (by transitivity of R), and $z \in \bar{y}$. Thus, $\bar{x} \subset \bar{y}$. By symmetry of R, we have yRx, and a symmetric argument gives $\bar{y} \subset \bar{x}$, whence $\bar{x} = \bar{y}$.

b. By reflexivity of R, xRx holds for each $x \in A$. But then $x \in \bar{x}$ for each $x \in A$, and $A \subset \bigcup_{x \in A} \bar{x} \subset A$, whence $A = \bigcup_{x \in A} \bar{x}$. Suppose, for $x,y \in A$, $\bar{x} \cap \bar{y} \neq \varnothing$. If $z \in x \cap y$, then zRx and zRy. But then, by a, $\bar{x} = \bar{y}$. It follows that the equivalence classes $\bar{x}$ $(x \in A)$ partition A.

We leave the remainder of the proof as an exercise. ▮

Of great importance among binary relations are the "maps."

Definition 1.4. Let A, B be sets, α a subset of $A \times B$ such that, for each $a \in A$ there is exactly one $b \in B$ for which $(a,b) \in \alpha$. Then α is a *map* (*mapping, function*) from A to B. The set A is the *domain* (Dom α) of α, the set B its *codomain*. We write $\alpha: A \to B$ if α is a map from A to B, and $\alpha: a \mapsto b$, or $b = \alpha(a)$, or simply $b = \alpha a$, if $(a,b) \in \alpha$.

The set $\alpha A = \text{Im}\,\alpha = \{b \in B \mid b = \alpha a \text{ for some } a \in A\}$ is the *image* (or *range*) of α. (Since $\varnothing \times B = \varnothing$ for any set B, the only map with domain $\varnothing$ is the empty set—referred to in this context as "the empty map.")

A map $\alpha: A \to B$ is

a. *Injective* (*one-to-one*) if $\alpha a_1 = \alpha a_2$ implies $a_1 = a_2$ $(a_1,a_2 \in A)$.

b. *Surjective* (*onto*) if $\text{Im}\,\alpha = B$.

c. *Bijective* (*one-to-one onto*) if it is both injective and surjective.

If $Y \subset \text{Im}\,\alpha$, then the subset $\overset{-1}{\alpha}\,Y$ of A defined by

$$\overset{-1}{\alpha}\,Y = \{a \in A \mid \alpha a \in Y\}$$

is the *complete inverse image of Y with respect to* α. For each $b \in \text{Im}\,\alpha$, we write $\overset{-1}{\alpha}\,b$ for the complete inverse image of $\{b\}$. ///

REMARKS.

surj. ⇒ $\phi \notin P$

1. If $\alpha: A \to B$ is a surjective map, then $P = \{\overset{-1}{\alpha}(b) \mid b \in B\}$ is a partition of A.

$a \in A \Rightarrow a \in \alpha^{-1}(\alpha a)$ $(\alpha a \in B)$ $\subseteq \bigcup_{b \in B} \alpha^{-1} b \subseteq A$

2. Let $\alpha_1: A \to B$ and $\alpha_2: A \to B$ be maps. Then $\alpha_1 = \alpha_2$ if and only if $\alpha_1 a = \alpha_2 a$ for all $a \in A$.

Then equal as subsets of $A \times B$

3. If $\alpha: A \to B$, $C \subset A$, then the set

$$\{(c,\alpha c) \mid c \in C\}$$

is a map, $\alpha|_C: C \to B$. This map is called the *restriction of* α *to* C.

$\alpha|_C =$

4. If $\alpha\colon A \to B$, and D is a subset of B containing $\operatorname{Im} \alpha$, then $\{(a,\alpha a) | a \in A\}$ is a map from A to D. This map is called the *corestriction of* α *to* D.

5. If A, B, C are sets, $\alpha\colon A \to B$, $\beta\colon B \to C$, then the set

$$\{(a,c) | c = \beta(\alpha(a))\}$$

is a map of A into C. This map is called the *composite of* β *and* α, denoted by $\beta \circ \alpha$ or simply $\beta\alpha$.

In this book, we make frequent use of diagrams such as the following to depict composition of maps:

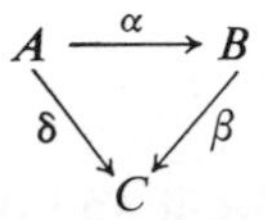

The diagram may be used to indicate that the map $\delta\colon A \to C$ is the composite of the maps $\alpha\colon A \to B$ and $\beta\colon B \to C$; i.e., $\delta = \beta\alpha$.

A diagram showing that a map is equal to the composite of several others, or that the composites of different sequences of maps are equal, is referred to as a "commutative diagram."

6. If A is a set, then the set

$$\{(a,a) | a \in A\}$$

is a bijection of A onto A. This bijection is called the identity map, $\iota_A\colon A \to A$, on A. If $B \subset A$, then the restriction of ι_A to B is an injection, called the *canonical injection* of B into A.

7. If $\alpha\colon A \to B$ and $\beta\colon B \to A$, then β is a *left inverse map* of α if $\beta\alpha = \iota_A$, and β is a *right inverse map* of α if $\alpha\beta = \iota_B$.

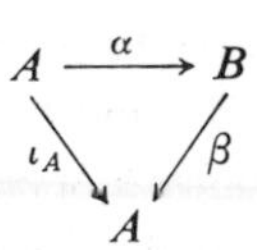

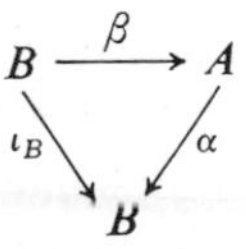

If β is both a right and a left inverse map of α, then β is a *two-sided inverse map* or, simply, an *inverse map*, of α.

8. Composition of maps is "associative"; i.e., if $\alpha: A \to B$, $\beta: B \to C$, $\delta: C \to D$, then

$$\delta(\beta\alpha) = (\delta\beta)\alpha$$

for

$$[\delta(\beta\alpha)](a) = \delta((\beta\alpha)(a)) = \delta(\beta(\alpha(a)))$$

and

$$[(\delta\beta)\alpha](a) = (\delta\beta)(\alpha(a)) = \delta(\beta(\alpha(a)))$$

for each $a \in A$.

9. It follows from 6, 7, and 8 that, if a map $\alpha: A \to B$ has a left inverse map $\beta': B \to A$ and a right inverse map $\beta'': B \to A$, then $\beta' = \beta''$. From this, it follows further that a given map $\alpha: A \to B$ has at most one two-sided inverse map.

10. A map $\alpha: A \to B$ is injective if and only if it has a left inverse map, surjective if and only if it has a right inverse map, and bijective if and only if it has a two-sided inverse map. (*Note:* The proof that every surjective map has a right inverse requires the use of the Axiom of Choice, which we shall discuss in Section 4.)

11. The composite of two injective (surjective, bijective) maps is injective (surjective, bijective).

12. If A, B are sets, we denote by A^B the set of all maps of B into A. (The exponent notation is natural if we consider that there are 5^3 maps from a set of three elements into a set of five elements: each of the three elements of the domain may be assigned any one of five images.)

In particular, we denote by 2^B the power set (set of all subsets) of B. In selecting a subset of B, we have two options regarding each element of B: We may *in*clude it or *ex*clude it. Thus, there is a one-to-one correspondence between the subsets of B and the maps of B to a set of two elements, e.g., the set {in,out}. This motivates the notation 2^B. (If B is a finite set, of n elements, then the number of its subsets is 2^n.)

13. If $\alpha \in A^B$, then for each $b \in B$ we may write a_b for αb. Thus the map α gives rise to an "indexing" of $\operatorname{Im} \alpha \subset A$. In some contexts, we find it convenient to write $\{a_b\}_{b \in B}$ for the map α; we refer to $\alpha = \{a_b\}_{b \in B}$ as a "family (or 'sequence') of elements of A indexed on B" and to B as an "index set." If B is the set $\{1,2,\ldots,n\}$ for some positive integer n, a family $\{a_b\}_{b \in B}$ is what is usually called an "n-tuple with components in B." Two families $\{a_b\}_{b \in B}$ and $\{a'_b\}_{b \in B}$, indexed on the same set B, are equal if and only if $a_b = a'_b$ for each $b \in B$. In this context, the empty map may be referred to as "the empty sequence."

If $\{A_b\}_{b \in B}$ is a family of sets, then the set of all families $\{a_b\}_{b \in B}$, where $a_b \in A_b$ for each $b \in B$, is the *Cartesian product*, $\times_{b \in B} A_b$, of the family $\{A_b\}_{b \in B}$. [In case $B = \{1,2\}$, we identify the 2-tuples $\{a_i\}_{i=1,2}$ with the ordered pairs (a_1,a_2) and equate $\times_{i=1,2} A_i$ with the Cartesian product $A_1 \times A_2$, previously introduced.]

2. Binary operations; Identities; Inverses; Homomorphisms

Of particular interest to us will be certain maps whose domain is a set of ordered pairs.

Definition 2.1. A map whose domain is a set of ordered pairs is a *binary operation.* In particular, if A is a set, then a *binary operation* (or *internal composition*) *in* A is a map whose domain is a subset of $A \times A$ and whose codomain is A. If $\circ$ is a binary operation in A, we generally write $a \circ b$ for $\circ\,(a,b)$. If $\circ$ is a binary operation in A whose domain is all of $A \times A$, we say that $\circ$ is a binary operation *on* A or that A is *closed under* $\circ$. If $\circ$ is a binary operation on A and $B \subset A$, we write $\circ|_B$ for the restriction of the map $\circ\colon A \times A \to A$ to the set $B \times B$, and refer to it as the "*restriction of the binary operation* $\circ$ *to the subset* B." Obviously, $\circ|_B$ is a binary operation on B if and only if $\circ|_B(B \times B) \subset B$. In this case we say that "*the subset* B *is closed under* $\circ$."

Another type of binary operation of interest to us is a map of the form $\mu\colon A \times X \to X$ (A, X sets). Such a map is a *scalar multiplication* (or *external composition*) on X, by A. We usually denote the elements $\mu(a,x)$ by ax or by xa. ///

Examples of internal compositions are addition and multiplication of integers, rational, real, or complex numbers; union and intersection of subsets of a given set; vector addition; and composition of maps of a given set into itself. Multiplication of vectors by real (or complex) scalars is the classical example of an external composition.

Definition 2.2. If $\circ$ is a binary operation on A, then $\circ$ is *commutative* if $a \circ b = b \circ a$ for all $a,b \in A$; $\circ$ is *associative* if $a \circ (b \circ c) = a \circ (b \circ c)$ for all $a,b,c \in A$. If $\circ$ and $\circ'$ are binary operations on A, then $\circ$ is *left-distributive* over $\circ'$ if $a \circ (b \circ' c) = (a \circ b) \circ' (a \circ c)$ for all $a,b,c \in A$; and $\circ$ is *right-distributive* over $\circ'$ if $(b \circ' c) \circ a = (b \circ a) \circ' (c \circ a)$ for all $a,b,c \in A$. ///

The reader is familiar with the commutative and associative operations + and · on integers, rational, real, or complex numbers, and with the distributivity of · over +. Two commutative and associative operations which are mutually distributive over each other are union and intersection, on the set of all subsets of a given set. Composition, defined on the set of all maps of a given set into itself, is associative but not commutative. Exponentiation on, say, the set of positive integers, is nonassociative $[2^{3^5} \neq (2^3)^5]$ and noncommutative $(2^3 \neq 3^2)$.

Definition 2.3. If A is a set, $\circ$ a binary operation on A, $e \in A$, then

a. e is a *right identity* for $\circ$ if $x \circ e = x$ for all $x \in A$.
b. e is a *left identity* for $\circ$ if $e \circ x = x$ for all $x \in A$.
c. e is a (*two-sided*) *identity* for $\circ$ if $e \circ x = x = x \circ e$ for all $x \in A$.

If $e \in A$ is a right, left, or two-sided identity for $\circ$, and $a,b \in A$, then

a. b is a *right inverse* of a if $a \circ b = e$.
b. b is a *left inverse* of a if $b \circ a = e$.
c. b is a *two-sided inverse* of a if $a \circ b = b \circ a = e$. ///

Theorem 2.1. *Let A be a set, $\circ$ a binary operation on A.*

a. *If e_1 is a left identity for $\circ$, and e_2 is a right identity for $\circ$, then $e_1 = e_2$.*
b. *A contains at most one two-sided identity for $\circ$.*

PROOF.

a. $e_1 = e_1 \circ e_2 = e_2$.
b. By a. ▮

Theorem 2.2. *Let A be a set, $\circ$ an associative binary operation on A, e a two-sided identity for $\circ$, and $a \in A$.*

a. *If $a_1 \in A$ is a left inverse of a and $a_2 \in A$ is a right inverse of a, then $a_1 = a_2$.*
b. *a has at most one two-sided inverse in A.*

PROOF.

a. $a_1 = a_1 \circ e = a_1 \circ (a \circ a_2) = (a_1 \circ a) \circ a_2 = e \circ a_2 = a_2$.
b. By a. ▮

We generally write a^{-1} for the inverse of an element $a \in A$. If + is used to denote the operation, we write $-a$ for the inverse of a, and $a - b$ for $a + (-b)$.

Definition 2.4. If A is a set, $\circ$ a binary operation on A such that

a. $\circ$ is associative,

b. A contains an identity for $\circ$,

then the ordered pair $\langle A,\circ\rangle$ is a *monoid.* (If $\langle A,\circ\rangle$ is a monoid, we usually refer to it simply as "the monoid A.") A subset B of a monoid A with identity e is a *submonoid* of A if $\langle B,\circ|_B\rangle$ is a monoid with identity e. ///

REMARK. If $\langle A,\circ\rangle$ is a monoid with identity e, then $B \subset A$ is a submonoid of A if and only if $e \in B$ and B is closed under $\circ$.

Example. Let X^X be the set of all maps of a set X into itself, and let $\circ$ be composition of maps. Then $\langle X^X,\circ\rangle$ is a monoid, with identity ι_X. For each subset Y of X, the set of all maps $\alpha: X \to X$ such that $\alpha Y \subset Y$ forms a submonoid of X^X. Not every subset B of X^X which forms a monoid under $\circ|_B$ necessarily forms a submonoid of X^X. For example, suppose that $a \in X$ and that X contains another element, different from a. Let $\alpha \in X^X$ be defined by $\alpha x = a$ for each $x \in X$, and let $B = \{\alpha\}$. Then $\langle B,\circ_B\rangle$ is a monoid with identity α, but B is not a submonoid of X^X, since $\alpha \neq \iota_X$.

Typical objects of study in algebra are mathematical systems consisting of sets together with internal or external compositions and maps which "preserve" these compositions. We give here a preliminary introduction to the basic notions and vocabulary connected with such "structure-preserving" maps, using the simple and basic case of monoids.

Definition 2.5. If $\langle A,\circ\rangle$, $\langle A',\circ'\rangle$ are monoids, $\alpha: A \to A'$ a map of A into A' such that $\alpha(a \circ b) = \alpha a \circ' \alpha b$ for each $a,b \in A$, then α is a *homomorphism* of the monoid A into the monoid A'.

If $\alpha: A \to A'$ is a homomorphism, then α is

a. a *monomorphism* if it is injective.

b. an *epimorphism* if it is surjective.

c. an *isomorphism* if it is bijective.

If $\langle A,\circ\rangle$ is a monoid, then a homomorphism of $\langle A,\circ\rangle$ into itself is an *endomorphism*; an isomorphism of $\langle A,\circ\rangle$ onto itself is an *automorphism.* ///

This terminology transfers readily to systems with more than one internal composition (e.g., rings—see Chapter 2); in the case of monoids on which a scalar multiplication is defined (e.g., operator groups, Chapter 1; modules, Chapter 3), homomorphisms are expected to commute with the scalar multiplication, and the terminology is modified slightly to indicate this fact (see Chapter 1, Definition 4.2).

Theorem 2.3. *Let $\langle A,\circ\rangle$, $\langle A',\circ'\rangle$ be monoids with respective identities e, e', and let $\alpha\colon A \to A'$ be a homomorphism. Then $\langle \alpha A,\circ'|_{\alpha A}\rangle$ is a monoid with identity αe.*

If $e' \in \alpha A$, then

a. *$\alpha e = e'$, and $\alpha A A$ is a submonoid of A'.*
b. *If $a,a^{-1} \in A$, then $\alpha a^{-1} = (\alpha a)^{-1}$ in A'.*
c. *$\overset{-1}{\alpha}\, e'$ is a submonoid of A.*

PROOF. αA is closed under $\circ'$ since $\alpha a \circ' \alpha b = \alpha(a \circ b) \in \alpha A$ for each $a,b \in A$. Obviously $\circ'|_{\alpha A}$ is associative. For each $a \in A$, $\alpha e \circ' \alpha A = \alpha(e \circ a) = \alpha a$ and $\alpha a \circ' \alpha e = \alpha(a \circ e) = \alpha a$. Thus, αe serves as identity for $\langle \alpha A,\circ'|_{\alpha A}\rangle$. Now suppose $e' \in \alpha A$. Since e' and αe are both identities for $\langle \alpha A,\circ'|_{\alpha A}\rangle$, $\alpha e = e'$, by Theorem 2.1. If $a,a^{-1} \in A$, then $\alpha(a \circ a^{-1}) = \alpha(a^{-1} \circ a) = \alpha e = e'$; hence $\alpha a \circ' \alpha a^{-1} = \alpha a^{-1} \circ' \alpha a = e'$, and $\alpha a^{-1} = (\alpha a)^{-1}$, by Theorem 2.2. Finally $\overset{-1}{\alpha}\, e'$ is a submonoid, for $e \in \overset{-1}{\alpha}\, e'$, and if $a,b \in \overset{-1}{\alpha}\, e'$, then $\alpha(a \circ b) = \alpha a \circ' \alpha b = e' \circ e' = e'$, whence $a \circ b \in \overset{-1}{\alpha}\, e'$. ▮

Corollary. *If $\langle A,\circ\rangle$ and $\langle A',\circ'\rangle$ are monoids,* and $\alpha\colon A \to A'$ is *an epimorphism, then $\alpha e = e'$; hence*

a. *If $a,a^{-1} \in A$, then $\alpha a^{-1} = (\alpha a)^{-1}$ in A'.*
b. *$\overset{-1}{\alpha}\, e'$ is a submonoid of A.* □

Definition 2.6. If $\langle A,\circ\rangle$, $\langle A',\circ'\rangle$ are monoids, and $\alpha\colon A \to A'$ is a homomorphism, then $\overset{-1}{\alpha}\,(\alpha e)$ is the *kernel*, Ker α, of α. ///

Ker α is a submonoid of A since $e \in$ Ker α and, for $a,b \in$ Ker α, $\alpha(a \circ b) = \alpha a \circ' \alpha b = \alpha e \circ' \alpha e = \alpha e$, whence $a \circ b \in$ Ker α.

If A, A' are monoids, $\alpha\colon A \to A'$ a monomorphism of A into A' such that αA is a submonoid of A', we refer to α as an *embedding* of A in A'. In the presence of such an embedding, we occasionally need the fact that A is actually a submonoid of a monoid isomorphic to A'.

Theorem 2.4. (Wraparound Lemma) *Let $\alpha\colon A \to A'$ be a monomorphism of monoid A into monoid A' such that αA is a submonoid of A'. Then there is a monoid $\bar{A}$ isomorphic to A', such that A is a submonoid of $\bar{A}$.*

PROOF. Form $\bar{A} = A \cup (A' - \alpha A)$, and define $\bar{\circ}\colon \bar{A} \times \bar{A} \to \bar{A}$ as follows:

a. For $a,b \in A$, let $a \mathbin{\bar{\circ}} b = a \circ b$.
b. For $a \in A$, $b \in A' - \alpha A$, let $a \mathbin{\bar{\circ}} b = \alpha a \circ' b$ if $\alpha a \circ' b \in A' - \alpha A$, or $a \mathbin{\bar{\circ}} b = \overset{-1}{\alpha}\,(\alpha a \circ' b)$ if $\alpha a \circ' b \in \alpha A$.

c. For $a \in A' - \alpha A$, $b \in A$, follow the rule in b, with obvious modifications.

d. For $a,b \in A' - \alpha A$, let $a \bar{\circ} b = a \circ' b$ if $a \circ' b \in A' - \alpha A$, and let $a \bar{\circ} b = \overset{-1}{\alpha}(a \circ' b)$ if $a \circ' b \in \alpha A$.

It is clear that, for each $a,b \in \bar{A}$, $a \bar{\circ} b$ is uniquely determined; i.e., $\bar{\circ}$ is a binary operation on $\bar{A}$. Define $\bar{\alpha}: \bar{A} \to A'$ by $\bar{\alpha}a = \alpha a$ for $a \in A$; $\bar{\alpha}a = a$ for $a \in A' - \alpha A$. Then $\bar{\alpha}$ is an injective map. We claim: If $a,b \in \bar{A}$, then $\bar{\alpha}(a \bar{\circ} b) = \bar{\alpha}a \bar{\circ} \bar{\alpha}b$.

CASE 1. $a,b \in A$.

$$\bar{\alpha}(a \bar{\circ} b) = \bar{\alpha}(a \circ b) = \alpha(a \circ b) = \alpha a \circ \alpha b = \bar{\alpha}a \bar{\circ} \bar{\alpha}b.$$

CASE 2. $a \in A$, $b \in A' - \alpha A$.

(a) $\alpha a \circ' b \in A' - \alpha A$:

$$\bar{\alpha}(a \bar{\circ} b) = \bar{\alpha}(\alpha a \circ' b) = \alpha a \circ' b = \bar{\alpha}a \bar{\circ} \bar{\alpha}b.$$

(b) $\alpha a \circ' b \in \alpha A$:

$$\bar{\alpha}(a \bar{\circ} b) = \bar{\alpha}(\overset{-1}{\alpha}\, a \circ' b) = \bar{\alpha}(a \circ \overset{-1}{\alpha}\, b) = \alpha(a \circ \overset{-1}{\alpha}\, b)$$
$$= \alpha a \circ b = \bar{\alpha}a \bar{\circ} \bar{\alpha}b.$$

CASE 3. $a \in A' - \alpha A$, $b \in A$, is similar to case 2.

CASE 4. $a,b \in A' - \alpha A$.

(a) $\bar{\alpha}(a \bar{\circ} b) = a \circ' b = \bar{\alpha}a \bar{\circ} \bar{\alpha}b$ if $a \circ' b \notin \alpha A$.

(b) $\bar{\alpha}(a \bar{\circ} b) = \bar{\alpha}\, \overset{-1}{\alpha}(a \circ' b) = \bar{\alpha}(\overset{-1}{\alpha}\, a \circ \overset{-1}{\alpha}\, b) = \alpha(\overset{1}{\alpha}\, a) \circ \alpha(\overset{-1}{\alpha}\, b)$
$= a \circ b = \bar{\alpha}a \bar{\circ} \bar{\alpha}b.$

Obviously, each $a' \in A'$ is $\bar{\alpha}a$ for some $a \in \bar{A}$; i.e., $\bar{\alpha}$ is surjective. Since $\bar{\alpha}$ is an operation preserving bijection of $\bar{A}$ onto A', $\langle \bar{A}, \bar{\circ} \rangle$ is a monoid isomorphic to $\langle A', \circ' \rangle$. $\langle A, \circ \rangle$ is a submonoid of $\langle A', \bar{\circ} \rangle$, for $A \subset \bar{A}$, $\circ = \bar{\circ}|_A$; since αA is a submonoid of A', $\alpha e = e'$, whence $e \bar{\circ} a = a = a \bar{\circ} e$ $(a \in A)$, and e is the identity of both $\bar{A}$ and A. ▮

3. Integers

We collect here some of the basic facts about the integers. We begin by postulating that the integers form a set, **Z**, on which are defined two binary operations, $+$ and $\cdot$, and a (total) order relation $<$ satisfying Axioms A_1 through A_4, M_1 through M_3, C, D, O_1, O_2, and WO:

A_1. $+$ is associative.

A_2. $+$ is commutative.

A_3. $\mathbf{Z}$ contains an identity, 0, for $+$.

A_4. Each $a \in \mathbf{Z}$ has an inverse, $-a$, relative to 0.

We write $a - b$ for $a + (-b)(a,b \in \mathbf{Z})$.

M_1. $\cdot$ is associative.

M_2. $\cdot$ is commutative.

M_3. $\mathbf{Z}$ contains an identity, $1 \neq 0$, for $\cdot$.

C. $ab = 0 \Rightarrow a = 0$ or $b = 0$ $(a,b \in \mathbf{Z})$.

D. $\cdot$ is distributive over $+$.

We let $\mathbf{N}' = \{c \in \mathbf{Z} | 0 < c\}$, i.e., the set of all "positive integers," and $\mathbf{N} = \mathbf{N}' \cup \{0\}$, the set of all nonnegative integers.

O_1. $a,b \in \mathbf{Z}$ and $a < b \Rightarrow a + c < b + c$ for all $c \in \mathbf{Z}$.

O_2. $a,b \in \mathbf{Z}$ and $a < b \Rightarrow ac < bc$ for all $c \in \mathbf{N}'$.

We write $a \leq b$ if $a < b$ or $a = b$. Obviously, $\leq$ is a partial order relation in $\mathbf{Z}$. If $X \subset \mathbf{Z}$ and $k \in X$ has the property $k \leq x$ $(x \leq k)$ for all $x \in X$, we call k a *least element, min X* (a *greatest element, max X*) *of X*. A subset X of $\mathbf{Z}$ has at most one least element, and at most one greatest element.

WO. Every nonempty subset of $\mathbf{N}$ has a least element (or $\mathbf{N}$ is *well-ordered* by $<$).

It is convenient to write $a < b$ or $b > a$ interchangeably.

By the trichotomy property of $<$, $\max\{a, -a\}$ exists for each $a \in \mathbf{Z}$. We use this fact in defining the *absolute value*, $|a|$, of an integer a: $|a| = \max\{a, -a\}$.

We leave to the reader the proofs of the following important theorems on integers:

Theorem 3.1. (Principle of Induction.) *If M is a subset of* $\mathbf{N}$ *such that*

a. $0 \in M$,

b. $n \in M \Rightarrow n + 1 \in M$,

then $M = \mathbf{N}$. ▯

Theorem 3.2. (Second Induction Principle.) *Let M be a subset of* $\mathbf{N}$ *such that $k \in M$ for all $k < n$ $(k,n \in \mathbf{N})$ implies $n \in M$. Then $M = \mathbf{N}$.* ▯

Theorem 3.3. (Finite Recursion Theorem.) *Let U be a set, $u \in U$ and $\beta: U \to U$. Then there is a unique map $\alpha: \mathbf{N} \to U$ such that*

$$\alpha(0) = u,$$
$$\alpha(n + 1) = \beta(\alpha(n)) \qquad \text{for each } n \in \mathbf{N}.$$

For a proof see [4, p. 48] or [3, p. 18]. ▯

Theorem 3.3 makes possible the recursive definition of functions with domain **N**. As an illustration, we define "exponentiation" in monoids. Let $\langle A,\circ\rangle$ be a monoid with identity e.

For $a \in A$, $k \in \mathbf{N}$, we "define a^k recursively" as follows:

$$a^0 = e,$$

$$a^{k+1} = a^k a \qquad \text{for each } k \in \mathbf{N}.$$

In this definition, we use Theorem 3.3, with $U = A$, $u = e$, and $\beta\colon U \to U$ the map defined by $x \mapsto xa$ $(x \in U)$.

(A stronger recursion theorem is needed in the definition of "products" of an arbitrary finite sequence of elements of a monoid. Generalized associative and commutative laws (for commutative monoids) may be proved using induction—see [3, Chap. 1].)

We turn now to divisibility properties of the integers.

Definition 3.1. If $a,b \in \mathbf{Z}$, then $a|b$ (*a divides b*) if $b = ac$ for some $c \in \mathbf{Z}$. If $a|b$, then a is a *proper divisor* of b if $a \neq \pm 1$, $a \neq \pm b$. An integer $p \neq 0$, $p \neq \pm 1$ is *prime* if it has no proper divisors. If $a,b \in \mathbf{Z}$, then $d \in \mathbf{Z}$ is a *greatest common divisor* of a and b if

$$d|a \quad \text{and} \quad d|b$$

and

$$e \in \mathbf{Z},\ e|a \text{ and } e|b \ \Rightarrow\ e|d.$$

If $a,b \in \mathbf{Z}$, then $m \in \mathbf{Z}$ is a *least common multiple* of a and b if

$$a|m \quad \text{and} \quad b|m$$

and

$$n \in \mathbf{Z},\ a|n \text{ and } b|n \ \Rightarrow\ m|n.$$

Two integers a and b are *relatively prime* if their only common divisors are ± 1. ///

REMARKS.

1. $a|a$ for each $a \in \mathbf{Z}$;

$$a|b \text{ and } b|a \Leftrightarrow a = \pm b \qquad (a,b \in \mathbf{Z});$$

$$a|b \text{ and } b|c \Rightarrow a|c \qquad (a,b,c \in \mathbf{Z}).$$

2. Let d_1 be a greatest common divisor of a and b. Then $d_2 \in \mathbf{Z}$ is another greatest common divisor of a and b if and only if $d_2 = \pm d_1$.

3. Let m_1 be a least common multiple of a and b. Then $m_2 \in \mathbf{Z}$ is another least common multiple of a and b if and only if $m_2 = \pm m_1$.

Theorem 3.4. (Division Algorithm.) *Let a, b be integers, $b \neq 0$. Then there is a unique pair of integers q, r such that*

$$a = bq + r, \qquad 0 \leq r < |b|.$$

PROOF. See [1, p. 16]. □

Theorem 3.5. *Every pair of integers a, b has a greatest common divisor, expressible as a linear combination of a and b.*

PROOF. See [1, p. 18]. □

By the second Remark following Definition 3.1, we conclude that every pair of integers a, b has a unique nonnegative greatest common divisor; we denote it by (a,b).

Corollary 1. *Two integers a and b are relatively prime if and only if there are integers s, t such that $sa + tb = 1$.* □

Corollary 2. *If $(a,b) = 1$ and $a|bc$, then $a|c$.*

PROOF. See [1, p. 19]. □

Corollary 3. (*Euclid*) *If p is a prime and $p|bc$, then $p|b$ or $p|c$.* □

Theorem 3.6. (Fundamental Theorem of Arithmetic.) *Every positive integer has a unique factorization as a product of powers of positive primes.*

PROOF. See [1, p. 21]. □

We now define on $\mathbf{Z}$ an equivalence relation which is of great importance in number theory and which enables us to introduce the classical models for two basic algebraic structures: factor groups and residue class rings (Chapter 1, p. 47, and Chapter 2, p. 15).

Definition 3.2. Let m be an integer. If $a,b \in \mathbf{Z}$, then $a \equiv b \bmod m$ (a is *congruent* to b *modulo* m) if $m|a - b$. ///

Theorem 3.7. *Let m be an integer. Then*

a. $\equiv \bmod m$ *is an equivalence relation on* $\mathbf{Z}$.

b. *If $m \neq 0$, the equivalence classes with respect to $\equiv \bmod m$ are the $|m|$ sets $\bar{r} = \{mq + r | q \in \mathbf{Z}\}$, $0 \leq r < |m|$. If $m = 0$, the equivalence classes with respect to $\equiv \bmod m$ are the sets $\bar{k} = \{k\}$, $k \in \mathbf{Z}$.*

c. *For $a,b,c \in \mathbf{Z}$, $a \equiv b \bmod m$ if and only if $a + c \equiv b + c \bmod m$.*

d. *If $a,b,c \in \mathbf{Z}$, and $a \equiv b \bmod m$, then $ac \equiv bc \bmod m$. If $(m,c) = 1$ and $ac \equiv bc \bmod m$, then $a \equiv b \bmod m$.*

PROOF.

1. $m|a - a$ for each integer a; if $a,b \in \mathbf{Z}$, then $m|a - b$ if and only if $m|b - a$; and if $m|a - b$ and $m|b - c$, then $m|a - c$ since $a - c = (a - b) + (b - c)$. Thus, $\equiv \bmod m$ is reflexive, symmetric, transitive.

2. Suppose $m \neq 0$. If $0 \leq r < |m|$, then the equivalence class, $\bar{r}$, of r is the set $\bar{r} = \{x \in \mathbf{Z} | x \equiv r \bmod m\} = \{mq + r | q \in \mathbf{Z}\}$. There are $|m|$ distinct classes belonging to such integers; i.e., if $0 \leq s < r < |m|$, then $\bar{s} \neq \bar{r}$. If a is an arbitrary integer, then by Theorem 3.4, $a = mq + r$ for some $q,r \in \mathbf{Z}$, $0 \leq r < |m|$, whence $a \in \bar{r}$ and $\bar{a} = \bar{r}$. Thus, there are exactly $|m|$ distinct equivalence classes, namely, the sets $\bar{r}$, $0 \leq r < |m|$.

If $m = 0$, then $a \equiv b \bmod m$ if and only if $0|a - b$; this is the case if and only if $a = b$. Thus, each equivalence class contains but one integer; the equivalence classes are the sets $\{k\}$, $k \in \mathbf{Z}$.

3. $m|a - b$ if and only if $m|[(a + c) - (b + c)]$.

4. If $m|a - b$, then $m|ac - bc$. Suppose $m|ac - bc$. Then $m|c(a - b)$. If $(m,c) = 1$, then, by Theorem 3.5, Corollary 2, $m|a - b$. ∎

The equivalence classes with respect to the relation $\equiv \bmod m$ ($m \in \mathbf{Z}$) are called the *residue classes* modulo m. We denote the set of all residue classes modulo m by $\mathbf{Z}_m$. On $\mathbf{Z}_m$, we can introduce two binary operations, $\oplus$ and $\circ$, which share many important properties with the operations $+$ and $\cdot$ on $\mathbf{Z}$.

Theorem 3.8. *Let m be an integer. For $\bar{h},\bar{k} \in \mathbf{Z}_m$, let $\bar{h} \oplus \bar{k} = \overline{h + k}$, $\bar{h} \circ \bar{k} = \overline{hk}$. Then*

a. $\oplus$ *and* $\circ$ *are binary operations on* $\mathbf{Z}_m$.

b. $\oplus$ *and* $\circ$ *are associative and commutative.*

c. $\bar{0}$ *serves as identity for $\oplus$ and $(\overline{-a})$ serves as inverse of a relative to* $\bar{0}$.

d. $\bar{1}$ *serves as identity for* $\circ$.

e. $\circ$ *is distributive over* $\oplus$.

f. *If* $m \neq 0$, *then every nonzero element of* $\mathbf{Z}_m$ *has an inverse relative to* $\circ$ *if and only if m is prime.*

g. *If* $m \neq 0$, *then* $\bar{a} \circ \bar{b} = \bar{0} \Rightarrow \bar{a} = \bar{0}$ *or* $\bar{b} = \bar{0}$ $(\bar{a},\bar{b} \in \mathbf{Z}_m)$ *if and only if m is prime.*

PROOF. Exercises 3.11 and 3.12. ▯

4. Axiom of Choice; Zorn's Lemma; Well-Ordering

In Section 5 we shall discuss the use of the nonnegative integers as cardinal and ordinal numbers, define finite and infinite sets, and introduce the basic concepts of transfinite arithmetic. We discuss first several equivalent versions of an axiom of set theory which we shall use repeatedly throughout this book.

We recall Axiom WO for the integers: Every nonempty subset of the set of nonnegative integers contains a least nonnegative integer. This axiom provides us with a "choice function" for the set of nonnegative integers, in the following sense.

Definition 4.1. Let X be a set and let $\mathscr{P}(X)$ be the set of all subsets (power set) of X. Then a *choice function* for X is a map $\theta: \mathscr{P}(X) - \{\varnothing\} \to X$ such that $\theta(Y) \in Y$ for each nonempty subset Y of X. ///

Example. Let $X = \mathbf{N}$, the set of all nonnegative integers. Define the "least element function" $\lambda: \mathscr{P}(\mathbf{N}) - \{\varnothing\} \to \mathbf{N}$ by: $\lambda(Y)$ is the least element of Y for each nonempty subset Y of $\mathbf{N}$. Then λ is a choice function for $\mathbf{N}$. Its existence is guaranteed by Axiom WO.

The question arises: Given an arbitrary set X, does there exist a choice function for X? It has been proved only recently that an answer to this question cannot be obtained using only a standard set of axioms (e.g., those of Zermelo–Frankel, see [8]) for basic set theory. It is convenient in many mathematical contexts to postulate the affirmative answer, Zermelo's

Axiom of Choice. Every set has a choice function; i.e., given a set X, there is a map $\theta: \mathscr{P}(X) - \{\varnothing\} \to X$ such that $\theta(Y) \in Y$ for each $Y \in \mathscr{P}(X) - \{\varnothing\}$.

In our example of the nonnegative integers, the existence of a "well-ordering" for $\mathbf{N}$ led to the definition of a particular choice function. The notion of well-ordering can be generalized to arbitrary sets.

Definition 4.2. Let R be a total order on a set X. Then R is a *well-ordering* for X (or R *well-orders* X) if every nonempty subset Y of X has an R-minimum. ///

It can be proved ([8, Chap. 8]) that, in the presence of the axioms of basic set theory, the Axiom of Choice is equivalent to the

Well-Ordering Principle. If X is a set, then there is a total order R on X which well-orders X.

Two other statements equivalent to the Axiom of Choice impose conditions on totally ordered subsets of partially ordered sets.

Zorn's Lemma (*First Version*)*:* If $\langle X,R\rangle$ is a partially ordered set such that every R-chain Y in X has an R-upper bound in X, then X has an R-maximal element.

The following, seemingly less general, version of Zorn's Lemma is actually equivalent to the first version.

Zorn's Lemma (*Second Version*)*:* If X is a nonempty set such that for every nonempty ascending chain Q of subsets of X, $\bigcup_{Y\in Q} Y \in X$, then X has a maximal element.

REMARK. Yet another equivalent version of Zorn's Lemma may be obtained from the first version by replacing R by a relation which is merely transitive ([6, Chap. 0]).

5. Finite and Infinite Sets

One of the most important uses of the natural numbers 0, 1, 2,... is "counting." When we count the elements of the set $\{a,b,c,d,e\}$ we "match them up with" the numbers 1, 2, 3, 4, 5. Our definition of "finite set" is inspired by this notion of counting. We first define, for each natural number n, the *initial segment*

$$I_n = \{k|0 \leq k < n\}.$$

(*Note:* $I_0 = \varnothing$.)

Definition 5.1. A set X is *finite* if there is a bijection of I_n onto X for some natural number n. ///

(*Note:* The empty map is a bijection of I_0 onto the empty set.)

If there exists a bijection of a set X onto a set Y, we shall say that X is equipotent to Y, and write $X \sim Y$.

The identity map is a bijection; the inverse map of a bijection is a bijection; and the composite of two bijections is a bijection; hence equipotence is an equivalence relation on any set of sets.

In this terminology, we can restate Definition 5.1: A set X is finite if it is equipotent to some initial segment of the natural numbers. Clearly, any set equipotent to a finite set is finite.

If X is equipotent to I_n, we say that X has n elements, or X has *cardinality* n. What makes this definition meaningful is the uniqueness of n; i.e., a set X cannot be equipotent to both I_m and I_n for $m \neq n$. This is a consequence of the following

Lemma. *An initial segment I_n ($n \in \mathbf{N}$) is not equipotent to any proper subset of itself.*

PROOF. By induction (see [1, p. 33]). □

Using this lemma, we obtain the more general

Theorem 5.1. *If X is a finite set, then X is not equipotent to a proper subset of itself.*

PROOF. Since X is finite, there is a bijection $\alpha: I_n \to X$ for some $n \in \mathbf{N}$. Suppose $Y \subsetneqq X$ and $\beta: X \to Y$ is a bijection. Then $\gamma = \alpha^{-1}\beta\alpha$ is an injection, $\gamma: I_n \to I_n$. Since $h \in \operatorname{Im} \gamma$ implies $\alpha h \in \operatorname{Im} \beta = Y$, $\operatorname{Im} \gamma \neq I_n$. Hence the corestriction of $\gamma: I_n \to I_n$ to $\operatorname{Im} \gamma$ is a bijection of I_n onto a proper subset, $\operatorname{Im} \gamma$, of I_n, in contradiction to the lemma. ∎

Corollary. *If X is a finite set, then every injection of X into X is a surjection.* □

We shall see that the condition of Theorem 5.1 is, in fact, equivalent to finiteness.

Definition 5.2. A set X is *denumerable* if it is equipotent to the set $\mathbf{N}$ of all natural numbers. If a set is either denumerable or finite, it is *countable*. ///

Since $k \mapsto k + 1$ defines a bijection of **N** onto a proper subset, $\mathbf{N} - \{0\}$, of **N**, **N** is not finite, by Theorem 5.1. Since any set equipotent to a finite set is finite, no denumerable set is finite. Using the Axiom of Choice and the Recursion Theorem, we can prove

Theorem 5.2. *Any set which is not finite has a denumerable subset.*

PROOF. See [1, p. 35]. ☐

Using Theorem 5.2, we easily obtain the converse of Theorem 5.1.

Theorem 5.3. *If a set X is not finite, then X is equipotent to a proper subset of itself.*

PROOF. By Theorem 5.2, X has a denumerable subset, Y. Let α be a bijection of **N** onto Y, $\beta: \mathbf{N} \to \mathbf{N}$, the map defined by $\beta k = k + 1$ ($k \in \mathbf{N}$). Let $\gamma_1: Y \to Y$ be defined by $\gamma_1 = \alpha\beta\alpha^{-1}$ and let $\gamma_2: X - Y \to X - Y$ be the identity map, ι_{X-Y}. Then $\gamma = \gamma_1 \cup \gamma_2$ is a bijection of X into $\operatorname{Im} \gamma$. Since $\alpha(0) \notin \operatorname{Im} \gamma$, $\operatorname{Im} \gamma$ is a proper subset of X. ▌

Corollary. *A set X is finite if and only if it is not equipotent to a proper subset of itself.* ☐

Definition 5.3. A set X is (*Dedekind*) *infinite* if it is equipotent to a proper subset of itself. ///

Corollary. *A set is (Dedekind) infinite if and only if it is not finite.* ☐

6. Cardinal and Ordinal Numbers

If X is a finite set, equipotent to I_n, then the number n serves as the cardinality (or the "cardinal number") of X. Two finite sets have the same cardinality if and only if they are equipotent. A finite set X equipotent to I_m is "smaller than" a finite set Y equipotent to I_n if and only if $m < n$. This comparison of finite cardinalities may be formulated directly in terms of equipotence.

Lemma. *If X, Y are finite sets of respective cardinalities m, n, then $m < n$ if and only if X is equipotent to some subset of Y, but Y is not equipotent to any subset of X.*

PROOF. Suppose $m < n$. Let $\alpha: I_m \to X$ and $\beta: I_n \to Y$ be bijections and let $\varepsilon: I_m \to I_n$ be the canonical injection. Then $\gamma = \beta\varepsilon\alpha^{-1}$ is an injection of X into Y, whence $X \sim \operatorname{Im} \gamma \subset Y$. If Y is equipotent to a subset of X, then there is an injection $\gamma: Y \to X$. But then $\alpha^{-1}\gamma\beta$ is an injection of I_n into I_m. Since $m < n$, there is a bijection of I_n onto a proper subset of I_n, in contradiction to Theorem 5.1.

Conversely, suppose X is equipotent to a subset of Y but Y is not equipotent to a subset of X. If $\alpha: I_m \to X$ and $\beta: I_n \to Y$ are bijections, and $\eta: X \to Y$ is an injection, then $\beta^{-1}\eta\alpha$ is an injection of I_m into I_n, whence $m \leq n$. Since Y is not equipotent to a subset of X, $m \neq n$. Thus, $m < n$. ▌

The condition "X is equipotent to a subset of Y" is independent of the finiteness of X and Y. We can use it to compare the "cardinalities" of arbitrary sets.

Definition 6.1. Let X, Y be sets; then X *is dominated by* Y ($X \preceq Y$) if X is equipotent to a subset of Y; X is *strictly dominated by* Y ($X \prec Y$) if $X \preceq Y$ but not $Y \preceq X$. ///

If X, Y are finite sets of cardinalities m, n, respectively, then by the lemma we have

(1)
$$m < n \Leftrightarrow X \prec Y,$$
$$m = n \Leftrightarrow X \sim Y.$$

We want cardinal numbers for arbitrary sets which behave according to (1). At the end of this section we indicate how a formal definition of cardinal number may be given in axiomatic set theory, based on the notion of ordinal number. At this point, we content ourselves with postulating the behavior of cardinal numbers with respect to equipotence and dominance.

C_1. For each set X, there is a unique cardinal number, card X.
C_2. card $X =$ card $Y \Leftrightarrow X \sim Y$.
C_3. card $X <$ card $Y \Leftrightarrow X \prec Y$.
C_4. If X is finite of cardinality n, then card $X = n$.

It follows quite easily from C_3 that $<$ is transitive, for $X \prec Y$ and $Y \prec Z$ implies $X \prec Z$. It is far from easy to prove that $<$ is trichotomous or, equivalently, that for two sets X, Y, exactly one of the following holds:

$$X \prec Y, \qquad X \sim Y, \qquad Y \prec X.$$

Using the Well-Ordering Principle, it may be shown that

Theorem 6.1. *If X, Y are sets, then, either $X \preceq Y$ or $Y \preceq X$.*

PROOF. See [8, p. 242]. □

Another important, and nontrivial, result is

Theorem 6.2. **(Schroeder–Bernstein.)** *If X, Y are sets such that $X \preceq Y$ and $Y \preceq X$, then $X \sim Y$.*

PROOF. See, for example, [8, p. 95]. □

Using Theorems 6.1 and 6.2, one obtains easily

Theorem 6.3. *If X, Y are sets, then exactly one of the following holds:*

$$X \prec Y, \qquad X \sim Y, \qquad Y \prec X.$$

PROOF. By definition of $\prec$ and $\sim$, the three alternatives are mutually exclusive. By Theorem 6.1, $X \preceq Y$ or $Y \preceq X$. Suppose $X \nsim Y$. Then, by Theorem 6.2, $X \preceq Y$ and $Y \preceq X$ cannot both hold. Thus, either $X \prec Y$ or $Y \prec X$. ∎

Corollary. *If a, b are cardinals, then exactly one of the following holds:*

$$a < b, \qquad a = b, \qquad b < a. \qquad \square$$

Thus, $<$ has the properties of a total order for cardinals. There is no greatest cardinal, for

Theorem 6.4. *If X is any set, $\mathscr{P}(X)$ the power set of X, then* card $X <$ card $\mathscr{P}(X)$.

PROOF. We must prove that $X \prec \mathscr{P}(X)$. By the Schroeder–Bernstein Theorem, it is sufficient to prove that $X \preceq \mathscr{P}(X)$ and $X \nsim \mathscr{P}(X)$. Clearly, $X \preceq \mathscr{P}(X)$, since the map $x \mapsto \{x\}$ is an injection of X into $\mathscr{P}(X)$. Suppose $\alpha: X \to \mathscr{P}(X)$ is a bijection. Let $K = \{x \in X | x \notin \alpha x\}$. Since $K \in \mathscr{P}(X)$, there is some $k \in X$ such that $K = \alpha k$. But then we are faced with the impossible situation: $k \in K \Leftrightarrow k \notin K$. Conclusion: No bijection $\alpha: X \to \mathscr{P}(X)$ exists. ∎

Since every infinite set has a denumerable subset (Theorem 5.2), every infinite set has a finite subset of cardinality n, for each natural number n. Thus, if a is an infinite cardinal, then $n < a$ for each finite cardinal n. We denote by $\aleph_0$ the cardinal of the set of all natural numbers (or, equivalently, of the set of all finite cardinals). Then every denumerable set has cardinal $\aleph_0$ and every infinite set has cardinal no less than $\aleph_0$. The set of all integers and the set of all rationals both have cardinal $\aleph_0$, but the cardinal, c, of the set of all real numbers is greater than $\aleph_0$ (see [8, p. 191]). The assertion $c = 2^{\aleph_0}$ is called the Continuum Hypothesis; it was recently proved to be independent of the Axiom of Choice and the basic axioms of set theory.

Guided by experience with the finite cardinals, one can, without difficulty, define arithmetic operations on cardinal numbers.

Definition 6.2. If a, b are cardinals, then $a + b = c$, where $c = \text{card } A \cup B$ for two sets A, B such that

$$a = \text{card } A,$$
$$b = \text{card } B,$$
$$A \cap B = \varnothing. \qquad ///$$

To make this definition meaningful, one must establish that given two cardinals, a and b, there exist two disjoint sets A, B whose respective cardinals are the given ones, and that card $(A \cup B)$ is independent of the particular choice of A and B. For details, we refer the reader to [8, p. 112].

Definition 6.3. If a, b are cardinals, then $ab = c$, where $c = \text{card}(A \times B)$ for two sets A, B such that

$$a = \text{card } A,$$
$$b = \text{card } B. \qquad ///$$

Again, the existence of such sets A, B and the independence of card$(A \times B)$ of the choice of A and B must be established (see [8, p. 114]).

Addition and multiplication of cardinals are both associative and commutative, and multiplication distributes over addition (see [8, p. 113–115]).

If a, b, c, d are cardinals such that $a \leq b$ and $c \leq d$, then $a + c \leq b + d$ and $ac \leq bd$.

Exponentiation is defined by

Definition 6.4. $a^b = c$, where $c = \text{card } A^B$ for two sets A, B such that $a = \text{card } A$, $b = \text{card } B$. ///

Exponentiation obeys the rules

$$a^{b+c} = a^b a^c,$$

$$(ab)^c = a^c b^c,$$

$$a^1 = a,$$

$$a^0 = 1,$$

$$0^0 = 1.$$

If X is any set, then the cardinal of its power set, 2^A, is $2^{\text{card } A}$ (see the discussion on p. 6).

As examples of cardinal arithmetic, we give a few basic results which are used later in this book.

Example 1. If a is an infinite cardinal, then $n + a = a$ for each finite cardinal n.

PROOF. Let X be a set such that card $X = a$, and $I_n \cap X = \varnothing$. By Theorem 5.2, X has a denumerable subset, $\bar{N}$. Let $k \mapsto \bar{k}$ be a bijection of $\mathbf{N}$ onto $\bar{N}$. Define $\alpha: I_n \cup X \to X$ as follows: $\alpha x = x$ for $x \in X - \bar{N}$; $\alpha\bar{k} = \overline{k + n}$ for each $\bar{k} \in \bar{N}$; and $\alpha k = \bar{k}$ for each $k \in I_n$. Then α is a bijection, and card$(I_n \cup X)$ = card X. Since $I_n \cap X = \varnothing$, card$(I_n \cup X) = n + a$; hence $n + a = a$. ▮

Example 2. If a is an infinite cardinal, then $a + a = a$.

PROOF. We first show that $\aleph_0 + \aleph_0 = \aleph_0$. Let X' and X'' be disjoint denumerable sets, $n \mapsto n'$ a bijection of $\mathbf{N}$ onto X', and $n \mapsto n''$ a bijection of $\mathbf{N}$ onto X''. Then

$$\left.\begin{aligned} 2n + 1 &\mapsto n' \\ 2n &\mapsto n'' \end{aligned}\right\} \text{ defines a bijection of } \mathbf{N} \text{ onto } X' \cup X''.$$

Hence $\aleph_0 + \aleph_0 = \aleph_0$.

Now let a be an arbitrary infinite cardinal, and let A be a set such that card $A = a$. For any set X, card$(X \times \{0,1\})$ = card$(X \times \{0\}) \cup$ card$(X \times \{1\})$ = card X + card X. In particular, for any denumerable subset X of A, card $(X \times \{0,1\}) = \aleph_0 + \aleph_0 = \aleph_0$ = card X; hence there is a bijection of $X \times \{0,1\}$ onto X.

Let $F = \{\alpha | \alpha$ is a bijection of $X \times \{0,1\}$ onto X for some $X \subset A\}$. By the preceding remark concerning denumerable subsets of A, F is not empty. On F, define a partial order "by extension"; i.e., $\alpha_1 < \alpha_2$ if $\alpha_1 = \alpha_2|_{\text{Dom } \alpha_1}$.

The union of any ascending chain $\{\alpha_j\}_{j\in J}$ in $F(\alpha_j\colon X_j \cup \{0,1\} \to X_j)$ is a bijection of $\bigcup_{j\in J} X_j \times \{0,1\}$ onto $\bigcup_{j\in J} X_j$, hence contained in F. But then, by Zorn's Lemma, F contains a maximal element, α^*. Let $X^* = \operatorname{Im} \alpha^*$. Then $X^* \sim X^* \times \{0,1\}$, whence card $X^* =$ card $X^* +$ card X^*. We claim that $A - X^*$ is finite. Otherwise, $A - X^*$ has a denumerable subset, Y, and α^* can be extended to a bijection of $X^* \cup Y \times \{0,1\}$ onto $X^* \cup Y$, in contradiction to the maximality of α^*. But then card $A =$ card $X^* +$ card$(A - X^*)$ $=$ card $X^* =$ card $X^* +$ card $X^* =$ card $A +$ card A, as required. ∎

Example 3. If a is any cardinal, and b is an infinite cardinal such that $a \le b$, then $a + b = b$.

PROOF. We have $a \le b$ and $b \le b$, whence $a + b \le b + b = b$. On the other hand, $b \le a + b$. But then, by Theorem 6.3, $a + b = b$. ∎

Example 4. If a is an infinite cardinal, then $a \cdot a = a$.

PROOF. First note that $\aleph_0 \cdot \aleph_0 = \aleph_0$. It is sufficient to establish that card$(\mathbf{N} \times \mathbf{N}) =$ card $\mathbf{N}$. This is accomplished by the well-known counting scheme indicated below:

$$\begin{array}{cccc} (0,0) & (0,1) & (0,2) & \cdots \\ (1,0) & (1,1) & (1,2) & \cdots \\ (2,0) & (2,1) & (2,2) & \cdots \\ \vdots & \vdots & \vdots & \vdots \end{array}$$

(The reader may find it amusing to write down an explicit formula for the bijection described in the diagram.)

Now suppose A is a set with card $A = a$, an infinite cardinal. Let

$$F = \{\alpha \mid \alpha \text{ is a bijection of } X \times X \text{ onto } X \text{ for some } X \subset A\}.$$

Since, for each denumerable subset of A, $X \times X \sim X$, $F \neq \varnothing$. Partially order F by extension, as in Example 2, and verify that the hypotheses of Zorn's Lemma are fulfilled. Conclude that there is a maximal bijection $\alpha^* \in F$, with $\operatorname{Im} \alpha^* = X^*$. Then card X^* card $X^* =$ card X^*, and we need only show that card $X^* =$ card A to complete the proof. Obviously, card $A =$ card $X^* +$ card$(A - X^*)$. If card $X^* \le$ card$(A - X^*)$, then there is a bijection of X^* onto a subset, Y, of $A - X^*$. But then $X^* \times X^*$, $X^* \times Y$, $Y \times X^*$, and $Y \times Y$ are disjoint infinite sets, each equipotent to Y. By Example 2, the union, U, of the sets $X^* \times Y$, $Y \times X^*$ and $Y \times Y$ is equipotent to Y. If β is a bijection of U onto Y, then $\alpha^* \cup \beta$ is a bijection of $(X^* \cup Y) \times (X^* \cup Y)$ onto $X^* \cup Y$, in contradiction to the maximality of α^*. It follows that $\operatorname{card}(A - X^*) < \operatorname{card} X^*$. But then, by Example 3, $\operatorname{card} A = \operatorname{card} X^* + \operatorname{card}(A - X^*) = \operatorname{card} X^*$, whence $\operatorname{card} A = \operatorname{card} A \cdot \operatorname{card} A$, as required. ▮

Example 5. If a is a nonzero cardinal and b is an infinite cardinal such that $a \leq b$, then $ab = b$.

PROOF. Let A, B be disjoint sets such that $\operatorname{card} A = a$, $\operatorname{card} B = b$. Then $a \cdot b \leq b \cdot b = b = a + b$. If $x \in A$ and $y \in B$, then

$$A \cup B \sim (A \times \{y\}) \cup (\{x\} \times B) \subset A \times B,$$

whence $a + b \leq a \cdot b$. Thus, $a \cdot b = a + b = b$. In particular, we have: for any infinite cardinal b, $\aleph_0 b = b$. ▮

Example 6. If $\{C_j\}_{j \in J}$ is a family of finite sets, indexed on an infinite set J, then $\operatorname{card} \bigcup_{j \in J} C_j \leq \operatorname{card} J$.

PROOF. We have $\operatorname{card} \bigcup_{j \in J} C_j \leq \operatorname{card} \bigcup_{j \in J} \bar{C}_j \leq \operatorname{card} \bigcup_{j \in J} N_j$, where the $\bar{C}_j$ are mutually disjoint finite sets, and the N_j are mutually disjoint denumerable sets. For each $j \in J$, there is a bijection $i \mapsto n_{ij}$ of $\mathbf{N}$ onto N_j. Since the sets N_j are mutually disjoint, $(i,j) \mapsto n_{ij}$ is a bijection of $N \times J$ onto $\bigcup_{j \in J} N_j$. Hence

$$\operatorname{card} \bigcup_{j \in J} C_j \leq \operatorname{card} \bigcup_{j \in J} N_j = \operatorname{card}(N \times J) = \aleph_0 \operatorname{card} J = \operatorname{card} J. \quad ▮$$

Example 7. If a is an infinite cardinal, then for each finite cardinal n, $a^n = a$.

PROOF. $a^n = \operatorname{card} A^n$, the set of all maps of I_n into a set A of cardinal a. Since $A^n \subset I_n \times A$, $a^n \leq na = a$. On the other hand, for each $a \in A$, the map $\alpha_a : i \mapsto a$ is an element of A^n. Hence $A \preceq A^n$ and $a \leq a^n$. It follows that $a^n = a$. ▮

Example 8. If A is a set of cardinal $a > 1$, then the cardinal of the set S of all n-tuples with components in A, where n ranges through $\mathbf{N}$, is $\aleph_0 \cdot a$. (If A is a finite set, this number is $\aleph_0$. If A is an infinite set, this number is a.)

PROOF. For each $n \in \mathbf{N}$, let S_n be the set of all n-tuples with components in A. The S_n are mutually disjoint, and $S = \bigcup_{n\in\mathbf{N}} S_n$. If A is finite, each S_n is a finite set, and card $S = \bigcup_{n\in\mathbf{N}} S_n \leq$ card $\bigcup_{n\in\mathbf{N}} X_n$, where the X_n are mutually disjoint denumerable sets. Since $\bigcup_{n\in\mathbf{N}} X_n \sim \mathbf{N} \times \mathbf{N}$, we have card $S \leq$ card$(\mathbf{N} \times \mathbf{N}) = \aleph_0 \times \aleph_0 = \aleph_0$. Since, for fixed $t \in A$, S contains maps α_i $(i \in \mathbf{N})$ such that

$$\alpha_i(j) = t \qquad \text{for } i = j,$$

$$\alpha_i(j) \neq t \qquad \text{for } i \neq j,$$

S is not finite, whence card $S = \aleph_0 = \aleph_0 \cdot a$.

Now suppose that A is infinite. By Example 7, for each $n \in \mathbf{N}$, card $S_n = a$, whence card $\bigcup_{n\in\mathbf{N}} S_n =$ card$(\mathbf{N} \times A) = \aleph_0 \cdot a = a$. ▌

We now give, as a very special application of Zorn's Lemma and of cardinal number theory, a theorem which embodies the common set-theoretic character of two algebraic theorems (Chapter 4, Theorem 1.1 and Chapter 5, Theorem 1.8) concerning "spanning functions."

Definition 6.5. If X is a set, then a map $\rho: 2^X \to 2^X$ is a *spanning function* for X if it satisfies each of the following conditions:

a. $S_1 \subset S_2 \Rightarrow \rho S_1 \subset \rho S_2$ $(S_1, S_2 \in 2^X)$.
b. If $\alpha \in \rho S$ $(S \in 2^X)$, then S has a finite subset, S', such that $\alpha \in \rho S'$.
c. $S \subset \rho S$ for each $S \in 2^X$.
d. $\rho S = \rho(\rho S)$ for each $S \in 2^X$.
e. Suppose $\alpha,\beta \in X$, $S \in 2^X$, $\beta \in \rho(S \cup \{\alpha\})$, and $\beta \notin \rho S$. Then $\alpha \in \rho(S \cup \{\beta\})$.

If ρ is a spanning function for X, $B \subset X$, then B is a *ρ-generating set* for X if $\rho B = X$; and B is a ρ-independent set for X if, for each $b \in B$, $b \notin \rho(B - \{b\})$. A ρ-independent ρ-generating set for X is a *ρ-basis* for X. ///

NOTE: Any ρ-basis B for X is a minimal ρ-generating set for X, since $b \in B$ implies $b \notin \rho(B - \{b\})$, whence $B - \{b\}$ is not a ρ-generating set for X. In fact, it can be shown that the following statements are equivalent:

1. B is a minimal ρ-generating set.
2. B is a maximal ρ-independent set.
3. B is a ρ-basis.

Theorem 6.5. (Spanning Lemma.) *Let ρ be a spanning function for a set X. Then*

a. *There exists at least one ρ-basis for X.*
b. *Any two ρ-bases for X are equipotent.*

PROOF.

a. Let $K = \{Y \in 2^X | Y \text{ is } \rho\text{-independent}\}$. Then $K \neq \varnothing$, since the empty set is vacuously a ρ-independent subset of X. Partially order K by inclusion ($\subset$). Let Γ be an ascending chain of subsets belonging to K, and let $U = \bigcup_{Y \in \Gamma} Y$. If Γ is finite, then U is equal to the "greatest" set in the chain; hence U is ρ-independent. Suppose Γ is infinite. Let $u \in U$. If $u \in \rho(U - \{u\})$, then, by b, there is a finite subset, $\overline{U}$, of U such that $u \in \rho(\overline{U} - \{u\})$. Since $\overline{U}$ is finite and Γ is infinite, there is some $V \in \Gamma$ such that $\overline{U} \subset V$, whence $\overline{U} - \{u\} \subset V - \{u\}$ and $\rho(\overline{U} - \{u\}) \subset \rho(V - \{u\})$, by a. Since $u \in \rho(\overline{U} - \{u\})$, $u \in \rho(V - \{u\})$, and, for all $W \in \Gamma$ such that $V \subset W$, $u \in \rho(W - \{u\})$, again by a. Since $u \in U = \bigcup_{Y \in \Gamma} Y$, there is some $T \in \Gamma$ such that $u \in T$, whence $u \in W$ for all $W \in \Gamma$ such that $T \subset W$. But then there is some $W \in \Gamma$ such that both $V \subset W$ and $T \subset W$, whence both $u \in W$ and $u \in \rho(W - \{u\})$, contrary to the hypothesis that each of the sets in Γ is ρ-independent. It follows that $u \notin \rho(U - \{u\})$. Thus, the set K satisfies the hypotheses of Zorn's Lemma, and there is a maximal ρ-independent subset, B, of X. We claim that B is a ρ-generating set for X. Suppose not. Then there is some $x \in X$ such that $x \notin \rho B$. Let $\overline{Y} = B \cup \{x\}$, and let $y \in \overline{Y}$. If $y = x$, then $y \notin \rho(\overline{Y} - \{y\})$ since $x \notin \rho B$. If $y \neq x$, then $y \in B$, hence $y \notin \rho(B - \{y\})$ since B is ρ-independent. But then, by e, $y \notin \rho(\overline{Y} - \{y\}) = \rho(B \cup \{x\}) - \{y\})$. It follows that $\overline{Y}$ is ρ-independent, in contradiction to the maximality of B. We conclude that $\rho B = X$, whence B is a ρ-basis for X.

b. Now suppose that both B and B' are ρ-bases of X.

CASE 1. card B' is infinite. If $x \in B$, then $x \in \rho B'$; hence there is some finite subset C_x of B' such that $x \in \rho C_x$. Let $C = \bigcup_{x \in B} C_x$. For each $x \in B$, $\rho C_x \subset \rho C$. But then $B \subset \rho C$, and $X = \rho B = \rho\rho C = \rho C \subset X$, whence $\rho C = X$. Thus, C is a ρ-generating set for X, contained in B'. Since B' is a ρ-independent ρ-generating set, it is a minimal ρ-generating set. It follows that $C = B'$. But then B is infinite. By Example 6, card B' = card $C \leq$ card B. A symmetric argument gives card $B \leq$ card B', and the equality follows.

CASE 2. card $B = n$ (finite). By case 1, card B' is finite, say card $B' = n'$. Suppose $B = \{b_1, \ldots, b_n\}$, $B' = \{b'_1, \ldots, b'_{n'}\}$. We show that the elements of B can be replaced, in turn, by elements of B' without losing the property that the sets so obtained from B are ρ-bases for X. Let $B_1 = B - \{b_1\}$. If $B' \subset \rho B_1$, then $X = \rho B' \subset \rho^2 B_1 = \rho B_1$, and $\rho B_1 = X$. This is impossible, since $B_1 \subsetneq B$ and B is a minimal ρ-generating set for X. Hence there is some $b'_i \in B'$ such that $b'_i \notin \rho B_1$. Since $b'_i \in \rho B = \rho(B_1 \cup \{b_1\})$, it follows by e that $b_1 \in \rho(B_1 \cup \{b'_i\})$. But then $B \subset \rho(B_1 \cup \{b'_i\})$, whence $\rho(B_1 \cup \{b'_i\}) = \rho B = X$;

i.e., $B_1 \cup \{b_i'\}$ is a ρ-generating set for X. Furthermore, $B_1 \cup \{b_i'\}$ is ρ-independent for we know that $b_i' \notin \rho(B_1) = \rho((B_1 \cup \{b_i'\}) - \{b_i'\})$. And if, for $j = 2,\ldots, n_1$, $b_j \in \rho((B_1 - \{b_j\}) \cup \{b_i'\})$, then, since $b_j \notin \rho(B_1 - \{b_j\})$, we have $b_i' \in \rho(B_1)$, by e, contrary to hypothesis. For simplicity, we may suppose (without loss of generality) that $b_i' = b_1'$. Proceeding inductively, we now assume that $\{b_1',\ldots,b_h',b_{h+1},\ldots,b_n\}$ is a ρ-basis for X $(1 \leq h < n)$. Let $B_{h+1} = \{b_1',\ldots,b_h',b_{h+2},\ldots,b_n\}$. Then, $\rho B_{h+1} \neq X$, since B_{h+1} is a minimal ρ-generating set for X. Hence there is some $b_i' \in B'$ such that $b_i' \notin \rho B_{h+1}$. Since, for $i = 1, \ldots, h$, $b_i' \in B_{h+1} \subset \rho B_{h+1}$, $i > h$. Without loss of generality, we may assume that $i = h + 1$. But then $\{b_1',\ldots,b_h',b_{h+1}',b_{h+2},\ldots,b_n\}$ is again a ρ-basis for X. By induction we find that each of the b_i may be thus replaced by a corresponding element b_i'. It follows that $n \leq n'$. A symmetric argument gives $n' \leq n$, whence $n' = n$. ▌

We note that, in the proof of part b, case 1, we used only the requirement that B and B' be minimal ρ-generating sets. We therefore have

Corollary. *Let* $\rho\colon 2^X \to 2^X$ *be a map satisfying conditions* a *through* d *for a spanning function of X. If B, B′ are minimal ρ-generating sets for X and if B is infinite, then* card B = card B'. □

[This corollary applies in the case of arbitrary free modules having an infinite basis (Chapter 3, Theorem 1.7), while the theorem, in general, does not.]

We conclude this section with a few informal remarks concerning ordinal numbers. The notion of cardinal number arises from the comparison of sets based on the existence or nonexistence of a bijection from one set into, or onto, another. The notion of ordinal number arises from the comparison of *well-ordered* sets based on the existence or nonexistence of *order-preserving* bijections. Two ordered sets $\langle A,R\rangle$, $\langle A',R'\rangle$ are *order equivalent* if there exists an order-preserving bijection of A onto A'. With each ordered set $\langle A,R\rangle$, where R is a well-ordering of A, one associates an *ordinal number*, ord$\langle A,R\rangle$, subject to the requirement that ord$\langle A,R\rangle$ = ord$\langle A',R'\rangle$ if and only if $\langle A,R\rangle$ and $\langle A',R'\rangle$ are order equivalent. If n is a finite cardinal, A a set with cardinal n, then any well-ordered set $\langle A,R\rangle$ is order-equivalent to $\langle I_n,<\rangle$, where $<$ is the natural order for I_n. Thus, to each finite cardinal n there corresponds a unique finite ordinal, also called n. On the other hand, to each infinite cardinal, there correspond "many" (in fact, infinitely many) ordinals.

As an example, consider $\aleph_0$. The set **N**, of cardinal $\aleph_0$, may be ordered in each of the following ways, no two of which are equivalent:

$$0, 1, 2, \ldots$$
$$1, 2, 3, \ldots; 0$$
$$2, 3, 4, \ldots; 0, 1$$
$$3, 4, 5, \ldots; 0, 1, 2$$
$$\vdots$$
$$0, 2, 4, 6, \ldots; 1, 3, 5, 7, \ldots$$
$$0, 3, 6, \ldots; 1, 4, 7, \ldots; 2, 5, 8, \ldots$$
$$0, 4, 8, \ldots; 1, 5, 9, \ldots; 2, 6, 10, \ldots; 3, 7, 11, \ldots$$
$$\vdots$$

Given two ordinals α and β, there are disjoint well-ordered sets $\langle A_1,R_1\rangle$ and $\langle A_2,R_2\rangle$ such that $\text{ord}\langle A_1,R_1\rangle = \alpha$, $\text{ord}\langle A_2,R_2\rangle = \beta$. We define $\alpha + \beta$ to be the ordinal of the well-ordered set $\langle \bar{A},\bar{R}\rangle$, where $\bar{A} = A_1 \cup A_2$ and $\bar{R}$ is defined by $\bar{R}|_{A_1} = R_1$, $\bar{R}|_{A_2} = R_2$, and $a_1\bar{R}a_2$ for each $a_1 \in A_1$, $a_2 \in A_2$. Addition of ordinals is associative but not commutative. If we denote by ω the ordinal, of $\langle \mathbf{N}, < \rangle$, where $<$ is the natural order on **N**, then the ordinals corresponding to the well-orderings of **N** in the preceding examples are, in turn, ω, $\omega + 1$, $\omega + 2$, $\omega + 3, \ldots$; $\omega + \omega$; $\omega + \omega + \omega$; $\omega + \omega + \omega + \omega$. Note that $1 + \omega = \omega$, but $\omega + 1 \neq \omega$. Using addition, one can define order for ordinals by $\alpha < \beta$ if $\beta = \alpha + \delta$ for some ordinal δ. For example, any finite ordinal is less than ω, since $n + \omega = \omega$ for each finite ordinal n. As one would wish, $<$ is both transitive and trichotomous.

Given two ordinals, α, β, there are well-ordered sets $\langle A_1,R_1\rangle$, $\langle A_2,R_2\rangle$ with respective ordinals α, β. The product, $\alpha\beta$, of α and β is the ordinal of the well-ordered set $\langle \tilde{A},\tilde{R}\rangle$, where $\tilde{A} = A_1 \times A_2$, and $\tilde{R}$ is antilexicographic; i.e., $(a_1,b_1)\tilde{R}(a_2,b_2)$ if $b_1 < b_2$ or if $b_1 = b_2$ and $a_1 < a_2$. Multiplication is associative, noncommutative, and left distributive over addition. Examples:

$$\omega \cdot 2 = \omega + \omega,$$
$$\omega \cdot 3 = \omega + \omega + \omega,$$
$$\omega^2 = \text{ord}(\mathbf{N} \times \mathbf{N}).$$

For each cardinal a, there is a least ordinal α such that there exists a well-ordered set $\langle A,R\rangle$ with $\text{ord}\, A = \alpha$ and $\text{card}\, A = a$. These least ordinals for given cardinals are called *initial ordinals*. If an ordinal α is equal to $\beta + 1$ for some ordinal β, then it is a *successor ordinal*—otherwise, a *limit ordinal*.

A model for the theory of ordinals and cardinals may be obtained in axiomatic set theory as follows: For any set X, define the successor, X', of X by $X' = X \cup \{X\}$. The sets $\varnothing$, $\varnothing'$, $\varnothing''$,... form a model for the finite ordinals, with

$$\begin{aligned}
0 &= \varnothing, \\
1 &= \varnothing' = \varnothing \cup \{\varnothing\} = \{\varnothing\} = \{0\}, \\
2 &= 1' = 1 \cup \{1\} = \{0,1\}, \\
3 &= 2' = 2 \cup \{2\} = \{0,1,2\}, \\
&\vdots
\end{aligned}$$

Thus, each nonzero finite ordinal is equal to the set consisting of all the preceding ones. We let ω denote the set of all finite ordinals, and form the sequence ω, ω', ω'',..., then the set, $\omega 2$, consisting of all preceding terms, and again the sequence of successors, etc., always alternating the formation of a successor sequence with the formation of the set of all preceding terms.

Each object α in the resulting collection has the properties

1. $x \in \alpha \Rightarrow x \subset \alpha$.
2. $x,y \in \alpha \Rightarrow x \in y$ or $y \in x$.

One may begin a formal development of transfinite arithmetic by defining an ordinal as a set α having properties 1 and 2. In the presence of suitable axioms, one can show that each ordinal is well-ordered by the membership relation ε. One then proceeds to define $+$, $\cdot$, and $<$ for ordinals in much the same way as we did in the preceding discussion. A cardinal can be defined as a special kind of ordinal: An ordinal α is a cardinal if $\alpha \leq \beta$ for any ordinal β equipotent to α. The detailed construction of the theory of cardinal numbers (see [8]) is one of the concerns of axiomatic set theory.

Bibliography

[1] G. Birkhoff and S. MacLane, *A Survey of Modern Algebra*. New York: Macmillan, 1956.

[2] N. Bourbaki, *Eléments de mathématique*, Première partie, Livre I, *Théorie des ensembles*, Chaps. I and II. Paris: Hermann, 1954.

[3] L. Cohen and G. Ehrlich, *The Structure of the Real Number System*. Princeton, N.J.: Van Nostrand, 1963.

[4] P. Halmos, *Naive Set Theory*. Princeton, N.J.: Van Nostrand, 1960.
[5] I. N. Herstein, *Topics in Algebra*. Waltham, Mass.: Blaisdell, 1964.
[6] J. L. Kelley, *General Topology*. Princeton, N.J.: Van Nostrand, 1955.
[7] W. Sierpinski, *Leçons sur les nombres transfinis*. Paris: Gauthiers-Villars, 1950.
[8] P. Suppes, *Axiomatic Set Theory*. Princeton, N.J.: Van Nostrand, 1960.

Chapter 1 / Groups

1. Preliminaries

Definition 1.1. Let G be a set, $\circ$ a binary operation on G. Then the system $\langle G,\circ\rangle$ is a *group* if

a. $\circ$ is associative,

b. G contains a two-sided identity, e, for $\circ$,

c. every element of G has a two-sided inverse with respect to e.

If $\circ$ is commutative, then $\langle G,\circ\rangle$ is a *commutative*, or *abelian*, group. The cardinality $|G|$ of the set G is called the *order* of $\langle G,\circ\rangle$. (If $\langle G,\circ\rangle$ is a group, we shall say that *G forms a group under* $\circ$, and refer informally to *the group G*.) ///

By Chapter 0, Theorems 2.1 and 2.2, a group contains exactly one identity, and each of its elements has exactly one inverse.

Requirements b and c of Definition 1.1 can be weakened either to

b_l. G contains a left identity, e, for $\circ$,

c_l. every element of G has a left inverse relative to e,

or to

b_r. G contains a right identity, e, for $\circ$,

c_r. every element of G has a right inverse relative to e.

We have

Theorem 1.1. *If G is a set, $\circ$ an associative binary operation on G, then the following statements are equivalent:*

1. *G is a group; i.e.,* b *and* c *of Definition 1.1 hold.*
2. b_l *and* c_l *hold.*
3. b_r *and* c_r *hold.*

PROOF. Obviously, 1 implies both 2 and 3. Suppose 2 holds. Let e_l be a left identity and let x_l be a left inverse of x in G. If, for $x,y,z \in G$, $x \circ y = x \circ z$, then

$$x_l \circ (x \circ y) = x_l \circ (x \circ z),$$

$$(x_l \circ x) \circ y = (x_l \circ x) \circ z,$$

$$e_l \circ y = e_l \circ z,$$

$$y = z.$$

Thus, we can left-cancel in G. Now, for each $a \in G$,

$$a_l \circ a = e_l = e_l \circ e_l = (a_l \circ a) \circ e_l = a_l \circ (a \circ e_l).$$

It follows that $a = a \circ e_l$ for each $a \in G$. But then e_l is also a right identity, hence a two-sided identity, for $\circ$.

If $a \in G$, then $a_l \circ e_l = e_l \circ a_l = (a_l \circ a) \circ a_l = a_l \circ (a \circ a_l)$, so that $e_l = a \circ a_l$, and a_l is a right, hence two-sided, inverse for a. Thus $\langle G,\circ\rangle$ is a group. The proof that c implies a is, of course, completely analogous. ▮

It is interesting to note that b_l and c_r, or b_r and c_l, do not suffice to make G a group. (See Exercise 1.1.)

Another important characterization of a group is obtained by replacing b and c of Definition 1.1 by the requirements

h. for every $a,b \in G$, there is some $x \in G$ such that $a \circ x = b$, and
k. for every $a,b \in G$, there is some $y \in G$ such that $y \circ a = b$.

(See Exercise 1.2.)

Familiar examples of groups are

1. The integers (rationals, reals, complex numbers) under addition.
2. The nonzero rationals (reals, complex numbers) under multiplication.

These groups are all infinite and abelian. We shall discuss an important class of finite non-abelian groups in Section 3. An example of a class of finite abelian groups appears in Exercise 1.3.

NOTATION. From now on, we use $\cdot$ or $+$ to denote the group operation. When we use $\cdot$, we write 1, or e, for the identity of the group, a^{-1} for the inverse of a. For $a \cdot b$ we usually write ab. When we use $+$, we write 0 for the identity of the group, $-a$ for the inverse of a. For the subset consisting of the identity only, we write E in multiplicative notation, 0 in additive notation.

In multiplicative notation, we use exponents according to the following definition: If G is a group, $a \in G$, then

$$a^0 = e,$$

$$a^1 = a,$$

$$\left.\begin{aligned} a^{k+1} &= a^k \cdot a \\ a^{-k} &= (a^k)^{-1} \end{aligned}\right\} k > 0 \text{ in } \mathbf{Z}.$$

In additive notation, coefficients take the place of exponents; i.e., if $a \in G$, then

$$0a = 0,$$

$$1a = a,$$

$$\left.\begin{aligned} (k+1)a &= ka + a \\ (-k)a &= -ka \end{aligned}\right\} k > 0 \text{ in } \mathbf{Z}.$$

We leave to the reader the verification of the following "laws of exponents" and the formulation of the corresponding "laws of coefficients":

1. If $a \in G$, then $a^{k+h} = a^k a^h$ for all $k,h \in \mathbf{Z}$.
2. If $a \in G$, then $(a^k)^h = a^{kh}$ for all $k,h \in \mathbf{Z}$.

(See Exercise 1.4.)

Warning: It is not, in general, the case that, if $a,b \in G$, $k \in \mathbf{Z}$, then $(a \cdot b)^k = a^k \cdot b^k$. In fact, this condition holds for all $a,b \in G$, all $k \in \mathbf{Z}$, if and only if G is abelian (Exercise 1.5). In this connection, we note that for $a,b \in G$ (G any group), $(a \cdot b)^{-1} = b^{-1}a^{-1}$.

2. Subgroups

Definition 2.1. If $\langle G,\circ\rangle$ is a group, H a subset of G, and $\circ_H$ the restriction of $\circ$ to H, then *H is a subgroup of G* if $\langle H,\circ_H\rangle$ is a group. ///

Obviously, any group G has G and E among its subgroups. A subgroup H of G which is different from these "trivial subgroups" is referred to as a *proper subgroup* of G.

The following theorem provides necessary and sufficient conditions that a subset of a group G be a subgroup of G.

Theorem 2.1. *Let $\langle G,\circ\rangle$ be a group, H a subset of G. Then the following statements are equivalent:*

a. *H is a subgroup of G.*
b. *$e \in H$,*
   $x^{-1} \in H$ if $x \in H$,
   $xy \in H$ if $x \in H$ and $y \in H$.
c. *$H \neq \varnothing$ and $xy^{-1} \in H$ for each $x,y \in H$.*
d. *$H \neq \varnothing$ and $x^{-1}y \in H$ for each $x,y \in H$.*

We leave the proof as an exercise (Exercise 2.1). □

Corollary. *The intersection of any nonempty set of subgroups of a group G is a subgroup of G.*

PROOF. Exercise 2.2. □

Every subset X of a group G is contained in a "smallest" subgroup of G, i.e., in the intersection of all subgroups of G which contain X. We use this fact in the following definition.

Definition 2.2. If X is any subset of a group G, then the intersection of all subgroups of G which contain X is *the subgroup*, $[X]$, *generated by* X. In particular, if X consists of just one element, a, then the subgroup generated by X is called *the cyclic subgroup*, $[a]$, *generated by* a. A group G is *cyclic* if $G = [a]$ for some $a \in G$. ///

It is easy to verify (Exercise 2.3) that the subgroup generated by a non-empty subset X of a group G consists of all products $a_1^{k_1} \cdots a_m^{k_m}$ ($a_i \in X$, $k_i \in \mathbf{Z}$, $m > 0$ in $\mathbf{Z}$). Hence, in particular, the cyclic subgroup $[a]$ generated by an element $a \in G$ is the set of all powers a^k ($k \in \mathbf{Z}$). If $X = \varnothing$, then $[X] = E$.

Definition 2.3. The order of the cyclic subgroup $[a]$ generated by an element a of a group G is called the *order*, $|a|$, *of the element* a. A group all of whose elements have finite order is a *torsion group*. (See Exercise 2.4.) ///

Theorem 2.2. *If G is a group, $a \in G$, and s is a positive integer, then the following statements are equivalent:*

1. *$s = \min\{t \mid a^t = e, t \in \mathbf{Z}, t > 0\}$.*
2. *The elements $e, a, \ldots, a^{s-1}$ are distinct, and $[a] = \{e,a,\ldots,a^{s-1}\}$.*
3. *a has order s.*
4. *$a^s = e$, and $s \mid t$ for all $t \in \mathbf{Z}$ such that $a^t = e$.*

PROOF. For $a = e$, the theorem holds since each of statements a through d is true if and only if $s = 1$.

Suppose $a \neq e$. We follow the proof scheme

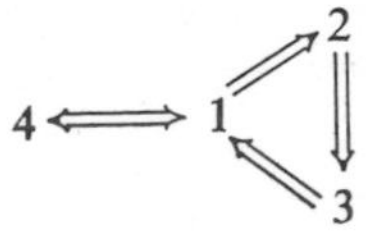

$1 \Rightarrow 2$. Since $s = \min\{t | a^t = e, t > 0 \text{ in } \mathbf{Z}\}$, the elements $e, a, \ldots, a^{s-1}$ are all distinct. They form a subgroup containing a. For, if $m,n \in \mathbf{Z}$ and $0 \leq m < n < s$, then $a^n a^{-m} = a^{n-m}$ $(0 < n - m < s)$; $a^m a^{-n} = a^{s+m-n}$ $(0 < s + m - n < s)$; and, if $m = n$, $a^m a^{-n} = a^0 = e$. But then, by Definition 2.2, $[a] \subset \{e,a,\ldots,a^{s-1}\}$. Since $[a] = \{a^k | k \in \mathbf{Z}\}$, the reverse inclusion holds, also, and equality follows.

$2 \Rightarrow 3$. By 2, $[a]$ has order s, whence a has order s.

$3 \Rightarrow 1$. If a has order s, then the set $[a]$ is finite. Hence there is a least positive integer k such that $a^k = e$. Since $1 \Rightarrow 2$, the elements $e, a, \ldots, a^{k-1}$ are all distinct, and $[a] = \{e,a,\ldots,a^{k-1}\}$. Thus, $k = s$, and

$$s = \min\{t | a^t = e, t \in \mathbf{Z}, t > 0\}.$$

$1 \Rightarrow 4$. By 1, $a^s = e$. Suppose $a^t = e$. There are integers q, r such that

$$t = sq + r, \qquad 0 \leq r < s.$$

Thus, $a^t = a^{sq+r} = (a^s)^q a^r = a^r = e$. But then, by 1, $r = 0$, and $s | t$.

$4 \Rightarrow 1$. By 4, $a^s = e$, and $s | t$ for all positive integers t such that $a^t = e$. But then $s = \min\{t | a^t = e, t > 0 \text{ in } \mathbf{Z}\}$. ▮

Corollary 1. *If G is a group, $a \in G$, then the following statements are equivalent:*

a. *a has infinite order.*

b. *The elements a^k $(k \in \mathbf{Z})$ are all distinct.*

c. *For all $k \in \mathbf{Z}$, $a^k \neq e$.* □

$k \neq 0$

Corollary 2. *If H is a finite nonempty subset of a group G, then H is a subgroup of G if and only if $ab \in H$ for all $a,b \in H$.*

PROOF. Exercise 2.5. □

Theorem 2.3.

a. *Every infinite cyclic group is isomorphic to the additive group* $\langle \mathbf{Z},+\rangle$ *of integers.*

b. *Every cyclic group of finite order s is isomorphic to the additive group* $\langle \mathbf{Z}_s,\oplus\rangle$ *of residue classes modulo s.* (*See p.* 15.)

PROOF. Let $G = [a]$. By the properties of exponents in G, the map $\alpha: x \mapsto a^x$ is a homomorphism of $\langle \mathbf{Z},+\rangle$ onto G if G is infinite, and the map $\bar{\alpha}: \bar{x} \mapsto a^x$ is a homomorphism of $\langle \mathbf{Z}_s,\oplus\rangle$ onto G if G has finite order s. In the finite case, it follows immediately that $\bar{\alpha}$ is an isomorphism. In the infinite case, α is one-to-one by Corollary 1 of Theorem 2.2, hence is an isomorphism. ▮

Every subgroup of a cyclic group is cyclic (Exercise 2.6). In particular, if H is a subgroup of the infinite cyclic group $\langle \mathbf{Z},+\rangle$, then $H = [m]$ for some $m \geq 0$ in $\mathbf{Z}$. (See Exercise 2.7.) The number-theoretic relation of congruence modulo m can be translated into group-theoretic language as follows: If $a,b \in \mathbf{Z}$, then $a \equiv b \bmod m$ if and only if $a - b \in [m]$. The equivalence classes with respect to this relation, i.e., the residue classes modulo m, form a partition of $\mathbf{Z}$. For each $a \in \mathbf{Z}$, the residue class $\hat{a}$ is the set $[m] + a = \{mk + a | k \in Z\}$. If we write $H = [m]$, then the residue class $\hat{a}$ is the set $H + a = \{h + a | h \in H\}$. For an arbitrary group G (written multiplicatively, and not necessarily commutative), we introduce the following terminology.

Definition 2.4. If H is a subgroup of G, and $a \in G$, then the sets $Ha = \{ha | h \in H\}$ and $aH = \{ah | h \in H\}$ are called, respectively, the *right and left cosets of H in G determined by a.* ///

Thus, the residue classes modulo m are the (right and left) cosets of $[m]$ in $\mathbf{Z}$. (Note that, if G is commutative, H a subgroup of G, then the right and left cosets of H determined by any element $a \in G$ are equal. We shall see that, in any group G, the subgroups having this property play a fundamental role: They are the "normal subgroups" which we introduce in Section 4.)

We now generalize the relation of congruence modulo a subgroup $[m]$ of $\mathbf{Z}$ by defining on an arbitrary group G the relations of right and left congruence modulo any subgroup H.

Definition 2.5. Let G be a group, H a subgroup of G. If $a,b \in G$, then $a \equiv_r b \bmod H$ if $ab^{-1} \in H$; and $a \equiv_l b \bmod H$ if $b^{-1}a \in H$. ///

Theorem 2.4. *If G is a group, H a subgroup of G, then*

a. $\equiv_r \bmod H$ *and* $\equiv_l \bmod H$ *are equivalence relations on G.*

b. *The equivalence classes with respect to* $\equiv_r \bmod H$ *are the right cosets of H in G; the equivalence classes with respect to* $\equiv_l \bmod H$ *are the left cosets of H in G.*

c. *The right (left) cosets of H in G form a partition of G; i.e., G is the union of all right (left) cosets of H, and distinct right (left) cosets are disjoint.*

d. *If $a,b \in G$, then $Ha = Hb \Leftrightarrow ab^{-1} \in H$ and $aH = bH \Leftrightarrow b^{-1}a \in H$.*

PROOF.

a. $\equiv_r \bmod H$ is reflexive since $aa^{-1} = e \in H$ for each $a \in G$, symmetric since $ab^{-1} \in H$ implies $(ab^{-1})^{-1} = ba^{-1} \in H$, and transitive since $ab^{-1} \in H$ and $bc^{-1} \in H$ implies $ab^{-1}bc^{-1} = ac^{-1} \in H$. Thus, $\equiv_r \bmod H$ is an equivalence relation on G. A similar argument applies to $\equiv_l \bmod H$.

b. For $a \in G$, the equivalence class of a with respect to $\equiv_r \bmod H$ is the set

$$\{x \mid x \underset{r}{\equiv} a \bmod H\} = \{x \mid xa^{-1} \in H\} = \{ha \mid h \in H\} = Ha;$$

the equivalence class of a with respect to $\equiv_l \bmod H$ is the set

$$\{x \mid x \underset{l}{\equiv} a \bmod H\} = \{x \mid a^{-1}x \in H\} = \{ah \mid h \in H\} = aH.$$

c and d follow immediately from b and the Fundamental Partition Theorem (Chapter 0, Theorem 1.1). ▮

Observe that the subgroup H is a right and left coset of itself; in fact, $H = Hh = hH$ for all $h \in H$. In particular, $H = eH = He$. We shall refer to the set of all right (left) cosets of H in G as the *right (left) quotient of G modulo H.*

Lemma 1. *If H is a subgroup of G, then $|H| = |Ha| = |aH|$ for each $a \in G$.*

PROOF. The mappings $\alpha: H \to Ha$ and $\beta: H \to aH$ defined by $\alpha(h) = ha$, $\beta(h) = ah$ $(h \in H)$ are bijections. ▮

Lemma 2. *Let $\mathscr{L}$ be the left quotient, $\mathscr{R}$ the right quotient of a group G modulo a subgroup H. Then $|\mathscr{L}| = |\mathscr{R}|$.*

PROOF. For $a,b \in G$,

$$aH = bH \Leftrightarrow b^{-1}a \in H \Leftrightarrow b^{-1}(a^{-1})^{-1} \in H \Leftrightarrow Ha^{-1} = Hb^{-1}.$$

Hence $aH \mapsto Ha^{-1}$ is a bijection of $\mathscr{L}$ onto $\mathscr{R}$. ▮

Definition 2.6. If H is a subgroup of G, then the cardinality of the left (right) quotient of G modulo H is called the *index*, $[G: H]$, *of* H *in* G. ///

Theorem 2.5. *If* H *is a subgroup of* G, *then* $|G| = |H|[G: H]$.

PROOF. This is an immediate consequence of Theorem 2.4c and Lemma 1. ▮

Note: This result is not restricted to finite groups. (See Chapter 0, Section 6.)

Theorem 2.6. (Lagrange.) *The order of any subgroup of a finite group divides the order of the group.* □

Corollary. *The order of any element of a finite group divides the order of the group.* □

3. Permutation Groups

Theorem 3.1. *If* X *is a nonempty set,* Γ_X *the set of all bijections of* X *onto itself, then* Γ_X *forms a group under composition.*

PROOF. Since the composite of two bijections is a bijection, composition is a binary operation on Γ_X. Composition is associative; the identity map ι_X belongs to Γ_X; and, if $\alpha \in \Gamma_X$, then its inverse map, α^*, belongs to Γ_X. Since $\alpha\alpha^* = \iota_X$, α^* serves as the (group) inverse of α in Γ_X. ▮

Theorem 3.2. (Cayley.) *Every group is isomorphic to a subgroup of the group of all bijections of some set* X *onto itself.*

PROOF. Let $\langle G,\circ\rangle$ be a group, and let X be the set G. Each element $a \in G$ determines a mapping $\gamma_a: G \to G$, defined by $\gamma_a x = ax$ for each $x \in G$. Let

$$T = \{\gamma_a | a \in G\}.$$

We first show that T is a subgroup of Γ_G, the group of all bijections of G onto G. Let $a \in G$. If $x,y \in G$ and $\gamma_a x = \gamma_a y$, then $ax = ay$, hence $x = y$. Thus, γ_a is an injection. If $z \in G$, then $z = a(a^{-1}z) = \gamma_a(a^{-1}z)$. Thus, γ_a is a bijection.

In particular, $\iota_G = \gamma_e \in T$. If $a,b \in G$, then for each $x \in G$, $\gamma_a\gamma_b x = \gamma_a(bx) = a(bx) = (ab)x = \gamma_{ab}x$, so that

$$\gamma_a\gamma_b = \gamma_{ab} \tag{1}$$

in T. Since $\gamma_a\gamma_{a^{-1}} = \gamma_e = \iota_G$, $(\gamma_a)^{-1} = \gamma_{a^{-1}} \in T$. Thus, T is a subgroup of Γ_G.

Now let $\alpha: G \to T$ be defined by

$$\alpha a = \gamma_a$$

for each $a \in G$. Then α is clearly a mapping of G onto T. By (1), α is an epimorphism. If $a,b \in G$ and $\alpha a = \alpha b$, then $\gamma_a e = \gamma_b e$, hence $a = b$. Thus, α is an isomorphism of G onto T. ▮

Definition 3.1. A bijection of a finite set X onto itself is a *permutation* of X. For any positive integer n, the group of all permutations of the set

$$X_n = \{1,2,\ldots,n\}$$

is the *symmetric group*, S_n, *of degree n*. ///

REMARK. If X is any set of n elements, then the group of all permutations of X is isomorphic to S_n.

From Theorem 3.2, we have

Corollary. *If G is a group of finite order n, then G is isomorphic to a subgroup of the symmetric group S_n.* □

We now investigate some of the basic properties of permutation groups. For each $\sigma \in S_n$, we define a binary relation on X_n by

$$x \sim y \bmod \sigma \Leftrightarrow x = \sigma^k y \qquad \text{for some } k \in \mathbf{Z}\ (x,y \in \mathbf{Z}).$$

It is easy to check (Exercise 3.1) that $\sim$ mod σ is an equivalence relation on X_n.

Definition 3.2. If $\sigma \in S_n$ ($n > 0$ in $\mathbf{Z}$), then the equivalence classes with respect to $\sim$ mod σ are the *orbits* of σ. ///

Example. If σ is the permutation in S_7 defined by

$$\begin{matrix} 1 & 2 & 3 & 4 & 5 & 6 & 7 \\ \downarrow & \downarrow & \downarrow & \downarrow & \downarrow & \downarrow & \downarrow \\ 6 & 2 & 7 & 3 & 5 & 1 & 4 \end{matrix}$$

then the orbits of σ are the sets $\{1,6\}$, $\{2\}$, $\{3,7,4\}$, and $\{5\}$.

We shall refer to orbits consisting of more than one element as *nontrivial* orbits. Obviously, a permutation $\sigma \in S_n$ has no nontrivial orbits if and only if it is the identity permutation, ι, on X_n.

Lemma. *If $\sigma \in S_n$ and $\mathcal{O}$ is one of the orbits of σ, then there is an integer $k \geq 0$ such that, for each $a \in \mathcal{O}$, the elements $\sigma^i a$ $(i = 0,\ldots,k-1)$ are all distinct and $\mathcal{O} = \{a,\sigma a,\ldots,\sigma^{k-1}a\}$.*

PROOF. Let $a \in \mathcal{O}$. Since $\mathcal{O}$ is a finite set, there is a least nonnegative integer k such that $\sigma^k a = a$. From the definition of k, it follows that the elements $a, \sigma a,\ldots, \sigma^{k-1}a$ are distinct elements of $\mathcal{O}$. If $b \in \mathcal{O}$, then $b \sim a \bmod \sigma$; i.e., $b = \sigma^h a$ for some $h \in \mathbf{Z}$. By the division algorithm, there is some r $(0 \leq r < k)$ such that $\sigma^h a = \sigma^r a = b$. But then $\mathcal{O} = \{a,\sigma a,\ldots,\sigma^{k-1}a\}$. Since k is the cardinality of the set $\mathcal{O}$, k is independent of the choice of a. ▌

Definition 3.3. A permutation $\sigma \in S_n$, $\sigma \neq \iota$, is a *cycle* if it has exactly one nontrivial orbit. The nontrivial orbit of a cycle σ is the *orbit of* σ; the cardinality of the orbit of σ is the *length* of σ. Two cycles in S_n are *disjoint* if their orbits are disjoint. ///

We use the notation $(a,\sigma a,\ldots,\sigma^{k-1}a)$ to designate a cycle σ whose orbit is the set $\{a,\sigma a,\ldots,\sigma^{k-1}a\}$.

REMARK. Disjoint cycles commute (Exercise 3.3).

Theorem 3.3. *Every permutation $\sigma \in S_n$, $\sigma \neq \iota$, is equal to the product of a unique set of disjoint cycles in S_n.*

PROOF. Since $\sigma \neq \iota$, σ has nontrivial orbits $\mathcal{O}_1,\ldots, \mathcal{O}_s$ $(s \geq 1$ in $\mathbf{Z})$. For each $i = 1,\ldots, s$, let σ_i be the permutation on X_n defined by

$$\sigma_i x = \begin{cases} \sigma x & \text{for } x \in \mathcal{O}_i, \\ x & \text{for } x \in X_n - \mathcal{O}_i. \end{cases}$$

Each σ_i is a cycle with orbit $\mathcal{O}_i$. Thus, the σ_i are disjoint cycles. Let $x \in X_n$. If $x \in \mathcal{O}_h$ for some h, then

$$\left(\prod_{i=1}^{s} \sigma_i\right)(x) = \sigma_h x = \sigma x.$$

If $x \in X_n - \bigcup_{i=1}^{s} \mathcal{O}_i$, then $(\prod_{i=1}^{s} \sigma_i)(x) = x = \sigma x$. But then $\sigma = \prod_{i=1}^{s} \sigma_i$, a product of disjoint cycles.

Suppose $\{\tau_1,\ldots,\tau_t\}$ is another set of disjoint cycles in S_n such that

$$\sigma = \prod_{j=1}^{t} \tau_j.$$

If $x \in X_n$ and $\sigma x \neq x$, then $\sigma x = \tau_j x$ for some $j = 1,\ldots, t$. It is easy to verify that $\sigma\tau_j = \tau_j\sigma$ and that $\sigma^k x = \tau_j^k x$ for each $k \in \mathbf{Z}$. But then the orbits of the cycles τ_j are precisely the orbits of σ. If $\mathcal{O}_i$ is the orbit of τ_j, then $\tau_j x = \sigma x = \sigma_i x$ for each $x \in \mathcal{O}_i$, and $\tau_j x = x = \sigma_i x$ for each $x \notin \mathcal{O}_i$, whence $\tau_j = \sigma_i$. In this way, we can define a bijection $\tau_j \mapsto \sigma_i$ of $\{\tau_j\}_{j=1}^t$ onto $\{\sigma_i\}_{i=1}^s$, where $\tau_j = \sigma_i$ for each $j = 1,\ldots, t$. This establishes the uniqueness claimed in the theorem. ▌

Example. The permutation $\sigma \in S_7$ defined in the example on page 40 can be expressed as a product of disjoint cycles as follows:

$$\sigma = (16)(374).$$

A cycle of length 2 is a *transposition*. Using Theorem 3.3, we easily obtain

Theorem 3.4. *Every permutation in S_n $(n > 1)$ is a product of transpositions.*

PROOF. Since every transposition has order 2 in S_n, the identity permutation is a product of transpositions. For $\sigma \neq \iota$ it is sufficient to prove that each cycle of σ is a product of transpositions. Let $(x_1 \cdots x_h)$ be a cycle in S_n. Then

$$(x_1 \cdots x_h) = (x_1x_h)\cdots(x_1x_3)(x_1x_2). \quad ▌$$

Definition 3.4. A permutation in S_n is *even* if it is the product of an even number of transpositions in S_n, *odd* if it is the product of an odd number of transpositions in S_n. ///

By Theorem 3.4, any permutation in S_n, $n > 1$, is even or odd, but it is not immediately clear that a permutation cannot be *both* even and odd.

Theorem 3.5. *A permutation cannot be both even and odd.*

PROOF. Suppose $\sigma \in S_n$, $n > 1$. For each n-tuple $(i_1,\ldots,i_n)$, $i_j \in X_n$, $j = 1,\ldots, n$, let

$$P(i_1,\ldots,i_n) = \prod_{h<k} (i_h - i_k).$$

If τ is the transposition $(i_r i_s)$, $1 \leq r < s \leq n$, then

$$P(\tau i_1,\ldots,\tau i_n) = \prod_{h<k} (\tau i_h - \tau i_k) = -P(i_1,\ldots,i_n),$$

since τ induces an odd number, $(2s - 2r - 1)$, of sign changes in the product. Hence, if $\sigma = \tau_1 \cdots \tau_k$, where each τ_i is a transposition, then

$$\begin{aligned} P(\sigma i_1,\ldots,\sigma i_n) &= P(\tau_1 \cdots \tau_k i_1,\ldots,\tau_1 \cdots \tau_k i_n) \\ &= -P(\tau_2 \cdots \tau_k i_1,\ldots,\tau_2 \cdots \tau_k i_n) = \cdots \\ &= (-1)^k P(i_1,\ldots,i_n). \end{aligned}$$

Thus, $P(\sigma i_1,\ldots,\sigma i_n)$ is equal to $P(i_1,\ldots,i_n)$ if k is even, and equal to $-P(i_1,\ldots,i_n)$ if k is odd. It follows that σ cannot be both even and odd. ▮

Theorem 3.6. *The even permutations in S_n, $n > 1$, form a subgroup of S_n, of index* 2. (This subgroup is called the *alternating group*, A_n, of degree n.) □

Theorem 3.7. *The order of a permutation $\sigma \neq \iota$ in S_n, $n > 1$, is equal to the least common multiple of the lengths of the disjoint cycles of σ.* □

We leave the proofs of Theorems 3.6 and 3.7 to the reader (Exercises 3.6 and 3.7).

4. Groups with Operators; Homomorphism and Isomorphism Theorems

In order to give a unified discussion of several important algebraic structures, we now introduce the concept of a group with operators.

Definition 4.1. Let $\langle G,\circ\rangle$ be a group, M a set, and μ a mapping $(m,x) \mapsto mx$ of $M \times G$ into G such that

$$m(x \circ y) = mx \circ my$$

for each $m \in M$, $x,y \in G$. Then the system $\langle G,M,\circ,\mu\rangle$ is called a *group with operator set M*. We shall say simply: G is a group with operator set M, or an *M-group*, with respect to μ. A subgroup H of G is an *M-subgroup of G* if $mx \in H$ for each $m \in M$, $x \in H$. ///

REMARK. If G is a group with operator set M, then for each $m \in M$, the mapping $\overline{m}$ defined by $\overline{m}(x) = mx$ for each $x \in G$ is an endomorphism of G. Thus, to the operator set M, there corresponds a set $\overline{M}$ of endomorphisms of G. (The map $m \mapsto \overline{m}$ of M into $\overline{M}$ is not, in general, injective.) If, on the other hand, $\overline{M}$ is a set of endomorphisms of G, then G is a group with operator set $\overline{M}$, where the external composition μ is defined by $(\overline{m},x) \mapsto \overline{m}(x)$ for each $x \in G$.

Examples. In each of the following, G is a group with operator set M, where $\mu: M \times G \to G$ is defined in the obvious way.

1. G any group, $M = \varnothing$. Every subgroup is an M-subgroup.
2. G any Abelian group, $M = \mathbf{Z}$. Every subgroup is an M-subgroup.
3. G any group, $M = \mathscr{E}$, the set of all endomorphisms of G.

The subgroups invariant under all the endomorphisms of G (i.e., the subgroups H such that $\alpha H \subset H$ for each $\alpha \in \mathscr{E}$) are the M-subgroups. (Such subgroups are called *fully invariant subgroups*.)

4. G any group, $M = \mathfrak{A}$, the set of all automorphisms of G. The subgroups invariant under all the automorphisms of G are the M-subgroups. (Such subgroups are called *characteristic* subgroups.)

We shall see later that rings, algebras, modules, and vector spaces can all be regarded as groups with operators.

By Chapter 0, Theorem 2.3, homomorphism of groups preserves identities and inverses. Hence, if G is a group with operator set M, $me = e$ and $ma^{-1} = (ma)^{-1}$ for all $m \in M$, $a \in G$.

Definition 4.2. If G, G' are groups with operator set M and α is a homomorphism of G into G' such that

$$\alpha(mx) = m(\alpha x)$$

for each $m \in M$, $x \in G$, then α is an *M-homomorphism* of G into G'. (Similarly, we speak of *M-endomorphisms*, *M-isomorphisms*, *M-automorphisms*, *M-monomorphisms*, and *M-epimorphisms*.) An M-homomorphism with domain G will often be referred to as an *M-homomorphism* of G. ///

Definition 4.3. If G, G' are M-groups, and α is a homomorphism of G into G', then the set

$$\{a \mid a \in G \quad \text{and} \quad \alpha a = e'\}$$

is the *kernel* (Ker α) of α. ///

Theorem 4.1. *Let G, G' be M-groups, α an (M)-homomorphism of G onto G', with* Ker $\alpha = H$. *Then*

a. *H is an (M)-subgroup of G.*
b. *$Ha = aH$ for each $a \in G$.*
c. *α is a monomorphism if and only if $H = E$.*

PROOF.

a. $H \neq \varnothing$ since $e \in H$. For $a,b \in H$, $\alpha(ab^{-1}) = \alpha a(\alpha b)^{-1} = e'(e')^{-1} = e'$, hence $ab^{-1} \in H$, and H is a subgroup of G. If α is an M-homomorphism, then for $m \in M$, $a \in h$, $\alpha(ma) = m(\alpha a) = me' = e'$, hence $ma \in H$. But then H is an M-subgroup of G.

b. Since, for $a,b \in G$, $ab^{-1} \in H$ if and only if $b^{-1}a \in H$, the relations $\equiv_r$ mod H and $\equiv_l$ mod H coincide. In fact, for $a \in G$, both aH and Ha are equal to $\overset{-1}{\alpha}(\alpha a)$:

$$aH = \{x|a^{-1}x \in H\} = \{x|\alpha a = \alpha x\} = \overset{-1}{\alpha}(\alpha a)$$

and

$$Ha = \{x|xa^{-1} \in H\} = \{x|\alpha a = \alpha x\} = \overset{-1}{\alpha}(\alpha a).$$

c. α is injective if and only if $\overset{-1}{\alpha}(\alpha a) = \{a\}$ for each $a \in G$. By b, this is the case if and only if $Ha = \{a\}$ for each $a \in G$; i.e., $H = \{e\}$. ▮

Definition 4.4. If G is an (M)-group, H an (M)-subgroup of G, then H is a *normal* (M)*-subgroup* of G ($H \lhd G$, or $G \rhd H$) if H is the kernel of some homomorphism of G. ///

Note: We shall see that an M-subgroup of an M-group G is normal in G if and only if it is the kernel of some M-homomorphism of G.

Among the homomorphisms of any M-group G are the trivial ones: the identity map on G and the map which sends every element of G to e. The corresponding kernels, E and G, are normal M-subgroups of G. Some M-groups have no nontrivial homomorphisms, and hence no proper normal M-subgroups.

Definition 4.5. A group is *simple* if it has no proper normal subgroups. An M-group is *M-simple* if it has no proper normal M-subgroups. ///

It is clear that every simple group is M-simple for any operator set M. On the other hand, a group which is M-simple for a given operator set M need not be a simple group. For example, the only simple abelian groups are the cyclic groups of prime order (Exercise 4.1); but there are many other examples of M-simple abelian M-groups, e.g., one-dimensional vector spaces, simple rings, etc.

If $H \lhd G$, we designate the (right and left) quotient of G modulo H by the symbol G/H. We now show that, for $H \lhd G$, G an M-group, the quotient G/H forms an M-group which is, itself, a homomorphic image of G:

Theorem 4.2. *Let G be an M-group, H a normal M-subgroup of G. Let G/H be the quotient of G modulo H. For each $a,b \in G$, let*

$$Ha \circ Hb = Hab$$

and, for each $m \in M$, $a \in G$, let

$$m(Ha) = Hma.$$

Then

a. $\circ$ *is a binary operation on G/H.*

b. $\langle G/H,\circ\rangle$ *is a group with operator set M.*

c. *The mapping $\nu: G \to G/H$ defined by $\nu a = Ha$ is an M-epimorphism of the M-group G onto the M-group G/H, with kernel H.*

PROOF.

a. Let $a,a',b,b' \in G$ be such that $Ha = Ha'$, $Hb = Hb'$. Then $a' = h_1a$, $b' = h_2b$ for some $h_1,h_2 \in H$; hence $a'b' = h_1ah_2b$. Since H is normal in G, $ah_2 = h_3a$ for some $h_3 \in H$. Hence $a'b' = h_1h_3ab \in Hab$. But then, by Theorem 3.5d, $Hab = Ha'b'$. It follows that $\circ$ is a binary operation on G/H.

b. Since $(Ha \circ Hb) \circ Hc = Hab \circ Hc = H(ab)c = Ha(bc) = Ha \circ Hbc = Ha \circ (Hb \circ Hc)$ for all $Ha,Hb,Hc \in G/H$, $\circ$ is associative. For each $a \in G$, $H \circ Ha = He \circ Ha = Hea = Ha$, and $Ha^{-1} \circ Ha = Ha^{-1}a = He = H$. Thus, H serves as a left identity for $\circ$ and, for each $a \in G$, Ha^{-1} is a left inverse for Ha relative to the identity H. By Theorem 1.1, it follows that $\langle G/H,\circ\rangle$ is a group. Since, for $m \in M$, $a,a' \in G$, $Ha = Ha'$ implies $Hma = Hma'$, $(m,Ha) \mapsto Hma$ is a map of $M \times G/H$ into G/H. For each $a,b \in G$, $m \in M$, $m(Ha \circ Hb) = mHab = Hm(ab) = Hmamb = Hma \circ Hmb = mHa \circ mHb$. Thus $\langle G/H,\circ\rangle$ is a group with operator set M.

c. It is clear that ν is a mapping of G onto G/H. Since, for each $a,b \in G$, $\nu(ab) = Hab = Ha \circ Hb = \nu a \circ \nu b$, ν is an epimorphism of G onto G/H. The kernel of ν is H, since

$$\operatorname{Ker} \nu = \{a \mid Ha = H\} = H.$$

Finally, ν is an M-epimorphism, since $m\nu a = mHa = Hma = \nu ma$ for each $a \in G$, $m \in M$. ▮

Definition 4.6. The M-group $\langle G/H, \circ \rangle$ of Theorem 4.2 is called the *M-factor group* (or *M-quotient group*) *of G modulo H*. The M-epimorphism ν is called the *natural* (or *canonical*) *M-epimorphism of G onto G/H.* ///

We have just seen that every quotient group of an M-group G is a homomorphic image of G. In fact, every homomorphic image of G is isomorphic to one of the factor groups of G.

Theorem 4.3. *Let G be an M-group, α an M-epimorphism of an M-group G onto an M-group G′, with kernel H. Then G′ is M-isomorphic to G/H.*

PROOF. The correspondence

$$\mu \colon Ha \mapsto \alpha a$$

is a one-to-one map of G/H into G', since, for $a,b \in G$,

$$Ha = Hb \Leftrightarrow ab^{-1} \in H \Leftrightarrow \alpha(ab^{-1}) = e' \Leftrightarrow \alpha a = \alpha b.$$

Since α is surjective, so is μ. For each $a,b \in G$,

$$\mu(HaHb) = \mu(Hab) = \alpha(ab) = \alpha a \alpha b = \mu(Ha)\mu(Hb)$$

and, for each $m \in M$,

$$\mu(mHa) = \mu Hma = \alpha(ma) = m(\alpha a) = m(\mu Ha).$$

Thus, α is an M-isomorphism of G/H onto G'. ▮

Theorem 4.3 is often referred to as the Fundamental Theorem of Homomorphism. We shall reserve this name for an expanded version of Theorem 4.3, which we prove later (Theorem 4.9).

We now give several equivalent characterizations of normality.

Theorem 4.4. *Let H be an M-subgroup of an M-group G. The following statements are equivalent:*

a. $H \lhd G$ (i.e., *H is the kernel of some homomorphism of G*).
b. $aH = Ha$ *for all* $a \in G$.
c. *H is the kernel of an M-homomorphism of G.*
d. $a^{-1}ha \in H$ *for all* $a \in G$, $h \in H$.
e. $a^{-1}Ha = H$ *for all* $a \in G$ (*where* $a^{-1}Ha = \{a^{-1}ha \mid h \in H\}$).

PROOF. a ⇒ b, by Theorem 4.1, b. In Theorem 4.2, the construction of the factor group G/H depends only on the condition $aH = Ha$ for all $a \in G$. Thus, if b holds, then $H = \text{Ker } \nu$, where ν is the natural M-epimorphism of G onto G/H. But then c holds. Obviously, c implies a. The equivalence of b, d and e is readily verified (Exercise 4.1). ▮

Corollary 1. *Every subgroup of an abelian group is normal.* □

Corollary 2. *An abelian group $G \neq E$ is simple if and only if it is cyclic of prime order.*

PROOF. Exercise 4.2. □

The significance of the fourth condition in Theorem 4.4 can be better appreciated in the light of the next theorem.

Theorem 4.5. *If G is a group, then for each $a \in G$, the mapping $\alpha_a: x \mapsto a^{-1}xa$ $(x \in G)$ is an automorphism of G.*

PROOF. Let $a \in G$. If $x,y \in G$, then $\alpha_a(xy) = a^{-1}xya = a^{-1}xaa^{-1}ya = \alpha_a x \cdot \alpha_a y$. Thus, α_a is an endomorphism of G. Since $\alpha_a x = a^{-1}xa = e$ only if $x = e$, α_a is a monomorphism of G into G. If $y \in G$, then $y = a^{-1}aya^{-1}a$, hence $y \in \text{Im } \alpha_a$. But then α_a is an automorphism of G. ▮

Definition 4.7. An automorphism α of a group G is called an *inner automorphism* of G if there is an element $a \in G$ such that $\alpha x = a^{-1}xa$ for each $x \in G$. ///

Corollary. *A subgroup H of a group G is normal in G if and only if it is invariant under every inner automorphism of G.* □

We note that, if G is any group, and M is the set of all inner automorphisms of G, then the M-subgroups of G are precisely the normal subgroups of G.

The following two theorems, whose proofs we leave to the reader (Exercises 4.6 and 4.7), serve to illustrate the concept of a quotient group.

Definition 4.8. If G is a group, $a,b \in G$, then the element $[a,b] = a^{-1}b^{-1}ab$ is called the *commutator* of a and b. The subgroup G^1 of G generated by the commutators $[a,b]$ for $a,b \in G$ is called the *commutator subgroup* of G. ///

Theorem 4.6. *Let G be a group, G^1 its commutator subgroup. Then*

a. *G^1 is fully invariant (i.e., G^1 is invariant under every endomorphism of G).*
b. *If $H \lhd G$, then G/H is Abelian if and only if $G^1 \subset H$.* □

Definition 4.9. If G is a group, then the set $C(G) = \{c \mid cx = xc, \text{ all } x \in G\}$ is called the *center* of G. ///

Theorem 4.7. *Let G be a group, $C(G)$ its center. Then*

a. *$C(G)$ is a characteristic subgroup of G [i.e., $C(G)$ is invariant under every automorphism of G].*
b. *The group $I(G)$ of all inner automorphisms of G is isomorphic to $G/C(G)$.* □

We now consider the following question: Suppose a group G' is a homomorphic image of a group G. If νG and $\nu' G'$ are homomorphic images, respectively, of G and G', under what conditions is $\nu' G'$ a homomorphic image of νG? The next theorem provides an answer to this question.

Theorem 4.8. (Rectangle Theorem.) *Let G, G' be M-groups, and let $\alpha: G \to G'$, $\nu: G \to \nu G$, and $\nu': G' \to \nu' G'$ be M-epimorphisms. Then*

a. *There is a (unique) M-epimorphism $\beta: \nu G \to \nu' G'$ such that $\beta\nu = \nu'\alpha$ if and only if* Ker $\nu' \supset \alpha(\text{Ker } \nu)$.
b. *There is a (unique) M-isomorphism $\beta: \nu G \to \nu' G'$ such that $\beta\nu = \nu'\alpha$ if and only if* Ker $\nu' = \alpha(\text{Ker } \nu)$ *and* Ker $\alpha \subset$ Ker ν.

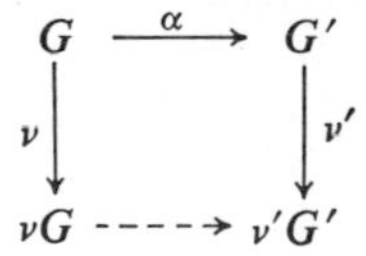

PROOF.

a. Suppose Ker $\nu' \supset \alpha(\text{Ker } \nu)$. We prove that $\beta: \nu a \mapsto \nu'(\alpha a)$ is the required M-epimorphism. To begin with, β is a map of νG into $\nu' G'$: If $a,b \in G$, $\nu a = \nu b \Rightarrow ab^{-1} \in \text{Ker } \nu \Rightarrow \alpha(ab^{-1}) \in \text{Ker } \nu' \Rightarrow \nu'(\alpha a) = \nu'(\alpha b)$. Since α, ν, ν' are surjective, β is a map of νG onto $\nu' G'$. For each $a,b \in G$, $\beta(\nu a \nu b) = \beta(\nu ab) = \nu'(\alpha ab) = \nu'\alpha a \, \nu'\alpha b = \beta a \beta b$, and, for each $a \in G$, $m \in M$, $\beta(m\nu a) = \beta(\nu ma) = \nu'(\alpha ma) = \nu'(m\alpha a) = m(\nu'\alpha a) = m\beta\nu a$. Thus, $\beta: \nu G \to \nu' G'$ is an M-epimorphism. From the definition of β, it follows immediately that $\beta\nu = \nu'\alpha$. If $\beta': \nu G \to \nu' G'$ is another map such that $\beta'\nu = \nu'\alpha$, then for each $a \in G$, $\beta'(\nu a) = (\beta'\nu)a = \nu'(\alpha a) = \beta(\nu a)$; hence $\beta' = \beta$. Under the hypothesis $\text{Ker}\,\nu' \supset \alpha(\text{Ker}\,\nu)$, we have established the existence and uniqueness of β.

Conversely, let us suppose the existence of an M-epimorphism $\beta: \nu G \to \nu' G'$ such that $\beta\nu = \nu'\alpha$. If $a \in \text{Ker}\,\nu$, then $\nu'(\alpha a) = (\nu'\alpha)a = (\beta\nu)a = \beta(\nu a) = \beta e_{\nu G} = e_{G'}$, whence $\alpha a \in \text{Ker}\,\nu'$. But then $\text{Ker}\,\nu' \supset \alpha(\text{Ker}\,\nu)$, as required.

b. Suppose $\text{Ker}\,\nu' = \alpha(\text{Ker}\,\nu)$ and $\text{Ker}\,\alpha \subset \text{Ker}\,\nu$. From part a, and the inclusion $\text{Ker}\,\nu' \supset \alpha(\text{Ker}\,\nu)$ follows the existence of a unique M-epimorphism $\beta: \nu G \to \nu' G'$ such that $\beta\nu = \nu'\alpha$. If $a \in G$ and $\beta(\nu a) = e_{\nu' G}$, then $a \in \text{Ker}\,\beta\nu = \text{Ker}\,\nu'\alpha$ and $\alpha a \in \text{Ker}\,\nu' \subset \alpha(\text{Ker}\,\nu)$. But then $\alpha a = \alpha b$ for some $b \in \text{Ker}\,\nu$; hence $ab^{-1} \in \text{Ker}\,\nu$, $a \in \text{Ker}\,\nu$, and $\nu a = e_{\nu G}$. Thus, β is an isomorphism.

Conversely, suppose there is an M-isomorphism $\beta: \nu' G' \to \nu G$ such that $\beta\nu = \nu'\alpha$. Then, by a, $\text{Ker}\,\nu' \supset \alpha(\text{Ker}\,\nu)$. If $a' \in \text{Ker}\,\nu'$, then $a' = \alpha a$ for some $a \in G$, and $\nu'\alpha a = \beta\nu a = e_{\nu' G'}$, whence $\nu a \in \text{Ker}\,\beta = \{e_{\nu G}\}$, and $a \in \text{Ker}\,\nu$. But then $a' = \alpha a \in \alpha(\text{Ker}\,\nu)$, and we have $\text{Ker}\,\nu' \subset \alpha(\text{Ker}\,\nu)$. Thus, $\text{Ker}\,\nu' = \alpha(\text{Ker}\,\nu)$. Finally, if $a \in \text{Ker}\,\alpha$, then $\nu'\alpha a = \beta\nu a = e_{\nu' G'}$, whence $\nu a = e_{\nu G}$ and $a \in \text{Ker}\,\nu$. Thus, $\text{Ker}\,\alpha \subset \text{Ker}\,\nu$. ∎

Theorem 4.8 yields a rich harvest of important results. We begin with an expanded version of Theorem 4.3.

Theorem 4.9. (Fundamental Theorem of Homomorphism for M-groups.) *Let G be an M-group, H a normal M-subgroup of G, and $\nu: G \to G/H$ the canonical M-epimorphism. Let $\alpha: G \to G'$ be an M-epimorphism. Then*

a. *There is a unique M-epimorphism $\beta: G/H \to G'$ such that $\beta\nu = \alpha$ if and only if $H \subset \text{Ker}\,\alpha$.*

b. *There is a unique M-isomorphism $\beta: G/H \to G'$ such that $\beta\nu = \alpha$ if and only if $H = \text{Ker}\,\alpha$.*

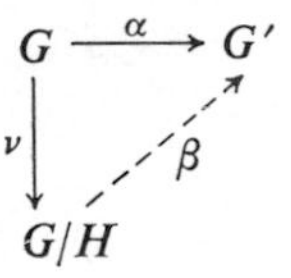

PROOF. First note that, in Theorem 4.8, the condition $\text{Ker}\,\nu' \supset \alpha(\text{Ker}\,\nu)$ is equivalent to the condition $\text{Ker}\,\nu \subset \text{Ker}\,\alpha$ in case $\text{Ker}\,\nu' = \{e_{G'}\}$; i.e., in case ν' is a monomorphism.

a. By Theorem 4.8a, with ν' the identity map on G', there is a unique M-epimorphism $\beta: G/H \to G'$ such that $\beta\nu = \alpha$ if and only if $H = \text{Ker}\,\nu \subset \text{Ker}\,\alpha$.

b. By Theorem 4.8b, with ν' the identity map on G', there is a unique M-isomorphism $\beta\colon G/H \to G'$ such that $\beta\nu = \alpha$ if and only if $H = \operatorname{Ker} \nu \subset \operatorname{Ker} \alpha$ and $\operatorname{Ker} \alpha \subset \operatorname{Ker} \nu$, i.e., if and only if $H = \operatorname{Ker} \alpha$. ▌

Remark. It will be instructive at this point to reformulate the property of factor groups expressed in Theorem 4.9a. For a fixed M-group G, and a fixed normal M-subgroup H of G, consider the set $\mathscr{C}$ of ordered pairs $\langle G',\alpha\rangle$, where G' is an M-group and $\alpha\colon G \to G'$ is an M-epimorphism such that $H \subset \operatorname{Ker} \alpha$. Clearly, $\langle G/H,\nu\rangle$ is an element of $\mathscr{C}$. According to Theorem 4.9a, the ordered pair $\langle G/H,\nu\rangle$ plays a very special role in $\mathscr{C}$:

(*) For each $\langle G',\alpha\rangle$ in $\mathscr{C}$ there is exactly one M-epimorphism $\beta\colon G/H \to G'$ such that $\beta\nu = \alpha$.

In language we shall introduce later (Section 14), (*) expresses the fact that $\langle G/H,\nu\rangle$ is a "universal object" in $\mathscr{C}$. This "universal object" is determined to within isomorphism; i.e., if $\langle Q,\nu'\rangle \in \mathscr{C}$ has the property

(†) For each $\langle G',\alpha\rangle$ in $\mathscr{C}$ there is exactly one M-epimorphism $\beta'\colon Q \to G'$ such that $\beta'\nu' = \alpha$,

then there is a unique M-isomorphism $\beta\colon G/H \to Q$ such that $\beta\nu = \nu'$.

The proof of this assertion may be outlined by considering consecutively diagrams (a) through (d).

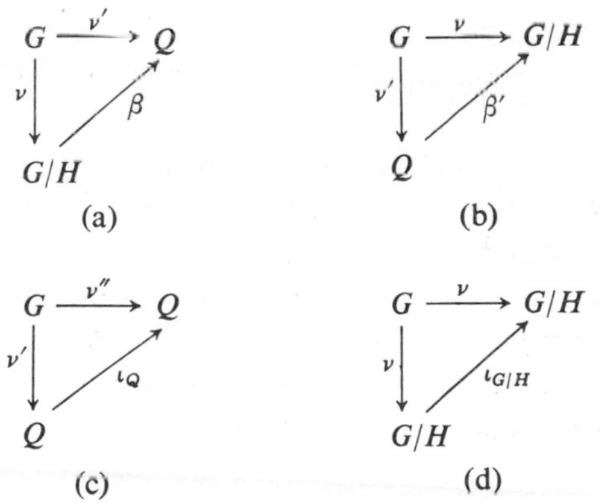

Conditions (*) and (†) provide the existence of M-homomorphisms β and β' in (a) and (b). The relations $\beta\nu = \nu'$ and $\beta'\nu' = \nu$ give rise to $\beta\beta'\nu' = \nu'$ and $\beta'\beta\nu = \nu$. The uniqueness requirement in Theorem 4.9a and a consideration of diagrams (c) and (d) leads to the identifications $\beta\beta' = \iota_Q$ and $\beta'\beta = \iota_{G/H}$. But then β is an isomorphism with the required properties.

Throughout this book, we shall introduce many algebraic structures as "universal objects," for example, free groups, products and coproducts, direct sums, quotient fields, and tensor products.

The next result we obtain using the Rectangle Theorem is the First Isomorphism Theorem.

Lemma. *Let $\alpha: G \to G'$ be an M-epimorphism of an M-group G onto an M-group G', H an M-subgroup of G such that* $\operatorname{Ker} \alpha \subset H$, *and H' an M-subgroup of G'. Then $\alpha H = H'$ if and only if $\overset{-1}{\alpha} H' = H$ (where $\overset{-1}{\alpha} H' = \{h \in G \mid \alpha h \in H'\}$).*

Proof. Let $K = \operatorname{Ker} \alpha$. Suppose that $\alpha H = H'$. Then the inclusion $H \subset \overset{-1}{\alpha} H'$ obviously holds. If $a \in \overset{-1}{\alpha} H'$, then $\alpha a \in H'$; hence $\alpha a = \alpha h$ for some $h \in H$. But then $ah^{-1} \in K$. Since $K \subset H$, $a \in H$. Thus, the inclusion $\overset{-1}{\alpha} H' \subset H$ also holds, and the equality follows.

The converse does not depend on the hypothesis: $K \subset H$. Suppose $\overset{-1}{\alpha} H' = H$. Then, certainly, $\alpha H \subset H'$. If $h' \in H'$, then $h' = \alpha h$ for some $h \in H$. Thus $\alpha H \supset H'$ and the equality follows. ▮

Theorem 4.10. (First Isomorphism Theorem.) *Let G be an M-group, $\alpha: G \to \alpha G$ an M-epimorphism with kernel K. Let S_K be the set of all M-subgroups of G which contain K, and let S' be the set of all M-subgroups of αG. Then*

a. *$\sigma: H \mapsto \alpha H$ is a one-to-one mapping of S_K onto S'.*
b. *If H is any normal M-subgroup of G, then $\alpha H \lhd \alpha G$; and, if $H \in S_K$ and $\alpha H \lhd \alpha G$, then $H \lhd G$.*
c. *If $H \lhd G$, then there exists a unique M-epimorphism β of G/H onto $\alpha G/\alpha H$ such that $\beta\nu = \nu'\alpha$, where ν is the natural M-epimorphism of G onto G/H, ν' the natural M-epimorphism of αG onto $\alpha G/\alpha H$. In particular, if $H \in S_K$, then β is an M-isomorphism.*

$$\begin{array}{ccc} G & \xrightarrow{\alpha} & \alpha G \\ {\scriptstyle \nu}\downarrow & & \downarrow{\scriptstyle \nu'} \\ G/H & \xrightarrow[\beta]{} & \alpha G/\alpha H \end{array}$$

PROOF.

a. We leave to the reader the verification that αH is an M-subgroup of αG for each M-subgroup H of G and that $\overset{-1}{\alpha} H'$ is an M-subgroup of G for each M-subgroup H' of αG (Exercise 4.3). Since $e' \in H'$ and $\overset{-1}{\alpha} \{e'\} = K$, $\overset{-1}{\alpha} H' \in S_K$. Then, clearly, σ is a mapping of S_K into S'. If $H' \in S'$ and $H = \overset{-1}{\alpha} H'$, then $H' = \alpha H = \sigma(H)$. Thus, σ maps S_K onto S'. By the lemma, if $H' = \sigma(H) = \alpha H$, then $H = \overset{-1}{\alpha} H'$. It follows that σ is one-to-one.

b. If H is any normal M-subgroup of G, then we may readily verify that αH is a normal M-subgroup of αG. Suppose αH is a normal M-subgroup of αG for some $H \in S_K$. Then for each $a \in G$, $h \in H$, $(\alpha a)^{-1}\alpha h \alpha a = \alpha(a^{-1}ha) \in \alpha H$. By the lemma, it follows that $a^{-1}ha \in H$. Thus, H is normal in G.

c. Let ν be the natural M-epimorphism of G onto G/H, ν' the natural M-epimorphism of αG onto $\alpha G/\alpha H$. Then Ker $\nu' = \alpha(\text{Ker } \nu)$ and, by Theorem 4.8, there exists a unique M-epimorphism $\beta: G/H \to \alpha G/\alpha H$ such that $\beta\nu = \nu'\alpha$. If $H \in S_K$, then $\text{Ker } \alpha = K \subset H = \text{Ker } \nu$ and $\text{Ker } \nu' = \alpha H = \alpha(\text{Ker } \nu)$. Therefore, once again by Theorem 4.8, there exists a unique M-isomorphism $\beta: G/H \to \alpha G/\alpha H$ such that $\beta\nu = \nu'\alpha$. ▮

Corollary 1. *If G is an M-group, K and H are M-subgroups of G such that $K \subset H$, $K \lhd G$, and $H \lhd G$, then $(G/K)/(H/K)$ is M-isomorphic to G/H.*

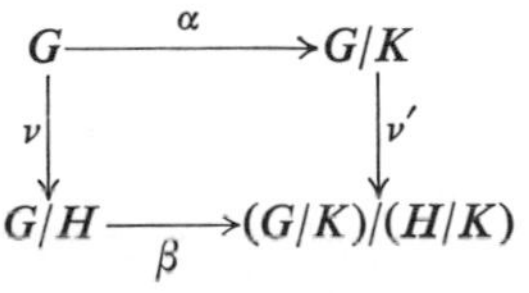

PROOF. The First Isomorphism Theorem, c, applies with $\alpha G = G/K$, $\alpha H = H/K$. ▮

Corollary 2. *If G is an M-group, H a normal M-subgroup of G, then G/H is M-simple if and only if H is a maximal normal M-subgroup of G.* □

Another important "isomorphism theorem" concerns intersections and products of subgroups. If H, K are M-subgroups of an M-group G, their intersection is always an M-subgroup. However, the set

$$HK = \{hk \mid h \in H, k \in K\}$$

does not, in general, form a subgroup. It does if one of the two subgroups is normal in G.

Lemma. *Let G be an M-group, H, K M-subgroups of G. Then*

a. *H ∩ K is an M-subgroup of G.*

b. *If K is normal in G, HK is an M-subgroup of G.*

PROOF. We leave to the reader the verification of a. To prove b we note first that $e = e \cdot e \in HK$. If $h_1 h_2 \in H$, $k_1, k_2 \in K$, then, by the normality of K in G, $h_1 k_1 (h_2 k_2)^{-1} = h_1 k_1 k_2^{-1} h_2^{-1} = h_1 h_2^{-1} \bar{k} \in HK$ for some $\bar{k} \in K$. If $m \in M$, $h \in H$, $k \in K$, then $m(hk) = mhmk \in HK$. Thus HK is an M-subgroup of G. ∎

$$h_1 k' h_2^{-1} = h_1 \left(h_2^{-1} h_2 \right) k' h_2^{-1}$$

Theorem 4.11. (Second Isomorphism Theorem.) *Let G be an M-group, H an M-subgroup, and K a normal M-subgroup of G. Then the factor groups H/H ∩ K and HK/K are M-isomorphic.*

PROOF. We note that $H \cap K \lhd H$ and $K \lhd HK$, by the normality of K in G. Consider the sequence of maps $H \overset{\varepsilon}{\to} HK \overset{\nu}{\to} HK/K$, where ε is the canonical embedding of H in HK and ν is the canonical M-epimorphism of HK onto HK/K. Clearly, $\varphi = \nu \varepsilon$ is an M-homomorphism of H into HK/K. In fact, φ is an epimorphism. For if $\bar{h} \in HK/K$, then there is some $hk \in HK$ ($h \in H$, $k \in K$) such that $\bar{h} = \nu(hk) = \nu h = \nu \varepsilon h = \varphi h$. Furthermore, $\text{Ker } \varphi = \overset{-1}{\varepsilon}(\text{Ker } \nu) = \overset{-1}{\varepsilon}(K) = H \cap K$. Hence, by Theorem 4.3, $H/H \cap K \cong HK/K$. ∎

5. Normal Series

Definition 5.1. Let G be an M-group. A descending chain of M-subgroups $G = G_0 \supset G_1 \supset \cdots$ is called a (descending) *normal chain* for G if $G_i \rhd G_{i+1}$ for each $i = 0, 1, \ldots$. A normal chain is *proper* if G_{i+1} is a proper normal M-subgroup of G_i for each $i = 0, 1, \ldots$. A finite normal chain

$$\gamma: G = G_0 \rhd G_1 \rhd \cdots \rhd G_k = E$$

is called a *normal series* for G. The M-subgroups G_i are the *terms* of γ, the factor groups G_i/G_{i+1} are its *factors*, and the integer k is its *length*. If γ and γ' are normal series for G, then γ is a *refinement* of γ' if every term of γ' occurs among the terms of γ. Let $\gamma: G = G_0 \rhd G_1 \rhd \cdots \rhd G_k = E$ and $\gamma': G = G_0' \rhd G_1' \rhd \cdots \rhd G_h' = E$. Then γ and γ' are *equivalent normal series* if $k = h$ and there is a bijection β of the set $\{0, 1, \ldots, k-1\}$ to itself such that G_i/G_{i+1} is M-isomorphic to $G_{\beta i}'/G_{\beta i+1}'$. A proper normal series is a *composition series* if all of its factors are M-simple. ///

We note that, by the First Isomorphism Theorem, a normal series $G = G_0 \triangleright G_1 \triangleright \cdots \triangleright G_k = E$ is a composition series if and only if, for each $i = 0, \ldots, k-1$, G_{i+1} is a maximal normal M-subgroup of G_i (i.e., there is no M-subgroup H of G such that $G_{i+1} \underset{\neq}{\triangleleft} H \underset{\neq}{\triangleleft} G_i$).

NOTATION. From now on, if H is a maximal normal M-subgroup of K, we write $H \mathrel{\cdot\!\!\triangleleft} K$ or $K \mathrel{\triangleright\!\!\cdot} H$.

While every M-group has at least one normal series (e.g., $G \triangleright E$), not every M-group has a composition series. In this section we prove the important Jordan–Hölder Theorem, which states that any two composition series of an M-group are equivalent. We also derive necessary and sufficient conditions for the existence of a composition series. For the case of an abelian M-group, these conditions reduce to the ascending and descending chain conditions on M-subgroups. Another interesting result (for which we outline a proof in Exercises 5.1 and 5.2) is the Schreier Refinement Theorem: Any two normal series of a given M-group have equivalent refinements. While the Jordan–Hölder Theorem is an immediate corollary of the Schreier Refinement Theorem, we choose to prove it directly.

Lemma 1. *Let G be an M-group. If there exists a positive integer r such that every proper normal series for G has length at most r, then G has a composition series.*

PROOF. If there is no composition series, then every normal series has a proper refinement; hence there exist proper normal series of arbitrary length, contrary to hypothesis. ∎

NOTE: From Lemma 1, it follows that every finite M-group has a composition series.

Lemma 2. *Let G be an M-group which has a composition series of length r. Then any proper normal series of G has length at most r.*

PROOF. Let $G = G_0 \mathrel{\triangleright\!\!\cdot} G_1 \mathrel{\triangleright\!\!\cdot} \cdots \mathrel{\triangleright\!\!\cdot} G_r = E$ be a composition series for G, and let $G = H_0 \triangleright H_1 \triangleright \cdots \triangleright H_s = E$ be a proper normal series for G. We proceed by induction on r. The assertion of the lemma obviously holds when $r = 1$. Suppose it holds for all M-groups which have a composition series of length less than r.

The M-subgroup G_1 has a composition series $G_1 \mathrel{\triangleright\!\!\cdot} G_2 \mathrel{\triangleright\!\!\cdot} \cdots \mathrel{\triangleright\!\!\cdot} G_r = E$ of length $r - 1$. If $G_1 = H_1$, then, by the induction hypothesis, the normal series $H_1 \triangleright \cdots \triangleright H_s = E$ is of length at most $r - 1$. Thus, in this case, $s - 1 \leq r - 1$, and hence $s \leq r$. If H_1 is properly contained in G_1, then, since $H_1 \triangleleft G$, $G_1 \triangleright H_1 \triangleright \cdots \triangleright H_s = E$ is a proper normal series for G_1, of length s. By the induction hypothesis, $s \leq r - 1$, hence certainly $s < r$. If H_1 is not contained in G_1, then $G_1H_1 \neq G_1$. But then, since G_1 is a maximal normal M-subgroup of G, $G_1H_1 = G$. Since $G_1H_1/H_1 \cong G_1/G_1 \cap H_1$ and $G_1H_1/G_1 \cong H_1/G_1 \cap H_1$, we have

$$G = G_1H_1 \mathrel{\dot{\triangleright}} G_1 \underset{\neq}{\triangleright} G_1 \cap H_1,$$

$$G = G_1H_1 \underset{\neq}{\triangleright} H_1 \mathrel{\dot{\triangleright}} G_1 \cap H_1.$$

By the induction hypothesis, every proper normal series for G_1 has length at most $r - 1$. Hence every proper normal series for $G_1 \cap H_1$ has length at most $r - 2$. By Lemma 1, $G_1 \cap H_1$ has a composition series of length at most $r - 2$. But then the chain $H_1 \mathrel{\dot{\triangleright}} G_1 \cap H_1$ can be completed to a composition series for H_1, of length at most $r - 1$. By the induction hypothesis, applied to H_1, the normal series $H_1 \triangleright \cdots \triangleright H_s = E$ has length at most $r - 1$. But then $s - 1 \leq r - 1$, and hence $s \leq r$, as required. ∎

Lemma 3. *If an M-group G has a composition series γ of length r, then*

a. *Every composition series has length r.*

b. *Every proper normal series of G can be refined to a composition series.*

PROOF.

a. If γ' is another composition series, of length r', then, by Lemma 2, we have $r' \leq r$ and also $r \leq r'$, so that $r' = r$.

b. Since the length of a normal series cannot exceed r, any proper normal series can be refined to a proper normal series of maximal length not exceeding r. Such a normal series is necessarily a composition series. ∎

Theorem 5.1. (Jordan–Hölder.) *Any two composition series of an M-group G are equivalent.*

PROOF. By Lemma 3, any two composition series for G have the same length. Thus, let

(1) $$G = G_0 \mathrel{\dot{\triangleright}} G_1 \mathrel{\dot{\triangleright}} \cdots \mathrel{\dot{\triangleright}} G_r = E$$

and

(2) $$G = H_0 \mathrel{\dot{\triangleright}} H_1 \mathrel{\dot{\triangleright}} \cdots \mathrel{\dot{\triangleright}} H_r = E$$

be composition series for G. We proceed by induction on r. The theorem certainly holds for $r = 1$. For $r > 1$, we assume the theorem to hold for $r - 1$. If $G_1 = H_1$, then the induction hypothesis, applied to H_1, ensures the equivalence of the series $H_1 = G_1 \trianglerighteq \cdots \trianglerighteq G_r = E$ and $H_1 \trianglerighteq \cdots \trianglerighteq H_r = E$, hence also of (1) and (2). Next, suppose $G_1 \neq H_1$. Since G_1 and H_1 are maximal normal M-subgroups of G, $G_1H_1 = G$. As in the proof of Lemma 2, we have

$$(3) \qquad G_1H_1/G_1 \cong H_1/G_1 \cap H_1 \quad \text{and} \quad G_1H_1/H_1 \cong G_1/G_1 \cap H_1.$$

Hence $G \trianglerighteq G_1 \trianglerighteq G_1 \cap H_1$ and $G \trianglerighteq H_1 \trianglerighteq G_1 \cap H_1$. By Lemma 3, since G_1 and H_1 have composition series of length $r - 1$, the normal series $G_1 \trianglerighteq G_1 \cap H_1 \trianglerighteq E$ and $H_1 \trianglerighteq G_1 \cap H_1 \trianglerighteq E$ can be refined to composition series

$$(4) \qquad G_1 \trianglerighteq G_1 \cap H_1 \trianglerighteq S_3 \trianglerighteq \cdots \trianglerighteq S_r = E$$

and

$$(5) \qquad H_1 \trianglerighteq G_1 \cap H_1 \trianglerighteq S_3 \trianglerighteq \cdots \trianglerighteq S_r = E,$$

both of length $r - 1$. By the induction hypothesis, (4) and (5) are, respectively, equivalent to the composition series

$$G_1 \trianglerighteq G_2 \trianglerighteq \cdots \trianglerighteq G_r = E$$

and

$$H_1 \trianglerighteq H_2 \trianglerighteq \cdots \trianglerighteq H_r = E.$$

But then the composition series

$$(6) \qquad G \trianglerighteq G_1 \trianglerighteq G_1 \cap H_1 \trianglerighteq S_3 \trianglerighteq \cdots \trianglerighteq S_r = E$$

and

$$(7) \qquad G \trianglerighteq H_1 \trianglerighteq G_1 \cap H_1 \trianglerighteq S_3 \trianglerighteq \cdots \trianglerighteq S_r = E$$

are, respectively, equivalent to (1) and (2). Because of the isomorphisms (3), the composition series (6) and (7) are equivalent to each other. It follows that the two given series (1) and (2) are equivalent. ▌

Theorem 5.2. *An M-group G has a composition series if and only if*

a. *every descending normal chain for G terminates, and*
b. *if H is a term in a normal series for G, then every ascending chain of normal M-subgroups of H terminates.*

PROOF. Suppose G has a composition series of length r.

a. For each positive integer k, the first k terms of a descending normal chain, together with E, form a normal series for G. Hence, by Lemma 2, a descending normal chain cannot contain more than r distinct terms. But then it terminates.

b. If H is a term in a normal series, then for each positive integer k, the first k terms of an ascending chain of normal subgroups of H form part of a normal series for G. Hence such a chain contains no more than r terms. But then it terminates.

Next, suppose that a and b hold. Then every M-subgroup $H \neq E$ which is a term in a normal series for G has a proper maximal normal M-subgroup. For, otherwise, we can construct an infinite ascending chain of normal M-subgroups of H, in contradiction to b. But then, by choosing G_{i+1} maximal normal in G_i for each $i = 0, 1, 2, \ldots$, we can construct a descending normal chain

$$G = G_0 \triangleright G_1 \triangleright \cdots$$

which must terminate, by a. Clearly, it terminates in E and, by construction, is a composition series for G. ∎

Corollary. *An Abelian M-group has a composition series if and only if it satisfies the ascending and descending chain conditions on M-subgroups.* □

Note that an abelian group (with $M = \varnothing$) has a composition series if and only if it is finite (Exercise 5.3).

Definition 5.2. If an M-group G has a composition series of length r, we say that r is the *length*, $l(G)$, of the M-group G. The length, $l(E)$, of E is 0. ///

Theorem 5.3. *If G is an M-group of length r, H a normal M-subgroup of G, then H and G/H both have composition series, and*

$$l(G) = l(H) + l(G/H).$$

PROOF. By Lemma 3, the normal series $G \triangleright H \triangleright E$ can be refined to a composition series for G from which a composition series for H can be extracted. If

$$G \triangleright G_1 \triangleright \cdots \triangleright G_s = H \triangleright H_1 \triangleright \cdots \triangleright H_t = E$$

is a composition series for G which passes through H, then, by the First Isomorphism Theorem, with ν the natural epimorphism of G onto G/H,

$$G/H = \nu G \triangleright \nu G_1 \triangleright \cdots \triangleright \nu G_s = \nu H = E$$

is a composition series for G/H. Since $l(H) = t$ and $l(G/H) = s$, we have

$$l(G) = l(H) + l(G/H),$$

as required. ▮

Corollary. *Let G be an M-group, and let H and K be normal M-subgroups of G. If G has a composition series, then*

$$l(KH) = l(K) + l(H) - l(K \cap H). \tag{1}$$

PROOF. Since both H and K are normal in G, KH is normal in G, hence has a composition series. By the Second Isomorphism Theorem, KH/K is isomorphic to $H/K \cap H$, hence $l(KH/K) = l(H/K \cap H)$. But then $l(KH) - l(K) = l(H) - l(K \cap H)$, and (1) follows immediately. ▮

6. Solvable Groups

In this section we let $M = \varnothing$. We make repeated use of the fact that, if $H \triangleleft G$, then G/H is abelian if and only if $a^{-1}b^{-1}ab \in H$ for each $a,b \in G$ (see Theorem 4.6).

Definition 6.1. A group G is *solvable* if it has a normal series all of whose factors are abelian. We shall refer to such a normal series as a *solvable series* for G. ///

The concept of a solvable group plays a key role in Galois Theory. The theorem of Galois–Abel that the generic equation of degree $n > 4$ is not solvable by radicals (Chapter 5) is based on the unsolvability of the symmetric group S_n for $n > 4$ (Theorem 6.4). In 1962, Thompson and Feit proved that every finite group of odd order is solvable. Their result yields a classification of all simple groups of odd order.

For a finite group $G \neq E$, solvability is equivalent to the requirement that all of the composition factors of G be cyclic of prime order. This follows from

Theorem 6.1. *A solvable group has a composition series if and only if it is finite and its composition factors are cyclic of prime order.*

Proof. Let G be a solvable group which has a composition series. Then $G \neq E$, and G has a solvable proper normal series

$$G = G_0 \triangleright G_1 \triangleright \cdots \triangleright G_n.$$

By Lemma 3 (p. 56), this normal series can be refined to a composition series, i.e., for each $i = 0, \ldots, n-1$, there are subgroups H_{ij} $(j = 0, \ldots, k_i, k_i \geq 1)$ such that

$$G_i = H_{i0} \mathrel{\dot{\triangleright}} H_{i1} \mathrel{\dot{\triangleright}} \cdots \mathrel{\dot{\triangleright}} H_{ik_i} = G_{i+1}.$$

Since G_i/G_{i+1} is Abelian, $a^{-1}b^{-1}ab \in G_{i+1}$ for each $a,b \in G_i$. In particular, for each $a,b \in H_{ij}$ $(j = 0, \ldots, k_i - 1)$, $a^{-1}b^{-1}ab \in G_{i+1} \subset H_{ij+1}$. But then H_{ij}/H_{ij+1} is abelian. Since H_{ij}/H_{ij+1} is simple, it is cyclic of prime order (Corollary 2, Theorem 4.4). The group G is finite since its order is the product of the orders of its composition factors.

The converse is obvious. ▮

Corollary. *A finite group $G \neq E$ is solvable if and only if its composition factors are cyclic of prime order.* □

Theorem 6.2. *Every subgroup, and every homomorphic image, of a solvable group G is solvable.*

Proof. If $G = E$, there is nothing to prove. Let $G \neq E$ be a solvable group, and let

$$G = G_0 \triangleright G_1 \triangleright \cdots \triangleright G_t = E$$

be a solvable series for G. If H is a subgroup of G, then $G_{i+1} \cap H$ is clearly a normal subgroup of $G_i \cap H$, for each $i = 1, \ldots, t-1$; hence

$$H = (G_0 \cap H) \triangleright (G_1 \cap H) \triangleright \cdots \triangleright (G_t \cap H) = E$$

is a normal series for H. For, $G_{i+1} \cap H$ is clearly a normal subgroup of $G_i \cap H$ since G_{i+1} is normal in G_i. Since G_i/G_{i+1} is abelian, $a^{-1}b^{-1}ab \in G_{i+1}$ for each $a,b \in G_i$. But, then, for each $a,b \in G_i \cap H$, $a^{-1}b^{-1}ab \in G_{i+1} \cap H$, and hence $(G_i \cap H)/(G_{i+1} \cap H)$ is abelian (Theorem 4.6b). Thus, H is solvable.

If α is an epimorphism of G onto G', and $G = G_0 \triangleright G_1 \triangleright \cdots \triangleright G_t = E$ is a solvable series for G, then, by Theorem 4.10b, $G' = G'_0 \triangleright G'_1 \triangleright \cdots \triangleright G'_t = E$, where $G'_i = \alpha(G_i)$ for each $i = 0, \ldots, t$ is a normal series for G'. Since, by Theorem 4.10c, G'_i/G'_{i+1} is a homomorphic image of the abelian group G_i/G_{i+1} for each i, G' is solvable. ∎

Theorem 6.3. *If H is normal in G, and H and G/H are solvable, then G is solvable.*

PROOF. Let ν be the natural epimorphism of G onto G/H, and write $G' = G/H$. Suppose $G' = G'_0 \triangleright G'_1 \triangleright \cdots \triangleright G'_r = E$ is a solvable normal series for G', and let $G_i = \overset{-1}{\nu}(G'_i)$ for each $i = 0, \ldots, r$. By Theorem 4.10b and c, $G_{i+1} \triangleright G_i$ for each i, and G_i/G_{i+1} is isomorphic to G'_i/G'_{i+1}, hence abelian. Since $G_r = \overset{-1}{\nu}(E) = H$ and H has a solvable normal series $H = H_0 \triangleright H_1 \triangleright \cdots \triangleright H_s = E$, the series $G = G_0 \triangleright G_1 \triangleright \cdots \triangleright G_r \triangleright H_1 \triangleright \cdots \triangleright H_s = E$ is a solvable normal series for G. ∎

Theorem 6.4. *For $n > 4$, the symmetric group S_n of order n is not solvable.*

PROOF. We first prove that if H is a subgroup of S_n which contains every 3-cycle and if $K \triangleleft H$ such that H/K is abelian, then K also contains every 3-cycle.

Let ν be the natural epimorphism of H onto H/K and let a, b, c, d, e be distinct natural numbers. Then, by hypothesis, $x = (abc)$ and $y = (cde)$ belong to H. Since H/K is abelian, $x^{-1}y^{-1}xy \in K$. But $x^{-1}y^{-1}xy = (cba)(edc)(abc)(cde) = (cbe)$. Since c, b, e were three arbitrary natural numbers, it follows that every 3-cycle belongs to K.

Now, if $S_n = H_0 \triangleright H_1 \triangleright \cdots \triangleright H_t = E$ were a solvable series for S_n, then each of the subgroups H_i, including $H_t = E$, would contain every 3-cycle, and this is clearly impossible. ∎

7. Conjugates; Centralizers; Normalizers

Definition 7.1. Let G be a group, x an element of G. For any subset S of G, the set $x^{-1}Sx$ is called the *conjugate of S via x*. For a single element $s \in G$, the element $x^{-1}sx$ is called the *conjugate of s via x*. If K is any subgroup of G, then conjugates via elements of K will sometimes be referred to as *K-conjugates*. For any subset S of G, the set

$$N_G(S) = \{x \in G | x^{-1}Sx = S\} = \{x \in G | Sx = xS\}$$

is the *normalizer of S in G*, and the set

$$C_G(S) = \begin{cases} \{x \in G | x^{-1}sx = s \text{ for all } s \in S\}, \\ \{x \in G | xs = sx \text{ for all } s \in S\} \end{cases}$$

is the *centralizer of S in G*. [If no confusion is likely, we write simply $N(S)$ and $C(S)$. If S consists of a single element s, its normalizer and centralizer coincide and we write either $C_G(s)$ or $N_G(s)$.] ///

REMARKS. For any subset S of G, both $C(S)$ and $N(S)$ are subgroups of G, and $C(S) \subset N(S)$. The centralizer of G is the center of G. If S is a subgroup of G, then $S \lhd N(S)$; and $S \lhd G$ if and only if $N(S) = G$. An element of G belongs to the center of G if and only if its centralizer is equal to G.

Theorem 7.1. *Let G be a group, K a subgroup of G. Then*

a. *The binary relation $\sim$ defined on G by $a \sim b$ if a is a K-conjugate of b is an equivalence relation on G.*
b. *The binary relation $\sim$ defined on the power set of G by $A \sim B$ if A is a K-conjugate of B is an equivalence relation on the power set of G.* □

We leave the proof as an exercise (Exercise 7.1).

***Definition* 7.2.** The equivalence classes relative to the relation $\sim$ are *classes of K-conjugate elements* or, simply, *conjugate classes* in case $K = G$.

The equivalence classes relative to the relation $\sim$ are *classes of K-conjugate subsets*, or simply *classes of conjugate subsets* in case $K = G$. ///

Any conjugate of a subgroup is a subgroup.

It is clear that the class of subgroups conjugate to a normal subgroup H contains H as its only element, and the class of elements conjugate to a central element c has c as its only element. More generally, we have

Theorem 7.2. *If G is a group, K a subgroup of G, then the cardinality of the class of subsets of G which are K-conjugate to a subset S of G is equal to* $[K: K \cap N_G(S)]$.

PROOF. If $x,y \in K$, then $x^{-1}Sx = y^{-1}Sy$ if and only if $Sxy^{-1} = xy^{-1}S$, i.e., if and only if $xy^{-1} \in K \cap N_G(S)$. Thus, $x^{-1}Sx = y^{-1}Sy$ if and only if the right cosets $[K \cap N_G(S)]x$ and $[K \cap N_G(S)]y$ are equal. It follows that the correspondence $x^{-1}Sx \mapsto [K \cap N_G(S)]x$ is a one-to-one mapping of the class of subsets K-conjugate to S onto the set of all right cosets of $K \cap N_G(S)$ in K. ∎

Corollary 1. *If S is a subset of G, then the cardinality of the class of subsets of G conjugate to S in G is $[G: N(S)]$.* □

Corollary 2. *If s is an element of a group G, then the cardinality of the conjugate class of s is $[G: N(s)] = [G: C(s)]$.* □

Corollary 3. *If G is a finite group, K a subgroup of G, then the cardinality of any class of K-conjugate subsets of G is a divisor of $|G|$. The cardinality of any class of K-conjugate elements of G is a divisor of $|G|$.* □

Corollary 4. *Let G be a group, A a complete set of representatives of the conjugate classes of G. Then*

$$|G| = \sum_{a \in A - C(G)} [G: C(a)] + |C(G)|.$$

PROOF. G is the union of disjoint conjugate classes. There are $|C(G)|$ conjugate classes belonging to central elements. ∎

8. Sylow Theorems; p-Groups

In Section 2 we saw (Exercise 2.8) that if G is a cyclic group of order n, then, for each divisor d of n, G has a unique subgroup of order d. The corresponding assertion for an arbitrary finite group G of order n is false: Given that $d|n$, we cannot guarantee that G has a subgroup of order d, nor can we guarantee uniqueness in case such a subgroup exists. For example, A_5 (of order 60) has no subgroup of order 30, but has 15 subgroups of order 2. We shall prove in this section that, for each prime power divisor p^m of $|G|$, G has a subgroup of order p^m (First Sylow Theorem). In particular, we shall examine subgroups of maximal prime-power order (Sylow subgroups) and study some of the properties of groups of prime-power order.

Lemma. *If G is an abelian group of finite order n, and p is a prime divisor of n, then G has an element of order p.*

PROOF. We proceed by induction on n. The theorem holds vacuously for $n = 1$. Suppose that, for $n > 1$, the theorem holds for all groups of order less than n. Let p be a prime divisor of n. If $p = n$, then G is cyclic of order p, hence has a generator of order p. If $p \neq n$, then n is composite; hence G has a proper subgroup H (Exercise 2.12). Let $|H| = m$, $1 < m < n$. If $p|m$, then, by the induction hypothesis, H has an element of order p, and so does G. If $p \nmid m$, then $p|(n/m)$. Since G is abelian, H is normal in G. Since $n/m < n$, the factor group G/H contains an element x' of order p. Let x be an element of G such that $\nu(x) = x'$, ν the natural epimorphism of G onto G/H, and let r be the order of x. Since $x^r = e$, $\nu(x^r) = (\nu x)^r = (x')^r = e' = (x')^p$. Thus, $p|r$. But then the cyclic subgroup of G, generated by x contains an element of order p, and so does G. ▌

Theorem 8.1. (First Sylow Theorem.) *If G is a group of order n, p a prime, and m a positive integer such that $p^m|n$, then G has a subgroup of order p^m.*

PROOF. We proceed by induction on n. The theorem holds vacuously for $n = 1$. For $n > 1$, suppose the theorem holds for all groups of order $k < n$.

CASE 1. G has a subgroup $H \neq G$ such that $p \nmid [G: H]$. Then $p^m|\ |H|$ and, by the induction hypothesis, H has a subgroup of order p^m.

CASE 2. For all subgroups $H \neq G$ of G, $p|[G: H]$. Since

$$|G| = \sum_{a \in A - C(G)} [G: C(a)] + |C|,$$

where $C = C(G)$ and A is a complete set of representatives of the conjugate classes of G, it follows that $p|\ |C|$. But C is abelian, hence, by the lemma, C has an element x of order p. Let $K = [x]$. Since $K \subset C$, $K \lhd G$. By Theorem 2.6, $p^{m-1}|\ |G/K|$. But then G/K has a subgroup S' of order p^{m-1}. (This is obviously the case if $m = 1$, and follows from the induction hypothesis if $m > 1$.) By the First Isomorphism Theorem (Theorem 4.10) $S' = S/K$ for some subgroup S of G. By Theorem 2.6, $|S| = p \cdot p^{m-1} = p^m$. ▌

Corollary. *If $p|\ |G|$, p prime, then G has an element of order p.* □

Definition 8.1. If G is a group, p a prime such that the order of every element of G is a power of p, then G is a *p-primary group* or, simply, a *p-group*. A group which is p-primary for some prime p is a *primary* group. If a subgroup of a group is a p-group, we refer to it as a *p-subgroup*. ///

Corollary. *If G is a finite group, p a prime, then G is p-primary if and only if $|G|$ is a power of p.*

PROOF. If G is a power of p, then G is p-primary, by Theorem 2.6. Conversely, suppose G is p-primary. If q is a prime different from p, and $q|\ |G|$, then by the corollary of Theorem 8.1, G has an element of order q. Contradiction! Thus, $|G|$ is a power of p. ▮

NOTE: A primary group need, by no means, be finite. For example, for any prime p, the multiplicative group of all complex p^kth roots of unity, $k = 0, 1, 2, \ldots$, is a p-primary group of infinite order.

Definition 8.2. If G is a finite group, p a prime, and m the largest non-negative integer such that $p^m|\ |G|$, then any subgroup of G of order p^m is a *Sylow p-subgroup* of G. ///

Clearly, every Sylow p-subgroup is p-primary. By Theorem 8.1, every finite group has a Sylow p-subgroup for each prime p. (If $p \nmid |G|$, then E is the only Sylow p-subgroup of G.)

To prove the other "Sylow Theorems", we need first

Theorem 8.2. *Let G be a finite group, p a prime such that $p|\ |G|$. If S is a Sylow p-subgroup, and P is any p-subgroup of G, then $P \cap N(S) = P \cap S$.*

PROOF. Since $S \subset N(S)$, $P \cap S \subset P \cap N(S)$. Let $P_1 = P \cap N(S)$. Then P_1 is a subgroup of $N(S)$ and S is a normal subgroup of $N(S)$. By the Second Isomorphism Theorem (Theorem 4.11), P_1S/S is isomorphic to $P_1/P_1 \cap S$, whence $|P_1S| = (|P_1|/|P_1 \cap S|)|S|$. Since P_1, S, and $P_1 \cap S$ are p-subgroups, P_1S is a p-subgroup containing S. But S is a p-subgroup of maximal order. Hence $P_1S = S$, and $P \cap N(S) = P_1 = P_1 \cap S \subset P \cap S$. It follows that $P \cap N(S) = P \cap S$. ▮

Theorem 8.3. *Let G be a finite group, S a Sylow p-subgroup of G. Then*

a. *Every p-subgroup of G is contained in a conjugate of S.*
b. *All Sylow p-subgroups are conjugate.*
c. *There are exactly* $[G: N(S)]$ *distinct Sylow p-subgroups of G.*
d. $[G: N(S)] \equiv 1 \bmod p$.

(Statements b and d are known, respectively, as Sylow's second and third theorem.)

PROOF.

a. Let $\mathscr{C}$ be the class of all subgroups of G which are G-conjugate to S. By Theorem 7.2, the number of subgroups belonging to $\mathscr{C}$ is $[G: N(S)]$. If P is an arbitrary p-primary subgroup, then $\mathscr{C}$ can be partitioned into classes $\mathscr{C}_i$ of P-conjugate subgroups: $\mathscr{C} = \mathscr{C}_1 \cup \cdots \cup \mathscr{C}_k$, $k \leq [G: N(S)]$. If $S_i \in \mathscr{C}_i$, $i = 1, \ldots, k$, then, by Theorems 7.2 and 8.2, the number of subgroups in $\mathscr{C}_i$ is $[P: P \cap N(S_i)] = [P: P \cap S_i]$. Hence

$$(*) \qquad [G: N(S)] = \sum_{i=1}^{k} [P: P \cap S_i].$$

Since P is a p-group, every term on the right is a power of p, possibly p^0. Since $S \subset N(S)$ and $p \nmid [G: S]$, it follows that $p \nmid [G: N(S)]$. But then, by (*), there is some i ($i = 1, \ldots, k$) such that $[P: P \cap S_i] = 1$, so that $P = P \cap S_i$, and $P \subset S_i$.

b. If S' is another Sylow p-subgroup of G, then, by a, S' is contained in, hence equal to, one of the conjugates of S. Thus, any two Sylow p-subgroups are conjugate.

c. Since every conjugate of a Sylow p-subgroup is a Sylow p-subgroup it follows from b that the class of all conjugates of S is the set of all Sylow p-subgroups. Hence the number of Sylow p-subgroups is $[G: N(S)]$.

d. In (*), we can choose the S_i so that exactly one of them, say S_1, is equal to S. Then, for $P = S$, we have

$$[G: N(S)] = \sum_{i=1}^{k} [S: S \cap S_i] = 1 + \sum_{i=2}^{k} [S: S \cap S_i].$$

Since $[S: S \cap S_i] = 1$ if and only if $S = S_i$, $[G: N(S)] \equiv 1 \bmod p$. ▌

Corollary. *If S is a Sylow p-subgroup of G, then $S \lhd G$ if and only if S is the only Sylow p-subgroup of G.* □

We close this section by proving several theorems concerned with elementary properties of p-groups.

Theorem 8.4. *If G is a finite p-group, $G \neq E$, then $C(G) \neq E$.*

PROOF. By Theorem 7.2, Corollary 3, $|G| - \sum_{a \in A - C(G)} [G: C(a)] = |C(G)|$, A a complete set of representatives of the conjugate classes of G. Each term on the left side in this equation is divisible by p, whence $p \mid |C(G)|$ and $C(G) \neq E$. ▌

Theorem 8.5. *If G is a p-group of finite order n and H is a subgroup of G, $H \neq G$, then $N_G(H) \neq H$.*

PROOF. We proceed by induction on n. The theorem is vacuously true if $n = 1$. For $n > 1$, assume that the theorem is true for all p-groups of order less than n.

If $C(G) \not\subset H$, then there exists $z \in C(G)$, $z \notin H$. But then $z \in N(H)$ and $z \notin H$, hence $N(H) \neq H$. Suppose next that $C(G) \subset H$. Let $\nu: G \to G/C(G)$ be the natural epimorphism of G to $G/C(G)$. Since $H \neq G$ and $H \supset \operatorname{Ker} \nu$, we have, by Theorem 4.10a, that $\nu H \neq \nu G$. The reader may verify that $\nu(N_G(H)) = N_{\nu G}(\nu H)$. By Theorem 8.4, $|\nu G| < n$; hence, by our induction assumption, $N_{\nu G}(\nu H) \neq \nu H$. Thus $\nu(N_G(H)) \neq \nu H$ and, again by Theorem 4.10a, $N_G(H) \neq H$. Therefore the theorem is true for G. ▮

Theorem 8.6. *Let p be a prime, and let G be a group of order p^n $(n > 0)$. If H is a subgroup of G, of order p^r $(0 \leq r < n)$, then G has a composition series*

$$E = G_0 \lhd \cdots \lhd G_r = H \lhd \cdots \lhd G_n = G,$$

with $[G_{i+1}: G_i] = p$ for each $i = 0, \ldots, n - 1$.

PROOF. We prove first that, for every subgroup L of G, $L \neq G$, there is a subgroup K of G such that $L \lhd K$ and $[K: L] = p$. We know that $L \lhd N_G(L)$ and, by Theorem 8.5, $N_G(L) \neq L$. Since $N_G(L)/L$ is a p-group, its order is divisible by p. By Theorem 8.1, $N_G(L)/L$ has a subgroup, $\bar{K}$, of order p. By Theorem 4.10, there is a subgroup K of $N_G(L)$ such that $L \lhd K$ and $\bar{K} = K/L$. But then $[K: L] = p$, and K is the required subgroup.

Now, starting with E, we first construct a sequence (G_i) of subgroups of H such that each subgroup G_i is normal, of index p, in its successor. Obviously, this sequence terminates with $G_r = H$, of order p^r. In the same way, we can now construct another sequence (G_j) of subgroups of G, starting with $H = G_r$, with each G_j normal, of index p, in its successor, terminating with $G_n = G$, of order p^n. But then

$$E = G_0 \lhd \cdots \lhd G_r = H \lhd \cdots \lhd G_n = E$$

is the required composition series. ▮

Corollary. *Every finite p-group is solvable.* □

9. Products; Coproducts; Direct Sums

In this section we examine several ways of "pasting together" the groups of a given family of M-groups so as to obtain a new M-group. Different "pastings" yield different groups: the "product," "coproduct," and "direct sum" of a family of M-groups. Our definitions of the latter groups are in terms of universal mapping properties (see the discussion in Section 4). The manner in which the "pasting" is accomplished becomes evident in the proofs of the existence of these groups (Theorems 9.2 and 9.4).

For practice, we consider first the case of two groups. Let G_1, G_2 be M-groups, $G = G_1 \times G_2$. On G, we define a binary operation $\cdot$ by $(a,b) \cdot (c,d) = (ac,bd)$, for each $(a,b),(c,d) \in G$. For each $m \in M$, $(a,b) \in G$, we let $m(a,b) = (ma,mb)$. Obviously, $\cdot$ is an associative binary operation on G; (e_1,e_2) serves as a two-sided identity for $\cdot$; (a^{-1},b^{-1}) is the inverse of (a,b) relative to (e_1,e_2); and $m(a,b)(c,d) = (mac,mbd) = m(a,b) \cdot m(c,d)$ for each $m \in M$, (a,b), $(c,d) \in G$. We now define "projection maps" $\pi_1: G \to G_1$ and $\pi_2: G \to G_2$ by $\pi_1(a,b) = a$, $\pi_2(a,b) = b$, for each $(a,b) \in G$. Clearly, π_1 and π_2 are M-homomorphisms; they are, in fact, M-epimorphisms. We claim that G and the projection maps π_1 and π_2 satisfy the following condition:

(*) If H is an M-group, $\xi_1: H \to G_1$ and $\xi_2: H \to G_2$ are M-homomorphisms, then there is a unique M-homomorphism $\tau: H \to G$ such that $\pi_1\tau = \xi_1$ and $\pi_2\tau = \xi_2$.

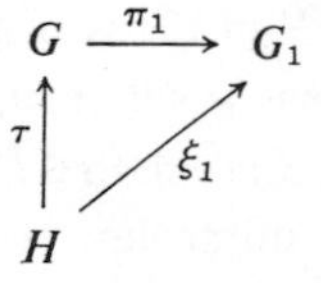

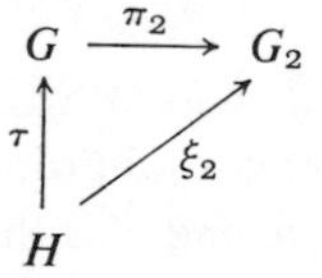

For, let $\tau: H \to G$ be defined as follows: For each $h \in H$, $\tau h = (\xi_1 h, \xi_2 h)$. Clearly, τ is an M-homomorphism. Since, for each $h \in H$, $\pi_1(\tau h) = \xi_1 h$ and $\pi_2(\tau h) = \xi_2 h$, we have $\pi_1\tau = \xi_1$ and $\pi_2\tau = \xi_2$, as required. If $\tau': H \to G$ is another M-homomorphism such that $\pi_1\tau' = \xi_1$, $\pi_2\tau' = \xi_2$, then $\tau' h = (\xi_1 h, \xi_2 h) = \tau h$ for each $h \in H$, and therefore $\tau = \tau'$.

We generalize this property of G and the projections π_1, π_2 in our definition of the "product" of an arbitrary family of groups.

Definition 9.1. Let G be an M-group, $\{G_i\}_{i \in J}$ a family of M-groups, and $\{\pi_i\}_{i \in J}$ a family of M-homomorphisms, $\pi_i: G \to G_i$. Then $\langle G, \{\pi_i\}_{i \in J}\rangle$ is a *product of* $\{G_i\}_{i \in J}$ if for every M-group H and every family $\{\xi_i\}_{i \in J}$ of M-homomorphisms, $\xi_i: H \to G_i$, there exists a unique M-homomorphism

$\tau: H \to G$ such that $\pi_i\tau = \xi_i$ for each $i \in J$; i.e., the following diagram commutes:

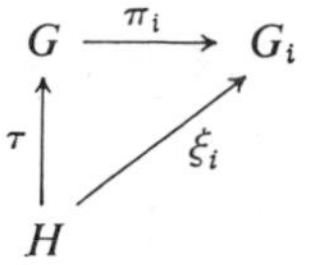

///

In the next theorem we see that an isomorphic image of a product of a family of M-groups is a product, and that a product, if it exists, is (in some precise sense) unique.

Theorem 9.1. *Let G and G' be M-groups, $\{G_i\}_{i\in J}$ a family of M-groups, $\{\pi_i\}_{i\in J}$ a family of M-homomorphisms, $\pi_i: G \to G_i$, and $\{\pi_i'\}_{i\in J}$ a family of M-homomorphisms, $\pi_i': G' \to G_i$.*

a. *If $\langle G, \{\pi_i\}_{i\in J}\rangle$ is a product of $\{G_i\}_{i\in J}$ and φ is an M-isomorphism of G' onto G, then $\langle G', \{\pi_i\varphi\}_{i\in J}\rangle$ is a product of $\{G_i\}_{i\in J}$.*
b. *If $\langle G, \{\pi_i\}_{i\in J}\rangle$ and $\langle G', \{\pi_i'\}_{i\in J}\rangle$ are both products of $\{G_i\}_{i\in J}$, then there is a unique M-isomorphism $\tau: G' \to G$ such that $\pi_i\tau = \pi_i'$ for each $i \in J$.*

PROOF.

a. Let $\langle G, \{\pi_i\}_{i\in J}\rangle$ be a product of $\{G_i\}_{i\in J}$, and let φ be an M-isomorphism of G' onto G. Then, for each $i \in J$, $\pi_i\varphi$ is an M-homomorphism of G' into G_i. If H is an M-group and $\{\xi_i\}_{i\in J}$ a family of M-homomorphisms, $\xi_i: H \to G_i$, then there exists a unique M-homomorphism $\tau: H \to G$ such that $\pi_i\tau = \xi_i$ for each $i \in J$. But then $\varphi^{-1}\tau$ is the unique M-homomorphism of H into G' such that $(\pi_i\varphi)(\varphi^{-1}\tau) = \xi_i$ $(i \in J)$, and $\langle G', \{\pi_i\varphi\}_{i\in J}\rangle$ is a product of $\{G_i\}_{i\in J}$.

b. Let $\langle G, \{\pi_i\}_{i\in J}\rangle$ and $\langle G', \{\pi_i'\}_{i\in J}\rangle$ be products of $\{G_i\}_{i\in J}$. By Definition 9.1 there is a unique M-homomorphism $\tau: G' \to G$ such that $\pi_i\tau = \pi_i'$ for each $i \in J$, and there is a unique M-homomorphism $\tau': G \to G'$ such that $\pi_i'\tau' = \pi_i$ for each $i \in J$. Then $\tau\tau'$ is an M-homomorphism of G into G, and $\pi_i\tau\tau' = \pi_i'\tau' = \pi_i$ for each $i \in J$. But then, by the uniqueness requirement of Definition 9.1, $\tau\tau' = \iota_G$, the identity map on G. By an analogous argument, $\tau'\tau = \iota_{G'}$. Hence τ is an M-isomorphism of G' onto G—the only M-isomorphism with the required property: $\pi_i\tau = \pi_i'$. The proof may be visualized by a commutative diagram.

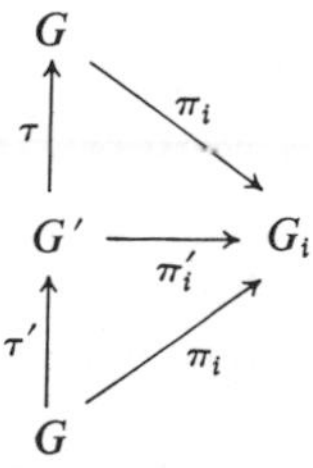

▮

We now consider the problem of the existence of a product of a family of M-groups.

Theorem 9.2. *For every family of M-groups, there exists a product.*

PROOF. Let J be a set, and let $\{G_i\}_{i\in J}$ be a family of M-groups. Consider the set

$$P = \{f \mid f: J \to \bigcup_{i\in J} G_i,\ f(i) \in G_i \text{ for each } i \in J\}.$$

For $f,g \in P$, $m \in M$, let $f \circ g = h$, where $h: J \to \bigcup_{i\in J} G_i$ and $h(i) = f(i)g(i)$ for each $i \in J$, and let $mf = k$, where $k: J \to \bigcup_{i\in J} G_i$ and $k(i) = m(f(i))$ for each $i \in J$. Then P is an M-group with respect to the compositions $\circ$ and $\mu: (m,f) \mapsto mf$.

For each $i \in J$, let $\pi_i: P \to G_i$ be the "projection" defined by $\pi_i(f) = f(i)$. Then π_i is a map of P into G_i. If $f,g \in P$, then $\pi_i(f \circ g) = (f \circ g)(i) = f(i)g(i) = (\pi_i f)(\pi_i g)$. For $m \in M$, $f \in P$, $\pi_i mf = (mf)(i) = m(f(i)) = m\pi_i f$. Thus, for each $i \in J$, π_i is an M-homomorphism of P into G_i. [We note parenthetically that, for each $i \in J$, π_i is an epimorphism. For, if $x \in G_i$, then P contains the mapping $f: J \to \bigcup_{i\in J} G_i$ such that $f(i) = x$ and $f(j) =$ identity of G_j for $j \neq i$. But then $x = \pi_i f$, and π_i is surjective.]

We show that $\langle P,\{\pi_i\}_{i\in J}\rangle$ is a product of $\{G_i\}_{i\in J}$. Let H be an M-group, and $\{\xi_i\}_{i\in J}$ a family of M-homomorphisms, $\xi_i: H \to G_i$. For each $x \in H$, let $\tau x = f$, where $f: J \to \bigcup_{i\in J} G_i$ and $\pi_i f = \xi_i x$ for each $i \in J$. Since, for each $x \in H$, there is exactly one such function f, $\tau: x \mapsto \tau x$ is a map of H into P. Since $\pi_i \tau x = \xi_i x$ for each $x \in H$, $i \in J$, $\pi_i \tau = \xi_i$ for each $i \in J$. For $x,y \in H$, let $\tau x = f$ and let $\tau y = g$. Then $\pi_i f = \xi_i x$ and $\pi_i g = \xi_i y$ for each $i \in J$. Hence $\pi_i(f \circ g) = \pi_i f \pi_i g = \xi_i x \xi_i y = \xi_i(xy)$. But then $\tau(xy) = f \circ g = \tau x \circ \tau y$, and τ is a homomorphism. If $m \in M$ and $x \in H$, let $\tau x = f$. Then $\pi_i f = \xi_i x$ for each $i \in J$; hence $\pi_i(mf) = m(\pi_i f) = m(\xi_i x) = \xi_i(mx)$ for each $i \in J$. But then $\tau(mx) = m\tau x$, and τ is an M-homomorphism. Suppose τ' is another M-homomorphism of H into P such that $\pi_i \tau' = \xi_i$ for each $i \in J$. If $x \in H$ and $\tau' x = f$, then $\pi_i f = \xi_i x$; hence $\tau x = f$. But then $\tau = \tau'$. Thus, τ is the only M-homomorphism such that $\pi_i \tau = \xi_i$. We conclude that $\langle P,\{\pi_i\}_{i\in J}\rangle$ is a product of $\{G_i\}_{i\in J}$.

NOTATION. We use $\prod_{i\in J} G_i$ to denote either the product $\langle P,\{\pi_i\}_{i\in J}\rangle$ or simply the group P.

Example 1. If $\{G_i\}_{i\in \mathbf{N}'}$ is a family of M-groups, and $\mathbf{N}'$ is the set of positive integers, then $\prod_{i\in \mathbf{N}'} G_i$ consists of all sequences s such that, for each $i \in \mathbf{N}'$, the ith component of s is in G_i. If $s = \langle s_1,s_2,\ldots\rangle$ and $t = \langle t_1,t_2,\ldots\rangle$ are sequences in $\prod_{i\in\mathbf{N}'} G_i$, then $s \circ t = \langle s_1t_1, s_2t_2, \ldots \rangle$, $ms = \langle ms_1, ms_2, \ldots \rangle$, and, for each $i \in \mathbf{N}'$, $\pi_i s = s_i$. If H is an M-group and $\{\xi_i\}_{i\in\mathbf{N}'}$ a family of M-homomorphisms $\xi_i\colon H \to G_i$, then the map $\tau\colon H \to \prod_{i\in\mathbf{N}'} G_i$ defined by $\tau(h) = \langle \xi_1(h), \xi_2(h), \ldots \rangle$ is the unique M-homomorphism of H into $\prod_{i\in\mathbf{N}'} G_i$ such that $\pi_i\tau = \xi_i$ for each $i \in \mathbf{N}$.

In general, if an object, for example a product, is defined by means of a universal mapping property "associated" with a commutative diagram D, then a "co-object" can be defined by the universal mapping property associated with the commutative diagram D^*, where D^* is the diagram obtained by reversing all the arrows in D. As an illustration we give

Definition 9.2. Let G be an M-group, $\{G_i\}_{i\in J}$ a family of M-groups, and $\{\eta_i\}_{i\in J}$ a family of M-homomorphisms $\eta_i\colon G_i \to G$. Then $\langle G, \{\eta_i\}_{i\in J} \rangle$ is a *coproduct of* $\{G_i\}_{i\in J}$ if for every M-group H and every family $\{\psi_i\}_{i\in J}$ of M-homomorphisms, $\psi_i\colon G_i \to H$, there exists a unique M-homomorphism $\sigma\colon G \to H$ such that $\sigma\eta_i = \psi_i$ for each $i \in J$; i.e., the following diagram commutes:

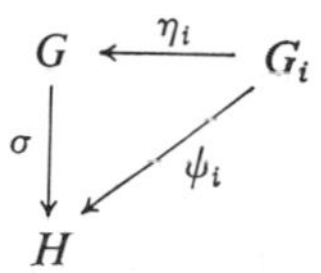

///

One can prove the uniqueness (up to isomorphism) and the existence of a coproduct (denoted by $\coprod_{i\in J} G_i$) for any family of M-groups $\{G_i\}_{i\in J}$. We limit our consideration of coproducts to the following example, the details of which are left to the reader (Exercise 9.2).

***Example* 2.** Let A and B be M-groups. A finite sequence of elements of $A \cup B$ is a *reduced sequence* if (a) it has no subsequence of the form aa' and bb' with $a,a' \in A$, $b,b' \in B$; (b) no term of the sequence, with the possible exceptions of the first or the last, is the identity of A or of B; (c) the sequence has an even number of terms; and (d) the first term of the sequence is an element of A. Let $A * B$ be the set of all reduced sequences, and define a binary operation $\circ$ on $A * B$ as follows: If $v = a_1b_1a_2b_2\cdots a_kb_k$ and $w = a_1'b_1'a_2'b_2'\cdots a_n'b_n'$, $v,w \in A * B$, then $v \circ w$ is the reduced sequence obtained by performing the obvious reductions and deletions (if any) in the sequence $a_1b_1\cdots a_kb_ka_1'b_1'\cdots a_n'b_n'$. For $v = a_1b_1\cdots a_kb_k \in A * B$ and $m \in M$, define mv to be the element in $A * B$ obtained by "reducing" the sequence $(ma_1)(mb_1)\cdots(ma_k)(mb_k)$. Finally, let $\eta_1\colon A \to A * B$ and $\eta_2\colon B \to A * B$ be the maps defined, respectively, by $\eta_1(a) = a1_B$ and $\eta_2(b) = 1_A b$, $a \in A$, $b \in B$. Then $\langle A * B, \{\eta_1, \eta_2\} \rangle$ is a coproduct of $\{A, B\}$.

Note that in the definition of a coproduct, $\langle G, \{\eta_i\}_{i \in J} \rangle$, of a family of M-groups $\{G_i\}_{i \in J}$, no condition is imposed on the images of the G_i in G under the M-homomorphisms $\eta_i: G_i \to G$. If in Definition 9.2 we require that for $i, j \in J$, $i \neq j$, the elements of $\eta_i(G_i)$ commute with the elements of $\eta_j(G_j)$, and state the universal mapping property accordingly, then we have the definition of a "direct sum" of a family of M-groups. Formally:

Definition 9.3. Let G be an M-group, $\{G_i\}_{i \in J}$ a family of M-groups, and $\{\eta_i\}_{i \in J}$ a family of M-homomorphisms $\eta_i: G_i \to G$ such that $\eta_i(x)\eta_j(y) = \eta_j(y)\eta_i(x)$ for $i, j \in J$, $i \neq j$, $x \in G_i$, $y \in G_j$. Then $\langle G, \{\eta_i\}_{i \in J} \rangle$ is a *direct sum of* $\{G_i\}_{i \in J}$ if for every M-group H and every family $\{\psi_i\}_{i \in J}$ of M-homomorphisms $\psi_i: G_i \to H$ such that $\psi_i(x)\psi_j(y) = \psi_j(y)\psi_i(x)$ for $i, j \in J$, $i \neq j$, $x \in G_i$, $y \in G_j$, there exists a unique M-homomorphism $\sigma: G \to H$ such that $\sigma\eta_i = \psi_i$ for each $i \in J$; i.e., the following diagram commutes:

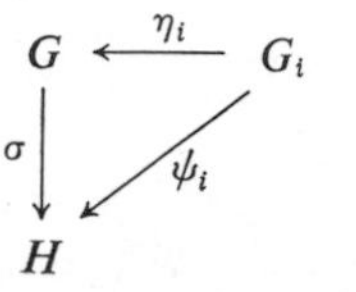

///

The next theorem states that an isomorphic image of a direct sum of a family of M-groups is a direct sum, and that a direct sum, if it exists, is unique up to isomorphism. The proof of this theorem is analogous to the proof of Theorem 9.1 and is left to the reader.

Theorem 9.3. *Let G, G' be M-groups, $\{G_i\}_{i \in J}$ a family of M-groups, $\{\eta_i\}_{i \in J}$ a family of M-homomorphisms, $\eta_i: G_i \to G$, and $\{\eta'_i\}_{i \in J}$ a family of M-homomorphisms, $\eta'_i: G_i \to G'$.*

a. *If $\langle G, \{\eta_i\}_{i \in J} \rangle$ is a direct sum of $\{G_i\}_{i \in J}$ and φ is an M-isomorphism of G onto G', then $\langle G', \{\varphi\eta_i\}_{i \in J} \rangle$ is a direct sum of $\{G_i\}_{i \in J}$.*
b. *If $\langle G, \{\eta_i\}_{i \in J} \rangle$ and $\langle G', \{\eta'_i\}_{i \in J} \rangle$ are both direct sums of $\{G_i\}_{i \in J}$, then there exists a unique M-isomorphism $\sigma: G \to G'$ such that $\sigma\eta_i = \eta'_i$ for each $i \in J$.* □

Theorem 9.4. *For every family of M-groups, there exists a direct sum.*

PROOF. Let $\{G_i\}_{i \in J}$ be a family of M-groups. Consider the set

$$S = \{f \mid f: J \to \bigcup_{i \in J} G_i,\ f(i) \in G_i \text{ for each } i \in J, \text{ and } f(i) = e_i$$
$$(e_i \text{ the identity of } G_i) \text{ for all but finitely many } i \in J\}.$$

For $f,g \in S$, $m \in M$, let $f \circ g = h$, where $h: J \to \bigcup_{i \in J} G_i$ and $h(i) = f(i)g(i)$ for each $i \in J$, and let $mf = k$, where $k: J \to \bigcup_{i \in J} G_i$ and $k(i) = m(f(i))$ for each $i \in J$. Then S is an M-group with respect to the compositions $\circ$ and $\mu: (m,f) \mapsto mf$. (Note that S is an M-subgroup of the M-group P discussed in the proof of Theorem 9.2. If J is a finite set, then $S = P$.)

For each $i \in J$, let $\eta_i: G_i \to S$ be the "injection" defined by $\eta_i(x) = f$, where, for $j \in J$,

$$f(j) = \begin{cases} x & j = i, \\ e_j & j \neq i. \end{cases}$$

We leave it to the reader to show that η_i is an M-homomorphism (actually an M-monomorphism) and that $\eta_i(x)\eta_j(y) = \eta_j(y)\eta_i(x)$ for $i,j \in J$, $i \neq j$, $x \in G_i$, $y \in G_j$.

We show that $\langle S, \{\eta_i\}_{i \in J}\rangle$ is a direct sum of $\{G_i\}_{i \in J}$. Let H be an M-group and $\{\psi_i\}_{i \in J}$ a family of M-homomorphisms $\psi_i: G_i \to H$ such that $\psi_i(x)\psi_j(y) = \psi_j(y)\psi_i(x)$ for $i,j \in J$, $i \neq j$, $x \in G_i$, $y \in G_j$. Define $\sigma: S \to H$ by

$$\sigma f = \prod_{\substack{j \in J \\ f(j) \neq e}} \psi_j f(j).$$

Since $\psi_j f(j) \neq e$ for but finitely many $j \in J$, and the $\psi_j G_j$ commute elementwise, the product on the right is well-defined; hence σ is a map. [From now on, we simply write $\prod_{j \in J} \psi_j f(j)$.]

If $i \in J$ and $x_i \in G_i$, then

$$\sigma\eta_i x_i = \prod_{j \in J} \psi_j[(\eta_i x_i)(j)] = \psi_i x_i.$$

Thus, $\sigma\eta_i = \psi_i$.

If $f,g \in S$, then

$$\begin{aligned} \sigma(f \circ g) &= \prod_{j \in J} \psi_j(f \circ g)(j) = \prod_{j \in J} \psi_j(f(j)g(j)) = \prod_{j \in J} \psi_j(f(j)) \prod_{j \in J} \psi_j(g(j)) \\ &= \sigma f \sigma g. \end{aligned}$$

Thus, σ is a homomorphism.

If $m \in M$, $f \in S$, then

$$\sigma(mf) = \prod_{j \in J} \psi_j mf(j) = \prod_{j \in J} m\psi_j(f(j)) = m \prod_{j \in J} \psi_j(f(j)) = m\sigma f.$$

Thus, σ is an M-homomorphism.

Finally, suppose that σ' is another M-homomorphism of S into H such that $\sigma'\eta_i = \psi_i$ for each $i \in J$. If $f \in S$, then $f = \eta_i x_{i_1} \circ \cdots \circ \eta_{i_n} x_{i_n}$ for some set $\{i_1,\ldots,i_n\} \subset J$, possibly empty, $x_{i_j} \in G_{i_j}$, $x_{i_j} \neq e_{i_j}$, $j = 1,\ldots, n$. But then

$$\sigma' f = \sigma'\eta_{i_1}x_{i_1}\cdots\sigma'\eta_{i_n}x_{i_n} = \psi_{i_1}x_{i_1}\cdots\psi_{i_n}x_{i_n} = \sigma\eta_{i_1}x_{i_1}\cdots\sigma\eta_{i_n}x_{i_n} = \sigma f.$$

Hence $\sigma' = \sigma$. We conclude that $\langle S,\{\eta_i\}_{i\in J}\rangle$ is a direct sum of $\{G_i\}_{i\in J}$. ▌

NOTATION. We use $\coprod'_{i\in J} G_i$ to denote the direct sum $\langle S,\{\eta_i\}_{i\in J}\rangle$ or simply the group S.

Example 3. If $\{G_i\}_{i\in \mathbf{N}'}$ is a family of M-groups, and $\mathbf{N}'$ is the set of positive integers, then $\coprod'_{i\in\mathbf{N}'} G_i$ consists of all sequences s such that, for each $i \in \mathbf{N}'$, the ith component of s is in G_i, and such that only finitely many components of s are different from the corresponding identity. If $s = \langle s_1,s_2,\ldots\rangle$ and $t = \langle t_1,t_2,\ldots\rangle$ are sequences in $\coprod'_{i\in\mathbf{N}'} G_i$, then $s \circ t = \langle s_1t_1,s_2t_2,\ldots\rangle$ and $ma = \langle ms_1,ms_2,\ldots\rangle$. For each $i \in \mathbf{N}'$, $s_i \in G_i$,

$$\eta_i s_i = \langle e_1,e_2,\ldots,e_{i-1},s_i,e_{i+1},e_{i+2},\ldots\rangle.$$

If H and $\{\psi\}_{i\in J}$ are as in the proof of Theorem 9.4, then the map $\sigma\colon \coprod'_{i\in\mathbf{N}'} G_i \to H$ defined by $\sigma\langle s_1,s_2,\ldots\rangle = \prod_{i\in\mathbf{N}'} \psi_i(s_i)$ is the unique M-homomorphism of $\coprod'_{i\in\mathbf{N}'} G_i$ into H such that $\sigma\eta_i = \psi_i$ for each $i \in \mathbf{N}'$.

REMARK. It is evident from our discussions above that $\coprod'_{i\in J} G_i$ is a subgroup of $\prod_{i\in J} G_i$ and that if J is finite, then $\coprod'_{i\in J} G_i = \prod_{i\in J} G_i$.

Definition 9.4. Let G be an M-group, $\{G_i\}_{i\in J}$ a family of M-subgroups of G, and $\varepsilon_i\colon G_i \to G$ the canonical embedding of G_i into G. If $\langle G,\{\varepsilon_i\}_{i\in J}\rangle$ is a direct sum of the family $\{G_i\}_{i\in J}$, then G is an *internal direct sum* of $\{G_i\}_{i\in J}$. (We write $G = \bigoplus_{i\in J} G_i$.) ///

Corollary. *Let $\langle G,\{\eta_i\}_{i\in J}\rangle$ be a direct sum of the family of M-groups $\{G_i\}_{i\in J}$. Then $G = \bigoplus_{i\in J} \eta_i(G_i)$.*

PROOF. Consider the following diagram:

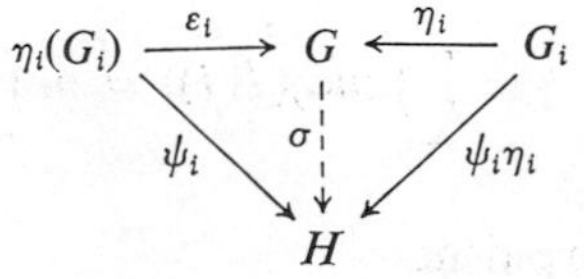

where H is an M-group, $\{\psi_i\}_{i\in J}$ is a family of M-homomorphisms satisfying the necessary commutativity conditions, and, for each $i \in J$, ε_i is the canonical embedding of $\eta_i(G_i)$ into G. Since $\langle G,\{\eta_i\}_{i\in J}\rangle$ is a direct sum of $\{G_i\}_{i\in J}$, there exists a unique M-homomorphism $\sigma: G \to H$ such that, for each $i \in J$, $\psi\,\eta_i = \sigma\eta_i = \sigma\varepsilon_i\eta_i$. Since, for each $x \in G_i$, $\psi_i(\eta_i x) = \sigma\varepsilon_i(\eta_i x)$, $\sigma: G \to H$ is the unique M-homomorphism such that $\psi_i = \sigma\varepsilon_i$. Hence $\langle G,\{\varepsilon_i\}_{i\in J}\rangle$ is a direct sum of the family $\{\eta_i(G_i)\}_{i\in J}$, and $G = \bigoplus_{i\in J} \eta_i(G_i)$. ∎

Theorem 9.5. *Let G be an M-group and let $\{G_i\}_{i\in J}$ be a family of M-subgroups of G. Then the assertions* a, b, *and* c *are equivalent.*

a. $G = \bigoplus_{i\in J} G_i$.

b. (1) $G_i \lhd G$ *for each* $i \in J$.

(2) $[\bigcup_{i\in J} G_i] = G$.

(3) *For each* $k \in J$, $G_k \cap [\bigcup_{i\in J, i\neq k} G_i] = E$.

c. (1) *For* $i,j \in J$, $i \neq j$, $xy = yx$ *for each* $x \in G_i$, $y \in G_j$.

(2) *For each* $x \neq e$ *in G, there is a unique nonempty finite subset* $J_x = \{i_1,\ldots,i_n\}$ *of J, and a unique nonempty finite subset* $P_x = \{x_{i_1},\ldots,x_{i_n}\}$ *of G, where* $x_{i_r} \neq e$, $x_{i_r} \in G_{i_r}$, $r = 1,\ldots, n$, *such that* $x = x_{i_1}\cdots x_{i_n}$.

PROOF. Suppose $G = \bigoplus_{i\in J} G_i$. Then $\langle G,\{\varepsilon_i\}_{i\in J}\rangle$ is a direct sum of the family $\{G_i\}_{i\in J}$. By Theorem 9.3, there exists an M-isomorphism $\sigma: \coprod'_{i\in J} G_i \to G$ such that $\sigma\eta_i = \varepsilon_i$. [Recall that $\eta_i(G_i) = \{f \mid f: J \to \bigcup_{i\in J} G_i,\ f(j) = e_j \text{ for } j \neq i,\ f(i) \in G_i\}$.] The reader may easily verify that $\eta_i(G_i) \lhd \coprod'_{i\in J} G_i$ for each $i \in J$, $[\bigcup_{i\in J} \eta_i(G_i)] = \coprod'_{i\in J} G_i$, and for each $k \in J$, $\eta_k(G_k) \cap [\bigcup_{i\in J, i\neq k} \eta_i(G_i)] = E$. But then $\sigma\eta_i(G_i) = \varepsilon_i(G_i) = G_i \lhd \sigma(\coprod'_{i\in J} G_i) = G$ for each $i \in J$, $[\bigcup_{i\in J} G_i] = G$, and for each $k \in J$, $G_k \cap [\bigcup_{i\in J, i\neq k} G_i] = E$. Hence a $\Rightarrow$ b.

Suppose b holds. Let $i,j \in J$, $i \neq j$, $x \in G_i$, and $y \in G_j$. By b(1),

$$(x^{-1}y^{-1}x)y = x^{-1}(y^{-1}xy) \in G_i \cap G_j.$$

Hence, by b(3), $x^{-1}y^{-1}xy = e$, and $xy = yx$. If $x \neq e$, $x \in G$, the existence of $J_x = \{i_1,\ldots,i_n\}$ and $P_x = \{x_{i_1},\ldots,x_{i_n}\}$ $(x_{i_j} \in G_{i_j},\ x_i \neq e)$ such that $x = x_{i_1}\cdots x_{i_n}$ is a consequence of b(2) and the uniqueness of J_x and P_x is a consequence of b(3). Hence b $\Rightarrow$ c.

Suppose c holds. For each $i \in J$, let $\varepsilon_i: G_i \to G$ be the canonical injection. By (1) of c, the M-homomorphisms ε_i satisfy the condition $\varepsilon_i x \varepsilon_j y = \varepsilon_j y \varepsilon_i x$ for $i \neq j$, $x \in G_i$, $y \in G_j$ $(i,j \in J)$. But then, by Definition 9.3, there is a unique M-homomorphism $\sigma: \coprod' G_i \to G$ such that $\sigma\eta_i = \varepsilon_i$ for each $i \in J$ (where the η_i are the M-homomorphisms associated with $\coprod' G_i$). For each $f \in \coprod'_{i\in J} G_i$, $\sigma f = \sigma \prod_{i\in J} \eta_i f(i) = \prod_{i\in J} \varepsilon_i f(i) = \prod_{i\in J} f(i)$. By (2) of c, σ is an isomorphism. But then, by Theorem 9.3a, $\langle G,\{\varepsilon_i\}\rangle$ is a direct sum of $\{G_i\}_{i\in J}$. Hence $G = \bigoplus_{i\in J} G_i$. ∎

Theorem 9.6. *Let G be an M-group and $\{G_i\}_{i\in J}$ a family of M-groups.*

a. *Suppose that $\{\pi_i\}_{i\in J}$ is a family of M-homomorphisms $\pi_i\colon G \to G_i$. Then $\langle G,\{\pi_i\}_{i\in J}\rangle$ is a product of $\{G_i\}_{i\in J}$ if and only if, for each $i \in J$, there exists an M-homomorphism $\eta_i\colon G_i \to G$ such that*
   (1) $\pi_i\eta_i = \iota_{G_i}$.
   (2) $\pi_i\eta_j = 0_{G_j\to G_i}$ *for $i \neq j$ (where $0_{G_j\to G_i}$ is the M-homomorphism which maps every element of G_j to the identity of G_i).*
   (3) *If $\{x_i\}_{i\in J}$ is a family of elements in $\bigcup_{i\in J} G_i$ ($x_i \in G_i$), then there exists a unique $x \in G$ such that, for each $i \in J$, $\pi_i x = x_i$.*

b. *Suppose that $\{\eta_i\}_{i\in J}$ is a family of M-homomorphisms, $\eta_i\colon G_i \to G$, such that, for $i \neq j$ and for all $x \in G_i$, $y \in G_j$, $\eta_i(x)\eta_j(y) = \eta_j(y)\eta_i(x)$. Then $\langle G,\{\eta_i\}_{i\in J}\rangle$ is a direct sum of $\{G_i\}_{i\in J}$ if and only if, for each $i \in J$, there exists an M-homomorphism $\pi_i\colon G \to G_i$ such that*
   (1) $\pi_i\eta_i = \iota_{G_i}$.
   (2) $\pi_i\eta_j = 0_{G_j\to G_i}$ *for $i \neq j$.*
   (3) *For each $x \in G$, $\pi_i(x) = e_i$ for all but finitely many $i \in J$, and $\prod_{i\in J} \eta_i\pi_i(x) = x$.*

PROOF OF b. Suppose that $\langle G,\{\eta_i\}_{i\in J}\rangle$ is a direct sum of $\{G_i\}_{i\in J}$. For $i,i_0 \in J$ let $\mathcal{O}_{i,i_0}\colon G_i \to G_{i_0}$ be the M-homomorphism defined by

$$\mathcal{O}_{i,i_0} = \begin{cases} \iota_{G_{i_0}} & \text{if } i = i_0, \\ 0_{G_i\to G_{i_0}} & \text{if } i \neq i_0. \end{cases}$$

Since $\langle G,\{\eta_i\}_{i\in J}\rangle$ is a direct sum, there exists an M-homomorphism $\pi_{i_0}\colon G \to G_{i_0}$ such that, for each $i \in J$, the diagram

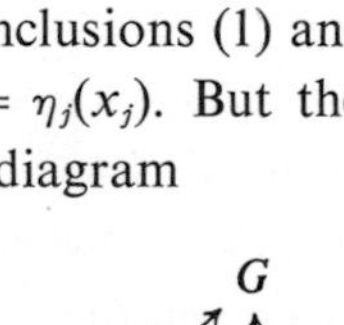

commutes. Note that $\pi_{i_0}\eta_{i_0} = \iota_{G_{i_0}}$ and $\pi_{i_0}\eta_i = 0_{G_i\to G_{i_0}}$ ($i \neq i_0$). But the choice of $i_0 \in J$ is arbitrary; hence conclusions (1) and (2) follow. Using (1) and (2) we see that $\prod_{i\in J} \eta_i\pi_i(\eta_j(x_j)) = \eta_j(x_j)$. But then, since ι_G is the unique M-homomorphism such that the diagram

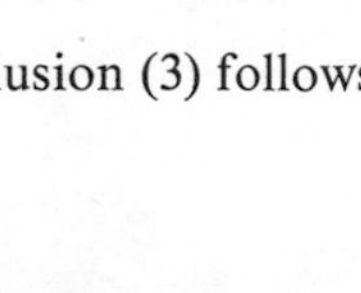

commutes for each $j \in J$, conclusion (3) follows.

Conversely suppose that (1), (2), and (3) are satisfied. If $\{\psi_i\}_{i\in J}$ is a family of M-homomorphisms, $\psi_i: G_i \to H$, of G_i to an M-group H such that, for all $i \neq j$ and for all $x \in G_i$, $y \in G_j$, $\psi_i(x)\psi_j(y) = \psi_j(y)\psi_i(x)$, then we see easily that the M-homomorphism $\tau: G \to H$ defined by $\tau(g) = \prod_{i\in J} \psi_i\pi_i(g)$ is the unique M-homomorphism such that $\tau\eta_i = \psi_i$ for all $i \in J$. Hence, $\langle G, \{\eta_i\}_{i\in J}\rangle$ is a direct sum.

The proof of a is similar. ∎

In the following four theorems, we give several useful properties of direct sums and products. For simplicity, we confine ourselves to the canonical direct sums $\coprod'$ and the canonical products $\prod$.

We first investigate the action of homomorphisms on direct sums and products.

NOTE. If $\{G_i\}_{i\in J}$, $\{H_i\}_{i\in J}$ are families of M-groups such that, for each $i \in J$, H_i is a subgroup of G_i, then the elements of $\prod_{i\in J} G_i$ are maps $f: J \to \bigcup_{i\in J} G_i$ and the elements of $\prod_{i\in J} H_i$ are maps $f: J \to \bigcup_{i\in J} H_i$. We identify each $f: J \to \bigcup G_i$ with its corestriction, $f: J \to \bigcup H_i$, and regard $\prod_{i\in J} H_i$ as a subgroup of $\prod_{i\in J} G_i$. Similarly, we regard $\coprod'_{i\in J} H_i$ as a subgroup of $\coprod_{i\in J} G_i$.

Theorem 9.7. *Let $\{G_i\}_{i\in J}$ and $\{H_i\}_{i\in J}$ be families of M-groups such that, for each $i \in J$, $H_i \lhd G_i$. Then*

a. $\prod_{i\in J} G_i/\prod_{i\in J} H_i \cong \prod_{i\in J} G_i/H_i$.

b. $\coprod'_{i\in J} G_i/\coprod'_{i\in J} H_i \cong \coprod'_{i\in J} G_i/H_i$.

If $G = \bigoplus_{i\in J} G_i$, then $\bigoplus_{i\in J} G_i/\bigoplus_{i\in J} H_i \cong \coprod' G_i/H_i$.

PROOF.

a. For each $i \in J$, let ν_i be the canonical M-epimorphism of G_i onto G_i/H_i, and let $\nu: \prod_{i\in J} G_i \to \prod_{i\in J} G_i/H_i$ be defined by $\nu f = \bar{f}$, where $\bar{f}(i) = \nu_i f(i)$ for each $i \in J$ ($f \in \prod_{i\in J} G_i$). Then ν is obviously an M-homomorphism. Since $f \in \operatorname{Ker} \nu$ if and only if $\nu_i f(i) = e_{G_i/H_i}$ for each $i \in J$, $\operatorname{Ker} \nu = \{f \mid f(i) \in H_i$ for each $i \in J\} = \prod_{i\in J} H_i$. But then, by the Fundamental Theorem of Homomorphism, $\prod_{i\in J} G_i/\prod_{i\in J} H_i$ is M-isomorphic to $\prod_{i\in J} G_i/H_i$.

b. A similar argument yields b. The assertion concerning internal direct sums follows from b. For, let $\varepsilon_i: G_i \to G$ be the canonical injections, $\eta_i: G_i \to \coprod'_{i\in J} G_i$ the M-monomorphisms associated with $\coprod'_{i\in J} G_i$. Then the M-isomorphism $\sigma: \coprod'_{i\in J} G_i \to G$ such that $\sigma\eta_i = \varepsilon_i$, for each $i \in J$, maps $\coprod_{i\in J} H_i$ onto $\bigoplus_{i\in J} H_i$. By the First Isomorphism Theorem, $\bigoplus_{i\in J} G_i/\bigoplus_{i\in J} H_i$ is M-isomorphic to $\coprod'_{i\in J} G_i/\coprod'_{i\in J} H_i$, hence M-isomorphic to $\coprod'_{i\in J} G_i/H_i$, by b. ∎

We leave the proofs of the other three theorems as exercises (Exercises 9.8, 9.9, and 9.10).

Theorem 9.8. *Let $\{J_j\}_{j\in K}$ be a set of pairwise disjoint sets. For each $j \in K$, let $\{G_i\}_{i\in J_j}$ be a family of M-groups. Then*

$$\prod_{j\in K}\Big(\prod_{i\in J_j} G_i\Big) \cong \prod_{\substack{i\in\cup J_j\\ j\in K}} G_i \quad \text{and} \quad \coprod_{j\in K}{}' \coprod_{i\in J_j}{}' G_i \cong \coprod_{\substack{i\in\cup J_j\\ j\in K}}{}' G_i. \qquad \square$$

Theorem 9.9. *Let $\{G_i\}_{i\in J}$ be a family of M-groups, and let σ be a bijection of J onto itself. Then*

$$\prod_{i\in J} G_i \cong \prod_{i\in J} G_{\sigma i} \quad \text{and} \quad \coprod_{i\in J}{}' G_i \cong \coprod_{i\in J} G_{\sigma i}. \qquad \square$$

Theorem 9.10. *If $\{G_i\}_{i\in J}$ is a family of M-groups, and $J' \subset J$, then*

$$\prod_{i\in J} G_i/\prod_{i\in J'} G_i \cong \prod_{i\in J-J'} G_i \quad \text{and} \quad \coprod_{i\in J}{}' G_i/\coprod_{i\in J'}{}' G_i \cong \coprod_{i\in J-J'}{}' G_i. \qquad \square$$

NOTE. In Theorem 9.10 we identify $\prod_{i\in J'} G_i$ ($\coprod'_{i\in J'} G_i$) with its isomorphic image in $\prod_{i\in J} G_i$ ($\coprod'_{i\in J} G_i$).

To illustrate the concept of internal direct sum, we prove the following theorem on abelian groups which will be useful to us later (Section 12).

Theorem 9.11. *Let G be an abelian torsion group* (*see Definition* 2.3), *and let $(p_i)_{i\in \mathbf{N}'}$ be the sequence of all* (*positive integer*) *primes, in increasing order. Then there is a unique sequence $(G_i)_{i\in\mathbf{N}'}$ of subgroups G_i of G such that G_i is p_i-primary for each $i \in \mathbf{N}'$, and $G = \bigoplus_{i\in\mathbf{N}'} G_i$.*

PROOF. For each $i \in \mathbf{N}'$, let G_i be the subgroup consisting of all elements of G whose order is a power of p_i. It is easy to check that each G_i forms a subgroup of G. By definition, each G_i is p_i-primary.

To prove that $G = \bigoplus_{i\in\mathbf{N}'} G_i$, we first show that $G = [\bigcup_{i\in\mathbf{N}'} G_i]$. It is sufficient to prove the following assertion: If $x \in G$ and $|x| = n = p_{i_1}^{k_1}\cdots p_{i_r}^{k_r}$, where the p_{i_j} ($j = 1,\ldots,r$) are distinct primes and the k_i are positive integers, then there are elements x_j ($j = 1,\ldots,r$) such that $x = x_1\cdots x_r$ and $x_j \in G_{i_j}$ for each $j = 1,\ldots, r$. We proceed by induction on r. If $r = 1$, then $x = x_1 \in G_{i_1}$. Suppose the assertion holds for elements whose order is a product of powers of fewer than r distinct primes. Let $n_r = n/p_{i_r}^{k_r}$, and let $q = p_{i_r}^{k_r}$. Since $(q,n_r) = 1$, there are integers s and t such that $1 = sq + tn_r$. Hence

$$x = x^{sq+tn_r} = x^{sq}x^{tn_r}.$$

Since the order of x^{sq} is a divisor of n_r, it is a product of powers of the $r - 1$ primes $p_{i_1}, \ldots, p_{i_{r-1}}$. Hence there are elements $x_1, \ldots, x_{r-1}$, $x_j \in G_{i_j}$, $j = 1, \ldots, r$, such that $x^{sq} = x_1 \cdots x_{r-1}$. Since $|x^{tn_r}|$ is a divisor of $q = p_{i_r}^{k_r}$, we let $x_r = x^{tn_r}$ and have $x = x_1 \cdots x_r$, with $x_j \in G_{i_j}$, $j = 1, \ldots, r$ as required.

It remains to be shown that, for each $j \in \mathbf{N}'$, $G_j \cap [\bigcup_{i \neq j} G_i] = E$. Suppose $x_j \in G_j \cap [\bigcup_{i \neq j} G_i]$. Then $x_j = x_1 \cdots x_r$, where $x_h \in G_{i_h}$, and the i_h are distinct indices different from j. Let t be the product of the orders of $x_1, \ldots, x_r$. Since G is abelian,

$$e = (x_1 \cdots x_r)^t = x_1^t \cdots x_r^t = x_j^t.$$

Since the order of x_j and the integer t are relatively prime, it follows that $x_j = e$.

We have proved that $G = \bigoplus_{i \in \mathbf{N}'} G_i$. Now suppose there is another sequence $(H_i)_{i \in \mathbf{N}'}$ of subgroups of G such that H_i is p_i-primary for each $i \in \mathbf{N}'$, and $G = \bigoplus_{i \in \mathbf{N}'} H_i$. By the definition of G_i, $H_i \subset G_i$ for each $i \in \mathbf{N}'$. If $x_i \in G_i$, $x_i \neq e$, then there are positive integers $i_1, \ldots, i_r$ and elements $h_1, \ldots, h_r$ such that $x_i = h_1 \cdots h_r$, $h_j \in H_{i_j}$, $j = 1, \ldots, r$. Since the order of x_i is a positive power of p_i and also a product of powers of $p_{i_1}, \ldots, p_{i_r}$, $p_{i_t} = p_i$ for some t ($t = 1, \ldots, r$) and $p_{i_j} = 1$ for $j \neq t$. But then $H_{i_t} = H_i$, and $x_i \in H_i$. It follows that $H_i \supset G_i$, and therefore $H_i = G_i$. Thus, the decomposition is unique. ▮

Corollary. *If G is an abelian group of order $|G| = p_1^{k_1} \cdots p_r^{k_r}$, where the p_i are distinct primes, $k_i \in \mathbf{N}'$ $(i = 1, \ldots, r)$, then $G = \bigoplus_{i=1}^r G_i$, where $|G_i| = p_i^{k_i}$ for each $i = 1, \ldots, r$. This decomposition is unique.* □

10. Indecomposable Groups; Krull–Schmidt Theorem

We have just seen that an abelian torsion group "decomposes" into a direct sum of primary groups and that this decomposition is unique. This theorem is a special case of a much more general theorem which we prove in this section; i.e., any decomposition of an M-group as a direct sum of "indecomposable" groups is unique to within isomorphism.

Definition 10.1. An M-group G is *decomposable* if there exist proper M-subgroups, G_1 and G_2, of G such that $G = G_1 \oplus G_2$. An M-group G is *indecomposable* if G is not decomposable, and $G \neq \{e\}$. ///

REMARK. If an M-group G is decomposable (indecomposable), then every M-isomorphic image of G is decomposable (indecomposable).

EXAMPLES.

1. Any infinite cyclic group is indecomposable. For, let g be a generator of an infinite cyclic group G, and suppose that $G = G_1 \oplus G_2$, with G_1, G_2 proper subgroups of G. Then there are nonzero integers k_1, k_2 such that $g^{k_1} \in G_1$, $g^{k_2} \in G_2$. But then $g^{k_1k_2} = (g^{k_1})^{k_2} = (g^{k_2})^{k_1} \in G_1 \cap G_2$, with $g^{k_1k_2} \neq e$, and we have a contradiction.
2. Any finite cyclic primary group is indecomposable (Exercise 10.1).

An M-group satisfies the ascending (descending) chain condition on [normal] M-subgroups if every ascending (descending) chain of [normal] M-subgroups terminates. We shall prove that if an M-group G satisfies the ascending and descending chain conditions on normal M-subgroups, then a decomposition of G into a direct sum of indecomposable M-groups is unique up to isomorphism. First, we prove two lemmas.

Lemma 1. *Let G be an M-group.*

a. *Let $\varphi: G \to G$ be an M-monomorphism of G into G. If G satisfies the descending chain condition on M-subgroups, then φ is an M-automorphism of G.*

b. *Let $\psi: G \to G$ be an M-epimorphism of G onto G. If G satisfies the ascending chain condition on normal M-subgroups, then ψ is an M-automorphism of G.*

PROOF.

a. The descending chain of M-subgroups of G, $G \supset \varphi(G) \supset \varphi^2(G) \supset \cdots$, must terminate. Hence there exists a positive integer, r, such that $\varphi^r(G) = \varphi^{r+1}(G)$. Let $g \in G$. Then there exists a $g' \in G$ such that $\varphi^r(g) = \varphi^{r+1}(g')$. It follows that $\varphi^r(g[\varphi(g')]^{-1}) = e$. Since φ is a monomorphism, so is φ^r. But then $g = \varphi(g')$. We conclude that φ is an M-epimorphism, hence an M-automorphism, as desired.

b. The ascending chain of normal M-subgroups of G, $\operatorname{Ker} \psi \subset \operatorname{Ker} \psi^2 \subset \cdots$, must terminate. Hence, there exists a positive integer, r, such that $\operatorname{Ker} \psi^r = \operatorname{Ker} \psi^{r+1}$. Let $g \in \operatorname{Ker} \psi$. Since ψ is an epimorphism, so is ψ^2. Hence, there exists $g' \in G$ such that $g = \psi^r(g')$. But then $e = \psi(g) = \psi^{r+1}(g')$, $g' \in \operatorname{Ker} \psi^{r+1}$, $g' \in \operatorname{Ker} \psi^r$ (since $\operatorname{Ker} \psi^r = \operatorname{Ker} \psi^{r+1}$), and $g = \psi^r(g') = e$. We have shown that $\operatorname{Ker} \psi = \{e\}$, whence ψ is an M-automorphism, as desired. ∎

REMARK. In part a of Lemma 1, if we assume that $\operatorname{Im} \varphi, \operatorname{Im} \varphi^2, \ldots$ are normal M-subgroups of G, then it is sufficient to require that G satisfies the descending chain condition on normal M-subgroups. For then $G \supset \varphi(G) \supset \varphi^2(G) \supset \cdots$ is a chain of normal M-subgroups and hence must terminate. The remainder of the proof of part a, without alteration, remains valid.

Lemma 2. *Let G be an indecomposable M-group which satisfies the ascending and descending chain conditions on normal M-subgroups. Let $\{\varphi_i\}_{i=1}^n$ be a family of M-endomorphisms of G, such that*

$$\varphi_i(x)\varphi_j(y) = \varphi_j(y)\varphi_i(x) \qquad \text{for } i \neq j \text{ and all } x, y \in G.$$

If the map $\theta: G \to G$ defined by $\theta(g) = \prod_{i=1}^n \varphi_i(g)$ is an M-automorphism of G, then there exists a k, $1 \le k \le n$, such that φ_k is an M-automorphism of G.

PROOF. We prove the lemma by induction on n. For $n = 1$, the lemma is trivially true. Assume that the lemma is true for any family of $s < n$ M-endomorphisms of G which satisfy the hypotheses of the lemma.

Let $\{\varphi_i\}_{i=1}^n$ be a family of M-endomorphisms satisfying the conditions of the lemma. We may, without loss of generality, assume that $\theta = \iota_G$. For, if θ is an M-automorphism, then $\{\theta^{-1}\varphi_i\}_{i=1}^n$ is a family of M-endomorphisms of G of the required type and $\prod_{i=1}^n (\theta^{-1}\varphi_i)(g) = g$ for all $g \in G$. We assume, therefore, that $\prod_{i=1}^n \varphi_i(g) = g$ for all $g \in G$.

Let $\tau: G \to G$ be defined by $\tau(g) = \prod_{i=2}^n \varphi_i(g)$ for $g \in G$. We see easily that τ is an M-endomorphism of G and that $\operatorname{Im} \tau, \operatorname{Im} \tau^2, \ldots$ are normal M-subgroups of G. If τ is a monomorphism, then (by Lemma 1a, Remark) τ is an automorphism; our induction assumption then implies that there exists a k, $2 \le k \le n$, such that φ_k is an M-automorphism of G. Suppose then that $\operatorname{Ker} \tau \neq \{e\}$. Then there exists $g_0 \in \operatorname{Ker} \tau$, $g_0 \neq e$, and $\varphi_1(g_0) = \varphi_1(g_0)\tau(g_0) = \prod_{i=1}^n \varphi_i(g_0) = g_0$. The descending chain $G \supset \varphi_1(G) \supset \varphi_1^2(G) \supset \cdots$ of normal M-subgroups of G must terminate. Hence there is an integer $r > 0$ such that $\varphi_1^r(G) = \varphi_1^{r+l}(G)$ for all positive integers l. Since $g_0 = \varphi_1^r(g_0) \in \varphi_1^r(G)$, $\varphi_1^r(G) \neq \{e\}$. Furthermore, from $\varphi_1^r(\varphi_1^r(G)) = \varphi_1^{2r}(G) = \varphi_1^r(G)$, it follows that $\varphi_1^r|_{\varphi_1^r(G)}$ is an M-epimorphism of $\varphi_1^r(G)$. By Lemma 1b,

$$\varphi_{1(G)}^r \cap \operatorname{Ker} \varphi_1^r \subset \varphi_1^r(G) \cap \operatorname{Ker} \varphi_1^{2r} \subset \varphi_1^r(G) \cap \operatorname{Ker} \varphi_1^{3r} \subset \cdots$$

is an ascending chain of normal M-subgroups of G. An argument similar to the one given in the proof of Lemma 1b shows that $\varphi_1^r|_{\varphi_1^r(G)}$ is an M-automorphism of $\varphi_1^r(G)$. Hence $G = \operatorname{Ker} \varphi_1^r \oplus \operatorname{Im} \varphi_1^r$. For if $g \in G$, then there is an $x \in \varphi_1^r(G)$ such that $\varphi_1^r(x) = \varphi_1^r(g)$. But then $g = (gx^{-1}) \cdot x$. Furthermore, $\operatorname{Ker} \varphi_1^r$ and $\operatorname{Im} \varphi_1^r$ are normal M-subgroups of G, and $\operatorname{Ker} \varphi_1^r \cap \operatorname{Im} \varphi_1^r = \{e\}$. We conclude that $G = \operatorname{Ker} \varphi_1^r \oplus \operatorname{Im} \varphi_1^r$. Since G is indecomposable and $\operatorname{Im} \varphi_1^r \neq \{e\}$, $\operatorname{Ker} \varphi_1^r = e$. But then φ_1^r is an M-automorphism of G, whence φ_1 is an M-automorphism of G, and the lemma follows by induction. ▮

Theorem 10.1. (Krull–Schmidt.) *Let G be an M-group which satisfies the ascending and descending chain conditions on normal M-subgroups. Let $\{G_i\}_{i=1}^m$ and $\{H_j\}_{j=1}^n$ be families of indecomposable M-subgroups of G such that $G = \bigoplus_{i=1}^m G_i = \bigoplus_{j=1}^n H_j$. Then $m = n$, and there exists a bijection β of the set $\{1,2,\ldots,m\}$ onto itself such that*

a. *G_i and $H_{\beta(i)}$ are M-isomorphic, $i = 1, 2,\ldots, m$.*

b. *$G = H_{\beta(1)} \oplus H_{\beta(2)} \oplus\cdots\oplus H_{\beta(k)} \oplus G_{k+1} \oplus G_{k+2} \oplus\cdots\oplus G_m$, for each $k = 1, 2,\ldots, m$.*

PROOF. Let ε_i, δ_j be the canonical embeddings of G_i and H_j, respectively, into G, $i = 1, 2,\ldots, m$, $j = 1, 2,\ldots, n$. By Theorem 9.6, there exist families of M-homomorphisms (projections) $\{\pi_i\}_{i=1}^m$, $\{\varphi_j\}_{j=1}^n$ associated with the decompositions $G = \bigoplus_{i=1}^m G_i$, $G = \bigoplus_{j=1}^n H_j$, respectively, such that (in particular) $\pi_1\varepsilon_1 = \iota_{G_1}$, and $\prod_{j=1}^n \delta_j\varphi_j(g) = g$ for all $g \in G$. From the last of these relations it follows that $\prod_{j=1}^n \pi_1\delta_j\varphi_j\varepsilon_1(x) = \pi_1\varepsilon_1(x) = x$ for all $x \in G_1$. Obviously, G_1 satisfies the ascending and descending chain conditions on normal M-subgroups; we leave it to the reader to verify that

$$\pi_1\delta_j\varphi_j\varepsilon_1(x)\pi_1\delta_k\varphi_k\varepsilon_1(y) = \pi_1\delta_k\varphi_k\varepsilon_1(y)\pi_1\delta_j\varphi_j\varepsilon_1(x)$$

for $j, k = 1, 2,\ldots, n$, $j \neq k$, and all $x,y \in G_1$. But then (by Lemma 2) there exists a j, say $j = \beta(1)$, such that $\pi_1\delta_{\beta(1)}\varphi_{\beta(1)}\varepsilon_1$ is an M-automorphism of G_1. We now show that $\varphi_{\beta(1)}\varepsilon_1: G_1 \to H_{\beta(1)}$ is an M-isomorphism. Since $\pi_1\delta_{\beta(1)}$ is an M-isomorphism of $\operatorname{Im}(\varphi_{\beta(1)}\varepsilon_1)$ onto G_1, $\operatorname{Im} \varphi_{\beta(1)}\varepsilon_1 \cap \operatorname{Ker} \pi_1\delta_{\beta(1)} = \{e\}$. Furthermore, if $x \in H_{\beta(1)}$, then $\pi_1\delta_{\beta(1)} \in G_1$ and there is a $y \in G_1$ such that $\pi_1\delta_{\beta(1)}\varphi_{\beta(1)}\varepsilon_1(y) = \pi_1\delta_{\beta(1)}(x)$. But then $x = (x\varphi_{\beta(1)}\varepsilon_1(y^{-1}))(\varphi_{\beta(1)}\varepsilon_1(y))$ with $x\varphi_{\beta(1)}\varepsilon_1(y^{-1}) \in \operatorname{Ker} \pi_1\delta_{\beta(1)}$ and $\varphi_{\beta(1)}\varepsilon_1(y) \in \operatorname{Im} \varphi_{\beta(1)}\varepsilon_1$. Hence $H_{\beta(1)} = \operatorname{Ker} \pi_1\delta_{\beta(1)} \oplus \operatorname{Im} \varphi_{\beta(1)}\varepsilon_1$. But $H_{\beta(1)}$ is indecomposable, and $\operatorname{Im} \varphi_{\beta(1)}\varepsilon_1 \neq \{e\}$, whence $H_{\beta(1)} = \operatorname{Im} \varphi_{\beta(1)}\varepsilon_1$, and $\varphi_{\beta(1)}\varepsilon_1: G_1 \to H_{\beta(1)}$, $\pi_1\delta_{\beta(1)}: H_{\beta(1)} \to G_1$ are M-isomorphisms.

The projection π_1 induces the trivial map on $G_2 \oplus G_3 \oplus\cdots\oplus G_m$ (i.e., π_1 takes every element into the identity), whereas π_1 induces an isomorphism of $H_{\beta(1)}$. Hence $H_{\beta(1)} \cap (G_2 \oplus G_3 \oplus\cdots\oplus G_m) = \{e\}$. Let G' be the M-subgroup of G generated by $H_{\beta(1)}$ and $G_2 \oplus G_3 \oplus\cdots\oplus G_m$. Then $G \rhd G' = H_{\beta(1)} \oplus G_2 \oplus\cdots\oplus G_m$. We define a map $\sigma: G \to G'$ as follows: Each element $x \in G$ has a unique representation $x = g_1g_2\cdots g_m$ with $g_i \in G_i$, and we put $\sigma(x) = \varphi_{\beta(1)}\varepsilon_1(g_1) \cdot g_2g_3\cdots g_m$. Then σ is an M-isomorphism of G onto G', and (by Lemma 1a, Remark) σ is an automorphism of G. But then $G = G' = H_{\beta(1)} \oplus G_2 \oplus G_3 \oplus\cdots\oplus G_m$.

An induction argument (which involves nothing more than an application of the above reasoning to the decompositions $G = H_{\beta(1)} \oplus\cdots\oplus H_{\beta(r)} \oplus$

$G_{r+1} \oplus \cdots \oplus G_m$ and $G = \oplus_{j=1}^{n} H_j$) proves that to each $i \in \{1,2,\ldots,m\}$ there corresponds a $\beta(i) \in \{1,2,\ldots,n\}$ such that $G_i \cong H_{\beta(i)}$, and $G = H_{\beta(1)} \oplus H_{\beta(2)} \oplus \cdots \oplus H_{\beta(k)} \oplus G_{k+1} \oplus G_{k+2} \oplus \cdots \oplus G_m$ for $k = 1, 2, \ldots, m$. Finally, from $G = H_{\beta(1)} \oplus H_{\beta(2)} \oplus \cdots \oplus H_{\beta(m)} = H_1 \oplus H_2 \oplus \cdots \oplus H_n$ we conclude that $m = n$ and β is bijective. ∎

11. Free Groups

In this section we let $M = \varnothing$.

While groups of small positive order may be conveniently described by means of their multiplication tables, this is clearly impractical for groups of larger finite order and impossible for groups of infinite order. Another way to describe a given group is by means of a set S of generators and a set D of defining relations. For example, we have

1. $G_1 = [b]$, the cyclic group of order 5:

$$S = \{b\}, \qquad D = \{b^5 = 1\}.$$

2. $F_1 = [a]$, the infinite cyclic group:

$$S = \{a\}, \qquad D = \varnothing.$$

3. $G_2 = V_4$, Klein's 4-group:

$$S = \{a,b\}, \qquad D = \{a^2 = 1, b^2 = 1, a^{-1}b^{-1}ab = 1\}.$$

We note that G_1 is a homomorphic image of F_1 (which is free of defining relations) under a homomorphism $\mu\colon a^t \mapsto b^t$ whose kernel is generated by a^5. It is natural to ask whether for G_2 there exists another group F_2 on two generators which is free of defining relations and has G_2 as a homomorphic image. More generally, given a group G which has a set of m generators subject to certain defining relations, does there exist a group on m generators which is free of defining relations and has G as a homomorphic image? We shall be able to formulate this question more precisely and give an affirmative answer after introducing the concept of a free group.

Definition 11.1. Let S be any set, F a group, and Φ a mapping of S into F. Then the pair $\langle F,\Phi\rangle$ is called a *free group on S* if for every group G and every mapping γ of S into G there exists a unique homomorphism μ of F into G such that $\gamma = \mu\Phi$. ///

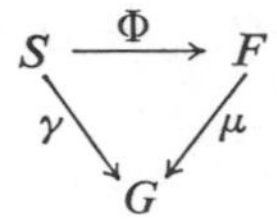

NOTE. $\langle E,\iota_E\rangle$ is a free group on $\varnothing$.

Theorem 11.1. *If $\langle F,\Phi\rangle$ is a free group on S, then*
a. *The mapping Φ is one-to-one.*
b. *$\Phi(S)$ is a set of generators for F.*

PROOF.
a. Suppose that for $a,b \in S$, $\Phi(a) = \Phi(b)$. We may choose G and γ so that $\gamma(a) \neq \gamma(b)$. Since $\gamma = \mu\Phi$, we have $\mu\Phi(a) \neq \mu\Phi(b)$. But this is impossible, since $\Phi(a) = \Phi(b)$.
b. Let $G = [\Phi(S)]$ and let ε be the inclusion homomorphism of G in F. Define $\gamma: S \to G$ by $\gamma(s) = \Phi(s)$ for each $s \in S$. Then $\varepsilon\gamma = \Phi$, and, by Definition 11.1, there is a homomorphism ν of F into G such that $\gamma = \nu\Phi$. Hence $\Phi = \varepsilon\gamma = \varepsilon\nu\Phi$, and $\varepsilon\nu$ is a homomorphism of F into F such that the diagram

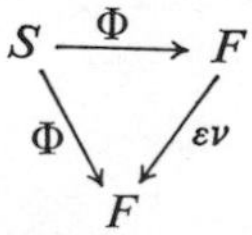

commutes. By Definition 11.1, there can be only one such homomorphism and, since the diagram

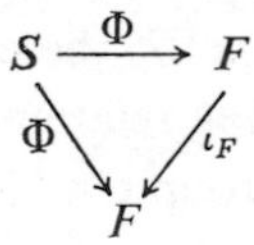

with ι_F the identity map on F, also commutes, $\iota_F = \varepsilon\nu$. But then $\operatorname{Im} \varepsilon = \operatorname{Im} \iota_F = F$, and so $G = F$, and F is generated by $\Phi(S)$. ∎

Theorem 11.2. (Uniqueness.) *If $\langle F,\Phi\rangle$ and $\langle F',\Phi'\rangle$ are free groups on the same set S, then there exists a unique isomorphism $\psi: F \to F'$ such that $\psi\Phi = \Phi'$.*

PROOF. Since $\langle F,\Phi\rangle$ is a free group on S, there exists a homomorphism $\psi: F \to F'$ such that $\Phi' = \psi\Phi$:

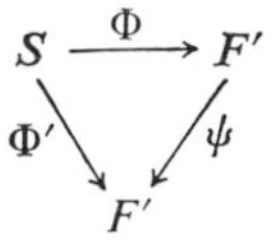

Since $\langle F',\Phi'\rangle$ is a free group on S, there exists a homomorphism $\psi': F' \to F$ such that $\Phi = \psi'\Phi'$:

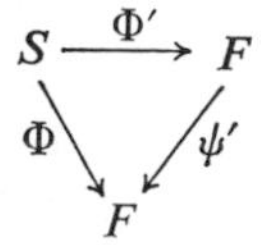

But then $\Phi = \psi'\Phi' = \psi'\psi\Phi$, and we have

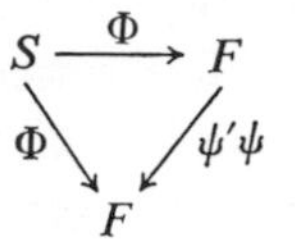

and

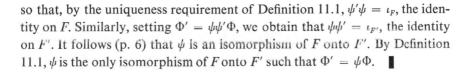

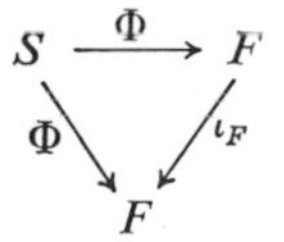

so that, by the uniqueness requirement of Definition 11.1, $\psi'\psi = \iota_F$, the identity on F. Similarly, setting $\Phi' = \psi\psi'\Phi$, we obtain that $\psi\psi' = \iota_{F'}$, the identity on F'. It follows (p. 6) that ψ is an isomorphism of F onto F'. By Definition 11.1, ψ is the only isomorphism of F onto F' such that $\Phi' = \psi\Phi$. ▌

Theorem 11.3. (Existence.) *For any set S, there exists a free group on S.*

PROOF. If $S = \varnothing$, the trivial group $\{e\}$ may serve as F and the empty map as Φ. Suppose $S \neq \varnothing$. For each $a \in S$, we denote by a^{-1} the ordered pair $(a,-1)$ and let $\bar{S} = \{a^{-1} | a \in S\}$. By a *word* on S we shall mean a finite sequence of elements from $S \cup \bar{S}$. We include the empty sequence (p. 6), which we refer to as the *empty word*. If a word has no subsequence of the form aa^{-1} or $a^{-1}a$, for $a \in S$, then we call it a *reduced word*. We denote by F the set of all reduced words on S.

From each word on S, we may obtain a reduced word by striking out all subsequences aa^{-1} or $a^{-1}a$, proceeding from left to right at each stage of the reduction. This process yields a unique reduced word for each word on S. We now define a binary operation $\circ$ on the set F of all reduced words as follows: If $w_1 = a_1 \cdots a_h$, $w_2 = b_1 \cdots b_k$ ($w_1, w_2 \in S$), we let $w_1 \circ w_2$ be the reduced word which results from the reduction of $a_1 \cdots a_h\, b_1 \cdots b_k$. (If w_1 is the empty word, then $w_1 \circ w_2 = w_2$, and if w_2 is the empty word, then $w_1 \circ w_2 = w_1$.) Thus, $\circ$ is a binary operation on F, and the empty word serves as two-sided identity for $\circ$.

For each $a \in S \cup \bar{S}$, write a^* for its "opposite"; i.e., if $a \in S$, then $a^* = a^{-1}$ and $(a^{-1})^* = a$. Clearly, for each reduced word $w = a_1 \cdots a_h$ ($h \geq 0$), the word $w^* = a_h^* \cdots a_1^*$ is reduced and serves as two-sided inverse for w. The operation $\circ$ is associative. For, let $w_1, w_2, w_3 \in F$. If one of the three words is empty, there is nothing to prove. Thus, suppose $w_1 = a_1 \cdots a_h$, $w_2 = b_1 \cdots b_k$, $w_3 = c_1 \cdots c_l$, with h, k, l positive integers. We proceed by induction on k, the length of the middle word. If $k = 1$, then $w_2 = b_1$ and there are three cases: (1) $b_1 \neq a_h^*$ and $b_1 \neq c_1^*$; (2) $b_1 = a_h^*$; (3) $b_1 = c_1^*$. In the first case, both products, $w_1 \circ (w_2 \circ w_3)$ and $(w_1 \circ w_2) \circ w_3$, are equal to the reduced word $a_1 \cdots a_h\, b_1 c_1 \cdots c_l$; in the second case, both are obtainable by reduction of $a_1 \cdots a_{h-1}\, c_1 \cdots c_l$; and in the third case both are obtainable by reduction of $a_1 \cdots a_h\, c_2 \cdots c_l$. Thus, associativity holds for $k = 1$. For $k > 1$, suppose associativity holds when the length of the middle word is $k - 1$, and let $w_2' = b_2 \cdots b_k$. Then

$$\begin{aligned} w_1 \circ (w_2 \circ w_3) &= w_1 \circ ((b_1 \circ w_2') \circ w_3) = w_1 \circ (b_1 \circ (w_2' \circ w_3)) \\ &= (w_1 \circ b_1) \circ (w_2' \circ w_3) \\ &= ((w_1 \circ b_1) \circ w_2') \circ w_3 \\ &= (w_1 \circ (b_1 \circ w_2')) \circ w_3 \\ &= (w_1 \circ w_2) \circ w_3. \end{aligned}$$

It follows that $\circ$ is associative.

Now let Φ be the mapping that associates with each $a \in S$ the word whose only term is a. Obviously, Φ is injective and $[\Phi S] = F$. Let G be any group, γ a map of S into G. We may define a map $\mu\colon S \cup \bar{S} \to G$ as follows: For each $a \in S$, let $\mu(\Phi a) = \gamma a$, $\mu(\Phi a)^{-1} = (\gamma a)^{-1}$. Since each element of F can be expressed in one and only one way as a product of elements of the form Φa and $(\Phi a)^{-1}$ ($a \in S$), we may extend μ so as to map products to corresponding products, and in this way obtain a homomorphism $\mu\colon F \to G$. By definition of μ, $\mu\Phi = \gamma$. If $\mu'\colon F \to G$ is another homomorphism such that $\mu'\Phi = \gamma$, then $\mu' = \mu$ since μ' and μ agree on ΦS and $[\Phi S] = F$. But then $\langle F, \Phi \rangle$ is a free group on S. ▌

Theorem 11.4. *If G is a group with generator set S, then G is a homomorphic image of a free group on S.*

PROOF. Let G be a group, S a set of generators for G, and let $\langle F,\Phi\rangle$ be a free group on S. If ε is the inclusion map of S in G,

$$\begin{array}{ccc} S & \xrightarrow{\Phi} & F \\ & \varepsilon\searrow \quad \swarrow\mu & \\ & G & \end{array}$$

then there exists a unique homomorphism μ of F into G such that $\varepsilon = \mu\Phi$. Hence $S = \varepsilon S \subset \mu\Phi(S) \subset \mu(F)$. But then, since S generates G, $\mu(F) = G$. Thus, μ is a homomorphism of F onto G, as required. ▌

Definition 11.2. Let G be a group with generator set S, $\langle F,\Phi\rangle$ a free group on S, and μ the homomorphism of Theorem 11.4. Then Ker μ is a *defining kernel for G with respect to S* and if T is a set of generators for Ker μ, then the set of equations $\mu(w) = 1$ for $w \in T$ is a *set of defining relations for G with respect to S.* ///

Corollary. *Let G_1 and G_2 be groups with the same generating set S. Let F be a free group on S and let K_1, K_2 be subgroups of F such that K_1 is a defining kernel for G_1 relative to S, and K_2 is a defining kernel for G_2 relative to S.*

a. *If $K_1 \subset K_2$, then G_2 is a homomorphic image of G_1.*
b. *If $K_1 = K_2$, then G_1 and G_2 are isomorphic.*

PROOF. By Definition 11.2, there are epimorphisms $\mu_i: F \to G_i$ such that Ker $\mu_i = K_i$ $(i = 1,2)$. Assertions a and b follow from Theorem 4.9. ▌

Part a of the corollary is known as Van Dyck's Theorem. Part b guarantees that a set S of generators and a corresponding set of defining relations on S determines a group to within isomorphism.

12. Free Abelian Groups

Definition 12.1. Let S be any set, A an abelian group and α a mapping of S into A. Then the pair $\langle A,\alpha\rangle$ is a *free abelian group on S* if, given any abelian group G, and any mapping γ of S into G, there exists a unique homomorphism μ of A into G such that $\gamma = \mu\alpha$.

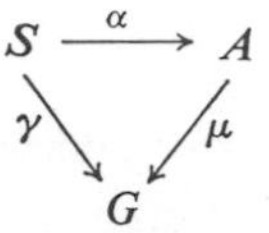

///

If A is an abelian group such that for some set S and some mapping α of S into A, $\langle A,\alpha\rangle$ is a free abelian group on S, we shall simply speak of A as a free abelian group.

As in the case of free groups, one can prove

Theorem 12.1. *If $\langle A,\alpha\rangle$ is a free abelian group on S, then α is one-to-one and $\alpha(S)$ generates A.* □

Theorem 12.2. (Uniqueness.)

a. *If $\langle A,\alpha\rangle$ and $\langle A',\alpha'\rangle$ are free abelian groups on the same set S, then there exists a unique isomorphism ψ of A onto A' such that $\alpha' = \psi\alpha$.*
b. *If $\langle A,\alpha\rangle$ is a free abelian group on S, A' a group, α' a mapping of S into A', and ψ an isomorphism of A onto A' such that $\alpha' = \psi\alpha$, then $\langle A',\alpha'\rangle = \langle\psi A,\psi\alpha\rangle$ is also a free abelian group on S.* □

Only slight modifications of the proofs of Theorems 11.1 and 11.2 are required to prove Theorem 12.1 and 12.2.

To establish the existence of a free abelian group on any set S, we make use of the free group on S.

Theorem 12.3. *For any set S, there exists a free abelian group on S.*

PROOF. Let $\langle F,\Phi\rangle$ be a free group on S, and let F^1 be the commutator subgroup of F. We shall show that the pair $\langle F/F^1,\nu\Phi\rangle$, where ν is the canonical epimorphism of F onto F/F^1, is a free abelian group on S. By Theorem 4.6 F/F^1 is abelian. Clearly $\nu\Phi$ is a mapping of S into F/F^1. Now let G be any abelian group, γ a mapping of S into G. Since F is a free group on S, there is a

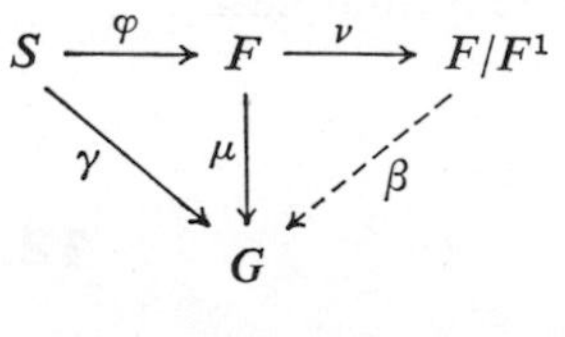

unique homomorphism $\mu: F \to G$ such that $\mu\varphi = \gamma$. By Theorem 4.6, since G is abelian, $F^1 \subset \operatorname{Ker} \mu$. Hence, by Theorem 4.9, there is a unique homomorphism $\beta: F/F^1 \to G$ such that $\beta\nu = \mu$. But then $\beta(\nu\varphi) = (\beta\nu)\varphi = \mu\varphi = \gamma$, as required. If $\beta': F/F^1 \to G$ is another homomorphism such that $\beta'(\nu\varphi) = (\beta'\nu)\varphi = \gamma$, then $\beta'\nu = \mu$, and therefore $\beta' = \beta$. It follows that $\langle F/F^1, \nu\varphi\rangle$ is a free abelian group on S. ▮

From Theorems 12.2 and 12.3 we have

Corollary. *Let S be a set, and let A be a group. Then A is a free abelian group on S if and only if A is isomorphic to F/F^1, where F is a free group on S and F^1 is the commutator subgroup of F.* ☐

NOTE. From this point on, we use additive notation in discussing abelian groups.

Another useful characterization of free abelian groups is based on the following theorem:

Theorem 12.4. *Let S be a set, $\alpha: S \to A$ a map of S into a group A. Then $\langle A, \alpha\rangle$ is a free abelian group on S if and only if $A = \bigoplus_{s\in S} [\alpha s]$, and each $[\alpha s]$ is an infinite cyclic group.*

PROOF. Suppose $A = \bigoplus_{s\in S} [\alpha s]$, where each $[\alpha s]$ is infinite cyclic. Then, for each $a \in A$, there is a unique finite subset $\{s_1, \ldots, s_n\}$ of S, and a unique set of integers, $\{k_1, \ldots, k_n\}$, such that $a = \sum_{i=1}^n k_i s_i$. If G is an abelian group, $\gamma: S \to G$ a map, we may define a map $\mu: A \to G$ by $\mu(\sum_{i=1}^n k_i s_i) = \sum_{i=1}^n k_i \gamma_i s_i$. Since G is abelian, μ is a homomorphism. Clearly, $\mu\alpha = \gamma$. If μ' is another homomorphism of A into G such that $\mu'\alpha = \gamma$, then μ' and μ agree on the set αS. Since $A = [\alpha S]$, $\mu' = \mu$. Thus, $\langle A, \alpha\rangle$ is free abelian on S.

Conversely, suppose that $\langle A, \alpha\rangle$ is free abelian on S. Let $G = \coprod'_{s\in S} [b_s]$, where each $[b_s]$ is infinite cyclic, and let $\{\eta_s\}_{s\in S}$ be the family of injection maps ($\eta_s: [b_s] \to G$) associated with this direct sum. Then $G = \bigoplus [\eta_s b_s]$. Define $\gamma: S \to G$ by $\gamma s = \eta_s b_s$ for each $s \in S$. By the first part of the proof, $\langle G, \gamma\rangle$ is free abelian on S. But then, by Theorem 12.2, there is an isomorphism $\psi: G \to A$ such that $\psi\gamma = \alpha$. It follows that $A = \bigoplus_{s\in S} [\alpha s]$ and that each $[\alpha s]$ is infinite cyclic. ▮

Corollary 1. *A group A is a free abelian group if and only if it is a direct sum of infinite cyclic subgroups.* ☐

Corollary 2. *If S is a subset of a group A, then the following conditions are equivalent:*

a. *$\langle A,\varepsilon\rangle$ is free abelian on S, where $\varepsilon: S \to A$ is the inclusion map.*
b. *$A = \bigoplus [s]$, where each $[s]$ is an infinite cyclic group.*
c. *$A = [S]$, and if $\sum_{i=1}^{n} k_i s_i = 0$ ($s_i \in S$, $k_i, n \in \mathbf{Z}$), then $k_i = 0$ for each $i = 1,\ldots, n$.*

PROOF. The equivalence of a and b is an immediate consequence of Theorem 12.4. The equivalence of b and c follows from Theorem 9.5. ∎

Definition 12.2. If $S \subset A$ and $\langle A,\varepsilon\rangle$ is a free abelian group on S ($\varepsilon: S \to A$ the inclusion map), then S is a *basis* for A. ///

Theorem 12.5. *Any two bases for a free abelian group A have the same cardinality.*

PROOF. Let $\mathscr{B}$ and $\mathscr{B}'$ be bases for A, of cardinality m and m', respectively. If neither m nor m' is finite, then card $A = m = m'$ (p. 6, Example 8).

Suppose m is finite. Let $B = 2A = \{a + a | a \in A\}$. Then $A = A_1 \oplus \cdots \oplus A_m$, where each $A_i = [a_i]$ is isomorphic to $\langle \mathbf{Z}, + \rangle$, and $B = B_1 \oplus \cdots \oplus B_m$, where $B_i = [2a_i]$ for each $i = 1,\ldots, m$. Let $\bar{A} = A/B$. By Theorem 9.7 $\bar{A}$ is isomorphic to $\coprod_{i=1}^{\prime m} \bar{A}_i$, where $\bar{A}_i = [\bar{a}_i]$, a cyclic group of order 2, for each $i = 1,\ldots, m$. But then $|\bar{A}| = 2^m$.

Now let $\mathscr{B}'$ be another basis for A, of cardinality m'. Then, by the same argument, $\bar{A}$ is a direct sum of m' cyclic groups of order 2; hence m' is finite. But then $|A/B| = 2^{m'} = 2^m$, and $m' = m$. ∎

Definition 12.3. If an abelian group A has a basis of cardinality m, then m is the *dimension* of A. ///

Corresponding to Theorem 11.4, we have

Theorem 12.6. *Every abelian group with generator set S is a homomorphic image of a free abelian group on S.*

The proof, based on Definition 12.1, is completely analogous to that of Theorem 11.4. □

13. Finitely Generated Abelian Groups

In Section 12 we saw that every free abelian group is a direct sum of cyclic groups. Since every abelian group is a homomorphic image of a free abelian group, it is natural to investigate which abelian groups inherit this property from the corresponding free groups. We shall prove here that every finitely generated abelian group is a direct sum of cyclic groups. While we confine ourselves in this section to the case $M = \varnothing$ (or, since the groups are abelian, $M = \mathbf{Z}$), our proofs will carry over almost verbatim to modules over an arbitrary Euclidean domain and, with some modifications, to modules over a principal ideal domain. In that more general setting, the theorem is intimately connected with the theory of similarity in linear algebra. (See Chapter 4, Section 4.)

If G is an abelian group with n generators, then G is the image under a homomorphism α of a free abelian group A of rank n; i.e., $G = \alpha([x_1] \oplus \cdots \oplus [x_n])$, where $\langle x_1,\ldots,x_n\rangle$ is a basis for A. Thus, $G = [\alpha x_1] + \cdots + [\alpha x_n]$. The difficulty lies in the fact that this sum, in general, is not direct.

To prove the theorem, we find bases $\langle u_1,\ldots,u_n\rangle$ for A and $\langle c_1u_1,\ldots,c_mu_m\rangle$ for Ker α such that $G = \oplus_{i=1}^{n} [u_i]/[c_iu_i]$, where $c_i = 0$ for $i = m + 1,\ldots, n$. That such a choice of bases is possible is a consequence of the following theorem.

Theorem 13.1. *If A is a free abelian group of dimension $n > 0$, and K is a subgroup of A, then K is a free abelian group of dimension $m \le n$ and there exist bases $\mathscr{B}_1 = \langle u_1,\ldots,u_n\rangle$ for A and $\mathscr{B}_2 = \langle v_1,\ldots,v_m\rangle$ for K such that, for each $i = 1,\ldots, m$, $v_i = c_iu_i$ for some positive integer c_i, and $c_i|c_{i+1}$ for each $i = 1,\ldots, m - 1$.*

PROOF. The assertion obviously holds for $K = 0$. Suppose $K \neq 0$. We proceed by induction on n. If $n = 1$, A and K are both cyclic and, if u is a generator for A, then cu will generate K for some positive integer c, and we can take $\mathscr{B}_1 = \langle u\rangle$ and $\mathscr{B}_2 = \langle cu\rangle$. If $n > 1$, suppose the assertion holds for $n - 1$. Let

$$S = \left\{ c \in \mathbf{N}' \;\middle|\; \begin{array}{l} \exists \text{ a basis } \langle a_1,a_2,\ldots,a_n\rangle \text{ for } A, \text{ and an } a \in K \text{ such that} \\ a = ca_1 + c_2a_2 + \cdots + c_na_n,\ (c_i \in \mathbf{Z}). \end{array} \right\}$$

Clearly, $S \neq \varnothing$; hence S has a least element, c_1, corresponding to some basis $\langle a_1,\ldots,a_n\rangle$. There exists an element $v_1 \in K$ such that

$$v_1 = c_1a_1 + k_2a_2 + \cdots + k_na_n, \qquad k_i \in \mathbf{Z},\quad i = 2,\ldots, n.$$

For each $i = 2,\ldots, n$, there exist integers q_i and r_i such that $k_i = c_1q_i + r_i$, $0 \le r_i < c_1$. Thus,

$$v_1 = c_1(a_1 + q_2a_2 + \cdots + q_na_n) + r_2a_2 + \cdots + r_na_n.$$

Let $u_1 = a_1 + q_2a_2 + \cdots + q_na_n$. Then $\mathscr{A}' = \langle u_1,a_2,\ldots,a_n\rangle$ is another basis for A, and $v_1 = c_1u_1 + r_2a_2 + \cdots + r_na_n$. By the definition of c_1, $r_2 = \cdots = r_n = 0$, and $v_1 = c_1u_1$. Now let $H = [a_2,\ldots,a_n]$. Then H is a free abelian group of dimension $n - 1$. By the induction hypothesis, its subgroup $K \cap H$ is a free abelian group of rank $m - 1 \leq n - 1$, and it is possible to choose a basis $\mathscr{B}_1' = \langle u_2,\ldots,u_n\rangle$ for H and a basis $\mathscr{B}_2' = \langle v_2,\ldots,v_m\rangle$ for $K \cap H$ such that $v_i = c_iu_i$, c_i a positive integer for each $i = 2,\ldots, m$, and $c_i|c_{i+1}$ for each $i = 2,\ldots, m - 1$. Since $\mathscr{A}' = \langle u_1,a_2,\ldots,a_n\rangle$ is a basis for A, the sum $[u_1] + H$ is direct and therefore $\mathscr{B}_1 = \langle u_1,u_2,\ldots,u_n\rangle$ is a basis for A.

We next prove that $\mathscr{B}_2 = \langle v_1,v_2,\ldots,v_m\rangle$ is a basis for K. It is sufficient to prove that (1) $[v_1] \cap (K \cap H) = 0$ and (2) $[v_1] + K \cap H = K$. The first statement follows from $v_1 = c_1u_1$, since $\langle u_1,a_2,\ldots,a_n\rangle$ is a basis for A. To prove the second statement, suppose $k \in K$. Since $\mathscr{A}' = \langle u_1,a_2,\ldots,a_n\rangle$ is a basis for A, $k = d_1u_1 + d_2a_2 + \cdots + d_na_n$, $d_i \in \mathbf{Z}$. Write $d_1 = c_1p_1 + s_1$, $c_1,s_1 \in \mathbf{Z}$, $0 \leq s_1 < c_1$. Then $k - p_1v_1 = s_1u_1 + d_2a_2 + \cdots + d_na_n \in K$. Because of the choice of c_1, $s_1 = 0$. Hence $k - p_1v_1 \in K \cap H$, and $k \in [v_1] + K \cap H$. It follows that $\mathscr{B}_2$ is a basis for K. Thus, K is a free abelian group of dimension $m \leq n$, and we have a basis $\mathscr{B}_1 = \langle u_1,\ldots,u_n\rangle$ for A and a basis $\mathscr{B}_2 = \langle v_1,\ldots,v_m\rangle$ for K such that $v_i = c_iu_i$ for each $i = 1,\ldots, m$, and $c_i|c_{i+1}$ for $i = 2,\ldots, m - 1$. To complete the proof, we need only verify that $c_1|c_2$. Write $c_2 = c_1q' + r', q',r' \in \mathbf{Z}, 0 \leq r' < c_1$, and let $w_1 = u_1 - q'u_2$. Then $\langle w_1,u_2,\ldots,u_n\rangle$ is also a basis of A. In terms of this basis, $v_2 - v_1 = (-c_1)w_1 + r'u_2$. But then, by the choice of c_1, it follows that $r' = 0$, and $c_1|c_2$. ∎

We are now ready to prove the main theorem.

Theorem 13.2. (Fundamental Theorem for Finitely Generated Abelian Groups.) *Every abelian group on n generators* ($n > 0$) *is a direct sum of n cyclic groups. In particular, there exist m* ($0 \leq m \leq n$) *finite cyclic subgroups* $G_1, G_2,\ldots, G_m$ *of G and* $n - m$ *infinite cyclic subgroups* $G_{m+1}, G_{m+2},\ldots, G_n$ *of G such that* $G = \bigoplus_1^n G_i$ *and such that for* $i = 1, 2,\ldots, m - 1$, $|G_i|\,|\,|G_{i+1}|$.

PROOF. Let G be an abelian group, S a set of n generators for G (n a positive integer). By Theorem 12.6, there exists a free abelian group A, on S, hence of dimension n, such that G is a homomorphic image of A. Let μ be an epimorphism of A onto G, and let $K = \text{Ker } \mu$. If $K = 0$, μ is an isomorphism, hence G is the direct sum of n infinite cyclic groups. Suppose $K \neq 0$. By the preceding theorem, K is a free abelian group of dimension $m \leq n$, and it is possible to choose a basis $\mathscr{B}_1 = \langle u_1,\ldots,u_n\rangle$ for A and a basis $\mathscr{B}_2 = \langle v_1,\ldots,v_m\rangle$ for K such that, for each $i = 1,\ldots, m$, $v_i = c_iu_i$ for some positive integer c_i, and

$c_i | c_{i+1}$ for each $i = 1,\ldots, m - 1$. But then $A = \bigoplus_{i=1}^{n} [u_i]$, and $K = \bigoplus_{i=1}^{n} [c_i u_i]$, where $c_i = 0$ for $i > m$. By Theorem 9.7 $G \cong A/K \cong \coprod_{i=1}^{\prime n} [u_i]/[c_i u_i]$. The groups $G_i' = [u_i]/[c_i u_i]$ satisfy the requirements of the theorem; i.e., for $i \leq m$, G_i' is finite cyclic of order c_i; for $i > m$, G_i' is infinite cyclic; and $c_i | c_{i+1}$ for $i = 1,\ldots, m - 1$. Hence there are subgroups G_i ($i = 1,\ldots,n$) of G such that $G = \bigoplus_{i=1}^{n} G_i$ and the G_i have the required properties. ▌

A certain number of initial c_i may be equal to 1, and the corresponding summands equal to zero. We shall refer to the nonzero segment of the decomposition in Theorem 13.2 as a *T-decomposition* for G. If c_{m-h} is the last of the c_i which is equal to 1, we shall let $t_j = c_{m-h+j}$ for each $j = 1,\ldots, h$.

By Theorem 9.11, the nonzero finite cyclic components in a T-decomposition of G are direct sums of primary cyclic subgroups of G. Hence we have

Theorem 13.3. *Every finitely generated abelian group is a direct sum of primary cyclic groups and infinite cyclic groups.* □

In the decomposition of Theorem 13.2, the components can be arranged so that all finite components precede all infinite components, the primes corresponding to the primary orders are nondecreasing and, for each prime, the exponents of the corresponding primary orders are nonincreasing. We shall call such a decomposition a *P-decomposition.*

Theorem 13.4. (Uniqueness.) *Let G be a finitely generated abelian group. Then*

a. *There is a unique integer $r \geq 0$ such that the number of infinite cyclic components in any decomposition of G as a direct sum of cyclic groups is equal to r.*
b. *There is a unique family of integers $P(G) = \{s_1,\ldots,s_l\}$, $l \geq 0$, such that in every P-decomposition of G, the primary cyclic components have orders $s_1,\ldots, s_l$.*
c. *There is a unique family of integers $T(G) = \{t_1,\ldots,t_h\}$, $h \geq 0$, such that in every T-decomposition of G, the nonzero, finite cyclic components have orders $t_1,\ldots, t_h$.*

PROOF.

a. In any decomposition of G as a direct sum of cyclic groups, the subgroup of G generated by the finite components is the torsion subgroup H of G, i.e., the subgroup consisting of all elements of G whose order is finite. Hence the subgroup generated by the infinite cyclic components is isomorphic to G/H.

But then G/H is a free abelian group, and the number r of infinite cyclic components in the decomposition of G is equal to the dimension of G/H. By Theorem 12.5, r is uniquely determined by G.

b. Since the primary cyclic summands in any P-decomposition of G are indecomposable summands of the torsion subgroup H of G, the Krull–Schmidt Theorem guarantees their uniqueness to within isomorphism. But then the family of orders $P(G) = \{s_1,\ldots,s_l\}$ of the primary summands is uniquely determined by G. (A direct proof, which does not involve the Krull–Schmidt Theorem, is outlined in Exercise 13.1.)

c. The nonzero finite cyclic components in any T-decomposition of G are summands in a direct decomposition of the torsion subgroup H of G. Let $\{t_1,\ldots,t_h\}$ be the family of orders of these summands, and let $p_1,\ldots, p_k$ be the distinct primes occurring in the primary factorization of $|H|$. Suppose

$$\begin{matrix} t_1 = p_1^{\alpha_{11}}\cdots p_k^{\alpha_{1k}} \\ \vdots \\ t_h = p_1^{\alpha_{h1}}\cdots p_k^{\alpha_{hk}} \end{matrix} \qquad \alpha_{ij} \geq 0 \text{ for each } i = 1,\ldots, h,\ j = 1,\ldots, k.$$

Since $t_i | t_{i+1}$ for each $i = 1,\ldots, m - 1$, $\alpha_{ig} \leq \alpha_{jg}$ if $1 \leq i \leq j \leq m, i \leq g \leq k$. For each $j = 1,\ldots, k$, there is a largest positive integer $l_j \leq m$ such that $\alpha_{ij} = 0$ for $i < l_j$. If, for each $i = 1,\ldots, m$, the ith summand is decomposed into its primary components, and the resulting primary cyclic groups are arranged to form a P-decomposition of G, then the family $P(G)$ of this P-decomposition is

$$\{p_1^{\alpha_{h1}},\ldots,p_1^{\alpha_{l_1 1}};\ p_2^{\alpha_{h2}},\ldots,p_2^{\alpha_{l_2 2}};\ldots;p_k^{\alpha_{hk}},\ldots,p_k^{\alpha_{l_k k}}\}.$$

By b, every T-decomposition must give rise to a P-decomposition with the same family $P(G)$ of prime-power orders. By the Fundamental Theorem of Arithmetic, it follows that the family of orders of the nonzero finite components in any T-decomposition of G is $\{t_1,\ldots,t_h\} = T(G)$. ▮

As a consequence of Theorem 2.3, we have

Corollary 1.

a. *If* $G = \bigoplus_{i=1}^{l} G_i$ *and* $G = \bigoplus_{i=1}^{l'} G_i'$ *are P-decompositions of G, then* $l = l'$ *and* G_i *is isomorphic to* G_i' *for each* $i = 1,\ldots, l$.

b. *If* $G = \bigoplus_{i=1}^{d} G_i$ *and* $G = \bigoplus_{i=1}^{d'} G_i'$ *are T-decompositions of G, then* $d = d'$, *and* G_i *is isomorphic to* G_i' *for each* $i = 1,\ldots, d$. □

If G is a finitely generated abelian group, we shall refer to $P(G)$ and $T(G)$, respectively, as the family of *elementary divisors* and the family of *invariant factors* (*torsion coefficients*) of G. The number r of infinite cyclic summands is the dimension in the sense of Definition 12.4, of the free abelian group G/H, where H is the torsion subgroup of G. We shall call it the *rank* of G.

In view of Theorem 13.4, we have

Corollary 2.

a. *Two finitely generated abelian groups are isomorphic if and only if they have the same rank and the same family of elementary divisors.*
b. *Two finitely generated abelian groups are isomorphic if and only if they have the same rank and the same family of invariant factors.* □

14. Categories

We have already encountered several kinds of mathematical objects, e.g., sets, ordered sets, monoids, groups, and groups with a given operator set. In each case, we were particularly interested in those maps between objects of the same kind which preserve the essential features of their structure, e.g., order, in the case of ordered sets; internal composition, in the case of monoids or groups. The consideration of a collection of "structured sets" and a corresponding collection of "structure-preserving maps" is a recurrent theme throughout mathematics. It may be described in very general terms, as follows:

Definition 14.1. A category C consists of a class, Ob C, of *objects*, and a class of *morphisms* (of objects into objects) such that

a. For any two objects X, Y, there is a set $\text{Mor}(X, Y)$ whose elements are the *morphisms of X into Y*.
b. For any three objects X, Y, Z, there is a map (law of composition) $(\alpha,\beta) \mapsto \beta \circ \alpha$ of $\text{Mor}(X,Y) \times \text{Mor}(Y,Z)$ into $\text{Mor}(X,Z)$.
c. $\text{Mor}(X,Y) \cap \text{Mor}(X',Y') = \varnothing$ if $X \neq X'$ or $Y \neq Y'$; $\text{Mor}(X,Y) = \text{Mor}(X',Y')$ if $X = X'$ and $Y = Y'$.
d. For each object X of C, there is a morphism $\iota_X \in \text{Mor}(X,X)$ such that for any object Y of C, $\iota_X\beta = \beta$ for each $\beta \in \text{Mor}(Y,X)$ and $\alpha\iota_X = \alpha$ for each $\alpha \in \text{Mor}(X,Y)$.
e. If X, Y, Z, T are objects of C, $\alpha \in \text{Mor}(X,Y)$, $\beta \in \text{Mor}(Y,Z)$, $\gamma \in \text{Mor}(Z,T)$, then $(\gamma \circ \beta) \circ \alpha = \gamma \circ (\beta \circ \alpha)$.

A morphism $\alpha \in \text{Mor}(X,Y)$ is an *isomorphism* if there is a morphism $\beta \in \text{Mor}(Y,X)$ such that $\alpha \circ \beta = \iota_Y$ and $\beta \circ \alpha = \iota_X$; a morphism $\alpha \in \text{Mor}(X,Y)$ is an *endomorphism* if $Y = X$; an endomorphism which is an isomorphism is an *automorphism*. ///

The conditions of Definition 14.1 are obviously fulfilled in the case of each of the following examples:

1. The category whose objects are sets and whose morphisms are maps; i.e., if X, Y are sets, $\mathrm{Mor}(X, Y)$ is the set of all maps of X into Y.
2. The category whose objects are ordered sets and whose morphisms are order-preserving maps.
3. The category whose objects are monoids and whose morphisms are homomorphisms.
4. The category whose objects are groups and whose morphisms are homomorphisms.
5. The category whose objects are M-groups, for a particular operator set M, and whose morphisms are M-homomorphisms (a special case is the category of $\mathbf{Z}$-groups, i.e., of abelian groups).

From a given category C, other categories may be derived. For example, for each object A of C, the morphisms $A \to X$, where X is any object of C, may be taken as the objects of a new category, C_A. For $\alpha, \beta \in \mathrm{Ob}(C_A)$, $\mathrm{Mor}(\alpha, \beta)$ consists of those morphisms φ of the original category C for which $\varphi\alpha = \beta$.

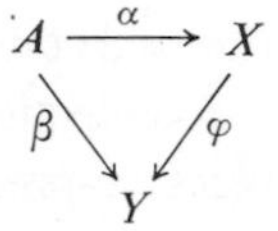

Another category C^A may be obtained using the morphisms $\alpha\colon X \to A$ of the original category as objects, and defining $\mathrm{Mor}(\alpha, \beta)$ as the set of morphisms φ of the original category C for which $\alpha\varphi = \beta$.

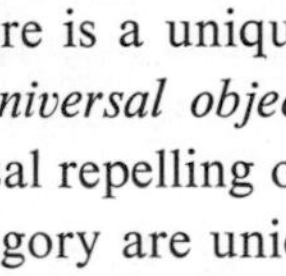

An object U of a given category C is a *universal repelling object* if, for each $X \in \mathrm{Ob}\, C$, there is a unique morphism $U \to X$, and a *universal attracting object* if for each $X \in \mathrm{Ob}\, C$ there is a unique morphism $X \to U$. (When no confusion is likely, the term *universal object* is used to designate either a universal attracting or a universal repelling object.)

Universal objects in any category are unique to within isomorphism. For suppose U_1, U_2 are, say, universal repelling objects in category C. Then there

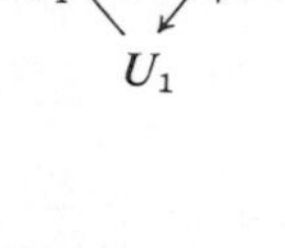

is a unique morphism $\alpha: U_1 \to U_2$ and a unique morphism $\beta: U_2 \to U_1$. Since the identity ι_{U_1} is the unique morphism $U_1 \to U_1$, we have $\beta\alpha = \iota_{U_1}$. Similarly, $\alpha\beta = \iota_{U_2}$. But then α is an isomorphism.

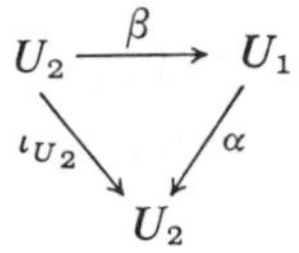

As an illustration, we characterize a free group on a set S as a universal repelling object. Let S be a set. We form a category C as follows: Let Ob C be the collection of ordered pairs $\langle G,\alpha\rangle$, where G is a group and α is a map of S into G. For $\langle G,\alpha\rangle,\langle H,\beta\rangle \in \text{Ob } C$, let $\text{Mor}(\langle G,\alpha\rangle,\langle H,\beta\rangle)$ be the set of all homomorphisms μ of G into H such that $\mu\alpha = \beta$.

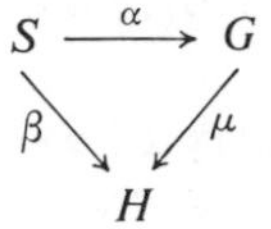

It is easy to check that C is a category. Clearly, $\langle G,\alpha\rangle$ is a free group on S according to Definition 11.1 if and only if $\langle G,\alpha\rangle$ is a universal repelling object in C. If $\langle G,\alpha\rangle$ and $\langle G',\alpha'\rangle$ are both free groups on a set S, then, by the uniqueness of universal objects in a given category, there is an isomorphism $\mu \in \text{Mor}(\langle G,\alpha\rangle,\langle G',\alpha'\rangle)$; i.e., there is a (unique) group isomorphism $\mu: G \to G'$ such that $\mu\alpha = \alpha'$. Replacing "group" by "abelian group" in the foregoing discussion, we may obtain a corresponding characterization of a free abelian group on S.

Products, coproducts, and direct sums may also be regarded as universal objects in suitably chosen categories. For example, given a family $\{G_i\}_{i\in J}$ of groups, we form a category C whose objects are ordered pairs $(G,\{\pi_i\}_{i\in J})$, where G is a group and $\{\pi_i\}_{i\in J}$ is a family of homomorphisms, $\pi_i: G \to G_i$, and whose morphisms $\alpha: (H,\{\delta_i\}_{i\in J}) \mapsto (G,\{\pi_i\}_{i\in J})$ are homomorphisms $\alpha: G \to H$ such that $\pi_i\alpha = \delta_i$ for each $i \in J$.

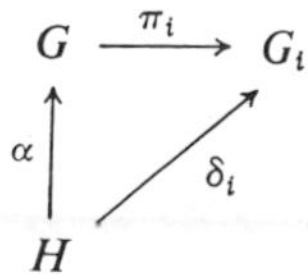

By Definition 9.1, $\langle G,\{\pi_i\}_{i\in J}\rangle$ is a product of $\{G_i\}_{i\in J}$ if and only if it is a universal attracting object in C. We leave it to the reader to give similar characterizations of coproduct and direct sum.

Given two categories C and C', a *functor* f from C to C' may be defined as follows: With each object, X, of C, we associate an object, $f(X)$, of C'; with each morphism α of C, we associate a morphism, $f(\alpha)$, of C', subject to the conditions

1. $f(\iota_X) = \iota_{f(X)}$ for each object X of C and *either*

2a. if α, β and $\beta\alpha$ are morphisms of C, then $f(\beta\alpha) = f(\beta)f(\alpha)$

or

2b. if α, β and $\beta\alpha$ are morphisms of C, then $f(\beta\alpha) = f(\alpha)f(\beta)$.

If a functor satisfies 1 and 2a, it is *covariant*; if it satisfies 1 and 2b, it is *contravariant.*

A simple example of a functor is the *stripping functor*. Let C be the category of groups, C' the category of sets. Define a functor f from C to C' as follows: For each group G, let $f(G)$ be the *set* G; for each homomorphism $\alpha: G \to H$, let $f(\alpha)$ be the *map* $\alpha: G \to H$. Clearly, f satisfies 1 and 2a; i.e., it is a covariant functor from C to C'.

Given an object A in a category C, we can define two functors, one covariant and one contravariant, as follows: In the first case, we let C' be the category, C_A, whose objects are the morphisms $A \to X$, where X is any object of C. We define a functor f_A such that, for each object X of C, $f_A(X) = \text{Mor}(A,X)$ and for each morphism $\gamma: X \to Y$ of C, $f_A(\gamma)$ is the morphism of $\text{Mor}(A,X)$ into $\text{Mor}(A,Y)$ such that, for each $\alpha \in \text{Mor}(A,X)$, $f_A(\gamma)(\alpha) = \gamma\alpha$.

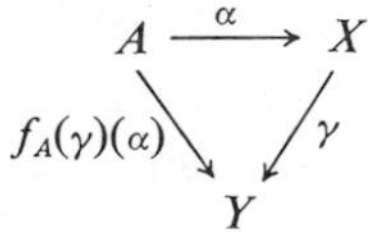

Obviously, $f_A(\iota_A) = \iota_{\text{Mor}(A,X)}$ and, for $\gamma: X \to Y$, $\delta: Y \to T$, $f_A(\delta\gamma)(\alpha) = (\delta\gamma)\alpha = \delta(\gamma\alpha) = f_A(\delta)(\gamma\alpha) = f_A(\delta)f_A(\gamma)(\alpha)$, for each $\alpha \in \text{Mor}(A,X)$. Thus, f_A is a covariant functor from C to C_A. Another functor, f^A, from the given category C to the category C^A whose objects are the morphisms $X \to A$ for objects X of C may be similarly defined by $f^A(X) = \text{Mor}(X,A)$, and for $\gamma: Y \to X$, $f^A(\gamma)$ is the morphism from $\text{Mor}(X,A)$ to $\text{Mor}(Y,A)$, such that, for each $\alpha \in \text{Mor}(X,A)$, $f^A(\gamma)(\alpha) = \alpha\gamma$.

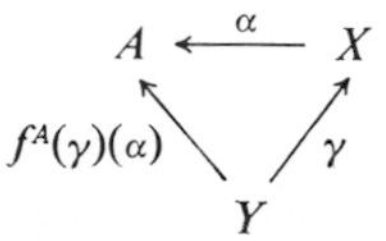

The functor f^A is contravariant, since, for $\gamma: Y \to X$ and $\delta: T \to Y$, $f^A(\gamma\delta)(\alpha) = \alpha(\gamma\delta) = (\alpha\gamma)\delta = f^A(\delta)(\alpha\gamma) = f^A(\delta)f^A(\gamma)(\alpha)$ for each $\alpha \in \text{Mor}(X,A)$. The two functors, f_A and f^A, are called *representation functors.*

As a final illustration of a functor, we give the functor $\mathrm{Hom}_{\mathbf{Z}}$ for abelian groups. If X, Y are abelian groups, denote by $\mathrm{Hom}_{\mathbf{Z}}(X,Y)$ the set of all homomorphisms of X into Y. For α,β in $\mathrm{Hom}_{\mathbf{Z}}(X,Y)$ we let $\alpha+\beta$ be the map of X into Y defined by $(\alpha+\beta)(x) = \alpha x + \beta x$ for each $x \in X$. If $x_1,x_2 \in X$, then $(\alpha+\beta)(x_1+x_2) = \alpha(x_1+x_2) + \beta(x_1+x_2) = \alpha x_1 + \alpha x_2 + \beta x_1 + \beta x_2 = \alpha x_1 + \beta x_1 + \alpha x_2 + \beta x_2 = (\alpha+\beta)x_1 + (\alpha+\beta)x_2$, since Y is abelian. Thus, $\alpha+\beta \in \mathrm{Hom}_{\mathbf{Z}}(X,Y)$. It is readily verified that $\langle \mathrm{Hom}_{\mathbf{Z}}(X,Y),+\rangle$ is an abelian group.

Define a category C whose objects are ordered pairs (X,Y) of abelian groups and whose morphisms $(X,Y) \mapsto (X',Y')$ are ordered pairs (μ,ν) of homomorphisms ($\mu\colon X' \to X$ and $\nu\colon Y \to Y'$), composed componentwise. Define another category C' whose objects are the sets $\mathrm{Hom}_{\mathbf{Z}}(X,Y)$ (X, Y abelian groups), and whose morphisms $\mathrm{Hom}_{\mathbf{Z}}(X,Y) \to \mathrm{Hom}_{\mathbf{Z}}(X',Y')$ are homomorphisms of $\mathrm{Hom}_{\mathbf{Z}}(X,Y)$ into $\mathrm{Hom}_{\mathbf{Z}}(X',Y')$, composed as usual. A functor $\mathrm{Hom}_{\mathbf{Z}}$ may now be defined as follows: With each object (X,Y) of C, associate the object $\mathrm{Hom}_{\mathbf{Z}}(X,Y)$ of C', and with each morphism (μ,ν) of C ($\mu \in \mathrm{Hom}_{\mathbf{Z}}(X',X)$, $\nu \in \mathrm{Hom}_{\mathbf{Z}}(Y',Y)$), associate the morphism $\alpha \mapsto \nu\alpha\mu$ of $\mathrm{Hom}_{\mathbf{Z}}(X,Y)$ into $\mathrm{Hom}_{\mathbf{Z}}(X',Y')$. One may verify that $\mathrm{Hom}_{\mathbf{Z}}$ is a covariant functor of C into C'.

Exercises

Section 1

1.1. Let $S = \{a,b\}$ be a set of two elements. Let $\alpha\colon S \to S$ and $\beta\colon S \to S$ be the mappings defined by:

$$\alpha(a) = a, \qquad \alpha(b) = a,$$
$$\beta(a) = b, \qquad \beta(b) = b.$$

Let $G = \{\alpha,\beta\}$, and let $\circ$ be the operation "composition of maps" on G. Show that $\langle G,\circ\rangle$ satisfies conditions a, b_r, and c_l (p. 32) but is not a group.

1.2. Let G be a set, $\circ$ an associative binary operation on G. Prove that G is a group if and only if the following two conditions are satisfied:

(h) For every $a,b \in G$, there is some $x \in G$ such that $a \circ x = b$.

(k) For every $a,b \in G$, there is some $y \in G$ such that $y \circ a = b$.

1.3. Let m be a nonzero integer and let $\mathbf{Z}/(m)$ be the set of all residue classes modulo m. Prove:

(a) $\mathbf{Z}/(m)$ forms an abelian group under addition of residue classes.

(b) For $m \neq 0$, $(\mathbf{Z}/(m)) - \{\bar{0}\}$ forms a monoid under multiplication of residue classes.

(c) The monoid $(\mathbf{Z}/(m)) - \{\bar{0}\}$ forms a group under multiplication of residue classes if and only if m is prime.

(d) If $\mathscr{R}_m$ is the set $\{0,1,\ldots,|m| - 1\}$, then $\langle \mathscr{R}_m, \oplus \rangle$ is a group isomorphic to $\langle \mathbf{Z}/(m), + \rangle$ and $\langle \mathscr{R}_m - \{0\}, \circ \rangle$ is a monoid isomorphic to $\langle (\mathbf{Z}/(m)) - \{\bar{0}\}, \cdot \rangle$, where $+$ and $\circ$ are defined by

$$a \oplus b = r, \quad r \equiv a + b \bmod m, \qquad 0 \leq r < |m|,$$

$$a \circ b = s, \quad s \equiv ab \bmod m, \qquad 0 \leq r < |m|.$$

1.4. Let G be a group. Prove

$$a^h a^k = a^{h+k},$$

$$(a^h)^k = a^{hk},$$

for all $a \in G$, $h,k \in \mathbf{Z}$.

1.5. Prove that the following conditions on a group G are equivalent:

(a) G is abelian.

(b) $(ab)^k = a^k b^k$ for all $a,b \in G$, $k \in \mathbf{Z}$.

(c) $(ab)^2 = a^2 b^2$ for all $a,b \in G$.

(d) $(ab)^{-1} = a^{-1}b^{-1}$ for all $a,b \in G$.

(c) $a^{-1}b^{-1}ab = e$ for all $a,b \in G$.

1.6. Let G be a finite set, $\circ$ an associative binary operation on G. Prove that $\langle G, \circ \rangle$ is a group if and only if the cancellation laws hold; i.e.,

(a) If $ac = bc$, then $a = b$
(b) If $ca = cb$, then $a = b$ $\Big\}(a,b,c \in G)$.

1.7. Let $\mathscr{P}(X)$ be the power set of a set X. Prove that $\langle \mathscr{P}(X), \cup \rangle$ and $\langle \mathscr{P}(X), \cap \rangle$ are monoids but not groups.

Section 2

2.1. Prove Theorem 2.1.

2.2. (a) The intersection of any set of subgroups of a group G is a subgroup of G.

(b) Let H, K be subgroups of a group G. Then $H \cup K$ is a subgroup of G if and only if $H \subset K$ or $K \subset H$.

2.3. If G is a group, X a nonempty subset of G, then

$$[X] = \{a_1^{k_1} \cdots a_m^{k_m} \mid a_i \in X,\ k_i \in \mathbf{Z},\ m \geq 0 \text{ in } \mathbf{Z}\}.$$

2.4. (a) The elements of finite order in any abelian group G form a subgroup. (This subgroup is called the *torsion subgroup* of G.)

(b) Give an example of a group in which the elements of finite order do not form a subgroup.

(c) Give an example of a non-abelian group in which the elements of finite order form a proper (nontrivial) subgroup.

2.5. A finite nonempty subset of a group G is a subgroup of G if and only if $ab \in G$ for each $a,b \in G$.

2.6. (a) Every subgroup of a cyclic group is cyclic.

(b) An infinite cyclic group is isomorphic to each of its nontrivial subgroups.

(c) If a non-trivial group is isomorphic to each of its nontrivial subgroups, then it is infinite cyclic.

2.7. (a) Let $G = [a]$ be cyclic of finite order n, and let m be an integer. Then $G = [a^m]$ if and only if $(m,n) = 1$.

(b) Let $G = [a]$ be infinite cyclic. Then $G = [a^m]$ if and only if $m = \pm 1$.

(c) Every subgroup of $\langle \mathbf{Z}, + \rangle$ has a nonnegative generator.

2.8. If G is a cyclic group of order n, then for each divisor d of n, G has a unique subgroup of order d.

2.9. If G is an infinite cyclic group, then G satisfies the ascending, but not the descending, chain condition on subgroups.

2.10. Let G be a group and let $C = \{c \in G | cx = xc \ \forall\ x \in G\}$. Prove: C forms a subgroup of G. (This subgroup is called the *center* of G.)

2.11. Prove that there are exactly two "abstract groups" of order 4. (This means: There exist two nonisomorphic groups such that any group of order 4 is isomorphic to one of them.)

2.12. A group $G \neq E$ has no proper subgroups if and only if it is finite, cyclic, of prime order.

2.13. If G is a group such that every $x \neq e$ $(x \in G)$ has order 2, then G is abelian.

2.14. If in an abelian group G the elements of infinite order, together with zero, form a nonzero subgroup of G, then G is torsionfree.

2.15. If G is a finitely generated group, then every proper subgroup of G is contained in a maximal proper subgroup.

Section 3

3.1. Prove that, for each permutation $\sigma \in S_n$, $\sim \bmod \sigma$ is an equivalence relation on $X_n = \{1,2,\ldots,n\}$.

3.2. For each $i \in X_n = \{1,2,\ldots,n\}$, the set $T_i = \{\alpha \in S_n | \alpha i = i\}$ forms a subgroup of S_n. Characterize the right and left cosets of T_i. Prove that, if $n \geq 3$, then T_i is not a normal subgroup of S_n.

3.3. If $n > 2$, then the center of S_n consists of the identity.

3.4. For $n > 2$, no subgroup of order 2 is normal in S_n.

3.5. Two permutations in S_n are conjugate if and only if they have the same cycle structure.

3.6. Prove Theorem 3.6.

3.7. Prove Theorem 3.7.

3.8. For $n \geq 3$, the subgroup of S_n generated by the 3-cycles of S_n is A_n. If a normal subgroup H of A_n contains a 3-cycle, then $H = A_n$. For $n > 5$, A_n is simple.

3.9. Given an integer n, find the smallest integer m for which the symmetric group S_m contains a cyclic subgroup of order n.

3.10. For $n > 2$, S_n is generated by (12) and $(12 \cdots n)$.

3.11. Let S be the group of all bijections of the set of all positive integers onto itself. For each of the theorems obtained in this section concerning S_n, obtain a corresponding theorem for S. In particular, note that the "even permutations" in S form a subgroup, A, of index 2, and that the procedure outlined in Exercise 3.8 can be used to prove that A is simple.

Section 4

4.1. Verify the equivalence of b, d, and e in Theorem 4.4.

4.2. A non-trivial abelian group is simple if and only if it is cyclic of prime order.

4.3. If G, G' are M-groups, $\alpha: G \to G'$ an M-homomorphism, then

(a) For each M-subgroup H of G, αH is an M-subgroup of G'.

(b) For each M-subgroup H' of αG, $\overset{-1}{\alpha} H'$ is an M-subgroup of G.

4.4. If G is an abelian group, H a subgroup of G such that H and G/H are both finitely generated, then G is finitely generated.

4.5. Let G be a group such that the only automorphism of G is the identity. Then G has order 1 or 2.

4.6. Prove Theorem 4.6.

4.7. Prove Theorem 4.7.

4.8. Determine all integers n for which the following statement is true for all groups G: If H is a subgroup of G such that $[G: H] = n$, then $H \lhd G$.

4.9. Let G be a group such that every subgroup of G is normal. Is G necessarily abelian?

4.10. Let H be a subgroup of G and let x be an element of G such that $x^{-1}Hx \subset H$. Prove: If $|H|$ is finite, then $x^{-1}Hx = H$. Prove that, if $|H|$ is infinite, the equality need not hold.

[*Hint:* Let G be the group of all bijections of $\mathbf{Z}$ onto itself, and let H be the subgroup of G generated by the transpositions $(n, n + 1)$ $(n > 0)$. If σ is the bijection on $\mathbf{Z}$ defined by $\sigma t = t - 1$ for each $t \in \mathbf{Z}$, then $\sigma^{-1}H\sigma \neq H$.]

4.11. Let G be an M-group, and let K be a normal M-subgroup of G. Let ν be the natural M-homomorphism of G with respect to K. If H is any subgroup of G, prove that $\nu^{-1}(\nu H) = [H,K]$, the subgroup of G generated by H and K.

4.12. A partially ordered set in which every pair of elements has a least upper bound and a greatest lower bound with respect to the given partial order is called a *lattice*. Prove that the subgroups of any M-group G form a lattice, $\mathscr{L}$, under set inclusion. Prove that the M-subgroups, the normal subgroups and the normal M-subgroups form sublattices of $\mathscr{L}$. (*Note:* In a sublattice, $\mathscr{S}$, the partial order is the restriction to $\mathscr{S}$ of the partial order in $\mathscr{L}$ and the least upper and greatest lower bounds for any pair of elements of $\mathcal{S}$ are the same as in $\mathcal{L}$.)

4.13. Let V be the set of all vectors in the plane and let $+$ be vector addition. Prove that $\langle V, + \rangle$ is an abelian group. For each vector $v \in V$, $T = \{av \mid a \in R\}$ forms a subgroup of V. Characterize geometrically the elements of V/T.

4.14. a. The center of a group G is invariant under all endomorphisms of G onto G.
b. Give an example of a group G whose center is not invariant under all endomorphisms of G into G.

4.15. Find the group of all automorphisms of a group G
(a) if G is infinite cyclic;
(b) if G is finite cyclic.

4.16. Prove that the group of all automorphisms of S_n $(n \geq 1)$ is isomorphic to S_n.

4.17. Let C^* be the multiplicative group of nonzero complex numbers $z = \rho(\cos\theta + i \sin\theta)$. Let $\mathbf{U} = \{z \mid \rho = 1\}$ and let $\mathbf{R}^* = \{z \mid \theta = 0, \rho \neq 0\}$. Characterize geometrically the elements of the factor groups $\mathbf{C}^*/\mathbf{U}$ and $\mathbf{C}^*/\mathbf{R}^*$. Prove that $\mathbf{C}^*/\mathbf{U}$ is isomorphic to the multiplicative group of non-zero real numbers and that $\mathbf{C}^*/\mathbf{R}^*$ is isomorphic to $\mathbf{R}/[2\pi]$, where $\mathbf{R}$ is the additive group of all real numbers.

4.18. Let G be the set of maps $\alpha_{a,b}: \mathbf{R} \to \mathbf{R}$ $(a,b \in \mathbf{R})$ defined by $\alpha_{a,b}x = ax + b$ for each $x \in \mathbf{R}$, and let $T = \{\alpha_{1,b} \mid b \in \mathbf{R}\}$. Prove that G forms a group under composition. Find a homomorphism of G onto $\langle R, + \rangle$, with kernel T and conclude: T is a normal subgroup of G.

4.19. Let G be a group, H a subgroup of G. Then the map $(Ha, Hb) \mapsto Hab$ is a binary operation on the set of right cosets of H in G if and only if $H \triangleleft G$.

4.20. Let G be an abelian group, T the torsion subgroup of G. Then
(a) G/T is torsion free.
(b) If $H \triangleleft G$ and G/H is torsion free, then $T \subset H$.
(c) If $\nu: G \to G/T$ is the canonical epimorphism, and $\alpha: G \to G'$ is a homomorphism such that G' is torsion free, then there is a unique homomorphism $\mu: G/T \to G'$ such that $\mu\nu = \alpha$.

4.21. If α is a homomorphism of a group G onto an abelian group G', then every subgroup of G which contains Ker α is normal.

4.22. If H is a cyclic subgroup of G such that $H \triangleleft G$, then every subgroup of H is normal in G.

4.23. If G is an M-group which satisfies the ascending chain condition on M-subgroups, and $\alpha: G \to G'$ is an M-homomorphism with Ker $\alpha \neq E$, then G' is not isomorphic to G. (See Exercise 8.8 or 11.9 for a counterexample in case the ascending chain condition is not assumed.)

4.24. An M-group G is isomorphic to a proper M-homomorphic image of itself if and only if there is an M-endomorphism of G onto G which is not an M-automorphism.

Section 5

5.1. Prove the Zassenhaus Lemma: If H, K, H', K' are M-subgroups of an M-group G such that $H' \lhd H$, $K' \lhd K$, then

(a) $H'(H \cap K') \lhd H'(H \cap K)$.

(b) $(H' \cap K)K' \lhd (H \cap K)K'$.

(c) $H'(H \cap K)/H'(H \cap K') \cong (H \cap K)K'/(H' \cap K)K'$.

(*Hint:* Consider the following diagram, where two lines going downward meet in a point which represents the intersection, and two lines going upward meet in a point which represents the product of two subgroups.

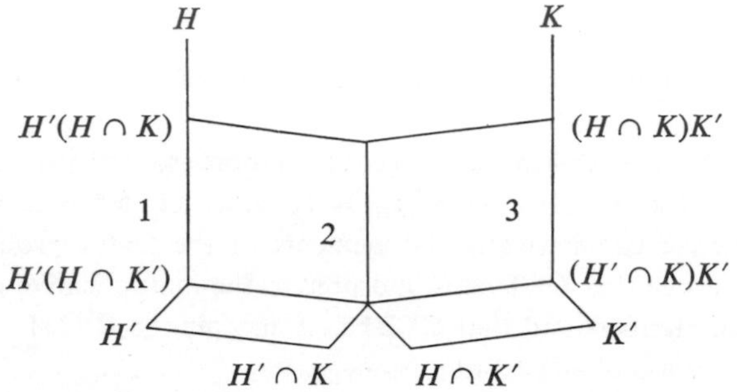

Prove that the factor group corresponding to the middle vertical line 2 is isomorphic to the factor group corresponding to 1, using Theorem 4.11. Complete the proof using symmetry.)

5.2. Use the Zassenhaus Lemma to prove: Any two normal series of an M-group G have equivalent refinements (Schreier Refinement Theorem).

[*Hint:* Given normal series

$$G = G_1 \rhd G_2 \rhd \cdots \rhd G_k = E,$$

$$G = H_1 \rhd H_2 \rhd \cdots \rhd H_l = E,$$

define $G_{ij} = G_{i+1}(H_j \cap G_i)$, $i = 1, \ldots, k-1$; $j = 1, \ldots, l$; and $H_{ji} = H_{j+1}(G_i \cap H_j)$, $j = 1, \ldots, l-1$; $i = 1, \ldots, k$.]

5.3. Obtain the Jordan–Hölder Theorem from the Schreier Refinement Theorem.

5.4. Apply the Jordan–Hölder Theorem to a finite cyclic group of order n to prove that n has a unique factorization as a product of primes.

5.5. If $G = G_1 \supset G_2 \supset \cdots \supset G_{k+1} = E$ is a normal series for G and if H is an M-subgroup of G, prove:

(a) $H = H \cap G_1 \supset H \cap G_2 \supset \cdots \supset H \cap G_{k+1} = E$ is a normal series for H.

(b) Each factor of the second series is isomorphic to a subgroup of some factor of the first series.

5.6. Obtain two distinct composition series for S_4 and establish their equivalence.

5.7. An abelian group has a composition series if and only if it is finite. Is the corresponding statement true for abelian M-groups?

Section 6

6.1. A group G is solvable if and only if it has a normal series

$$G \supset G' \supset G'' \supset \cdots \supset G^{(i)} \supset \cdots \supset E,$$

where each group $G^{(i)}$ is the commutator subgroup of its predecessor.

6.2. If a solvable group G has a composition series, then every normal series for G has a solvable refinement.

6.3. Let G be a group, and let $\{C_n\}_{n \in \mathbf{N}}$ be the sequence of subgroups of G defined by

$$C_0 = E,$$
$$C_{n+1} = \{x \in G \mid x^{-1}y^{-1}xy \in C_n \text{ for all } y \in G\}.$$

($\{C_n\}$ is called the *upper central series* for G.) Prove (a) $C_n \lhd G$ for each $n \in \mathbf{N}$ and (b) C_{n+1}/C_n is the center of G/C_n.

6.4. A group G is *nilpotent* if its upper central series terminates, i.e., if there is an integer n such that $C_n = G$. Prove that every nilpotent group is solvable.

6.5. The alternating group of degree 4 is not a normal subgroup of the alternating group of degree 5.

Section 7

7.1. Prove Theorem 7.1.

7.2. Let G be a group.

(a) If S is a subset of G, then $C_G(S)$ and $N_G(S)$ are subgroups of G, and $C_G(S) \subset N_G(S)$.

(b) If S_1, S_2 are subsets of G, then $C_G(C_G(S)) \supset S$, and $C_G(C_G(C_G(S))) = C_G(S)$.

(c) If H is a subgroup of G, then $S \lhd N_G(H)$.

(d) $H \lhd G$ if and only if $N_G(H) = G$.

7.3. If G is a group such that $G/C(G)$ is cyclic, then G is abelian.

7.4. If a group G contains exactly one element, a, of order n, then $n = 2$ and a is in the center of G.

7.5. The center of a group G is equal to the intersection of the centralizers of the elements of G.

7.6. If $\nu: G \to G'$ is an epimorphism, H a subgroup of G, with $H \supset \operatorname{Ker} \nu$, then $N_{\nu G}(\nu H) = \nu(N_G(H))$.

7.7. (a) If G is a group, H a subgroup of G, then the cardinality of the set of all subgroups of G which are isomorphic to H is greater than, or equal to, $[G: N_G(H)]$.

(b) If $G = S_4$ and H is any subgroup of order 3 or 8, then the number of subgroups isomorphic to H is equal to $[G: N_G(H)]$.

7.8. If, in a group G, the elements of finite order form a finite subgroup, then this subgroup is normal.

7.9. Let S be a subset of a group G. The intersection of all normal subgroups of G which contain S is called the *normal subgroup of G generated by S*. Prove that the normal subgroup generated by S is equal to the subgroup generated by $\bigcup_{x \in G} x^{-1}Sx$.

Section 8

8.1. Prove that there are five abstract groups of order 8, three abelian and two non-abelian.

8.2. There is no simple group of order 12, 28, 42, 56.

8.3. If a Sylow p-subgroup of a group G is normal, then it is fully invariant (i.e., invariant under all endomorphisms of G).

8.4. Let $n = pq$, where p, q are primes and $q > p$. Prove:

(a) If $q \not\equiv 1 \bmod p$, then any group of order pq is cyclic.

(b) If $q \equiv 1 \bmod p$, then there are exactly two "abstract groups" of order pq. (See Exercise 2.11.)

8.5. Every finite p-group is nilpotent (hence solvable). (See Exercises 6.3 and 6.4.)

8.6. If G is a finite abelian group with elements $x_1 \cdots x_n$, prove:

(a) If G has no element of order 2, or more than one element of order 2, then $\prod_{i=1}^{n} x_i = e$.

(b) If G has a unique element, a, of order 2, then $\prod_{i=1}^{n} x_i = a$.

Use the preceding result to prove Wilson's Theorem: If p is a prime, then $(p - 1)! \equiv -1 \bmod p$.

8.7. Let p be a prime, and let G be an infinite p-primary group. Prove:

(a) The order of every finite subgroup of G is a power of p.

(b) If G has a finite subgroup of maximal order p^k, then G has a subgroup of order p^h for each positive integer $h \leq k$.

(c) If G does not have a subgroup of maximal finite order, then G has a subgroup of order p^h for each positive integer h.

8.8. For a given prime p, let G be the set of all complex p^kth roots of 1, where k ranges through $\mathbf{N}$. Prove:

(a) Under multiplication, G forms a p-primary group of infinite order.

(b) For each $k \in \mathbf{N}$, G has a unique cyclic subgroup G_k of order p^k.

(c) Every proper subgroup of G is cyclic of order p^k for some $k \in \mathbf{N}$.

(d) $G = \bigcup_{k \in \mathbf{N}} G_k$.

(c) G satisfies the descending, but not the ascending chain condition on subgroups.

(f) Every nontrivial homomorphic image of G is isomorphic to G.

(*Note:* A group which is isomorphic to G is called a "group of type p^∞," "quasicyclic," or a "Prüfer group.")

8.9. For a given prime p, let $\mathbf{Q}_p$ be the additive group of all rational numbers x

whose denominator (in lowest-term representation) is a power of p. Prove that $\mathbf{Q}_p/\mathbf{Z}$ is a group of type p^∞. (See Exercise 8.8.)

8.10. A group G is of type p^∞ if and only if G contains a finite cyclic group of order p^n for each $n = 0, 1, 2, \ldots$, but no proper subgroup of G has this property.

8.11. Let $\mathscr{U}$ be the multiplicative group of all complex roots of 1. Prove that a group G is isomorphic to $\mathscr{U}$ if and only if it has a finite cyclic subgroup of order n for each $n = 0, 1, 2, \ldots$, but no proper subgroup of $\mathscr{U}$ has this property.

8.12. If an abelian group G does not contain two distinct isomorphic subgroups, then it is isomorphic to a subgroup of the multiplicative group $\mathscr{U}$ of all complex roots of 1.

Section 9

9.1. If H is a direct summand of an M-group G, then every M-homomorphism of H into G can be extended to an M-endomorphism of G; every M-monomorphism of H into G can be extended to an M-automorphism of G.

9.2. Carry out the details of Example 2 (p. 71) establishing the existence of the coproduct of two M-groups.

9.3. $\coprod'_{i\in J} G_i$ is a p-group if and only if each G_i is a p-group. Does the corresponding assertion hold if $\coprod'$ is replaced by $\prod$?

9.4. Let G_1, G_2 be groups such that each is isomorphic to a subgroup of the other. Are G_1 and G_2 necessarily isomorphic?

9.5. If a finitely generated group G has a unique maximal subgroup, then G is cyclic of prime-power order. (*Hint:* Use Exercise 2.15.)

9.6. Let $\mathbf{Q}$ be the additive group of rationals, $\mathbf{Z}$ the additive group of integers. Prove:

(a) $\mathbf{Q}/\mathbf{Z}$ is a torsion group.

(b) For each prime p, the p-primary component of $\mathbf{Q}/\mathbf{Z}$ is $\mathbf{D}_p/\mathbf{Z}$, where $\mathbf{D}_p$ is the set of all rationals whose denominator (in lowest terms) is a power of p.

9.7. Let G be a finite abelian group of order $n = \prod_{i=1}^{k} p_i^{\alpha_i}$, where the p_i are distinct primes. Then $G = \prod_{i=1}^{k} G_i$, where each G_i is p_i-primary. If G is cyclic, then each G_i is cyclic of order $p_i^{\alpha_i}$.

9.8. Prove Theorem 9.8.

9.9. Prove Theorem 9.9.

9.10. Prove Theorem 9.10.

9.11. The multiplicative group of nonzero complex numbers is isomorphic to a direct product of the multiplicative group of positive reals and the multiplicative group of complex numbers of absolute value 1.

9.12. Suppose $H_1 \lhd G_1$, $H_2 \lhd G_2$. Are any of the following statements true?

(a) $G_1 \cong G_2$ and $H_1 \cong H_2 \Rightarrow G_1/H_1 \cong G_2/H_2$.

(b) $G_1 \cong G_2$ and $G_1/H_1 \cong G_2/H_2 \Rightarrow H_1 \cong H_2$.

(c) $H_1 \cong H_2$ and $G_1/H_1 \cong G_2/H_2 \Rightarrow G_1 \cong G_2$.

9.13. Let G, H be direct sums of cyclic groups. Prove: $G \oplus G \cong H \oplus H$ implies $G \cong H$. Prove that $G \oplus G \oplus \cdots \oplus G \cong H \oplus H \oplus \cdots \oplus H$ does not, in general, imply $G \cong H$.

9.14. If G is a finite abelian group and $m \mid |G|$, then
(a) G has a subgroup of order m, and
(b) G has a factor group of order m.

Section 10

10.1. A finite abelian group is indecomposable if and only if it is cyclic of prime-power order.

10.2. Let G be an M-group and let $\alpha: G \to G$ be an M-endomorphism.
(a) If G satisfies the ascending chain condition on normal M-subgroups, then there is a least positive integer k such that Ker α^k = Ker α^{k+p} for each $p \geq 1$.
(b) If G satisfies the descending chain condition on M-subgroups, then there is a least positive integer l such that $\alpha^l G = \alpha^{l+p} G$ for each $p \geq 1$.
(c) If G satisfies the ascending chain condition on normal M-subgroups, and the descending chain condition on M-subgroups, then $k = l$, $G = \alpha^k G$. Ker α^k, $\alpha^k G \cap \text{Ker } \alpha^k = E$, $\alpha|_{\alpha^k G}$ is an automorphism, and $\alpha|_{\text{Ker } \alpha^k}$ is nilpotent.

(*Note:* An endomorphism $\beta: X \to X$ is *nilpotent* if $\beta^s = 0_X$ for some positive integer s, where 0_X is the endomorphism mapping every element of X to the identity.)

10.3. An M-endomorphism of an M-group G is *normal* if it commutes with every inner automorphism of G. (*Note:* If $\alpha: G \to G$ is a normal M-endomorphism of G, then $\alpha^i G \lhd G$ for each $i = 1, 2, \ldots$.)

From Exercise 10.2 deduce Fitting's Lemma: If G is an M-group which satisfies both chain conditions on normal M-subgroups and $\alpha: G \to G$ is a normal M-endomorphism, then
(a) There is a positive integer k such that $G = \alpha^k G \oplus \text{Ker } \alpha^k$.
(b) $\alpha|_{\alpha^k G}$ is an automorphism and $\alpha|_{\text{Ker } \alpha^k}$ is nilpotent.

10.4. Let G be an indecomposable M-group satisfying both chain conditions on (normal) M-subgroups, and let $\alpha: G \to G$ be a (normal) M-endomorphism. Then α is either an automorphism or a nilpotent endomorphism.

10.5. Each of the following groups is indecomposable:
(a) The additive group of rationals.
(b) Any finite cyclic group of prime-power order.
(c) Any group of type p^∞ for some prime p.
(d) Any simple group.

Section 11

11.1. Obtain a system of generators and defining relations for each of the five groups of order 8. (See Exercise 8.1.)

11.2. (a) Let G be a group with generating set

$$S = \{c_1, c_2, \ldots\}$$

and set of defining relations

$$\{c_1 = e, c_2^2 = c_1, c_3^3 = c_2, \ldots, c_n^n = c_{n-1}, \ldots\}.$$

Prove that G is isomorphic to the additive group $\mathbf{Q}$ of all rational numbers.

(b) Prove that the additive group $\mathbf{Q}$ is equal to the union of the ascending chain

$$[1] \subset \left[\frac{1}{2!}\right] \subset \cdots \subset \left[\frac{1}{n!}\right] \subset \cdots.$$

11.3. Let G be a group with generating set

$$S = \{c_1, c_2, \ldots\}$$

and set of defining relations

$$\{pc_1 = e, pc_2 = c_1, \ldots, pc_{n+1} = c_n, \ldots\}.$$

Prove that G is of type p^ω. (See Exercises 8.8, 8.9, and 8.10.)

11.4. A free group $\neq E$ is abelian if and only if it is cyclic.

11.5. Let F be a free group, with generating set $S \subset F$. Prove: If $X \subsetneqq S$, then the subgroup of F generated by X is properly contained in the normal subgroup generated by X.

11.6. Let F be a free group on a set of more than one element. Then

(a) The center of F consists of the identity only.

(b) The commutator subgroup of F has infinite order.

11.7. If F is a free group, then

(a) F is indecomposable.

(b) F has no composition series.

(c) F is not solvable unless it is cyclic.

11.8. Let k be any cardinal number. Prove: If F is a free group on a set of cardinality k, then F is a homomorphic image of every free group on a set of cardinality h, where $k \leq h$.

11.9. If F is a free group on infinitely many generators, then F is isomorphic to a proper homomorphic image of itself (or, equivalently, there is an endomorphism of F onto F which is not an automorphism).

11.10. (a) The group of all inner automorphisms of a free group on more than one generator is free.

(b) Prove or disprove: The group of all automorphisms of a free group on more than one generator is free.

Section 12

12.1. A free abelian group is a free group if and only if it is cyclic.

12.2. If F is a free group on a set S of cardinality a, then F/F^1 is a free abelian group of rank a.

12.3. If F_1 is a free group on a set S_1, F_2 a free group on a set S_2, then $F_1 \cong F_2$ if and only if S_1 and S_2 have the same cardinality.

12.4. (a) A free abelian group $\neq E$ has a subgroup of index n for each positive integer n.

(b) A free group $\neq E$ has a normal subgroup of index n for each positive integer n.

(c) If F is a free (abelian) group, $\neq E$, then the number of nonisomorphic factor groups of F, of order n, is at most $n!$.

12.5. The multiplicative group of positive rationals is a free abelian group on a countable generating set. The multiplicative group of nonnegative rationals is a direct sum of a free abelian group and a group of order 2.

12.6. The additive group of rationals is a torsion-free abelian group but is not a free abelian group.

12.7. Let $\{G_i\}_{i \in J}$ be a family of free abelian groups. Prove that $\coprod_{i \in J} G_i$ is a free abelian group. (*Note:* $\prod_{i \in J} G_i$ need not be a free abelian group. For an example, see [9, p. 168].)

Section 13

13.1. Let G be a finitely generated p-primary abelian group. Prove: If $G = H_1 \oplus \cdots \oplus H_s = K_1 \oplus \cdots \oplus K_t$ $(s,t \in \mathbf{Z})$, where the H_i, K_j are cyclic, with $|H_i| = p^{\alpha_i}$ $(i = 1,\ldots,s)$, $|K_j| = p^{\beta_j}$ $(j = 1,\ldots,t)$, and $\alpha_1 \geq \alpha_2 \geq \cdots \geq \alpha_s$, $\beta_1 \geq \beta_2 \geq \cdots \geq \beta_k$, then $s = t$ and $|H_i| \cong |K_i|$ $(i = 1,\ldots,s)$. Use this result to prove the uniqueness of the family of orders of the finite cyclic subgroups in any p-decomposition of G. (*Hint:* First prove that the subgroup P of G formed by 0 and the elements of order p has order $p^s = p^t$, whence $s = t$. Next suppose that there is a positive integer h such that $\alpha_h < \beta_h$ and $\alpha_i = \beta_i$ for $i < h$. Compute the order of $p^{\alpha_h}G$, using each of the two decompositions, to produce a contradiction.)

13.2. If G is a finitely generated abelian group of rank n and H is a subgroup of G of rank m, then the rank of G/H is $n - m$.

13.3. A finitely generated abelian group is not isomorphic to any proper homomorphic image of itself.

13.4. An infinite abelian group is cyclic if and only if its subgroups $\neq E$ are all of finite index.

13.5. (a) Every subgroup of a finitely generated abelian group is finitely generated.

(b) A finitely generated non-abelian group may have a subgroup which is not finitely generated.

(c) A finitely generated abelian M-group may have an M-subgroup which is not finitely generated.

13.6. If $n = \prod_{i=1}^{k} p_i^{e_i}$ (p_i distinct primes, $e_i \geq 1$), then a maximal set of non-isomorphic abelian groups of order n has cardinality $\prod_{i=1}^{k} p(e_i)$, where $p(e_i)$ is the number of (additive) partitions of e_i, for each $i = 1, \ldots, k$.

Section 14

14.1. Let M be a class and let $\circ$ be a binary operation on a subclass of M. (Thus, $\alpha \circ \beta$ is not necessarily defined for all $\alpha, \beta \in M$.) An element $e \in M$ is an *identity* if, for $\alpha, \beta \in M$, $e \circ \alpha = \alpha$ and $\beta \circ e = \beta$ whenever the compositions are defined. Suppose that for $\alpha, \beta, \gamma \in M$, the following statements are true:

(a) If one of $\alpha \circ (\beta \circ \gamma)$, $(\alpha \circ \beta) \circ \gamma$ is defined, then so is the other, and the two are equal.

(b) If $e \in M$ is an identity, and $\alpha \circ e$ and $e \circ \beta$ are defined, then $\alpha \circ \beta$ is defined.

(c) There are identities $e, f \in M$ such that $e \circ \alpha$ and $\alpha \circ f$ are defined.

(d) For any pair e, f of identities in M, $\{\alpha \in M \mid (e \circ \alpha) \circ f \text{ is defined}\}$ is a set.

Show that to any such class M there corresponds a category; and conversely, to every category there corresponds such a class M.

14.2. From the category of groups to the category of sets, construct two functors, one covariant, the other contravariant, such that to each group G corresponds the set of all subgroups of G.

14.3. An object $\mathscr{Z}$ in a category C is a zero object if for all objects A in C each of the sets $\text{Mor}(\mathscr{Z}, A)$, $\text{Mor}(A, \mathscr{Z})$ consists of a single element. Let C be a category with a zero object $\mathscr{Z}$; for objects A, B in C, $0 \in \text{Mor}(A,B)$ is a zero morphism if 0 factors through $\mathscr{Z}$; i.e., 0 is the unique morphism $\omega_{\mathscr{Z},D}\omega_{A,\mathscr{Z}}$, where $\{\omega_{A,\mathscr{Z}}\} = \text{Mor}(A, \mathscr{Z})$ and $\{\omega_{\mathscr{Z},D}\} = \text{Mor}(\mathscr{Z}, B)$.

Prove: An object $\mathbf{Z}$ in the category Ablgp of abelian groups is isomorphic to the additive group of integers if and only if

(a) for every object $G \in$ Ablgp, G not a zero object, $|\text{Mor}(\mathbf{Z}, G)| > 1$, and

(b) if $\eta \in \text{Mor}(\mathbf{Z}, \mathbf{Z})$ is such that $\eta\eta = \eta$, then η is a zero map, or $\eta = \iota_{\mathbf{Z},\mathbf{Z}}$.

14.4. Let A, B, C be objects in a category. A morphism $\mu \in \text{Mor}(B,C)$ is *monic* if, for $\alpha, \beta \in \text{Mor}(A,B)$, $\alpha = \beta$ whenever $\mu\alpha = \mu\beta$. A morphism $\xi \in \text{Mor}(A,B)$ is *epic* if, for $\gamma, \delta \in \text{Mor}(B,C)$, $\gamma = \delta$ whenever $\gamma\xi = \delta\xi$.

(a) Give an example of a monic morphism μ, in some category, such that μ is not an injective map.

(b) Give an example of an epic morphism ξ, in some category, such that ξ is not a surjective map.

(c) Show that, in the category of groups, μ is monic if and only if μ is an injective map.

(d) Show that, in the category of groups ξ is epic if and only if ξ is a surjective map.

Chapter 2 / Rings; Integral Domains

1. Preliminaries

Definition 1.1. Let A be a set, $+$, $\cdot$ binary operations on A. Then $\langle A,+,\cdot\rangle$ is a *ring* if

a. $\langle A,+\rangle$ is an abelian group.

b. $\cdot$ is associative.

c. $\cdot$ is left and right distributive with respect to $+$.

Briefly, if $\langle A,+,\cdot\rangle$ is a ring, we say that A is a ring.

If $\cdot$ is commutative, then A is a *commutative ring*; if A contains an identity for $\cdot$, then A is a *ring with identity*.

A ring A with identity $1 \neq 0$ is a *division ring* if every nonzero element of A has a multiplicative inverse in A. A commutative division ring is a *field*.

A commutative ring A with identity $1 \neq 0$ is an *integral domain* if $ab = 0$ $(a,b \in A)$ implies $a = 0$ or $b = 0$.

[A nonzero element a of a ring A such that $ax = 0$ or $xa = 0$ for some $x \neq 0$ in A is referred to as a (left or right) *zero divisor*. Thus, a commutative ring with identity $1 \neq 0$ is an integral domain if and only if it has no zero divisors.]

In any ring A with identity, an element which has a multiplicative inverse is a *unit* in A. ///

REMARKS.

1. The following computational rules for rings are easy consequences of the definition (see Exercise 1.1).

If $\langle A,+,\cdot\rangle$ is a ring and $a,b,c \in A$, then

a. $0 \cdot a = 0 = a \cdot 0$.

b. $(-a)b = -ab = a(-b)$.

c. $(-a)(-b) = ab$.

d. $c(a - b) = ca - cb$, $(a - b)c = ac - bc$.

2. It is clear that every field is an integral domain. For, if A is a field, $a,b \in A$, $ab = 0$, and $a \neq 0$, then $b = (a^{-1}a)b = a^{-1}(ab) = a^{-1}0 = 0$.

3. In the definition of "integral domain," the condition "$ab = 0$ implies $a = 0$ or $b = 0$" can be replaced by either of the two multiplicative cancellation laws "$ac = bc$, $c \neq 0$, implies $a = b$" or "$ca = cb$, $c \neq 0$, implies $a = b$." (See Exercise 1.2.)

Definition 1.2. If $\langle A,+,\cdot\rangle$ is a ring, then B is a *subring* of A if $B \subset A$ and $\langle B,+_B,\cdot_B\rangle$ is itself a ring. ///

Theorem 1.1. *If $\langle A,+,\cdot\rangle$ is a ring, $B \subset A$, then B is a subring of A if and only if*

a. $B \neq \varnothing$

b. $x - y \in B$ *for each* $x,y \in B$

} *i.e., B is a subgroup of $\langle A,+\rangle$,*

c. $xy \in B$ *for each* $x,y \in B$.

PROOF. Exercise 1.3. □

A role analogous to that of the normal subgroups in the theory of groups is played in the theory of rings by the "ideals."

Definition 1.3. If $\langle A,+,\cdot\rangle$ is a ring, $K \subset A$ such that

a. $K \neq \varnothing$

b. $x - y \in K$ for each $x,y \in K$

} i.e., K is a subgroup of $\langle A,+\rangle$,

then K is a *right ideal* of A if $xa \in K$ for each $x \in K$, $a \in A$; K is a *left ideal* of A if $ax \in K$ for each $x \in K$, $a \in A$; and K is a *two-sided ideal* of A if $ax \in K$ and $xa \in K$ for each $x \in K$, $a \in A$.

A right, left, or two-sided ideal K of A is *proper* if $K \neq A$ and $K \neq 0$. ///

It is clear that, in any ring A, both 0 and A form (right, left, and two-sided) ideals. Not every ring has proper ideals. It is quite easy to verify that a division ring has no proper one-sided ideals, hence certainly no proper two-sided ideals (Exercise 1.4). Nonexistence of proper one-sided ideals is a very strong condition: To satisfy it, a ring must be either a division ring or a "zero ring," i.e., a ring in which all products are zero (Exercise 1.5). For any ring A and positive integer n, the $n \times n$ matrices with elements in A form a ring, A_n, with respect to the usual matrix addition and multiplication. If A is not a zero ring, then for $n > 1$, A_n is noncommutative and has proper right and left ideals (Exercise 1.6). If, in particular, A is a division ring, then the matrix ring A_n is a ring without proper two-sided ideals (Exercise 1.7) in which every descending chain of right (left) ideals must terminate (Chapter 8, Section 4). One of the important theorems of ring theory (the Wedderburn Structure Theorem for Simple Rings) asserts that, except in the case of zero rings, the converse is true: Every "simple ring", i.e., every ring without proper two-sided ideals which is not a zero ring and which satisfies the descending chain condition on right (left) ideals is isomorphic, for some n, to the ring of all $n \times n$ matrices with elements in some division ring (Chapter 8, Theorem 4.2). The simple rings are among the basic building blocks in the structure theory of rings (see Chapter 8, Theorem 5.1, Corollary 2; the Artin–Wedderburn Structure Theorem for Semisimple Rings).

REMARK. If A is a ring, then the intersection of any nonempty set of subrings of A is again a subring; the intersection of any nonempty set of right, left, or two-sided ideals is, respectively, a right, left, or two-sided ideal.

Definition 1.4. If A is a ring, S a nonempty subset of A, then the intersection of all subrings of A containing S is the *subring* $[S]$ *generated by* S; the intersection of all right, left, or two-sided ideals of A containing S is, respectively, the *right, left, or two-sided ideal* $(S)_r$, $(S)_l$, *or* (S) *generated by* S. In particular, the right, left, or two-sided ideal generated by the set consisting of a single element x is called the *principal right, left, or two-sided ideal* $(x)_r$, $(x)_l$, *or* (x), *generated by* x. ///

REMARK. If A is a ring with identity, $x \in A$, then the right ideal $(x)_r$ generated by x is the set $xA = \{xa | a \in A\}$, the left ideal $(x)_l$ generated by x is the set $Ax = \{ax | a \in A\}$, and the two-sided ideal (x) generated by x is the set of all sums of elements of the form axb, ax, and xb $(a,b \in A)$.

In the absence of an identity, $(x)_r = \{xa + kx | a \in A, k \in \mathbf{Z}\}$; $(x)_l = \{xa + kx | a \in A, k \in \mathbf{Z}\}$, and (x) is the set of all sums of elements axb, ax, and xb $(a,b \in A)$, and elements $kx, k \in \mathbf{Z}$. (See Exercise 1.8.)

The definitions of isomorphism, automorphism, homomorphism, endomorphism, epimorphism, and monomorphism (Chapter 0, Definition 2.5) apply to rings with respect to the two operations $+$ and $\cdot$, e.g., if $\langle A,+,\cdot\rangle$ and $\langle A',+',\cdot'\rangle$ are rings and α is a mapping of A into A', then α is a homomorphism of A into A' if $\alpha(a + b) = \alpha a +' \alpha b$, and $\alpha(ab) = \alpha a \cdot' \alpha b$, for all $a,b \in A$. It is easy to check that Im α is a subring of A', with $\alpha 0 = 0'$, the additive identity of A'.

Definition 1.5. If A, A' are rings and α is a homomorphism of A into A', then the *kernel* of α is the set Ker $\alpha = \{a \in A | \alpha a = 0'\}$. ///

The analogy between normal subgroups and two-sided ideals stems from the fact that the kernel of any ring homomorphism is a two-sided ideal.

Theorem 1.2. *If $\langle A,+,\cdot\rangle$, $\langle A',+',\cdot'\rangle$ are rings, and if α is a homomorphism of A into A', with kernel K, then K is a two-sided ideal of A.*

PROOF. Since α is a homomorphism of $\langle A,+\rangle$ into $\langle A',+'\rangle$, its kernel K is a subgroup of $\langle A,+\rangle$. If $a \in K$, $x \in A$, then $\alpha(ax) = \alpha a \alpha x = 0' \cdot' \alpha x = 0'$; $\alpha(xa) = \alpha x \alpha a = \alpha x \cdot' 0'$; hence $ax \in K$, $xa \in K$, and K is a two-sided ideal of A. ∎

In analogy to the construction of the factor group of a group with respect to a normal subgroup, we now construct the "residue class ring" of a ring with respect to a two-sided ideal.

Theorem 1.3. *Let A be a ring, K a two-sided ideal in A. Let A/K be the set of all additive cosets of A modulo K. On A/K, define $\oplus$ as coset addition:*

(1) $$(K + a) \oplus (K + b) = K + (a + b)$$

and define $\circ$ by

(2) $$(K + a) \circ (K + b) = K + ab.$$

Then

a. *$\langle A/K,\oplus,\circ\rangle$ is a ring.*
b. *The mapping $\nu: a \rightarrow K + a$ is an epimorphism of the ring $\langle A,+,\cdot\rangle$ onto the ring $\langle A/K,\oplus,\circ\rangle$, with kernel K.*

PROOF.

a. Because of the definition of $\oplus$, $\langle A/K,\oplus\rangle$ is simply the factor group of $\langle A,+\rangle$ with respect to K. Clearly, $\langle A/K,\oplus\rangle$ is abelian. We must prove that (2) defines a binary operation $\circ$ on A/K. For each $a,b \in A$, $K + ab \in A/K$. Thus, we need only show that, if $a,a',b,b' \in A$, and $K + a = K + a'$, $K + b = K + b'$, then $K + ab = K + a'b'$. We have $ab - a'b' = ab - ab' + ab' -$

$a'b' = a(b - b') + (a - a')b'$. Since $a - a' \in K$, $b - b' \in K$, and K is a two-sided ideal, it follows that $ab - a'b' \in K$, hence $K + ab = K + a'b'$. The associativity of $\circ$, and its distributivity with respect to $\oplus$, are easily checked; and so $\langle A/K, \oplus, \circ \rangle$ is a ring.

b. By Chapter 1, Theorem 4.2, we know that ν is an epimorphism of $\langle A, + \rangle$ onto $\langle A/K, \oplus \rangle$, with kernel K. Since, for each $a,b \in A$, $\nu(ab) = K + ab = (K + a) \circ (K + b) = \nu a \circ \nu b$, ν is an epimorphism of the ring $\langle A, +, \cdot \rangle$ onto the ring $\langle A/K, \oplus, \circ \rangle$, as required. ∎

The mapping ν of Theorem 1.3 is called the canonical (ring) epimorphism of A onto the residue class ring A/K.

Corollary. *If A is a ring, K a subset of A, then K is a two-sided ideal of A if and only if K is the kernel of some ring homomorphism of A.* □

In analogy to Chapter 1, Theorem 4.9, we now have

Theorem 1.4. (Fundamental Theorem of Homomorphism for Rings.) *Let A, A' be rings, H an ideal in A, and $\nu: A \to A/H$ the canonical ring epimorphism. Let $\alpha: A \to A'$ be a ring epimorphism. Then*

a. *There is a unique ring epimorphism $\beta: A/H \to A'$, with $\beta\nu = \alpha$, if and only if $H \subset \text{Ker } \alpha$.*

b. *There is a unique ring isomorphism $\beta: A/H \to A'$, with $\beta\nu = \alpha$, if and only if $H = \text{Ker } \alpha$.*

PROOF. By Chapter 1, Theorem 4.9a, we know that there is a unique epimorphism β of $\langle A, + \rangle$ onto $\langle A', +' \rangle$ such that $\beta\nu = \alpha$ if and only if $H \subset \text{Ker } \alpha$. This epimorphism is a *ring* epimorphism, since, for each $\nu a, \nu b \in A/H$, $\beta(\nu a \circ \nu b) = \beta(\nu ab) = \beta\nu(ab) = \alpha(ab) = \alpha a \cdot' \alpha b = (\beta\nu)a \cdot' (\beta\nu)b = \beta(\nu a) \cdot' \beta(\nu b)$.

By Chapter 1, Theorem 4.9b, β is a one-to-one mapping, and therefore a ring isomorphism, of A/H onto A', if and only if $H = \text{Ker } \alpha$. ∎

The examples of "residue class rings" which give rise to the name are the rings $\mathbf{Z}/(m)$, where m is any integer. Every ideal in $\mathbf{Z}$ is of the form (m) for some integer m, since every subgroup of $\langle \mathbf{Z}, + \rangle$ is cyclic and forms an ideal.

Explicitly, for $m > 1$, the elements of $\mathbf{Z}/(m)$ are the cosets $(m) + i = \{x \mid x \equiv i \bmod m\} = \nu i$ for each $i = 0, 1, \ldots, m - 1$, where ν is the natural epimorphism of $\mathbf{Z}$ with respect to (m). It is easy to verify directly (Exercise 1.9) that $\mathbf{Z}/(m)$ is a field if and only if m is prime. We shall see presently that this statement is a consequence of a much more general result on commutative rings.

Definition 1.6. If A is a ring, $K \neq A$ an ideal in A, then

a. K is a *maximal ideal* in A if, for every ideal H in A such that $K \subset H$, either $H = K$ or $H = A$.

b. K is a *prime ideal* in A if for all $x,y \in A$ such that $xy \in K$, either $x \in K$ or $y \in K$. ///

In the ring of integers, both the nonzero maximal ideals and the nonzero prime ideals are precisely the ideals generated by primes (Exercise 1.10). However, as we shall see, the two concepts "maximal ideal" and "prime ideal" do not, in general, coincide.

Theorem 1.5.

a. *If A is a commutative ring with identity* 1, *and K is a maximal ideal in A, then A/K is a field.*

b. *If A is a ring, K an ideal in A such that A/K is a division ring, then K is a maximal ideal in A.*

PROOF.

a. Let ν be the natural epimorphism of A onto A/K. Then, clearly, $\nu A = A/K$ is a commutative ring with identity $\nu 1$. From the definition of "maximal ideal" it follows that $K \neq A$, hence $1 \notin K$. But then $\nu 1 \neq \nu 0$. To complete the proof that νA is a field we need only show that every nonzero element of νA has a multiplicative inverse in νA. Thus, suppose $\nu a \neq \nu 0$, $a \in A$. Then $a \notin K$, and hence $(K \cup \{a\}) \neq K$. Since K is a maximal ideal, $(K \cup \{a\}) = A$. Since A is a commutative ring with identity, $(K \cup \{a\}) = \{k + xa | k \in K, x \in A\}$. Hence, in particular, there are elements $k_1 \in K$, $x_1 \in A$ such that $1 = k_1 + x_1 a$. But then $\nu 1 = \nu k_1 + \nu x_1 \nu a = \nu x_1 \nu a$, so that νx_1 serves as multiplicative inverse of νa. It follows that $\nu A = A/K$ is a field.

b. Since A/K is a division ring, it consists of more than one element, hence $K \neq A$.

Let H be an ideal in A such that $K \subset H$. Let ν and μ be, respectively, the natural epimorphisms of A with respect to K and H. Then, by Theorem 1.4a, there is a unique epimorphism β: $A/K \to A/H$ such that $\beta\nu = \mu$.

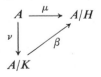

Since A/K is a division ring, it has no proper ideals. Hence either $\operatorname{Ker}\beta = A/K$ or $\operatorname{Ker}\beta = \{0_{A/K}\}$. In the first case, since β is an epimorphism of A/K onto A/H, it follows that A/H consists of a single element, hence $H = A$. In the second case, β is an isomorphism and, by Theorem 1.4b, $H = K$. Thus, K is a maximal ideal in A. ∎

Observe that Theorem 1.5a is weaker than the converse of Theorem 1.5b. The converse of Theorem 1.5b does not hold: If A is not commutative, or does not have an identity, then A/K (K a maximal ideal) need not be a division ring (Exercise 1.11).

As a corollary of Theorem 1.5 we have

Corollary. *If A is a commutative ring with identity, K an ideal in A, then K is a maximal ideal in A if and only if A/K is a field.* □

Theorem 1.6. *If A is a ring, $K \neq A$ an ideal in A, then A/K has no zero divisors if and only if K is a prime ideal in A.*

PROOF. Let ν be the natural epimorphism of A with respect to K. Suppose A/K has no zero divisors. If $ab \in K (a,b \in A)$, then $\nu a \nu b = \nu 0$, hence either $\nu a = \nu 0$ or $\nu b = \nu 0$. But then either $a \in K$ or $b \in K$, and so K is a prime ideal.

Conversely, suppose K is a prime ideal. If $\nu a \nu b = \nu 0$ $(a,b \in A)$, then $ab \in K$, hence either $a \in K$ or $b \in K$. But then either $\nu a = \nu 0$ or $\nu b = \nu 0$, and so A/K has no zero divisors. ∎

Corollary 1. *If A is a commutative ring with identity, K an ideal in A, then K is a prime ideal if and only if A/K is an integral domain.* □

Since every field is an integral domain, we immediately have

Corollary 2. *If A is a commutative ring with identity, then every maximal ideal in A is a prime ideal in A.* □

Without commutativity or the existence of an identity, a ring may have maximal ideals which are not prime (Exercise 1.12). In Section 2 we shall investigate further the relation between prime and maximal ideals in connection with divisibility properties in integral domains.

We have, so far, obtained results on homomorphisms of rings directly, using the definition of a ring as a system with two internal binary operations.

It is natural to ask whether rings can be regarded in some suitable way as groups with operators, so that the theorems on homomorphism and isomorphism for operator groups proved in Chapter 1 could carry over without further proof to rings. This can indeed be done, in several ways (some of which we tabulate below), in which the left, right, or two-sided ideals serve as the operator invariant subgroups. In the table, we use M and μ to denote, respectively, the operator set and the external composition. If A is any ring, $a \in A$, we denote by l_a the mapping of A into A defined by $l_a x = ax$ for all $x \in A$ (*left multiplication by a*), and by r_a the mapping of A into A defined by $r_a x = xa$ for all $x \in A$ (*right multiplication by a*). We write $\mathscr{L}_A = \{l_a | a \in A\}$ and $\mathscr{R}_A = \{r_a | a \in A\}$.

If A is a ring, then $\langle A, + \rangle$ can be made into an operator group in each of the following ways:

M	$\mu: M \times A \to A$	M-subgroups
A	$(a,x) \mapsto a \cdot x$	Left ideals
A	$(x,a) \mapsto x \cdot a$	Right ideals
$\mathscr{L}_A$	$(l_a,x) \mapsto a \cdot x$	Left ideals
$\mathscr{R}_A$	$(r_a,x) \mapsto x \cdot a$	Right ideals
$\mathscr{L}_A \cup \mathscr{R}_A$	$\left.\begin{matrix}(l_a,x) \mapsto a \cdot x \\ (r_a,x) \mapsto x \cdot a\end{matrix}\right\}$	Two-sided ideals

In order to make the theorems of Chapter 1, Section 4, carry over to rings, we may proceed as follows. Let A, A' be rings and let α be a homomorphism of the group $\langle A, + \rangle$ into the group $\langle A', +' \rangle$. We make $\langle A, + \rangle$ into an A-group by the first method indicated in the table; i.e., we let $\mu(a,x)$ be $a \cdot x$ for each $a \in A$, $x \in A$. To make $\langle A', +' \rangle$ into an A-group, we define $\mu' : A \times A' \to A'$ by $\mu'(a,x') = \alpha a \cdot' x'$ for each $a \in A$, $x' \in A'$. Then, in the usual notation, i.e., with "ax" for $\mu(a,x)$, "ax'" for $\mu'(a,x')$, we have

$$a(x' +' y') = \alpha a \cdot' (x' +' y') = \alpha a \cdot' x' +' \alpha a \cdot' y' = a(x') +' a(y'),$$

for each $a \in A$, $x',y' \in A'$, as required. For each $a,x \in A$, $a(\alpha x) = \alpha(ax)$ if and only if $\alpha a \cdot' \alpha x = \alpha(a \cdot x)$. Hence α is a ring homomorphism of A into A' if and only if α is an A-homomorphism of the A-group A into the A-group A'. (Note that, even if $A = A'$, the two A-groups defined here are, in general, distinct. A similar construction may be performed using the definitions $ax = x \cdot a$ and $ax' = x' \cdot' \alpha a$.) From Chapter 1, Theorem 4.8 we now obtain

Theorem 1.7. (Rectangle Theorem for Rings.) *Let A, A' be rings, and let $\alpha: A \to A'$, $\nu: A \to \nu A$, $\nu': A' \to \nu' A'$ be ring epimorphisms. Then*

a. *There is a (unique) ring epimorphism $\beta: \nu A \to \nu' A'$ such that $\beta\nu = \nu'\alpha$ if and only if* $\operatorname{Ker} \nu' \supset \alpha \operatorname{Ker} \nu$.

b. *There is a (unique) ring isomorphism $\beta: \nu A \to \nu' A'$ such that $\beta\nu = \nu'\alpha$ if and only if* $\operatorname{Ker} \nu' = \alpha \operatorname{Ker} \nu$ *and* $\operatorname{Ker} \alpha \subset \operatorname{Ker} \nu$. □

The Fundamental Theorem of Homomorphism (Theorem 1.4), which we obtained directly, is a corollary of Theorem 1.7. With left (right) ideals as M-subgroups, and normal M-subgroups replaced by two-sided ideals, the Isomorphism Theorems (Chapter 1, Theorem 4.10 and 4.11) for operator groups yield the following Isomorphism Theorems for rings:

Theorem 1.8. (First Isomorphism Theorem for Rings.) *Let A be a ring, $\alpha: A \to \alpha A$ a ring epimorphism of A onto αA, with kernel K. Let S_k be the set of all left (right) ideals of A which contain K, and let S' be the set of all left (right) ideals of αA. Then*

a. *$\sigma: H \mapsto \alpha H$ is a one-to-one mapping of S_k onto S'.*

b. *If H is any two-sided ideal of A, then αH is a two-sided ideal of αG; and, if $H \in S_k$ and αH is a two-sided ideal of αA, then H is a two-sided ideal of A.*

c. *If H is a two-sided ideal of A, then there exists a unique ring epimorphism β of A/H onto $\alpha A/\alpha H$ such that $\beta\nu = \nu'\alpha$, where ν is the canonical ring epimorphism of αA onto $\alpha A/\alpha H$. In particular, if $H \in S_k$, then β is an isomorphism.* □

Theorem 1.9. (Second Isomorphism Theorem for Rings.) *Let A be a ring, H a subring, and K a two-sided ideal of A. Then the residue class rings $H/H \cap K$ and $(H + K)/K$ are isomorphic.* □

We leave to the reader the formulation for rings of theorems analogous to those on normal series for M-groups.

2. Embeddings; Quotient Rings

In Section 1 we discussed particular kinds of subrings of a given ring. We now consider the problem of extending a ring to another ring which has special properties or bears a special relationship to the given ring.

Definition 2.1. If A, B are rings and α is a monomorphism of A into B, then $\langle B,\alpha\rangle$ is an *extension of* A. Informally, we call the ring B itself an extension of A. The mapping α is an *embedding* of A in B. ///

The three problems we shall consider here are:

1. Embedding any ring in a ring with identity.
2. Embedding a commutative ring A with identity in a ring of polynomials "in n indeterminates" ($n > 0$), with coefficients in A.
3. Embedding an integral domain in its quotient field.

As a generalization of 3, we give the construction of the quotient ring of an arbitrary commutative ring with identity relative to a multiplicative system.

Theorem 2.1. *Every ring can be embedded in a ring with identity.*

PROOF. Let A be a ring and let $\bar{A} = A \times \mathbf{Z}$. Define addition in $\bar{A}$ componentwise, and define multiplication in $\bar{A}$ by $(a,m)\cdot(b,n) = (ab + mb + na, mn)$ for all $a,b \in A$, $m,n \in \mathbf{Z}$. It is easy to check that $\bar{A}$ forms a ring with respect to these operations, that $(0,1)$ serves as multiplicative identity for $\bar{A}$, and that the mapping $\bar{\alpha}\colon A \to \bar{A}$ defined by $\bar{\alpha}a = (a,0)$ for each $a \in A$ is a monomorphism of A into $\bar{A}$. ∎

REMARK. If $\{x\}$ is a set of one element, disjoint from A, the mapping $\bar{\alpha}\colon A \to \bar{A}$ of Theorem 2.1 can be extended to a mapping $\alpha\colon A \cup \{x\} \to \bar{A}$ by defining $\alpha(x) = (0,1)$, $\alpha a = (a,0)$ for each $a \in A$. The pair $\langle \bar{A},\alpha\rangle$ satisfies the following universal mapping condition: For every ring B with identity 1_B and every mapping $\beta\colon A \cup \{x\} \to B$ such that $\beta|_A$ is a homomorphism of A into B, and $\beta x = 1_B$, there is a unique homomorphism $\mu\colon \bar{A} \to B$ such that $\mu\alpha = \beta$, i.e., such that the following diagram commutes:

$$\begin{array}{ccc} A \cup \{x\} & \xrightarrow{\alpha} & \bar{A} \\ & {\scriptstyle\beta}\searrow \quad \swarrow{\scriptstyle\mu} & \\ & B & \end{array}$$

From this, it can be deduced that α is an injection, $[\alpha(A \cup \{x\})] = \bar{A}$, and every ring B with identity 1_B such that $B = [A \cup \{1_B\}]$ is a homomorphic image of $\bar{A}$ (Exercise 2.1).

We now turn to the second problem:

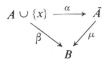

Theorem 2.2. *Let A be a commutative ring with identity, and let $P(A)$ be the set of all sequences (a_n), with $a_n \in A$ for each $n = 0, 1, 2, \ldots$ and only finitely many terms different from* 0. *For each $(a_n),(b_n) \in P(A)$, define*

$$(a_n) + (b_n) = (c_n), \qquad \text{where } c_n = a_n + b_n \text{ for each } n = 0, 1, 2, \ldots,$$

$$(a_n) \cdot (b_n) = (c_n), \qquad \text{where } c_n = \sum_{i+j=n} a_i b_j \text{ for each } n = 0, 1, 2, \ldots.$$

Then

a. $\langle P,+,\cdot\rangle$ *is a commutative ring with identity* $(1,0,0,\ldots)$.
b. *The mapping* $\alpha\colon A \to P(A)$ *defined by* $\alpha a = \bar{a} = (a,0,0,\ldots)$ *is a monomorphism of A into $P(A)$.*
c. *If* $x = (0,1,0,\ldots)$, *then* $x^k = (0,0,\ldots,\underset{k+1}{1},0,\ldots)$ *for each positive integer k.*
d. *For every element $f \neq 0$ in $P(A)$, there is a unique finite sequence* $\langle a_0,\ldots,a_n\rangle$, $a_i \in A$ $(i = 0,\ldots,n)$, $a_n \neq 0$, *such that* $f = \bar{a}_0 + \bar{a}_1 x + \cdots + \bar{a}_n x^n$.

The proof is left as an exercise (Exercise 2.2). ▯

We note that, if we identify the elements of A with their images under the monomorphism α, then every element $f \in P(A)$, $f \neq 0_{P(A)}$, can be represented in exactly one way as a "polynomial in x, with coefficients in A": $f = a_0 + a_1 x + \cdots + a_n x^n$, $a_n \neq 0$. The ring $P(A)$ is usually referred to as "the ring of all polynomials over A, in the indeterminate x" and is denoted by the symbol $A[x]$. If $a_n \neq 0$ for some nonnegative integer n, then the polynomial $f = a_0 + a_1 x + \cdots + a_n x^n$ has "*degree n*." (We write $\deg f = n$.) The "zero polynomial," i.e., the sequence all of whose terms are zero, has no degree. If $a_n = 1$, then f is *monic*.

Since $P(A)$ is again a commutative ring with identity, we may repeat the construction in Theorem 2.2, using $P(A)$ in place of A. We can thus define recursively, for any commutative ring A with identity, polynomial rings $P^n(A)$ of order $n = 0, 1, 2, \ldots$ by

$$\begin{aligned} P^0(A) &= A, \\ A[x_1] = P^1(A) &= P(A), \\ A[x_1][x_2] = P^2(A) &= P(P^1(A)), \\ &\vdots \\ A[x_1][x_2]\cdots[x_n] = P^n(A) &= P(P^{n-1}(A)) \qquad \text{for each } n = 1, 2, \ldots. \end{aligned}$$

Another way to generalize the construction in Theorem 2.2 is to introduce, for an arbitrary positive integer n, "polynomials in n indeterminates" over A

as functions from the set of all n-tuples of nonnegative integers into A. We shall prove that the resulting ring $A[x_1,\ldots,x_n]$ is isomorphic to the ring $A[x_1]\cdots[x_n]$, which we have defined recursively above (corollary of Theorem 2.4).

In plain language: A polynomial in the indeterminates, say x_1, x_2, x_3, with coefficients in A, may be regarded as a polynomial in x_3 whose coefficients are polynomials in x_2 whose coefficients are polynomials in x_1, over A.

We shall characterize the ring of all polynomials in n indeterminates over A by means of a universal mapping property as a "free commutative ring of rank n over A".

Definition 2.2. Let A be a commutative ring with identity, Y a set disjoint from A. If B is a commutative ring, $\alpha\colon A \cup Y \to B$ a mapping of $A \cup Y$ into B such that $\alpha|_A$ is a homomorphism of A into B, then $\langle B,\alpha\rangle$ is a *free commutative ring over A, with respect to Y*, if B and α satisfy the following condition: For every commutative ring C and every mapping $\gamma\colon A \cup Y \to C$ such that $\gamma|_A$ is a homomorphism, there is a unique homomorphism $\mu\colon B \to C$ such that $\mu\alpha = \gamma$:

$$\begin{array}{ccc} A \cup Y & \xrightarrow{\alpha} & B \\ & \gamma\searrow \quad \swarrow\mu & \\ & C & \end{array}$$

If B is a commutative ring such that for some set Y of cardinality σ ($Y \cap A = \varnothing$) and some mapping $\alpha\colon A \cup Y \to B$, $\langle B,\alpha\rangle$ is a free commutative ring over A with respect to Y, then B is a *free commutative ring of rank σ over A*. We write $B = A[Y]$. ///

Exactly as in the case of free groups, the following statements are immediate consequences of Definition 2.2:

Corollary 1. *Let A be a commutative ring wtih identity.*

a. *If $\langle B,\alpha\rangle$ is a free commutative ring over A, with respect to a set Y, then*
   (1) *α is an injection, and*
   (2) *$[\alpha(A \cup Y)] = B$.*

b. *If $\langle B,\alpha\rangle$, $\langle B',\alpha'\rangle$ are both free commutative rings over A, then there is a unique isomorphism $\mu\colon B \to B'$ such that $\mu\alpha = \alpha'$.* □

From b, we have

Corollary 2. *If B and B' are free commutative rings of rank σ over A (A commutative with identity), then B and B' are isomorphic.* □

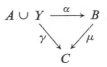

Given any commutative ring A with identity, we now prove that, for each positive integer n, there is a free commutative ring of rank n over A. (For clarity of exposition, we confine ourselves to the case of finite cardinals. However, Theorem 2.3 may be generalized without difficulty to the infinite case; see Exercise 2.3.)

Theorem 2.3. *Let A be a commutative ring with identity. Let $\langle H,+\rangle$ be the set of all n-tuples of nonnegative integers together with the operation "componentwise addition." Let $P = P(n,A)$ be the set of all mappings $f\colon H \to A$ such that $f(\eta) = 0$ for all but finitely many $\eta \in H$. On P, define $+$ and $\cdot$ by*

$f + g = h\ (f,g \in P)$, *where h is the element of P such that $h(\eta) = f(\eta) + g(\eta)$ for each $\eta \in H$,*

$f \cdot g = h\ (f,g \in P)$, *where h is the element of P such that*

$$h(\eta) = \sum_{\substack{\delta+\gamma=\eta \\ \delta,\gamma\in H}} f(\delta)g(\gamma).$$

Then $\langle P(n,A),+,\cdot\rangle$ is a free commutative ring of rank n over A.

PROOF.

1. It is easy to verify that $\langle P,+,\cdot\rangle$ is a commutative ring.
2. For each $i = 1,\ldots,n$, denote by ε_i the n-tuple $(0,\ldots,0,\underset{\text{ith}}{1},0,\ldots,0)$ in H, and let $\varepsilon_0 = (0,0,\ldots,0)$. Let $Y = \{y_1,\ldots,y_n\}$ be a set of n elements disjoint from A. Note that the function $f \in P$ defined by $f(\varepsilon_0) = 1$, $f(\eta) = 0$ for $\eta \neq \varepsilon_0$ in P serves as multiplicative identity for P. Denote this function by 1_P. For each $f \in P$, $a \in A$, denote by af the function $af\colon H \to A$ defined by $af(\eta) = a \cdot f(\eta)$ for each $\eta \in H$.

Now define $\alpha\colon A \cup Y \to P$ as follows: For $a \in A$, let $\alpha a = a1_P$. For each $i = 1,\ldots, n$, let $\alpha y_i = x_i$, where

$$x_i(\varepsilon_i) = 1,$$
$$x_i(\eta) = 0 \qquad \text{for } \eta \neq \varepsilon_i.$$

Then $\alpha|_A$ is a monomorphism of A into P. For each $i = 1, 2,\ldots, n$, $x_i^0 = 1_P$ and, for $k > 0$, $x_i^k(k\varepsilon_i) = 1$, $x_i^k(\eta) = 0$ if $\eta \neq k\varepsilon_i$. Hence, if $k_1,\ldots, k_n$ are nonnegative integers, then $x_1^{k_1}\cdots x_n^{k_n}(k_1\varepsilon_1 + \cdots + k_n\varepsilon_n) = 1$, while $x_1^{k_1}\cdots x_n^{k_n}(\eta) = 0$ for $\eta \neq k_1\varepsilon_1 + \cdots + k_n\varepsilon_n$. Now suppose $f \in P$. Then there are finitely many elements of H, say, $\eta_1,\ldots,\eta_m$ such that $f(\eta_i) \neq 0$

$(i = 1,\ldots,m)$. Since for each η_i there is a unique set of nonnegative integers $k_{i1},\ldots, k_{in}$ such that $\eta_i = k_{i1}\varepsilon_1 + \cdots + k_{in}\varepsilon_n$,

$$f = a_1x_1^{k_{11}}\cdots x_n^{k_{1n}} + a_2x_1^{k_{21}}\cdots x_n^{k_{2n}} + \cdots + a_mx_1^{k_{m1}}\cdots x_n^{k_{mn}},$$

where $a_i = f(k_{i1},\ldots,k_{in})$ for each $i = 1,\ldots, m$. Thus, f can be written as a "polynomial in $x_1,\ldots, x_n$" and $P = [\alpha(A \cup Y)]$. It is easy to see that only one polynomial in $x_1,\ldots, x_n$ can represent a given function $f \in P$.

To prove that P is a free commutative ring of rank n over A, suppose R is a commutative ring, $\gamma\colon A \cup Y \to R$ a mapping such that $\gamma|_A$ is a homomorphism. Define $\mu\colon P \to R$ as follows: If $f = \sum_{i=1}^{m} a_ix_1^{k_{i1}}\cdots x_n^{k_{in}}$, k_{ij} nonnegative integers $(j = 1,\ldots,n;\ i = 1,\ldots,m)$, let $\mu f = \sum_{i=1}^{m} \gamma a_i(\gamma y_1)^{k_{i1}}\cdots(\gamma y_n)^{k_{in}}$. Then, because of the uniqueness of the representation of f as a polynomial in the x_i, μ is a map. Because R is commutative and $\gamma|_A$ is a homomorphism, μ is a homomorphism. For each $a \in A$, $\mu\alpha a = \mu\ (ax_1^0\cdots x_n^0) = \gamma a$, and for each $i = 1,\ldots, n$, $\mu\alpha y_i = \mu x_i = \gamma y_i$. Thus, $\mu\alpha = \gamma$. Since $[\alpha(A \cup Y)] = P$, μ is the only such homomorphism of P into R. ▮

We shall refer to the ring we have just constructed as the *ring of all polynomials in n indeterminates,* $x_1,\ldots, x_n$, *over A*, and we denote this ring from now on by $A[x_1,\ldots,x_n]$. Note that the construction coincides with that of Theorem 2.2 in case $n = 1$ if we identify each nonnegative integer k with the 1-tuple (k).

The isomorphism of $A[x_1,\ldots,x_n]$ with the recursively defined ring $A[x_1]\cdots[x_n]$ is an immediate consequence of the following theorem:

Theorem 2.4. *Let A be a commutative ring with identity and let S, T be sets such that* $A \cap S = A \cap T = S \cap T = A[S] \cap T = \varnothing$. *Then* $A[S][T]$ *is isomorphic to* $A[S \cup T]$.

Proof. Suppose that $\langle A[S],\alpha\rangle$ is a free commutative ring over A with respect to S, $\langle A[S][T],\beta\rangle$ is a free commutative ring over $A[S]$ with respect to T, and $\langle A[S \cup T],\gamma'\rangle$ a free commutative ring over A with respect to $S \cup T$ $(\alpha\colon A \cup S \to A[S],\ \beta\colon A[S] \cup T \to A[S][T],\ \gamma'\colon A \cup S \cup T \to A[S \cup T])$.

Let $\gamma\colon A \cup S \to A[S \cup T]$ be the mapping $\gamma'|_{A\cup S}$. Then there is a unique homomorphism $\mu\colon A[S] \to A[S \cup T]$ such that $\mu\alpha = \gamma$:

$$\begin{array}{ccc} A \cup S & \xrightarrow{\alpha} & A[S] \\ & {\scriptstyle\gamma}\searrow \quad \swarrow{\scriptstyle\mu} & \\ & A[S \cup T] & \end{array} \tag{1}$$

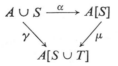

Let $\alpha'\colon A \cup S \cup T \to A[S] \cup T$ be the mapping such that $\alpha'|_{A \cup S} = \alpha$ and $\alpha'|_T = \iota_T$ and let $\mu'\colon A[S] \cup T \to A[S \cup T]$ be the mapping such that $\mu'|_{A[S]} = \mu$ and $\mu'|_T = \gamma'$. Then

(2) $$\mu'\alpha' = \gamma'.$$

Since μ' is a mapping of $A[S] \cup T$ into $A[S \cup T]$ such that $\mu'|_{A[S]}$ is a homomorphism, there is a unique homomorphism $\nu\colon A[S][T] \to A[S \cup T]$ such that $\nu\beta = \mu'$:

(3) $$\begin{array}{ccc} A[S] \cup T & \xrightarrow{\beta} & A[S][T] \\ & {}_{\mu'}\searrow \quad \swarrow_{\nu} & \\ & A[S \cup T] & \end{array} .$$

Hence

(4) $$\nu\beta\alpha' = \mu'\alpha' = \gamma'. \qquad \begin{array}{ccc} A \cup S \cup T & \xrightarrow{\beta\alpha'} & A[S][T] \\ & {}_{\gamma'}\searrow \quad \swarrow_{\nu} & \\ & A[S \cup T] & \end{array} .$$

Now, since $A[S][T]$ is a commutative ring and $(\beta\alpha')|_A$ is a homomorphism, there is a unique homomorphism $\bar{\nu}\colon A[S \cup T] \to A[S][T]$ such that $\bar{\nu}\gamma' = \beta\alpha'$:

(5) $$\begin{array}{ccc} A \cup S \cup T & \xrightarrow{\gamma'} & A[S \cup T] \\ & {}_{\beta\alpha'}\searrow \quad \swarrow_{\bar{\nu}} & \\ & A[S][T] & \end{array} .$$

But then, by (4) and (5),

(6) $$\bar{\nu}\nu\beta\alpha' = \beta\alpha',$$

(7) $$\nu\bar{\nu}\gamma' = \nu\beta\alpha' = \gamma'.$$

By the uniqueness requirement in Definition 2.2, it follows from (6) that $\bar{\nu}\nu = \iota_{A[S][T]}$ and from (7) that $\nu\bar{\nu} = \iota_{A[S \cup T]}$. But then ν is an isomorphism. ∎

Corollary. *If A is a commutative ring with identity, then the polynomial ring $A[x_1,\ldots,x_n]$ in n indeterminates $x_1,\ldots,x_n$ is isomorphic to the recursively defined polynomial ring $A[x_1][x_2]\cdots[x_n]$.* □

We shall sometimes denote the elements f of $A[x_1,\ldots,x_n]$ by $f(x_1,\ldots,x_n)$. If $\langle B,\beta\rangle$ is an extension of A, $f = \sum_{i=1}^{m} a_i x_1^{k_{i1}}\cdots x_n^{k_{in}}$ a polynomial in $A[x_1,\ldots,x_n]$, we shall write βf or $\beta f(x_1,\ldots,x_n)$ for the polynomial $\sum_{i=1}^{m} \beta a_i x_1^{k_{i1}}\cdots x_n^{k_{in}}$ in $B[x_1,\ldots,x_n]$.

One of the most common elementary operations on polynomials is the substitution of "values" for the indeterminates. In the context of our discussion, such substitutions may be described as follows:

Theorem 2.5. *Let A be a commutative ring with identity, $A[x_1,\ldots,x_n]$ the ring of all polynomials in the indeterminates $x_1,\ldots,x_n$. over A. Let $\langle B,\beta\rangle$ be an extension of A, where B is a commutative ring, β a monomorphism of A into B. For each $f(x_1,\ldots,x_n) = \sum_{i=1}^{m} a_i x_1^{k_{i1}}\cdots x_n^{k_{in}}$ in $A[x_1,\ldots,x_n]$, let $\beta f(b_1,\ldots,b_n) = \sum_{i=1}^{m} \beta a_i b_1^{k_{i1}}\cdots b_n^{k_{in}}$ in B. Then the mapping $\varphi\colon A[x_1,\ldots,x_n] \to B$ defined by*

$$\varphi(f(x_1,\ldots,x_n)) = \beta f(b_1,\ldots,b_n) \qquad \text{for each } f \in A[x_1,\ldots,x_n]$$

is a homomorphism of $A[x_1,\ldots,x_n]$ into B.

Proof. If $\langle A[x_1,\ldots,x_n],\alpha\rangle$ is a free commutative ring over A, with respect to a set $X = \{x_1,\ldots,x_n\}$, let $\gamma\colon A \cup X \to B$ be defined by $\gamma|_A = \beta$ and $\gamma x_i = b_i$ for each $i = 1,\ldots,n$. Then φ is simply the homomorphism $\mu\colon A[x_1,\ldots,x_n] \to B$ guaranteed to exist by Definition 2.2. ∎

We now turn to the problem of embedding an integral domain in a field. Let A be an integral domain and let $X = A \times (A - \{0\})$. On X, define a binary relation $\sim$ by

$$(a,b) \sim (c,d) \qquad \text{if } ad = cb.$$

Then $\sim$ is an equivalence relation on X. Reflexivity and symmetry of $\sim$ are immediate consequences of the corresponding properties of $=$. To prove transitivity, suppose that $(a,b) \sim (c,d)$ and $(c,d) \sim (e,f)$, where $(a,b),(c,d),(e,f) \in X$. From $ad = cb$ and $cf = ed$, we have $adf = cbf$, hence $afd = ebd$ and, since $d \neq 0$, $af = eb$. But then $(a,b) \sim (e,f)$.

We denote by a/b the equivalence class of (a,b) with respect to $\sim$ and let F be the set of all equivalence classes. On F, we define binary operations $+$ and $\cdot$ by

$$\left.\begin{aligned}\frac{a}{b}+\frac{c}{d}&=\frac{ad+cb}{bd}\\ \frac{a}{b}\cdot\frac{c}{d}&=\frac{ac}{bd}\end{aligned}\right\}\ \frac{a}{b},\frac{c}{d}\in F.$$

We claim

Theorem 2.6. *If A is an integral domain, F, $+$, and $\cdot$ are as defined above, then*

a. $\langle F,+,\cdot\rangle$ *is a field.*
b. *If $\alpha\colon A\to F$ is defined by $\alpha a = a/1$ for each $a\in A$, then α is a monomorphism of A into F.*
c. $F=\{\alpha a(\alpha b)^{-1}\mid a\in A,\ b\neq 0 \text{ in } A\}$, *the subfield of F generated by αA.*
d. $\langle F,\alpha\rangle$ *satisfies the following universal mapping condition: If F' is a field, $\alpha'\colon A\to F'$ a monomorphism, then there is a unique homomorphism $\mu\colon F\to F'$ such that $\mu\alpha=\alpha'$.*

PROOF.

a. We must first show that $+$ and $\cdot$ are binary operations on F. Thus, suppose a/b, $c/d\in F$. Since A is an integral domain, $bd\neq 0$, and $(ad+cb)/bd$, $ac/bd\in F$. If

$$\frac{a}{b}=\frac{a'}{b'},\qquad \frac{c}{d}=\frac{c'}{d'}\left(\frac{a}{b},\frac{c}{d},\frac{a'}{b'},\frac{c'}{d'}\in F\right),$$

then from $ab'=a'b$, $cd'=c'd$ we easily obtain

$$\frac{ad+cb}{bd}=\frac{a'd'+c'b'}{b'd'},\qquad \frac{ac}{bd}=\frac{a'c'}{b'd'},$$

Thus, for each $x,y\in F$, $x+y$ and $x\cdot y$ are uniquely determined elements of F. We leave to the reader the verification that $\langle F,+,\cdot\rangle$ is a field, noting only that $0/1$ and $1/1$ serve, respectively, as additive and multiplicative identities, 0_F and 1_F, for F; $-a/b$ serves as additive inverse for a/b, and b/a serves as multiplicative inverse for a/b, provided $a/b\neq 0_F$.

b. If $\alpha: A \to F$ is defined by $\alpha a = a/1$, then α is a one-to-one map, since $\alpha a = \alpha b$ if and only if $(a,1) \sim (b,1)$, i.e., if and only if $a = b$. Since, for each $a,b \in A$,

$$\alpha(a + b) = \frac{a + b}{1} = \frac{a}{1} + \frac{b}{1} \quad \text{and} \quad \alpha(a \cdot b) = \frac{ab}{1} = \frac{a}{1} \cdot \frac{b}{1},$$

α is a monomorphism of A into F.

c. If $x = a/b \in F$, then $x = (a/1) \cdot (1/b) = \alpha a(\alpha b)^{-1}$. Hence

$$F = \{\alpha a(\alpha b)^{-1} | a \in A,\, b \neq 0 \text{ in } A\}.$$

d. Let F' be a field, α' a monomorphism of A into F'. Define $\mu: F \to F'$ by $\mu(\alpha a(\alpha b)^{-1}) = \alpha' a(\alpha' b)^{-1}$. Then μ is a map of F into F'. For, by c, every element of F is of the form $\alpha a(\alpha b)^{-1}$ for some $a,b \neq 0$, in A. If $\alpha a_1(\alpha b_1)^{-1} = \alpha a_2(\alpha b_2)^{-1}$, then $\alpha a_1 \alpha b_2 = \alpha a_2 \alpha b_1$, and therefore $a_1 b_2 = a_2 b_1$, since α is a monomorphism. But then $\alpha'(a_1 b_2) = \alpha'(a_2 b_1)$ and $\alpha' a_1(\alpha' b_1)^{-1} = \alpha' a_2(\alpha' b_2)^{-1}$, since α' is a monomorphism. The mapping $\mu: F \to F'$ is a homomorphism:

$$\begin{aligned}
\mu(\alpha a(\alpha b)^{-1} + (\alpha c)(\alpha d)^{-1}) &= \mu((\alpha a \alpha d + \alpha c \alpha b)(\alpha b \alpha d)^{-1}) \\
&= \mu(\alpha(ad + cb)(\alpha(bd))^{-1}) \\
&= \alpha'(ad + cb)(\alpha'(bd))^{-1} \\
&= \alpha' a(\alpha' b)^{-1} + \alpha' c(\alpha' d)^{-1} \\
&= \mu(\alpha a(\alpha b)^{-1}) + \mu(\alpha c(\alpha d)^{-1}), \\
\mu(\alpha a(\alpha b)^{-1} \cdot \alpha c(\alpha d)^{-1}) &= \mu(\alpha a \alpha c \cdot (\alpha b)^{-1}\ (\alpha d)^{-1}) \\
&= \mu(\alpha a \alpha c(\alpha b \alpha d)^{-1}) \\
&= \mu(\alpha(ac)[\alpha(bd)]^{-1}) \\
&= \alpha'(ac)[\alpha'(bd)]^{-1} \\
&= \alpha' a(\alpha' b)^{-1} \cdot \alpha' c(\alpha' d)^{-1} \\
&= \mu(\alpha a(\alpha b)^{-1}) \cdot \mu(\alpha c(\alpha d)^{-1}).
\end{aligned}$$

From the definition of μ, it follows immediately that $\mu\alpha = \alpha'$. If $\bar{\mu}: F \to F'$ is any homomorphism of F into F' such that $\bar{\mu}\alpha = \alpha'$, then

$$\bar{\mu}[\alpha a(\alpha b)^{-1}] = \bar{\mu}[\alpha(ab^{-1})] = \alpha'(ab^{-1}) = \alpha' a(\alpha' b)^{-1} = \mu(\alpha a(\alpha b)^{-1})$$

for each $a,b \neq 0$ in A. But then, since $F = \{\alpha a(\alpha b)^{-1} | a \in A,\, b \neq 0 \text{ in } A\}$, it follows that $\bar{\mu} = \mu$. ∎

We note that, if we "identify" A with its image αa in F, and $a,b \in A$ ($b \neq 0$) with their images $a/1$, $b/1$, then, by Theorem 2.6c, $a/b = ab^{-1}$, a *quotient* of elements of A. This suggests calling F a "quotient field." The following definition of a quotient field is in terms of the universal mapping property in Theorem 2.6d.

Definition 2.3. If A is an integral domain, F a field, and $\alpha: A \to F$ a monomorphism of A into F, then $\langle F,\alpha \rangle$ is a *quotient field* of A if it satisfies the following condition: For every field F' and every monomorphism $\alpha': A \to F'$, there is a unique homomorphism $\mu: F \to F'$ such that $\mu\alpha = \alpha'$. ///

Corollary 1. *Every integral domain has a quotient field.* ▯

Corollary 2. *Let A be an integral domain.*

a. *If $\langle F,\alpha \rangle$ and $\langle F',\alpha' \rangle$ are quotient fields of A, then there is a unique isomorphism $\mu: F \to F'$ such that $\mu\alpha = \alpha'$.*
b. *Let $\langle F,\alpha \rangle$ be a quotient field of A. If F' is a field, α' a monomorphism of A into F', and $\mu: F \to F'$ an isomorphism such that $\mu\alpha = \alpha'$, then $\langle F',\alpha' \rangle$ is a quotient field of A.*
c. *If E is a field such that $A \subset E$ and $E = \{ab^{-1} | a,b \in A, b \neq 0\}$, then $\langle E,\varepsilon \rangle$ is a quotient field of A, where ε is the inclusion map of A in E.*
d. *If A is a field, then $\langle A,\iota_A \rangle$ is a quotient field of A.*

We leave the proof to the reader. ▯

A natural generalization of the construction of the quotient field of an integral domain is the construction of "quotient rings" from an arbitrary commutative ring with identity. Let A be a commutative ring with identity, S a subset of A such that

$$1 \in S,$$

$$a,b \in S \Rightarrow ab \in S.$$

(We shall refer to such a subset S of a ring A as a *multiplicative system* in A.)

Form $A \times S = \{(a,b) | a \in A, b \in S\}$. On $A \times S$, define a binary relation $\sim$ by $(a,b) \sim (c,d)$ if and only if

$$s(ad - cb) = 0$$

for some $s \in S$. It is easy to verify that $\sim$ is an equivalence relation on $A \times S$ (Exercise 2.4). We denote by a/b the equivalence class of (a,b)

($a \in A$, $b \in S$), and let B be the set of all equivalence classes with respect to $\sim$. On B, we define $+$ and $\cdot$ by

$$\frac{a}{b} + \frac{c}{d} = \frac{ad + cb}{bd},$$

$$\frac{a}{b} \cdot \frac{c}{d} = \frac{ac}{bd}$$

($a/b, c/d \in B$). We leave as an exercise the verification that $+$ and $\cdot$ are binary operations on B and that $\langle B,+,\cdot\rangle$ is a commutative ring with identity. We shall refer to it as the *quotient ring*, AS^{-1}, of A with respect to S. (*Note*: If $0 \in S$, AS^{-1} consists of just one element.) If A is an integral domain and $S = A - \{0\}$, then the quotient ring of A with respect to S coincides with the quotient field of A.

Theorem 2.7. *Let A be a commutative ring with identity, S a multiplicative system in A. Let B be the quotient ring AS^{-1} of A with respect to S and define $\alpha_S: A \to B$ by $\alpha_S a = a/1$ for each $a \in A$. Then*

a. *α_S is a homomorphism of A into B such that, for each $s \in S$, $\alpha_S(s)$ is a unit in B.*

b. *$B = \{\alpha_S a(\alpha_S b)^{-1} | a \in A, b \in S\}$.*

c. *The pair $\langle B,\alpha_s\rangle$ satisfies the following universal mapping condition: If B' is a commutative ring with identity, $\alpha': A \to B'$ a homomorphism such that $\alpha' s$ is a unit in B' for each $s \in S$, then there is a unique homomorphism $\mu: B \to B'$ such that $\mu\alpha_s = \alpha'$.*

d. *If A is an integral domain and $0 \notin S$, then α_S is a monomorphism.*

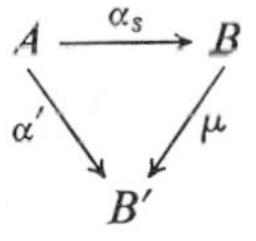

PROOF.

a. α_S is obviously a homomorphism. For $s \in S$, $[\alpha_S]^{-1} = 1/s \in B$.

b. If $x = a/b \in B$, then $x = (a/1) \cdot (1/b) = \alpha_s a(\alpha_s b)^{-1}$, hence $B = \{\alpha_s a(\alpha_s b)^{-1} | a \in A, b \in S\}$.

c. Let B' be a ring with identity, α' a homomorphism of A into B' such that $\alpha' s$ is a unit for each $s \in S$. Define $\mu: B \to B'$ by $\mu(a/b) = \alpha' a(\alpha' b)^{-1}$. μ is a map, for if $a_1/b_1 = a_2/b_2$, then $s(a_1b_2 - a_2b_1) = 0$ for some $s \in S$, and $\alpha' s\alpha'(a_1b_2 - a_2b_1) = 0$. Since α' is a homomorphism and $\alpha' s$ is a unit, we have $\alpha'\alpha_1\alpha' b_2 = \alpha' a_2\alpha' b_1$, whence $\alpha' a_1(\alpha' b_1)^{-1} = \alpha' a_2(\alpha' b_2)^{-1}$. The verification that μ is a homomorphism is completely straightforward. From the definition of μ it is clear that $\mu\alpha_S = \alpha'$, and the uniqueness of μ may be shown in the usual manner.

d. Suppose A is an integral domain, and $0 \notin S$. If $\alpha a_1 = \alpha a_2$ $(a_1,a_2 \in A)$, then $(a_1,1) \sim (a_2,1)$, whence $s(a_1 - a_2) = 0$ for some $s \in S$. Since $s \neq 0$ and A is an integral domain, it follows that $a_1 = a_2$. Thus, α_s is a monomorphism. ∎

A particularly interesting type of quotient ring is the "local ring at a prime ideal" of a commutative ring with identity. Let A be a ring, P a prime ideal in A. Let $S = A - P$. Since $P \neq A$, $1 \in S$. If $a,b \in S$, then $a \notin P$, $b \notin P$, hence $ab \notin P$; i.e., $ab \in S$. Thus S is a multiplicative system in A.

Theorem 2.8. *If A is a commutative ring with identity and $S = A - P$, where P is a prime ideal in A, then the quotient ring AS^{-1} of A with respect to S has a unique maximal ideal, $M = \{a/b \mid a \in P\}$. The set $AS^{-1} - M$ is the set of all units in AS^{-1}.*

PROOF. First note that, if $a/b = c/d$ and $a \in P$, then $c \in P$. For, $s(ad - cb) = 0$ for some $s \in S$. Since $0 \in P$ and $s \notin P$, we have $ad - bc \in P$. Since $a \in P$, we have $ad \in P$, and therefore $bc \in P$. But then, since $b \notin P$, $c \in P$. Thus, $M = \{a/b \mid a \in P\}$ is a well-defined set of equivalence classes. M is an ideal: If $a/b, c/d \in M$, then

$$\frac{a}{b} - \frac{c}{d} = \frac{ad - cb}{bd} \in M;$$

and if $a/b \in M$, $x/y \in AS^{-1}$, then

$$\frac{a}{b} \cdot \frac{x}{y} = \frac{ax}{by} \in M.$$

Since $P \neq A$, $M \neq AS^{-1}$, and M contains no units. If $e/f \notin M$, then $e \in S$, and therefore $f/e = [e/f]^{-1} \in AS^{-1}$; i.e., every element of AS^{-1} which is not in M is a unit. But then $AS^{-1} - M$ is the set of all units of AS^{-1}. It follows immediately that M is a maximal ideal in AS^{-1}, and that every ideal of AS^{-1} which is different from the whole ring must be contained in M. But then M is the only maximal ideal of AS^{-1}. ∎

Definition 2.4. A ring which has exactly one maximal ideal is a *local ring*. If A is a commutative ring with identity, P a prime ideal of A, then the quotient ring AS^{-1}, where $S = A - P$ is the *local ring*, A_P, *of A at P*. ///

Examples.

1. The quotient field of an integral domain A is the local ring of A at the prime ideal 0.

2. If $A = \mathbf{Z}$, the ring of integers, and $P = (p)$, where p is a prime, then the local ring, $\mathbf{Z}_p$, of $\mathbf{Z}$ at P consists of "quotients" a/b, where $p \nmid b$. Its maximal ideal M is the set of quotients a/b, where $p|a$ and $p \nmid b$. The quotients e/f, where $p \nmid e$, $p \nmid f$ are the units in $\mathbf{Z}_p$.

We shall return to these concepts in Chapter 6 in connection with valuations on a field.

3. Integral Domains

We first consider the polynomial domains $A[x]$, where A is an integral domain.

Theorem 3.1. *Let A be an integral domain.*

a. *If f, g are nonzero polynomials in $A[x]$, then* $\deg fg = \deg f + \deg g$.

b. *$A[x]$ is an integral domain.*

PROOF.

a. Let $f = a_0 + a_1x + \cdots + a_nx^n$, $a_n \neq 0$, and $g = b_0 + b_1x + \cdots + b_mx^m$, $b_m \neq 0$. Since A is an integral domain, $a_nb_m \neq 0$, hence the degree of fg is $m + n$.

b. Is an immediate consequence of a. ▮

If, in particular, F is a field, then the following "division algorithm" holds in $F[x]$:

Theorem 3.2. (Division Algorithm.) *Let F be a field, and let $g \neq 0$ and f be polynomials in $F[x]$. Then there is exactly one pair of polynomials $p,r \in F[x]$ such that $f = gp + r$, where either $r = 0$ or* $\deg r < \deg g$.

PROOF. If $f = 0$, we let $p = r = 0$ to satisfy the conditions of the theorem. For $f \neq 0$, we proceed by induction on the degree of f. Thus, suppose $f = a_0 + a_1x + \cdots + a_nx^n$, $a_n \neq 0$, and $g = b_0 + b_1x + \cdots + b_mx^m$, $b_m \neq 0$. If $n = 0$ and $m \neq 0$, use $p = 0$ and $r = f$. If n and m are both zero, use $p = g^{-1}f$ and $r = 0$. Now assume that, for $n > 0$, the theorem is known to hold for polynomials of degree less than n. If $n < m$, use $p = 0$ and $r = f$. Finally, if $n \geq m$, form

$$f_1 = f - a_n b_m^{-1} x^{n-m} g.$$

If $f_1 = 0$, use $p = a_n b_m^{-1} x^{n-m}$ and $r = 0$. If $f_1 \neq 0$, then $\deg f_1 < n$ and the induction hypothesis implies the existence of $p,r \in F[x]$ such that $f_1 = p_1 g + r$, where either $r = 0$ or $\deg r < \deg g$. But then $f = pg + r$, where $p = a_n b_m^{-1} x^{n-m} + p_1$, and r has the required properties.

To prove the uniqueness of p and r, suppose there is another pair, $\bar{p}$ and $\bar{r}$, of polynomials in $F[x]$ such that $f = \bar{p}g + \bar{r}$, where either $\bar{r} = 0$ or $\deg \bar{r} < \deg g$. Then $(p - \bar{p})g = \bar{r} - r$. If $r \neq \bar{r}$, then $p \neq \bar{p}$ and $0 \leq \deg(\bar{r} - r) < \deg g$, while $\deg(p - \bar{p})g = \deg(p - \bar{p}) + \deg g \geq \deg g$—a contradiction. It follows that $r = \bar{r}$ and $p = \bar{p}$, as required. ▮

We recall that, in the division algorithm for integers (Chapter 0, Theorem 3.4), the absolute value played a role somewhat similar to that of the degree in Theorem 3.2. The domain of integers and the polynomial domains over a field are "Euclidean domains" in the sense of the following definition:

Definition 3.1. Let A be an integral domain, $\delta: A \to \mathbf{Z}$ a mapping of A into $\mathbf{Z}$ such that

a. $\delta a \geq 0$ for all $a \in A$,
   $\delta a = 0$ if and only if $a = 0$ $(a \in A)$.
b. $\delta(ab) = \delta a \, \delta b$ for all $a,b \in A$.
c. If $a,b \in A$, $b \neq 0$, then there are elements $p,r \in A$ such that

$$a = bp + r,$$

   where $0 \leq \delta r < \delta b$.

Then δ is a *Euclidean norm* on A and $\langle A,\delta \rangle$ is a *Euclidean domain.* ///

It is clear that the absolute-value function serves as a Euclidean norm for $\mathbf{Z}$, so that $\langle \mathbf{Z}, |\ | \rangle$ is a Euclidean domain. The degree of polynomials in $F[x]$, F a field, cannot be used directly as a Euclidean norm. However, the difficulty is easily remedied.

If F is a field, $f \in F[x]$, let $\delta f = 0$ if $f = 0$, and let $\delta f = 2^{\deg f}$ if $f \neq 0$. Then δ clearly satisfies a and b. It also satisfies c, since from $f = gp + r$ and $r = 0$ or $\deg r < \deg g$, $(f,g,p,r \in F[x], g \neq 0)$ we have $\delta r = 0$ or $2^{\deg r} < 2^{\deg g}$, whence $0 \leq \delta r < \delta g$.

Other examples of Euclidean domains are found among the "rings of integers in quadratic number fields." These rings may be described as follows: Let d be a square free integer, and let

$$\theta = \begin{cases} \sqrt{d} & \text{if } d \equiv 2,3 \bmod 4, \\ \dfrac{1+\sqrt{d}}{2} & \text{if } d \equiv 1 \bmod 4. \end{cases}$$

Then $A = \{a + b\theta | a,b \in \mathbf{Z}\}$ is the ring of algebraic integers of the "quadratic field" consisting of the elements $a + b\theta$, $a,b \in \mathbf{Q}$. It can be shown that, for d negative, A is a Euclidean domain if and only if $d = -1, -2, -3, -7$, or -11. In particular, if A is Euclidean, then $\delta: A \to \mathbf{Z}$ defined by

$$\delta(a + b\theta) = \begin{cases} a^2 - db^2 & \text{if } d \equiv 2,3 \bmod 4, \\ a^2 + ab + b^2\dfrac{1-d}{4} & \text{if } d \equiv 1 \bmod 4 \end{cases}$$

serves as a Euclidean norm. There are only finitely many positive values of d for which A is Euclidean (see [11] of the Bibliography).

We prove next that, just as in the special case of the domain of integers, every ideal in an arbitrary Euclidean domain is generated by a single element.

Definition 3.2. An integral domain A is a *principal ideal domain* if every ideal in A is a principal ideal. ///

Theorem 3.3. *Every Euclidean domain is a principal ideal domain.*

PROOF. Let $\langle A,\delta\rangle$ be a Euclidean domain, and let K be an ideal in A. If $K = 0$, then $K = (0)$, a principal ideal. If $K \neq 0$, then K contains elements of positive norm and therefore contains an element k of least positive norm δk; i.e., $0 < \delta k \leq \delta x$ for all $x \in K$. Certainly, $(k) \subset K$. If $x \in K$, $x \neq 0$, then there are $p,r \in A$ such that $x = pk + r$, where $0 \leq \delta r < \delta k$. But $r = x - pk \in K$. Hence, if $\delta r > 0$, then, by the choice of k, $\delta k \leq \delta r$—a contradiction. It follows that $\delta r = 0$, whence $r = 0$ and $x = pk$. But then $K \subset (k)$, so that, in fact, $K = (k)$, a principal ideal. ▮

Corollary. *If F is a field, then $F[x]$ is a principal ideal domain. Every ideal $K \neq 0$ in $F[x]$ has a unique monic generator.* □

Theorem 3.3 suggests a strong connection between divisibility properties and the ideal structure of an integral domain. We will investigate this connection further, and show how the ideal structure of a principal ideal domain implies a "unique factorization" theorem which is a natural generalization of the Fundamental Theorem of Arithmetic (Chapter 0, Theorem 3.6).

First, we collect some of the necessary terminology:

Definition 3.3. Let A be an integral domain, $a,b \in A$. Then

1. *a divides b* $(a|b)$ if $b = ac$ for some $c \in A$.
2. If a has a multiplicative inverse, a^{-1}, in A, then a is a *unit* of A.
3. If $a = ub$, u a unit of A, then a is an *associate* of b in A $(a \sim b)$. (It is easy to check that $\sim$ is an equivalence relation.)
4. If $a|b$ and a is neither a unit nor an associate of b, then a is a *proper divisor* of b.
5. If $a \neq 0$ is not a unit in A, then a is *irreducible in A* if a has no proper divisor in A. If a is not zero, not a unit, and has a proper divisor in A, then a is *properly reducible in A*.
6. If $a \neq 0$ is not a unit, then a is *prime* if $a|bc$ $(b,c \in A)$ implies $a|b$ or $a|c$. An element of A which is a power of a prime is *primary*.
7. An element $d \in A$ such that (i) $d|a$ and $d|b$, and (ii) if $c|a$ and $c|b$ $(c \in A)$, then $c|d$, is a *greatest common divisor* of a and b.

   More generally, if X is any nonempty subset of A and $d \in A$ such that (i) $d|x$ for each $x \in X$, and (ii) if $e \in A$ and $e|x$ for each $x \in X$, then $e|d$, then d is a *greatest common divisor for X*.
8. An element $m \in A$ such that (i) $a|m$ and $b|m$, and (ii) if $a|n$ and $b|n$, then $m|n$, is a *least common multiple* of a and b.

   More generally, if X is any nonempty subset of A and $m \in A$ such that (i) $x|m$ for each $x \in X$, and (ii) if $n \in A$ and $x|n$ for each $x \in X$, then $m|n$, then m is a least common multiple for X. ///

We can now make a dictionary which translates the vocabulary of Definition 3.3 into the language of ideals:

Theorem 3.4. *If A is an integral domain, a,b ∈ A, then*

a. $a|b \Leftrightarrow (b) \subset (a)$.

b. u *is a unit* $\Leftrightarrow (u) = A$.

c. $a \sim b \Leftrightarrow a|b$ *and* $b|a \Leftrightarrow (a) = (b)$.

d. *a is a proper divisor of b* $\Leftrightarrow (b) \subsetneqq (a) \subsetneqq A$.

e. *a is prime* $\Leftrightarrow (a)$ *is a nonzero prime ideal.*

We leave the proof as an exercise (Exercise 3.1). □

As a Corollary of Theorem 3.4c, we have

Corollary 1. *Let A be an integral domain, $a,b \in A$. Then* (1) *any two greatest common divisors* (*least common multiples*) *of a and b are associates, and* (2) *any associate of a greatest common divisor* (*least common multiple*) *of a and b is itself a greatest common divisor* (*least common multiple*) *of a and b.* □

Observe that Definition 3.3 distinguishes between "irreducible elements" and "primes" in an integral domain. We shall see that these concepts do not coincide in general but *do* coincide in principal ideal domains.

From Definition 3.3 and Theorem 3.4c, we have

Corollary 2. *In an integral domain, every prime is irreducible.*

PROOF. If $p \in A$ is prime, and $p = hk$ for some $h,k \in A$, then $p|hk$, hence $p|h$ or $p|k$. But $h|p$ and $k|p$. By Theorem 3.4c we have $p \sim h$ or $p \sim k$, and so p is irreducible. ▮

If A is a principal ideal domain then we can add another entry to our dictionary (sec a in thc following theorem):

Theorem 3.5. *Let A be a principal ideal domain, $a \in A$. Then*

a. *a is irreducible $\Leftrightarrow$ (a) is maximal.*
b. *a is prime if and only if it is irreducible.*
c. *An ideal $K \neq 0$ in A is prime if and only if it is maximal.*

PROOF.

a. If (a) is a maximal ideal, then (a) is a prime ideal (Corollary 2, p. 118); hence a is prime (Theorem 3.4) and therefore irreducible. Suppose a is irreducible. Then a is not a unit, so $(a) \neq A$. If there is an ideal H in A such that $(a) \subset H$, then $H = (h)$ for some $h \in A$ and so, by Theorem 3.4a, $h|a$. But then, since a is irreducible, either h is a unit or $h \sim a$; hence, by Theorem 3.4b and c, either $(h) = A$ or $(h) = (a)$. It follows that (a) is a maximal ideal.

b. If a is irreducible, then (a) is maximal, and so (a) is prime, by Corollary 2, p. 118. But then a is prime, by Theorem 3.4e. The converse holds in any integral domain, as we have shown.

c. If K is an ideal in A, then $K = (a)$ for some $a \in A$, and we have

$$(a) \text{ maximal} \Leftrightarrow a \text{ irreducible} \Leftrightarrow a \text{ prime} \Leftrightarrow (a) \text{ prime.}$$ ▮

None of the assertions of Theorem 3.5 holds in arbitrary integral domains. For example, the first assertion fails in the integral domain $F[x,y]$ (F a field) since the polynomial x is irreducible but $(x) \subsetneq (x,y) \subsetneq (1)$ so that (x) is not maximal. The second assertion fails in the integral domain formed by the complex numbers $a + b\sqrt{-5}$, $a,b \in \mathbf{Z}$: 3 is irreducible but not prime (see Exercise 3.2). The third assertion fails in $F[x,y]$ (F a field): (x) is a prime ideal but not a maximal ideal.

Theorem 3.6. *In a principal ideal domain, every pair of elements has a greatest common divisor and a least common multiple.*

PROOF. Let A be a principal ideal domain, $a,b \in A$. Then there is an element $d \in A$ such that $(d) = (a,b)$. But then $d|a$ and $d|b$, and if $c|a$ and $c|b$ ($c \in A$), then $(a) \subset (c)$ and $(b) \subset (c)$, whence $(d) \subset (c)$ and so $c|d$. Thus, d is a greatest common divisor of a and b. [Observe that, since $(a,b) = \{sa + tb | s,t \in A\}$, there are elements $s_0,t_0 \in A$ such that $d = s_0a + t_0b$.]

There is also an element $m \in A$ such that $(m) = (a) \cap (b)$. Since $(m) \subset (a)$ and $(m) \subset (b)$, we have $a|m$ and $b|m$. If $a|n$ and $b|n$ ($n \in A$), then $(n) \subset (a)$ and $(n) \subset (b)$, hence $(n) \subset (m) = (a) \cap (b)$, and so $m|n$. Thus, m is a least common multiple of a and b. ▮

Theorem 3.6 extends readily to arbitrary nonempty subsets of A (Exercise 3.3).

Our next task is to prove that "unique factorization" holds in principal ideal domains.

Definition 3.4. If A is an integral domain and $\{a_i\}_{i=1}^n$ and $\{b_j\}_{j=1}^m$ ($n > 1$, $m > 1$) are families of nonunits of A, then the products $\prod_{i=1}^n a_i$ and $\prod_{j=1}^n b_j$ are *equivalent* if $m = n$ and there is a permutation σ of $\{1,2,\ldots,n\}$ such that $a_i \sim b_j$ if $\sigma i = j$. ///

Definition 3.5. An integral domain A is *Gaussian* if every properly reducible element is equal to a product of irreducible elements of A, and any two products representing the same element a are equivalent. ///

(Note that a field is trivially a Gaussian domain since it has no properly reducible elements.)

We want to prove that every principal ideal domain is Gaussian. The existence of a factorization for every nonunit $a \neq 0$ will follow if we can show that every descending chain of divisors terminates. By Theorem 3.4a this is equivalent to showing that every ascending chain of ideals terminates:

Theorem 3.7. *Every principal ideal domain satisfies the ascending chain condition on ideals.*

PROOF. Let $(k_1) \subset (k_2) \subset \cdots$ be an ascending chain of ideals in A. Form $K = \bigcup_{i \in \mathbf{N}'} (k_i)$. It is easy to check that K is an ideal. Hence there is some element $k \in A$ such that $K = (k)$. Now, $k \in (k_n)$ for some $n \in \mathbf{N}'$; hence $(k) \subset (k_n) \subset (k)$ and $(k) = (k_n)$. But then, for each $p \in \mathbf{N}'$, $(k_n) \subset (k_{n+p}) \subset (k) = (k_n)$, and so $(k_{n+p}) = (k_n)$. Thus, the chain $(k_1) \subset (k_2) \subset \cdots$ terminates. ▮

The following lemma is a generalization of the induction principle for integers. We shall employ it in the proof of the unique factorization theorem much as the induction principle is used in the proof of the Fundamental Theorem of Arithmetic. (In fact, this lemma and the induction principle are both special cases of a more general theorem on partially ordered sets—see Exercise 3.4.)

Lemma. *Let A be an integral domain satisfying the ascending chain condition on ideals, and let M be a nonempty subset of A satisfying the condition: If $x \in A$ and all proper divisors of x are in M, then $x \in M$. Then $M = A$.*

PROOF. Let $\overline{M} = A - M$, and suppose $M \neq A$; i.e., $\overline{M} \neq \varnothing$. If $x_1 \in \overline{M}$, then x_1 has a proper divisor $x_2 \in \overline{M}$, since, otherwise, $x_1 \in M$. For the same reason, x_2 has a proper divisor, x_3, in $\overline{M}$ and, continuing in this way, we obtain a sequence (x_n) of elements of $\overline{M}$ such that x_{n+1} is a proper divisor of x_n for each $n = 1, 2, \ldots$. Corresponding to this sequence, we have the ascending chain of ideals $(x_1) \subset (x_2) \subset \cdots$, with each inclusion proper. But A satisfies the ascending chain condition on ideals—a contradiction! It follows that $M = A$. ▮

We are now ready to prove

Theorem 3.8. *Every principal ideal domain is Gaussian.*

PROOF. We first prove that every properly reducible element of A is equal to a product of irreducible elements of A. Let $M = \{x \mid x \text{ is not properly reducible, or } x \text{ is a product of irreducible elements of } A\}$. Suppose $a \in A$ and all proper divisors of a are in M. If a is not properly reducible, then, of course, $a \in M$. If a is properly reducible, there are elements $y,z \in A$ such that $a = yz$, where y and z are both proper divisors of a. Then y and z are elements of M which are neither zero nor units. Hence each of y, z is either irreducible or a product of irreducible elements. But then a is a product of irreducible elements, and so $a \in M$. Thus, M satisfies the hypotheses of the lemma, and therefore $M = A$. It follows that every properly reducible element of A is a product of irreducible elements.

We must now prove that any two products of irreducible elements which represent the same properly reducible element of A are equivalent. We again employ the lemma. Let $M = \{x | x \text{ is not properly reducible, or any two products of irreducible elements representing } x \text{ are equivalent}\}$. Suppose $a \in A$ has all its proper divisors in M. If a is not properly reducible, then certainly $a \in M$. If a is properly reducible, then, by the first part of the proof, a is a product of irreducible elements of A. Now suppose $p_1, \ldots, p_s$ and $q_1, \ldots, q_t$ $(s > 1, t > 1)$ are irreducible elements of A such that

$$a = p_1 \cdots p_s = q_1 \cdots q_t.$$

Since A is a principal ideal domain, every irreducible element of A is prime (Theorem 3.5). Hence $p_1 | q_i$ for some $i = 1, \ldots, t$. Since A is commutative, we may assume without loss of generality that $i = 1$, i.e., $p_1 | q_1$. Since p_1 is not a unit and q_1 is irreducible, it follows that $p_1 \sim q_1$, say $up_1 = q_1$, where u is a unit in A. From $p_1 p_2 \cdots p_s = up_1 q_2 \cdots q_t$ we have $a' = p_2 p_3 \cdots p_s = (uq_2) q_3 \cdots q_t$. If $s = 2$, then $t = 2$ and $p_2 = uq_2$, so that $p_2 \sim q_2$ and therefore the products $p_1 p_2 \cdots p_s$ and $q_1 q_2 \cdots q_t$ are, in this case, equivalent. If $s > 2$, then a' is a properly reducible proper divisor of a and therefore a properly reducible element of M. But then the products $p_2 p_3 \cdots p_s$ and $(uq_2) q_3 \cdots q_t$ are equivalent. It follows that the products $p_1 p_2 \cdots p_s$ and $q_1 q_2 \cdots q_t$ are equivalent, and so, by the lemma, $M = A$. Hence, if a is any properly reducible element of A, then any two products of irreducible elements representing a are equivalent. ▮

Corollary. *If F is a field, then $F[x]$ is a Gaussian integral domain.* □

Not every Gaussian domain is a principal ideal domain. For example, as we shall see, the polynomial domain $F[x,y]$ (F a field) is Gaussian (Corollary of Theorem 3.11), but the ideal (x,y) is not principal. For the only common divisors of x are y are units in $F[x,y]$. Hence, if $f \in F[x,y]$ and $(x,y) = (f)$, then f is a unit and so $(x,y) = F[x,y]$, which is clearly false, since all polynomials in (x,y) have zero constant term.

Also, not every integral domain is Gaussian. For example, the integral domain formed by the complex numbers $a + b\sqrt{-5}$ $(a,b \in \mathbf{Z})$ is not

Gaussian, since 9 is a properly reducible element of this domain which has two nonequivalent representations as a product of irreducible elements:

$$9 = 3 \cdot 3,$$

$$9 = (2 + \sqrt{-5})(2 - \sqrt{-5}).$$

(See Exercise 3.2.)

Let $\mathfrak{E}$, $\mathfrak{P}$, $\mathfrak{G}$, and $\mathfrak{D}$ denote, respectively, the class of Euclidean, principal ideal, Gaussian, and arbitrary integral domains. We have seen that $\mathfrak{E} \subset \mathfrak{P} \subset \mathfrak{G} \subset \mathfrak{D}$. Each of these class inclusions is strict, as the following examples show:

1. An integral domain which is not Gaussian:

$$A = \{a + b\sqrt{-5} \mid a,b \in \mathbf{Z}\}.$$

2. A Gaussian domain which is not a principal ideal domain:

$$A = F[x,y], \qquad F \text{ a field.}$$

3. A principal ideal domain which is not Euclidean:

$$A = \left\{a + b\left(\frac{1 + \sqrt{-19}}{2}\right) \middle| a,b \in \mathbf{Z}\right\}.$$

Several of the properties of principal ideal domains which we have discussed hold in all Gaussian domains. We state some of these properties in the following theorems, whose proofs we leave to the reader.

Theorem 3.9. *If A is a Gaussian domain, $a \in A$, then a is prime if and only if a is irreducible.* □

Note that, since the ideal generated by an irreducible element need not be maximal in a Gaussian domain [e.g., the ideal (x) in $F[x,y]$, F a field], Theorem 3.9 does not imply that, in an arbitrary Gaussian domain, an ideal is prime if and only if it is maximal [e.g., the ideal (x) in $F[x,y]$, F a field, is prime but not maximal].

Theorem 3.10. *If A is a Gaussian domain, $a,b \in A$, then a and b have a greatest common divisor and a least common multiple in A. In particular, if*

$a \sim p_1^{\alpha_1}\cdots p_h^{\alpha_h}$, $b \sim p_1^{\beta_1}\cdots p_h^{\beta_h}$, where, for each $i = 1,\ldots,h$, p_i is a prime in A, and α_i, β_i are nonnegative integers, then

$$d = p_1^{\delta_1}\cdots p_h^{\delta_h}, \qquad \delta_i = \min\{\alpha_i,\beta_i\}, \qquad i = 1,\ldots,h,$$
$$m = p_1^{\mu_1}\cdots p_h^{\mu_h}, \qquad \mu_i = \max\{\alpha_i,\beta_i\}, \qquad i = 1,\ldots,h$$

are, respectively, a greatest common divisor and a least common multiple of a and b.

PROOF. Exercise 3.7. ∎

What cannot be asserted for arbitrary Gaussian domains is that, if d and m are, respectively, a greatest common divisor and a least common multiple for a and b, then $(d) = (a,b)$ and $(m) = (a) \cap (b)$—a statement which holds in the special case of principal ideal domains. In general, only the inclusions $(d) \supset (a,b)$ and $(m) \subset (a) \cap (b)$ are valid. (See Exercise 3.6.) Consequently, a greatest common divisor of two elements cannot, in general, be expressed as a linear combination of the elements.

We note that Theorem 3.10 can be extended to arbitrary subsets X of a Gaussian domain A except that, when X contains infinitely many nonassociate elements, the only least common multiple of X is 0 (Exercise 3.7).

We have seen that, for F a field, $F[x]$ is a Gaussian integral domain. We have also made the claim that, for F a field, $F[x,y]$ is Gaussian. Both of these assertions are consequences of the following theorem which we now set out to prove: If A is Gaussian domain, then so is $A[x]$. The proof requires some preparation.

Definition 3.6. Let A be an integral domain, $f \in A[x]$. Then f is a *primitive polynomial* in $A[x]$ if f has positive degree and the only common divisors of all the coefficients of f are units in A. ///

In proving the following lemmas, two rather trivial remarks will be helpful:

1. If A is an integral domain, $a \in A$ and $f \in A[x]$, then $a|f$ in $A[x]$ if and only if a is a divisor in A of every coefficient of f.
2. If A is an integral domain, $f \in A[x]$, then f is a unit of $A[x]$ if and only if $f \in A$ and f is a unit of A.

Lemma 1. *Let A be a Gaussian domain, f a polynomial of positive degree in $A[x]$. Then*

a. *$f = dp$ for some $d \in A$, p a primitive polynomial in $A[x]$.*
b. *If $f = d_1p_1 = d_2p_2$, $d_1,d_2 \in A$, p_1, p_2 primitive polynomials in $A[x]$, then $d_1 \sim d_2$ in A and $p_1 \sim p_2$ in $A[x]$.*

PROOF.

a. Since A is Gaussian, the coefficients of f have a greatest common divisor, d, in A, and $f = dp$ for some polynomial $p \in A[x]$, where $\deg p = \deg f > 0$. If p is not primitive, then the coefficients of p have a prime factor q and dq is a divisor of f, hence a divisor of all coefficients of f. But then $dq|d$, whence q is a unit in A, contrary to hypothesis. Thus, p is primitive.

b. Suppose $f = d_1p_1 = d_2p_2$, $d_1,d_2 \in A$, p_1, p_2 primitive in $A[x]$. Since p_2 is primitive, each primary divisor of d_1 must be a divisor of d_2 in A (see Exercise 3.8) and therefore, since A is Gaussian, $d_1|d_2$ in A. Similarly, $d_2|d_1$ in A, and so $d_1 \sim d_2$ in A. If $d_2 = ud_1$, u a unit in A, then $d_1p_1 = ud_1p_2$, hence $p_1 = up_2$, and $p_1 \sim p_2$ in $A[x]$. ▌

Lemma 2. *Let A be a Gaussian domain, f, g primitive polynomials in $A[x]$. Then $h = f \cdot g$ is a primitive polynomial in $A[x]$.*

PROOF. Let

$$f = a_0 + a_1x + \cdots + a_mx^m, \ a_m \neq 0, \ a_i \in A \qquad (i = 0,\ldots,m),$$

$$g = b_0 + b_1x + \cdots + b_nx^n, \ b_n \neq 0, \ b_j \in A \qquad (j = 0,\ldots,m).$$

Then there are elements $c_i \in A$ $(i = 0,\ldots,m + n)$ such that $h = c_0 + c_1x + \cdots + c_{m+n}x^{m+n}$, $c_{m+n} \neq 0$. Suppose h is not primitive. Then there is a prime element $q \in A$ such that $q|c_i$ for each $i = 0, 1,\ldots, m + n$. Since f and g are primitive, there is a least integer $s \geq 0$ such that $q \nmid a_s$ and there is a least integer $t \geq 0$ such that $q \nmid b_t$. Now,

$$c_{s+t} = a_0b_{s+t} + a_1b_{s+t-1} + \cdots + a_sb_t + \cdots + a_{s+t-1}b_1 + a_{s+t}b_0.$$

By the choice of s and t, $q|a_ib_j$ for $i < s$ or $j < t$. Since $q|c_{s+t}$, q also divides a_sb_t. But then, being prime, q divides either a_s or b_t, contrary to hypothesis. We conclude that $h = fg$ is a primitive polynomial. ▌

Lemma 3. *Let A be a Gaussian integral domain, F a quotient field of A such that $A \subset F$. If f is a primitive polynomial in $A[x]$, then f is an irreducible element of $A[x]$ if and only if it is an irreducible element of $F[x]$.*

PROOF. If f is irreducible in $F[x]$, then f has no proper divisor in $F[x]$, hence f has no divisor g in $F[x]$ such that $0 < \deg g < \deg f$. Thus every proper divisor k of f in $A[x]$ has degree 0; i.e., $k \in A$. But then k is a divisor of all the coefficients of f, and so, since f is primitive, k is a unit in A, hence a unit in

$A[x]$, and therefore not a proper divisor of f—a contradiction! It follows that f is irreducible in $A[x]$.

If, on the other hand, f is irreducible in $A[x]$, suppose there are polynomials $g,h \in F[x]$ such that $f = gh$, where g and h are both proper divisors of f in $F[x]$. There are elements $a,b \in A$ such that ag and bh are both elements of $A[x]$. (For example, if the coefficients of f and g are written as quotients of elements of A, a may be taken equal to a least common multiple of the denominators of the coefficients of f, and b equal to a least common multiple of the denominators of the coefficients of g.) By Lemma 1, there are elements $a_1,b_1 \in A$ and primitive polynomials $g_1,h_1 \in A[x]$ such that $ag = a_1g_1$ and $bh = b_1h_1$. Hence $abf = a_1b_1g_1h_1$ and, by Lemma 2, g_1h_1 is a primitive polynomial in $A[x]$. Since f is also a primitive polynomial in $A[x]$, $f \sim g_1h_1$ in $A[x]$, by Lemma 1. But then $g_1|f$ in $A[x]$ and, since $0 < \deg g = \deg g_1 < \deg f$, g_1 is a proper divisor of f, contrary to the hypothesis that f is irreducible in $A[x]$. Thus, f is irreducible in $F[x]$. ▮

Lemma 4. *Let A be a Gaussian integral domain, F a quotient field of A such that $A \subset F$. Then two primitive polynomials f, g in $A[x]$ are associates in $A[x]$ if and only if they are associates in $F[x]$.*

PROOF. Suppose $f \sim g$ in $F[x]$, say $f = ag$, where a is a unit in $F[x]$. Then $a = c/d$ for some $c,d \in A$ and so $df = cg$. By Lemma 1, since f and g are primitive, $f \sim g$ in $A[x]$.

Conversely, suppose $f \sim g$ in $A[x]$, say $f = ug$, u a unit in $A[x]$. Since $u \neq 0$, u is a unit in F, hence in $F[x]$, and $f \sim g$ in $F[x]$. ▮

We are now ready to prove our theorem.

Theorem 3.11. *If A is a Gaussian integral domain, then $A[x]$ is also a Gaussian integral domain.*

PROOF. We know that $A[x]$ is an integral domain. Let F be a quotient field of A such that $A \subset F$. We know that $F[x]$ is Gaussian. Let f be a properly reducible element of $A[x]$ and suppose first that f is a primitive polynomial in $A[x]$. Since $f \in F[x]$ and is properly reducible in $F[x]$, there are irreducible polynomials $\bar{p}_1,\ldots,\bar{p}_s$ in $F[x]$ such that $f = \bar{p}_1\bar{p}_2\cdots\bar{p}_s$. For each $i = 1,\ldots,s$, there are elements $a_i,b_i \in A$ such that $a_i\bar{p}_i = b_ip_i \in A[x]$, where p_i is primitive. Then $af = bp_1\cdots p_s$, where $a = a_1a_2\cdots a_s$, $b = b_1\cdots b_s$. Since, for each $i = 1,\ldots,s$, $\bar{p}_i$ is irreducible in $F[x]$, p_i is also irreducible in $F[x]$, and so, by Lemma 3, p_i (being primitive) is irreducible in $A[x]$. By Lemma 2, $p_1\cdots p_s$ is a primitive polynomial in $A[x]$ and so, by Lemma 1, $f \sim p_1\cdots p_s$ in $A[x]$.

Hence $f = p_1'p_2 \cdots p_s$, where $p_1' \sim p_1$ in A. We have thus represented f as a product of irreducible elements of $A[x]$.

Now let g be any properly reducible element of $A[x]$. If $g \in A$, then, since A is Gaussian, there are irreducible elements $a_1, \ldots, a_h \in A$ such that $g = a_1 \cdots a_h$, and any two products of elements of A representing g are equivalent in A, hence in $A[x]$. Since g can have no factors of degree greater than zero, the conclusion of the theorem holds for $g \in A$.

If $g \notin A$, then $g = df$, where $a \in A$ and f is a primitive polynomial in $A[x]$. By the first part of the proof, there are irreducible (primitive) polynomials $p_1, \ldots, p_s$ of positive degree in $A[x]$ such that $f = p_1 \cdots p_s$. Since A is Gaussian, there are irreducible elements $d_1, \ldots, d_h \in A$ such that $d = d_1 \cdots d_h$. Thus, $g = d_1 \cdots d_h p_1 \cdots p_s$, a product of irreducible elements of $A[x]$. Now suppose $e_1, \ldots, e_k \in A$ and $q_1, \ldots, q_t \in A[x] - A$ are irreducible elements of $A[x]$ such that $g = e_1 \cdots e_k q_1 \cdots q_t$. Then the q_j are primitive ($j = 1, \ldots, t$) and so, by Lemma 3, the product $q_1 \cdots q_t$ is primitive. By Lemma 1, $d_1 \cdots d_h \sim e_1 \cdots e_k$ in A. Since A is Gaussian, the products $d_1 \cdots d_h$ and $e_1 \cdots e_k$ are equivalent in A, hence in $A[x]$. Again by Lemma 1, $p_1 \cdots p_s \sim q_1 \cdots q_t$ in $A[x]$. Hence, by Lemma 4, $p_1 \cdots p_s \sim q_1 \cdots q_t$ in $F[x]$. But then the products $p_1 \cdots p_s$ and $q_1 \cdots q_t$ are equivalent, by Theorem 3.8, in $F[x]$, and, by Lemma 4, in $A[x]$. It now follows that the products $d_1 \cdots d_h\, p_1 \cdots p_s$ and $e_1 \cdots e_k\, q_1 \cdots q_t$ are equivalent in $A[x]$, and the theorem is proved. ▌

Corollary. *If F is a field, then for each positive integer n, the polynomial domain $F[x_1x_2, \ldots, x_n]$ in n indeterminates over F is Gaussian,* □

We conclude this chapter by proving some of the elementary facts about polynomial equations with coefficients in a field. In Chapter 5 we shall return to this subject for a more extensive investigation.

Definition 3.7. Let F be a field, $\langle E,\alpha\rangle$ an extension field of F, $f = a_0 + a_1x + \cdots + a_nx^n$, ($a_i \in F$) a polynomial of positive degree in $F[x]$, and u an element of E. Then u is a *root of* f in $\langle E,\alpha\rangle$ if $\alpha f(u) = \alpha a_0 + \alpha a_1 u + \cdots + \alpha a_n u^n = 0_E$ in E. ///

Theorem 3.12. *If F is a field, f a polynomial of positive degree in $F[x]$, then F has an extension field in which f has a root.*

PROOF. Since $F[x]$ is a Gaussian integral domain, there are polynomials $p,q \in F[x]$ such that $f = pq$ and p is irreducible. Since $F[x]$ is a principal ideal domain, (p) is a maximal ideal and so, by Theorem 1.5, $E = F[x]/(p)$ is a field. Let ν be the natural homomorphism of $F[x]$ with respect to (p), and let

$\alpha = \nu|_F$. Then α is a monomorphism of F into E, since, for $a \in F$, $\alpha a = 0$ implies $a \in (p)$, hence $a = 0$. Thus, $\langle E,\alpha\rangle$ is an extension field of F.

Now let $u = \nu x$. If $p = a_0 + a_1x + \cdots + a_nx^n$ $(a_i \in F, i = 0,1,\ldots,n)$, then

$$\begin{aligned}\alpha p(u) = \alpha p(\nu x) &= \alpha a_0 + \alpha a_1 \nu x + \cdots + \alpha a_n(\nu x)^n \\ &= \nu a_0 + \nu a_1 \nu x + \cdots + \nu a_n(\nu x)^n \\ &= \nu(a_0 + a_1 x + \cdots + a_n x^n) = \nu p = \nu 0 = 0_E.\end{aligned}$$

Thus, $u = \nu x$ is a root of p. But then

$$\alpha f(u) = \alpha p(u)\alpha q(u) = 0_E$$

and therefore u is a root of f. ▮

Theorem 3.13. *Let F be a field, $\langle E,\alpha\rangle$ an extension field of F.*

a. *If $f \in F[x]$, $u \in E$, then u is a root of f if and only if $(x - u)|\alpha f$ in $E[x]$.*

b. *If f is a polynomial of degree n in $F[x]$, then f has at most n roots in E.*

PROOF.

a. Follows easily from the division algorithm.

b. May be proved inductively, using a. ▮

Exercises

Section 1

1.1. Prove that the computational rules given in Remark 1 (p. 113) hold in any ring.

1.2. In any ring A, the following conditions are equivalent:

(a) $ab = 0 \Rightarrow a = 0$ or $b = 0$.

(b) $ac = bc$ $(c \neq 0) \Rightarrow a = b$.

(c) $ca = cb$ $(c \neq 0) \Rightarrow a = b$.

1.3. Prove Theorem 1.1.

1.4. (a) A division ring has no proper one-sided ideals.

(b) If a ring with identity has no proper right (or no proper left) ideals, then it is a division ring.

1.5. If a ring A (with or without identity) has no proper one-sided ideals, then either $A^2 = 0$ or A is a division ring.

1.6. If A is a ring such that $A^2 \neq 0$, then for each $n > 1$,

(a) A_n is noncommutative.

(b) A_n has proper right and left ideals.

(c) A_n has zero divisors.

1.7. If A is a division ring, then for $n \geq 1$, A_n has no proper two-sided ideals. (*Hint:* For $n > 1$, define "matrix units" E_{ij}, with 1 in the ij position, 0's elsewhere. Show that

$$E_{ij}E_{kl} = \delta_{jk}E_{il} \qquad \text{where } \delta_{jk} = 1 \text{ if } j = k, \quad \delta_{jk} = 0 \text{ if } j \neq k.$$

Use the E_{ij} to prove that every two-sided ideal K of A_n contains I_n, the identity of A_n.)

1.8. Verify the details of the remark following Definition 1.4. Obtain corresponding characterizations for the right, left, or two-sided ideal generated by an arbitrary subset of a ring.

1.9. Verify directly that $\mathbf{Z}/(m)$ is a field if and only if m is prime.

1.10. In $\mathbf{Z}$, the following statements concerning an ideal K are equivalent:

(a) K is maximal.

(b) K is prime.

(c) $K = (p)$, where p is a prime.

1.11. Let $A = \mathbf{Z}_n$, the ring of all $n \times n$ matrices over $\mathbf{Z}$.

(a) Characterize the maximal ideals in A.

(b) Prove that, if K is any maximal ideal in A, then A/K is not a division ring.

1.12. (a) If A is a division ring, then the 0-ideal in A_n ($n > 1$) is maximal but not prime.

(b) If A is a ring such that the group $\langle A, + \rangle$ is of prime order and $ab = 0$ for all $a,b \in A$, then the 0-ideal in A is maximal but not prime.

1.13. Find an example of a commutative ring A such that, for some maximal ideal K of A, A/K is not a field.

1.14. (a) Every finite integral domain is a field.

(b) In a commutative ring with identity, every prime ideal of finite index is a maximal ideal.

1.15. An ideal $\mathfrak{a}$ in a commutative ring A is a prime ideal if and only if there is a multiplicative system S in A such that $\mathfrak{a} \cap S = \varnothing$ and $\mathfrak{a}$ is not properly contained in any ideal of A which is disjoint from S (i.e., $\mathfrak{a}$ is prime $\Leftrightarrow$ $\mathfrak{a}$ is maximal in the set of ideals disjoint from S).

1.16. Let A be a commutative ring with 1.

(a) Let S be a multiplicative system in A and let $\mathfrak{a}$ be an ideal in A such that $\mathfrak{a} \cap S = \varnothing$. Then there is an ideal $\mathfrak{p}$ in A such that $\mathfrak{p} \supset \mathfrak{a}$, $\mathfrak{p} \cap S = \varnothing$, and every ideal which contains $\mathfrak{p}$ properly meets S. Such an ideal $\mathfrak{p}$ is prime.

(b) If $\mathfrak{a}$ is an ideal in A such that $\mathfrak{a} \neq A$, then there is a maximal ideal $\mathfrak{m}$ in A such that $\mathfrak{m} \supset \mathfrak{a}$.

1.17. Let $\{\mathfrak{p}_\alpha\}_{\alpha \in J}$ be a chain of prime ideals in a commutative ring. Then $\bigcup_{\alpha \in J} \mathfrak{p}_\alpha$ and $\bigcap_{\alpha \in J} \mathfrak{p}_\alpha$ are prime ideals.

1.18. An element e of a ring A is idempotent if $e^2 = e$. Prove:

(a) The only idempotents in a division ring are 0 and 1.

(b) If a ring A without zero divisors has an idempotent $e \neq 0$, then e is a (two-sided) identity for A.

1.19. Let A be a ring with identity, e, f idempotents in A. Then $eA = fA$ if and only if $f = e + ex(1 - e)$ for some $x \in A$.

1.20. An element a of a ring A is *nilpotent* if $a^k = 0$ for some $k \in \mathbf{N}'$. Prove that, if A is commutative, the nilpotent elements of A form an ideal, $\mathfrak{N}$, which is equal to the intersection of all maximal ideals of A.

prime (or assume $A \ni 1$)

1.21. Let A be a ring. Prove:

(a) If $a \in A$, then the sets

$$\{x | xa = 0\} \quad \text{and} \quad \{x | ax = 0\}$$

are, respectively, left and right ideals of A.

(b) If K is a left ideal of A, then the set $\{x | xk = 0 \; \forall \, k \in K\}$ is a two-sided ideal of A.

1.22. In a ring A with identity 1, the following conditions are equivalent:

(a) $xy = 1 \Rightarrow yx = 1$ $(x, y \in A)$.

(b) Every left unit of A is a unit of A.

(c) Every right unit of A is a unit of A.

1.23. Let A be a ring with identity, u an element of A which has a right inverse. Then the following are equivalent:

(a) u has more than one right inverse.

(b) u is not a unit.

(c) u is a left zero divisor.

1.24. In a ring with identity, without left (or right) zero divisors, every one-sided unit is a unit.

1.25. If an element of a ring with identity has more than one right inverse, then it has infinitely many.

1.26. If a ring has only one left identity 1_l, then 1_l is a two-sided identity.

1.27. Let A be a ring, and let K be a (right, left, two-sided) ideal in the matrix ring A_n. Then the set $A(K)$ of elements of A which are entries of matrices in K forms a (right, left, two-sided) ideal in A.

The map $K \mapsto A(K)$ of the set of (right, left, two-sided) ideals of A_n into the set of (right, left, two-sided) ideals of A is inclusion preserving, surjective, but not injective.

1.28. If A_n is the ring of all $n \times n$ matrices over a ring A, then the "scalar matrices"

$$(a) = \begin{pmatrix} a & 0 & \cdots & 0 \\ 0 & a & & \vdots \\ \vdots & & \ddots & 0 \\ 0 & & & a \end{pmatrix}$$

form a subring of A_n, isomorphic to A under the map $a \mapsto (a)$. The map $(a,B) \mapsto (a)B$ of $A \times A_n$ into A_n is a scalar multiplication on A_n, which makes $\langle A_n, + \rangle$ into an A-group.

1.29. Let $\mathfrak{A}$ be the set of all 2×2 matrices with complex elements, of form

$$\begin{pmatrix} z & w \\ -\bar{w} & \bar{z} \end{pmatrix},$$

where $\bar{w}$ and $\bar{z}$ are the complex conjugates of w and z.

(a) Prove that $\mathfrak{A}$ forms a subring of the 2×2 matrix ring $\mathbf{C}_2$.

(b) Prove that $\mathfrak{A}$ is a division ring.

(c) Let

$$1 = \begin{pmatrix} 1 & 0 \\ 0 & 1 \end{pmatrix}, \quad i = \begin{pmatrix} \sqrt{-1} & 0 \\ 0 & -\sqrt{-1} \end{pmatrix}, \quad j = \begin{pmatrix} 0 & 1 \\ -1 & 0 \end{pmatrix},$$

$$k = \begin{pmatrix} 0 & \sqrt{-1} \\ \sqrt{-1} & 0 \end{pmatrix}.$$

Prove that each element of $\mathfrak{A}$ may be represented uniquely in the form $a_0 1 + a_1 i + a_2 j + a_3 k$, where $a_i \in \mathbf{R}$.

(d) Prove that $i^2 = j^2 = k^2 = -1$ and

$$\begin{aligned} ij &= -ji = k, \\ jk &= -kj = i, \\ ki &= -ik = j. \end{aligned}$$

(e) Prove that the subgroup of the multiplicative group of $\mathfrak{A}$ generated by i, j, k is non-abelian, of order 8 (see Chapter 1, Exercise 8.1).

($\mathfrak{A}$ is the *ring of real quaternions*; the multiplicative subgroup generated by i, j, k is the *quaternion group*.)

1.30. If F is any field, then the additive group of F is not isomorphic to the multiplicative group of F.

1.31. (Cartan Brauer–Hua Theorem.) Let A be a division ring, B a subring of A such that $a^{-1}Ba \subset A$ for all $a \neq 0$ in A. Prove: B is contained in the center of A. (*Hint:* Verify and use Hua's identity:

$$t = [x^{-1} - (t-1)^{-1}x^{-1}(t-1)][t^{-1}x^{-1}t - (t-1)^{-1}x^{-1}(t-1)]^{-1},$$

where x, t, and $t - 1$ are nonzero elements of A.)

Section 2

2.1. Carry out the details in the Remark following Theorem 2.1.

2.2. Prove Theorem 2.2.

2.3. Generalize Theorem 2.3 to the case where n is an arbitrary cardinal.

2.4. Verify that the binary relation $\sim$ on $A \times S$ defined in the discussion preceding Theorem 2.7 is an equivalence relation.

2.5. Let A be an integral domain, F a quotient field of A such that $A \subset F$. Prove: If A' is an integral domain, $A \subset A' \subset F$, then F is a quotient field of A'.

2.6. Let A be an integral domain, S a multiplicative system of A not containing 0. Then

(a) AS^{-1} is an integral domain.

(b) If A is a principal ideal domain, then AS^{-1} is a principal ideal domain.

(c) If A is a Gaussian domain, then AS^{-1} is a Gaussian domain.

2.7. A nonzero homomorphic image of an integral domain need not be an integral domain—but every nonzero homomorphic image of a local ring is local.

2.8. The following two conditions on a subdomain A of $\mathbf{Q}$ are equivalent:

(a) A is a maximal subdomain with quotient field $\mathbf{Q}$.

(b) A is the local ring $\mathbf{Z}_{(p)}$ for some prime p.

Generalize this result to the quotient field F of an arbitrary principal ideal domain.

Section 3

3.1. Prove Theorem 3.4.

3.2. Prove that, in the integral domain $D = \{a + b\sqrt{-5} \mid a,b \in \mathbf{Z}\}$,

$$9 = (2 + \sqrt{-5})(2 - \sqrt{-5}),$$

$$9 = 3 \cdot 3$$

are nonequivalent factorizations of 9 as a product of irreducible elements. Conclude that the irreducible elements 3, $2 + \sqrt{-5}$, and $2 - \sqrt{-5}$ are not prime.

3.3. Extend Theorem 3.6 to arbitrary subsets of an integral domain.

3.4. Let $\langle X, \prec \rangle$ be a partially ordered set in which every $\prec$-chain terminates, and suppose $M \in X$ satisfies the condition: If $a \in A$ and $x \in M$ for all x with $a \prec x$, then $a \in M$. Prove that $M = A$.

3.5. An integral domain D is Gaussian if and only if every nonzero prime ideal in D contains a nonzero prime ideal which is principal.

3.6. Give an example of a Gaussian domain A and two elements $a,b \in A$ such that

(a) $(d) \supsetneqq (a,b)$ (d a greatest common divisor of a and b).

(b) $(m) \subsetneqq (a) \cap (b)$ (m a least common multiple of a and b).

3.7. (a) Prove Theorem 3.10.
(b) Extend Theorem 3.10 to arbitrary subsets X of a Gaussian domain A. Prove that, if X is infinite, the only least common multiple of X is zero.

3.8. Prove the Irreducibility Criterion of Eisenstein: Let A be a Gaussian domain, F its quotient field, and let

$$f(x) = a_0 + a_1x + \cdots + a_nx^n \in A[x].$$

If there is a prime $p \in A$ such that

$$a_n \not\equiv 0 \bmod p,$$

$$a_i \equiv 0 \bmod p \qquad \text{for all } i < n,$$

$$a_0 \not\equiv 0 \bmod p^2,$$

then $f(x)$ is irreducible in $F[x]$.

3.9. A polynomial $f \in A[x_1,\ldots,x_n]$ (A commutative with identity) is *symmetric* if, for each $\tau \in S_n$, $f(x_{\tau 1},\ldots,x_{\tau n}) = f(x_1,\ldots,x_n)$. Prove:
(a) The polynomials

$$\sigma_1 = \sum x_ix_j, \qquad 1 \le i < j \le n,$$

$$\sigma_2 = \sum x_ix_jx_k, \qquad 1 \le i < j < k \le n,$$

$$\vdots$$

$$\sigma_n = x_1x_2\cdots x_n$$

are symmetric. (These are the *elementary symmetric polynomials* in $A[x_1,\ldots,x_n]$.)
(b) If f is a symmetric polynomial in $A[x_1,\ldots,x_n]$, then $f \in A[\sigma_1,\ldots,\sigma_n]$.

3.10. Let $f = x^n + a_{n-1}x^{n-1} + \cdots + a_0 \in F[x]$, with roots $u_1,\ldots, u_n$ (contained in some extension field E of F). Prove: $a_{n-i} = (-1)^i\sigma_i(u_1,\ldots,u_n)$, $i = 1,\ldots, n$, where the σ_i are the elementary symmetric polynomials in $E[x_1,\ldots,x_n]$ (see Exercise 3.9).

3.11. Let $A = \{z \in \mathbf{C} | z = a + bi,\ a,b \in \mathbf{Z}\}$. Prove that A forms an integral domain under the usual addition and multiplication of complex numbers. Prove that $\delta: a + bi \mapsto a^2 + b^2$ is a Euclidean norm on A.

3.12. Let F be a field, $f \in F[x]$, $f \neq 0$. Consider the map $\bar{f}$: $a \mapsto f(a)$ of F into F. Prove that if card $F > \deg f$, then $\bar{f} \neq 0$. Give an example of a field F and a polynomial $f \in F[x]$ such that $f \neq 0$ and $\bar{f} = 0$.

3.13. A Gaussian integral domain satisfies the descending chain condition on ideals if and only if it is a field.

3.14. Let $n = 2^e p_1^{e_1} p_2^{e_2} \cdots p_s^{e_s}$ $(e, e_i \ge 0)$ be the factorization of the positive integer n into a product of distinct primes. Let $[\mathbf{Z}/(n)]^*$ denote the multiplicative group of invertible elements of $\mathbf{Z}/(n)$. Prove:

(a) $[\mathbf{Z}/(n)]^*$ is isomorphic to a product of the groups $[\mathbf{Z}/(2^e)]^*$ and $[\mathbf{Z}/(p_i^{e_i})]^*$, $i = 1, 2, \ldots, s$.

(b) If p is an odd prime, $[\mathbf{Z}/(p^e)]^*$ is cyclic of order $p^{e-1}(p - 1)$.

(c) $[\mathbf{Z}/(2^2)]^*$ is cyclic of order 2, and for $e > 2$, $[\mathbf{Z}/(2^e)]$ is a product of a cyclic group of order 2^{e-2} and a cyclic group of order 2.

(d) $[\mathbf{Z}/(n)]^*$ is isomorphic to a product of a cyclic group of order 2 (if $e > 1$), a cyclic group of order 2^{e-2} (if $e > 2$), and cyclic groups of order $p^{e_i-1}(p_i - 1)$, $i = 1, 2, \ldots, s$.

3.15. Let n be a positive integer, and let $\varphi(n)$ be the number of positive integers which are less than n and relatively prime to n. [Then $\varphi(n)$ is the order of the multiplicative group $[\mathbf{Z}/(n)]^*$ of invertible elements in the ring $\mathbf{Z}/(n)$.] Prove:

(a) If $m,n \in \mathbf{N}'$, and $(m,n) = 1$, then $\varphi(mn) = \varphi(m)\varphi(n)$.

(b) If p is a positive prime, and e is a positive integer, then $\varphi(p^e) = p^{e-1}(p - 1)$.

(c) If n is an integer greater than 1, then

$$\varphi(n) = n \prod_{\substack{p \mid n \\ p \text{ prime}}} \left(1 - \frac{1}{p}\right).$$

Chapter 3 / Modules

1. Preliminaries

In this chapter we consider an important type of operator group, in which the operator set is a ring.

Definition 1.1. Let A be a ring, $\langle X,+\rangle$ an abelian A-group. Then X is a *left A-module* if for all $a,b \in A$, $x \in X$,

a. $(a + b)x = ax + bx$.

b_l. $(ab)x = a(bx)$.

If X satisfies a and

b_r. $(ab)x = b(ax)$

for all $a,b \in A$, $x \in X$, then X is a *right A-module*. [Condition b_r appears more natural when the operators are indicated on the right. In that case, b_r reads $x(ab) = (xa)b$. If A is commutative, the distinction between b_l and b_r vanishes altogether and we write ax and xa interchangeably.]

If A is a ring with identity 1, then an A-module X such that $1x = x$ ($x1 = x$) for all $x \in X$ is a *unitary A-module.*

If A is a division ring, then a left (right) unitary A-module X is a left (right) *vector space* over A. ///

In the following, unless we specify otherwise, the term "A-module" will refer to a left A-module. If A has an identity, it will be understood that an A-module is unitary.

We have encountered several examples of modules in Chapters 1 and 2. For instance, every abelian group is a **Z**-module. The additive group of any ring A can be made into a left (right) A-module, X, by defining the action of A on X as left (right) multiplication; i.e., $ax = a \cdot x$ ($ax = x \cdot a$) for each $a,x \in A$. We shall denote the resulting A-modules, respectively, by A_l and A_r, and refer to them as the *left-regular* and *right-regular* A-modules.

It is clear that any A-subgroup of an A-module, X, forms an A-module under the operations of X. This justifies

Definition 1.2. Let X be an A-module. Then the A-subgroups of X are the submodules of X. If Y is a subset of X, then the A-subgroup $[Y]$ generated by Y is the *submodule*, $[Y]$, generated by Y. In particular, if $y \in X$, then the A-subgroup $[y]$ generated by y is the *cyclic submodule*, $[y]$, generated by y. If $X = [x]$ for some $x \in X$, then X is a cyclic A-module. ///

(Note that the submodule $[Y]$ generated by a subset Y of X is the intersection of all submodules of X of which Y is a subset. Thus, $[\varnothing] = 0$, the submodule consisting of 0 only.)

It is easy to check that, if X is an A-module, $Y \subset X$, $Y \neq \varnothing$, then

$$[Y] = \left\{ \sum_{i=1}^{k} a_i y_i + \sum_{j=1}^{h} n_j z_j \middle| h,k \in \mathbf{N}', y_i,z_j \in Y, a_i \in A, n_j \in \mathbf{Z} \right\}$$

and, for $y \in X$,

$$[y] = \{ay + ny | a \in A, n \in \mathbf{Z}\}.$$

If A has an identity and X is unitary, then $[Y]$ is simply the set $AY = \{\sum_{i=1}^{k} a_i y_i | a_i \in A, y_i \in Y, k \in \mathbf{N}'\}$ and $[y]$ is the set $Ay = \{ay | a \in A\}$.

NOTATION. If $\{X_i\}_{i \in J}$ is a family of submodules of an A-module X, we shall write $\sum_{i \in J} X_i$ for the submodule of X generated by $\bigcup_{i \in J} X_i$.

The definitions of Chapter 1 concerning M-groups, i.e., the definitions of M-homomorphism, M-factor groups, direct product, and coproduct of M-groups, carry over immediately to modules. The image of an A-module under an A-homomorphism is, itself, an A-module. The kernel of an A-homomorphism of an A-module X is a submodule of X. The A-factor group X/Y determined by a submodule Y of X is an A-module, referred to as the difference (or factor) module of X with respect to Y. The Rectangle, Homomorphism, and Isomorphism Theorems (Chapter 1, Theorems 4.8 through

4.11) for operator groups apply directly to modules. Direct products and coproducts of A-modules are, themselves, A-modules.

For a fixed ring A, we may define a category whose objects are left (right) A-modules, and whose morphisms are A-homomorphisms of left (right) A-modules. The definitions of direct product and coproduct can be translated into the language of categories in complete analogy to the case of M-groups which we discussed in Chapter 1, Section 14. (Within the category of A-modules, coproduct and direct sum coincide; in particular $\coprod = \coprod'$.)

For each ring A, the category of right A-modules and the category of left A-modules are subcategories of the category of A-groups. The category of $\mathbf{Z}$-modules coincides with that of abelian groups (Chapter 1, Section 14).

If a is an element of a group G, then the integers k such that $ka = 0$ form an ideal in $\mathbf{Z}$. The nonnegative generator of this ideal is the order of a (see Chapter 1, Theorem 2.2). A natural extension of the concept of order to modules is based on the observation that, for any nonempty subset Y of an A-module X, the set $T_Y = \{a \mid a \in A, ay = 0 \text{ for all } y \in Y\}$ forms a left ideal in A.

Definition 1.3. If X is an A-module, Y a nonempty subset of X, then the left ideal $T_Y = \{a \mid a \in A, ay = 0 \text{ for all } y \in Y\}$ is the *annihilator of* Y. If Y consists of a single element y, then the annihilator of y is the *order ideal*, T_y, *of* y; if T_y is principal, then any generator of T_y is an *order for* y. (We note that, if A is a commutative ring with identity, then the *order ideal of the cyclic submodule* Ay is equal to the order ideal of y. In this case, we shall sometimes refer to an order for y as *an order for* Ay.) If $x \in X$, then x is a *torsion element* if its order ideal is different from zero, and x is *torsion free* if its order ideal is equal to zero.

If A is a ring without zero divisors, X an A-module, then X is a *torsion module* if all its elements are torsion elements, and X is *torsion free* if all its elements are torsion free. ///

For any ring A, the cyclic A-modules bear an intimate relationship to the left and right regular A-modules A_l and A_r.

Theorem 1.1. *Let A be a ring, and let X be a cyclic left A-module, generated by $x \in X$. Then the mapping μ_x: $a \mapsto ax$ ($a \in A$) is an A-homomorphism of the left regular A-module A_l into X. If x is torsion free, then μ_x is a monomorphism. If A is a ring with identity and X is unitary, then μ_x is an epimorphism. Thus, if A is a ring with identity and X is a unitary A-module generated by a torsion-free element x, then X is equal to Ax and is isomorphic to A_l.* □

A completely analogous theorem holds for any cyclic right A-module X, the right regular A-module A_r, and the mapping $\nu_x: a \mapsto xa$ of A_r into X.

The concept of a free abelian group generalizes readily to modules.

Definition 1.4. Let X be an A-module, S a set, and $\alpha: S \to X$ a mapping of S into X. Then $\langle X,\alpha\rangle$ is a *free A-module on S* if it satisfies the following condition: For every A-module Y, and every mapping $\gamma: S \to Y$, there is a unique A-homomorphism $\mu: X \to Y$ such that $\mu\alpha = \gamma$.

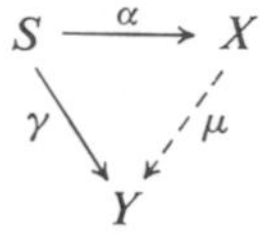

(If X is an A-module such that, for some set S and some mapping $\alpha: S \to X$, $\langle X,\alpha\rangle$ is a free A-module, we shall refer to X itself as a "free A-module" or "a free A-module on S.") ///

From Definition 1.4, we have, as usual, the following immediate corollaries:

Corollary 1. *If $\langle X,\alpha\rangle$ is a free A-module on a set S, then α is a one-to-one map and $[\alpha S] = X$.* □

Corollary 2.

a. *If $\langle X,\alpha\rangle$ and $\langle X',\alpha'\rangle$ are free A-modules on a set S, then there is a unique A-isomorphism $\mu: X \to X'$ such that $\mu\alpha = \alpha'$.*
b. *Every isomorphic image of a free A-module is free. More precisely: Let $\langle X,\alpha\rangle$ be a free A-module on S, $\alpha': S \to X'$ a mapping of S into X', and $\mu: X \to X'$ an A-isomorphism such that $\mu\alpha = \alpha'$. Then $\langle X',\alpha'\rangle$ is also a free A-module on S.* □

REMARK. As in the case of free groups, we can translate our definition of "free module" into the language of categories. Suppose A is a ring, S a set. We define a category C as follows: The objects of C are the ordered pairs (Y,γ), where Y is an A-module, $\gamma: S \to Y$ a map of S into Y; the morphisms $(Y,\gamma) \mapsto (Y',\gamma')$ are A-homomorphisms $\varphi: Y \to Y'$ such that $\varphi\gamma = \gamma'$. Then $\langle X,\alpha\rangle$ is a free A-module on S, in the sense of Definition 1.4, if and only if $\langle X,\alpha\rangle$ is a universal repelling object in C.

Theorem 1.2. (Existence). *For every set S and every ring A, there exists a free A-module on S.*

PROOF. If $S = \varnothing$, then the 0-module serves as a free A-module on S. Suppose $S \neq \varnothing$. We consider first the case where A has an identity 1. Let $\{X'_s\}_{s\in S}$ be a family of A-modules, each isomorphic to A_l. By Chapter 1, Theorem 9.2 and the corollary of Definition 9.4, the direct sum $X = \coprod_{s\in S} X'_s$ exists and is equal to an internal direct sum of submodules X_s, each isomorphic to A_l. Let 1_s be the element in X_s corresponding to 1 under the appropriate isomorphism. Define $\alpha\colon S \to X$ by $\alpha s = 1_s$ for each $s \in S$. Then $\langle X,\alpha\rangle$ is a free A-module on S. For, suppose Y is an A-module, $\gamma\colon S \to Y$ a mapping of S into Y. Every element of X has a unique representation as $\sum_{i=1}^m a_i 1_{s_i}$ ($m \in \mathbf{N}'$). Define $\mu\colon X \to Y$ by $\mu(\sum_{i=1}^m a_i 1_{s_i}) = \sum_{i=1}^m a_i \gamma s_i$. Then μ is a map. It is easy to check that μ is an A-homomorphism. Clearly $\mu\alpha = \gamma$. Since $[\alpha S] = X$, μ is the only such homomorphism. Thus $\langle X,\alpha\rangle$ is a free A-module on S.

Now suppose A has no identity. By Chapter 2, Theorem 2.1, there is a ring B with identity, containing A as a subring, which can be made into an A-module via left multiplications. As in the first part of the proof, we may infer that there exists an A-module $X = \bigoplus_{s\in S} X_s$, where each X_s is an A-module isomorphic to the A-module B. Again, we write 1_s for the element in X_s which corresponds to 1 in B, and define $\alpha\colon S \to X$ such that $\alpha s = 1_s$ for each $s \in S$. We note that every element of X can be expressed uniquely in the form $\sum_{i=1}^m a_i 1_{s_i} + \sum_{i=1}^m n_i 1_{s_i}$ ($m \in \mathbf{N}'$). Given an A-module Y and a map $\gamma\colon S \to Y$, we may define $\mu\colon X \to Y$ by

$$\mu\left(\sum_{i=1}^m a_i 1_{s_i} + \sum_{i=1}^m n_i 1_{s_i}\right) = \sum_{i=1}^m a_i \gamma s_i + \sum_{i=1}^m n_i \gamma s_i.$$

Again, one may easily verify that μ is the unique A-homomorphism of X into Y such that $\mu\alpha = \gamma$. But then $\langle X,\alpha\rangle$ is a free A-module on S. ∎

Corollary. *Every A-module is a homomorphic image of a free A-module.* □

If A is a ring with identity, then the free A-modules can be characterized as direct sums:

Theorem 1.3. *Let A be a ring with identity, X an A-module, S a set, and $\alpha\colon S \to X$ a mapping of S into X. Then $\langle X,\alpha\rangle$ is a free A-module on S if and only if $X = \bigoplus_{s\in S} A\alpha s$ and, for each $s \in S$, αs is torsion free.*

PROOF. The theorem holds trivially if $S = \varnothing$. For $S \neq \varnothing$, suppose $\langle X,\alpha\rangle$ is a free A-module on S. For each $s \in S$, let $X_s = [\alpha s] = A\alpha s$. Since $[\alpha S] = X$, $X = \sum_{s\in S} X_s$. Suppose there is an $\bar{s} \in S$ such that $X_{\bar{s}} \cap \sum_{s\neq\bar{s}} X_s \neq 0$. If

$y \neq 0$, $y \in X_{\bar{s}} \cap \sum_{s \neq \bar{s}} X_s$, then $y = a\alpha\bar{s} = \sum_{i=1}^{k} a_i \alpha s_i$ ($a_i, a \in A$, $a \neq 0$, $s_i \in S$, $k \in \mathbf{N}'$). Define $\gamma: S \to A$ by $\gamma\bar{s} = 1$, $\gamma s = 0$ for $s \neq \bar{s}$. If $\mu: X \to A_l$ is the A-homomorphism such that $\mu\alpha = \gamma$, then $\mu y = \sum_{i=1}^{k} a_i \mu\alpha s_i = \sum_{i=1}^{n} a_i \gamma s_i = 0$. On the other hand, $\mu y = a\mu\alpha\bar{s} = a\gamma\bar{s} = a \neq 0$. Contradiction! It follows that $X_{\bar{s}} \cap \sum_{s \neq \bar{s}} X_s = 0$. But then $X = \bigoplus_{s \in S} X_s$. For each $s \in S$, αs is torsion free. For suppose that for some $\bar{s} \in S$, $a\alpha\bar{s} = 0$ ($a \neq 0$ in A). Then, with γ and μ as defined before, we have $0 = \mu(a\alpha\bar{s}) = a(\mu\alpha\bar{s}) = a(\gamma\bar{s}) = a1 = a \neq 0$—a contradiction!

To prove the converse, note that, by Theorem 1.1, each $A\alpha s$ is isomorphic to the left regular A-module A_l, and proceed as in the proof of Theorem 1.2. ▮

By Theorem 1.1, we have

Corollary 1. *Let A be a ring with identity, X an A-module. Then X is a free A-module if and only if, for some set S, $X = \bigoplus_{s \in S} X_s$, where each X_s is a submodule isomorphic to A_l.* □

Corollary 2. *Let A be a ring with identity, containing no zero divisors, and let X be an A-module. Then X is a free A-module if and only if X is a direct sum of torsion-free cyclic submodules.*

PROOF. We need only note that $A_l = A1$ is torsion free if A has no zero divisors. ▮

It is easy to verify that, if $\langle X,\alpha \rangle$ is a free A-module on a set S and $\varepsilon: \alpha S \to X$ is the inclusion map of αS in X, then $\langle X,\varepsilon \rangle$ is a free A-module on αS. Thus, if X is a free A-module on some set, then X is a free A-module on one of its own generating sets. This suggests the following definition.

Definition 1.5. A subset $\mathscr{B}$ of an A-module X is a *basis* for X if $\langle X,\varepsilon \rangle$ is a free A-module on $\mathscr{B}$, where ε is the inclusion map of $\mathscr{B}$ in X.

More generally, a subset $\mathscr{B}$ of an A-module X is a *free set* for X if $\mathscr{B}$ is a basis for $[\mathscr{B}]$. ///

We note that the empty set is a basis for the A-module 0.

From Definition 1.4, Corollary 1, it follows that, if $\mathscr{B}$ is a basis for X, then $[\mathscr{B}] = X$. Thus, a basis of an A-module $X \neq 0$ is a free generating set for X. In the case of modules over rings with identity, free sets can be characterized in a particularly simple way:

Theorem 1.4. *Let A be a ring with identity, X a (unitary) A-module. Then a subset $\mathscr{B}$ of X is a free set if and only if it satisfies the following condition:*

(1) $\sum_{i=1}^{n} a_i x_i = 0$ *$(a_i \in A,\ x_i \in \mathscr{B},\ n \in \mathbf{N}')$ implies $a_i = 0$ for each $i = 1, \ldots, n$.*

PROOF. Let $Y = [\mathscr{B}]$ and let ε be the inclusion map of $\mathscr{B}$ in Y. Then $\mathscr{B}$ is free if and only if $\langle Y, \varepsilon \rangle$ is a free A-module on $\mathscr{B}$. By Theorem 1.3, this is the case if and only if $Y = \bigoplus_{x \in \mathscr{B}} A\varepsilon x = \bigoplus_{x \in \mathscr{B}} Ax$, where each x is torsion free—a condition which is easily seen to be equivalent to (1). ∎

If X is an A-module, then a generating set $\mathscr{B}$ of X is *minimal* if, for all $x \in \mathscr{B}$, $[\mathscr{B} - \{x\}] \neq X$; and a free set $\mathscr{B}$ of X is *maximal* if, for all $x \in X - \mathscr{B}$, the set $\mathscr{B} \cup \{x\}$ fails to be free.

Theorem 1.5. *If A is a ring with identity, then any basis $\mathscr{B}$ of a free A-module $X \neq 0$ is both a minimal generating set and a maximal free set of X.*

PROOF. Suppose $x \in \mathscr{B}$ and $[\mathscr{B} - \{x\}] = X$. Then there are elements $x_1, \ldots, x_n \in \mathscr{B} - \{x\}$, and elements $a_1, \ldots, a_n \in A$, such that $\sum_{i=1}^{n} a_i x_i = x$. But then $1x + \sum_{i=1}^{n} (-a_i)x_i = 0$, and so $\mathscr{B}$ is not a free set. Contradiction! Thus, $\mathscr{B}$ is a minimal generating set of X.

Now suppose $x \in X - \mathscr{B}$. Since $[\mathscr{B}] = X$, there are elements $x_1, \ldots, x_n \in \mathscr{B}$, $a_1, \ldots, a_n \in A$ such that $x = \sum_{i=1}^{n} a_i x_i$. Hence $1x + \sum (-a_i x_i) = 0$ and so $\mathscr{B} \cup \{x\}$ is not a free set. Thus, $\mathscr{B}$ is a maximal free set of X. ∎

In general, a maximal free set, or a minimal generating set, of an A-module X need not be a basis for X (Exercise 1.1). However, in the special case where A is a division ring, we have

Theorem 1.6. *Let $X \neq 0$ be a vector space over a division ring A, $\mathscr{B}$ a subset of X. Then the following statements are equivalent:*

a. *$\mathscr{B}$ is a basis for X.*
b. *$\mathscr{B}$ is a minimal generating set for X.*
c. *$\mathscr{B}$ is a maximal free set for X.*

PROOF. In view of Theorem 1.5, we need only prove b $\Rightarrow$ a and c $\Rightarrow$ a.

b $\Rightarrow$ a. Suppose $\mathscr{B}$ is a minimal generating set for X. Then $\mathscr{B}$ is free. For, suppose $\sum_{i=1}^{n} a_i x_i = 0$ $(x_i \in \mathscr{B}, a_i \in A; i = 1, \ldots, n)$. If $a_h \neq 0$ for some h $(h = 1, \ldots, n)$, then, since A is a division ring,

$$x_h = a_h^{-1} \sum_{i \neq h} -a_i x_i.$$

But then $\mathscr{B} - \{x_h\}$ is a generating set for X, contrary to the hypothesis that $\mathscr{B}$ is minimal. It follows that $a_i = 0$ for each $i = 1,\ldots,n$. Thus, $\mathscr{B}$ is a free set, and therefore a basis, for X.

c $\Rightarrow$ a. Suppose $\mathscr{B}$ is a maximal free set in X. Then $[\mathscr{B}] = X$. For, suppose $x \in X$. By the maximality of $\mathscr{B}$, the set $\mathscr{B} \cup \{x\}$ is not a free set. Hence there are elements $x_1,\ldots, x_n \in \mathscr{B}$, and elements $a_0, a_1,\ldots, a_n \in A$, not all zero, such that

$$a_0x + \sum_{i=1}^{n} a_ix_i = 0.$$

Since $\mathscr{B}$ is a free set, $a_0 \neq 0$. But then, since A is a division ring,

$$x = -a_0^{-1} \sum_{i=1}^{n} a_ix_i$$

and so $x \in [\mathscr{B}]$. Thus, $\mathscr{B}$ is a generating set, and therefore a basis, for X. ▌

If A is a ring with identity, X an A-module, it is immediate from Theorem 1.4 that the union of an ascending chain of free subsets is itself free. Hence, by Zorn's Lemma, every A-module which has a free subset contains a maximal free subset. Thus, Theorem 1.6 implies the important result:

Corollary. *Every vector space has a basis. In other words: If A is a division ring, then every A-module is free.* □

The converse also holds, although it is more complicated to prove: If A is any ring having the property that every A-module is free, then A is a division ring. (See Chapter 8, Exercise 5.1.)

REMARK. In Chapter 4, Theorem 1.1, we give another proof that every vector space has a basis, using the Spanning Lemma (Chapter 0, Theorem 6.5), which conveniently provides the additional result that any two bases of a vector space have the same cardinality. For vector spaces having an infinite basis, this latter result will also be a special case of Theorem 1.7; for vector spaces having a finite basis, it is an easy consequence of the Jordan–Hölder Theorem (Chapter 1, Theorem 5.1), applied to the normal series $[x_1] \subset [x_1,x_2] \subset \cdots \subset [x_1,\ldots,x_n]$, where $\{x_i\}_{i=1}^{n}$ is a basis (Exercise 1.2).

Definition 1.6. If A is a ring, X a free A-module such that all bases of X have the same cardinality, then X is *dimensional* and the cardinality of any basis of X is the *dimension* of X. A ring A which has the property that every free A-module is dimensional is a *dimensional ring.* ///

We have remarked that every vector space is dimensional; i.e., every division ring is a dimensional ring. It is natural to ask whether, perhaps, *all* free modules are dimensional. The answer is: All infinitely based free modules are dimensional (Theorem 1.7), but there exist free modules having finite bases of different cardinalities (Exercise 1.3). We shall prove (Theorem 1.8) that a ring A with identity is a dimensional ring if and only if some nonzero homomorphic image of A is a dimensional ring. This will enable us to find a wide class of dimensional rings including, in particular, all commutative rings with identity and, in fact, all rings with identity which can be mapped homomorphically onto nonzero commutative rings or division rings.

We prove first:

Theorem 1.7. *If A is a ring with identity, X a free A-module having an infinite basis, then X is dimensional.*

PROOF. Let $\mathscr{B}$, $\mathscr{B}'$ be bases for X, with $\mathscr{B}$ an infinite set. The map $\rho: 2^X \to 2^X$ defined by $\rho(Y) = [Y]$ for each subset Y of X obviously satisfies conditions a through d for a spanning function (Chapter 0, Definition 6.5). By Theorem 1.5, any basis for X is a minimal generating set of X. But then, by the corollary of the Spanning Lemma (Chapter 0, Theorem 6.5), it follows that card $\mathscr{B}$ = card $\mathscr{B}'$. (*Note:* Chapter 0, case 1 of Theorem 6.5b, is all that is needed to prove the corollary.) ▮

To prove Theorem 1.8 and its Corollaries, we need two lemmas:

Lemma 1. *If $A \neq 0$ is a ring with identity 1, then A has a maximal ideal.*

PROOF. Let S be the set of all ideals K of A, $K \neq A$. Then $S \neq \varnothing$. If $\{K_i\}_{i \in J}$ is an ascending chain of ideals of A, $K_i \neq A$ $(i = 1,2,\ldots)$, then $\bigcup_{i \in J} K_i$ is itself an ideal of A. If $\bigcup_{i \in J} K_i = A$, then $1 \in K_h$ for some $h \in J$, hence $K_h = A$, contrary to hypothesis. Thus, $\bigcup_{i \in J} K_i \in S$, and S satisfies the hypotheses of Zorn's Lemma. But then A has a maximal ideal. ▮

The same argument may be used to establish the existence of maximal one-sided ideals in rings with identity.

Lemma 2. *Let A be a ring with identity, and let X be a free A-module with basis $\{x_i\}_{i \in J}$. If $K \neq A$ is an ideal in A, then X/KX is a free A/K-module with basis $\{\nu x_i\}_{i \in J}$, where ν is the natural A-epimorphism of X onto X/KX.*

PROOF. We have $X = \bigoplus_{i \in J} Ax_i$ and $KX = \bigoplus_{i \in J} Kx_i$, with each x_i torsion free; hence by Chapter 1, Theorem 9.8 (Corollary), the A-module X/KX is isomorphic to the A-module $\bigoplus_{i \in J} Ax_i/Kx_i = \bigoplus_{i \in J} A(\nu x_i)$, where ν is the natural A-epimorphism of X with respect to KX. Let μ be the natural epimorphism of the ring A onto the ring A/K. Then X/KX can be made into an A/K-module by defining $\mu a \nu x$ to be equal to $a\nu x$ for each $a \in A$, $x \in X$. We note that the correspondence $(\mu a, \nu x) \to a\nu x$ is an external composition on X/K. For, suppose $a,b \in A$, $x,y \in X$ such that $\mu a = \mu b$, $\nu x = \nu y$. Then $a - b \in K$, hence $(a - b)x \in KX$ and so $\nu[(a - b)x] = (a - b)\nu x = a\nu x - b\nu x = 0$, whence $a\nu x = b\nu x = b\nu y$. It is trivial to check that, with respect to this external composition, X/KX is an A/K-module, generated by $\{\nu x_i\}_{i \in J}$. To complete the proof, we need only show that $\{\nu x_i\}_{i \in J}$ is a free set over A/K. Thus, suppose $\sum_{j=1}^{n} \mu a_j \nu x_{i_j} = 0$ in X/KX. Now, $\sum_{j=1}^{n} \mu a_j \nu x_{i_j} = \sum_{j=1}^{n} a_j \nu x_{i_j} = \sum_{j=1}^{n} \nu a_j x_{i_j} = \nu \sum_{j=1}^{n} a_j x_{i_j} = 0$, whence $\sum_{j=1}^{n} a_j x_{i_j} \in KX$. Thus, $\sum_{j=1}^{n} a_j x_{i_j} = \sum_{l=1}^{m} b_l x_{h_l}$ for some set $\{h_1, \ldots, h_m\} \subset J$, and some set $\{b_1, \ldots, b_m\} \subset K$. Since the A-module X is equal to $\bigoplus_{i \in J} Ax_i$ and each x_i is torsion free, it follows that each a_j $(j = 1, \ldots, n)$ is equal to one of the b_l $(l = 1, \ldots, m)$, and therefore belongs to K. But then $\mu a_j = 0$ for each $j = 1, \ldots, n$, and $\{\nu x_i\}_{i \in J}$ is, indeed, a free set over A/K. ∎

Theorem 1.8. *Let A be a ring with identity, α a nonzero homomorphism of A such that every αA-module is dimensional. Then every A-module is dimensional.*

PROOF. Let $H = \operatorname{Ker} \alpha$, and let X be a free A-module. By Lemma 2, X/HX is a free A/H-module and every basis for the A-module X is equipotent with a basis for the A/H-module X/HX. Since A/H is isomorphic to αA, the A/H-module X/HX is dimensional, hence so is the A-module X. ∎

Corollary 1. *If a ring A with identity has a homomorphic image which is a division ring, then A is a dimensional ring.*

PROOF. By Theorem 1.7, and the Jordan–Hölder Theorem (see Exercise 1.2), division rings are dimensional. ∎

Corollary 2. *Every commutative ring A with identity is a dimensional ring.*

PROOF. By Lemma 1, A has a maximal ideal K. By Chapter 2, Theorem 1.7, A/K is a field. Hence, by Corollary 1, A is dimensional. ∎

Corollary 3. *If a ring A with identity has a nonzero homomorphic image which is commutative, then A is a dimensional ring.* □

2. Exact Sequences; Projective and Injective Modules

If X, Y, Z are A-modules, and $\alpha: X \to Y$, $\beta: Y \to Z$ are A-homomorphisms such that $\operatorname{Ker} \beta = \operatorname{Im} \alpha$, then (α,β) is an "exact sequence" of A-homomorphisms. More generally:

Definition 2.1. Let A be a ring, and let J be the set of all ordinals less than a given ordinal γ. If $\{X_i\}_{i \in J}$ is a sequence of A-modules and $\{\alpha_i\}_{i \in J}$ is a sequence of A-homomorphisms, $\alpha_i: X_i \to X_{i+1}$, such that $\operatorname{Ker} \alpha_{i+1} = \operatorname{Im} \alpha_i$ for each i, $i + 1 \in J$, then $\{\alpha_i\}_{i \in J}$ is an *exact sequence of A-homomorphisms.* (If $\{\alpha_i\}_{i \in J}$ is an exact sequence, we shall say that the diagram

$$\cdots \longrightarrow X_i \xrightarrow{\alpha_i} X_{i+1} \xrightarrow{\alpha_{i+1}} \cdots$$

is "exact." We may omit the designation of the homomorphisms when the choice is unique, obvious from the context, or immaterial.) ///

Exact sequences may be used to describe properties of a single homomorphism:

Theorem 2.1 *If X, Y are A-modules and α: $X \to Y$ is an A-homomorphism, then*

a. *α is injective if and only if*

$$0 \longrightarrow Y \xrightarrow{\alpha} X$$

is exact.

b. *α is surjective if and only if*

$$Y \xrightarrow{\alpha} X \longrightarrow 0$$

is exact.

c. *α is bijective if and only if*

$$0 \longrightarrow Y \xrightarrow{\alpha} X \longrightarrow 0$$

is exact.

(*Note:* The homomorphisms which are left unnamed here are the only possible ones, from 0 into Y, and from X into 0.)

PROOF.

a. Let ε be the (unique) map of 0 into Y. Then α is injective if and only if $\text{Ker}\ \alpha = 0 = \text{Im}\ \varepsilon$.

b. Let ω be the (unique) map of X into 0. Then α is surjective if and only if $\text{Im}\ \alpha = X = \text{Ker}\ \omega$.

c. Follows from a and b. ▮

Corollary 1. *Let X be an A-module, Y a submodule of X. Then*

$$0 \longrightarrow Y \xrightarrow{\ \varepsilon\ } X \xrightarrow{\ \nu\ } X/Y \longrightarrow 0$$

is exact, where ε is the canonical injection of Y into X and ν is the natural epimorphism of X onto X/Y.

PROOF. ε is injective, ν is surjective, and $\text{Ker}\ \nu = Y = \text{Im}\ \varepsilon$. ▮

Corollary 2. *If X, Y are A-modules and $\alpha: X \to Y$ is an A-homomorphism, then*

$$0 \longrightarrow \text{Ker}\ \alpha \xrightarrow{\ \varepsilon\ } X \xrightarrow{\ \alpha\ } Y \xrightarrow{\ \nu\ } Y/\alpha(X) \longrightarrow 0$$

is exact, where ε is the inclusion map of Ker α *into X and ν is the natural epimorphism of Y onto $Y/\alpha(X)$.* □

Definition 2.2. An exact sequence (α,β) such that

$$0 \longrightarrow Y \xrightarrow{\ \alpha\ } X \xrightarrow{\ \beta\ } Z \longrightarrow 0$$

is a *short exact sequence.* ///

Note that, if $0 \to Y \xrightarrow{\alpha} X \xrightarrow{\beta} Z \to 0$ is exact, then Z is isomorphic to $X/\alpha(Y)$ and $\alpha(Y)$ is isomorphic to Y.

If Y is a submodule of an A-module X, then Y may, or may not, be a direct summand of X (Exercise 1.9).

Theorem 2.2.

a. *If X, Z are A-modules and β is an A-homomorphism such that*

$$X \xrightarrow{\ \beta\ } Z \longrightarrow 0$$

is exact, then Ker β *is a direct summand of X if and only if there is an A-homomorphism $\beta': Z \to X$ such that $\beta\beta' = \iota_Z$. In this case, $X =$* $\text{Ker}\ \beta \oplus \text{Im}\ \beta'$.

b. *If Y, Z are A-modules and α is an A-homomorphism such that*

$$0 \longrightarrow Y \xrightarrow{\alpha} X$$

is exact, then $\operatorname{Im} \alpha$ *is a direct summand of X if and only if there is an A-homomorphism $\alpha': X \to Y$ such that $\alpha'\alpha = \iota_Y$. In this case,* $X = \operatorname{Im} \alpha \oplus \operatorname{Ker} \alpha'$.

PROOF.

a. Suppose $\operatorname{Ker} \beta$ is a direct summand of X, and X' is a submodule of X such that $\operatorname{Ker} \beta \oplus X' = X$. Then $\beta|_{X'}$ is an isomorphism of X' onto Z. The mapping $\beta': Z \to X$ defined by $\beta' z = [\beta|_{X'}]^{-1} z$ for each $z \in Z$ is an A-homomorphism such that $\beta\beta' = \iota_Z$.

Conversely, suppose $\beta': Z \to X$ is an A-homomorphism such that $\beta\beta' = \iota_Z$. Let $X' = \operatorname{Im} \beta'$. If $t \in X' \cap \operatorname{Ker} \beta$, then $t = \beta' z$ for some $z \in Z$, and $0 = \beta t = \beta\beta' z = z$, whence $t = 0$. Thus, $\operatorname{Ker} \beta \cap X' = 0$. If $x \in X$, let $x' = \beta'\beta x$, and let $x'' = x - x'$. Then $\beta x'' = \beta x - \beta\beta'\beta x = \beta x - \beta x = 0$, hence $x'' \in \operatorname{Ker} \beta$ and $x \in \operatorname{Ker} \beta + X'$. But then $X = \operatorname{Ker} \beta \oplus X' = \operatorname{Ker} \beta \oplus \operatorname{Im} \beta'$.

b. Suppose $\operatorname{Im} \alpha$ is a direct summand of X and X' is a submodule of X such that $X = \operatorname{Im} \alpha \oplus X'$. Let $\alpha': X \to Y$ be the mapping defined by

$$\alpha'(x') = 0 \qquad \text{for } x' \in X',$$

$$\alpha'(x) = y \qquad \text{for } x = \alpha(y) \in \operatorname{Im} \alpha.$$

Then α' is an A-homomorphism such that $\alpha'\alpha = \iota_Y$.

Conversely, suppose $\alpha': X \to Y$ is an A-homomorphism such that $\alpha'\alpha = \iota_Y$. Let $X' = \operatorname{Ker} \alpha'$. If $t \in \operatorname{Im} \alpha \cap X'$, then $t = \alpha y$ for some $y \in Y$, and $0 = \alpha' t = \alpha'\alpha y = y$, whence $t = 0$. Thus, $\operatorname{Im} \alpha \cap X' = 0$. If $x \in X$, let $x' = \alpha\alpha' x$ and let $x'' = x - x'$. Then $\alpha' x'' = \alpha' x - \alpha'\alpha\alpha' x = \alpha' x - \alpha' x = 0$, hence $x'' \in \operatorname{Ker} \alpha' = X'$, and $x = x' + x'' \in \operatorname{Im} \alpha \oplus X'$. But then $X = \operatorname{Im} \alpha \oplus X' = \operatorname{Im} \alpha \oplus \operatorname{Ker} \alpha'$. ∎

REMARK. Any surjective map has right inverses and any injective map has left inverses. Theorem 2.2 provides necessary and sufficient conditions for a surjective (injective) A-homomorphism to have an A-homomorphism among its right (left) inverse maps.

Definition 2.3. If β is an A-homomorphism such that $X \xrightarrow{\beta} Z \to 0$ is exact and $\beta': Z \to X$ is an A-homomorphism such that $\beta\beta' = \iota_Z$, then β' is a *splitting homomorphism* for $X \xrightarrow{\beta} Z \to 0$ and $X \xrightarrow{\beta} Z \to 0$ is *split exact.*

If α is an A-homomorphism such that $0 \to Y \xrightarrow{\alpha} X$ is exact and $\alpha': X \to Y$ is an A-homomorphism such that $\alpha'\alpha = \iota_Y$, then α' is a *splitting homomorphism* for $0 \to Y \xrightarrow{\alpha} X$ and $0 \to Y \xrightarrow{\alpha} X$ is *split exact.*

A short exact sequence $0 \to Y \xrightarrow{\alpha} X \xrightarrow{\beta} Z \to 0$ is *split exact* if either $0 \to Y \xrightarrow{\alpha} X$ or $X \xrightarrow{\beta} Z \to 0$ is split exact.

(If an exact sequence is split exact, we shall usually say simply that it *splits.*) ///

Theorem 2.3. *Let X, Y, Z be A-modules, α, β A-homomorphisms such that*

$$0 \longrightarrow Y \xrightarrow{\ \alpha\ } X \xrightarrow{\ \beta\ } Z \longrightarrow 0$$

is exact. Then the following statements are equivalent:

a. $0 \to Y \xrightarrow{\alpha} X$ *splits.*

b. $X \xrightarrow{\beta} Z \to 0$ *splits.*

c. $0 \to Y \xrightarrow{\alpha} X \xrightarrow{\beta} Z \to 0$ *splits.*

PROOF.

a $\Rightarrow$ b. Let $\alpha': X \to Y$ be a splitting homomorphism such that $\alpha'\alpha = \iota_Y$. As in the proof of Theorem 2.2b, we have $X = \operatorname{Ker} \alpha' \oplus \operatorname{Im} \alpha = \operatorname{Ker} \alpha' \oplus \operatorname{Ker} \beta$. But then, by Theorem 2.2b, $X \xrightarrow{\beta} Z \to 0$ is split exact.

b $\Rightarrow$ a. If $\beta': Z \to X$ is a splitting homomorphism such that $\beta\beta' = \iota_Z$, then (Theorem 2.2a) $X = \operatorname{Ker} \beta \oplus \operatorname{Im} \beta' = \operatorname{Im} \alpha \oplus \operatorname{Im} \beta'$, whence $0 \to Y \xrightarrow{\alpha} X$ is split exact (Theorem 2.2b).

From Definition 2.3, it now follows that c is equivalent to each of a and b. ∎

Corollary. If $0 \to Y \xrightarrow{\alpha} X \xrightarrow{\beta} Z \to 0$ *is split exact, then X is isomorphic to a direct sum of Y and Z.*

PROOF. Let α' be a splitting homomorphism for $0 \to Y \xrightarrow{a} X$. Then $X = \operatorname{Im} \alpha \oplus \operatorname{Ker} \alpha'$. Since $\operatorname{Im} \alpha = \operatorname{Ker} \beta$, $\operatorname{Ker} \alpha' \cong X/\operatorname{Ker} \beta \cong Z$. Since α is injective, $\operatorname{Im} \alpha \cong Y$. But then X is isomorphic to the external direct sum of Y and Z. ∎

Note that, if $X = Y \oplus Z$, $\varepsilon: Y \to X$ is the canonical injection of Y into X, and $\pi: X \to Z$ is the projection of X onto Z, then $0 \to Y \xrightarrow{\varepsilon} X \xrightarrow{\pi} Z \to 0$ is split exact.

In Section 1 we saw that every A-module is a homomorphic image of a free A-module. We now characterize a class of modules which are direct summands of free A-modules.

Definition 2.4. An A-module P is *projective* if it has the following property: Given two A-modules X, Y, an A-homomorphism $\gamma: P \to Y$ and an A-epimorphism $\beta: X \to Y$, there is an A-homomorphism $\mu: P \to X$ such that $\beta\mu = \gamma$.

In other words, P is projective if every diagram of the form

$$\begin{array}{ccccc} & & P & & \\ & & \downarrow{\scriptstyle\gamma} & & \\ X & \xrightarrow[\beta]{} & Y & \longrightarrow & 0 \text{ (exact)} \end{array}$$

can be embedded in a commutative diagram

$$\begin{array}{ccccc} & & P & & \\ & {\scriptstyle\mu}\swarrow & \downarrow{\scriptstyle\gamma} & & \\ X & \xrightarrow[\beta]{} & Y & \longrightarrow & 0 \text{ (exact).} \end{array} \qquad ///$$

Theorem 2.4. *The following conditions on an A-module P are equivalent:*

a. *P is projective.*

b. *Every exact sequence $X \xrightarrow{\beta} P \to 0$ splits.*

c. *P is a direct summand of a free A-module.*

PROOF.

a $\Rightarrow$ b. Let X be an A-module and let β be an A-homomorphism such that

$$X \xrightarrow{\ \beta\ } P \longrightarrow 0$$

is exact. Since P is projective, there is an A-homomorphism $\beta': P \to X$ satisfying the commutative diagram

$$\begin{array}{ccccc} & & P & & \\ & {\scriptstyle\beta'}\swarrow & \downarrow{\scriptstyle\iota_P} & & \\ X & \xrightarrow[\beta]{} & P & \longrightarrow & 0 \text{ (exact).} \end{array}$$

Since $\beta\beta' = \iota_P$, $X \xrightarrow{\beta} P \to 0$ splits.

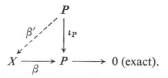

b $\Rightarrow$ c. By Theorem 1.2, there is a free A-module $\bar{F}$ on the set P. By the Corollary of Theorem 1.2, there is an A-epimorphism $\mu: \bar{F} \to P$. By b, the exact sequence $\bar{F} \xrightarrow{\mu} P \to 0$ splits; i.e., there is an A-homomorphism $\mu': P \to \bar{F}$ such that $\mu\mu' = \iota_P$. But then μ' is an A-monomorphism, $\bar{F} = \operatorname{Im} \mu' \oplus \operatorname{Ker} \mu$, and $P \cong \operatorname{Im} \mu'$. By the technique employed in the proof of the Wraparound Lemma (Chapter 0, Theorem 2.4), we can obtain a free A-module F containing P as an (internal) direct summand.

c $\Rightarrow$ a. Let X, Y be A-modules, and let β, γ be A-homomorphisms satisfying the diagram

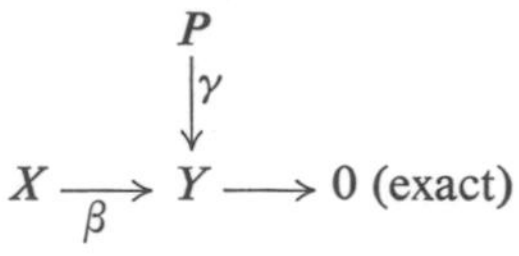

Since c holds, there is a free A-module, F, and a submodule, Q, of F such that $F = P \oplus Q$. The mapping γ can be extended to an A-homomorphism γ' of F into Y such that $\gamma'|_Q = 0$ and $\gamma'|_P = \gamma$. Let S be a basis for F, and let $s \in S$. Since β is surjective, the set $X_s = \{x \in X | \beta x = \gamma' s\}$ is nonempty. By the Axiom of Choice, there is a mapping α: $S \to X$ such that $\alpha s \in X_s$, i.e., $\beta(\alpha s) = \gamma' s$, for each $s \in S$. By Definition 1.4, there is a (unique) A-homomorphism μ': $F \to X$ such that $\mu'\varepsilon = \alpha$ (ε the canonical injection of S into F).

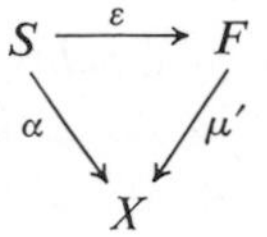

For each $s \in S$, $\gamma' s = \beta\alpha s = \beta\mu'\varepsilon s = \beta\mu' s$, whence $\gamma' = \beta\mu'$. Let $\mu = \mu'|_P$. Since $\gamma = \gamma'|_P$, we have $\gamma = \beta\mu$, as required.

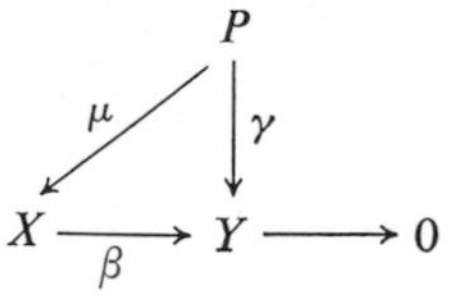

∎

Corollary 1. *Every free A-module is projective.*

PROOF. Every free A-module is a direct summand of itself. ∎

By Corollary 1 and the Corollary of Theorem 1.2, we have

Corollary 2. *Every A-module is a homomorphic image of a projective A-module.* □

Reversing the arrows in Definition 2.4 gives a "dual" concept:

Definition 2.5. An A-module Q is *injective* if it has the following property:

(*) Given two A-modules X, Y, an A-homomorphism $\gamma\colon Y \to Q$ and an A-monomorphism $\alpha\colon Y \to X$, there is an A-homomorphism $\mu\colon X \to Q$ such that $\mu\alpha = \gamma$.

In other words: An A-module Q is injective if every diagram of the form

$$\begin{array}{ccccl} 0 & \longrightarrow & Y & \xrightarrow{\alpha} & X \text{ (exact)} \\ & & {\scriptstyle\gamma}\downarrow & & \\ & & Q & & \end{array}$$

can be embedded in a commutative diagram

$$\begin{array}{ccccl} 0 & \longrightarrow & Y & \xrightarrow{\alpha} & X \text{ (exact)} \\ & & \downarrow & \swarrow{\scriptstyle\mu} & \\ & & Q & & \end{array} \qquad . \qquad ///$$

REMARK. Condition (*) in Definition 2.5 is equivalent to:

(†) Given two A-modules X, Y such that $Y \subset X$, and an A-homomorphism $\gamma\colon Y \to Q$, there is an A-homomorphism $\mu\colon X \to Q$ such that $\mu\varepsilon = \gamma$, where $\varepsilon\colon Y \to X$ is the inclusion map (i.e., such that μ is an extension of γ).

[(*) obviously implies (†). Conversely, if Q satisfies (†), $\alpha\colon Y \to X$ is an A-monomorphism and $\gamma\colon Y \to Q$ an A-homomorphism, we can produce the desired map by using αY in place of Y in (†).]

For convenient reference, we state

Definition 2.5a. An A-module Q is injective if it satisfies (†). ///

To prove an injective analogue of Theorem 2.4, we require certain preliminaries.

We consider first the case of injective $\mathbf{Z}$-module, i.e., injective abelian groups.

Definition 2.6. An abelian group G is *divisible* if $mG = G$ for each nonzero integer m. ///

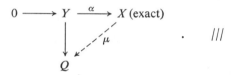

It is clear that G is divisible if and only if, for each nonzero integer m and each $x \in G$, there is some $y \in G$ such that $x = my$.

For example, the additive group of rationals is divisible, while the additive group of integers is not.

The concepts "injective" and "divisible" are equivalent for abelian groups:

Theorem 2.5. *A* **Z**-*module G is injective if and only if it is divisible.*

PROOF. Suppose G is injective. Let $n \neq 0$ be an integer and let $x \in G$. Then $\gamma: \mathbf{Z}n \to G$ defined by $\gamma(kn) = kx$ $(k \in \mathbf{Z})$ is a homomorphism of $\mathbf{Z}n$ into G. Since G is injective, there is a homomorphism $\mu: \mathbf{Z} \to G$ such that $\mu\varepsilon = \gamma$, where $\varepsilon: \mathbf{Z}n \to \mathbf{Z}$ is the inclusion map. Then

$$x = \gamma(n) = \mu(n) = \mu(n \cdot 1) = n\mu(1).$$

Thus, G is divisible.

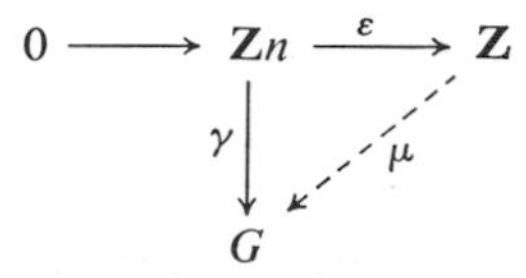

Conversely, suppose that G is divisible. We use Definition 2.5a of "injective module." Thus, suppose X, Y are **Z**-modules, $Y \subset X$, and $\gamma: Y \to G$ is a homomorphism:

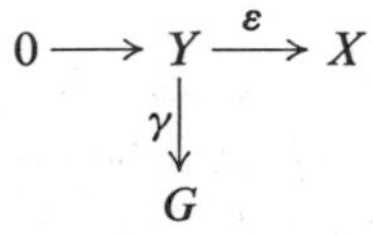

Our problem is to find a **Z**-homomorphism μ of X into G which extends γ. We use Zorn's Lemma. Let Σ be the set of all ordered pairs (T,τ), where T is a **Z**-module such that $Y \subset T \subset X$ and $\tau: T \to G$ is a homomorphism which extends γ. Let $\prec$ be the binary relation defined on Σ by $(T_1,\tau_1) \prec (T_2,\tau_2)$ if $T_1 \subset T_2$ and τ_2 is an extension of τ_1. Clearly, Σ is inductively ordered. By Zorn's Lemma, there is a maximal pair $(T^*,\tau^*) \in \Sigma$. We prove that $T^* = X$. Indeed, suppose $T^* \neq X$. Let $x_0 \in X - T^*$. If the sum $T' = T^* + \mathbf{Z}x_0$ is direct, then the homomorphism $\tau': T' \to G$ such that $\tau'|_{T^*} = \tau^*$, $\tau'|_{\mathbf{Z}x_0} = 0$ is a proper extension of τ^*, hence certainly an extension of γ. But then the pair (T',τ') properly "contains" (T^*,τ^*), in contradiction to the maximality of (T^*,τ^*). Thus, the sum $T' = T^* + \mathbf{Z}x_0$ is not direct, and $T^* \cap \mathbf{Z}x_0 \neq 0$.

We shall show that we can, nevertheless, produce an extension of τ^* to a homomorphism of T'. Let k be the least positive integer such that $kx_0 \in T^*$. Since G is divisible, there is some $y \in G$ such that $\tau^* kx_0 = ky$. For $t^* \in T^*, n \in \mathbf{Z}$, let $\tau''(t^* + nx_0) = \tau^* t^* + ny$. Then $\tau'' : t^* + nx_0 \mapsto \tau^* t^* + ny$ is a map. For, if $t_1^* + n_1 x_0 = t_2^* + n_2 x_0$, then $t_1^* - t_2^* = (n_2 - n_1)x_0$. From the definition of k (via the division algorithm) it follows that $n_2 - n_1 = ks$ for some $s \in \mathbf{Z}$. Hence $\tau^*(t_1^* - t_2^*) = \tau^* ksx_0 = sky$, and $\tau^* t_1^* + n_1 y = \tau^* t_2^* + sky + n_1 y = \tau^* t_2^* + n_2 y$. Clearly, τ'' is a homomorphism of T' into G, properly extending τ^*. But then $(T',\tau'') \in \Sigma$, in contradiction to the maximality of (T^*,τ^*). It follows that $T^* = X$, and that $\mu = \tau^*$ is the desired extension of γ. Thus, G is injective. ∎

We have seen that every A-module is a homomorphic image of a projective A-module. Finally, we now prove: Every A-module can be embedded in an injective A-module. We start with the case of a $\mathbf{Z}$-module.

Lemma 1. *Every $\mathbf{Z}$-module can be embedded in an injective $\mathbf{Z}$-module.*

PROOF. Let G be a $\mathbf{Z}$-module, $\{x_i\}_{i \in J}$ a generating set for G. Form the free $\mathbf{Z}$-module, F, and the free $\mathbf{Q}$-module, $\bar{F}$, on $\{x_i\}_{i \in J}$. By Chapter 1, Theorem 11.4, $F \simeq \coprod_{i \in J} \mathbf{Z}x_i$ and $\bar{F} \cong \coprod_{i \in J} \mathbf{Q}x_i$. Clearly, $\bar{F}$ is also a $\mathbf{Z}$-module, and F is $\mathbf{Z}$-isomorphic to a submodule of the $\mathbf{Z}$-module $\bar{F}$. Let η be a monomorphism of F into $\bar{F}$ and let δ be an epimorphism of F onto G. Let $\bar{G} = \bar{F}/\eta \operatorname{Ker} \delta$ and let $\bar{\delta}$ be the natural epimorphism of $\bar{F}$ onto $\bar{G}$. Then there is a monomorphism μ such that the diagram

$$\begin{array}{ccc} F & \xrightarrow{\eta} & \bar{F} \\ \delta \downarrow & & \downarrow \bar{\delta} \\ G & \xrightarrow{\mu} & \bar{G} \end{array}$$

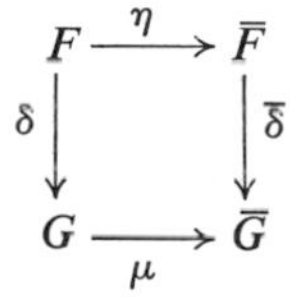

commutes.

Since each of the $\mathbf{Q}x_i$ is divisible, $\bar{F} = \coprod_{i \in J} \mathbf{Q}x_i$ is divisible. But then $\bar{\delta}\bar{F} = \bar{G}$ is divisible, hence injective. Thus, μ is an embedding of G in the injective $\mathbf{Z}$-module $\bar{G}$. ∎

Lemma 2. *If G is an injective $\mathbf{Z}$-module and A is a ring with identity, then* $\operatorname{Hom}_{\mathbf{Z}}(A,G)$ (see p. 99) *is an injective left A-module.*

PROOF. For each $a \in A$, $\alpha \in \operatorname{Hom}_{\mathbf{Z}}(A,G)$, let $a\alpha$ be the homomorphism defined by

$$a\alpha(b) = \alpha(ba)$$

for each $b \in A$. Then $\mathrm{Hom}_{\mathbf{Z}}(A,G)$ is a left A-module with respect to the scalar multiplication $(a,\alpha) \mapsto a\alpha$, since

$$[(ca)\alpha](b) = \alpha(b(ca)) = (a\alpha)(bc) = [c(a\alpha)](b)$$

for each a, b, $c \in A$, $\alpha \in \mathrm{Hom}_{\mathbf{Z}}(A,G)$. We prove that this left A-module $\mathrm{Hom}_{\mathbf{Z}}(A,G)$ is injective. Suppose that X, Y are A-modules ($Y \subset X$) and that $\gamma\colon Y \to \mathrm{Hom}_{\mathbf{Z}}(A,G)$ is an A-homomorphism.

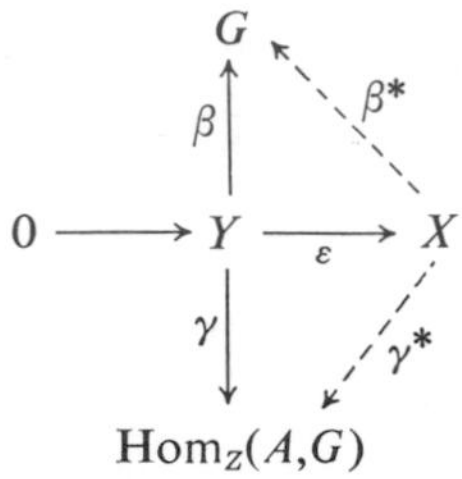

For each $y \in Y$, $\gamma(y) \in \mathrm{Hom}_{\mathbf{Z}}(A,G)$, and $[\gamma(y)](1) \in G$. The correspondence $y \mapsto [\gamma(y)](1)$ defines a $\mathbf{Z}$-homomorphism, β, of Y into G. Since G is an injective $\mathbf{Z}$-module, there is a $\mathbf{Z}$-homomorphism $\beta^*\colon X \to G$ such that $\beta^*\varepsilon = \beta$. For each $x \in X$, let $\gamma^*(x)$ be the $\mathbf{Z}$-homomorphism of A into G defined by $[\gamma^*(x)](a) = \beta^*(ax)$ $(a \in A)$. Then $\gamma^*\colon x \mapsto \gamma^*(x)$ is, clearly, a $\mathbf{Z}$-homomorphism of X into $\mathrm{Hom}_{\mathbf{Z}}(A,G)$. It is also an A-homomorphism: If $x \in X$, $c \in A$; then $\gamma^*(cx)(a) = \beta^*(a(cx)) = \beta^*((ac)(x)) = \gamma^*(x)(ac) = c(\gamma^*(x)(a))$. [The last equality results from our definition of the scalar multiplication on $\mathrm{Hom}_{\mathbf{Z}}(A,G)$.] Since, for each $y \in Y$, and each $a \in A$, $[\gamma^* \varepsilon y](a) = \beta^*(a\varepsilon y) = \beta^*\varepsilon(ay) = \beta(ay) = [\gamma(ay)](1) = [a\gamma(y)](1) = \gamma(y)(a)$, we have $\gamma^*\varepsilon = \gamma$, as desired. ▮

We are now ready to prove:

Theorem 2.6. *Let A be a ring with identity. Then every A-module can be embedded in an injective A-module.*

PROOF. Let X be an A-module. The A-homomorphisms of A_l into X form an abelian group, $\mathrm{Hom}_A(A,X)$, which can be made into a (left) A-module with scalar multiplication defined by

$$(a\alpha)(b) = \alpha(ba) \qquad (a,b \in A,\ \alpha \in \mathrm{Hom}_A(A,X)).$$

The A-module X is A-isomorphic to the A-module $\mathrm{Hom}_A(A,X)$ under the mapping $\varphi\colon x \mapsto \alpha_x$, where α_x is the A-homomorphism of A into X which sends 1 to x.

By Lemma 1, X (considered as a $\mathbf{Z}$-module) can be embedded in an injective $\mathbf{Z}$-module G. For convenience, we may assume $X \subset G$. We now have

$$X \xrightarrow{\varphi} \mathrm{Hom}_A(A,X) \xrightarrow{\varepsilon_1} \mathrm{Hom}_{\mathbf{Z}}(A,X) \xrightarrow{\varepsilon_2} \mathrm{Hom}_{\mathbf{Z}}(A,G),$$

where φ is the mapping defined in the first paragraph, ε_1 is the appropriate inclusion map and ε_2 associates with each $\sigma \in \mathrm{Hom}_{\mathbf{Z}}(A, X)$ the homomorphism in $\mathrm{Hom}_{\mathbf{Z}}(A, G)$ which has the same graph as σ. The mapping $\varepsilon_2\varepsilon_1\varphi$ is an A-monomorphism of X into the A-module $\mathrm{Hom}_{\mathbf{Z}}(A,G)$. By Lemma 2, $\mathrm{Hom}_{\mathbf{Z}}(A,G)$ is an injective A-module. ∎

Corresponding to Theorem 2.4 on projective modules, we now have

Theorem 2.7. *Let A be a ring with identity. Then the following conditions on an A-module Q are equivalent:*

a. *Q is injective.*
b. *Every exact sequence $0 \to Q \xrightarrow{\alpha} X$ splits.*
c. *Q is a direct summand of every A-module X of which it is a submodule.*

PROOF.

a ⇒ b. Suppose Q is injective. Let $0 \to Q \xrightarrow{\alpha} X$ be exact. Then there is an A-homomorphism $\mu: X \to Q$ such that the diagram

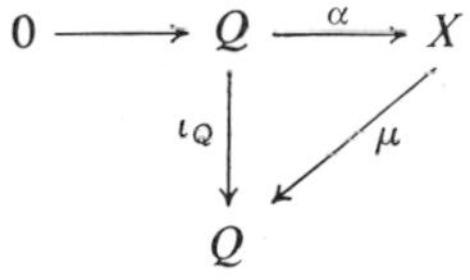

commutes. Since $\mu\alpha = \iota_Q$, μ is a splitting homomorphism for $0 \to Q \xrightarrow{\alpha} X$.

b ⇒ c. Suppose b holds. Let X be an A-module containing Q as a submodule. If $\varepsilon: Q \to X$ is the inclusion map, then $0 \to Q \xrightarrow{\varepsilon} X$ splits; i.e., there is an A-homomorphism $\varepsilon': X \to Q$ such that $\varepsilon'\varepsilon = \iota_Q$. By Theorem 2.2b, $X = \mathrm{Im}\,\varepsilon \oplus \mathrm{Ker}\,\varepsilon' = Q \oplus \mathrm{Ker}\,\varepsilon'$.

c ⇒ a. Assume c. By Theorem 2.6, there is an injective module T of which Q is a submodule, hence a direct summand. But then Q is, itself, injective. For, suppose $T = Q \oplus Q'$. Let X, Y be A-modules ($Y \subset X$); let $\gamma: Y \to Q$

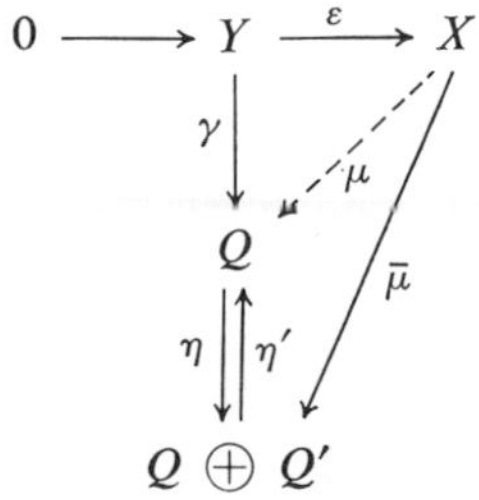

be an A-homomorphism, and let $\varepsilon\colon Y \to X$ and $\eta\colon Q \to Q \oplus Q'$ be the inclusion maps. Then there is an A-homomorphism $\bar{\mu}\colon X \to Q \oplus Q'$ such that $\bar{\mu}\varepsilon = \eta\gamma$. Let η' be the projection of $Q \oplus Q'$ onto Q. Then $\eta'\bar{\mu}$ is an A-homomorphism, μ, of X into Q. Since $\bar{\mu}\varepsilon = \eta\gamma$, $\mu\varepsilon = \eta'\bar{\mu}\varepsilon = \eta'\eta\gamma = \gamma$. Thus, Q is injective. ▮

3. Modules of Homomorphisms

If X, Y are A-modules, we denote by $\mathrm{Hom}_A(X, Y)$ the set of all A-homomorphisms of the A-module X into the A-module Y. If $X = Y$, we write $\mathrm{End}_A(X)$ for $\mathrm{Hom}_A(X, X)$, the set of all A-endomorphisms of the A-module X.

It is easy to verify that:

1. $\mathrm{Hom}_A(X, Y)$ is an abelian group under the operation $+$ defined by $(\alpha + \beta)x = \alpha x + \beta x$ for all $\alpha, \beta \in \mathrm{Hom}_A(X, Y)$, all $x \in X$.
2. $\mathrm{End}_A(X)$ is a ring, with addition defined as in 1, with multiplication defined as composition of maps, and with identity ι_X, the identity map on X.
3. The automorphisms of the A-module X form the unit group of the ring $\mathrm{End}_A(X)$ [we denote this group by $\mathrm{Aut}_A(X)$].
4. $\mathrm{Hom}_A(X, Y)$ is a right A-module, with scalar multiplication defined by $\alpha a(x) = \alpha(ax)$ ($\alpha \in \mathrm{Hom}_A(X, Y)$, $a \in A$, $x \in X$).
5. $\mathrm{Hom}_A(X, Y)$ is a left module over $\mathrm{End}_A(Y)$, with scalar multiplication defined by $(\gamma, \alpha) \mapsto \gamma \circ \alpha$ ($\alpha \in \mathrm{Hom}_A(X, Y)$, $\gamma \in \mathrm{End}_A(Y)$, $\circ$: composition of maps).
6. $\mathrm{Hom}_A(X, Y)$ is a right module over $\mathrm{End}_A(X)$, with scalar multiplication defined by $(\gamma, \alpha) \mapsto \alpha \circ \gamma$ ($\alpha \in \mathrm{Hom}_A(X, Y)$, $\gamma \in \mathrm{End}_A(X)$, $\circ$: composition of maps).

(Analogous remarks apply if X and Y are right A-modules.)

If X, X', Y, Y' are A-modules, and $\mu\colon X' \to X$, $\nu\colon Y \to Y'$ are A-homomorphisms, then, for each $\alpha \in \mathrm{Hom}_A(X, Y)$, the mapping $\nu\alpha\mu$ is an element of $\mathrm{Hom}_A(X', Y')$,

$$\begin{array}{ccc} X & \xrightarrow{\ \alpha\ } & Y \\ {\scriptstyle\mu}\uparrow & & \downarrow{\scriptstyle\nu} \\ X' & \xrightarrow{\ \nu\alpha\mu\ } & Y' \end{array}$$

and $\alpha \mapsto \nu\alpha\mu$ is a $\mathbf{Z}$-homomorphism of the abelian group $\mathrm{Hom}_A(X, Y)$ into the abelian group $\mathrm{Hom}_A(X', Y')$. We denote this homomorphism by $\mathrm{Hom}_A(\mu, \nu)$, or simply by $\mathrm{Hom}(\mu, \nu)$.

REMARK. We leave to the reader the verification of the following statements: If X, X', Y, Y' are A-modules, $\mu,\mu_1,\mu_2,\mu' \in \mathrm{Hom}_A(X',X)$, $\nu,\nu_1,\nu_2,\nu' \in \mathrm{Hom}_A(Y,Y')$, then

1. $\mathrm{Hom}(\mu_1 + \mu_2,\nu) = \mathrm{Hom}(\mu_1,\nu) + \mathrm{Hom}(\mu_2,\nu)$.
2. $\mathrm{Hom}(\mu,\nu_1 + \nu_2) = \mathrm{Hom}(\mu,\nu_1) + \mathrm{Hom}(\mu,\nu_2)$.
3. $\mathrm{Hom}(\mu \circ \mu', \nu' \circ \nu) = \mathrm{Hom}(\mu',\nu') \circ \mathrm{Hom}(\mu,\nu)$.

If μ and ν are isomorphisms, then $\mathrm{Hom}(\mu,\nu)$ is an isomorphism, with inverse $\mathrm{Hom}(\mu^{-1},\nu^{-1})$.

If X, X' are A-modules and μ is an A-homomorphism of X' into X, then, for each A-module Y, the mapping $\bar{\mu} = \mathrm{Hom}(\mu,\iota_Y)$ is a homomorphism of the **Z**-module $\mathrm{Hom}_A(X,Y)$ into the **Z**-module $\mathrm{Hom}_A(X',Y)$. Similarly, if Y, $Y'$are A-modules, and ν is an A-homomorphism of Y into Y', then, for each A-module X, the mapping $\bar{\nu} = \mathrm{Hom}(\iota_X,\nu)$ is a homomorphism of the **Z**-module $\mathrm{Hom}_A(X,Y)$ into the **Z**-module $\mathrm{Hom}_A(X',Y)$. In particular, if μ is an endomorphism of X, then $\bar{\mu}$ is simply the right multiplication of $\mathrm{End}_A(X)$ by μ; and, if ν is an endomorphism of Y, then $\bar{\nu}$ is simply the left multiplication of $\mathrm{End}_A(Y)$ by ν.

We may translate our definitions of the **Z**-modules $\mathrm{Hom}_A(X,Y)$ and of the **Z**-homomorphisms $\mathrm{Hom}_A(\mu,\nu)$ into the language of categories and functors: For a fixed ring A, we form a category C whose objects are ordered pairs (X,Y) of (left) A-modules, and whose morphisms $(X,Y) \mapsto (X',Y')$ are ordered pairs (μ,ν) of A-homomorphisms ($\mu: X' \to X$, $\nu: Y \to Y'$), combined under componentwise composition. We define a functor Hom_A from C to the category of **Z**-modules as follows: With each object (X,Y) of C, we associate the **Z**-module $\mathrm{Hom}_A(X,Y)$; with each morphism (μ,ν) of C we associate the **Z**-homomorphism $\mathrm{Hom}_A(\mu,\nu)$: $\mathrm{Hom}_A(X,Y) \to \mathrm{Hom}_A(X',Y')$ defined by $\alpha \mapsto \nu\alpha\mu$ ($\alpha \in \mathrm{Hom}_A(X,Y)$). It is easy to verify that Hom_A is a covariant functor on C. The **Z**-modules $\mathrm{Hom}_A(X,Y)$ and the **Z**-homomorphisms $\mathrm{Hom}_A(\mu,\nu)$ which we defined above are the images, respectively, of the objects (X,Y) and the morphisms (μ,ν) under the functor Hom_A.

We now investigate the behavior of the functor Hom_A in relation to exact sequences. (We omit the subscript A and write Hom when no confusion is likely.)

Theorem 3.1. *Let X, X', X'' be A-modules, and let $\mu: X' \to X$ and $\nu: X \to X''$ be A-homomorphisms. Then*

(1) $$X' \xrightarrow{\mu} X \xrightarrow{\nu} X'' \longrightarrow 0$$

is an exact sequence of A-homomorphisms if and only if for each A-module Y,

$$(2)\qquad 0 \longrightarrow \mathrm{Hom}(X'', Y) \xrightarrow{\bar{\nu}} \mathrm{Hom}(X, Y) \xrightarrow{\bar{\mu}} \mathrm{Hom}(X', Y)$$

is an exact sequence of **Z***-homomorphisms, where* $\bar{\mu} = \mathrm{Hom}(\mu, \iota_Y)$ *and* $\bar{\nu} = \mathrm{Hom}(\nu, \iota_Y)$.

PROOF. Suppose $X' \xrightarrow{\mu} X \xrightarrow{\nu} X'' \to 0$ is exact. If $\alpha \in \mathrm{Hom}(X'', Y)$ and $\bar{\nu}\alpha = 0$, then $\iota_Y \alpha \nu = \alpha\nu = 0$, whence $\alpha = 0$, since ν is surjective. Thus, $\bar{\nu}$ is injective and $0 \to \mathrm{Hom}(X'', Y) \xrightarrow{\bar{\nu}} \mathrm{Hom}(X, Y)$ is exact.

Since $\mathrm{Ker}\,\nu = \mathrm{Im}\,\mu$, $\nu\mu = 0$. But $\bar{\mu}\bar{\nu} = \mathrm{Hom}(\nu\mu, \iota_Y)$, hence $\bar{\mu}\bar{\nu} = 0$ and $\mathrm{Im}\,\bar{\nu} \subset \mathrm{Ker}\,\bar{\mu}$. On the other hand, suppose $\alpha \in \mathrm{Ker}\,\bar{\mu}$. Then $\bar{\mu}\alpha = \iota_Y \alpha\mu = 0$, hence $\alpha\mu = 0$ and $\mathrm{Im}\,\mu \subset \mathrm{Ker}\,\alpha$. But $\mathrm{Im}\,\mu = \mathrm{Ker}\,\nu$, so that $\mathrm{Ker}\,\nu \subset \mathrm{Ker}\,\alpha$. Since $\nu\colon X \to X''$ is an epimorphism, there is an A-homomorphism $\alpha'\colon X'' \to Y$ such that $\alpha'\nu = \alpha$ (Chapter 1, Theorem 4.9).

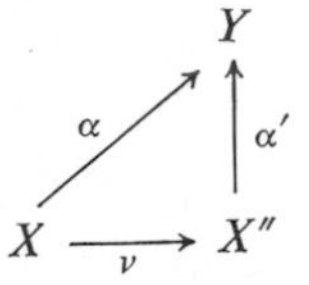

But then $\bar{\nu}(\alpha') = \alpha$, and therefore $\mathrm{Ker}\,\bar{\mu} \subset \mathrm{Im}\,\bar{\nu}$. It follows that $\mathrm{Ker}\,\bar{\mu} = \mathrm{Im}\,\bar{\nu}$, and that the sequence (2) is exact.

Conversely, suppose that (2) is exact for any A-module Y. Since $\bar{\mu}\bar{\nu} = 0$, $\alpha\nu\mu = 0$ for each $\alpha \in \mathrm{Hom}(X'', Y)$, for any A-module Y. Hence in particular for $Y = X''$ and $\alpha = \iota_{X''}$, we have $\nu\mu = 0$. Thus, $\mathrm{Im}\,\mu \subset \mathrm{Ker}\,\nu$.

Now let $Y = X/\mathrm{Im}\,\mu$, and let φ be the canonical homomorphism of X onto Y. Then $\varphi\mu = 0 = \bar{\mu}\varphi$. Thus, $\varphi \in \mathrm{Ker}\,\bar{\mu} = \mathrm{Im}\,\bar{\nu}$, and therefore there is some $\psi \in \mathrm{Hom}(X'', Y)$ such that $\varphi = \bar{\nu}\psi = \psi\nu$. But then $\mathrm{Im}\,\mu = \mathrm{Ker}\,\varphi \supset \mathrm{Ker}\,\nu$. Thus, $\mathrm{Im}\,\mu = \mathrm{Ker}\,\nu$.

Finally, ν is surjective. For, if $Y = X''/\mathrm{Im}\,\nu$ and φ' is the canonical homomorphism of X'' onto Y, then $\varphi'\nu = 0 = \bar{\nu}\varphi'$. Thus, $\varphi' \in \mathrm{Ker}\,\bar{\nu} = 0$, and therefore $\mathrm{Im}\,\nu = X''$. ▌

Reversing the arrows in the preceding theorem (and relabeling) yields a dual theorem:

Theorem 3.2. *Let X, X′, X″ be A-modules, and let* $\mu\colon X' \to X$, $\nu\colon X \to X''$ *be A-homomorphisms. Then*

$$(3)\qquad 0 \longrightarrow X' \xrightarrow{\mu} X \xrightarrow{\nu} X''$$

is an exact sequence of A-homomorphisms if and only if, for each A-module Y,

$$(4)\qquad 0 \longrightarrow \operatorname{Hom}(Y,X') \xrightarrow{\bar{\mu}} \operatorname{Hom}(Y,X) \xrightarrow{\bar{\nu}} \operatorname{Hom}(Y,X'')$$

is an exact sequence of **Z**-*homomorphisms, where* $\mu = \operatorname{Hom}(\iota_Y,\mu)$ *and* $\bar{\nu} = \operatorname{Hom}(\iota_Y,\nu)$.

PROOF. Suppose that (3) is exact, and let Y be an A-module. Since $\operatorname{Im}\mu = \operatorname{Ker}\nu$, $\nu\mu = 0$ and therefore $\bar{\nu}\bar{\mu} = \operatorname{Hom}(\iota_Y,\nu\mu) = 0$. Thus, $\operatorname{Im}\bar{\mu} \subset \operatorname{Ker}\bar{\nu}$. On the other hand, if $\gamma \in \operatorname{Ker}\bar{\nu}$, then $\bar{\nu}\gamma = \nu\gamma = 0$, hence $\operatorname{Im}\gamma \subset \operatorname{Ker}\nu = \operatorname{Im}\mu$. Let μ_1 be the homomorphism of X' onto $\operatorname{Im}\mu$ such that $\mu_1 x' = \mu x'$ for each $x' \in X'$. Since μ is injective, μ_1 is an isomorphism. Since $\operatorname{Im}\gamma \subset \operatorname{Im}\mu$, the domain of μ_1^{-1}, we can form $\alpha = \mu_1^{-1}\gamma$. Then $\alpha \in \operatorname{Hom}(Y,X')$, and $\gamma = \mu\alpha = \bar{\mu}\alpha$. Thus, $\gamma \in \operatorname{Im}\bar{\mu}$, and we have $\operatorname{Ker}\bar{\nu} = \operatorname{Im}\bar{\mu}$. Since $\bar{\mu}$ is clearly injective, it follows that (4) is exact.

Conversely, suppose (4) is exact for any A-module Y. Then $\bar{\nu}\bar{\mu} = \operatorname{Hom}(\iota_Y,\nu\mu) = 0$, for any A-module Y. Let $Y = X'$. Then $\nu\mu\iota_{X'} = \nu\mu = 0$, and therefore $\operatorname{Im}\mu \subset \operatorname{Ker}\nu$. Next, let $Y = \operatorname{Ker}\nu$. If $y \in Y$, then $\nu y = \nu\iota_Y(y) = 0$, whence $\bar{\nu}\iota_Y = 0$ and $\iota_Y \in \operatorname{Ker}\bar{\nu} = \operatorname{Im}\bar{\mu}$. But then $\iota_Y = \bar{\mu}\beta = \mu\beta$ for some $\beta \in \operatorname{Hom}(Y,X')$ and therefore $y = \iota_Y(y) = \mu\beta(y) \in \operatorname{Im}\mu$. Thus, $\operatorname{Ker}\nu = \operatorname{Im}\mu$. Clearly, $\bar{\mu}$ is injective. It follows that (3) is exact. ∎

Despite Theorems 3.1 and 3.2, the exactness of the sequence

$$(5)\qquad 0 \longrightarrow X' \xrightarrow{\mu} X \xrightarrow{\nu} X'' \longrightarrow 0$$

does not, in general, imply exactness for either of the sequences

$$(6)\quad 0 \longrightarrow \operatorname{Hom}(X'',Y) \xrightarrow{\bar{\nu}} \operatorname{Hom}(X,Y) \xrightarrow{\bar{\mu}} \operatorname{Hom}(X',Y) \longrightarrow 0$$
$$(\bar{\nu} = \operatorname{Hom}(\nu,\iota_Y),\ \bar{\mu} = \operatorname{Hom}(\mu,\iota_Y));$$

$$(7)\quad 0 \longrightarrow \operatorname{Hom}(Y,X') \xrightarrow{\bar{\mu}} \operatorname{Hom}(Y,X) \xrightarrow{\bar{\nu}} \operatorname{Hom}(X,X'') \longrightarrow 0$$
$$(\bar{\mu} = \operatorname{Hom}(\iota_Y,\mu),\ \bar{\nu} = \operatorname{Hom}(\iota_Y,\nu)).$$

(See Exercise 3.2.) However, if (5) is split exact, then both (6) and (7) are exact for all Y. In fact, we have:

Theorem 3.3.

a. *If* (5) *is split exact, then* (6) *is split exact for all A-modules Y.*

Conversely, if (6) *is exact for all A-modules Y, then* (5) *is split exact.*

b. *If* (5) *is split exact, then* (7) *is split exact for all A-modules Y. Conversely, if* (7) *is exact for all A-modules Y, then* (5) *is split exact.*

PROOF.

a. Suppose (5) is split exact. Let Y be an A-module. By Theorem 3.1, the sequence

$$0 \longrightarrow \text{Hom}(X'', Y) \xrightarrow{\bar{\nu}} \text{Hom}(X, Y) \xrightarrow{\bar{\mu}} \text{Hom}(X', Y)$$

is exact. To prove that (6) is exact, we need only verify that $\bar{\mu}$ is surjective. Since (5) splits there is a homomorphism $\mu': X \to X'$ such that $\mu'\mu = \iota_{X'}$. Let $\bar{\mu}' = \text{Hom}(\mu', \iota_Y)$. Then $\bar{\mu}'$ is a homomorphism of $\text{Hom}(X', Y)$ into $\text{Hom}(X, Y)$ such that $\bar{\mu}\bar{\mu}' = \text{Hom}(\mu'\mu, \iota_Y) = \text{Hom}(\iota_{X'}, \iota_Y) = \iota_{\text{Hom}(X', Y)}$. But then $\bar{\mu}$ is surjective, and therefore (6) is exact. By Theorem 2.3, (6) is split exact.

Now suppose that (6) is exact for all A-modules Y. By Theorem 3.1, the sequence

$$X' \xrightarrow{\mu} X \xrightarrow{\nu} X'' \longrightarrow 0$$

is exact. To prove that (5) is exact, we need only verify that μ is injective. Let $Y = X$. By our hypothesis, there is a homomorphism $\bar{\mu}': \text{Hom}(X', X) \to \text{Hom}(X, X)$ such that $\bar{\mu}\bar{\mu}' = \text{Hom}(\mu'\mu, \iota_X) = \iota_{\text{Hom}(X', X)}$. But then $\mu'\mu = \iota_{X'}$, and therefore μ is injective and (5) is exact. By Theorem 2.3, (5) is split exact.

b. The proof is left to the reader (Exercise 3.3). ▌

Projective and injective modules can be characterized in this context as follows:

Theorem 3.4.

a. *An A-module Y is injective if and only if, for each exact sequence of A-homomorphisms,*

$$(5) \qquad 0 \longrightarrow X' \xrightarrow{\mu} X \xrightarrow{\nu} X'' \longrightarrow 0,$$

the corresponding sequence of **Z**-*homomorphisms,*

$$(6) \quad 0 \longrightarrow \text{Hom}(X'', Y) \xrightarrow{\bar{\nu}} \text{Hom}(X, Y) \xrightarrow{\bar{\mu}} \text{Hom}(X', Y) \longrightarrow 0,$$

is also exact.

b. *An A-module Y is projective if and only if, for each exact sequence of A-homomorphisms,*

$$(5) \qquad 0 \longrightarrow X' \xrightarrow{\mu} X \xrightarrow{\nu} X'' \longrightarrow 0,$$

the corresponding sequence of **Z**-*homomorphisms,*

$$(7) \quad 0 \longrightarrow \operatorname{Hom}(Y,X') \xrightarrow{\bar{\mu}} \operatorname{Hom}(Y,X) \xrightarrow{\bar{\nu}} \operatorname{Hom}(Y,X'') \longrightarrow 0,$$

is also exact.

PROOF.

a. Suppose that, for each exact sequence of A-homomorphisms,

$$0 \longrightarrow X' \xrightarrow{\mu} X \xrightarrow{\nu} X'' \longrightarrow 0,$$

the corresponding sequence of Z-homomorphisms,

$$0 \longrightarrow \operatorname{Hom}(X'', Y) \xrightarrow{\bar{\nu}} \operatorname{Hom}(X, Y) \xrightarrow{\bar{\mu}} \operatorname{Hom}(X', Y) \longrightarrow 0,$$

is also exact.

Let X, X' be A-modules, $\mu: X' \to X$ a monomorphism, and $\gamma: X' \to Y$ a homomorphism. Then the sequence

$$0 \longrightarrow X' \xrightarrow{\mu} X \xrightarrow{\nu} X/\operatorname{Im} \mu \longrightarrow 0$$

is exact, where ν is the natural epimorphism of X onto $X/\operatorname{Im} \mu$. Hence the sequence

$$0 \longrightarrow \operatorname{Hom}(X/\operatorname{Im} \mu, Y) \xrightarrow{\bar{\nu}} \operatorname{Hom}(X, Y) \xrightarrow{\bar{\mu}} \operatorname{Hom}(X', Y) \longrightarrow 0$$

is exact, and therefore $\bar{\mu}: \operatorname{Hom}(X, Y) \to \operatorname{Hom}(X', Y)$ is surjective. Thus, there is some $\alpha \in \operatorname{Hom}(X, Y)$ such that $\gamma = \bar{\mu}\alpha = \alpha\mu$. By Definition 2.5, Y is injective.

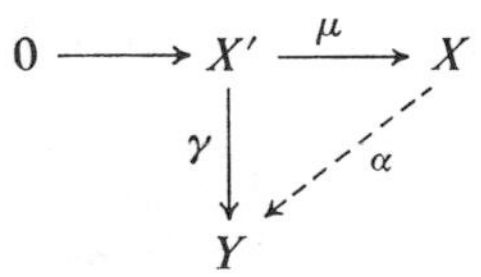

Conversely, suppose that Y is an injective A-module. Let

$$0 \longrightarrow X' \xrightarrow{\mu} X \xrightarrow{\nu} X'' \longrightarrow 0$$

be an exact sequence. If γ is a homomorphism of X' into Y, then, since Y is injective, there is a homomorphism $\alpha\colon X \to Y$ such that $\gamma = \alpha\mu = \bar{\mu}\alpha$. Hence $\bar{\mu}\colon \mathrm{Hom}(X, Y) \to \mathrm{Hom}(X', Y)$ is surjective. But then, by Theorem 3.1, the sequence

$$0 \longrightarrow \mathrm{Hom}(X'', Y) \xrightarrow{\bar{\nu}} \mathrm{Hom}(X, Y) \xrightarrow{\bar{\mu}} \mathrm{Hom}(X', Y) \longrightarrow 0$$

is exact.

b. Suppose that, for each exact sequence of A-homomorphisms,

$$0 \longrightarrow X' \xrightarrow{\mu} X \xrightarrow{\nu} X'' \longrightarrow 0,$$

the corresponding sequence

$$0 \longrightarrow \mathrm{Hom}(Y, X') \xrightarrow{\bar{\mu}} \mathrm{Hom}(Y, X) \xrightarrow{\bar{\nu}} \mathrm{Hom}(Y, X'') \longrightarrow 0$$

is also exact.

Let X, X'' be A-modules, ν an epimorphism of X onto X''. Then the sequence

$$0 \longrightarrow \mathrm{Ker}\,\nu \xrightarrow{\mu} X \xrightarrow{\nu} X'' \longrightarrow 0$$

is exact, with μ the inclusion map of $\mathrm{Ker}\,\nu$ into X. It follows that the sequence

$$0 \longrightarrow \mathrm{Hom}(Y, \mathrm{Ker}\,\nu) \xrightarrow{\bar{\mu}} \mathrm{Hom}(Y, X) \xrightarrow{\bar{\nu}} \mathrm{Hom}(Y, X'') \longrightarrow 0$$

is exact, and therefore $\bar{\nu}\colon \mathrm{Hom}(Y, X) \to \mathrm{Hom}(Y, X'')$ is surjective. Thus, given $\gamma \in \mathrm{Hom}(Y, X'')$ there is some $\alpha \in \mathrm{Hom}(Y, X)$ such that $\gamma = \bar{\nu}\alpha = \nu\alpha$. By Definition 2.4, Y is projective.

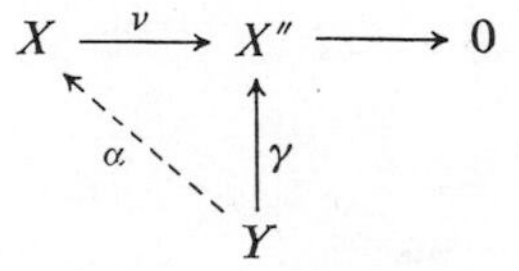

Conversely, suppose that Y is a projective A-module. Let

$$0 \longrightarrow X' \xrightarrow{\mu} X \xrightarrow{\nu} X'' \longrightarrow 0$$

be an exact sequence of A-homomorphisms. If γ is a homomorphism of Y into X'' then, since Y is projective, there is an A-homomorphism $\alpha\colon Y \to X$ such that $\gamma = \nu\alpha = \bar{\nu}\alpha$. Thus, $\bar{\nu}\colon \text{Hom}(Y,X) \to \text{Hom}(Y,X'')$ is surjective. But then, by Theorem 3.2, the sequence

$$0 \longrightarrow \text{Hom}(Y,X') \xrightarrow{\bar{\mu}} \text{Hom}(Y,X) \xrightarrow{\bar{\nu}} \text{Hom}(Y,X'') \longrightarrow 0$$

is exact. ▌

4. Tensor Products

Homomorphisms of a vector space are traditionally referred to as "linear maps" ("linear transformations"). This language carries over to arbitrary A-modules; i.e., the homomorphisms of an A-module are referred to as "(A-)linear maps."

If A is a ring, T, X, and Y are left (right) A-modules, and $\alpha\colon X \times Y \to T$ is a mapping of the Cartesian product of X and Y into T such that $\alpha(a_1x_1 + a_2x_2,y) = a_1\alpha(x_1,y) + a_2\alpha(x_2,y)$ and $\alpha(x_1,b_1y_1 + b_2y_2) = b_1\alpha(x,y_1) + b_2\alpha(x,y_2)$ for all $x,x_1,x_2 \in X$, $y,y_1,y_2 \in Y$, $a_1,a_2 \in A$, $b_1,b_2 \in B$, then α is referred to as a(n) (A-)bilinear map. [In an analogous way, (A-) multilinear maps can be defined for arbitrary families of left (right) A-modules.]

In Section 3 we constructed from two given left A-modules (or from two given right A-modules) the **Z**-module $\text{Hom}_A(X, Y)$ consisting of all A-linear maps of X into Y. We now begin with a pair of modules X and Y, where X is a right A-module, Y a left A-module, and construct a **Z**-module $X \otimes_A Y$, the tensor product of X and Y. One of the most important features of the tensor product will be its usefulness in reducing considerations involving bilinear maps of the Cartesian product $X \times Y$ to considerations involving linear maps of $X \otimes_A Y$. We build this feature into its definition.

If G is a **Z**-module, we shall refer to a map $\gamma\colon X \times Y \to G$ as an *A-balanced map* if

1. γ is **Z**-bilinear, i.e.,

$$\left.\begin{aligned} \gamma(x_1 + x_2,y) &= \gamma(x_1,y) + \gamma(x_2,y) \\ \gamma(x,y_1 + y_2) &= \gamma(x,y_1) + \gamma(x,y_2) \end{aligned}\right\} \quad \text{for all } x,x_1,x_2 \in X,\ y,y_1,y_2 \in Y.$$

2. $\gamma(xa,y) = \gamma(x,ay)$ for all $x \in X, y \in Y, a \in A$.

(Note that 1 and 2 are equivalent in case $A = \mathbf{Z}$.)

Definition 4.1. Let A be a ring. Let X be a right A-module, and let Y be a left A-module. Let T be a $\mathbf{Z}$-module, $\theta: X \times Y \to T$ an A-balanced map of the Cartesian product $X \times Y$ into T. Then the ordered pair $\langle T,\theta \rangle$ is a *tensor product* of X and Y if it satisfies the following condition:

(*) For every $\mathbf{Z}$-module G, and every A-balanced map $\gamma: X \times Y \to G$, there is a unique $\mathbf{Z}$-homomorphism $\mu: T \to G$ such that $\mu\theta = \gamma$.

$$\begin{array}{ccc} X \times Y & \xrightarrow{\theta} & T \\ & \gamma \searrow \quad \swarrow \mu & \\ & G & \end{array}$$

///

We leave to the reader the verification of the usual uniqueness theorem:

Theorem 4.1. *Let X be a right A-module, Y a left A-module.*

a. *If $\langle T,\theta \rangle$ and $\langle T',\theta' \rangle$ are both tensor products of X and Y, then there is a unique $\mathbf{Z}$-isomorphism $\mu: T \to T'$ such that $\mu\theta = \theta'$.*

b. *If $\langle T,\theta \rangle$ is a tensor product of X and Y, T' is a $\mathbf{Z}$-module, $\theta': X \times Y \to T'$ an A-balanced map, and $\mu: T \to T'$ a $\mathbf{Z}$-isomorphism such that $\mu\theta = \theta'$, then $\langle T',\theta' \rangle$ is also a tensor product of X and Y.* □

REMARK. We may translate Definition 4.1 into categorical language as follows: Let A be a ring, X a right A-module, Y a left A-module. Form a category C whose objects are ordered pairs (G,γ), where G is a $\mathbf{Z}$-module, $\gamma: X \times Y \to G$ an A-balanced map, and whose morphisms $(G,\gamma) \mapsto (G',\gamma')$ are $\mathbf{Z}$-homomorphisms $\varphi: G \to G'$ such that $\varphi\gamma = \gamma'$. Then $\langle T,\theta \rangle$ is a tensor product of X and Y, in the sense of Definition 4.1, if and only if $\langle T,\theta \rangle$ is a universal repelling object in C.

Later (p. 188) we shall interpret the tensor product categorically in another way, as a functor.

Our next problem is, of course, that of existence. We proceed as follows: Given a right A-module X and a left A-module Y, we form a free abelian group, F, on $X \times Y$, with $X \times Y \subset F$. Let $T = F/[S]$, where $[S]$ is the subgroup of F generated by the set, S, of elements of form

$$(x_1 + x_2, y) - (x_1,y) - (x_2,y),$$
$$(x, y_1 + y_2) - (x,y_1) - (x,y_2),$$
$$(xa,y) - (x,ay)$$

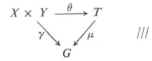

($x,x_1,x_2 \in X$, $y,y_1,y_2 \in Y$, $a \in A$). Let ν be the natural **Z**-homomorphism of F onto $F/[S]$, $\varepsilon: X \times Y \to F$ the inclusion map of $X \times Y$ into F, and let $\theta = \nu\varepsilon$. We claim:

Theorem 4.2. *If A is a ring, X a right A-module, Y a left A-module, and T, θ are as defined above, then $\langle T,\theta\rangle$ is a tensor product for X and Y.*

PROOF. By Definition, T is a **Z**-module, and θ is an A-balanced map since ν vanishes on S. Suppose G is an abelian group, $\gamma: X \times Y \to G$ an A-balanced map. By Chapter 1, Definition 12.1, there is a **Z**-homomorphism $\eta: F \to G$ such that $\eta\varepsilon = \gamma$.

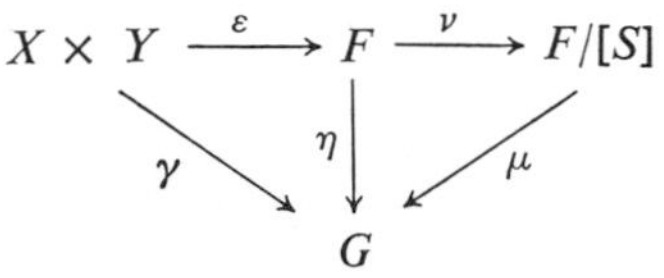

Since γ vanishes on S, Ker $\eta \supset [S] =$ Ker ν. Hence, by Chapter 1, Theorem 4.9, there is a **Z**-homomorphism $\mu: F/[S] \to G$ such that $\mu\nu = \eta$. But then $\gamma = \eta\varepsilon = \mu\nu\varepsilon = \mu\theta$, as required. The uniqueness of μ follows from the fact that Im θ generates $F/[S]$. ▮

In view of Theorem 4.1, we refer to $\langle T,\theta\rangle$ as "the" tensor product of X and Y. Somewhat inaccurately, we shall call T itself "the tensor product of X and Y." We write $X \otimes_A Y$ or simply $X \otimes Y$ for T, and $x \otimes y$ for $\theta(x,y)$ ($(x,y) \in X \times Y$).

REMARK 1. The following computational rules are immediate consequences of the definitions:

$$(x_1 + x_2) \otimes y = x_1 \otimes y + x_2 \otimes y,$$

$$x \otimes (y_1 + y_2) = x \otimes y_1 + x \otimes y_2,$$

$$xa \otimes y = x \otimes ay$$

($x,x_1,x_2 \in X$, $y,y_1,y_2 \in Y$, $a \in A$). From these rules it follows easily that $x \otimes 0 = 0 \otimes y = 0$ for all $x \in X$, $y \in Y$.

For each $k \in \mathbf{Z}$, $kx \otimes y = x \otimes ky = k(x \otimes y)$ ($x \in X$, $y \in Y$). If $\langle T,\theta\rangle$ is a tensor product, then by the proof of Theorems 4.2 and 4.1 (or directly from Definition 4.1) we have $T = [\theta\{x \otimes y | x \in X, y \in Y\}]$. Thus each element of T has the form $\sum_i k_i(x_i' \otimes y_i) = \sum_i k_i x_i' \otimes y_i = \sum_i x_i \otimes y_i$ ($x_i \in X$, $y_i \in Y$).

REMARK 2. The tensor product of two nonzero modules may be zero. For example, if m is any positive integer and X, Y are the $\mathbf{Z}$-modules $\mathbf{Z}/(m+1)$ and $\mathbf{Z}/(m)$, respectively, then for each $x \in X$, $y \in Y$, we have $x \otimes y = (m+1)(x \otimes y) - m(x \otimes y) = ((m+1)x \otimes y) - (x \otimes my) = 0 \otimes y - x \otimes 0 = 0$. Thus, $X \otimes_{\mathbf{Z}} Y = 0$.

REMARK 3. If X is a right A-module, Y a left A-module, then X and Y are both $\mathbf{Z}$-modules, and $X \otimes_A Y$ is isomorphic to the factor group $X \otimes_{\mathbf{Z}} Y/[L]$, where $[L]$ is the subgroup generated by the set, L, of elements of the form $(xa \otimes y) - (x \otimes ay)$ $(x \in X, y \in Y, a \in A)$.

We have defined the tensor product of a right A-module and a left A-module as an abelian group, i.e., a $\mathbf{Z}$-module. We shall now investigate circumstances under which the tensor product can be made into an A-module.

Definition 4.2. If B, A are rings, and Q is a left B-module as well as a right A-module, then Q is a *(B,A)-bimodule* provided $b(qa) = (bq)a$ for all $b \in B$, $a \in A$, $q \in Q$. ///

REMARK. If A is commutative, Q a left A-module, then Q is a right A-module with scalar multiplication defined by $qa = aq$ $(a \in A, q \in Q)$. Since $b(qa) = b(aq) = (ba)q = (ab)q = a(bq) = (bq)a$ for all $a,b \in A$, $q \in Q$, Q is an (A,A)-bimodule. We shall tacitly assume any module over a commutative ring A to be endowed with an (A,A)-bimodule structure in this way.

Theorem 4.3. *Let A, B be rings.*

a. *If X is a (B,A)-bimodule and Y is a left A-module, then $X \otimes_A Y$ is a left B-module.*
b. *If X is a right A-module and Y is an (A,B)-bimodule, then $X \otimes_A Y$ is a right B-module.*

PROOF.

a. Suppose X is a (B,A)-bimodule, Y a left A-module. Then, for each $b \in B$, $(x,y) \in X \times Y$, the mapping $\varphi_b\colon X \times Y \to X \otimes_A Y$ defined by $\varphi_b(x,y) = bx \otimes y$ is A-balanced. Hence there is a unique endomorphism $\mu_b\colon X \otimes_A Y \to X \otimes_A Y$ such that $\mu_b(x \otimes y) = bx \otimes y$ for each $x \in X$, $y \in Y$. Since every element of $X \otimes_A Y$ is equal to a sum of the form $\sum_{i=1}^n (x_i \otimes y_i)$, we can define a scalar multiplication on $X \otimes_A Y$ by setting $b(\sum_{i=1}^n (x_i \otimes y_i)) = \mu_b(\sum_{i=1}^n (x_i \otimes y_i)) = \sum_{i=1}^n bx_i \otimes y_i$ for each $b \in B$. This scalar multiplication makes $X \otimes_A Y$ into a left B-module.

b. An analogous discussion applies, in this case, to the mapping $\psi_b\colon X \times Y \to X \otimes_A Y$ defined by $\psi_b(x,y) = x \otimes yb$. ▮

Corollary 1. *If A is commutative, then $X \otimes_A Y$ is an A-module, with scalar multiplication defined by* $a(\sum_{i=1}^n x_i \otimes y_i) = \sum_{i=1}^n ax_i \otimes y_i = \sum_{i=1}^n x_i \otimes y_i a$ *for each* $a \in A$, $\sum_{i=1}^n (x_i \otimes y_i) \in X \otimes_A Y$.

PROOF. X and Y are both (A,A)-bimodules (see Remark following Definition 4.2) and, for each $a \in A$, $(x,y) \in X \times Y$,

$$ax \otimes y = xa \otimes y = x \otimes ay = x \otimes ya. \quad \blacksquare$$

Corollary 2. *Let A be commutative and let X, Y be A-modules. Then $\langle T,\theta\rangle$ is a tensor product for X and Y if and only if T is an A-module, and $\theta\colon X \times Y \to T$ is an A-bilinear map satisfying the condition*

(†) *For each A-module G and each A-bilinear map $\gamma\colon X \times Y \to G$ there is a unique A-homomorphism $\mu\colon T \to G$ such that $\mu\theta = \gamma$.*

PROOF. Suppose $\langle T,\theta\rangle$ is a tensor product for X and Y. By Corollary 1, T is an A-module and θ is an A-bilinear map, since, for $x \in X$, $y \in Y$, $a \in A$,

$$a\theta(x,y) = a(x \otimes y) = xa \otimes y = x \otimes ay;$$

that is,

$$a\theta(x,y) = \theta(xa,y) = \theta(x,ay).$$

Given an A-module G and an A-bilinear map $\gamma\colon X \times Y \to G$, there is a unique $\mathbf{Z}$-homomorphism $\mu\colon X \otimes_A Y \to G$ such that $\mu\theta = \gamma$. This mapping μ is, in fact, an A-homomorphism. For

$$\mu(a\theta(x,y)) = \mu(ax \otimes y) = \gamma(ax,y) = a\gamma(x,y) = a\mu\theta(x,y) \qquad ((x,y) \in X \times Y, a \in A).$$

Since any A-homomorphism is also a $\mathbf{Z}$-homomorphism, the uniqueness of μ, as an A-homomorphism, is assured. Thus, $\langle T,\theta\rangle$ satisfies (†).

Conversely, suppose $\langle T,\theta\rangle$ satisfies (†). Then T is certainly a $\mathbf{Z}$-module, and θ is a balanced map of $X \times Y$ into T. By Theorem 4.2, there exists a tensor product $\langle T',\theta'\rangle$ for X and Y. By the first part of the proof, $\langle T',\theta'\rangle$ satisfies (†). The usual uniqueness theorem (analogous to Theorem 4.1) applies to (†) and provides an A-isomorphism $\mu\colon T \to T'$ such that $\mu\theta = \theta'$. This A-isomorphism is also a $\mathbf{Z}$-isomorphism and therefore, by Theorem 4.1b, $\langle T,\theta\rangle$ is a tensor product for X and Y, according to Definition 4.1. $\blacksquare$

In view of Corollary 2, condition (*) in Definition 4.1 can be replaced by condition (†) in case A is commutative.

It is natural to inquire whether (and in what sense) the tensor product, considered as a "binary operation" on modules, is "associative" or "commutative."

Theorem 4.4. (Associativity.) *Let X be a right A-module, Y an $(A,B$-) bimodule, and Z a left B-module, where A, B are rings. Then there exists a unique* **Z**-*isomorphism μ of $(X \otimes_A Y) \otimes_B Z$ onto $X \otimes_A (Y \otimes_B Z)$ such that*

$$\mu((x \otimes y) \otimes z) = x \otimes (y \otimes z) \tag{1}$$

for each $x \in X$, $y \in Y$, $z \in Z$.

PROOF. By Theorem 4.3, $X \otimes_A Y$ is a right B-module and $Y \otimes_B Z$ is a left A-module. Thus, the two tensor products, $(X \otimes_A Y) \otimes_B Z$ and $X \otimes_A (Y \otimes_B Z)$, exist. Given $x \in X$, let $\alpha_x \colon Y \times Z \to (X \otimes_A Y) \otimes_B Z$ be the mapping defined by

$$\alpha_x(y,z) = (x \otimes y) \otimes z.$$

Clearly, α_x is a B-balanced map; hence there is a **Z**-homomorphism $\mu_x \colon Y \otimes_B Z \to (X \otimes_A Y) \otimes_B Z$ such that $\mu_x \theta_{Y,Z} = \alpha_x$ (where $\theta_{Y,Z}$ is the canonical B-balanced map associated with $Y \otimes_B Z$). Now the map $\alpha \colon X \times (Y \otimes_B Z) \to (X \otimes_A Y) \otimes_B Z$ defined by $\alpha(x,t) = \mu_x(t)$ $(x \in X, t \in Y \otimes_B Z)$ is an A-balanced map; hence there is a **Z**-homomorphism $\mu \colon X \otimes_A (Y \otimes_B Z) \to (X \otimes_A Y) \otimes_B Z$ such that $\mu\theta = \alpha$ [where θ is the canonical A-balanced map associated with $X \otimes_A (Y \otimes_B Z)$]. For each $x \in X$, $y \in Y$, $z \in Z$, we have

$$\mu(x \otimes (y \otimes z)) = \alpha(x,(y \otimes z)) = \mu_x(y \otimes z) = \alpha_x(y,z) = (x \otimes y) \otimes z.$$

Since the elements of form $x \otimes (y \otimes z)$ generate $X \otimes_A (Y \otimes_B Z)$, μ is the only **Z**-homomorphism of $X \otimes_A (Y \otimes_B Z)$ into $(X \otimes_A Y) \otimes_B Z$ satisfying (1). An analogous argument shows that there exists a unique **Z**-homomorphism $\mu' \colon (X \otimes_A Y) \otimes_B Z \to X \otimes_A (Y \otimes_B Z)$ such that $\mu'((x \otimes y) \otimes z) = x \otimes (y \otimes z)$. The mapping μ' serves as a two-sided inverse for μ, and therefore μ is an isomorphism. ∎

Before considering "commutativity," we note that, given a ring A, we can form the ring A° opposite to A by defining on the set A the same addition as for ring A, and reversing products, i.e., defining $a \circ b$ in A° to be the element

$ba \in A$. Given a right (left) A-module M, we can define an "opposite" left (right) A^o-module M^o by setting ax in M^o (xa in M^o) equal to xa in M (ax in M).

Theorem 4.5. (Commutativity.) *Let A be a ring, X a right A-module and Y a left A-module. Then there is a unique* **Z**-*isomorphism $\mu\colon X \otimes_A Y \to Y^o \otimes_{A^o} X^o$ such that $\mu(x \otimes y) = y \otimes x$ for each $x \in X$, $y \in Y$.*

PROOF. Since Y^o is a right A^o-module and X^o is a left A^o-module, the tensor product $Y^o \otimes_{A^o} X^o$ exists. The mapping $\alpha\colon X \times Y \to Y^o \otimes_{A^o} X^o$ defined by $\alpha(x,y) = y \otimes x$ is, clearly, an A-balanced map. Hence there is a unique **Z**-homomorphism $\mu\colon X \otimes_A Y \to Y^o \otimes_{A^o} X^o$ such that $\mu(x \otimes y) = y \otimes x$ for each $x \in X$, $y \in Y$. By symmetry, there is a (unique) **Z**-homomorphism $\mu'\colon Y^o \otimes_{A^o} X^o \to X \otimes_A Y$ such that $\mu'(y \otimes x) = x \otimes y$. Since μ' serves as a two-sided inverse for μ, μ is a **Z**-isomorphism. ▮

If X, Y are A-modules over a commutative ring A, then $A = A^o$, X and Y are (A,A)-bimodules (see p. 184 Remark), hence $X \otimes_A Y$ and $Y \otimes_A X$ are A-modules, and we have

Corollary. *If X, Y are A-modules, A commutative, then there is a unique A-isomorphism $\mu\colon X \otimes_A Y \to Y \otimes_A X$ such that $\mu(x \otimes y) = y \otimes x$ for each $x \in X$, $y \in Y$.* □

Another basic result is

Theorem 4.6. *Let A be a ring with identity, X a left A-module. Then there is a unique A-isomorphism $\mu\colon A_r \otimes_A X \to X$ such that $\mu(a \otimes x) = ax$ for each $a \in A$, $x \in X$.*

PROOF. The mapping $\varphi\colon A_r \times X \to X$ defined by $\varphi(a,x) = ax$ ($a \in A$, $x \in X$) is A-balanced. Hence there is a unique **Z**-homomorphism $\mu\colon A_r \otimes_A X \to X$ such that $\mu(a \otimes x) = \varphi(a,x) = ax$. Since A_r is an (A,A)-bimodule, $A_r \otimes_A X$ is a left A-module. For each $b \in A$,

$$\mu(b(a \otimes x)) = \mu(ba \otimes x) = \varphi(ba,x) = (ba)x = b(ax) = b\mu(a \otimes x),$$

μ is an A-homomorphism. On the other hand, the mapping $\mu'\colon X \to A_r \otimes_A X$ defined by $\mu'(x) = 1 \otimes x$ ($x \in X$) is, clearly, an A-homomorphism. Since $\mu\mu'(x) = \mu(1 \otimes x) = 1x = x$ for each $x \in X$, and $\mu'\mu(a \otimes x) = \mu'(ax) = 1 \otimes ax = a \otimes x$ for each $x \in X$, $a \in A$, μ is an isomorphism. ▮

Suppose now that X and X' are right A-modules, Y and Y' left A-modules. If $\alpha \in \mathrm{Hom}_A(X,X')$, $\beta \in \mathrm{Hom}_A(Y,Y')$, then the mapping $(x,y) \mapsto \alpha x \otimes \beta y$ of $X \times Y$ into $X' \otimes_A Y'$ is balanced and induces a **Z**-homomorphism $\mu_{\alpha,\beta}: X \otimes_A Y \to X' \otimes_A Y'$ such that $\mu_{\alpha,\beta}(x \otimes y) = \alpha x \otimes \beta y$.

The mapping $(\alpha,\beta) \mapsto \mu_{\alpha,\beta}$ of $\mathrm{Hom}_A(X,X') \times \mathrm{Hom}_A(Y,Y')$ into $\mathrm{Hom}_{\mathbf{Z}}(X \otimes_A Y, X' \otimes_A Y')$ is balanced and induces a **Z**-homomorphism, λ, of $\mathrm{Hom}_A(X,X') \otimes \mathrm{Hom}_A(Y,Y')$ into $\mathrm{Hom}_{\mathbf{Z}}(X \otimes_A Y, X' \otimes_A Y')$ which sends $\alpha \otimes \beta$ to $\mu_{\alpha,\beta}$ ($\alpha \in \mathrm{Hom}_A(X,X')$, $\beta \in \mathrm{Hom}_A(Y,Y')$). Even though this mapping is not, in general, injective, we shall write $\alpha \otimes \beta$ for $\mu_{\alpha,\beta}: x \otimes y \mapsto \alpha x \otimes \beta y$ when no confusion is likely. If A is commutative, the **Z**-modules involved are A-modules, the balanced maps are A-balanced, and the **Z**-homomorphisms are A-homomorphisms.

We now translate the preceding remarks into the language of categories and functors.

For a fixed ring A, we form a category C whose objects are ordered pairs (X,Y) (X a right A-module, Y a left A-module) and whose morphisms $(X,Y) \mapsto (X',Y')$ are ordered pairs (α,β) of A-homomorphisms ($\alpha: X \to X'$, $\beta: Y \to Y'$), combined under componentwise composition. We define a functor $\otimes$ of C into the category of **Z**-modules as follows: With each object (X,Y) of C we associate the **Z**-module $X \otimes_A Y$; and with each morphism (α,β) of C we associate the **Z**-homomorphism $\alpha \otimes \beta: X \otimes_A Y \to X' \otimes_A Y'$ defined by $(\alpha \otimes \beta)(x \otimes y) = \alpha x \otimes \beta y$.

It is easy to verify that $\otimes$ is a covariant functor of C into the category of **Z**-modules. The **Z**-modules $X \otimes_A Y$ and the **Z**-homomorphisms $\alpha \otimes \beta$, as previously defined, are the images assigned by the functor $\otimes$ to the objects (X,Y) and to the morphisms (α,β), of the category C.

The following theorem expresses the behavior of the tensor product in relation to direct sums:

Theorem 4.7. *Let A be a ring, Y a left A-module, and X a right A-module equal to a direct sum of a family $\{X_i\}_{i \in J}$ of right A-modules. Then the* **Z**-*module $X \otimes_A Y$ is a direct sum of the family $\{X_i \otimes_A Y\}_{i \in J}$ of* **Z**-*modules. (If A is commutative, then the A-module $X \otimes_A Y$ is a direct sum of the family $\{X_i \otimes_A Y\}_{i \in J}$ of A-modules.)*

PROOF. By Chapter 1, Theorem 9.6b, there is a family $\{\pi_i\}_{i \in J}$ of A-homomorphisms, $\pi_i: X \to X_i$, and a family $\{\eta_i\}_{i \in J}$ of A-homomorphisms, $\eta_i: X_i \to X$, such that

1. $\pi_i \eta_i = \iota_{X_i}$ for each $i \in J$.
2. $\pi_i \eta_j = 0_{X_j \to X_i}$ for $i \neq j$.

3. For each $x \in X$, $\pi_i x = 0_i$ for all but finitely many $i \in J$, and $\sum_{i \in J} \eta_i \pi_i(x) = x$.

Let $\bar{\pi}_i = \pi_i \otimes \iota_Y$, $\bar{\eta}_i = \eta_i \otimes \iota_Y$, for each $i \in J$. Then $\bar{\pi}_i\colon X \otimes_A Y \to X_i \otimes_A Y$ and $\bar{\eta}_i\colon X_i \otimes_A Y \to X \otimes_A Y$ are **Z**-homomorphisms satisfying 1, 2, and 3.

1. For each $x_i \in X_i$, $y \in Y$, $\bar{\pi}_i \bar{\eta}_i(x_i \otimes y) = \bar{\pi}_i \bar{\eta}_j x_i \otimes y = x_i \otimes y$. Hence $\bar{\pi}_i \bar{\eta}_i = \iota_{X_i \otimes Y}$.

2. For each $x_j \in X_j$, $y \in Y$, $i \neq j$, $\pi_i \eta_j(x_j \otimes y) = \pi_i \eta_j x_j \otimes y = 0_i \otimes y = 0_{X_i \otimes Y}$. Hence $\bar{\pi}_i \bar{\eta}_j = 0_{X_j \otimes Y \to X_i \otimes Y}$.

3. If $x \in X$, $y \in Y$, then for all but finitely many $i \in J$, $\bar{\pi}_i(x \otimes y) = (\pi_i \otimes \iota_Y)(x \otimes y) = \pi_i x \otimes y = 0 \otimes y = 0$ in $X_i \otimes_A Y$; and $\sum_{i \in J} \bar{\eta}_i \bar{\pi}_i(x \otimes y) = \sum_{i \in J} \eta_i \pi_i x \otimes y = x \otimes y$.

Since every element $t \in X \otimes_A Y$ is a finite sum of elements of form $x \otimes y (x \in X, y \in Y)$, it follows that for each $t \in X \otimes_A Y$, $\bar{\pi}_i t = 0$ for all but finitely many $i \in J$, and $\sum_{i \in J} \bar{\eta}_i \bar{\pi}_i(t) = t$. By Chapter 1, Theorem 9.6b, $X \otimes_A Y$ is a direct sum of $\{X_i \otimes_A Y\}_{i \in J}$. If A is commutative, the $\bar{\pi}_i$ and $\bar{\eta}_i$ are A-homomorphisms, and the A-module $X \otimes_A Y$ is a direct sum of the A-modules $X_i \otimes_A Y$. ∎

We employ the techniques of Theorems 4.6 and 4.7 to "lift" a free module over a commutative ring A to a free module over a commutative ring B containing A as a subring.

Theorem 4.8. *Let B be a commutative ring with identity and let A be a subring of B with the same identity. If X is a free A-module with basis $\{x_i\}_{i \in J}$, then $B \otimes_A X$ is a free B-module with basis $\{1_B \otimes x_i\}_{i \in J}$. The A-module X is A-isomorphic to a submodule of $B \otimes_A X$, considered as an A-module.*

PROOF. Since A is a subring of B, B is a (B,A)-bimodule and $B \otimes_A X$ is a B-module. For each $i \in J$, let T_i be the B-submodule of $B \otimes_A X$ generated by $1_B \otimes x_i$, and let X_i be the A-submodule Ax_i of the A-module X. Then $X = \bigoplus_{i \in J} X_i$, and there are A-epimorphisms $\pi_i\colon X \to X_i$ such that, for η_i the canonical injections (A-monomorphisms), $\eta_i\colon X_i \to X$:

1. $\pi_i \eta_i = \iota_{X_i}$ for each $i \in J$.
2. $\pi_i \eta_j = 0_{X_j \to X_i}$ for $i \neq j$.
3. For each $x \in X$, $\pi_i x = 0_i$ for all but finitely many $i \in J$, and $\sum_{i \in J} \eta_i \pi_i(x) = x$.

For each $i \in J$, $\bar{\pi}_i = \iota_B \otimes \pi_i$ is a B-epimorphism of $B \otimes_A X$ onto T_i, and $\bar{\eta}_i = \iota_B \otimes \eta_i$ is a B-monomorphism equal to the canonical injection of T_i into $B \otimes_A X$. As in the proof of Theorem 4.7, it is easily checked that the families $\{\bar{\pi}_i\}_{i \in J}$ and $\{\bar{\eta}_i\}_{i \in J}$ satisfy 1, 2, and 3.

By Chapter 1, Theorem 9.6, $B \otimes_A X = \bigoplus_{i \in J} T_i$. For each $i \in J$, T_i is B-isomorphic to $B \otimes_A Ax_i$ and there is a B-isomorphism $\mu\colon T_i \to B$ such that

$\mu(b \otimes x_i) = b$. Hence, for each $i \in J$, T_i is a one-dimensional B-module generated by $1 \otimes x_i$, and $B \otimes_A X$ is a free B-module with basis $\{1_B \otimes x_i\}_{i \in J}$.

$B \otimes_A X$ may also be regarded as an A-module. The map $\gamma: x \mapsto 1_B \otimes x$ is an A-monomorphism of X into $B \otimes_A X$. It is clear that γ is an A-homomorphism. We show that γ is a monomorphism. Suppose $1_B \otimes x = 0$ for some $x \in X$. If $x = \sum_{j=1}^{n} c_j x_j$ $(c_j \in A, n \in \mathbf{N}')$, then $1_B \otimes x = \sum_{j=1}^{n} c_j(1_B \otimes x_j) = 0$. Since the $1_B \otimes x_j$ form a B-free set, they certainly form an A-free set. Hence $c_j = 0$ for each $j = 1, \ldots, n$, and $x = 0$. ▮

In the following, we investigate the action of the functor $\otimes$ on exact sequences.

Theorem 4.9. *Let X, X', X'' be right A-modules and let Y be a left A-module. Suppose*

$$X' \xrightarrow{\mu} X \xrightarrow{\nu} X'' \longrightarrow 0 \tag{1}$$

is an exact sequence of A-homomorphisms and set $\bar{\mu} = \mu \otimes \iota_Y$, $\bar{\nu} = \nu \otimes \iota_Y$. Then

$$X' \otimes_A Y \xrightarrow{\bar{\mu}} X \otimes_A Y \xrightarrow{\bar{\nu}} X'' \otimes_A Y \longrightarrow 0 \tag{2}$$

is an exact sequence of $\mathbf{Z}$-homomorphisms. Conversely, if (2) *is exact for all left A-modules Y, then* (1) *is exact.*

PROOF. Since (1) is exact, $\nu\mu = 0$; hence $\bar{\nu}\bar{\mu} = (\nu \otimes \iota_Y)(\mu \otimes \iota_Y) = \nu\mu \otimes \iota_Y = 0$ and $\operatorname{Im} \bar{\mu} \subset \operatorname{Ker} \bar{\nu}$. Let $\gamma: X \otimes_A Y \to (X \otimes_A Y)/\operatorname{Im} \bar{\mu}$ be the natural $\mathbf{Z}$-homomorphism with respect to $\operatorname{Im} \bar{\mu}$. By Chapter 1, Theorem 4.5, there is a unique $\mathbf{Z}$-homomorphism $\varphi: (X \otimes_A Y)/\operatorname{Im} \bar{\mu} \to X'' \otimes_A Y$ such that $\varphi\gamma = \bar{\nu}$. To prove that $\operatorname{Im} \bar{\mu} = \operatorname{Ker} \bar{\nu}$, we need only verify that φ is an isomorphism (Chapter 1, Theorem 4.5), i.e., that φ has a two-sided inverse. We first define a balanced map, β, of $X'' \times Y$ into $(X \otimes_A Y)/\operatorname{Im} \bar{\mu}$: If $(x'', y) \in X'' \times Y$, let $\beta(x'', y) = \gamma(x \otimes y)$, where x is chosen from $\overset{-1}{\nu}(x'')$. [Since ν is surjective, $\overset{-1}{\nu}(x'') \neq \varnothing$ for all $x'' \in X''$.] If $x_1, x_2 \in X$, $y \in Y$, and $\nu x_1 = \nu x_2$, then $x_1 - x_2 \in \operatorname{Ker} \nu = \operatorname{Im} \mu$, hence $(x_1 - x_2) \otimes y \in \operatorname{Im} \bar{\mu}$, and therefore $\gamma(x_1 \otimes y) = \gamma(x_2 \otimes y)$. Thus, $\beta: (x'', y) \mapsto \gamma(x \otimes y)$ is a map. It now follows easily that β is balanced. Hence there is a unique $\mathbf{Z}$-homomorphism $\psi: X'' \otimes_A Y \to (X \otimes_A Y)/\operatorname{Im} \bar{\mu}$ such that $\psi(x'' \otimes y) = \beta(x'', y) = \gamma(x \otimes y)$ for each $x'' \in X''$ $y \in Y$, and all $x \in \overset{-1}{\nu}(x'')$. But then $\varphi\psi(x'' \otimes y) = \varphi\gamma(x \otimes y) = \bar{\nu}(x \otimes y) = (\nu x \otimes y) = x'' \otimes y$ for each $x'' \in X''$, $y \in Y$, $x \in \overset{-1}{\nu}(x'')$, and $\psi\varphi(\gamma(x \otimes y)) =$

$\psi\bar{\nu}(x \otimes y) = \psi(\nu x \otimes y) = \gamma(x \otimes y)$, for each $x \in X$, $y \in Y$. Since every element of $X'' \otimes_A Y$ is a sum of elements $x'' \otimes y$ ($x'' \in X, y \in Y$), and every element of $(X \otimes_A Y)/\text{Im}\,\bar{\mu}$ is a sum of elements $\gamma(x \otimes y)$ ($x \in X, y \in Y$), it follows that $\varphi\psi = \iota_{X'' \otimes_A Y}$ and $\psi\varphi = \iota_{(X \otimes_A Y)/\text{Im}\,\bar{\mu}}$. Thus, $\varphi: (X \otimes_A Y)/\text{Im}\,\bar{\mu} \to X'' \otimes Y$ is a $\mathbf{Z}$-isomorphism, as required. We conclude that $\text{Im}\,\bar{\mu} = \text{Ker}\,\bar{\nu}$. Finally, the $\mathbf{Z}$-homomorphism $\bar{\nu}$ is clearly surjective, since ν is surjective. It follows that (2) is exact. Conversely, if (2) is exact for all left A-modules Y, we need only let $Y = A_l$ and use Theorem 4.6 to infer that (1) is exact. ▌

Corollary. *If X', X, X'' are left A-modules,*

(3) $$X' \xrightarrow{\mu} X \xrightarrow{\nu} X'' \longrightarrow 0$$

is an exact sequence of A-homomorphisms, and Y is a right A-module, then the corresponding sequence of $\mathbf{Z}$-homomorphisms

(4) $$Y \otimes_A X' \xrightarrow{\bar{\mu}} Y \otimes_A X \xrightarrow{\bar{\nu}} Y \otimes_A X'' \longrightarrow 0$$

($\bar{\mu} = \iota_Y \otimes \mu, \bar{\nu} = \iota_Y \otimes \nu$) *is exact. Conversely, if* (4) *is exact for all right A-Modules Y, then* (3) *is exact.* □

REMARK. If

(1) $$0 \longrightarrow X' \xrightarrow{\mu} X \xrightarrow{\nu} X'' \longrightarrow 0$$

is an exact sequence of A-homomorphisms (X', X, X'' right A-modules), and Y is a left A-module, then the corresponding sequence of $\mathbf{Z}$-homomorphisms,

(2) $$0 \longrightarrow X' \otimes Y \xrightarrow{\bar{\mu}} X \otimes Y \xrightarrow{\bar{\nu}} X'' \otimes Y \longrightarrow 0$$

($\bar{\mu} = \mu \otimes \iota_Y, \bar{\nu} = \nu \otimes \iota_Y$), need not be exact. For example, let $A = \mathbf{Z}$, $X' = n\mathbf{Z}$, $X = \mathbf{Z}$, $Y = X/n\mathbf{Z}$ (n a positive integer), and let μ be the inclusion map of X' in X. (The choice of ν and X'' is immaterial.) Then $\bar{\mu} = \mu \otimes \iota_Y$ is not a monomorphism. For, $\text{Im}\,\bar{\mu}$ is generated by the elements $\bar{\mu}(x' \otimes y) = nx \otimes y = x \otimes ny = x' \otimes 0 = 0$ ($x' = nx \in X'$, $x \in X$, $y \in Y$); hence $\text{Im}\,\bar{\mu} = 0$. But $X' \otimes Y$ is not the 0-module, since X' is isomorphic to X, hence $X' \otimes Y$ is isomorphic to $X \otimes Y$, which, by Theorem 4.6, is isomorphic to Y. Thus, $\bar{\mu}$ is not injective. A left A-module Y with the property that, for each exact sequence of form (1), the corresponding sequence (2) is also exact is known as a "flat" left A-module. [A right A-module Y is "flat" if, for each exact sequence of form (3) (see the corollary of Theorem 4.9), the corresponding sequence (4) is also exact.] Flat modules bear a similar relationship to the tensor product as injective and projective modules bear to Hom.

We now investigate further the relationship between the functors $\otimes$ and Hom. On page 188 we discussed the **Z**-homomorphism, λ, of $\text{Hom}_A(X,X') \otimes_A \text{Hom}_A(Y,Y')$ into $\text{Hom}_{\mathbf{Z}}(X \otimes_A Y, X' \otimes_A Y')$ which sends $\alpha \otimes \beta$ to $\alpha \otimes \beta$, i.e., to the mapping $\mu_{\alpha,\beta}: (x \otimes y) \mapsto \alpha x \otimes \beta y$. If A is commutative, $\text{Hom}_A(X,X') \otimes_A \text{Hom}_A(Y,Y')$ and $\text{Hom}_A(X \otimes_A Y, X' \otimes_A Y')$, are A-modules, $\text{Im}\,\lambda = \text{Hom}_A(X \otimes_A Y, X' \otimes_A Y')$, and λ "is" an A-homomorphism.

In the following theorem, we confine ourselves to the commutative case:

Theorem 4.10. *Let A be a commutative ring, and let X, Y, M be A-modules. Then the following structures are isomorphic A-modules:*

$\text{Hom}_A(X \otimes_A Y, M)$,

$\text{Hom}_A(Y, \text{Hom}_A(X,M))$,

$\text{Hom}_A(X, \text{Hom}_A(Y,M))$,

$\text{Bil}_A(X, Y; M)$, *the set of all A-bilinear maps of $X \times Y$ into M.*

PROOF. Since A is commutative, the four structures are defined, and each of them is an A-module.

(1) $$\text{Bil}_A(X,Y;M) \cong \text{Hom}_A(X \otimes Y, M).$$

To each $\alpha \in \text{Bil}_A(X,Y;M)$, associate the induced A-homomorphism $\mu_\alpha: X \otimes_A Y \to M$ such that $\alpha(x,y) = \mu_\alpha(x \otimes y)$. By the uniqueness requirement in Definition 4.1, $\alpha \mapsto \mu_\alpha$ defines a map. Each $\alpha \in \text{Bil}_A(X,Y;M)$ is completely determined by its induced map μ_α; i.e., $\alpha \mapsto \mu_\alpha$ is injective. Since, for each $\mu \in \text{Hom}_A(X \otimes_A Y, M)$, we can define an A-bilinear map $\alpha: X \times Y \to X \otimes_A Y$ such that $\alpha(x,y) = \mu(x \otimes y) = \mu_\alpha(x \otimes y)$ for each $(x,y) \in X \times Y$, $\alpha \mapsto \mu_\alpha$ is surjective. Since A is commutative, $\alpha \mapsto \mu_\alpha$ is an A-isomorphism of $\text{Bil}_A(X,Y;M)$ onto $\text{Hom}_A(X \otimes_A Y, M)$.

(2) $$\text{Bil}_A(X,Y;M) \cong \text{Hom}_A(X, \text{Hom}_A(Y,M)).$$

For each $\alpha \in \text{Bil}_A(X,Y;M)$, let $\alpha_x: Y \to M$ be the A-homomorphism defined by

$$\alpha_x(y) = \alpha(x,y) \qquad (y \in Y),$$

and let $\beta_\alpha: X \to \text{Hom}_A(Y,M)$ be the A-homomorphism defined by

$$\beta_\alpha(x) = \alpha_x \qquad (x \in X).$$

Then $\alpha \mapsto \beta_\alpha$ is an A-homomorphism of $\mathrm{Bil}_A(X,Y;M)$ into

$$\mathrm{Hom}_A(X, \mathrm{Hom}_A(Y,M)).$$

If $\beta_\alpha = \beta_{\bar{\alpha}}(\alpha, \bar{\alpha} \in \mathrm{Bil}_A(X,Y;M))$, then $\alpha_x = \bar{\alpha}_x$ for each $x \in X$, whence $\alpha(x,y) = \alpha_x(y) = \bar{\alpha}_x(y) = \bar{\alpha}(x,y)$ for each $(x,y) \in X \times Y$, and $\alpha = \bar{\alpha}$. Thus, $\alpha \mapsto \beta_\alpha$ is injective. For each $\beta \in \mathrm{Hom}_A(X, \mathrm{Hom}_A(Y,M))$, there is an $\alpha \in \mathrm{Bil}_A(X,Y;M)$ such that $\alpha_x = \beta(x) = \beta_\alpha(x)$ for each $x \in X$. Thus, $\alpha \mapsto \beta_\alpha$ is surjective, and is therefore an A-isomorphism.

3. From (1) and (2) it follows that

$$\mathrm{Hom}_A(X \otimes_A Y, M),$$
$$\mathrm{Bil}_A(X,Y;M),$$
$$\mathrm{Hom}_A(X, \mathrm{Hom}_A(Y,M))$$

are isomorphic. By symmetry, $\mathrm{Hom}_A(Y, \mathrm{Hom}_A(X,M))$ is isomorphic to $\mathrm{Hom}_A(Y \otimes_A X, M)$. Since A is commutative, $X \otimes_A Y$ is isomorphic to $Y \otimes_A X$ (Corollary of Theorem 4.5); hence $\mathrm{Hom}_A(X \otimes_A Y, M)$ is isomorphic to $\mathrm{Hom}_A(Y \otimes_A X, M)$. But then $\mathrm{Hom}_A(Y, \mathrm{Hom}_A(X,M))$ is isomorphic to each of the other three structures, as required. ∎

5. Determinant; Dual Module; Trace

If A is a commutative ring, the definition of the tensor product is easily extended to apply to arbitrary finite families of A-modules: If $\{X_i\}_{i=1}^n$ is a family of A-modules, T is an A-module and $\theta: X_1 \times \cdots \times X_n \to T$ an A-n-linear map, then $\langle T, \theta \rangle$ is a tensor product of $\{X_i\}_{i=1}^n$ if :

$(\dagger)_n$ For each A-module Y, and each A-n-linear map $\gamma: X_1 \times \cdots \times X_n \to Y$, there is a unique A-homomorphism $\mu: T \to Y$ such that $\mu\theta = \gamma$.

The uniqueness and existence proofs carry over in an obvious way. We write $x_1 \otimes \cdots \otimes x_n$ for $\theta(x_1, \ldots, x_n)$ $(x_i \in X_i)$.

As an application of the "n-fold tensor product," we now define the determinant of a linear map.

Let A be a commutative ring with identity 1, and with the property $a + a \neq 0$ for each $a \neq 0$ in A. (The case where $a + a$ may be zero for some nonzero $a \in A$ is treated in Exercise 5.1.) Let X be a free A-module of dimension n, and let τ be a linear transformation on X; i.e., $\tau \in \mathrm{Hom}_A(X,X)$. Form $T = X \otimes_A \cdots \otimes_A X$, the n-fold tensor product, over A, of n copies of

X. Let S_n be the symmetric group of degree n. Make T into an S_n-group by defining

$$\sigma(x_1 \otimes \cdots \otimes x_n) = x_{\sigma 1} \otimes \cdots \otimes x_{\sigma n}$$

($x_1 \otimes \cdots \otimes x_n \in T$, $\sigma \in S_n$) and make $\langle A,+\rangle$ into an S_n-group by defining $\sigma a = a$ for σ even, $\sigma a = -a$ for σ odd ($a \in A$, $\sigma \in S_n$). An A-homomorphism $\alpha: T \to A_l$ is an S_n-homomorphism provided that, for each $x_1 \otimes \cdots \otimes x_n \in T$, $\sigma \in S_n$,

$$\alpha(x_1 \otimes \cdots \otimes x_n) = \alpha(x_{\sigma 1} \otimes \cdots \otimes x_{\sigma n}) \qquad \text{for } \sigma \text{ even},$$

$$\alpha(x_1 \otimes \cdots \otimes x_n) = -\alpha(x_{\sigma 1} \otimes \cdots \otimes x_{\sigma n}) \qquad \text{for } \sigma \text{ odd}.$$

We write $\mathrm{Hom}_{S_n,A}(T,A_l)$ for the set of all those A-homomorphisms of T into A_l which are also S_n-homomorphisms.

Theorem 5.1. *Let A be a commutative ring with identity* 1 *($a + a \neq 0$ for $a \neq 0$ in A), and let X be an n-dimensional A-module. Then*

a. *$\mathrm{Hom}_{S_n,A}(T,A_l)$ is a one-dimensional A-module, isomorphic to A_l.*

b. *For each $\tau \in \mathrm{End}_A(X)$, there is a unique element $d_\tau \in A$ such that*

$$\alpha(\tau x_1 \otimes \cdots \otimes \tau x_n) = d_\tau \alpha(x_1 \otimes \cdots \otimes x_n)$$

for each $x_1 \otimes \cdots \otimes x_n \in T$, $\alpha \in \mathrm{Hom}_{S_n,A}(T,A_l)$.

c. *$\tau \mapsto d_\tau$ is a multiplicative homomorphism of $\mathrm{End}_A(X)$ into A.*

PROOF.

a. $\mathrm{Hom}_{S_n,A}(T,A_l)$ is obviously an A-module. Let $\{e_i\}_{i=1}^n$ be a basis for X. Then the elements $e_{i_1} \otimes \cdots \otimes e_{i_n}$ ($1 \leq i_j \leq n$) form a basis for the A-module T. There is a unique map $\eta \in \mathrm{Hom}_{S_n,A}(T,A_l)$ such that

$$\eta(e_1 \otimes e_2 \otimes \cdots \otimes e_n) = 1.$$

Clearly, $\eta(e_{i_1} \otimes \cdots \otimes e_{i_n}) = 0$ if $i_j = i_k$ for some $j \neq k$:

$$\eta(e_{\sigma 1} \otimes \cdots \otimes e_{\sigma n}) = \left\{\begin{array}{ll} 1 & \text{if } \sigma \text{ is even} \\ -1 & \text{if } \sigma \text{ is odd} \end{array}\right\} \sigma \in S_n.$$

If $\alpha \in \mathrm{Hom}_{S_n,A}(T,A_l)$, then (since $a \neq -a$ for $a \neq 0$ in A), $\alpha(e_{i_1} \otimes \cdots \otimes e_{i_n}) = 0$ if $i_j = i_k$ for some $j \neq k$. If $\sigma \in S_n$ and $\alpha(e_1 \otimes \cdots \otimes e_n) = a$, then

$$\alpha(e_{\sigma 1} \otimes \cdots \otimes e_{\sigma n}) = \begin{cases} a & \text{if } \sigma \text{ is even}, \\ -a & \text{if } \sigma \text{ is odd}. \end{cases}$$

But then $\alpha = a\eta$. Thus, $\{\eta\}$ serves as a basis for $\text{Hom}_{S_n,A}(T,A_l)$, and $\text{Hom}_{S_n,A}(T,A_l)$ is a one-dimensional A-module. The A-homomorphism determined by $\eta \mapsto 1$ is an isomorphism of $\text{Hom}_{S_n,A}(T,A_l)$ onto A_l.

b. If τ is a linear transformation on X, i.e., $\tau \in \text{Hom}_A(X,X)$, then the correspondence

$$\mu_\tau\colon x_1 \otimes \cdots \otimes x_n \mapsto \tau x_1 \otimes \cdots \otimes \tau x_n$$

determines an A-endomorphism of T which commutes with each $\sigma \in S_n$. But then

$$\alpha \mapsto \alpha\mu_\tau \qquad (\alpha \in \text{Hom}_{S_n,A}(T,A_l))$$

is an A-homomorphism of $\text{Hom}_{S_n,A}(T,A_l)$. Since $\text{Hom}_{S_n,A}(T,A_l)$ is a one-dimensional A-module, there is a unique element $d_\tau \in A$ such that $\alpha\mu_\tau = d_\tau\alpha$ for each $\alpha \in \text{Hom}_{S_n,A}(T,A_l)$, i.e., $\alpha(\tau x_1 \otimes \cdots \otimes \tau x_n) = d_\tau\alpha(x_1 \otimes \cdots \otimes x_n)$ for each $x_1 \otimes \cdots \otimes x_n \in T$.

c. For each $\tau \in \text{End}_A(X)$, the element $d_\tau \in A$ is uniquely determined. If $\tau_1,\tau_2 \in \text{End}_A(X)$, then $\mu_{\tau_1\tau_2} = \mu_{\tau_1}\mu_{\tau_2}$, hence $d_{\tau_1\tau_2} = d_{\tau_1}\,d_{\tau_2}$. Thus $\tau \mapsto d_\tau$ is a multiplicative homomorphism of $\text{End}_A(X)$ into A. ▌

Definition 5.1. If X is an n-dimensional A-module over a commutative ring A with identity ($a + a \neq 0$ for $a \neq 0$ in A) and τ is an A-linear map of X, then the element $d_\tau \in A$ corresponding to τ is *the determinant*, det τ, of τ. ///

Corollary 1. *If* $\{e_i\}_{i=1}^n$ *is a basis for* X *and* $\eta\colon T \to A_l$ *is the A-homomorphism in* $\text{Hom}_{S_n,A}(T,A_l)$ *determined by*

$$\eta(e_1 \otimes \cdots \otimes e_n) = 1,$$

then, for each $\tau \in \text{Hom}_A(X,X)$,

$$\det \tau = \eta(\tau e_1 \otimes \cdots \otimes \tau e_n).$$

PROOF. This follows immediately from Theorem 5.1b. ▌

Definition 5.2. Let X be a set, α a map of $X \times \cdots \times X$ into A, where A is a ring with identity. Then α is *symmetric* if $\alpha(x_{\sigma 1},\ldots,x_{\sigma n}) = \alpha(x_1,\ldots,x_n)$ for all $\sigma \in S_n$, $(x_1,\ldots,x_n) \in X \times \cdots \times X$; and α is *alternating* if for $\sigma \in S_n$, $(x_1,\ldots,x_n) \in X \times \cdots \times X$, $\alpha(x_{\sigma 1},\ldots,x_{\sigma n}) = s\alpha(x_1,\ldots,x_n)$, where $s = 1$ if σ is even $s = -1$ if σ is odd. ///

Corollary 2. *Let X be an n-dimensional A-module (A a commutative ring with identity, $a + a \neq 0$ for $a \neq 0$ in A), and let $\mathscr{B} = \{e_i\}_{i=1}^n$ be a basis for X. Then $(\tau e_1,\ldots,\tau e_n) \mapsto \det \tau$ ($\tau \in \operatorname{End}_A(X)$) is an A-n-linear alternating map of the Cartesian product $X \times \cdots \times X$ into A.*

PROOF. For each n-tuple $(x_1,\ldots,x_n)$ in $X \times \cdots \times X$, there is a unique linear map $\tau \in \operatorname{End}_A(X)$ such that $x_i = \tau e_i$ for each $i = 1,\ldots, n$. Hence

$$\gamma_{\mathscr{B}}: (\tau e_1,\ldots,\tau e_n) \mapsto \det \tau$$

is a map of $X \times \cdots \times X$ into A_l. Let $\eta: T \to A_l$ be defined as in Corollary 1. Since $(\tau e_1,\ldots,\tau e_n) \mapsto \tau e_1 \otimes \cdots \otimes \tau e_n$ is A-n-linear and symmetric, and $\eta \in \operatorname{Hom}_{A,S_n}(T,A_l)$, the composite map $\gamma_{\mathscr{B}}$ is A-n-linear and alternating. ▌

We illustrate Corollary 1 in the following example:

Example. Let X be a two-dimensional vector space over $\mathbf{Q}$. Let $\{e_i\}_{i=1,2}$ be a basis for X, and let τ be the linear transformation on X defined by

$$\tau e_1 = a_{11}e_1 + a_{12}e_2,$$
$$\tau e_2 = a_{21}e_1 + a_{22}e_2.$$

If $\eta \in \operatorname{Hom}_{S_n,\mathbf{Q}}(X \otimes_{\mathbf{Q}} X, \mathbf{Q})$ maps $e_1 \otimes e_2$ to 1, then

$$\eta(e_2 \otimes e_1) = -1,$$
$$\eta(e_1 \otimes e_1) = \eta(e_2 \otimes e_2) = 0,$$

$$\begin{aligned} \det \tau &= \eta(\tau e_1 \otimes \tau e_2) = \eta((a_{11}e_1 + a_{12}e_2) \otimes (a_{21}e_1 + a_{22}e_2)) \\ &= a_{11}a_{21}\eta(e_1 \otimes e_1) + a_{12}a_{21}\eta(e_2 \otimes e_1) \\ &\quad + a_{11}a_{22}\eta(e_1 \otimes e_2) + a_{12}a_{22}\eta(e_2 \otimes e_2) \\ &= a_{11}a_{22} - a_{12}a_{21}. \end{aligned}$$

We leave to the reader (Exercise 5.2) the verification of the general computational rule for determinants: If $\{e_i\}_{i=1}^n$ is a basis for the n-dimensional A-module X ($a + a \neq 0$ for $a \neq 0$ in A), $\tau \in \operatorname{End}_A(X,X)$, $\tau e_i = \sum_j a_{ij}e_j$ ($i = 1,\ldots,n$), then

(1) $$\det \tau = \sum_{\sigma \in S_n} s(\sigma)a_{1,\sigma 1}\cdots a_{n,\sigma n},$$

where $s(\sigma) = 1$ for σ even, $s(\sigma) = -1$ for σ odd. The proof is a straightforward generalization of our example for the case $n = 2$.

In the final paragraphs of this chapter we shall introduce another homomorphism which associates with each linear transformation its "trace." First, we define the dual of a module. Let A be a ring with identity, not necessarily commutative. If X is a left A-module, then $\mathrm{Hom}_A(X,A_l)$ can be made into a right A-module by defining αa to be the A-homomorphism $x \mapsto (\alpha x)a$ for each $\alpha \in \mathrm{Hom}_A(X,A_l)$, each $a \in A$. Note that, for $a,b \in A$, $\alpha \in \mathrm{Hom}_A(X,A_l)$, $x \in X$,

$$\alpha(ab)(x) = (\alpha x)(ab) = ((\alpha x)a)b = [(\alpha a(x)]b = [(\alpha a)b](x).$$

Thus, $\alpha(ab) = (\alpha a)b$. Similarly, for X a right A-module, $\mathrm{Hom}_A(X,A_r)$ can be made into a left A-module.

Definition 5.3. If X is a left (right) A-module, then the right (left) A-module $\mathrm{Hom}_A(X,A_l)$ ($\mathrm{Hom}_A(X,A_r)$) is the *dual module*, X^*, of X. The elements of X^* are the (A-)*linear functionals* on X. ///

If X is a left A-module, $x \in X$, $x^* \in X^*$, we denote by $\langle x,x^*\rangle$ the function value $x^*(x) \in A$. The following formulas are readily verified:

(1) $$\langle x + y, x^*\rangle = \langle x,x^*\rangle + \langle y,x^*\rangle,$$

(2) $$\langle x, x^* + y^*\rangle = \langle x,x^*\rangle + \langle x,y^*\rangle,$$

(3) $$\langle ax,x^*\rangle = a\langle x,x^*\rangle,$$

(4) $$\langle x,x^*a\rangle = \langle x,x^*\rangle a$$

($x,y \in X$, $x^*, y^* \in X^*$, $a \in A$).

[If X is a right A-module, we write $\langle x^*,x\rangle$ for $x^*(x)$. In this case, we have $\langle x^*,xa\rangle = \langle x^*,x\rangle a$ and $\langle ax^*,x\rangle = a\langle x^*,x\rangle$ in place of (3) and (4).]

Associated with each left A-module X is the map $\beta\colon X \times X^* \to A_l$ defined by

$$\beta(x,x^*) = \langle x,x^*\rangle.$$

By virtue of formulas (1) through (4), β is an A-bilinear map of $X \times X^*$ into A_l. We refer to β as the canonical A-bilinear map of $X \times X^*$ into A_l. For each linear functional $x^* \in X^*$, and each $x \in X$, we have $x^*(x) = \beta(x,x^*)$.

Suppose now that X, Y are left A-modules. If $\mu: X \to Y$ is an A-homomorphism, then the mapping $\mathrm{Hom}(\mu,\iota_{A_l})$: $y^* \mapsto y^*\mu$ of Y^* into X^* is an A-homomorphism, since $(y^*\mu)a = y^*(\mu a)$ for each $a \in A$.

$$\begin{array}{ccc} Y & \xrightarrow{\;y^*\;} & A_l \\ {\scriptstyle\mu}\uparrow & & \downarrow{\scriptstyle\iota_{A_l}} \\ X & \xrightarrow[\;y^*\mu\;]{} & A_l \end{array}$$

Definition 5.4. If X, Y are left A-modules and $\mu \in \mathrm{Hom}_A(X, Y)$, then the A-homomorphism $\mathrm{Hom}(\mu,\iota_{A_l})$: $y^* \mapsto y^*\mu$ of the right A-module Y^* into the right A-module X^* is called the *transpose*, μ^T, of μ. ///

It follows immediately from this definition that, for each $\mu \in \mathrm{Hom}_A(X, Y)$, μ^T is the A-homomorphism defined by

$$\langle \mu(x), y^* \rangle = \langle x, \mu^T(y^*) \rangle$$

for each $x \in X$, each $y^* \in Y^*$.

From the properties of the functor Hom, we deduce that, for X, Y, Z left A-modules,

$$(\mu_1 + \mu_2)^T = \mu_1^T + \mu_2^T$$

($\mu_1, \mu_2 \in \mathrm{Hom}_A(X, Y)$), and

$$(\mu\nu)^T = \nu^T\mu^T$$

($\mu \in \mathrm{Hom}_A(X, Y)$, $\nu \in \mathrm{Hom}_A(Y,Z)$). Suppose $X^* \neq 0$. Then, clearly, $(\iota_X)^T = \iota_{X^*}$. It follows that μ has a right (left) inverse if and only if μ^T has a left (right) inverse. In particular, μ is invertible if and only if μ^T is invertible; in this case, $(\mu^T)^{-1} = (\mu^{-1})^T$. The mapping $\mu \mapsto \mu^T$ is a monomorphism of the group $\mathrm{Aut}_A(X)$ into the group $\mathrm{Aut}_A(X^*)$.

If A is a ring with identity, X a free A-module with basis $\{e_i\}_{i\in J}$, then the functionals $\{e_j^*\}_{j\in J}$ defined by

$$e_j^*(e_i) = \langle e_i, e_j^* \rangle = \delta_{ij} \qquad \text{for each } i,j \in J \qquad \left(\delta_{ij} = \begin{cases} 0 & \text{for } i \neq j \\ 1 & \text{for } i = j \end{cases}\right)$$

form a free set in X^*. For, suppose

$$\sum_{h=1}^{n} e_j^* a_h = 0 \qquad (a_h \in A).$$

Then

$$\left(\sum_{h=1}^{n} e_{j_h}^* a_h\right)(e_i) = \sum_{h=1}^{n} a_h e_{j_h}^*(e_i) = \sum_{h=1}^{n} a_h \delta_{ij_h} = 0$$

for each $i \in J$. But then, setting i, in turn, equal to each of the j_h ($h = 1,\ldots,n$), we obtain $a_h = 0$ for each $h = 1,\ldots, n$.

In general, the functionals e_j^* ($j \in J$) need not form a basis for X^*—in fact, X^* need not be a free A-module (Exercise 5.3). For X finite dimensional, we have

Theorem 5.2. *If $\{e_i\}_{i=1}^n$ is a basis for an A-module X, then the functionals $e_j^* \in X^*$ defined by $e_j^*(e_i) = \delta_{ij}$ ($i,j = 1,\ldots,n$) form a basis for the dual A-module X^*.*

PROOF. By the remarks preceding the theorem, the e_j^* ($j = 1,\ldots,n$) form a free set in X^*. If $x^* \in X$, then for each $i = 1,\ldots, n$

$$x^*(e_i) = \sum_{j=1}^{n} e_j^*\langle e_j,x^*\rangle(e_i),$$

hence

$$x^* = \sum_{j=1}^{n} e_j^*\langle e_j,x^*\rangle.$$

Thus, $\{e_j^*\}_{j=1}^n$ is a basis for X^*. ∎

The basis $\{e_j^*\}_{j=1}^n$ for X^* is the *dual basis* corresponding to the basis $\{e_i\}_{i=1}^n$ for X.

Corollary 1. *Let A be a ring, X a left A-module of finite dimension n. Let $\{e_i\}_{i=1}^n$ be a basis for X, $\{e_i^*\}_{i=1}^n$ the dual basis for X^*. If $x = \sum_{i=1}^n a_i e_i \in X$ ($a_i \in A$), and $x^* = \sum_{j=1} e_j^* b_j \in X^*$ ($b_j \in A$), then*

$$\langle x,x^*\rangle = \sum_{i=1}^{n} a_i b_i.$$

PROOF.

$$\langle x,x^*\rangle = \sum_{j=1}^{n} e_j^* b_j\left(\sum_{i=1}^{n} a_i e_i\right) = \sum_{i,j=1}^{n} a_i\langle e_i,e_j^*\rangle b_j$$

$$= \sum_{i=1}^{n} a_i b_i. \quad ∎$$

Corollary 2. *If A is a commutative ring, X an A-module of finite dimension n, then X, X^*, and X^{**} are isomorphic A-modules. A particular isomorphism $\varphi: X \to X^{**}$ is given by $\varphi: x \mapsto \varphi_x$ $(x \in X)$, where $\varphi_x \in X^{**}$ is such that*

$$\varphi_x(x^*) = \langle x,x^* \rangle \tag{1}$$

for each $x^* \in X$.

PROOF. If $\{e_i\}_{i=1}^n$ is a basis for X, then (by Theorem 5.2) $\{e_i^*\}_{i=1}^n$ is a basis for X^*. Hence X^* is an n-dimensional A-module and we may, again, employ Theorem 5.2 to infer that $\{e_i^{**}\}_{i=1}^n$ is a basis for X^{**}, whence X^{**} is an n-dimensional A-module. It follows immediately that the three A-modules X, X^*, and X^{**} are isomorphic. We now produce the special isomorphism $\varphi: X \to X^{**}$, which satisfies (1) and is thus independent of the choice of bases.

For each $x \in X$, there is a unique mapping $\varphi_x: X^* \to A_l$ such that, for each $x^* \in X^*$, $\varphi_x(x^*) = \langle x,x^* \rangle$. It is easy to check that φ_x is an A-homomorphism; i.e., $\varphi_x \in X^{**}$ for each $x \in X$. The mapping $\varphi: x \mapsto \varphi_x$ is an A-homomorphism of X into X^{**}. Since φ maps any basis $\{e_i\}_{i=1}^n$ for X to the corresponding basis $\{e_i^{**}\}_{i=1}^n$ for X^{**}, φ is an isomorphism. ▮

If X is a vector space, not necessarily finite-dimensional, $\{e_i\}_{i \in J}$ a basis for X, then the free set $\{e_j^*\}_{j \in J}$ is contained in a basis for X^*, hence $\dim X^* \geq \dim X$. For examples where the strict inequality holds, see Exercise 5.4.

In Theorem 4.8 we discussed some homomorphisms relating $\otimes$ and Hom. We give here another such map which involves the dual of a module, and which will be useful to us in defining the trace of a linear transformation.

Theorem 5.3. *Let A be a commutative ring, and let X, Y be A-modules. Then*

a. *There is a unique A-homomorphism*

$$\gamma: X^* \otimes_A Y \to \mathrm{Hom}_A(X,Y)$$

such that $\gamma(x^* \otimes y) = \tau_{y,x^*}$, where τ_{y,x^*} is the A-linear map defined by

$$\tau_{y,x^*}(z) = \langle z,x^* \rangle y$$

for each $z \in X$ $(x^* \in X^*, y \in Y)$.

b. *If X, Y are A-modules of finite dimensions m and n, respectively, then $X^* \otimes_A Y$ and $\mathrm{Hom}_A(X,Y)$ are both mn-dimensional A-modules, hence isomorphic. In particular, the A-homomorphism γ defined in part* a *is an isomorphism.*

PROOF.

a. Since A is commutative, $X^* \otimes_A Y$ and $\mathrm{Hom}_A(X, Y)$ are both A-modules. It is easy to check that

$$(x^*, y) \mapsto \tau_{y,x^*}$$

is an A-bilinear map of the Cartesian product $X^* \times Y$ into the A-module $\mathrm{Hom}_A(X, Y)$. Hence there is a unique A-linear map $\gamma: X^* \otimes_A Y \to \mathrm{Hom}_A(X, Y)$ such that $\gamma(x^* \otimes y) = \tau_{y,x^*}$.

b. Let $\{e_i\}_{i=1}^m$ be a basis for X, $\{e_i^*\}_{i=1}^m$ the corresponding dual basis for X^*, and let $\{f_j\}_{j=1}^n$ be a basis for Y. A straightforward verification shows that the mn elements $e_i^* \otimes f_j$ $(i = 1,\ldots,m; j = 1,\ldots,n)$ form a basis for $X^* \otimes_A Y$ (Exercise 5.5), and the mn A-linear maps ε_{ij} $(i = 1,\ldots,m; j = 1,\ldots,n)$ of X into Y defined by

$$\varepsilon_{ij}(e_i) = f_j,$$
$$\varepsilon_{ij}(e_k) = 0 \qquad \text{for } k \neq i$$

form a basis for $\mathrm{Hom}_A(X, Y)$. Thus, $X^* \otimes_A Y$ and $\mathrm{Hom}_A(X, Y)$ are isomorphic A-modules of dimension mn. In particular, our homomorphism

$$\gamma: (x^* \otimes y) \mapsto \tau_{y,x^*}$$

is an isomorphism of $X^* \otimes_A Y$ onto $\mathrm{Hom}_A(X, Y)$. We prove this by exhibiting an inverse for γ. Let $\gamma': \mathrm{Hom}_A(X, Y) \to X^* \otimes_A Y$ be the A-homomorphism defined by

$$\gamma': \beta \mapsto \sum_{i=1}^{n} (e_i^* \otimes \beta e_i)$$

for each $\beta \in \mathrm{Hom}_A(X, Y)$. Then, for each $x^* \in X^*$, each $y \in Y$,

$$\gamma'\gamma(x^* \otimes y) = \gamma'\tau_{y,x^*} = \sum_{i=1}^{n} (e_i^* \otimes \langle e_i, x^* \rangle y)$$
$$= \sum_{i=1}^{n} e_i^* \langle e_i, x^* \rangle \otimes y = x^* \otimes y.$$

Thus, $\gamma'\gamma = \iota_{X^* \otimes Y}$. On the other hand, for each $\beta \in \mathrm{Hom}_A(X, Y)$,

$$\gamma\gamma'\beta = \gamma\left(\sum_{i=1}^{n} e_i^* \otimes \beta e_i\right) = \sum_{i=1}^{n} \tau_{\beta,e_i e_i^*} = \beta.$$

Thus, $\gamma\gamma' = \iota_{\mathrm{Hom}_A(X,Y)}$. It follows that γ and γ' are isomorphisms, with $\gamma' = \gamma^{-1}$. ∎

For X an n-dimensional A-module (A a commutative ring with identity) we have defined a multiplicative homomorphism of $\mathrm{End}_A(X)$ into A, which associates with each A-linear map τ on X its determinant, det τ.

We now define an A-homomorphism of $\mathrm{Hom}_A(X,X)$ into A_l, which associates with each A-linear map τ on X its "trace," tr τ.

Theorem 5.4. *Let X be an n-dimensional A-module (A commutative). Then there is a unique A-homomorphism β: $\mathrm{Hom}_A(X,X) \to A_l$ such that, for every basis $\{e_i\}_{i=1}^n$ of X,*

$$\beta(\tau) = \sum_{i=1}^{n} \langle \tau e_i, e_i^* \rangle,$$

where $\{e_i^*\}_{i=1}^n$ is the dual basis corresponding to $\{e_i\}_{i=1}^n$.

PROOF. By Theorem 5.3b, $X^* \otimes_A X$ and $\mathrm{Hom}_A(X,X)$ are isomorphic n^2-dimensional A-modules. We first define an A-homomorphism η: $X^* \otimes_A X \to A_l$, then combine it with the isomorphism γ^{-1} of Theorem 5.3b to produce the required homomorphism β.

The map of $X^* \times X$ into A_l defined by $(x^*,x) \mapsto \langle x,x^* \rangle$ is clearly A-bilinear. Hence there is a unique A-homomorphism η: $X^* \otimes_A X \to A_l$ such that $\eta(x^* \otimes x) = \langle x,x^* \rangle$ for each $x \in X$, $x^* \in X^*$.

Let $\beta = \eta\gamma^{-1}$, where γ: $X^* \otimes_A X \to \mathrm{Hom}_A(X,X)$ is the map defined in Theorem 5.3. Then β is an A-homomorphism of $\mathrm{Hom}_A(X,X)$ into A_l. If $\{e_i\}_{i=1}^n$ is a basis for X, $\{e_i^*\}_{i=1}^n$ the corresponding dual basis for X^*, then

$$\beta(\tau) = \eta\left(\sum_{i=1}^{n} (e_i^* \otimes \tau e_i)\right) = \sum_{i=1}^{n} \langle \tau e_i, e_i^* \rangle,$$

as required.

Now suppose that β': $\mathrm{Hom}_A(X,X) \to A$ is an A-homomorphism such that, for some particular basis $\{e_i\}_{i=1}^n$, $\beta'(\tau) = \sum_{i=1}^n \langle \tau e_i, e_i^* \rangle$ for each $\tau \in \mathrm{Hom}_A(X,X)$. Then for each i, j ($i = 1,\ldots,n; j = 1,\ldots,n$),

$$\beta'\gamma(e_i^* \otimes e_j) = \beta'\tau_{e_j,e_i^*} = \sum_{k=1}^{n} \langle \tau_{e\,,e_i} e_k, e_k^* \rangle$$

$$= \sum_{k=1}^{n} \langle \langle e_k, e_i^* \rangle e_j, e_k^* \rangle = \langle e_j, e_i^* \rangle = \eta(e_i^* \otimes e_j)$$

(where the notation is that of Theorem 5.3). But then $\beta'\gamma = \eta$, and $\beta' = \eta\gamma^{-1} = \beta$. This establishes the uniqueness claimed for β. ▮

Definition 5.5. For each $\tau \in \mathrm{Hom}_A(X,X)$ we refer to the element $\beta(\tau)$ as the *trace*, $\mathrm{tr}\,\tau$, of τ. ///

Corollary. *Let A be a commutative ring with identity, X an A-module. If $\tau \in \mathrm{Hom}_A(X,X)$ is given relative to a particular basis $\{e_i\}_{i=1}^n$ by*

$$\tau e_i = \sum_{j=1}^{n} a_{ij}e_j$$

for each $i = 1,\ldots,n$, then $\mathrm{tr}\,\tau = \sum_{i=1}^n a_{ii}$.

PROOF.
$$\mathrm{tr}\,\tau = \sum_{i=1}^{n} \langle \tau e_i, e_i^* \rangle = \sum_{i,j} \langle a_{ij}e_j, e_i^* \rangle = \sum_{i=1}^{n} a_{ii}.$$ ▮

The determinant and the trace of a particular linear transformation $\tau \in \mathrm{Hom}_A(X,X)$ may be computed with respect to any given basis, but they are both independent of the choice of basis; i.e., they are "invariants of τ with respect to change of basis." In Chapter 4 we consider the special case where X is a finite-dimensional vector space over a field, and we obtain sets of polynomial invariants for any linear transformation τ. The determinant and the trace of τ appear as (plus or minus) two of the coefficients of the "characteristic polynomial" of τ. (See Chapter 4, Theorem 4.2h, and Corollary of Theorem 4.2.)

Exercises

Section 1

1.1. (a) If $G = [a]$ is a finite cyclic group, then $\{a\}$ is a minimal generating set, but not a free set, for the $\mathbf{Z}$-module G.
(b) If G is the additive group of rationals, then for each $a \in G$ such that $a \neq 0$, $a \neq 1/k$ ($k \in \mathbf{Z}$), $\{a\}$ is a maximal free set, but not a generating set, for the $\mathbf{Z}$-module G.

1.2. Use the Jordan–Holder Theorem to prove: If a vector space X has a finite basis of n elements, then every basis of X has n elements.

1.3. Let X be an A-module with a countable basis $\{e_i\}_{i\in\mathbf{N}'}$ and let B be the set of all A-endomorphisms of X. Then B is a ring with identity ι_X. Prove: For every positive integer n, B_l has a basis of n elements.

(*Hint* (Bourbaki): $\{\iota_X\}$ forms a basis for B_l. Let α and β be the A-homomorphisms defined by

$$\left.\begin{array}{ll} \alpha e_{2n} = e_n, & \beta e_{2n} = 0 \\ \alpha e_{2n-1} = 0, & \beta e_{2n-1} = e_n \end{array}\right\} \text{ for each } n \in \mathbf{N}'.$$

Prove that $\{\alpha,\beta\}$ is a basis for X. Hence prove that B_l is a direct sum of n torsion-free cyclic submodules, for each positive integer n.)

1.4. Let A be a ring with identity, and let X be an A-module with an infinite, not necessarily countable, basis. Prove that the conclusions of Exercise 1.4 are valid for the endomorphism ring B of X.

1.5. If an A-module X (A a ring with identity) has one basis of n elements and another basis of $n + 1$ elements, then X has a basis of m elements for each $m \geq n$ ($m,n \in \mathbf{N}'$).

1.6. Let A be a ring with identity and let X be a free A-module of dimension n. Prove:

(a) If every free set of X of cardinality n is a basis for X, then every one-sided unit of $\operatorname{End}_A X$ is a unit.

(b) If every generating set of X of cardinality n is a basis of X, then every one-sided unit of $\operatorname{End}_A X$ is a unit.

1.7. If A is an integral domain, X an A-module, then the set of all torsion elements of X forms a submodule, $T(X)$, of X. The A-module $X/T(X)$ is torsion free. [We refer to $T(X)$ as the "torsion submodule" of X.]

1.8. Give an example of an A-module X, A commutative, such that the torsion elements of X do not form a submodule of X.

1.9. A ring A is (*left*) *dependent* if for each pair of elements $a,b \in A$, there are elements c, d, not both zero, such that $ca + db = 0$. Prove: If A is a dependent ring without zero divisors, then A_l has no proper direct summand (i.e., A_l is indecomposable).

1.10. If A is a dependent ring with identity, without zero divisors, then A is dimensional.

1.11. If A is a ring with identity, having no one-sided units, then A_l (A_r) does not have a basis of more than one element.

Section 2

2.1. Let A be an integral domain, X', X, X'' A-modules, and $\alpha: X' \to X$, $\beta: X \to X''$ A-homomorphisms. Denote by $T(X')$, $T(X)$, $T(X'')$ the torsion submodules of X', X, X'', respectively, and let $\alpha_T: T(X') \to T(X'')$, $\beta_T: T(X) \to T(X'')$ be the maps such that $\alpha_T(x') = \alpha|_{T(X')}(x')$ for each $x' \in T(X')$, $\beta_T(x) = \beta|_{T(X)}(x)$ for each $x \in T(X)$. Prove: If

$$0 \longrightarrow X' \xrightarrow{\alpha} X \xrightarrow{\beta} X''$$

is exact, then so is

$$0 \longrightarrow T(X') \xrightarrow{\alpha_T} T(X) \xrightarrow{\beta_T} T(X'').$$

2.2. If D is a division ring, then every D-module is both projective and injective.

2.3. Every finitely generated projective $\mathbf{Z}$-module is a direct sum of infinite cyclic groups.

2.4. A finitely generated $\mathbf{Z}$-module cannot be both projective and injective.

2.5. Let A be a ring with identity, X a free left A-module. Then

(a) The annihilator of any nonzero element of X consists of left zero divisors.

(b) If A has no left zero divisors, then every element of a free left A-module is free.

(c) If A has no left zero divisors, then every element of a projective left A-module is free.

2.6. Prove that the following groups are divisible:

(a) Any group of type p^∞.

(b) The additive group of rationals.

2.7. Prove:

(a) Every homomorphic image of a divisible group is divisible.

(b) If $G = \prod_{i \in J} G_i$, then G is divisible if and only if each G_i is divisible.

2.8. Let G be an abelian group. Prove:

(a) G has a maximal divisible subgroup, D.

(b) $G = D \oplus R$, where R is a "reduced group"; i.e., R has no divisible subgroups.

2.9. If G is a divisible abelian group, then $G = T \oplus A$, where T is the maximal torsion subgroup of G and A is a torsion-free subgroup.

2.10. Any torsion-free divisible abelian group G is equal to a direct sum of (additive) rational groups. (*Hint:* Prove that G is a vector space over the rational field.)

2.11. Any p-primary divisible abelian torsion group G is a direct sum of groups of type p^∞.

[*Hint:* Apply Zorn's Lemma to the set Σ of all independent sets of subgroups, each of type p^∞. (A set of subgroups is independent if their sum is direct.) Use Theorem 2.7c to conclude that the sum of any maximal set in Σ is equal to G.]

2.12. Any divisible group is a direct sum of quasicyclic (see Chapter 1, Exercise 8.8) and rational groups. (*Hint:* Use Exercises 2.9, 2.10, and 2.11.)

2.13. Every abelian group is the union of a countable ascending sequence of direct sums of cyclic groups. (Use Exercise 2.12; Chapter 3, Theorem 2.7; and Chapter 1, Exercises 11.2b and 8.8.)

2.14. Let M_i and N_i ($i = 1, 2, 3, 4$) be A-modules. Suppose that the diagram

$$\begin{array}{ccccccc} M_1 & \longrightarrow & M_2 & \xrightarrow{\alpha} & M_3 & \longrightarrow & M_4 \\ \downarrow{\scriptstyle \varphi_1} & & \downarrow{\scriptstyle \varphi_2} & & \downarrow{\scriptstyle \varphi_3} & & \downarrow{\scriptstyle \varphi_4} \\ N_1 & \longrightarrow & N_2 & \xrightarrow[\beta]{} & N_3 & \longrightarrow & N_4 \end{array}$$

is commutative, and that the rows are exact. Prove: If φ_1 is an epimorphism, and φ_4 is a monomorphism, then $\operatorname{Ker}\varphi_3 = \alpha(\operatorname{Ker}\varphi_2)$, and $\operatorname{Im}\varphi_2 = \beta^{-1}(\operatorname{Im}\varphi_3)$.

2.15. Let M_i and N_i ($i = 1, 2, 3, 4, 5$) be A-modules. Suppose that the diagram

$$\begin{array}{ccccccccc} M_1 & \longrightarrow & M_2 & \longrightarrow & M_3 & \longrightarrow & M_4 & \longrightarrow & M_5 \\ \downarrow{\scriptstyle\varphi_1} & & \downarrow{\scriptstyle\varphi_2} & & \downarrow{\scriptstyle\varphi_3} & & \downarrow{\scriptstyle\varphi_4} & & \downarrow{\scriptstyle\varphi_5} \\ N_1 & \longrightarrow & N_2 & \longrightarrow & N_3 & \longrightarrow & N_4 & \longrightarrow & N_5 \end{array}$$

is commutative, and that the rows are exact. Prove:

(a) $\left.\begin{array}{l}\varphi_1 \text{ is an epimorphism} \\ \varphi_2, \varphi_4 \text{ are monomorphisms}\end{array}\right\} \Rightarrow \varphi_3$ is a monomorphism.

(b) $\left.\begin{array}{l}\varphi_5 \text{ is a monomorphism} \\ \varphi_2, \varphi_4 \text{ are epimorphisms}\end{array}\right\} \Rightarrow \varphi_3$ is an epimorphism.

Section 3

3.1. Let X be an M-group, $\operatorname{Hom}_M(X,X)$ the set of all M-endomorphisms of X. For $\alpha,\beta \in \operatorname{Hom}_M(X,X)$, set $\alpha + \beta = \gamma$, where $\gamma: X \to X$ is defined by

$$\gamma x = \alpha x \beta x \qquad \text{for each } x \in X.$$

Prove that, for each $\alpha,\beta \in \operatorname{Hom}_M(X,X)$, γ commutes with each $m \in M$ but is not necessarily a homomorphism. Prove that $\langle \operatorname{Hom}_M(X,X), + \rangle$ is a group if and only if X is a commutative M-group.

3.2. Give an example of an exact sequence of A-homomorphisms

$$0 \longrightarrow X' \xrightarrow{\mu} X \xrightarrow{\nu} X'' \longrightarrow 0$$

and an A-module Y such that either the sequence

(a) $0 \longrightarrow \operatorname{Hom}(X'', Y) \xrightarrow{\bar{\nu}} \operatorname{Hom}(X, Y) \xrightarrow{\bar{\mu}} \operatorname{Hom}(X', Y) \longrightarrow 0$

($\bar{\nu} = \operatorname{Hom}(\nu,\iota_Y)$, $\bar{\mu} \in \operatorname{Hom}(\mu,\iota_Y)$) or the sequence

(b) $0 \longrightarrow \operatorname{Hom}(Y,X') \xrightarrow{\bar{\mu}} \operatorname{Hom}(Y,X) \xrightarrow{\bar{\nu}} \operatorname{Hom}(Y,X'') \longrightarrow 0$

($\bar{\mu} = \operatorname{Hom}(\iota_Y,\mu)$, $\bar{\nu} = \operatorname{Hom}(\iota_Y,\nu)$) is not exact.

3.3. Complete the proof of Theorem 3.3.

3.4. If $X = \coprod_{i \in J} X_i$ ($\{X_i\}_{i \in J}$ a family of A-modules), prove that, for each A-module Y,

$$\mathrm{Hom}_A(X, Y) = \coprod_{i \in J} \mathrm{Hom}_A(X_i, Y).$$

Prove the corresponding assertion for $\prod$.

3.5. Let m, n be positive integers. Consider the **Z**-modules $\mathbf{Z}/(m)$ and $\mathbf{Z}/(n)$. Show that $\mathrm{Hom}_{\mathbf{Z}}(\mathbf{Z}/(m), \mathbf{Z}/(n)) \simeq \mathbf{Z}/(m,n)$.

3.6. Let A be a ring, X a left A-module equal to a direct sum of a family $\{X_i\}_{i \in J}$ of left A-modules, and Y a left A-module equal to a product of a family $\{Y_j\}_{j \in K}$ of left A-modules. Show that

$$\mathrm{Hom}_A\Big(\coprod_{i \in J} X_i, Y\Big) \simeq \prod_{i \in J} \mathrm{Hom}_A(X_i, Y),$$

$$\mathrm{Hom}_A\Big(X, \prod_{j \in K} Y_j\Big) \simeq \prod_{j \in K} \mathrm{Hom}_A(X, Y_j).$$

Section 4

4.1. Let X be a right A-module, Y a left A-module, X_1 a submodule of X, and Y_1 a submodule of Y. Prove that

$$X/X_1 \otimes_A Y/Y_1 \simeq (X \otimes_A Y)/P(X_1, Y_1),$$

where $P(X_1, Y_1)$ is the **Z**-submodule of $X \otimes_A Y$ generated by the elements $x_1 \otimes y$ and $x \otimes y_1$ ($x_1 \in X_1$, $y \in Y$, $x \in X$, $y_1 \in Y_1$).

4.2. Let H be a right ideal in A, Y a left A-module. Then the **Z**-module $A/H \otimes_A Y$ is isomorphic to the **Z**-module Y/HY, where HY is the **Z**-submodule of Y generated by the elements hy ($h \in H$, $y \in Y$).

4.3. Let A be a commutative ring, H, K ideals in A. Then $A/H \otimes_A A/K$ is A-isomorphic to $A/(H + K)$.

4.4. Determine the structure of $X \otimes_{\mathbf{Z}} Y$ (where X, Y are **Z**-modules) in each of the following cases:
(a) X, Y infinite cyclic.
(b) X, Y finite cyclic.
(c) X finite cyclic, Y infinite cyclic.
(d) X, Y finitely generated abelian.
(e) X, Y free abelian.

4.5. Let A be a commutative ring with identity, X a free A-module with basis $\{x_i\}_{i \in J}$, Y a free A-module with basis $\{y_h\}_{h \in H}$. Then $X \otimes_A Y$ is a free A-module with basis $\{x_i \otimes y_h\}_{i \in J, h \in H}$.

4.6. Let X, Y be free A-modules, A an integral domain. Then $x \otimes y = 0$ ($x \in X$, $y \in Y$) implies $x = 0$ or $y = 0$.

4.7. Let A be a ring and let R, S be rings which are also (A,A)-bimodules such that $ar = ra$ and $as = sa$ for all $a \in A$, $r \in R$, $s \in S$. Define a "multiplication" on $R \otimes_A S$ by $(\sum_i r_i \otimes s_i)(\sum_j r'_j \otimes s'_j) = \sum_{i,j} r_i r'_j \otimes s_i s'_j$. Prove: $R \otimes_A S$ is a ring (and also an A-module).

4.8. Let A, R, S be as in Exercise 4.7. Let T be a ring and an (A,A)-bimodule with $at = ta$ for all $a \in A$, $t \in T$. Let $\varphi_1: R \to T$ and $\varphi_2: S \to T$ be A-homomorphisms of the rings R and S, respectively, into T. Suppose that $\varphi_1(r)\varphi_2(s) = \varphi_2(s)\varphi_1(r)$ for all $r \in R$, $s \in S$. Prove: There is an A-homomorphism φ of the ring $R \otimes_A S$ into T such that $\varphi(\sum_i r_i \otimes s_i) = \sum_i \varphi_1(r_i)\varphi_2(s_i)$.

Section 5

5.1. Define "determinant" for the case where A is a commutative ring with identity such that $a + a = 0$ for each $a \in A$.

5.2. Verify (1) (p. 196). Prove that (1) holds also in the case where $a + a = 0$ for all $a \in A$. Give a simpler version of (1) for this case.

5.3. Give an example of an A-module X with basis $\{e_i\}_{i \in J}$ such that the functionals $\{e_j^*\}_{j \in J}$ defined on page 198 do not form a basis for the dual module X^*.

5.4. Let F be a field, X an infinite set, and V the free F-module based on X.

(a) Show that $\mathrm{Hom}_F(V,F) \cong F^X$, where F^X is the vector space over F of all functions with domain X and range in F.

(b) Show that $\dim F^X/F = |F|^{|X|}$.

(c) Conclude that if V is an infinite-dimensional vector space over F, then $\dim V^*/F > \dim V/F$.

5.5. Let A be a commutative ring and let X, Y be finite-dimensional A-modules. If $\{e_i\}_{i=1}^m$ and $\{f_j\}_{j=1}^n$ are bases for X, Y, respectively, then

$$\{e_i \otimes f_j | i = 1,\ldots,m, j = 1,\ldots,n\}$$

is a basis for the A-module $X \otimes_A Y$. (Thus $X \otimes_A Y$ is a free A-module of dimension mn.)

5.6. Let A be a commutative ring and let X be a finite-dimensional free A-module. If $\mu_1,\mu_2 \in \mathrm{End}_A(X)$, then

$$\mathrm{tr}\ \mu_1\mu_2 = \mathrm{tr}\ \mu_2\mu_1.$$

More generally, if $\mu_1,\ldots, \mu_k \in \mathrm{End}_A(X)$, then

$$\mathrm{tr}(\mu_1\mu_2\cdots\mu_k) = \mathrm{tr}(\mu_i\mu_{i+1}\cdots\mu_k\mu_1\cdots\mu_{i-1}).$$

(However, the trace of a product of endomorphisms is not invariant under arbitrary permutation of the factors.)

Chapter 4 / Finite-Dimensional Vector Spaces

1. Bases; Linear Transformations

In Chapter 3, Section 1, we obtained the result that every vector space has a basis (Theorem 1.6, Corollary 1) and that any two bases of a vector space have the same cardinality (see Theorem 1.7 and the Remark, p. 160). We have also seen that, for vector spaces, the notions of basis, maximal free set, and minimal generating set are equivalent (Chapter 3, Theorem 1.6). We give here another proof that every vector space has a basis and that any two bases of a vector space have the same cardinality.

Theorem 1.1.

a. *Every vector space has a basis.*

b. *Any two bases of a vector space have the same cardinality.*

PROOF. Let X be a vector space over a division ring A. Define a "spanning function" $\rho: 2^X \to 2^X$ by $\rho S = [S]$ for each $S \in 2^X$. Then ρ satisfies conditions a through e of Chapter 0, Theorem 6.5:

a. If $S_1 \subset S_2$, then $\rho S_1 = [S_1] \subset [S_2] = \rho S_2 (S_1, S_2 \in 2^X)$.

b. If $\alpha \in \rho S$ $(S \in 2^X)$, then S has a finite subset S' such that $\alpha \in \rho S'$. For, if $\alpha \in [S]$, then $\alpha = \sum_{i=1}^{n} a_i s_i$ $(a_i \in A,\ s_i \in S)$, hence $\alpha \in S' = \{s_1, \ldots, s_n\} \subset S$.

c. If $S \in 2^X$, then $S \subset [S] = \rho S$.
d. If $S \in 2^X$, then $\rho(\rho S) = [[S]] = [S] = \rho S$.
e. Suppose $\alpha,\beta \in X$, $S \in 2^X$, $\beta \in \rho(S \cup \{\alpha\})$, and $\beta \notin \rho S$. Then $\beta = \sum_{i=1}^{n} a_i s_i + a\alpha$, $a,a_i \in A$, $a \neq 0$. Hence

$$\alpha = a^{-1}\left[\beta - \sum_{i=1}^{n} a_i s_i\right] \in \rho(S \cup \{\beta\}).$$

By Chapter 0, Theorem 6.5, it now follows that X has a minimal generating set which, by Chapter 3, Theorem 1.6, is a basis for X. By Chapter 0, Theorem 6.5, and Chapter 3, Theorem 1.6, it also follows that any two bases of X have the same cardinality. ▮

Observe that conditions a through d are satisfied by any module over an arbitrary ring A with identity. Only the proof of e required the additional hypothesis that A is a division ring.

NOTATION. We shall write "dim X" for the dimension of a vector space X. If a basis $\mathscr{B}$ is indexed with respect to some index set J, we use the same letter $\mathscr{B}$ to designate the resulting family, e.g., $\mathscr{B} = \{e_i\}_{i \in J}$. When the indexing is essential in a given context, we may refer to $\mathscr{B}$ as an "ordered basis."

Corollary 1.
a. *Every free set of a vector space X is contained in a basis for X.*
b. *Every generating set of a vector space X contains a basis for X.*

PROOF.
a. By Zorn's Lemma, every free set of X is contained in a maximal free set of X which, by Chapter 3, Theorem 1.6, is a basis for X.
b. If Y is a generating set of X, then the free set $\varnothing$ is a subset of Y. By Zorn's Lemma, there is a free subset, $\mathscr{B}$, of Y which is maximal among the free subsets of Y. But then $Y \subset [\mathscr{B}]$, and $\mathscr{B}$ is a generating set, hence a basis, for X. ▮

Corollary 2. *Let X be a vector space. Then the cardinality of any free set of X is less than or equal to* dim X, *and the cardinality of a generating set of X is greater than or equal to* dim X. □

Corollary 3. *If X is a vector space of finite dimension n, and $\mathscr{B}$ is a subset of X, then the following statements are equivalent:*
a. *$\mathscr{B}$ is a basis for X.*
b. *$\mathscr{B}$ is a free set of cardinality n.*
c. *$\mathscr{B}$ is a generating set of cardinality n.*

PROOF. Of course, $1 \Rightarrow 2$ and $1 \Rightarrow 3$. By Corollary 1, $2 \Rightarrow 1$ and $3 \Rightarrow 1$. ▮

The submodules of a vector space are called *subspaces*.

Corollary 4. *If Y is a subspace of a vector space X, then* $\dim Y \leq \dim X$.

PROOF. Any basis for Y, being a free set of X, can be extended to a basis for X (Corollary 1). ▮

Corollary 5. *If X is a finite-dimensional vector space, Y a subspace of X such that* $\dim Y = \dim X$, *then* $Y = X$.

PROOF. This follows from Corollaries 1 and 4. ▮

Corollary 6. *If X is a vector space over a division ring D, then X is a direct sum of one-dimensional subspaces, each isomorphic to D_l.*

PROOF. $X = \bigoplus_{i \in J} De_i$, where $\{e_i\}_{i \in J}$ is a basis for X. Each De_i is isomorphic to D_l. ▮

Corollary 7. *Two vector spaces over a division ring D are isomorphic if and only if they have the same dimension.*

PROOF. This follows immediately from Corollary 6. ▮

NOTE: If X is a vector space of finite dimension n, then each ordered basis $\{e_i\}_{i=1}^n$ determines an isomorphism $\sum_{i=1}^n a_i e_i \mapsto (e_i)_{i=1}^n$, onto the vector space, $V_n(D)$, formed by the n tuples over D, under componentwise addition and scalar multiplication.

Corollary 8. *If Y is a subspace of a vector space X, then Y is a direct summand of X; i.e., there is a subspace Y' of X such that $Y \oplus Y' = X$.*

PROOF. Let $\mathscr{B}$ be a basis for Y. By Corollary 1 there is a free set $\mathscr{B}'$ of X such that $\mathscr{B} \cup \mathscr{B}'$ is a basis for X. The subspace Y' generated by $\mathscr{B}'$ serves as a complement for X; i.e., $X = Y \oplus Y'$. ▮

Corollary 9. *If X is a vector space of finite dimension n and Y is a submodule of X, of dimension m, then* $\dim X/Y = n - m$.

PROOF. The subspace Y has a complement, Y', isomorphic to X/Y. The dimension of Y' is, clearly, $n - m$, and isomorphism preserves dimension. ▮

Corollary 10. *If Y, Z are subspaces of a vector space X, then* $\dim(Y+Z) = \dim Y + \dim Z - \dim Y \cap Z$.

PROOF. Start with a basis for $Y \cap Z$, extend it to a basis for Y, extend this basis to a basis for $Y + Z$, and count. *Or:* Use the isomorphism $(Y + Z)/Z \simeq Y/Y \cap Z$ (Chapter 1, Theorem 4.11) and Corollary 9. ▮

We shall usually refer to the homomorphisms of vector spaces as linear transformations.

Definition 1.1. If τ is a linear transformation then $\dim(\text{Im}\,\tau)$ is the *rank* of τ, and $\dim(\text{Ker}\ \tau)$ is the *nullity* of τ.

Theorem 1.2. *If τ is a linear transformation on a vector space X, then* $\text{rank}\ \tau \leq \dim X$, *and*

$$\text{rank}\ \tau + \text{nullity}\ \tau = \dim X.$$

PROOF. Since $\text{Im}\ \tau \simeq X/\text{Ker}\ \tau$, $\text{rank}\ \tau = \dim \text{Im}\ \tau = \dim X - \text{nullity}\ \tau$, by Corollary 9 of Theorem 1.1. ▮

Theorem 1.3. *Let X and X' be vector spaces of the same finite dimension n, over a division ring D, and let τ be a linear transformation of X into X'. Then the following statements are equivalent:*

a. $\text{rank}\ \tau = n$.
b. *τ is surjective* (*an epimorphism*).
c. $\text{nullity}\ \tau = 0$.
d. *τ is injective* (*a monomorphism*).
e. *τ is bijective* (*an isomorphism*).
f. *τ maps any basis of X to a basis of X'.*
g. *There is a linear transformation $\sigma: X' \to X$ such that $\sigma\tau = \iota_X$ and $\tau\sigma = \iota_{X'}$.*
h. *There is a linear transformation σ of X into X' such that $\sigma\tau = \iota_X$.*
i. *There is a linear transformation σ' of X' into X such that $\tau\sigma' = \iota_{X'}$.*

PROOF.

a $\Rightarrow$ b. This follows from Theorem 1.1, Corollary 5.

b $\Rightarrow$ c. This follows from Theorem 1.2.

c $\Rightarrow$ d. $\text{Ker}\ \tau = 0$; hence τ is injective.

d $\Rightarrow$ e. If τ is injective, $\text{Ker}\ \tau = 0$, $\text{nullity}\ \tau = 0$, hence $\text{rank}\ \tau = n$. But then τ is surjective, hence bijective.

e $\Rightarrow$ f. Since τ is an isomorphism, Im $\tau = X'$. If $\mathscr{B}$ is a basis for X, then $\tau\mathscr{B}$ is a generating set for Im τ. But card $\tau\mathscr{B}$ = card $\mathscr{B}$ = dim X'. By Corollaries 3 and 5 of Theorem 1.1, $\tau\mathscr{B}$ is a basis for X'.

f $\Rightarrow$ g. By Theorem 1.1, X has a basis, $\mathscr{B}$. Since $\tau\mathscr{B}$ is a basis for X', Im $\tau = X'$; i.e., τ is surjective. We have shown that b $\Rightarrow$ e. Thus, τ is bijective. Hence there is a map $\sigma: X' \to X$ such that $\sigma\tau = \iota_X$ and $\tau\sigma = \iota_{X'}$. If $a,b \in D$, $x',y' \in X'$, then $\sigma(ax' + by') = \sigma(a\tau\sigma x' + b\tau\sigma y') = \sigma\tau(a\sigma x' + b\sigma y') = a\sigma x' + b\sigma y'$. Thus, σ is linear. (Note that it is sufficient to assume that τ maps a *single* basis of X to a basis of X'.)

g $\Rightarrow$ h. Obvious.

h $\Rightarrow$ i. If σ is a linear transformation such that $\sigma\tau = \iota_X$, then τ is injective, hence bijective (d $\Rightarrow$ e), and σ is a two-sided inverse for τ.

i $\Rightarrow$ a. If $\tau\sigma = \iota_X$, then τ is surjective, hence rank $\tau = n$. ▮

If $X' = X$, then a linear transformation on X satisfying one of the conditions of Theorem 1.3 is an automorphism of X. The automorphisms of a vector space are also referred to as *nonsingular* linear transformations.

It is evident that a linear transformation of a vector space X is determined by its action on a basis of X, and that any mapping whose domain is a given basis can be extended to a linear transformation of X. Thus, if $\{x_1,\ldots,x_n\}$ is a basis for X, and $\{y_1,\ldots,y_n\}$ is a set of elements of X, then there is a linear transformation τ of X such that $\tau x_i = y_i$ for each $i = 1,\ldots, n$. If the y_i themselves form a basis for X, then τ is nonsingular.

2. Matrices

Let X, Y left be vector spaces of dimensions n and m, respectively, over a division ring D. Let $\{e_i\}_{i=1}^n$ be a basis for X and let $\{f_j\}_{j=1}^m$ be a basis for Y. If τ is a linear transformation of X into Y, then for each $i = 1,\ldots, n$, $\tau e_i = \sum_{j=1}^m t_{ij}f_j$ ($t_{ij} \in D$). The coefficients t_{ij} can be arranged in a rectangular array of n rows and m columns—an $n \times m$ *matrix* $T = (t_{ij})$. We shall refer to T as *the matrix of the linear transformation* τ *relative to the pair of* (ordered) *bases* $\{e_i\}$ *and* $\{f_j\}$. (If $X = Y$ and $\{e_i\} = \{f_j\}$, we shall say that T is *the matrix of* τ *relative to* $\{e_i\}$.)

We leave to the reader the verification of the following remarks:

REMARKS.

1. Let X, Y, Z be vector spaces over a division ring D, with bases $\{e_i\}_{i=1}^n$, $\{f_j\}_{j=1}^m$, and $\{g_k\}_{k=1}^p$, respectively. If $\tau \in \mathrm{Hom}_D(X,Y)$ has matrix $T = (t_{ij})$

relative to $\{e_i\}_{i=1}^n$, $\{f_j\}_{j=1}^m$ and $\sigma \in \mathrm{Hom}_D(Y,Z)$ has matrix $S = (s_{jk})$ relative to $\{f_j\}_{j=1}^m$ and $\{g_k\}_{k=1}^p$, then the matrix of $\sigma\tau \in \mathrm{Hom}_D(X,Z)$ relative to $\{e_i\}_{i=1}^n$, $\{g_k\}_{k=1}^p$ is the $n \times p$ matrix (u_{ik}), where $u_{ik} = \sum_j t_{ij}s_{jk}$, for each $i = 1,\ldots, n$; $k = 1,\ldots, p$.

The $n \times p$ matrix $(u_{ik}) = (\sum_j t_{ij}s_{jk})$ is the *product*, TS, of the $n \times m$ matrix $T = (t_{ij})$ and the $m \times p$ matrix $S = (s_{jk})$.

Let X, Y be vector spaces over a division ring D with bases $\{e_i\}_{i=1}^n$, $\{f_j\}_{j=1}^m$, respectively. If $\tau,\sigma \in \mathrm{Hom}_D(X, Y)$ have matrices $T = (t_{ij})$ and $S = (s_{ij})$ relative to $\{e_i\}$, $\{f_j\}$, then the matrix of $\tau + \sigma \in \mathrm{Hom}_D(X, Y)$ relative to $\{e_i\}$, $\{f_j\}$ is (v_{ij}), where $v_{ij} = t_{ij} + s_{ij}$ for each $i = 1,\ldots, n; j = 1,\ldots, m$.

The $n \times m$ matrix $(v_{ij}) = (t_{ij} + s_{ij})$ is the *sum*, $T + S$, of the $n \times m$ matrices T and S.

As noted in Chapter 2, Exercise 1.6, the $n \times n$ matrices $(n \geq 1)$ with elements in a ring A form a ring, A_n, under the operations of matrix addition and matrix multiplication.

2. If τ is a linear transformation of X into Y, with matrix (t_{ij}) relative to a given pair of (ordered) bases $\{e_i\}_{i=1}^n$ and $\{f_j\}_{j=1}^m$ and $x = \sum_{i=1}^n c_ie_i$, then the coefficients c_i form the $1 \times n$ matrix (c_i); the coefficients of τx relative to $\{f_j\}$ form the $1 \times m$ matrix $(c_i)(t_{ij})$. In particular, for each fixed i_0 ($i_0 = 1,\ldots,n$), the coefficients of τe_{i_0} form the $1 \times m$ matrix (t_{i_0j}) whose entries are those in the i_0th row of (t_{ij}).

For each $t \in D$, the *scalar matrix* $\mathrm{diag}(t,\ldots,t)$ represents the linear transformation which multiplies the components (relative to $\{e_i\}$) on the right by t. If D is commutative, this transformation is equal to the scalar multiplication $x \mapsto tx$.

3. From the associativity of multiplication of mappings, it follows that matrix multiplication is associative.

For fixed n, the $n \times n$ matrices with elements in D form a ring, D_n. If X is an n-dimensional vector space over D, then every basis $\{e_i\}_{i=1}^n$ for X determines a mapping $\mu: \tau \mapsto T$, where T is the matrix of τ relative to $\{e_i\}$. By virtue of Remark 1, this mapping preserves addition and reverses multiplication; i.e., it is an antihomomorphism of the ring $\mathrm{End}_D(X)$ into D_n. Since every matrix $T = (t_{ij})$ corresponds to one, and only one, linear transformation τ relative to $\{e_i\}$ (i.e., the transformation τ given by $\tau e_i = \sum_{j=1}^n t_{ij}e_j$), μ is an antiisomorphism.

The matrix corresponding under μ to the identity transformation on X is the $n \times n$ unit matrix, $I_n = \mathrm{diag}(1,\ldots,1)$. The matrix T of a linear transformation τ is a unit in D_n if and only if τ is nonsingular. In this case, T is called a *nonsingular matrix*. From Theorem 1.3 it follows that a matrix $T \in D_n$ has a right inverse in D_n if and only if it has a left inverse in D_n.

Theorem 2.1.

a. *Let X, Y be vector spaces over a division ring D, of finite dimensions m and n, respectively, and let τ be a linear transformation of X into Y. If T is the matrix of τ relative to a given pair of ordered bases for X and Y, then T' is the matrix of τ relative to another pair of ordered bases if and only if $T' = PTQ$, where $P \in D_n$ and $Q \in D_m$ are nonsingular matrices.*

b. *In particular, if τ is a linear transformation of X, and T is the matrix of τ relative to a (single) given ordered basis for X, then T' is the matrix of τ relative to another ordered basis for X if and only if $T = PTP^{-1}$ for some $P \in D_n$.*

PROOF. To facilitate this proof, we adopt the following notation: If σ is a linear transformation of X into Y, $\mathscr{U}$ is an ordered basis for X, and $\mathscr{V}$ is an ordered basis for Y, we write ${}_{\mathscr{U}}\sigma_{\mathscr{V}}$ for the matrix of σ relative to $(\mathscr{U},\mathscr{V})$.

Let $\mathscr{A}$, $\mathscr{A}'$ be ordered bases for X, and let $\mathscr{B}$, $\mathscr{B}'$ be ordered bases for Y. Let $T = {}_{\mathscr{A}}\tau_{\mathscr{B}}$ and let $T' = {}_{\mathscr{A}'}\tau_{\mathscr{B}'}$. Since $\tau = \iota_Y\tau\iota_X$, $T' = {}_{\mathscr{A}'}\tau_{\mathscr{B}'} = {}_{\mathscr{A}'}(\iota_Y\tau\iota_X)_{\mathscr{B}'} = {}_{\mathscr{A}'}(\iota_X)_{\mathscr{A}} \cdot {}_{\mathscr{A}}\tau_{\mathscr{B}} \cdot {}_{\mathscr{B}}(\iota_Y)_{\mathscr{B}'} = PTQ$, where $P = {}_{\mathscr{A}'}(\iota_X)_{\mathscr{A}} \in D_m$, with inverse $P^{-1} = {}_{\mathscr{A}}(\iota_X)_{\mathscr{A}'} \in D_m$, and $Q = {}_{\mathscr{B}}(\iota_Y)_{\mathscr{B}'} \in D_n$, with inverse $Q^{-1} = {}_{\mathscr{B}'}(\iota_Y)_{\mathscr{B}} \in D_n$. In particular, if $X = Y$, $\mathscr{A} = \mathscr{B}$ and $\mathscr{A}' = \mathscr{B}'$, then

$$T' = {}_{\mathscr{A}'}\tau_{\mathscr{A}} = {}_{\mathscr{A}'}(\iota_X)_{\mathscr{A}} \cdot {}_{\mathscr{A}}\tau_{\mathscr{A}} \cdot {}_{\mathscr{A}}(\iota_Y)_{\mathscr{A}'} = PTP^{-1}.$$

Conversely, suppose $T = {}_{\mathscr{A}}\tau_{\mathscr{B}}$ and $T' = PTQ$, where $P \in D_m$ and $Q \in D_n$ are nonsingular. Let $\pi\colon X \to X$ be the linear transformation such that ${}_{\mathscr{A}}\pi_{\mathscr{A}} = P$, and let $\rho\colon Y \to Y$ be the linear transformation such that ${}_{\mathscr{B}}\rho_{\mathscr{B}} = Q^{-1}$. Then $\mathscr{A}' = \pi\mathscr{A}$ is a basis for X, $\mathscr{B}' = \rho\mathscr{B}$ is a basis for Y, and

$$P = {}_{\mathscr{A}'}(\iota_X)_{\mathscr{A}}, \qquad Q = {}_{\mathscr{B}}(\iota_Y)_{\mathscr{B}'},$$

whence $T' = PTQ = {}_{\mathscr{A}'}(\iota_X)_{\mathscr{A}} \cdot {}_{\mathscr{A}}\tau_{\mathscr{B}} \cdot {}_{\mathscr{B}}(\iota_Y)_{\mathscr{B}'} = {}_{\mathscr{A}'}\tau_{\mathscr{B}'}$, as required. In particular, if $X = Y$, $T = {}_{\mathscr{A}}\tau_{\mathscr{A}}$ and $T' = PTP^{-1}$, then $P = {}_{\mathscr{A}'}(\iota_X)_{\mathscr{A}}$, $P^{-1} = {}_{\mathscr{A}}(\iota_Y)_{\mathscr{A}'}$, and

$$T' = {}_{\mathscr{A}'}(\iota_X)_{\mathscr{A}} \cdot {}_{\mathscr{A}}\tau_{\mathscr{A}} \cdot {}_{\mathscr{A}}(\iota_Y)_{\mathscr{A}'} = {}_{\mathscr{A}'}\tau_{\mathscr{A}'}. \quad ▮$$

Definition 2.1. If D is a division ring, n a positive integer, $S,T \in D_n$, then S is *equivalent* to T (over D) if $S = PTQ$ where P, Q are nonsingular matrices in D_n; S is *similar to* T (over D) if $S = PTP^{-1}$ for some (nonsingular) matrix S in D_n. ///

Obviously, equivalence and similarity are both equivalence relations and the usual terminology is "S and T are equivalent" or "S and T are similar."

Corollary. *Two matrices T, T' in D_n are similar if and only if they represent the same linear transformation $\tau \in \mathrm{Hom}_D(X,X)$ with respect to two ordered bases $\{e_i\}$, $\{e_i'\}$ of X.* □

Theorem 2.2.

a. *If τ is a linear transformation of rank r, $\tau \in \mathrm{Hom}_D(X,X)$, then one of the matrices representing τ relative to a pair of ordered bases for X is $I_{r,n} = \mathrm{diag}(\underbrace{1,\ldots,1}_{r},0,\ldots,0) \in D_n$.*

b. *If τ is a linear transformation of rank r, $\tau \in \mathrm{Hom}_D(X,X)$, then every matrix in D_n which represents τ relative to a pair of ordered bases for X is equivalent to $I_{r,n}$.*

c. *If $T \in D_n$ is equivalent to $I_{r,n}$ $(0 \le r \le n)$, then every linear transformation in $\mathrm{Hom}_D(X,X)$ represented by T relative to a pair of bases for X has rank r.*

d. *Every matrix $T \in D_n$ is equivalent to $I_{r,n}$ for exactly one r $(0 \le r \le n)$.*

PROOF.

a. Since rank $\tau = r$, nullity $\tau = n - r$, and Ker τ has a basis, $\{e_{r+1},\ldots,e_n\}$, which can be extended to a basis $\{e_i\}_{i=1}^n$ for X. The vectors $\{\tau e_i\}_{i=1}^n$ form a generating set for Im τ. Since $\tau e_{r+1} = \cdots = \tau e_n = 0$, the r vectors τe_i $(i = 1,\ldots,r)$ form a generating set of r elements, hence a basis for the r-dimensional subspace Im τ. This basis for Im τ can be extended to a basis, $\{f_i\}_{i=1}^n$, for X such that $f_i = \tau e_i$ for $i = 1,\ldots, r$. The matrix of τ relative to the pair of bases $\{e_i\}_{i=1}^n$, $\{f_i\}_{i=1}^n$ is $I_{r,n}$.

b. This follows immediately from a and Theorem 2.1.

c. If $\tau \in \mathrm{Hom}_D(X)$ is represented by $I_{r,n}$ relative to a pair of bases $\{e_i\}_{i=1}^n$, $\{f_i\}_{i=1}^n$, then $\tau e_i = f_i$ for $i = 1,\ldots, r$ and $\tau e_i = 0$ for $i = r + 1,\ldots, n$. Thus, rank $\tau = \dim(\mathrm{Im}\ \tau) = r$.

d. If $T \in D_n$, then there is a linear transformation $\tau \in \mathrm{Hom}_D(X,X)$ such that T represents τ relative to some pair of bases. By b, T is equivalent to $I_{r,n}$. If T is also equivalent to $I_{s,n}$ $(0 \le s \le n)$, then τ has rank s, by c. But then $r = s$. ▮

By virtue of Theorem 2.2, we can now define the rank of a matrix:

***Definition* 2.2.** If $T \in D_n$, then T has *rank* r if it represents a linear transformation $\tau \in \mathrm{Hom}_D(X,X)$ of rank r. ///

Corollary 1. *Two matrices in D_n have the same rank if and only if they are equivalent.* □

The matrices $I_{r,n}$ are idempotents in the ring D_n; i.e., $(I_{r,n})^2 = I_{r,n}$ for each $r = 0, \ldots, n$.

Corollary 2. *Every matrix in D_n is equivalent to an idempotent matrix.* □

3. Modules over Principal Ideal Domains

Our results on the structure of abelian torsion groups and on finitely generated abelian groups (Chapter 1, Section 12) can be generalized almost verbatim to the case of modules over arbitrary Euclidean domains. We treat here, in full, the more general case of modules over principal ideal domains. In Section 4 we shall apply these results to the theory of linear transformations on finite-dimensional vector spaces.

Definition 3.1. If A is a principal ideal domain, p a prime in A, and X an A-module such that every element of X is annihilated by a power of p, then X is a *p-primary A-module*.

If $\mathscr{P}$ is a family of primes from A such that $\mathscr{P}$ contains an associate of every prime in A, and no two primes in $\mathscr{P}$ are associates, then we shall call $\mathscr{P}$ a *representative family of primes* from A. ///

Theorem 3.1. *Let A be a principal ideal domain, X a torsion A-module. If $\mathscr{P} = \{p_i\}_{i\in J}$ is a representative family of primes from A, then there is a unique family $(X_i)_{i\in J}$ of submodules of X such that $X = \bigoplus_{i\in J} X_i$ and X_i is p_i-primary for each $i \in J$.* □

The proof, completely parallel to that of Chapter 1, Theorem 9.12, on abelian torsion groups, is left to the reader.

We now turn our attention to free modules over principal ideal domains. It is easy to see that, if A is an arbitrary integral domain, every free A-module is torsion free (Exercise 3.2a). On the other hand, for every integral domain A which is not a field, there are torsion-free A-modules which are not free (Exercise 3.2b).

Theorem 3.2. *Let A be a principal ideal domain, X a free A-module, and $Y \neq 0$ a submodule of X. Then Y is also a free A-module, and rank $Y \leq$ rank X.*

PROOF. Let $\{x_\alpha\}_{\alpha \in J}$ be a basis for X. For each subset $H \subset J$, let

$$Y_H = Y \cap [\{x_h | h \in H\}].$$

Let Σ be the set of all ordered pairs $(H,\mathscr{B})$, where $H \subset J$ and $\mathscr{B}$ is a basis for Y_H with $|\mathscr{B}| \leq |H|$. The set Σ is not empty. For, let H be the subset consisting of a single element $h \in J$. Then the set of all $a \in A$ such that $ax_h \in Y$ is an ideal which, since A is a principal ideal domain, is generated by an element $a_h \in A$. If $a_h = 0$, then $Y_H = \{0\}$, and $\mathscr{B} = \varnothing$ is a basis for Y_H, with $0 = |\mathscr{B}| \leq |H|$. Thus $(H,\mathscr{B}) \in \Sigma$. If $a_h \neq 0$, then $Y_H = [a_h x_h] \neq 0$, and $\mathscr{B} = \{a_h x_h\}$ is a basis for Y_H, with $|\mathscr{B}| = 1 = |H|$. Again, $(H,\mathscr{B}) \in \Sigma$. On Σ, define a partial order $\prec$ by $(H_1,\mathscr{B}_1) \prec (H_2,\mathscr{B}_2)$ if $H_1 \subset H_2$, $\mathscr{B}_1 \subset \mathscr{B}_2$. Let $\{(H_i,\mathscr{B}_i)\}_{i \in I}$ be a family of elements of Σ, totally ordered by $\prec$, and let $\tilde{H} = \bigcup_{i \in I} H_i$, $\tilde{\mathscr{B}} = \bigcup_{i \in I} \mathscr{B}_i$. Then $(\tilde{H},\tilde{\mathscr{B}})$ is itself an element of Σ. For $\tilde{\mathscr{B}}$ is a free subset of $Y_{\tilde{H}}$ and, if $y \in Y_{\tilde{H}}$, then $y \in H_i$ for some $i \in I$; hence $y \in [\mathscr{B}_i] \subset [\tilde{\mathscr{B}}]$. Thus, $\tilde{\mathscr{B}}$ is a basis for $Y_{\tilde{H}}$. Since $|\mathscr{B}_i| \leq |H_i|$ for each $i \in I$, $|\tilde{\mathscr{B}}| \leq |\tilde{H}|$. But then $(\tilde{H},\tilde{\mathscr{B}}) \in \Sigma$. Since $(\tilde{H},\tilde{\mathscr{B}})$ is clearly an upper bound for $\{(H_i,\mathscr{B}_i)\}_{i \in I}$, it follows that $(\Sigma,\prec)$ satisfies the conditions of Zorn's Lemma, and therefore Σ contains a maximal element $(H^*,\mathscr{B}^*)$. We shall prove that $H^* = J$.

Suppose there is some $j \in J$ such that $j \notin H^*$. Let $\bar{H} = H^* \cup \{j\}$. If $Y_H = Y_{H^*}$, then $(\bar{H},\mathscr{B}^*) \in \Sigma$, contrary to the hypothesis that $(H^*,\mathscr{B}^*)$ is maximal in Σ. On the other hand, if $Y_H \neq Y_{H^*}$, then there is some $y \in Y_{\bar{H}} - Y_{H^*}$ such that

$$y = a_1 x_{h_1} + \cdots + a_n x_{h_n} + a x_j,$$

where $a_i \in A$, $h_i \in H^*$ $(i = 1,\ldots,n)$, and $a \neq 0$ in A. Hence the set $A_j = \{a | y - ax_j \in Y_{H^*}, y \in Y_{\bar{H}}, a \in A\}$ is a nonzero ideal in A, generated by some nonzero element $a_j \in A$. Let $\bar{y}$ be an element of $Y_{\bar{H}}$ such that $\bar{y} - a_j x_j \in Y_{H^*}$ and let $\bar{\mathscr{B}} = \mathscr{B}^* \cup \{\bar{y}\}$. Then $\bar{\mathscr{B}}$ is a basis for $Y_{\bar{H}}$. For, suppose $y \in Y_{\bar{H}}$. Then, for some $c \in A$, $y - cx_j \in Y_{H^*}$. Since $c \in A_j$, $c = da_j$ for some $d \in A$. But then $y - d\bar{y} \in Y_{H^*}$, and $y \in [Y_{H^*} \cup \{\bar{y}\}] = [\bar{\mathscr{B}}]$. Thus, $\bar{\mathscr{B}}$ is a generating set for $Y_{\bar{H}}$. Since $a_j \neq 0$, $b\bar{y} \notin Y_H$ for all $b \neq 0$ in A. Hence $\mathscr{B}^* \cup \{\bar{y}\} = \bar{\mathscr{B}}$ is a free set, and therefore a basis, for $Y_{\bar{H}}$. Since $|\mathscr{B}^*| \leq |H^*|$, we have $|\bar{\mathscr{B}}| \leq |\bar{H}|$, and so $(\bar{H},\bar{\mathscr{B}}) \in \Sigma$. This is impossible, since $(H^*,\mathscr{B}^*)$ is maximal in Σ.

It follows that $H^* = J$. But then $Y_{H^*} = Y_J = Y$, and therefore $\mathscr{B}^*$ is a basis for Y. Thus, Y is a free A-module, and rank $Y = |\mathscr{B}^*| \leq |H^*| = |J| \leq$ rank X. ∎

We are now ready to study the structure of finitely generated modules over principal ideal domains. Our aim is to prove that every finitely generated module over a principal ideal domain A is a direct sum of finitely many cyclic submodules. As in the case of abelian groups, we shall accomplish this by regarding the given A-module as a homomorphic image of a free A-module. The key to the proof will be a judicious choice of bases for the free A-module and the submodule which serves as the kernel of the appropriate homomorphism. The following theorem sharpens the result of Theorem 3.2 in case Y is a finitely generated submodule of a free A-module X, and provides precisely the right choice of bases.

Theorem 3.3. *Let A be a principal ideal domain, X a free A-module, and Y a submodule of X, of finite rank $n \geq 0$. Then there is a basis, $\mathscr{B}$, of X, a subset $\{u_1,\ldots,u_n\}$ of $\mathscr{B}$, and a subset $\{c_1,\ldots,c_n\}$ of A such that*

a. *$\{c_1u_1,\ldots,c_nu_n\}$ is a basis for Y.*
b. *$c_i | c_{i+1}$ for each $i = 1,\ldots, n - 1$.*

PROOF. We proceed by induction on n. If $n = 0$, then $Y = 0$, $\mathscr{B} = \varnothing$ is a basis for Y, and there is nothing to prove.

For $n > 0$, suppose the theorem to hold for submodules of rank $n - 1$. We first produce elements u_1 in X and c_1u_1 in Y such that $[u_1]$ is a direct summand of X, and $[c_1u_1]$ is a direct summand of Y.

Consider the set of all A-homomorphisms of the A-module X into the A-module A. For each linear functional $\varphi \in X^*$, $\varphi' Y$ is a principal ideal in A. Since the principal ideal domain A satisfies the ascending chain condition on ideals the set of all ideals φY ($\varphi \in X^*$) contains a maximal ideal $\varphi_1 Y = (c_1)$ ($\varphi_1 \in X^*$, $c_1 \in A$). Since $Y \neq 0$, and X^* contains all the "coordinate maps" relative to any basis of X, $\varphi Y \neq 0$ for some $\varphi \in X$. Hence $\varphi_1 Y = (c_1) \neq 0$ and $c_1 \neq 0$. Let v be an element of Y such that $c_1 = \varphi_1 v$. We shall prove that, for all $\varphi \in X^*$, $\varphi v \in (c_1)$. If $b = \varphi v$, then the ideal (c_1,b) is generated by some element $d \in A$ and we have $la_1 + mb = d$ for some $l,m \in A$. Let $\psi = l\varphi_1 + m\varphi$. Then $d = \psi v \in \psi Y$, and therefore $(c_1) \subset (d) \subset \psi Y$. But then, by the maximality of (c_1), we have $(c_1) = (d) = \psi Y$, and so $b = \varphi v \in (c_1)$.

It follows that, in particular, all the coordinates of v relative to a given basis $\{x_i\}_{i\in J}$ belong to the ideal (c_1). Hence there is an element $u_1 \in X$ such that $v = c_1u_1$. Since $\varphi_1 v = c_1 = c_1\varphi_1 u_1$, we have $\varphi_1 u_1 = 1$. Let $X_1 = \operatorname{Ker} \varphi_1$. Then $X = [u_1] \oplus X_1$. For, if $x \in X$, then $x = \varphi_1(x)u_1 + (x - \varphi_1(x)u_1)$. But $\varphi_1(x - \varphi_1(x)u_1) = \varphi_1(x) - \varphi_1(x) \cdot 1 = 0$. Hence $x \in [u_1] + \operatorname{Ker} \varphi_1 = [u_1] + X_1$, and so $X = [u_1] + X_1$. If $x \in [u_1] \cap X_1$, $x = au_1$ for some $a \in A$, whence $0 = \varphi x = a\varphi u_1 = a$, and $x = 0$. Thus, $[u_1] \cap X_1 = \{0\}$, and $X = [u_1] \oplus X_1$.

Now let $Y_1 = Y \cap \operatorname{Ker} \varphi_1$. Then $Y = [c_1u_1] \oplus Y_1$. (Since $[c_1u_1] \subset [u_1]$

and $Y_1 \subset X_1$, we have $[c_1u_1] \cap Y_1 = \{0\}$. If $y \in Y$, then $\varphi_1 y = ac_1$ for some $a \in A$. Hence $\varphi_1(y - ac_1u_1) = \varphi_1 y - ac = 0$, and

$$y = ac_1u_1 - (y - ac_1u_1) \in [c_1u_1] + Y_1.$$

Thus, $Y = [c_1u_1] \oplus Y_1$.)

Now, Y_1 is a submodule of X_1, of rank $n - 1$, and we can apply the induction hypothesis. Thus, there is a basis $\mathscr{B}_1$ of X_1, a subset $\{u_2,\ldots,u_n\}$ of $\mathscr{B}_1$, and a subset $\{c_2,\ldots,c_n\}$ of A such that $\{c_2u_2,\ldots,c_nu_n\}$ is a basis for Y_1, with $c_i | c_{i+1}$ for each $i = 2,\ldots, n - 1$. Clearly, $\mathscr{B} = \{u_1\} \cup \mathscr{B}_1$ is a basis for X, and $\{c_1u_1,c_2u_2,\ldots,c_nu_n\}$ is a basis for Y. Thus, we need only convince ourselves that $c_1 | c_2$. Let φ be the homomorphism in X^* defined by $\varphi(u_2) = 1$ and $\varphi(x) = 0$ for all $x \in \mathscr{B}$, $x \neq u_2$. Since $\varphi \in X^*$, $(c_2) = \varphi Y \subset \varphi_1 Y = (c_1)$. Thus, $c_1 | c_2$. ▌

The next theorem is an extension of Chapter 1, Theorem 13.2, on abelian groups.

Theorem 3.4. *If A is a principal ideal domain, then every A-module X on n generators ($n \in \mathbf{N}$) is a direct sum of n cyclic submodules. In particular, there exist m ($0 \leq m \leq n$) cyclic torsion submodules $Ay_1,\ldots, Ay_m$ of X, and $n - m$ torsion-free cyclic submodules $Ay_{m+1},\ldots, Ay_n$ of X such that $X = \bigoplus_{i=1}^n Ay_i$ and, for each $i = 1, 2,\ldots, m - 1$, the order ideal of Ay_i contains the order ideal of Ay_{i+1}.*

PROOF. If S is a set of n generators for X, then there exists a free A-module $\bar{X}$ on S such that X is a homomorphic image of $\bar{X}$. Let $\mu: \bar{X} \to X$ be an epimorphism of $\bar{X}$ onto X, and let $K = \operatorname{Ker} \mu$. By Theorem 3.2, K is a free A-module of rank $m \leq n$. By Theorem 3.3, there is a basis $\{u_i\}_{i=1}^n$ of X such that $\{c_iu_i\}_{i=1}^m$ forms a basis for K, where $c_i \in A$ ($i = 1,\ldots,m$) and $c_i | c_{i+1}$ for $i = 1,\ldots, m - 1$. Since $Ac_iu_i \subset Au_i$ for each $i = 1,\ldots, m$, and $K = \bigoplus_{i=1}^m Ac_iu_i$, it follows from Chapter 1, Theorem 9.7 that X is isomorphic to $\coprod_{i=1}^n Au_i/Ac_iu_i$, where $c_i = 0$ for $i > m$. The first m summands are cyclic torsion A-modules Ay_i, where y_i has order ideal (c_i); the last $n - m$ summands are torsion-free cyclic modules, each isomorphic to the A-module A. For each $i = 1,\ldots, m - 1$, $(c_i) \supset (c_{i+1})$. ▌

A certain number of initial c_i may be equal to 1 and the corresponding summands equal to zero.

Following the terminology of Chapter 1, Section 13, we shall call the nonzero segment of the decomposition in Theorem 3.4 a T-decomposition of the A-module X. By Theorem 3.1, each of the cyclic torsion components in a T-decomposition is a direct sum of primary cyclic submodules, and we have

Theorem 3.5. *If A is a principal ideal domain, then every finitely generated A-module is a direct sum of finitely many cyclic submodules, some primary cyclic, some torsion free.* □

Relative to a representative family $\mathscr{P}$ of primes from A, we shall refer to a decomposition of an A-module into primary and torsion-free cyclic summands as a *P-decomposition* if all the torsion components precede all the torsion-free components, and if for each prime in $\mathscr{P}$, the exponents of the corresponding primary orders are nondecreasing.

Theorem 3.6. (Uniqueness.) *Let A be a principal ideal domain, X a finitely generated A-module. Then*

a. *There is a unique integer $r \geq 0$ such that the number of torsion-free summands in any decomposition of X as a direct sum of cyclic submodules is equal to r.*

b. *There is a unique family $P_{\mathscr{P}}(X) = \{\mathfrak{Q}_1,\ldots,\mathfrak{Q}_l\}$, $l \geq 0$, of ideals of A such that, in every P-decomposition of X relative to $\mathscr{P}$, the primary cyclic components have order ideals $\mathfrak{Q}_1,\ldots,\mathfrak{Q}_l$.*

c. *There is a unique family $T(X) = \{\mathfrak{T}_1,\ldots,\mathfrak{T}_h\}$, $h \geq 0$, such that, in every T-decomposition of X, the nonzero cyclic torsion components have order ideals $\mathfrak{T}_1,\ldots,\mathfrak{T}_h$.* □

The proof is almost word for word the same as that of Chapter 1, Theorem 13.4.

As a consequence of Theorem 3.6, we have

Corollary 1. *Let A be a principal ideal domain, X an A-module, and $\mathscr{P}$ a representative family of primes from A.*

a. *If $X = \bigoplus_{i=1}^{l} X_i$ and $X = \bigoplus_{i=1}^{l'} X_i'$ are P-decompositions of X relative to $\mathscr{P}$, then $l = l'$, and X_i is isomorphic to X_i' for each $i = 1,\ldots,l$.*

b. *If $X = \bigoplus_{i=1}^{d} X_i$ and $X = \bigoplus_{i=1}^{d'} X_i'$ (X_i, $X_i' \neq 0$) are T-decompositions of X, then $d = d'$ and X_i is isomorphic to X_i' for each $i = 1,\ldots,d$.* □

If X is a finitely generated A-module (A a principal ideal domain), we shall refer to $P(X)$ and $T(X)$, respectively, as the family of *primary invariants* and the family of *torsion invariants* of X. The number r of torsion-free cyclic summands is the dimension, in the sense of Chapter 3, Definition 1.6, of the free A-module X/Y, where Y is the torsion submodule of X. We shall call it the *rank* of X. In the special case where A is the ring of integers, the (unique) positive generators of the primary invariants are the elementary divisors of X, and the (unique) positive generators of the torsion invariants are the invariant factors (torsion coefficients) of X (Chapter 1, Section 13). We extend this terminology to another special case, where A is the polynomial domain $F[\lambda]$ over a field F by referring to the (unique) monic generators of the primary invariants as the *elementary divisors* of X and to the (unique) monic generators of the torsion invariants as the *invariant factors* (*torsion coefficients*) of X.

In view of Theorem 3.6, we have

Corollary 2. *Let A be a principal ideal domain, $\mathscr{P}$ a representative family of primes from A.*

a. *Two finitely generated A-modules are isomorphic if and only if they have the same rank and the same family of primary invariants relative to $\mathscr{P}$.*
b. *Two finitely generated A-modules are isomorphic if and only if they have the same rank and the same family of torsion invariants.* □

4. Decomposition of a Vector Space with Respect to a Given Linear Transformation

In this section we apply our results on modules over principal ideal domains to obtain canonical decompositions of a vector space determined by a single linear transformation.

Throughout this section we shall deal with finite-dimensional vector spaces over a commutative division ring, i.e., a field.

If X is a vector space over a field F, $\tau \in \operatorname{Hom}_F(X,X)$ and $g = a_0 + a_1\lambda + \cdots + a_k\lambda^k \in F[\lambda]$, then $g(\tau) = a_0\iota_X + a_1\tau + \cdots + a_k\tau^k \in \operatorname{Hom}_F(X,X)$. (From now on, for simplicity, we shall write a_0 for $a_0\iota_X$.) The mapping $\alpha: g \mapsto g(\tau)$ is an F-homomorphism of the F-space $F[\lambda]$ into the F-space $\operatorname{Hom}_F(X,X)$ (Exercise 4.1). For each $x \in X$, the mapping α_x: $g \mapsto g(\tau)(x)$ is an F-homomorphism of $F[\lambda]$ into X.

Theorem 4.1. *Let X be a vector space of finite dimension n over a field F, and let τ be a linear transformation on X. Then*

a. *For each $x \in X$, there is a unique monic polynomial $m_x \in F[\lambda]$ of least degree* $\deg m_x \leq n$ *such that $m_x(\tau)(x) = 0$.*
b. *There is a unique monic polynomial $m \in F[\lambda]$ of least degree such that $m(\tau) = 0$.*
c. *$m_x | m$ for all $x \in X$.*

PROOF.

a. The F-homomorphism α_x: $g \mapsto g(\tau)(x)$ of $F[\lambda]$ into X is obviously not an F-monomorphism, since $F[\lambda]$ is an infinite-dimensional F-space (Exercise

4.1) while X is finite-dimensional. Thus, Ker $\alpha_x \neq 0$, and the monic generator of Ker α_x (see Chapter 2, Theorem 3.3, Corollary) is the required polynomial m_x. In particular, Ker α_x contains a polynomial of degree n. For, since the $n + 1$ elements $x, \tau x, \ldots, \tau^n x \in X$ are linearly dependent (e.g., by Chapter 3, Theorem 1.6), there are elements $a_0, a_1, \ldots, a_n \in F$, not all zero, such that $a_0 + a_1 \tau x + \cdots + a_n \tau^n x = 0$. But then the nonzero polynomial $g = a_0 + a_1 \lambda + \cdots + a_n \lambda^n \in$ Ker α_x. Since $m_x | g$, deg $m_x \leq n$.

b. The F-space $\mathrm{Hom}_F(X,X)$ has finite dimension n^2 (Chapter 3, Theorem 5.3b). Hence the F-homomorphism $\alpha: g \mapsto g(\tau)$ of $F[\lambda]$ into $\mathrm{Hom}_F(X,X)$ is not an F-monomorphism; i.e., Ker $\alpha \neq 0$. The monic generator of Ker α is the required polynomial m.

c. Clearly, Ker $\alpha \subset$ Ker α_x for each $x \in X$. Hence, for each $x \in X$, $m_x | m$. ▮

We shall prove later (corollary of Theorem 4.4) that deg $m \leq n$.

Definition 4.1. Let X be a vector space over a field F, τ a linear transformation on X. Then, for each $x \in X$, the monic polynomial m_x of least degree in $F[\lambda]$ such that $m_x(\tau)(x) = 0$ is the *relative minimal polynomial of* τ *with respect to* x. The monic polynomial m of least degree in $F[\lambda]$ such that $m(\tau) - 0$ is the *minimal polynomial*, m_τ, of τ. ///

We shall say that a subspace Y of a vector space X is an *invariant subspace of a linear transformation* τ (or a τ*-subspace*) if $\tau Y \subset Y$. It is clear that, for each $x \in X$, the subspace, $X(\tau,x)$, of X generated by the elements $\tau^i x$ ($i \in N$) is a τ-subspace. We shall call it the *cyclic* τ-subspace generated by x. It is quite easy to see that the relative minimal polynomial m_x of τ with respect to x serves as the minimal polynomial of the restriction of τ to $X(\tau,x)$. If deg $m_x = k$, then the vectors $x, \tau x, \ldots, \tau^{k-1} x$ form a basis for $X(\tau,x)$. Hence deg $m_x =$ dim $X(\tau,x)$. More generally, if Y is any τ-subspace of X, we shall refer to the minimal polynomial of the restriction $\tau|_Y$ as the *relative minimal polynomial of* τ *with respect to* Y.

We now show how a finite-dimensional vector space over a field may be represented, relative to a given linear transformation τ, as a direct sum of cyclic τ-subspaces.

Given a vector space X over a field F, and a linear transformation τ on X, we can make the abelian group X into a module over the principal ideal domain $F[\lambda]$ by defining scalar multiplication as follows:

$$fx = f(\tau)x$$

for each $x \in X$, $f \in F[\lambda]$.

Since every generating set of the vector space X is also a generating set for the $F[\lambda]$-module X, the $F[\lambda]$-module X is finitely generated if the vector space X is finite-dimensional. This enables us to apply the decomposition theorems of Section 3 to the $F[\lambda]$-module X, and to obtain corresponding decompositions for the vector space.

Theorem 4.2. *Let X be a vector space over a field F, of finite dimension n, and let τ be a linear transformation on X. Then for some integer $h \leq n$, there are vectors $x_1, \ldots, x_h$ $(h \leq n)$ in X such that*

$$X = \bigoplus_{i=1}^{h} X(\tau, x_i)$$

and $t_i | t_{i+1}$ for each $i = 1, \ldots, h - 1$, where t_i is the relative minimal polynomial, m_{x_i}, of τ with respect to x_i. The integer h and the family $\langle t_1, \ldots, t_h \rangle$ are uniquely determined by τ.

Proof. By Theorem 3.4, the $F[\lambda]$-module X has a T-decomposition $X = \bigoplus_{i=1}^{q} F[\lambda]x_i$. By Theorem 4.1, the order ideal $\mathfrak{T}_i = (t_i)$ of each of the x_i is different from zero, hence q is equal to h, the number of torsion invariants of the $F[\lambda]$-module X, and $t_i | t_{i+1}$ for each $i = 1, \ldots, h - 1$. For each $i = 1, \ldots, h$, $F[\lambda]x_i = \{f(\tau)x_i | f \in F[\lambda]\} = X(\tau, x_i)$ and therefore the vector space X is equal to $\bigoplus_{i=1}^{h} X(\tau, x_i)$. If, for each $i = 1, \ldots, h$, the polynomial t_i is taken to be the unique monic generator of the order ideal of x_i, then t_i is the relative minimal polynomial, m_{x_i}, of τ with respect to x_i. Thus, we have the required decomposition for the vector space X. If X has another decomposition $X = \bigoplus_{i=1}^{h} X(\tau, x_i')$, with t_i' the relative minimum polynomial of τ with respect to x_i', and $t_i' | t_{i+1}'$ for $i = 1, \ldots, h' - 1$, then the $F[\lambda]$-module X is equal to $\bigoplus_{i=1}^{n} F[\lambda]x_i'$, the t_i' serving as invariant factors for X. Hence, by Theorem 3.6, $h = h'$ and $t_i = t_i'$ for each $i = 1, \ldots, h$. ∎

The family of polynomials $\{t_i\}_{i=1}^{h}$ is called the family of *invariant factors of the linear* transformation τ.

Corollary 1. *If $\{t_i\}_{i=1}^{h}$ is the family of invariant factors of a linear transformation τ, then t_h is the minimal polynomial m_τ of τ.*

Proof. If $x \in X$, then $x = c_1x_1 + \cdots + c_hx_h$ $(c_i \in F)$, where x_i has order ideal (t_i) $(i = 1, \ldots, h)$. Because of the divisibility conditions on the t_i, $t_h(\tau)(x) = 0$. Thus, if m_τ is the minimal polynomial of τ, then $m_\tau | t_h$. Since, in particular, $m_\tau(\tau)(x_h) = 0$, $t_h | m_\tau$. It follows that $m_\tau = t_h$. ∎

Corollary 2. *If τ is a linear transformation on an n-dimensional vector space X, and m_τ is the minimal polynomial of τ, then* $\deg m_\tau \leq n$. □

From the primary decomposition of the A-module X (Theorem 3.5), we obtain

Theorem 4.3. *Let X be a vector space over a field F, of finite dimension n, τ a linear transformation on X, and $\mathscr{P}$ a representative family of monic irreducible polynomials in $F[\lambda]$. Then there is a sequence $\{x_i\}_{i=1}^l$ of elements of X such that*

$$X = \bigoplus_{i=1}^{l} X(\tau, x_i),$$

where the relative minimal polynomial, $\mathfrak{q}_i$, of each x_i is monic primary, with the exponents decreasing for each prime in $\mathscr{P}$ The family $\{\mathfrak{q}_i\}_{i=1}^l$ of primary polynomials is uniquely determined by τ.

We leave the proof to the reader. □

The family of monic primary polynomials in Theorem 4.3 is called the family of *elementary divisors of the linear transformation, τ, relative* to $\mathscr{P}$.

We have seen that the "last" of the invariant factors of a linear transformation τ is the minimal polynomial, m_τ, of τ. Another important polynomial associated with a linear transformation τ is the product of its invariant factors.

Definition 4.2. The product of the invariant factors of a linear transformation τ on a vector space X is the *characteristic polynomial*, p_τ, of τ. ///

Theorem 4.4. *Let X be a vector space over a field F, of finite dimension n. If p_τ is the characteristic polynomial of $\tau \in \text{Hom}_F(X,X)$ then*

a. *p_τ is a monic polynomial of degree n.*
b. *$m_\tau | p_\tau$ (m_τ the minimal polynomial of τ).*
c. *$p_\tau(\tau) = 0$.*
d. *If q is an irreducible divisor of p_τ, then q is a divisor of m_τ.*
e. *If c is a root of p_τ ($c \in F$), then c is a root of m_τ.*
f. *If c is a root of p_τ ($c \in F$), then the linear transformation $\tau - c\iota \in \text{Hom}_F(X,X)$ is not an automorphism (ι the identity map on X).*
g. *For each root c of p_τ ($c \in F$), there are vectors $x \in X$ such that $\tau x = cx$; these vectors form a subspace of X. Conversely, if $\tau x = cx$ for some $c \in F$, $x \neq 0$ in X, then c is a root of p_τ.*
h. *The constant term, a_0, of p_τ is equal to* $(-1)^n \det \tau$.

PROOF.

a. Let $\{t_i\}_{i=1}^h$ be the family of invariant factors of τ. Then $p_\tau = \prod_{i=1}^h t_i$ is clearly monic. Its degree is n, since the degrees of the invariant factors are equal to the dimensions of the corresponding cyclic summands in a direct decomposition of the n-dimensional space X.

b. Since $m_\tau = t_h$, $m_\tau | p_\tau$.

c. Since $m_\tau | p_\tau$, $p_\tau(\tau) = 0$.

d. If q is an irreducible divisor of $p_\tau = \prod_{i=1}^h t_i$, then $q | t_i$ for some $i = 1,\ldots, h$. But then q is a divisor of $t_h = m_\tau$.

e. If c is a root of p_τ ($c \in F$), then $\lambda - c$ is an irreducible divisor of p_τ, hence (by d) divides m_τ. But then $m_\tau(c) = 0$.

f. If c is a root of p_τ ($c \in F$), then there is a greatest integer $k > 0$ such that $m_\tau(\lambda) = (\lambda - c)^k g(\lambda)$ ($g(\lambda) \neq 0$ in $F[\lambda]$). Since $m_\tau(\lambda)$ is the minimal polynomial of τ, $(\tau - c\iota)^{k-1}g(\tau) \neq 0$, and there is some $\mu \in X$ such that $(\tau - c\iota)^{k-1}g(\tau)(\mu) \neq 0$. Let $x = (\tau - c\iota)^{k-1}g(\tau)(\mu)$. Then $(\tau - c\iota)(x) = 0$, $x \neq 0$.

g. If c is a root of p_τ, then, by f, there is a vector $x \neq 0$ in X such that $\tau x = cx$. The set $X_c = \{x | \tau x = cx\}$ is obviously a subspace of X; i.e., $X_c = \operatorname{Ker}(\tau - c\iota)$.

If $c \in F$ and $x \neq 0$ in X are such that $\tau x = cx$, then $(\tau - c\iota)x = 0$, hence $\lambda - c$ is the relative minimal polynomial of τ with respect to x. But then $(\lambda - c) | m_\tau$. Since $m_\tau | p_\tau$, c is a root of p_τ.

h. Let $\{t_i\}_{i=1}^h$ be the family of invariant factors of τ. For each i, let $t_i = a_0^{(i)} + a_i^{(i)}\lambda + \cdots + \lambda^{k_i - 1}$, and let $\{e_i, \tau e_i, \ldots, \tau e_i^{k_i - 1}\}$ be a τ-cyclic basis for the τ-invariant subspace W_i corresponding to t_i. If η: $W_i \otimes \cdots \otimes W_i \to F$ is the S_{k_i}-homomorphism defined by $\eta(e_i \otimes \tau e_i \otimes \cdots \otimes \tau^{k_i - 1}e_i) = 1$, then

$$\begin{aligned}\det(\tau|_{W_i}) &= \eta(\tau e_i \otimes \tau^2 e_i \otimes \cdots \otimes \tau^{k_i} e_i)\\ &= \eta(\tau e_i \otimes \cdots \otimes \tau^{k_i - 1} e_i \otimes (-a_0^{(i)} - a_1^{(i)}\tau - a_{k_i-1}^{(i)}\tau^{k_i - 1})e_i)\\ &= (-1)^{k_i} a_0^{(i)}.\end{aligned}$$

Since $\tau = \tau_1 \cdots \tau_r$, where $\tau_i = \tau|_{W_i} \cup \iota_{X - W_i}$,

$$\det \tau = \prod_{i=1}^{r} \det \tau_i = (-1)^{k_1 + \cdots + k_r} \prod_{i=1}^{r} a_0^{(i)} = (-1)^n a_0. \quad \blacksquare$$

Definition 4.3. If $\tau \in \operatorname{Hom}_F(X,X)$ and $x \neq 0$ in X, and $c \in F$ such that $\tau x = cx$, then x is a *characteristic vector* (*eigenvector*) *of* τ and c is a *characteristic root* (*eigenvalue*) *of* τ *in F.* ///

By Theorem 4.4g, the characteristic roots in F of a linear transformation $\tau \in \text{Hom}_F(X,X)$ are the roots in F of the characteristic polynomial $p_\tau \in F[\lambda]$.

Theorem 4.4h is also a consequence of the following theorem on characteristic polynomials, whose proof we outline in Exercise 4.5.

Theorem 4.5. *Let X be an n-dimensional vector space over a field F, and let τ be a linear transformation on X, with characteristic polynomial p_τ. Lift X to an $F[\lambda]$-module, and let $\lambda\iota - \tau$ be the $F[\lambda]$-linear transformation defined by $x \mapsto \lambda x - \tau x$. Then $p_\tau = \det(\lambda\iota - \tau)$.*   ☐

Corollary 1. (Hamilton–Cayley.) *If τ is a linear transformation of a finite-dimensional vector space over a field F, then τ is a root of the polynomial $\det(\lambda\iota - \tau) \in F[\lambda]$.*   ☐

Corollary 2. *If the characteristic polynomial of a linear transformation τ is $p_\tau = \sum_{i=0}^{n-1} a_i\lambda^i + \lambda^n$, then*

$$\text{tr}(\tau) = -a_{n-1}. \quad ☐$$

5. Canonical Matrices for a Linear Transformation

Suppose that X is a vector space of finite dimension n over a field F. Let $\tau \in \text{Hom}_F(X,X)$ and let Y be a τ-invariant subspace of X, of dimension $k \le n$. Then $\tau|_Y \in \text{Hom}_F(Y,Y)$. Since every basis for Y can be extended to a basis for X, we may choose a basis $\mathscr{B} = \{x_i\}_{i=1}^n$ for X such that $\mathscr{B}_Y = \{x_i\}_{i=j+1}^{j+k}$ is a basis for Y, for some positive integer $j \le n - k$. If the matrix of $\tau|_Y$ relative to $\mathscr{B}_Y$ is $T_Y \in F_k$, then the matrix of τ relative to $\mathscr{B}$ has T_Y as a "submatrix," formed by the elements in the $(j + 1)$st to $(j + k)$th rows and columns of T.

$$
\begin{array}{c}
\quad\quad (j+1)\ (j+k) \\
\begin{array}{c} j+1 \\ \\ j+k \end{array}
\left(
\begin{array}{c|c|c}
\ & \ & \ \\ \hline
\ & T_Y & \ \\ \hline
\ & \ & \
\end{array}
\right) = T.
\end{array}
$$

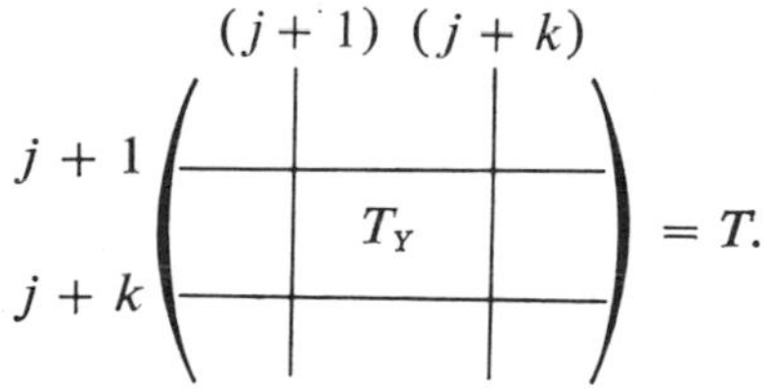

Now suppose $X = Y_1 \oplus \cdots \oplus Y_q$, where each Y_i is a τ-invariant subspace. For each $i = 1, \ldots, n$, let $\tau_i \in \text{Hom}_F(X,X)$ be defined by

$$
\tau_i x = \begin{cases} \tau x & \text{for } x \in Y_i, \\ 0 & \text{for } x \notin Y_i. \end{cases}
$$

Then $\tau = \tau_1 + \cdots + \tau_n$. Let $\mathscr{B} = \mathscr{B}_1 \cup \cdots \cup \mathscr{B}_q$ be a basis for X such that $\mathscr{B}_i$ is a basis for Y_i ($i = 1,\ldots,q$). If T_i is the matrix of $\tau|_{Y_i}$ relative to $\mathscr{B}_i$, then the matrix of τ relative to $\mathscr{B}$ has the q submatrices T_i arranged along its diagonal and is zero elsewhere:

$$T = \begin{pmatrix} T_1 & \cdots & 0 \\ \vdots & \ddots & \vdots \\ 0 & \cdots & T_q \end{pmatrix} = \mathrm{Diag}(T_1,\ldots,T_q).$$

We shall refer to $\mathrm{Diag}(T_1,\ldots,T_q)$ as *the direct sum* of the submatrices T_i.

We now consider the case where Y is the cyclic τ-subspace, $Y = X(\tau,x)$, generated by some $x \in X$. Let $m_x(\lambda) = a_0 + a_1\lambda + \cdots + a_{k-1}\lambda^{k-1} + \lambda^k$ be the relative minimal polynomial of τ with respect to x. Then $\mathscr{B}_Y = \{\tau^i x\}_{i=0}^{k-1}$ is a basis for Y, and $\tau^k = -a_0 - a_1\tau - \cdots - a_{k-1}\tau^{k-1}$. The matrix of $\tau|_Y$ relative to $\mathscr{B}_Y$ is

$$T_Y = \begin{pmatrix} 0 & 1 & 0 & \cdots & 0 & 0 \\ 0 & 0 & 1 & \cdots & 0 & 0 \\ \vdots & \vdots & \vdots & & \vdots & \vdots \\ 0 & 0 & 0 & \cdots & 0 & 1 \\ -a_0 & -a_1 & -a_2 & \cdots & -a_{k-2} & -a_{k-1} \end{pmatrix}.$$

Definition 5.1. If $f(\lambda) = a_0 + a_1\lambda + \cdots + a_k\lambda^k \in F[\lambda]$, then the $k \times k$ matrix

$$\begin{pmatrix} 0 & 1 & 0 & \cdots & 0 & 0 \\ 0 & 0 & 1 & \cdots & 0 & 0 \\ \vdots & \vdots & \vdots & & \vdots & \vdots \\ 0 & 0 & 0 & \cdots & 0 & 1 \\ -a_0 & -a_1 & -a_2 & \cdots & -a_{k-2} & -a_{k-1} \end{pmatrix}$$

is the *companion matrix*, $C(f)$, of the polynomial f. ///

The matrix T_Y, above, is $C(m_x)$, the companion matrix of the relative minimal polynomial of τ with respect to x.

We now apply these observations to our results of Section 4.

Theorem 5.1. *Let X be a vector space of finite dimension n over a field F, and let $\tau \in \mathrm{Hom}_F(X,X)$. Suppose that $\{s_i\}_{i=1}^{l}$ is the family of elementary divisors and $\{t_j\}_{j=1}^{h}$ is the family of invariant factors of τ. Then*

a. *X has a basis relative to which the matrix of* τ *is* $\text{Diag}(C(s_1),\ldots,C(s_l))$, *the direct sum of the companion matrices of the elementary divisors of* τ.
b. *X has a basis relative to which the matrix of* τ *is* $\text{Diag}(C(t_1),\ldots,C(t_h))$, *the direct sum of the companion matrices of the invariant factors of* τ.

PROOF.
a. Apply the preceding remarks to a P-decomposition of X relative to τ.
b. Do the same for a T-decomposition. ▮

Suppose that T is any matrix in F_n. Then all linear transformations in $\text{Hom}_F(X,X)$ which may be represented by T relative to some basis have the same elementary divisors and the same invariant factors. For, suppose T represents τ relative to some basis $\mathscr{B}$ and τ has elementary divisors $\{s_1,\ldots,s_l\}$. Then T is similar to $\text{Diag}(C(s_1),\ldots,C(s_l))$ (Chapter 4, Theorem 2.1). If τ' is another linear transformation represented by T relative to some basis, then there is another basis, $\mathscr{B}'$, relative to which the matrix of τ' is $\text{Diag}(C(s_1),\ldots, C(s_l))$. But then $\mathscr{B}' = \mathscr{B}_1 \cup \cdots \cup \mathscr{B}_l$, where each $\mathscr{B}_j$ is of the form $\mathscr{B}_j = \{e_j,\tau' e_j,\ldots,(\tau')^{k_j-1}e_j\}$ ($j = 1,\ldots,l$; k_j the degree of s_j). Hence $[\mathscr{B}_j] = X(\tau',e_j)$ for each $j = 1,\ldots, l$, and $X = \bigoplus_{j=1}^{l} [\mathscr{B}_j]$ is a P-decomposition for X, relative to τ', whence, by Theorem 4.3, $\{s_1,\ldots,s_l\}$ is the family of elementary divisors of τ'. A similar argument applies to the invariant factors. We can therefore define elementary divisors and invariant factors *of a matrix* as follows:

Definition 5.2. If $T \in F_n$, then the family of elementary divisors (invariant factors) of any linear transformation of X which may be represented by T relative to some basis of X *is the family of elementary divisors (invariant factors) of the matrix T.* ///

Corollary
a. *Two matrices in* F_n *are similar if and only if they have the same family of elementary divisors.*
b. *Two matrices in* F_n *are similar if and only if they have the same family of invariant factors.* □

If F is an algebraically closed field (Chapter 5, Definition 2.1), e.g., the complex field, then every polynomial in $F[\lambda]$ is a product of powers of first-degree polynomials in $F[\lambda]$; hence the elementary divisors of a linear transformation $\tau \in \text{Hom}_F(X,X)$ are all of the form $(\lambda - c)^{\alpha}$, $c \in F$, α a positive integer. In this case, bases can be chosen for the primary cyclic components in a P-decomposition of X in such a way as to give a canonical matrix simpler than the matrix $\text{Diag}(C(s_1),\ldots,C(s_t))$ of Theorem 5.1a.

Let τ be a linear transformation on X whose relative minimal polynomial with respect to a τ-invariant subspace Y is $(\lambda - c)^r$. Let σ be the linear transformation on X which agrees with $\tau - c\iota$ on Y and is zero elsewhere. Then the relative minimal polynomial of σ with respect to Y is λ^r. Relative to a σ-cyclic basis $\mathscr{B} = \{\sigma^i e\}_{i=0}^{r-1}$ for Y, the matrix of $\sigma|_Y$ is the $r \times r$ companion matrix

$$(\lambda)^r = \begin{pmatrix} 0 & 1 & 0 & \cdots & 0 & 0 \\ 0 & 0 & 1 & \cdots & 0 & 0 \\ \vdots & \vdots & \vdots & & \vdots & \vdots \\ 0 & 0 & 0 & \cdots & 0 & 1 \\ 0 & 0 & 0 & \cdots & 0 & 0 \end{pmatrix}.$$

Since $\tau|_Y = (\sigma + c\iota)|_Y$, the matrix of $\tau|_Y$ relative to the basis $\mathscr{B}_\sigma$ is

$$\begin{pmatrix} c & 1 & 0 & \cdots & 0 & 0 \\ 0 & c & 1 & \cdots & 0 & 0 \\ \vdots & \vdots & \vdots & & \vdots & \vdots \\ 0 & 0 & 0 & \cdots & c & 1 \\ 0 & 0 & 0 & \cdots & 0 & c \end{pmatrix} = J(c,r).$$

The matrix $J(c,r)$ is called an *elementary Jordan matrix.*

Theorem 5.2. *If F is an algebraically closed field, X an n-dimensional vector space over F, and $\tau \in \text{Hom}_F(X,X)$, then there is a basis for X relative to which the matrix of τ is the direct sum of the elementary Jordan matrices corresponding to the elementary divisors of τ.*

PROOF. We need only choose, for each component Y in a P-decomposition of X, the basis relative to which the matrix of $\tau|_Y$ is the elementary Jordan matrix corresponding to the relative minimum polynomial of τ with respect to Y. ∎

The canonical matrix of Theorem 5.2 is referred to as the *Jordan canonical matrix of τ.*

Example. Let X be eight-dimensional over the complex field $\mathbf{C}$, and let τ be a linear transformation on X, with elementary divisors $(\lambda - c_1)^3$, $(\lambda - c_1)^2$; $(\lambda - c_2)^2$, $(\lambda - c_2)$. Then the Jordan canonical matrix of τ is

$$\left(\begin{array}{ccc|cc|cc|c} c_1 & 1 & 0 & & & & & \\ 0 & c_1 & 1 & & & & & \\ 0 & 0 & c_1 & & & & & \\ \hline & & & c_1 & 1 & & & \\ & & & 0 & c_1 & & & \\ \hline & & & & & c_2 & 1 & \\ & & & & & 0 & c_2 & \\ \hline & & & & & & & c_2 \end{array}\right)$$

Corollary 1. *If F is algebraically closed, then every matrix in F_n $(n \geq 1)$ is similar to a Jordan canonical matrix. This matrix is determined to within the order of its elementary Jordan sub-matrices.* ☐

Note that the Jordan canonical matrix is diagonal if and only if all the elementary divisors are of the first degree. Since every diagonal matrix is in Jordan form, we have

Corollary 2. *If F is algebraically closed, $T \in F_n$ $(n \geq 1)$, then T is similar to a diagonal matrix if, and only if, each of the elementary divisors of T is of the form $\lambda - c$, for some $c \in F$.* ☐

Exercises

Section 1

1.1. The subspaces of a vector space X form a lattice $\mathscr{L}$ (see Chapter 1, Exercise 4.12) under set inclusion, with $Y + Z$ and $Y \cap Z$ serving as least upper and greatest lower bound, respectively, for $Y, Z \in \mathscr{L}$, and X, 0 serving as least upper and greatest lower bound, respectively, for the entire lattice $\mathscr{L}$. Prove:

(a) $\mathscr{L}$ is *complemented*; i.e., for each $Y \in \mathscr{L}$ there is some $Z \in \mathscr{L}$ such that $Y + Z = X$, $Y \cap Z = 0$.

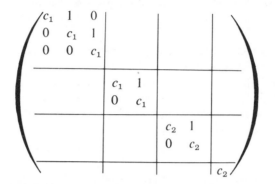

(b) $\mathscr{L}$ is *modular*; i.e., if $X,Y,Z \in \mathscr{L}$ and $Z \subset X$, then $X \cap (Y \cup Z) = (X \cap Y) \cup Z$.

(c) If X is infinite-dimensional, then $\mathscr{L}$ satisfies neither the ascending nor the descending chain condition.

1.2. If X is a vector space of infinite dimension δ, then X has infinitely many proper subspaces of dimension ν, for each cardinal ν such that $0 \le \nu \le \delta$.

1.3. Prove:

(a) If X is a vector space over a division ring A, then X is both a projective and an injective A-module.

(b) Deduce from a: If X, Y are vector spaces over a division ring A, $\tau \in \text{Hom}_A(X,Y)$, then τ is a monomorphism if and only if it has a right inverse in $\text{Hom}_A(Y,X)$, and τ is an epimorphism if and only if it has a left inverse in $\text{Hom}_A(Y,X)$.

1.4. Let X be an infinite-dimensional vector space over a division ring A. Prove that

(a) There is a linear transformation $\tau \in \text{Hom}_A(X,X)$ which is a monomorphism but not an epimorphism.

(b) There is a linear transformation $\tau \in \text{Hom}_A(X,X)$ which is an epimorphism but not a monomorphism.

(c) The endomorphism ring $\text{End}_A(X)$ has one-sided units.

1.5. Let X be a finite-dimensional vector space over a division ring D.

(a) Infer from Theorem 1.3 that the endomorphism ring $\text{End}_D(X)$ has no one-sided units.

(b) Make the same inference using Lemma 1 of Chapter 1, Section 10.

1.6. Let X, Y, Z be vector spaces over a division ring D, $\tau \in \text{Hom}_D(X,Y)$, $\sigma \in \text{Hom}_D(Y,Z)$. Prove that rank $\sigma\tau \le \min\{\text{rank } \sigma, \text{rank } \tau\}$.

1.7. If X, Y are vector spaces over a division ring D and $\sigma,\tau \in \text{Hom}_D(X,Y)$, then $\text{rank}(\sigma + \tau) \le \text{rank } \sigma + \text{rank } \tau$.

Section 2

2.1. Verify Remarks 1, 2, and 3 on pages 213–214.

2.2. For any ring $\langle A,+,\cdot\rangle$, the *opposite ring* $\langle A^0,\oplus,\circ\rangle$ is defined by $A^0 = A$, $\oplus = +$, and, for each $x,y \in A^0$, $x \circ y = y \cdot x$ (obviously, A^0 is a ring anti-isomorphic to A). Prove that, for each positive integer n, $(A^0_n) = (A_n)^0$.

2.3. Let X be an n-dimensional left vector space over a division ring D. Prove:

(a) X forms a right vector space, X^0, over D^0, with scalar multiplication defined by $xa = ax$ ($a \in D^0 = D$, $x \in X^0 = X$).

(b) $\text{End}_{D^0} X^0 \cong (D^0)_n = D^0_n$.

(c) $\text{End}_D X = \text{End}_{D^0} X^0$.

(d) $\text{End}_D X \cong (D^0)_n$.

Note that, if D is commutative, then $D = D^0$ and $D^0_n = D$ for each $n \ge 1$.

2.4. For A a commutative ring, define the *transpose* of an $m \times n$ matrix $S = (s_{ij})$, $i = 1, \ldots, m$, $j = 1, \ldots, n$ $(s_{ij} \in A)$ to be the $n \times m$ matrix $S^T = (s_{ji})$, $i = 1, \ldots, m, j = 1, \ldots, n$. Prove that, if S, T are $m \times n$ matrices over A, then

(a) $(S + T)^T = S^T + T^T$.

(b) $(ST)^T = T^T S^T$.

In particular, if $m = n$, then

(c) $(S^T)^T = S$ for each $S \in A_n$.

(d) $S \to S^T$ is an antiautomorphism of the ring A_n.

2.5. Let X be a finite-dimensional vector space over a field F, and let $\{e_i\}_{i=1}^n$ and $\{e_i^*\}_{i=1}^n$ be dual bases for X and X^*, respectively. If $\sigma \in \mathrm{Hom}_A(X,X)$ has matrix $S = (s_{ij})$ relative to $\{e_i\}_{i=1}^n$, prove that the transpose $\sigma^T \in \mathrm{Hom}_A(X^*,X^*)$ has matrix S^T relative to $\{e_i^*\}_{i=1}^n$.

2.6. Let X be a vector space of finite dimension n over a field F, and let $\tau \in \mathrm{Hom}_F(X,X)$. Prove that rank τ = rank τ^T.

2.7. If F is a field, T a matrix in F_n, $r,n \in N$, $1 \leq r \leq n$, then the following statements are equivalent:

(a) T has rank r.

(b) T has exactly r linearly independent rows.

(c) The largest nonzero determinant of a submatrix of T has order r.

(d) T has exactly r linearly independent columns.

(e) T^T has rank r.

2.8. For every matrix $T \in D_n$ (D a division ring) there is a nonsingular matrix $Q \in D_n$ such that $TQT = T$. (*Hint:* Use Theorem 2.2, Corollary 2.)

2.9. Prove that every $n \times n$ matrix over a division ring D is similar to a matrix of the form

$$\begin{pmatrix} A & 0 \\ 0 & B \end{pmatrix},$$

where A is a nonsingular matrix in D_m for some $m \leq n$, and $B \in D_{n-m}$ is nilpotent. [*Hint:* Use Fitting's Lemma (Chapter 1, Exercise 10.3) and the corollary of Theorem 2.1.]

Section 3

3.1. Carry out the details of the proofs of Theorems 3.1. and 3.6.

3.2. (a) If A is an integral domain, every free A-module is torsion free.

(b) For every integral domain A which is not a field, there are torsion-free A-modules which are not free.

3.3. Generalize to modules over principal ideal domains the results of Chapter 1, Exercises 13.1 through 13.5.

3.4. An A-module over a principal ideal domain satisfies the ascending chain condition on submodules if and only if it is finitely generated.

Section 4

4.1. Let X be a finite-dimensional vector space over a field F, $\tau \in \text{Hom}_F(X,X)$.
(a) $\alpha: g \to g(\tau)$ is an F-homomorphism of $F[\lambda]$ into $\text{Hom}_F(X,X)$.
(b) For each $x \in X$, $\alpha_x: g \to g(\tau)(x)$ is an F-homomorphism of $F[\lambda]$ into X.
(c) $F[\lambda]$ is infinite dimensional over F; hence α_x $(x \in X)$ is not a monomorphism.

4.2. Let V be a vector space over a field F of finite dimension n. Let $\sigma \in \text{Hom}_F(V,V)$ and let m_σ be the minimum polynomial of σ. Prove: V is a cyclic σ-space if and only if $\deg m_\sigma = n$.

4.3. Let V, F, σ be as in Exercise 4.2. Prove: Every element in $\text{Hom}_F(V,V)$ which commutes with σ is a polynomial in σ if and only if V is a cyclic σ-space.

4.4. Let V, F, σ be as in Exercise 4.2, and let $\tau \in \text{Hom}_F(V,V)$. Prove: If τ commutes with every linear transformation which commutes with σ, then τ is a polynomial in σ.

4.5. Prove Theorem 4.5. [*Hint:* Proceed as in the proof of Theorem 4.4h. Find bases for the cyclic subspaces of $\lambda\iota - \tau$ which are appropriately related to the bases for the cyclic subspaces of τ. Compute $\det(\lambda\iota - \tau)$ as a product of the determinants of the restrictions of $\lambda\iota - \tau$ to the cyclic subspaces.]

4.6. Let V be a finite-dimensional vector space over the complex field **C**. Prove: If $\sigma\tau = \tau\sigma$, where $\sigma,\tau \in \text{Hom}_F(V,V)$, then there is a nonzero vector in V which is a characteristic vector for σ and for τ.

Section 5

5.1. If the matrix A has characteristic roots $\lambda_1, \lambda_2, \ldots, \lambda_n$ (with repetitions possible), and if f is a polynomial, then $f(A)$ has characteristic roots $f(\lambda_1), f(\lambda_2), \ldots, f(\lambda_n)$.

5.2. Give a method for finding a polynomial h each of whose roots is a polynomial f in a root of a polynomial g [i.e., the roots of h are $f(\lambda_1), f(\lambda_2), \ldots, f(\lambda_n)$, where $\lambda_1, \lambda_2, \ldots, \lambda_n$ are the roots of g].

5.3. Consider the linear recursive relation $x_{n+2} = x_{n+1} + x_n$. Note that

$$\begin{pmatrix} x_{n+1} \\ x_{n+2} \end{pmatrix} = \begin{pmatrix} 0 & 1 \\ 1 & 1 \end{pmatrix} \begin{pmatrix} x_n \\ x_{n+1} \end{pmatrix}.$$

Let

$$A = \begin{pmatrix} 0 & 1 \\ 1 & 1 \end{pmatrix}.$$

Note that

$$\begin{pmatrix} x_n \\ x_{n+1} \end{pmatrix} = A^n \begin{pmatrix} x_0 \\ x_1 \end{pmatrix}.$$

The minimum polynomial of A is $x^2 - x - 1$, and the characteristic roots of A are $\lambda_1 = (1 + \sqrt{5})/2$ and $\lambda_2 = (1 - \sqrt{5})/2$. Verify that

$$A^n = \frac{\lambda_1^n - \lambda_2^n}{\lambda_1 - \lambda_2} A + \frac{\lambda_1 \lambda_2^n - \lambda_2 \lambda_1^n}{\lambda_1 - \lambda_2} I.$$

Conclude that

$$x_n = \frac{1}{\lambda_1 - \lambda_2} [(\lambda_1 \lambda_2^n - \lambda_2 \lambda_1^n) x_0 + (\lambda_1^n - \lambda_2^n) x_1].$$

In particular, if $x_0 = 0$ and $x_1 = 1$, then $x_n = (1/\sqrt{5})(\lambda_1^n - \lambda_2^n)$.

5.4. Generalize the method of Exercise 5.3 to a general linear recursive relation. (Care must be exercised if the corresponding matrix has repeated roots.)

5.5. Let F be a field and E a field containing F. Let A and B be matrices with coefficients in F. If there is an invertible matrix C with entries in E such that $C^{-1}AC = B$, then there is an invertible matrix D with coefficients in F such that $D^{-1}AD = B$. (In other words: If A and B are similar over E, then they are similar over F.)

5.6. Show that two idempotent matrices are similar if and only if they have the same rank.

Chapter 5 / Field Theory

1. Fields; Transcendental and Algebraic Field Extensions

We recall (Chapter 2, Definition 1.1) that a field is a commutative ring with identity $1 \neq 0$ in which every nonzero element has a multiplicative inverse.

Definition 1.1.

a. A subring F of a field E is a *subfield* of E if F is itself a field. A subfield F of a field E is a *proper subfield* of E if $F \neq E$.

b. Let F be a field. Then $\langle E/F,\varepsilon \rangle$ is an *extension field* (or, simply, an *extension*) of F if E is a field and $\varepsilon: F \to E$ is a monomorphism of the field F into the field E. An extension $\langle E/F,\varepsilon \rangle$ of F is a *proper extension* if $\varepsilon(F) \neq E$.

c. A *prime field* is a field which has no proper subfields. ///

If $\langle E/F,\varepsilon \rangle$ is an extension of F, and $\langle K/E,\kappa \rangle$ is an extension of E, then $\langle K/F,\kappa\varepsilon \rangle$ is an extension of F. In order to simplify our exposition we shall sometimes "identify" E with the subfield $\kappa(E)$ of K, the field F with the subfield $\kappa\varepsilon(F)$ of K, we write $K \supset E \supset F$, and say that E is an extension of F and K an extension of E (and F). These considerations may be applied in a similar way to any tower of fields $E_1 \supset E_2 \supset \cdots \supset E_n \supset F$.

A problem which appears as a recurrent theme in algebra is the following: Given an algebraic structure, to what extent does knowledge about the homomorphisms of this structure yield information about the structure itself? The following very simple theorem, whose proof we leave to the reader, illustrates a trivial relationship between a field and its homomorphisms.

Theorem 1.1. *Let F be a commutative ring with identity $1 \neq 0$. Then F is a field if and only if for every ring A, every nonzero homomorphism of F into A is a monomorphism.* □

For any field F, the mapping $\varphi: \mathbf{Z} \to F$ defined by $\varphi(n) = n \cdot 1$ (1 the identity of F) is a homomorphism of the ring of integers into F. Since $\operatorname{Im} \varphi$ is a subring of the field F, $\operatorname{Im} \varphi$ is an integral domain. Furthermore, $\operatorname{Im} \varphi \cong \mathbf{Z}/\operatorname{Ker} \varphi$. It follows (Chapter 2, Theorem 1.6) that $\operatorname{Ker} \varphi$ is a prime ideal of $\mathbf{Z}$. Hence, $\operatorname{Ker} \varphi$ is generated by 0 or by a positive prime $p \in \mathbf{Z}$.

Definition 1.2. Let F be a field and let $\varphi: \mathbf{Z} \to F$ be the map defined by $\varphi(n) = n \cdot 1$. Then the *characteristic of F*, Char F, is the nonnegative generator of $\operatorname{Ker} \varphi$. ///

In view of the discussion preceding the definition, for any field F, Char F is either 0 or a positive prime $p \in \mathbf{Z}$. Obviously, all subfields and all extension fields of a field F have the same characteristic as F.

The following theorem is left as an exercise (Exercise 1.2):

Theorem 1.2.

a. *Every field F contains a unique prime field, namely the intersection of all the subfields of F.*
b. *If F is a prime field of characteristic 0, then F is isomorphic to the field $\mathbf{Q}$ of rational numbers.*
c. *If F is a prime field of characteristic p, then F is isomorphic to $\mathbf{Z}/(p)$.* □

If $E \supset F$, then E has the structure of an F-module; i.e., E is a vector space over F.

Definition 1.3. Let $E \supset F$. The *degree of E over F*, denoted by $[E: F]$, is the dimension of E considered as a vector space over F. (More generally, if V is an F-subspace of E, we write $[V: F]$ for the dimension of V over F.) ///

Theorem 1.3. *Suppose that K, E, and F are fields with $K \supset E \supset F$. Then $[K: F] = [K: E][E: F]$. In particular, if $\{\eta_i\}_{i \in I}$ is a basis for E over F and $\{\kappa_j\}_{j \in J}$ is a basis for K over E, then $\{\eta_i \kappa_j\}_{i \in I, j \in J}$ is a basis for K over F.*

PROOF. Let $\{\eta_i\}_{i \in I}$ be a basis for E over F, $\{\kappa_j\}_{j \in J}$ a basis for K over E, with I and J chosen so that $|I| = [E: F]$ and $|J| = [K: E]$. We shall show that $\{\eta_i \kappa_j\}_{i \in I, j \in J}$ is a basis for K over F, and from this the conclusion of the theorem follows.

First note that $\{\eta_i \kappa_j\}_{i \in I, j \in J}$ is a set of generators for K over F. In fact, if $\alpha \in K$, then there exist $j_1, j_2, \ldots, j_m$ in J and $\varepsilon_1, \varepsilon_2, \ldots, \varepsilon_m$ in E such that $\alpha = \sum_{r=1}^{m} \varepsilon_r \kappa_{j_r}$. Furthermore, to each of these ε_r there correspond $i_{r1}, i_{r2}, \ldots, i_{rn_r}$ in I and $a_{r1}, a_{r2}, \ldots, a_{rn_r}$ in F such that $\varepsilon_r = \sum_{s=1}^{n_r} a_{rs} \eta_{i_{rs}}$. Hence $\alpha = \sum_{r=1}^{m} \sum_{s=1}^{n_r} a_{rs} \eta_{i_{rs}} \kappa_{j_r}$.

It remains to show that $\{\eta_i \kappa_j\}_{i \in I, j \in J}$ is a free set over F. Suppose that I' and J' are finite subsets of I and J, respectively, and that, for $i \in I'$ and $j \in J'$, there exist $a_{ij} \in F$ such that $\sum_{i \in I, j \in J'} a_{ij} \eta_i \kappa_j = 0$. Then $\sum_{j \in J'} (\sum_{i \in I'} a_{ij} \eta_i) \kappa_j = 0$, and since $\{\kappa_j\}_{j \in J}$ is free over E, it follows that for each $j \in J'$, $\sum_{i \in I'} a_{ij} \eta_i = 0$. Since $\{\eta_i\}_{i \in I}$ is free over F, it follows that, for each $i \in I'$ and each $j \in J'$, $a_{ij} = 0$; whence $\{\eta_i \kappa_j\}_{i \in I, j \in J}$ is free over F, as desired. ▮

Definition 1.4. If F is a subfield of K, S a subset of K, then the subfield

$$F(S) = \bigcap_{\substack{E \supset S \\ K \supset E \supset F}} E$$

is the *subfield of K obtained by the adjunction of S to F*, or alternatively, the *subfield of K generated by F and S*. The subset S is a *system of generators* for $F(S)$ over F. An extension $\langle K/F, \varepsilon \rangle$ of F such that $\varepsilon F = F'$ is a *simple extension* if $K = F'\{\alpha\}$ for some $\alpha \in K$. ///

NOTATION. We shall write "$F(\alpha)$" for the simple extension $F(\{\alpha\})$.

We now have the following trivial

Theorem 1.4. *If $E \supset F$, E and F fields, and if S_1, S_2 are subsets of E, then $F(S_1 \cup S_2) = F(S_1)(S_2) = F(S_2)(S_1)$.*

PROOF. Clearly, $F(S_1 \cup S_2)$ contains F, S_1, and S_2, whence $F(S_1 \cup S_2)$ contains $F(S_1)$ and S_2. It follows that $F(S_1 \cup S_2) \supset F(S_1)(S_2)$. On the other hand, $F(S_1)(S_2)$ contains $F(S_1)$ and S_2, whence $F(S_1)(S_2)$ contains F and $S_1 \cup S_2$. It follows that $F(S_1)(S_2) \supset F(S_1 \cup S_2)$. But then $F(S_1 \cup S_2) = F(S_1)(S_2) = F(S_2 \cup S_1) = F(S_2)(S_1)$. ▮

NOTATION. We write $F(S_1,S_2)$ for $F(S_1 \cup S_2)$. If $K \supset E_1 \supset F$ and $K \supset E_2 \supset F$, we write E_1E_2 or $E_1 \cup E_2$ for $F(E_1 \cup E_2)$.

Theorem 1.5. *Let $K \supset F$ and let S be a subset of K.*

a. *If $\alpha \in F(S)$, then there exists a finite subset S' of S such that $\alpha \in F(S')$.*

b. $F(S) = \bigcup_{\substack{S' \subset S \\ S' \text{ finite set}}} F(S')$.

PROOF.

a. Let $E = \{\alpha \in F(S) | \alpha \in F(S') \text{ for some finite subset } S' \text{ of } S\}$. It is easy to verify that E is a subfield of K, $E \supset S$, and $E \supset F$. Thus it follows from Definition 1.4 that $F(S) \subset E$. Since $E \subset F(S)$, we have $E = F(S)$.

b. Follows immediately from a. ∎

We shall now give a coarse classification for the elements of a field. Let us recall (Chapter 2, Theorem 2.5) that if $F[x]$ is the polynomial domain in one indeterminate over the field F and if α is an element of a field $E \supset F$, then there exists an F-homomorphism $\varphi_{\alpha/F}: F[x] \to E$ defined by $\varphi_{\alpha/F}(f(x)) = f(\alpha)$. Denote $\varphi_{\alpha/F}(F[x])$ by $F[\alpha]$; then $F[\alpha] \cong F[x]/\text{Ker } \varphi_{\alpha/F}$. Since $F[\alpha]$ is contained in E, $F[\alpha]$ is an integral domain. It follows (Chapter 2, Theorem 1.6) that Ker $\varphi_{\alpha/F}$ is a prime ideal. Since $F[x]$ is a principal ideal domain, Ker $\varphi_{\alpha/F} = (0)$ or Ker $\varphi_{\alpha/F} = (m_{\alpha/F}(x))$, where $m_{\alpha/F}(x)$ is a monic irreducible polynomial in $F[x]$.

Definition 1.5. Let F be a subfield of a field E, $\alpha \in E$.

a. α is *transcendental over F* if Ker $\varphi_{\alpha/F} = (0)$.

b. α is *algebraic over F* if Ker $\varphi_{\alpha/F} = (m_{\alpha/F}(x)) \neq 0$.

c. If α is algebraic over F, then $m_{\alpha/F}(x)$ is the *minimum polynomial* of α over F, and the *degree* of α over F is $[\alpha: F] = \deg m_{\alpha/F}(x)$.

d. An extension $\langle K/F,\varepsilon\rangle$ is an *algebraic extension* of F (or *algebraic over F*) if every element of K is algebraic over $\varepsilon(F)$.

e. An extension $\langle K/F,\varepsilon\rangle$ is a *transcendental extension* of F (or *transcendental over F*) if there exists an element in K which is transcendental over $\varepsilon(F)$. ///

In analogy to Theorem 1.1, we can characterize the property of a field's being an algebraic extension of another field F in terms of a property of certain F-endomorphisms. (We note that if $F \subset K$ and $\varphi: K \to K$ is a field endomorphism, then φ is an F-endomorphism if and only if $\varphi a = a$ for each $a \in F$.)

Theorem 1.6. *Let $E \supset F$. E is an algebraic extension of F if and only if, for every field K such that $E \supset K \supset F$, every F-monomorphism of K into K is an F-automorphism of K.*

PROOF. Suppose that E is an algebraic extension of F, that K is a field with $E \supset K \supset F$, and that $\sigma: K \to K$ is an F-monomorphism of K to K. We must show that σ is an epimorphism. Let $\alpha \in K$. By assumption, α is algebraic over F, whence Ker $\varphi_{\alpha/F} \neq (0)$ and there exists a nonzero polynomial $f(x) \in F[x]$, say of degree n, such that $f(\alpha) = 0$. Since σ is an F-endomorphism, $f(\sigma^m(\alpha)) = 0$ for every positive integer m. Since $f(x)$ may factor over K into a product of at most n linear factors, it follows that there exist at most n distinct $\sigma^i(\alpha)$. Therefore, there exist positive integers k, l with $k > l$ such that $\sigma^k(\alpha) = \sigma^l(\alpha)$. Since σ is a monomorphism, so is σ^l. Hence $\sigma^{k-l}(\alpha) = \alpha$ and $\sigma(\beta) = \alpha$, with $\beta = \sigma^{k-l-1}(\alpha)$. Hence σ is an epimorphism, as desired.

Now suppose that E is a transcendental extension of F. We must find a field K, $E \supset K \supset F$, and an F-monomorphism of K to K which is not an automorphism. Since E is transcendental over F, it contains an element α which is transcendental over F. Consider the diagram

$$\begin{array}{ccc} F[x] & \xrightarrow{\varphi_{\alpha/F}} & F[\alpha] \\ \Big\downarrow \iota & & \Big\downarrow \iota^* \\ F[x] & \xrightarrow[\varphi_{\alpha^2/F}]{} & F[\alpha^2] \end{array}$$

where ι is the identity map on $F[x]$ and $\varphi_{\alpha/F}$, $\varphi_{\alpha^2/F}$ are as defined above. Since α is transcendental over F, Ker $\varphi_{\alpha/F} =$ Ker $\varphi_{\alpha^2/F} = (0)$ and therefore there exists (Chapter 2, Theorem 1.5) an F-monomorphism $\iota^*: F[\alpha] \to F[\alpha^2]$. The map ι^* extends to an F-monomorphism, σ, of the quotient field $F(\alpha)$ of $F[\alpha]$ to the quotient field $F(\alpha^2)$ of $F[\alpha^2]$. Clearly $F(\alpha^2) \subset F(\alpha)$; furthermore, from the fact that α is transcendental over F it follows that $F(\alpha^2) \neq F(\alpha)$. Let $\varepsilon: F(\alpha^2) \to F(\alpha)$ be the natural inclusion of $F(\alpha^2)$ in $F(\alpha)$. Then $\varepsilon\sigma: F(\alpha) \to F(\alpha)$ is an F-monomorphism with $E \supset F(\alpha) \supset F$, and $\varepsilon\sigma$ is not an automorphism. ▮

The discussion which preceded Theorem 1.6 and which involved only a single element $\alpha \in E$ can be carried through almost verbatim for any finite set of elements. In particular, let F be a subfield of a field E and let $\{\alpha_i\}_1^n$ be a set of n elements of E. If $F[x_1,x_2,\ldots,x_n]$ is the polynomial domain in n indeterminates over F, then there exists a homomorphism $\varphi_{(\alpha_1,\ldots,\alpha_n)/F}: F[x_1,\ldots,x_n] \to E$ defined by $\varphi_{(\alpha_1,\ldots,\alpha_n)/F}(f(x_1,\ldots,x_n)) = f(\alpha_1,\ldots,\alpha_n)$. Denote $\varphi_{(\alpha_1,\ldots,\alpha_n)/F}(F[x_1,\ldots,x_n])$ by $F[\alpha_1,\ldots,\alpha_n]$.

Definition 1.6.

a. $\{\alpha_i\}_1^n$ is an *algebraically independent set* over F if Ker $\varphi_{(\alpha,\ldots,\alpha_n)/F} = (0)$.

b. $\{\alpha_i\}_1^n$ is an *algebraically dependent set* over F if Ker $\varphi_{(\alpha_1,\ldots,\alpha_n)/F} \neq (0)$.

c. Let S be a set of elements of E. Then S is a *transcendence set* of E over F if every finite subset of S is an algebraically independent set over F.

d. A subset B of E is a *transcendence base* for E over F if B is a transcendence set of E over F and E is an algebraic extension of $F(B)$.

e. E is a *pure transcendental extension* of F if there exists a subset T of E such that T is a transcendence set over F and $E = F(T)$. ///

We shall show below that, if F is a subfield of E, then there exists a transcendence base for E over F, and any two transcendence bases for E over F have the same cardinality. We first consider some elementary properties of algebraic extensions.

Theorem 1.7. *Let $K \supset E \supset F$ be a tower of fields, $\alpha,\beta \in K$ and S a subset of K.*

a. *The statements*
   (1) $[F[\alpha]: F]$ *is finite*, (2) α *is algebraic over* F, *and* (3) $F(\alpha) = F[\alpha]$ *are equivalent.*

b. *If α is algebraic over $F(S)$, then there exists a finite subset S' of S such that α is algebraic over $F(S')$.*

c. *If α is algebraic over F, then α is algebraic over E.*

d. *If E is algebraic over F and if K is algebraic over E, then K is algebraic over F.*

e. *If β is algebraic over $F(\alpha)$, and if β is transcendental over F, then α is algebraic over $F(\beta)$.*

PROOF.

a. Recall that $F[\alpha] = \varphi_{\alpha/F}(F[x])$, where $\varphi_{\alpha/F}: F[x] \to K$ is the F-homomorphism defined by $\varphi_{\alpha/F}(f(x)) = f(\alpha)$. If $[F[\alpha]: F]$ is finite, then, since $F[x]$ is an infinite-dimensional vector space over F, Ker $\varphi_{\alpha/F} \neq (0)$. But then α is algebraic over F. Thus if $[F[\alpha]: F]$ is finite, then α is algebraic over F.

By definition,

$$F(\alpha) = \bigcap_{\substack{L \text{ subfield of } K \\ \alpha \in L \\ K \supset L \supset F}} L.$$

Clearly, every such field L contains $F[\alpha]$. Therefore, whether or not α is algebraic, $F(\alpha) \supset F[\alpha]$. Now assume that α is algebraic over F. Then Ker $\varphi_{\alpha/F}$ is a proper prime ideal in $F[x]$ and is therefore also a maximal ideal (Chapter 2, Theorem 3.5) in $F[x]$. Hence, $F[\alpha]$ is a subfield of K (Chapter 2, Theorem 1.5) such that $\alpha \in F[\alpha]$ and $K \supset F[\alpha] \supset F$. It follows that $F[\alpha] \supset F(\alpha)$. We have shown: If α is algebraic over F, then $F(\alpha) = F[\alpha]$.

Suppose that $F(\alpha) = F[\alpha]$. Since $F[x]$ is not a field, while $F(\alpha) = F[\alpha] = \varphi_{\alpha/F}(F[x])$ is a field, it follows that $\operatorname{Ker} \varphi_{\alpha/F} = (m_{\alpha/F}(x)) \neq 0$. Now, if $f(x) \in F[x]$, then there exists (Chapter 2, Theorem 3.2) $q(x),r(x) \in F[x]$ such that $f(x) = q(x)m_{\alpha/F}(x) + r(x)$, where $r(x) = 0$ or degree $r(x) < n = \deg m_{\alpha/F}(x)$. Hence $\varphi_{\alpha/F}(f(x)) = r(\alpha)$, and therefore $\{1,\alpha,\ldots,\alpha^{n-1}\}$ spans $F[\alpha]$ over F. [In fact, $\{1,\alpha,\ldots,\alpha^{n-1}\}$ is a basis for $F[\alpha]$ over F (Exercise 1.4).] We have shown: If $F(\alpha) = F[\alpha]$, then $[F[\alpha]: F]$ is finite. This completes the proof of statement a of the theorem.

b. Assume that α is algebraic over $F(S)$ and let $m_{\alpha/F(S)}(x)$ be the minimum polynomial of α over $F(S)$. For each of the coefficients c_i, $i = 1, 2,\ldots, n$, of $m_{\alpha/F(S)}(x)$, there exists, by Theorem 1.5a, a finite subset S_i of S such that $c_i \in F(S_i)$. Let $S' = \bigcup_{i=1}^{n} S_i$. Then S' is a finite subset of S and $m_{\alpha/F(S)}(x) \in F(S')[x]$; hence the kernel of $\varphi_{\alpha/F(S')}: F(S')[x] \to K$ is not zero and α is algebraic over $F(S')$.

c. If $E \supset F$, then $E[x] \supset F[x]$ and for $K \supset E \supset F$, $\alpha \in K$, we have $\operatorname{Ker} \varphi_{\alpha/E} \supset \operatorname{Ker} \varphi_{\alpha/F}$. If α is algebraic over F, then $\operatorname{Ker} \varphi_{\alpha/F} \neq (0)$, whence $\operatorname{Ker} \varphi_{\alpha/E} \neq (0)$ and α is algebraic over E.

d. Suppose that $\alpha \in K$. We must show that α is algebraic over F. In view of part a of this theorem, it is sufficient to show that $[F(\alpha): F]$ is finite. By assumption, α is algebraic over $E = F(E)$. From part b of this theorem it follows that there exists a finite subset $\{\beta_i\}_1^n$ of E such that α is algebraic over $F(\beta_1,\ldots,\beta_n)$. Since E is algebraic over F and $\beta_i \in E$ we have, by a, c, and iterated use of Theorem 1.3, that $[F(\beta_1,\ldots,\beta_n): F] = [F(\beta_1,\ldots,\beta_n) : F(\beta_1,\ldots,\beta_{n-1})][F(\beta_1,\ldots,\beta_{n-1}): F(\beta_1,\ldots,\beta_{n-2})]\cdots[F(\beta_1,\beta_2): F(\beta_1)][F(\beta_1): F]$ is finite; whence $[F(\alpha,\beta_1,\ldots,\beta_n): F] = [F(\alpha,\beta_1,\ldots,\beta_n): F(\beta_1,\ldots,\beta_n)] \times [F(\beta_1,\ldots,\beta_n): F]$ is finite. On the other hand, $[F(\alpha,\beta_1,\ldots,\beta_n): F] = [F(\alpha,\beta_1,\ldots,\beta_n): F(\alpha,\beta_1,\ldots,\beta_{n-1})]\cdots[F(\alpha,\beta_1): F(\alpha)][F(\alpha): F]$, from which it follows that $[F(\alpha): F]$ is finite.

e. We are given that β is algebraic over $F(\alpha)$ and that β is transcendental over F. Consider the following diagram:

$$\begin{array}{ccc} F[x,y] & \xrightarrow{\ \sigma\ } & F(\alpha)[y] \\ {\scriptstyle\tau}\downarrow & & \downarrow{\scriptstyle\varphi_{\beta/F(\alpha)}} \\ F(\beta)[x] & \xrightarrow[\varphi_{\alpha/F(\beta)}]{} & F(\alpha,\beta) \end{array}$$

where, for $f(x,y) \in F[x,y]$, σ and τ are homomorphisms defined by $\sigma(f(x,y)) = f(\alpha,y)$ and $\tau(f(x,y)) = f(x,\beta)$. Clearly $\varphi_{\alpha/F(\beta)}\tau = \varphi_{\beta/F(\alpha)}\sigma$. Since β is algebraic over $F(\alpha)$, $\operatorname{Ker} \varphi_{\beta/F(\alpha)} \neq (0)$. Furthermore, if $g(y) \in F(\alpha)[y]$, then $g(y) = \sum_{i=0}^{r} (a_i/b_i)y^i$, where $a_i,b_i \in \operatorname{Im} \sigma \cap F(\alpha)$. Thus, if $g(y) \in \operatorname{Ker} \varphi_{\beta/F(\alpha)}$, then

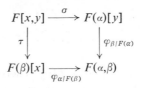

$(\prod_1^r b_i)g(y) \in \operatorname{Ker} \varphi_{\beta/F(\alpha)} \cap \operatorname{Im} \sigma$. Therefore, $\operatorname{Ker} \varphi_{\beta/F(\alpha)} \cap \operatorname{Im} \sigma \neq (0)$. Since β is transcendental over F, $\operatorname{Ker} \tau = (0)$. From the commutativity of the diagram it now follows that $\operatorname{Ker} \varphi_{\alpha/F(\beta)} \neq (0)$. We have shown that if β is algebraic over $F(\alpha)$ and β is transcendental over F, then α is algebraic over $F(\beta)$. ▮

A simple consequence of Theorems 1.3 and 1.7a and c is

Corollary. *Let E be an extension of a field F. Then $E_a = \{\alpha \in E | \alpha$ algebraic over $F\}$ is a subfield of E.* □

We are now ready to prove that if F is a subfield of E, then there exists a transcendence base for E over F, and any two transcendence bases for E over F have the same cardinality. The proof of these results is analogous to the proof that every vector space has a basis and that the cardinal numbers of any two bases are equal: We define a map on the set of subsets of E, prove that this map has the properties of a "spanning map" (see Chapter 0, Definition 6.5) and apply the conclusions of Chapter 0, Theorem 6.5. We start with

Lemma. *Let $E \supset F$ and let $\rho: 2^E \to 2^E$ be defined by $\rho(S) = \{\alpha \in E | \alpha$ algebraic over $F(S)\}$. Then a subset B of E is a transcendence base for E over F if and only if*

a. $\rho(B) = E$,

and

b. *if $\beta \in B$, then $\beta \notin \rho(B - \{\beta\})$.*

PROOF. Suppose that B is a transcendence base for E over F. Then E is algebraic over $F(B)$, whence $\rho(B) = E$, and a holds. We must show that if $\beta \in B$, then $\beta \notin \rho(B - \{\beta\})$. Assume the contrary; i.e., there exists $\beta \in B$ such that $\beta \in \rho(B - \{\beta\})$. Then, by Theorem 1.7b, there exists a finite subset $\{\gamma_i\}_1^r$ of $B - \{\beta\}$ such that $\beta \in \rho(\{\gamma_1, \ldots, \gamma_r\})$. But then $\{\beta, \gamma_1, \ldots, \gamma_r\}$ is an algebraically dependent subset of B, contrary to the assumption that B is a transcendence set over F. Hence also b holds.

Now suppose that B is a subset of E such that (1) $\rho(B) = E$ and (2) if $\beta \in B$, then $\beta \notin \rho(B - \{\beta\})$. Since $\rho(B) = E$, E is algebraic over $F(B)$. We must show that B is a transcendence set over F. Assume the contrary. Then there exists a nonvoid finite subset S of B which is algebraically dependent, and there exists a maximal algebraically independent subset T of S. Since S is algebraically dependent, $S - T \neq \varnothing$, hence there exists a $\beta_0 \in S$, $\beta_0 \notin T$. We claim that $\beta_0 \in \rho(T)$. In fact, suppose $T = \{\beta_1,\ldots,\beta_n\}$ and consider the following diagram:

$$\begin{array}{ccc} F[x_0,x_1,\ldots,x_n] & \xrightarrow{\sigma} & F(T)[x_0] \\ & {\scriptstyle \varphi_{(\beta_0,\beta_1,\ldots,\beta_n)/F}} \searrow \quad \swarrow {\scriptstyle \varphi_{\beta_0/F(T)}} & \\ & F(\beta_0,\beta_1,\ldots,\beta_n) & \end{array}$$

where for $f(x_0,x_1,\ldots,x_n) \in F[x_0,x_1,\ldots,x_n]$, and $\sigma(f(x_0,x_1,\ldots,x_n)) = f(x_0,\beta_1,\ldots,\beta_n)$. Then $\varphi_{(\beta_0,\beta_1,\ldots,\beta_n)/F} = \varphi_{\beta_0/F(T)}\sigma$. Since $\{\beta_1,\ldots,\beta_n\}$ is a maximal algebraically independent subset of S, Ker $\sigma = (0)$ and Ker $\varphi_{(\beta_0,\beta_1,\ldots,\beta_n)/F} \neq (0)$. From the commutativity of the diagram it now follows that Ker $\varphi_{\beta_0/F(T)} \neq (0)$, whence β_0 is algebraic over $F(T)$. Thus $\beta_0 \in \rho(T)$, as claimed. Since $T \subset B - \{\beta_0\}$, we have $\beta_0 \in \rho(B - \{\beta_0\})$. Hence the assumption that B is not a transcendence set over F implies that there exists $\beta_0 \in B$ such that $\beta_0 \in \rho(B - \{\beta_0\})$, and this contradicts assumption (2). ▮

Theorem 1.8. *Let $E \supset F$. Then there exists a transcendence base for E over F. If B_1 and B_2 are transcendence bases for E over F, then $|B_1| = |B_2|$.*

PROOF. Define a mapping $\rho: 2^E \to 2^E$ by $\rho(S) = \{\alpha \in E | \alpha$ algebraic over $F(S)\}$. We now use Theorem 1.7 to prove that ρ has the following properties:

1. If $S_1 \subset S_2$, then $\rho(S_1) \subset \rho(S_2)$. This follows from Theorem 1.7c.
2. If $\alpha \in \rho(S)$, then there exists a finite subset S' of S such that $\alpha \in \rho(S')$. This follows from Theorem 1.7b.
3. $S \subset \rho(S)$. This follows from the trivial observation that if β is any element of a field K, then β is algebraic over K.
4. $\rho(\rho(S)) = \rho(S)$. From property 3 we have $\rho(S) \subset \rho(\rho(S))$. If $\alpha \in \rho(\rho(S))$, then α is algebraic over $F(\rho(S))$. Also, $F(\rho(S))$ is algebraic over $F(S)$. For, if $\beta \in F(\rho(S))$, then, by Theorem 1.5a, there exist $\beta_1,\ldots,\beta_r \in \rho(S)$ such that $\beta \in F(\beta_1,\ldots,\beta_r)$; since each β_i is algebraic over $F(S)$, it follows, by iterated use of Theorem 1.7c and d, that β is algebraic over $F(S)$; whence $F(\rho(S))$ is algebraic over $F(S)$. Therefore, if $\alpha \in \rho(\rho(S))$, then α is algebraic over $F(S)$, and thus $\alpha \in \rho(S)$. Hence we have $\rho(\rho(S)) \subset \rho(S)$ and property 4 holds.
5. If $\beta \in \rho(S \cup \{\alpha\})$ and $\beta \notin \rho(S)$, then $\alpha \in \rho(S \cup \{\beta\})$. Property 5 is merely a restatement of Theorem 1.7e.

Since ρ has properties 1 through 5, it follows from Chapter 0, Theorem 6.5, that there exists a subset B_1 of E such that

a. $\rho(B_1) = E$.
b. If $\beta \in B_1$, then $\beta \notin \rho(B_1 - \{\beta\})$.
c. If B_2 is another subset satisfying a and b, then $|B_2| = |B_1|$.

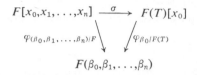

Since, by the lemma, B is a transcendence base for E over F if and only if a and b hold, our theorem is proved. ▮

Definition 1.7. Let $E \supset F$ and let B be a transcendence base for E over F. The *transcendence degree of E over F* = tr.d. $E/F = |B|$, where $|B|$ is the cardinality of B. ///

Note that from Theorem 1.8 it follows that tr.d. E/F is independent of the choice of a transcendence base for E over F.

Theorem 1.9. *Let $K \supset E \supset F$. Then* tr.d. K/F = tr.d. K/E + tr.d. E/F.

PROOF. Let B_1 and B_2 be transcendence bases for K over E and for E over F, respectively. We shall show that $B_1 \cap B_2 = \varnothing$ and that $B_1 \cup B_2$ is a transcendence base for K over F, and from this the theorem follows immediately.

If $\beta \in B_2$, then $\beta \in E$ and β is algebraic over E. Since B_1 is a transcendence set over E, $\beta \notin B_1$. Hence $B_1 \cap B_2 = \varnothing$.

We first show that K is algebraic over $F(B_1 \cup B_2)$. For, E is algebraic over $F(B_2)$, hence also over $F(B_1 \cup B_2)$. It follows, as the reader may verify by using Theorems 1.5a and 1.7d, that $E(B_1)$ is algebraic over $F(B_1 \cup B_2)$. Since K is algebraic over $E(B_1)$, it follows by Theorem 1.7d that K is algebraic over $F(B_1 \cup B_2)$.

We now show that $B_1 \cup B_2$ is a transcendence set over F. Let $\{\beta_1,\ldots,\beta_m, \gamma_1,\ldots,\gamma_n\}$ be a finite subset of $B_1 \cup B_2$, where $\beta_i \in B_2$ for $i = 1, 2,\ldots, m$ and $\gamma_i \in B_1$ for $i = 1, 2,\ldots, n$. Consider the following diagram:

$$\begin{array}{ccc} F[x_1,\ldots,x_m,y_1,\ldots,y_n] & \xrightarrow{\ \sigma\ } & F(\beta_1,\ldots,\beta_m)[y_1,\ldots,y_n] \\ \tau = \varphi_{(\beta_1,\ldots,\beta_m,\gamma_1,\ldots,\gamma_n)/F} \searrow & & \swarrow \varphi_{(\gamma_1,\ldots,\gamma_n)/F(\beta_1,\ldots,\beta_m)} = \rho \\ & F(\beta_1,\ldots,\beta_m,\gamma_1,\ldots,\gamma_n) & \end{array}$$

where, for $f(x_1,\ldots,x_m,y_1,\ldots,y_n) \in F[x_1,\ldots,x_m,y_1,\ldots,y_n]$,

$$\sigma(f(x_1,\ldots,x_m,y_1,\ldots,y_n)) = f(\beta_1,\ldots,\beta_m,y_1,\ldots,y_n).$$

We see that $\rho\sigma = \tau$. Furthermore, since $\{\beta_i\}_1^m$ is a subset of B_2 and B_2 is a transcendence set over F, Ker $\sigma = (0)$. Similarly, Ker $\rho = (0)$. Therefore, Ker $\tau = (0)$, and $B_1 \cup B_2$ is a transcendence set over F. ▮

2. Algebraically Closed Fields; Algebraic Closure of a Field; Extension of Isomorphisms

We have seen in Section 1 that every extension of a field F is an algebraic extension of a pure transcendental extension of F. Every field F admits a pure transcendental extension, e.g., the quotient field of the polynomial domain $F[x]$. However, we shall see that there exist fields which admit no algebraic extensions of degree greater than 1.

Definition 2.1. A field C is *algebraically closed* if it has no proper algebraic extension, i.e., if $\tau(C) = E$ for every monomorphism $\tau: C \to E$, where E is algebraic over $\tau(C)$. ///

We note that, of course, an isomorphic image of an algebraically closed field is algebraically closed.

The following theorem is an immediate consequence of Chapter 2, Theorem 3.13. Its proof and the proof of the corollary are left to the reader.

Theorem 2.1. *Let C be a field. The following statements are equivalent:*

a. *C is algebraically closed.*
b. *If $f(x)$ is an irreducible polynomial in $C[x]$, then* $\deg f(x) = 1$.
c. *If $f(x)$ is a polynomial in $C[x]$ of degree $n > 0$, then there exist $\alpha_i \in C$, $i = 0, 1, 2, \ldots, n$, such that $f(x) = \alpha_0 \prod_{i=1}^{n} (x - \alpha_i)$.*
d. *If $f(x)$ is a polynomial in $C[x]$ of degree greater than 0, then there exists an $\alpha \in C$ such that $f(\alpha) = 0$; i.e., every polynomial in $C[x]$, of degree greater than 0, has a root in C.* □

Corollary. *Suppose that $C \supset F$ and C is algebraically closed. If $C_0 = \{\alpha \in C \mid \alpha$ algebraic over $F\}$, then C_0 is algebraic over F and is an algebraically closed subfield of C.* □

Definition 2.2. C is an *algebraic closure* of a field F if C is an algebraic extension of F and C is an algebraically closed field. ///

By the corollary, above, we have

REMARK. Let C be an algebraically closed field and suppose that C is an extension of a field F. Then

$$C_0 = \{\alpha \in C \mid \alpha \text{ is algebraic over } F\}$$

is an algebraic closure of F.

The next theorem characterizes an algebraic closure of a field F as an algebraic extension of F in which every algebraic extension of F can be isomorphically embedded. Stated another way: An algebraic extension C of F is an algebraic closure of F if and only if for every algebraic extension E of F there exists a monomorphism ρ of E into C. In fact, we have

Theorem 2.2. *Let $\langle C/F,\varepsilon\rangle$ be an algebraic extension of F. Then C is an algebraic closure of F if, and only if, given any algebraic extension $\langle E/F,\sigma\rangle$ of F, there exists a monomorphism $\rho\colon E \to C$, such that $\rho\sigma = \varepsilon$.*

$$\begin{array}{ccc} F & \xrightarrow{\sigma} & E \\ & {\scriptstyle\varepsilon}\searrow \quad \swarrow{\scriptstyle\rho} & \\ & C & \end{array}$$

In the proof of the theorem, we use the following lemma.

Lemma. *Let $\tau\colon F_1 \to F_2$ be an isomorphism of a field F_1 onto a field F_2 and let $\tau'\colon F_1[x] \to F_2[x]$ be the isomorphism extending τ to $F_1[x]$. Suppose that $f_1(x)$ is an irreducible polynomial in $F_1[x]$ and that $f_2(x) = \tau'(f_1(x))$. If α_1, α_2 are elements in extension fields of F_1 and F_2, respectively, such that $f_i(\alpha_i) = 0$ for $i = 1, 2$, then there is a unique isomorphism $\psi\colon F_1(\alpha_1) \to F_2(\alpha_2)$ such that $\psi(\alpha_1) = \alpha_2$, and ψ is an extension of τ.*

PROOF OF LEMMA. For $i = 1, 2$, let ν_i be the natural homomorphism of $F_i[x]$ onto $F_i[x]/(f_i(x))$ and $\varphi_{\alpha_i/F_i}\colon F_i[x] \to F_i(\alpha_i)$ the substitution map defined by $g(x) \mapsto g(\alpha_i)$. By Chapter 2, Theorems 1.4 and 1.7, there exist unique isomorphisms ρ_1, ρ_2, $(\tau')^*$, and ψ such that the following diagrams commute:

$$\begin{array}{ccc} F_1[x] & \xrightarrow{\nu_1} & F_1[x]/(f_1(x)) \\ & {\scriptstyle\varphi_{\alpha_1/F_1}}\searrow \quad \swarrow{\scriptstyle\rho_1} & \\ & F_1(\alpha_1) & \end{array} \qquad \begin{array}{ccc} F_2[x] & \xrightarrow{\nu_2} & F_2[x]/(f_2(x)) \\ & {\scriptstyle\varphi_{\alpha_2/F_2}}\searrow \quad \swarrow{\scriptstyle\rho_2} & \\ & F_2(\alpha_2) & \end{array}$$

$$\begin{array}{ccccc} F_1[x] & \xrightarrow{\nu_1} & F_1[x]/(f_1(x)) & \xrightarrow{\rho_1} & F_1(\alpha_1) \\ {\scriptstyle\tau'}\downarrow & & \downarrow{\scriptstyle(\tau')^*} & & \downarrow{\scriptstyle\psi} \\ F_2[x] & \xrightarrow[\nu_2]{} & F_2[x]/(f_2(x)) & \xrightarrow[\rho_2]{} & F_2(\alpha_2) \end{array}$$

Since $\psi\rho_1\nu_1 = \rho_2\nu_2\tau'$, $\rho_1\nu_1 = \varphi_{\alpha_1/F_1}$, and $\rho_2\nu_2 = \varphi_{\alpha_2/F_2}$, we have $\psi\varphi_{\alpha_1/F_1} = \varphi_{\alpha_2/F_2}\tau'$. Hence $\psi\varphi_{\alpha_1/F_1}(x) = \varphi_{\alpha_2/F_2}\tau'(x)$ and $\psi(\alpha_1) = \alpha_2$, as desired. ▌

PROOF OF THEOREM. Suppose that $\langle C/F,\varepsilon\rangle$ is an algebraic closure of F. Let $\langle E/F,\sigma\rangle$ be an algebraic extension of F. We wish to show that there exists a monomorphism $\rho\colon E \to C$ such that $\rho\sigma = \varepsilon$. To this end we define

$$S = \left\{\langle K,K',\psi\rangle \;\middle|\; \begin{array}{l} E \supset K \supset \sigma(F),\ C \supset K' \supset \varepsilon(F),\ \psi\colon K \to K' \text{ an} \\ \text{isomorphism of } K \text{ onto } K' \text{ such that } \psi\sigma = \varepsilon. \end{array}\right\}.$$

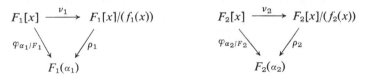

Note that $\langle\sigma(F),\varepsilon(F),\varepsilon\sigma^{-1}\rangle \in S$, whence $S \neq \varnothing$. Our procedure will be as follows: We shall introduce a partial ordering on S with the property that every totally ordered subset of S has an upper bound in S. It will then follow, by Zorn's Lemma (Chapter 0, Section 4), that S has a maximal element, say $\langle K_0,K'_0,\psi_0\rangle$. Finally, we shall show that $K_0 = E$, whence ψ_0 yields a monomorphism $\rho: E \to C$ such that $\rho\sigma = \varepsilon$.

Define a partial ordering on S as follows: $\langle K_1,K'_1,\psi_1\rangle \leq \langle K_2,K'_2,\psi_2\rangle$ if and only if $K_1 \subset K_2$ and $\psi_2|_{K_1} = \psi_1$ (where $\psi_2|_{K_1}$ denotes the map which is the restriction of ψ_2 to K_1). Now let $T = \{\langle K_i,K'_i,\psi_i\rangle\}_{i\in J}$ be a totally ordered subset of S. Then T has an upper bound in S. In fact, let $K = \bigcup_{i\in J} K_i$ and $K' = \bigcup_{i\in J} K'_i$. Clearly, K and K' are fields such that $E \supset K \supset \sigma(F)$ and $C \supset K' \supset \varepsilon(F)$. Before defining an isomorphism $\psi: K \to K'$ we note that if $\alpha \in K$, then there exists an $i \in J$ such that $\alpha \in K_i$; furthermore, if for $\alpha \in K$ we have $\alpha \in K_i$ and $\alpha \in K_j$, then from the assumption that T is a totally ordered set it follows that $\psi_i(\alpha) = \psi_j(\alpha)$. For $\alpha \in K$ define $\psi(\alpha) = \psi_i(\alpha)$, where $i \in J$ and $\alpha \in K_i$. Then, as we may easily verify, ψ is an isomorphism of K onto K', $\langle K,K',\psi\rangle \in S$, and $\langle K,K',\psi\rangle$ is an upper bound for T. Thus every totally ordered subset of S has an upper bound in S. Therefore, by Zorn's Lemma, S has a maximal element.

Let $\langle K_0,K'_0,\psi_0\rangle$ be a maximal element of S. We now show that $K_0 = E$. Clearly $E \supset K_0$. Suppose that $\alpha \in E$. Let $m_\alpha(x)$ be the minimum polynomial of α over K_0. Then ψ_0 extends to an isomorphism ψ'_0 of $K_0[x]$ onto $K'_0[x]$ and we have $\psi'_0(m_\alpha(x)) = m'_\alpha(x) \in K'_0[x] \subset C[x]$. Since C is algebraically closed, $m'_\alpha(x)$ has a root α' in C. By the lemma, ψ_0 extends to an isomorphism ψ_1 of $K_0[\alpha]$ onto $K'_0[\alpha']$. But then $\langle K_0[\alpha],K'_0[\alpha'],\psi_1\rangle \in S$ and $\langle K_0,K'_0,\psi_0\rangle \leq \langle K_0[\alpha],K'_0[\alpha'],\psi_1\rangle$. Since $\langle K_0,K'_0,\psi_0\rangle$ is a maximal element of S, we have $K_0 = K_0[\alpha]$ and hence $\alpha \in K_0$. Thus $K_0 \supset E$, whence $K_0 = E$, as desired.

Suppose now that C is an algebraic extension of F which has the property that if E is any algebraic extension of F, then there exists a monomorphism $\rho: E \to C$ such that $\rho\sigma = \varepsilon$, where ε and σ are the monomorphisms of F into C and E, respectively. We must show that C is an algebraic closure of F. Suppose that E is an algebraic extension of C and that $\tau: C \to E$ is the monomorphism of C into E. We then have $F \xrightarrow{\varepsilon} C \xrightarrow{\tau} E$ and, by Theorem 1.7d, E is an algebraic extension of F. Our assumption concerning C implies that there exists a monomorphism $\rho: E \to C$ such that $\rho\tau\varepsilon = \varepsilon$. But then $\tau\rho$ is a $\tau\varepsilon(F)$-monomorphism of E to E, and since E is algebraic over $\tau\varepsilon(F)$ it follows from Theorem 1.6 that $\tau\rho$ is an automorphism of E, whence τ is an epimorphism. Thus $\tau(C) = E$ and C is an algebraic closure of F. ▌

Corollary. *Let $\langle C_1/F_1,\varepsilon_1\rangle$ be an algebraic extension of F_1. Then C_1 is an algebraic closure of F_1 if and only if for every isomorphism $\mu: F \to F_1$ of a field*

F onto F_1 and for every algebraic extension $\langle E/F,\varepsilon\rangle$ of F, there exists a monomorphism $\rho: E \to C_1$ such that the following diagram commutes:

$$\begin{array}{ccc} F & \xrightarrow{\varepsilon} & E \\ {\scriptstyle\mu}\big\downarrow & & \big\downarrow{\scriptstyle\rho} \\ F_1 & \xrightarrow[\varepsilon_1]{} & C_1 \end{array}$$

(i.e., C_1 is an algebraic closure of F_1 if and only if every isomorphism of a field F onto F_1 extends to a monomorphism of E into C_1, where E is any algebraic extension of F).

PROOF. The corollary follows easily once we observe that if F, E, μ, and ε are as given, then $\varepsilon\mu^{-1}: F_1 \to E$ is a monomorphism of F_1 into E and we can apply the theorem with $\sigma = \varepsilon\mu^{-1}$. ▮

Theorem 2.3. *Any two algebraic closures of a field are isomorphic. In particular, if $\langle C_1/F_1,\varepsilon_1\rangle$ and $\langle C_2/F_2,\varepsilon_2\rangle$ are algebraic closures of F_1 and F_2, respectively, and if $\mu: F_1 \to F_2$ is an isomorphism of F_1 and F_2, then there exists an isomorphism $\rho: C_1 \to C_2$ such that $\rho\varepsilon_1 = \varepsilon_2\mu$.*

PROOF. Consider the diagram:

$$\begin{array}{ccc} F_1 & \xrightarrow{\varepsilon_1} & C_1 \\ {\scriptstyle\mu}\big\downarrow & & \big\downarrow{\scriptstyle\rho} \\ F_2 & \xrightarrow[\varepsilon_2]{} & C_2 \end{array}$$

By the Corollary to Theorem 2.2, there exist monomorphisms $\rho: C_1 \to C_2$ and $\tau: C_2 \to C_1$ such that $\rho\varepsilon_1 = \varepsilon_2\mu$ and $\tau\varepsilon_2 = \varepsilon_1\mu^{-1}$. But then, for $a \in F_2$, $\rho\tau\varepsilon_2(a) = \rho\varepsilon_1\mu^{-1}(a) = \varepsilon_2(a)$ and $\rho\tau: C_2 \to C_2$ is an $\varepsilon_2(F_2)$-monomorphism of C_2 to C_2. Since C_2 is algebraic over $\varepsilon_2(F_2)$, it follows from Theorem 1.6 that $\rho\tau$ is an automorphism of C_2, whence ρ is an epimorphism. Thus $\rho: C_1 \to C_2$ is an isomorphism such that $\rho\varepsilon_1 = \varepsilon_2\mu$, as desired. ▮

We proceed to prove that every field has an algebraic closure. In doing so, we shall make use of the following two lemmas.

Lemma 1. *Let F be a field and $f \in F[x]$ with $\deg f = n$, $n \geq 1$. Then there exists an algebraic extension K of F such that $K \supset F$, $[K: F] \leq n!$, and f factors into a product of linear factors in $K[x]$.*

PROOF. We proceed by induction on n. For $n = 1$, the lemma holds, with $K = F$. For $n > 1$, suppose the lemma holds for polynomials g of degree less than n ($g \in E[x]$, E a field). Let F be a field, $f \in F[x]$ a polynomial of degree n, and let $p \in F[x]$ be an irreducible factor of f. Then (Chapter 2, Theorem 3.12) $\bar{E} = F[x]/(p)$ is a field; if $\nu: F \to \bar{K}$ is the canonical epimorphism, then $\nu|_F$ is a monomorphism, and $\bar{E} = \nu F(\nu x)$. By the technique employed in the proof of Chapter 0, Theorem 2.4, we can "wrap around" F a field $E \supset F$ such that there is an isomorphism $\mu: \bar{E} \to E$ and $E = F(\alpha)$, where $\alpha = \mu(\nu x)$. Since $\deg p(y) \leq \deg f(y)$, it follows from Theorem 1.7a that $[F(\alpha): F] \leq n$, Since $p(\alpha) = 0$, there is a polynomial $q(x) \in F(\alpha)[x]$ such that $p(x) = (x - \alpha)q(x)$. Hence there is some $r(x) \in F(\alpha)[x]$ such that $f(x) = (x - \alpha)r(x)$, where $\deg r(x) = n - 1$. By our induction assumption, there exists an algebraic extension $K \supset F(\alpha)$ such that $[K: F(\alpha)] \leq (n - 1)!$ and $r(x)$ factors into a product of linear factors in $K[x]$. But then $K \supset F$, $[K: F] = [K: F(\alpha)] \times [F(\alpha): F] \leq n!$, and $f(x)$ factors into a product of linear factors in $K[x]$. The lemma follows by induction. ▮

Lemma 2. *Let E be an algebraic extension of F. Then $|E| \leq \aleph_0|F|$. If F is infinite, then $|E| = |F|$.*

PROOF. By Chapter 0, Section 6, Example 8, $|F[x]| = \aleph_0|F|$. Every element u of E is a root of some polynomial $f \in F[x]$. Let P be the set of all polynomials in $F[x]$ which have a root in E. Then $|E| \leq |P|$. (For, we may partition E into finite subsets, E_α, where $E_\alpha = \{\beta \in E | m_{\alpha/F} = m_{\beta/F}\}$. If $E_\alpha = \{\alpha_1, \ldots, \alpha_n\}$ ($\alpha_1 = \alpha \in E$), then $\varphi_\alpha: E_\alpha \to P$ defined by $\varphi_\alpha(\alpha_i) = (x - 1)^i m_{\alpha/F}$ is a one-to-one map of E_α into P, and $\varphi: E \to P$ defined by: $\varphi|_{E_\alpha} = \varphi_\alpha$ is a one-to-one map of E into P.) Thus $|E| \leq |P| \leq \aleph_0|F|$.

If F is infinite, then

$$|E| \leq \aleph_0|F| = |F| \leq |E|, \qquad \text{whence } |E| = |F|. \quad ▮$$

We are now ready to prove

Theorem 2.4.

a. *Every field has an algebraic closure.*

b. *If C is an algebraic closure of a field F, then $|C| = \aleph_0|F|$.*

c. *If C_1 and C_2 are algebraic closures of F with $C_1 \supset F$ and $C_2 \supset F$, then C_1 and C_2 are F-isomorphic.*

PROOF. Let B be a set such that $F \subset B$, and $|B| > \aleph_0|F|$. Let $S = \{E \subset B | E \supset F$ and E is an algebraic extension of $F\}$. Define a partial order, $\prec$, on S as follows: For $E_1, E_2 \in S$, $E_1 \prec E_2$ if E_1 is a subfield of E_2. Since $F \in S$, $S \neq \varnothing$. It is easy to see that Zorn's Lemma applies. Hence S has a maximal element, C.

Suppose C is not algebraically closed. Then there is some irreducible polynomial $g \in C[x]$, with $\deg g > 1$. By Lemma 1, there is an algebraic extension K of C, with $K \supsetneqq C$, over which g splits. By Lemma 2, $|K| \leq \aleph_0|C| \leq \aleph_0\aleph_0|F| = \aleph_0|F| < B$. But then B has a subset, $\bar{K}$, such that $|\bar{K}| = |K|$, and $C \subsetneqq \bar{K}$. By suitably extending the operations in C we can make $\bar{K}$ into a field C-isomorphic to K. Since C is algebraic over F, so is $\bar{K}$; but then $\bar{K} \in S$, and $\bar{K} \supsetneqq C$, in contradiction to the maximality of C in S. It follows that C is algebraically closed, and is therefore an algebraic closure of F.

Since $C \supset F$, we have $|F| \leq |C| \leq \aleph_0|F|$. If $|F|$ is an infinite cardinal, then $\aleph_0|F| = |F|$, and hence $|C| = \aleph_0|F|$. We show that if L is a field with $|L|$ finite, then L is not algebraically closed; it follows that in the case where $|F|$ is finite we also have $|C| = \aleph_0|F|$. If $\{\alpha_i\}_1^{n-1}$ are the nonzero elements of a field L with $|L| = n$, then $x^n + \prod_{i=1}^{n-1}(x - \alpha_i)$ does not factor into linear factors in $L[x]$, whence L is not algebraically closed.

Finally, from Theorem 2.3 it follows that any two algebraic closures of F, each containing F, are F-isomorphic. The proof of the theorem is complete. ∎

We have seen (in Theorem 2.3) that every isomorphism of a field F_1 onto a field F_2 extends to an isomorphism of an algebraic closure, C_1, of F_1 onto an algebraic closure, C_2, of F_2. We now generalize this result to the case where the C_i are algebraically closed extensions (but not necessarily algebraic closures) of the F_i such that $\text{tr.d. } C_1/F_1 = \text{tr.d. } C_2/F_2$.

Theorem 2.5. *For $i = 1, 2$, let $\langle C_i/F_i, \eta_i\rangle$ be an algebraically closed extension of F_i. Let $\psi: F_1 \to F_2$ be an isomorphism of F_1 onto F_2. If* $\text{tr.d. } C_1/\eta_1(F_1) = \text{tr.d. } C_2/\eta_2(F_2)$, *then there exists an isomorphism $\rho: C_1 \to C_2$ such that $\rho\eta_1 = \eta_2\psi$; i.e., the following diagram commutes:*

$$\begin{array}{ccc} F_1 & \xrightarrow{\eta_1} & C_1 \\ {\scriptstyle\psi}\downarrow & & \downarrow{\scriptstyle\rho} \\ F_2 & \xrightarrow[\eta_2]{} & C_2 \end{array}$$

PROOF. Denote $\eta_i(F_i)$ by $\bar{F}_i$ and let B_i be a transcendence base for C_i over $\bar{F}_i$, $i = 1, 2$. To prove the theorem, it is sufficient to prove that there exists an isomorphism $\sigma: \bar{F}_1(B_1) \to \bar{F}_2(B_2)$ such that the diagram

$$\begin{array}{ccc} F_1 & \xrightarrow{\eta_1} & \bar{F}_1(B_1) \\ {\scriptstyle\psi}\downarrow & & \downarrow{\scriptstyle\sigma} \\ F_2 & \xrightarrow[\eta_2]{} & \bar{F}_2(B_2) \end{array}$$

commutes. For, since C_i is algebraically closed, and B_i is a transcendence base for C_i over $\bar{F}_i$, C_i is an algebraic closure of $\bar{F}_i(B_i)$. It follows from Theorem 2.3 that there exists an isomorphism $\rho: C_1 \to C_2$ such that the diagram

$$\begin{array}{ccc} \bar{F}_1(B_1) & \xrightarrow{\varepsilon_1} & C_1 \\ {\scriptstyle\sigma}\downarrow & & \downarrow{\scriptstyle\rho} \\ \bar{F}_2(B_2) & \xrightarrow[\varepsilon_2]{} & C_2 \end{array}$$

commutes, where $\varepsilon_i: \bar{F}_i(B_i) \to C_i$ is the inclusion map of $\bar{F}_i(B_i)$ into C_i, $i = 1, 2$. Finally, from $\rho\varepsilon_1 = \varepsilon_2\sigma$, $\sigma\eta_1 = \eta_2\psi$, $\varepsilon_1\eta_1 = \eta_1$, and $\varepsilon\eta_2 = \eta_2$, it follows that $\rho\eta_1 = \eta_2\psi$.

We now show that there exists an isomorphism $\sigma: \bar{F}_1(B_1) \to \bar{F}_2(B_2)$ such that $\sigma\eta_1 = \eta_2\psi$. By assumption, tr.d. $C_1/\eta_1(F_1) =$ tr.d. $C_2/\eta_2(F_2)$. Hence, $|B_1| = |B_2|$ and, without loss of generality, we may write $B_1 = \{\alpha_i\}_{i\in J}$, $B_2 = \{\beta_i\}_{i\in J}$. Let $\bar{F}_1[\{x_i\}_{i\in J}]$ and $\bar{F}_2[\{x_i\}_{i\in J}]$ be the polynomial domains, over $\bar{F}_1$ and $\bar{F}_2$, respectively, in the indeterminates $x_i \in J$. Consider the diagram

$$\begin{array}{ccccccccc} F_1 & \xrightarrow{\eta_1} & \eta_1(F_1) = \bar{F}_1 & \xrightarrow{\varepsilon_1} & \bar{F}_1[\{x_i\}_{i\in J}] & \xrightarrow{\varphi_1} & \bar{F}_1[\{\alpha_i\}_{i\in J}] & \xrightarrow{\varepsilon_1'} & \bar{F}_1(\{\alpha_i\}_{i\in J}) \\ {\scriptstyle\psi}\downarrow & & \downarrow{\scriptstyle\bar{\psi}} & & \downarrow{\scriptstyle\bar{\psi}'} & & \vdots{\scriptstyle\sigma_1} & & \vdots{\scriptstyle\sigma} \\ F_2 & \xrightarrow[\eta_2]{} & \eta_2(F_2) = \bar{F}_2 & \xrightarrow[\varepsilon_2]{} & \bar{F}_2[\{x_i\}_{i\in J}] & \xrightarrow[\varphi_2]{} & \bar{F}_2[\{\beta_i\}_{i\in J}] & \xrightarrow[\varepsilon_2]{} & \bar{F}_2(\{\beta_i\}_{i\in J}) \end{array}$$

where ε_i, ε_i' $(i = 1,2)$ are natural embeddings, $\bar{\psi}$ is the isomorphism of $\bar{F}_1$ onto $\bar{F}_2$ which is defined by $\bar{\psi}\eta_1(a) = \eta_2\psi(a)$, $\bar{\psi}'$ is the isomorphism extending $\bar{\psi}$ to $\bar{F}_1[\{x_i\}_{i\in J}]$, $\varphi_1(f(x_{i_1},x_{i_2},\ldots,x_{i_n})) = f(\alpha_{i_1},\alpha_{i_2},\ldots,\alpha_{i_n})$, and $\varphi_2(f(x_{i_1},x_{i_2},\ldots,x_{i_n})) = f(\beta_{i_1},\beta_{i_2},\ldots,\beta_{i_n})$. Since B_i is a transcendence set over $\bar{F}_i$, φ_i is an isomorphism, $i = 1, 2$. It follows (Chapter 2, Theorem 1.7) that there exists an isomorphism σ_1 such that $\sigma_1\varphi_1 = \varphi_2\bar{\psi}'$. The isomorphism σ_1 extends to an isomorphism σ of the quotient field of $\bar{F}_i[\{\alpha_i\}_{i\in J}]$ onto the quotient field of

$\bar{F}_2[\{\beta_i\}_{i \in J}]$. Finally, since each of the "subdiagrams" commutes, and since $\varepsilon'_1\varphi_i\varepsilon_i\eta_i = \eta_i$ for $i = 1, 2$, it follows that the diagram

$$\begin{array}{ccc} F_1 & \xrightarrow{\eta_1} & \bar{F}_1(B_1) \\ {\scriptstyle\psi}\downarrow & & \downarrow{\scriptstyle\sigma} \\ F_2 & \xrightarrow[\eta_2]{} & \bar{F}_2(B_2) \end{array}$$

commutes, as desired. ▮

An immediate consequence of the theorem is

Corollary 1. *Suppose that C, E, and F are fields such that C is algebraically closed and $C \supset E \supset F$. If φ is an F-automorphism of E, then φ extends to an F-automorphism of C.* □

Another consequence is

Corollary 2. *Suppose that C, E, and F are fields such that C is algebraically closed, $C \supset E \supset F$, and* tr.d. *E/F is finite. If φ is an F-monomorphism of E into C, then φ extends to an F-automorphism of C.*

PROOF. In view of Theorem 2.5 it is sufficient to prove that tr.d. $C/E =$ tr.d. $C/\varphi(E)$. We note that, since φ is an F-monomorphism, tr.d. $\varphi(E)/F =$ tr.d. E/F and is finite. Consider the field towers

$$F \subset E \subset C,$$

$$F \subset \varphi(E) \subset C.$$

By Theorem 1.9, we have tr.d. $C/F =$ tr.d. $C/E +$ tr.d. $E/F =$ tr.d. $C/\varphi(E) +$ tr.d. $\varphi(E)/F$. Since tr.d. E/F and tr.d. $\varphi(E)/F$ are equal and finite, we conclude that tr.d. $C/E =$ tr.d. $C/\varphi(E)$. ▮

3. Splitting Fields; Normal Extensions; Elements Conjugate over a Field

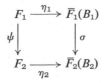

Let C, E, and F be fields such that C is algebraically closed, and $C \supset E \supset F$. Let G be the set of all F-monomorphisms of E into C. Later in this chapter we shall see that, under certain conditions, G is a group and there is an intimate relationship between the set of subgroups of G and the set of subfields of E containing F. In this section we shall, among other things, characterize those algebraic extensions E of F for which G is a group under composition of maps, i.e., the algebraic extensions E of F such that every F-monomorphism of E into C is an automorphism of E. In particular, we shall see that, if E is an algebraic extension of F, then G is a group if and only if E is generated over F by all the roots, in C, of a set of polynomials in $F[x]$. This characterization fails if E is a transcendental extension of F (Exercise 3.1).

NOTATION. If $\varepsilon: F \to E$ is a mapping of a field F into a field E, then ε extends to a mapping $\varepsilon': F[x] \to E[x]$ defined by $\varepsilon'(\sum_j \alpha_j x^j) = \sum_j \varepsilon(a_j)x^j$. For $f \in F[x]$ we shall denote $\varepsilon'(f)$ by f^ε.

Definition 3.1. Let E be a field and let $g(x) \in E[x]$. Then $g(x)$ *splits over* E if $g(x)$ factors into linear factors in $E[x]$; i.e., there exist $\alpha_j \in E, j = 0, 1, \ldots, n$, such that $g(x) = \alpha_0 \prod_{j=1}^{n} (x - \alpha_j)$.

Let F be a field and S a set of polynomials in $F[x]$. An extension $\langle E/F,\varepsilon\rangle$ is a *splitting field for S over F* if it satisfies the following two conditions:

a. For each $f \in S$, f^ε splits over E.
b. If $\langle K/F,\kappa\rangle$ is an extension such that, for each $f \in S$, f^κ splits over K, then there exists a monomorphism $\sigma: E \to K$ such that $\sigma\varepsilon = \kappa$; i.e., the diagram

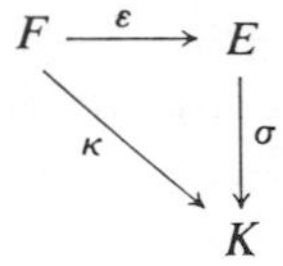

commutes.

If $f \in F[x]$ and $S = \{f\}$, then we shall refer to a splitting field for S as a *splitting field for f*. ///

Informally: E is a splitting field for S over F if every polynomial in S splits completely in $E[x]$, and if E can be embedded appropriately in any field over which all the elements of S split completely.

REMARKS.

1. If $\langle E/F,\varepsilon\rangle$ is a splitting field for S over F, then E is an algebraic extension of F. For, let E_a be the set of all elements of E which are algebraic over $\varepsilon(F)$. Then for every element $f \in S$, f^ε splits completely in $E_a[x]$ and, therefore, there exists an $\varepsilon(F)$-monomorphism of E into E_a. But then $E = E_a$.

2. If $\langle E/F,\varepsilon\rangle$ is a splitting field for S over F, then $\langle E/\varepsilon(F),\iota\rangle$ is a splitting field for $S' = \{f^\varepsilon | f \in S\}$ over $\varepsilon(F)$, with ι the natural inclusion of $\varepsilon(F)$ in E.

Theorem 3.1. *Let F be a field and S a set of polynomials in $F[x]$. A splitting field for S over F is unique up to isomorphism; i.e., if $\langle E_i/F,\varepsilon_i\rangle$, $i = 1, 2$, are splitting fields of S over F, then there exists an isomorphism, σ_1 of E_1 onto E_2 such that $\sigma_1\varepsilon_1 = \varepsilon_2$.*

PROOF. From the definition of splitting field for S over F it follows that there exist monomorphisms $\sigma_1: E_1 \to E_2$, and $\sigma_2: E_2 \to E_1$ such that $\sigma_1\varepsilon_1 = \varepsilon_2$ and $\sigma_2\varepsilon_2 = \varepsilon_1$. But then $\sigma_1\sigma_2\varepsilon_2 = \varepsilon_2$ and $\sigma_1\sigma_2$ is an $\varepsilon_2(F)$-monomorphism of E_1 to E_2. Since E_2 is algebraic over $\varepsilon_2(F)$, $\sigma_1\sigma_2$ is an automorphism of E_2 (Theorem 1.6); hence σ_1 is an epimorphism and is therefore an isomorphism of E_1 onto E_2. ▮

Corollary. *If $\langle E/F,\varepsilon\rangle$ is a splitting field for S over F and if $\varphi: E \to K$ is a monomorphism of E into K, then $\langle\varphi(E)/F,\varphi\varepsilon\rangle$ is a splitting field for S over F.* □

In the last theorem we considered uniqueness of a splitting field. In the next theorem we address ourselves to the problem of the existence of a splitting field.

Theorem 3.2. *Let $\langle C/F,\varepsilon\rangle$ be an algebraically closed extension of a field F, and let S be a set of polynomials in $F[x]$. Let R be the subset of C defined by $R \to \{\alpha \in C \mid f^{\varepsilon}(\alpha) = 0 \text{ for some } f \in S\}$ and let $E' = \varepsilon F(R)$. Then*

a. *$\langle E'/F,\varepsilon\rangle$ is a splitting field for S over F.*
b. *E' is the intersection of all subfields K of C such that $\varepsilon F \subset K$ and f^{ε} splits over K for all $f \in S$.*
c. *For any subfield, K, of C containing εF, $\langle K/F,\varepsilon\rangle$ is a splitting field for S over F if and only if $K = E'$.*

PROOF.

a. Clearly, every f^{ε}, with $f \in S$, splits over E'. Thus, to prove a it is sufficient to show that, if $\langle K/F,\kappa\rangle$ is an extension of F over which every f^{κ}, $f \in S$, factors into linear factors, then there exists a monomorphism $\sigma: E' \to K$ such that $\sigma\varepsilon = \kappa$. To this end, let K_a be the subfield of K consisting of all elements of K which are algebraic over $\kappa(F)$, let $\langle C'/K_a,\mu\rangle$ be an algebraic closure of K_a, and let C_a be the set of elements of C which are algebraic over εF. Then $\langle C'/F,\mu\kappa\rangle$ and $\langle C_a/F,\varepsilon\rangle$ are algebraic closures of F. Consider the diagram

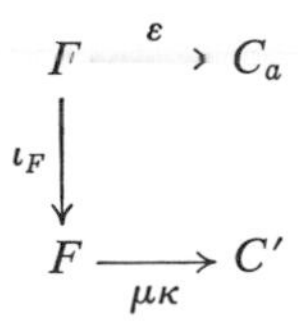

By Theorem 2.3, there exists an isomorphism $\tau\colon C_a \to C'$ such that $\tau\varepsilon = \mu\kappa$. Using the fact that, for each $f \in S$, f^{κ} factors into linear factors over K_a, we see easily that $\tau(E') \subset \mu(K_a)$. Let $\lambda\colon \mu(K_a) \to K_a$ be the monomorphism such that $\lambda \cdot \mu|_{K_a} = \iota_{K_a}$ and let $\sigma = \lambda \cdot \tau|_{E'}$. Then σ is a monomorphism of E' to $K_a \subset K$ and $\sigma\varepsilon = \kappa$.

b. and c. The proofs are easy and are left to the reader. ▌

Definition 3.2. If $F \subset E \subset C$, with C an algebraic closure of E, then E *is normal over* F if E is algebraic over F and every F-monomorphism of E into C is an F-automorphism of E; i.e., the F-monomorphisms of E into C form a group.

More generally, if $\langle E/F,\varepsilon\rangle$ is an extension of F, $E \subset C$ (C an algebraic closure of E), then E is a *normal extension* of F if E is normal over $\varepsilon(F)$, in the sense defined above. ///

NOTE: Our definition of normality, while stated in terms of a particular algebraic closure, is independent of the choice of algebraic closure. For, suppose $F \subset E \subset C$, and $F \subset E \subset C'$, where C and C' are both algebraic closures of E. Let $\rho\colon C' \to C$ be an isomorphism which extends ι_E. Suppose every F-monomorphism $\alpha\colon E \to C$ is an F-automorphism of E. Let $\alpha'\colon E \to C'$ be an F-monomorphism. Then $\alpha = \rho\alpha'$ is an F-monomorphism of E into C', hence an F-automorphism of E. But then $\alpha' x = \rho^{-1}\alpha x = \alpha x$ for each $x \in E$, whence $\alpha' = \alpha$, an F-automorphism of E.

Theorem 3.3. *Let $\langle E/F,\varepsilon\rangle$ be an extension of a field F. The following statements are equivalent:*

a. *There exists a set, S, of polynomials in $F[x]$ such that E is a splitting field for S over F.*
b. *E is a normal extension of F.*
c. *E is algebraic over F and, if $f \in F[x]$ is an irreducible polynomial such that f^{ε} has a root in E, then f^{ε} splits over E.*

PROOF. Let C be an algebraic closure of E containing E as a subfield. Let $F' = \varepsilon(F)$.

a $\Rightarrow$ b. Suppose that E is a splitting field for S over F, $S \subset F[x]$. Then, by the corollary to Theorem 3.1 and Theorem 3.2, $E = F'(R)$, where $R = \{\alpha \in C \mid f^{\varepsilon}(\alpha) = 0 \text{ for some } f \in S\}$. If φ is any F'-monomorphism of E into C, then $\varphi(R) \subset R$. Therefore, φ is an F'-monomorphism of E into E, and, by Theorem 1.6, φ is an F'-automorphism of E. But then, by definition, E is a normal extension of F.

b $\Rightarrow$ c. Let f be an irreducible polynomial in $F[x]$, and let $\alpha \in E$ be a root of f^{ε}. It is sufficient to prove that if $\beta \in C$ is any root of f^{ε}, then $\beta \in E$. By the lemma given in the proof of Theorem 2.2, there exists an F'-isomorphism, φ, of $F'(\alpha)$ onto $F'(\beta)$ such that $\varphi(\alpha) = \beta$. By Corollary 2 of Theorem 2.5, φ extends to an F'-automorphism, $\bar{\varphi}$, of C. Now if E is a normal extension of F, then $\bar{\varphi}(E) = E$ and $\bar{\varphi}(\alpha) = \varphi(\alpha) = \beta \in E$, as desired.

c $\Rightarrow$ a. It is sufficient to show that if c holds, then there exists a set, S', of polynomials in $F'[x]$ such that E is a splitting field for S' over F'. If we assume c, then E is algebraic over F' and, furthermore, the minimal polynomial $m_{\alpha/F'}(x)$, over F' of any element $\alpha \in E$ factors, over E, into a product of linear factors. Let $S' = \{m_{\alpha/F'}(x)\}_{\alpha \in E}$ and $R' = \{\alpha \in C |$ there is some $f \in S'$ such that $f(\alpha) = 0\}$. Then $R' = E$ and $E = F'(R')$. But then, by Theorem 3.2a, E is a splitting field for S' over F'. ▌

Corollary 1. *E is normal over F and $[E: F]$ is finite if and only if there exists an $f \in F[x]$ such that E is a splitting field for f over F.*

PROOF. If E is normal over F, then E is a splitting field for a set, S, of polynomials over F. If, in addition, $[E: F]$ is finite, then there exists a finite subset T of S such that E is a splitting field for T over F. Let $f(x) = \prod_{g(x) \in T} g(x)$. Then E is a splitting field for f over F.

The converse is obvious. ▌

Corollary 2. *Let $C \supset E \supset F$ be a tower of fields where C is an algebraic closure of E. If E is algebraic over F, then there exists a unique minimal subfield, K, of C which contains E and which is normal over F; if $[E: F]$ is finite, then $[K: F]$ is finite.*

PROOF. There exists a subset $\{\alpha_i\}_{i \in J}$ of C such that $E = F(\{\alpha_i\}_{i \in J})$. Suppose E is algebraic over F. Let $S = \{m_{\alpha_i/F}(x)\}_{i \in J}$, and let K be the subfield of C which is a splitting field for S over F. Then K is normal over F, contains E, and is contained in every subfield of C which contains E and which is normal over F. If $[E: F]$ is finite, then there is a finite subset $\{\alpha_i\}_{i \in J}$ of C such that $E = F(\{\alpha_i\}_{i \in J})$. But then S is a finite set and, by Theorems 3.2a and 1.3, $[K: F]$ is finite. ▌

The union and intersection of normal extensions of a field F are normal over F. A normal extension, E, of F is also normal over every field lying between E and F. Formally, we have

Theorem 3.4. *For $i \in J$, let $C \supset E_i \supset F$ be a tower of fields with E_i normal over F and C an algebraic closure of E, and let K be a subfield of C containing F. Then*

a. *$F(\bigcup_{i \in J} E_i)$ is normal over F.*
b. *$F(\bigcap_{i \in J} E_i)$ is normal over F.*
c. *If E is normal over F, then $E(K)$ is normal over K. In particular, if $E \supset K \supset F$, then E is normal over K.*

PROOF. Since each E_i, $i \in J$, is algebraic over F, $F(\bigcap_{i\in J} E_i)$ is algebraic over F, and, by Theorem 1.7c and d, $F(\bigcup_{i\in J} E_i)$ is algebraic over F. If φ is any F-monomorphism of $F(\bigcup_{i\in J} E_i)$ into C, then $\varphi F(\bigcup_{i\in J}(E_i)) = F(\bigcup_{i\in J} \varphi(E_i)) = F(\bigcup_{i\in J} E_i)$, and φ is an F-automorphism of $F(\bigcup_{i\in J} E_i)$. Now suppose ψ is an F-monomorphism of $F(\bigcap_{i\in J} E_i)$ into C. Since C is an algebraic closure of F, ψ can be extended to an F-automorphism, $\bar{\psi}$, of C (Theorem 2.5, Corollary 2). Then $\bar{\psi}|_{E_i}$ is an F-automorphism of E_i for each $i \in J$, and $\psi(F(\bigcap_{i\in J} E_i)) = F(\bigcap_{i\in J} \bar{\psi}E_i) = F(\bigcap_{i\in J} E_i)$, whence ψ is an F-automorphism of $F(\bigcap_{i\in J} E_i)$. This proves a and b.

To prove c we note that, by Theorem 1.7c, $E_i(K)$ is algebraic over K and that, if φ is any K-monomorphism of $E_i(K)$ into C, then $\varphi|_{E_i}$ is an F-monomorphism of E_i into C; since E_i is normal over F, $\varphi(E_i) = E_i$, whence $\varphi(E_i(K)) = E_i(K)$ and φ is a K-automorphism of $E_i(K)$. ▮

REMARK. The reader may have discerned from Theorem 3.4 that the normal subgroups of groups behave, relative to union and intersection, in a way which is similar to the behavior of fields normal over a field F. Normal subgroups and normal extensions behave analogously in another way: Just as it is true that a normal subgroup of a normal subgroup is not necessarily a normal subgroup, so it is true that a normal extension of a normal extension is not necessarily a normal extension. We give an example: $\mathbf{Q}(\sqrt{2})$ is a splitting field of $\{x^2 - 2\}$ over the rational field $\mathbf{Q}$. Thus $\mathbf{Q}(\sqrt{2})$ is normal over $\mathbf{Q}$. $\mathbf{Q}(\sqrt[4]{2})$ is a splitting field of $\{x^2 - \sqrt{2}\}$, over $\mathbf{Q}(\sqrt{2})$, and hence is normal over $\mathbf{Q}(\sqrt{2})$. However, $\mathbf{Q}(\sqrt[4]{2})$ is not normal over $\mathbf{Q}$. For $x^4 - 2$, which is irreducible over $\mathbf{Q}$, has a root in $\mathbf{Q}(\sqrt[4]{2})$ but does not factor over $\mathbf{Q}(\sqrt[4]{2})$ into a product of linear factors. ($\sqrt[4]{2}$ denotes the positive real fourth root of 2.)

We close this section with a definition and two theorems whose proofs we leave to the reader (Exercises 3.5 and 3.6).

Definition 3.3. Let C be an algebraically closed field containing a field F. Two subfields, E_i, $i = 1, 2$, of C which contain F are *conjugate over F*, or *F-conjugate*, if there exists an F-automorphism of C such that $\varphi(E_1) = E_2$. Two elements, α_i, $i = 1, 2$, of C are *conjugate over F*, or *F-conjugate*, if there exists an F-automorphism of C such that $\varphi(\alpha_1) = \alpha_2$. ///

Theorem 3.5. *Let C be an algebraically closed field containing a field F, and let α and β be elements of C. Then α and β are conjugate over F if and only if*

a. *α and β are both transcendental over F, or*
b. *α and β are both algebraic over F, and $m_{\alpha/F}(x) = m_{\beta/F}(x)$ (i.e., they have the same minimum polynomial).* □

Corollary. *An element $\alpha \in C$ is algebraic over F if and only if the number, N, of distinct F-conjugates of α in C is finite. If $\alpha \in C$ is algebraic over F, then*

a. $N \leq [\alpha: F]$.
b. *N is equal to the number of distinct roots of $m_{\alpha/F}(x)$ in C.*
c. *N is equal to the number of distinct F-monomorphisms of $F[\alpha]$ into C.* □

Theorem 3.6. *Let C be an algebraically closed field containing a field F and let S be a set of elements of C, each algebraic over F. If $S_1 = \{\alpha \in C | \alpha$ F-conjugate to an element of $S\}$, then $F(S_1)$ is the unique smallest subfield of C which contains $F(S)$ and which is normal over F.* □

4. Purely Inseparable and Separable Extensions

Let F be a subfield of an algebraically closed field C. In this section we study two types of subfields of C containing F: (1) those which admit "very few" F-monomorphisms into C, and (2) those which admit "very many" F-monomorphisms into C. We begin with an example.

Example. Let F be the quotient field of the polynomial domain in one transcendental element u over the prime field of characteristic $p \neq 0$, i.e., $F = (\mathbf{Z}/(p))(u)$, and let C be an algebraically closed field containing F. Let θ be a root, in C, of $x^p - u \in F[x]$, and let $E = F(\theta)$. Since $x^p - u$ is irreducible, $[E: F] = p$. Over C, $x^p - u = (x - \theta)^p$. Now, every F-monomorphism of E into C must map θ to a root of $x^p - u$. Since θ is the only root of $x^p - u$ in C, every F-monomorphism of E into C leaves θ fixed, and is therefore the identity map on E. Hence, the only F-monomorphism of E into C is the identity map.

Definition 4.1. Let $C \supset E \supset F$ be a tower of fields with C algebraically closed. E is *purely inseparable over F* if the only F-monomorphism of E into C is the one which acts as the identity on E. An element $\alpha \in C$ is *purely inseparable over F* if the field $F(\alpha)$ is purely inseparable over F. ///

NOTE: This definition is independent of the choice of C. For, suppose $F \subset E \subset C$ (C algebraically closed), and suppose every F-monomorphism $\alpha: E \to C$ is the identity on E. Let C' be another algebraically closed field such that $F \subset E \subset C'$, and let $\alpha': E \to C'$ be an F-monomorphism. There exist algebraic closures $\overline{C}, \overline{C}'$ of E such that $E \subset \overline{C} \subset C$ and $\alpha'E \subset \overline{C}' \subset C'$. By Theorem 2.3, there is an E-isomorphism $\sigma: \overline{C} \to \overline{C}'$. The map $\alpha: E \to C$ defined by $\alpha x = \sigma^{-1}\alpha'\sigma x$ for each $x \in E$ is an F-monomorphism, hence equal to the identity on E. But then, for each $x \in E$, $\alpha' x = \sigma\alpha x = \sigma x = x$, and so α' is the identity on E.

REMARK. If E is purely inseparable over F, then E is algebraic over F. For, suppose there exists an $x \in E$ which is transcendental over F. Then the F-monomorphism $\varphi: F(x) \to F(x^2)$ defined by $f(x) \mapsto f(x^2)$ extends to an F-automorphism, $\hat{\varphi}$, of any algebraically closed field $C \supset E$ (Theorem 2.5, Corollary 2). But then $\hat{\varphi}|_E$ is an F-monomorphism of E into C which does not act as the identity on E and we have a contradiction.

Theorem 4.1. *Let $C \supset E \supset F$ be a tower of fields with C algebraically closed and $E \neq F$. The following statements are equivalent:*

a. *E is purely inseparable over F.*
b. *Every element of E is purely inseparable over F.*
c. *The characteristic of F is $p > 0$ and the minimum polynomial over F of every $\alpha \in E$ is of the form $m_{\alpha/F}(x) = x^{p^n} - a$, $n \geq 0$, $a \in F$.*
d. *E is generated over F by a set of elements each purely inseparable over F.*

PROOF.

a $\Rightarrow$ b. Let $\alpha \in E$. By Theorem 2.5, Corollary 2, every F-monomorphism $\varphi: F(\alpha) \to C$ extends to an F-automorphism $\hat{\varphi}$ of C. Since E is purely inseparable over F, $\hat{\varphi}|_E$ acts as the identity on E. But then, $\hat{\varphi}|_{F(\alpha)} = \varphi$ acts as the identity on $F(\alpha)$, and α is purely inseparable over F.

b $\Rightarrow$ c. Let $\alpha \in E$, $\alpha \notin F$. By the Remark preceding the theorem, α is algebraic over F. Furthermore, the only F-conjugate of α in C is α; for otherwise there exists an F-automorphism of C which moves α. Therefore, there exists $k \in \mathbf{N}$ such that $m_{\alpha/F}(x) = (x - \alpha)^k = x^k - k\alpha x^{k-1} + \cdots + (-1)^k\alpha^k$. It follows that $k\alpha \in F$; but since $\alpha \notin F$, we are forced to conclude that Char F is a prime dividing k. Suppose $k = p^n r$, $(r,p) = 1$. Then $m_{\alpha/F}(x) = (x - \alpha)^{p^n r} = (x^{p^n} - \alpha^{p^n})^r$ and we claim that $\alpha^{p^n} \in F$. For, otherwise, reasoning as we did in the case of $(x - \alpha)^k$, we infer that $p|r$, contrary to the assumption $(r,p) = 1$. Hence $\alpha^{p^n} \in F$, and so $m_{\alpha/F}(x) = x^{p^n} - \alpha^{p^n}$.

c $\Rightarrow$ d. If Char $F = p > 0$ and the minimum polynomial over F of an element $\alpha \in E$ is $x^{p^n} - a$, $n \in \mathbf{N}$, $a \in F$, then α is purely inseparable over F. For, over C, $x^{p^n} - a = (x - \alpha)^{p^n}$, and the only F-conjugate of α in C is α. But then every F-monomorphism of $F(\alpha)$ into C must act as the identity on $F(\alpha)$ and α is purely inseparable over F. It follows that if c holds, then E is a set of purely inseparable elements over F which generates E over F.

d $\Rightarrow$ a. If E is generated over F by a set of purely inseparable elements over F, then every F-monomorphism of E into C must fix each of the generators, hence must act as the identity on E. But then, E is purely inseparable over F. ▮

Another example of a purely inseparable extension is contained in

Theorem 4.2. *Let F be a subfield of an algebraically closed field C, and let F_0 be the set of all elements fixed by every F-automorphism of C; i.e., $F_0 = \{\alpha \in C | \varphi(\alpha) = \alpha$ for every F-automorphism φ of $C\}$. Let $C_a = \{\alpha \in C | \alpha$ algebraic over $F\}$. Then*

a. *F_0 is purely inseparable over F.*
b. *$F_0 = \{\alpha \in C_a | \psi(\alpha) = \alpha$ for every F-automorphism ψ of $C_a\}$.*
c. *$F_0 = F$ if* Char $F = 0$; *$F_0 = \{\alpha \in C_a | \exists n \in \mathbf{Z}, n \geq 0$, such that $\alpha^{p^n} \in F\}$ if* Char $F = p > 0$.

PROOF.

a. If $\alpha \in F_0$, then every F-monomorphism of $F(\alpha)$ into C acts as the identity on $F(\alpha)$. For otherwise, there exists an F-monomorphism $\varphi: F(\alpha) \to C$ which moves α. φ extends to an F-automorphism $\hat{\varphi}$ of C. But then $\hat{\varphi}(\alpha) \neq \alpha$, and we have a contradiction to $\alpha \in F_0$. Hence every element of F_0 is purely inseparable over F, and, by Theorem 4.1, F_0 is purely inseparable over F.

b. Follows easily from the observations that F_0 is algebraic over F, that the restriction to C_a of every F-automorphism of C is an automorphism of C_a (Theorem 3.5), and that every F-automorphism of C_a extends to an F-automorphism of C (Theorem 2.5, Corollary 1).

c. We have seen that F_0 is purely inseparable over F. It follows from Theorem 4.1 that if $F_0 \neq F$, then Char $F = p > 0$ and for each $\alpha \in F_0$ there exists an $n \geq 0$ such that $\alpha^{p^n} \in F_0$. On the other hand, if Char $F = p > 0$ and α is an element of C_a such that $\alpha^{p^m} \in F$ for some $m \geq 0$, then for every F-automorphism ψ of C_a, $\alpha^{p^m} = \psi(\alpha^{p^m}) = [\psi(\alpha)]^{p^m}$, $0 = \alpha^{p^m} - [\psi(\alpha)]^{p^m} = [\alpha - \psi(\alpha)]^{p^m}$, and $\alpha = \psi(\alpha)$. But then α is fixed by every F-automorphism of C_a, and $\alpha \in F_0$. ▌

Before turning our attention to fields $E \supset F$ which admit "many" F-monomorphisms into an algebraically closed field $C \supset E$, we shall try to get some idea about the "size" of the set of F-monomorphisms of E into C.

Theorem 4.3. (Artin.) *Let $C \supset E \supset F$ be a tower of fields. If $\{\varphi_j\}_{j \in J}$ is a set of distinct F-monomorphisms of E into C, then $\{\varphi_j\}_{j \in J}$ is a free set over C: i.e., if $\{\varphi_1, \varphi_2, \ldots, \varphi_n\}$ is any finite subset of $\{\varphi_j\}_{j \in J}$ for which there exist $a_1, a_2, \ldots, a_n$ in C such that $\sum_{i=1}^{n} a_i \varphi_i(\alpha) = 0$ for all $\alpha \in E$, then $a_1 = a_2 = \cdots = a_n = 0$.*

PROOF. To prove the theorem, it is sufficient to show that every finite set of F-monomorphisms of E into C is free over C. Clearly, a set consisting of a single F-monomorphism of E into C is free over C. For $k > 1$, assume that every set of fewer than k distinct F-monomorphisms of E into C is free over C.

Let $\{\varphi_i\}_{i=1}^k$ be a set of k distinct F-monomorphisms of E into C and suppose that this set is dependent over C. Then there exist $a_i \in C$, $i = 1, 2, \ldots, k$, such that $\sum_{i=1}^k a_i\varphi_i(\alpha) = 0$ for all $\alpha \in E$. From our induction assumption it follows that each of the a_i is different from 0. Hence,

$$(*) \qquad \sum_{i=1}^{k=1} b_i\varphi_i(\alpha) + \varphi_k(\alpha) = 0 \qquad \text{for all } \alpha \in E,$$

where $b_i = a_i/a_k \neq 0$, $i = 1, 2, \ldots, k - 1$. Since φ_1 and φ_k are distinct, there exists $\beta \in E$ such that $\varphi_1(\beta) \neq \varphi_k(\beta)$. From equation (*) it follows that $\sum_{i=1}^{k-1} b_i\varphi_i(\beta\alpha) + \varphi_k(\beta\alpha) = 0$ for all $\alpha \in E$. Hence

$$(\dagger) \qquad \sum_{i=1}^{k-1} (\varphi_k(\beta))^{-1}b_i\varphi_i(\beta)\varphi_i(\alpha) + \varphi_k(\alpha) = 0 \qquad \text{for all } \alpha \in E.$$

If we combine the relations in (*) and (†) appropriately we conclude that

$$\sum_{i=1}^{k-1} [b_i - [\varphi_k(\beta)]^{-1}b_i\varphi_i(\beta)]\varphi_i(\alpha) = 0 \qquad \text{for all } \alpha \in E.$$

Since $\varphi_1(\beta) \neq \varphi_k(\beta)$ and $b_1 \neq 0$, the coefficient of $\varphi_1(\alpha)$ in the last equation is not equal to zero, whence $\{\varphi_i\}_{i=1}^{k-1}$ is a dependent set over C. But this contradicts our induction assumption. Hence every finite set of distinct F-monomorphisms of E into C is free over C. ▮

NOTATION. Let F be a subfield of C and consider C as an F-space. Let V be an F-subspace of C. The set $\text{Hom}_F(V,C)$ of all F-homomorphisms of V into the F-space C is a C-space, with scalar multiplication defined by: $(c\varphi)(\alpha) = c(\varphi\alpha)$ $(c \in C, \varphi \in \text{Hom}_F(V,C), \alpha \in V)$.

We denote by $\text{Aut}_F C$ the set of all field automorphisms of C which leave each element of F fixed. Note that $\text{Aut}_F C$ is a subset of the C-space $\text{Hom}_F(C,C)$. If A is any subset of $\text{Aut}_F C$, we shall write $[A]$ for the C-subspace of $\text{Hom}_F(C,C)$ generated by A. For V an F-subspace of C, we denote by $[A|_V]$ the C-subspace of $\text{Hom}_F(V,C)$ generated by the set $\{\varphi|_V \mid \varphi \in A\}$.

If $F \subset E \subset C$ is a field tower, we write $\text{Mon}_F(E,C)$ for the set of all field monomorphisms of E into C which leave each element of F fixed. We use the symbol $[V\colon F]$ to designate the dimension of any F-subspace V of C.

REMARK. If V is a finite-dimensional F-subspace of C, then $[\text{Hom}_F(V,C)\colon C] = [V\colon F]$. For, let $\{\alpha_j\}_{j=1}^n$ be a basis for V over F. For each $i = 1, \ldots, n$, define $\varepsilon_i\colon V \to V$ by: $\varepsilon_i(\alpha_j) = \delta_{ij}$ for each $j = 1, \ldots, n$. Then $\{\varepsilon_i\}_{i=1}^n$ is a basis for the C-space $\text{Hom}_F(V,C)$.

From Artin's Theorem, we have:

Corollary 1. *Let $C \supset E \supset F$ be a field tower with $[E: F]$ finite. Then* $|\mathrm{Mon}_F(E,C)| \leq [E: F]$.

Proof. By the Remark preceding Corollary 1, $[\mathrm{Hom}_F(E,C): C] = [E: F]$. By the Theorem, $\mathrm{Mon}_F(E,C)$ is a C-free subset of $\mathrm{Hom}_F(E,C)$. Hence $\mathrm{Mon}_F(E,C) \leq [\mathrm{Hom}_F(E,C): C] = [E: F]$. ▌

Another consequence of the theorem is

Corollary 2. *Let F be a subfield of a field C, A a subset of* $\mathrm{Aut}_F(C)$, *and V an F-subspace of C. Then $[|A|_V]: C] = |A|_V|$, the cardinality of the set $A|_V$. In particular,* $[[\mathrm{Aut}_F C|_V]: C] = |\mathrm{Aut}_F\, C|_V|$.

Proof. The theorem applies, with E equal to the F-subspace of C generated by V. ▌

Corollary 3. *Let $C \supset E \supset F$ be a tower of fields with C algebraically closed and* tr.d. *E/F finite. Then*

$$|\mathrm{Mon}_F(E,C)| = |\mathrm{Aut}_F\, C|_E| = [[\mathrm{Aut}_F\, C|_E]: C].$$

Proof. Clearly $\mathrm{Aut}_F\, C|_E \subset \mathrm{Mon}_F(E,C)$. Since tr.d. E/F is finite, every F-monomorphism of E into C extends to an F-automorphism of C (Theorem 2.5, Corollary 2). But then, $\mathrm{Mon}_F(E,C) \subset \mathrm{Aut}_F\, C|_E$, and $|\mathrm{Mon}_F(E,C)| = |\mathrm{Aut}_F\, C|_E|$. The remaining equality follows from Corollary 2. ▌

The upper bound given in Corollary 1 is, in many situations, actually attained. We recall part of the corollary to Theorem 3.5: Let F be a subfield of an algebraically closed field C, and let α be an element of C which is algebraic over F. Then $|\mathrm{Mon}_F(F(\alpha),C)| = [F(\alpha): F]$ if and only if $m_{\alpha/F}(x)$ has no repeated root in C; i.e., $m_{\alpha/F}(x)$ factors into a product of distinct linear factors over C. As we have seen (in the Example preceding Definition 4.1), there are fields $C \supset E \supset F$ such that $|\mathrm{Mon}_F(E,C)| < [E: F]$.

Our next theorem will yield another expression for $[[\mathrm{Aut}_F\, C|_V]: C]$.

If A is a set of monomorphisms of a field E into a field $C \supset E$, then the set of all elements $\alpha \in E$ which are fixed under all monomorphisms in A is a subfield of E.

Definition 4.2. If E is a subfield of a field C, and A is a set of monomorphisms of E into C, then the set $\{\alpha \in E | \varphi(\alpha) = \alpha \text{ for all } \varphi \in A\}$ is the *fixed field* $\mathfrak{f}(A)$, of A. ///

(Recall that, for C an algebraically closed field, $F \subset C$, we have characterized $\mathfrak{f}(\mathrm{Aut}_F\, C)$ in Theorem 4.2c: If Char $F = 0$, then $\mathfrak{f}(\mathrm{Aut}_F\, C) = F$, and if Char $F = p > 0$, then $\mathfrak{f}(\mathrm{Aut}_F\, C) = \{\alpha \in C \mid \alpha^{p^k} \in F \text{ for some integer } k \geq 0\}$.)

Theorem 4.4. *Let C be a field, let A be a nonempty set of automorphisms of C closed under composition of maps, and let K be the fixed field of A. If V is a K-subspace of C such that either $[V: K]$ or $[[A|_V]: C]$ is finite, then $[V: K] = [[A|_V]: C]$.*

PROOF. Since $A|_V$ is a subset of $\mathrm{Hom}_K(V,C)$, $[[A|_V]: C]$ is less than or equal to the dimension of the C-space $\mathrm{Hom}_K(V,C)$. For finite-dimensional V, $[\mathrm{Hom}_K(V,C): C] = [V: K]$; hence $[[A|_V]: C] \leq [V: K]$, and $[A|_V]$ is finite dimensional over C if V is finite dimensional over K. It is therefore sufficient to prove that if $[[A|_V]: C] = n$, then $[V: K] \leq n$.

Let $\{\varphi_i\}_{i=1}^n$ be a subset of A such that $\{\varphi_i|_V\}_{i=1}^n$ is a basis for $[A|_V]$ over C. We prove that any set of $n + 1$ elements of V is dependent over K. Let $\alpha_j \in V$, $j = 1, 2, \ldots, n + 1$. Consider the $n \times (n + 1)$ matrix $T = (\varphi_i(\alpha_j))$, $i = 1, 2, \ldots, n$; $j = 1, 2, \ldots, n + 1$. There exists a nonzero vector

$$w = \begin{pmatrix} c_1 \\ c_2 \\ \vdots \\ c_{n+1} \end{pmatrix} \qquad \text{with } c_j \in C,$$

such that $Tw = 0$. From the nonempty set $\{v \mid Tv = 0, v \neq 0\}$ choose one, say v_0, having the least number of nonzero components. Since, if necessary, we may relabel the φ_i and the α_j, we may suppose that

$$v_0 = \begin{pmatrix} a_1 \\ a_2 \\ \vdots \\ a_{r-1} \\ a_r \\ 0 \\ 0 \\ \vdots \\ 0 \end{pmatrix},$$

with $a_j \in C$, $a_r = 1$, $a_j \neq 0$, $j = 1, 2, \ldots, r - 1$.

In order to prove that $\{\alpha_j\}_{j=1}^{n+1}$ is dependent over K, it is sufficient to prove that every component of v_0 is in K. For, if $a_j \in K$ for each j, then for each $i = 1, 2, \ldots, n$,

$$0 = \sum_{j=1}^{r} a_j\varphi_i(\alpha_j) = \sum_{j=1}^{r} \varphi_i(a_j\alpha_j) = \varphi_i\left(\sum_{j=1}^{r} a_j\alpha_j\right), \quad \sum_{j=1}^{r} a_j\alpha_j = 0,$$

and $\{\alpha_j\}_{j=1}^{n+1}$ is dependent over K.

Suppose that, say, $a_1 \notin K$. Since K is the fixed field of A, there exists $\varphi \in A$ such that $\varphi(a_1) \neq a_1$. Since $Tv_0 = 0$,

$$((\varphi\varphi_i)(\alpha_j)) \begin{pmatrix} \varphi(a_1) \\ \varphi(a_2) \\ \vdots \\ \varphi(a_{r-1}) \\ 1 \\ 0 \\ 0 \\ \vdots \\ 0 \end{pmatrix} = 0.$$

We write the last equation as $(\varphi T)\varphi(v_0) = 0$. Since A is closed under composition of maps, there exist $b_{ij} \in C$ such that $(\varphi\varphi_i)|_V = \sum_{j=1}^{n} b_{ij}\varphi_j|_V$, $i = 1, 2, \ldots, n$. Thus, $\varphi T = BT$, and $(\varphi T)\varphi(v_0) = BT\varphi(v_0) = 0$, where $B = (b_{ij})$. It is easy to see that $\{(\varphi\varphi_i)|_V\}_{i=1}^{n}$ is a basis for $[A|_V]$ over C. The matrix B therefore has an inverse. From $Tv_0 = 0$, $BTv_0 = 0$, and $BT\varphi(v_0) = 0$, we conclude that $BT(\varphi(v_0) - v_0) = 0$. Since B has an inverse, $T(\varphi(v_0) - v_0) = 0$; since $\varphi(a_1) \neq a_1$ and $\varphi(a_r) = a_r = 1$, $\varphi(v_0) - v_0$ is a nonzero vector with fewer nonzero terms than v_0. But, by the choice of v_0, this is impossible, whence every component of v_0 is in K, and $\{\alpha_j\}_{j=1}^{n+1}$ is a dependent set over K. ▌

Corollary 1. *Let F be a subfield of a field C, let F_0 be the fixed field of $\mathrm{Aut}_F\, C$, and let V be an F_0-subspace of C. Then V is an F-subspace of C and $[V: F_0] \leq [V: F]$. If $[V: F_0]$ or $[V: F]$ is finite, then*

$$|\mathrm{Aut}_F\, C|_V| = [V: F_0] \leq [V: F].$$

PROOF. It is obvious that V is an F-subspace of C and that $[V: F_0] \leq [V: F]$. The remainder of the corollary follows from Theorem 4.3, Corollary 2, and the theorem. ▌

Another consequence of Theorem 4.3, Corollary 3, and the theorem is

Corollary 2. *Let $F \subset E \subset C$ be a field tower, with C algebraically closed, and let $F_0 = \mathfrak{f}(\mathrm{Aut}_F\, C)$. If either $[E(F_0): F_0]$ or $[E: F]$ is finite, then $|\mathrm{Mon}_F(E,C)| = [E(F_0): F_0] \leq [E: F]$.*

PROOF. By Theorem 4.2c, we know that $F_0 = F$ if Char $F = 0$, and $F_0 = \{a \in C | a^{p^n} \in F$ for some $n \geq 0\}$ if Char $F = p$. Thus, F_0 is algebraic over F. It follows that if $[E(F_0): F_0]$ or $[E: F]$ is finite, then $E(F_0)$ is algebraic over F_0 (and over F). But then $E(F_0) = E[F_0] = F_0[E]$, and $E(F_0)$ has an F_0-basis consisting of elements in E. Since $F \subset F_0$, every F_0-free set in E is F-free. Hence if $[E(F_0): F_0]$ or $[E: F]$ is finite, then $[E(F_0): F_0] \leq [E: F]$.

Suppose that at least one of the cardinals $[E(F_0): F_0]$, $[E: F]$ is finite. Then $E(F_0)$ is algebraic over F, and (by Theorem 4.3, Corollary 3, and Theorem 4.4)

$$|\mathrm{Mon}_F(E(F_0),C)| = [E(F_0): F_0] \leq [E: F].$$

We claim that $|\mathrm{Mon}_F(E(F_0),C)| = |\mathrm{Mon}_F(E,C)|$. If $\varphi \in \mathrm{Mon}_F(E(F_0),C)$, then (by Theorem 2.5), φ extends to an F-automorphism of C, hence to an F-monomorphism of E into C. Since $F_0 = \mathfrak{f}(\mathrm{Aut}_F\, C)$, distinct F-monomorphisms of $E(F_0)$ into C induce distinct F-monomorphisms of E into C. Hence

$$|\mathrm{Mon}_F(E(F_0),C)| \leq |\mathrm{Mon}_F(E,C)|.$$

Since $E(F_0)$ is algebraic over F, we have E algebraic over F, and a similar argument yields

$$|\mathrm{Mon}_F(E,C)| \leq |\mathrm{Mon}_F(E(F_0),C)|.$$

Thus,

$$|\mathrm{Mon}_F(E,C)| = [E(F_0): F_0] \leq [E: F]. \quad \blacksquare$$

We can use Corollary 1 to formalize the notion: A field $E \supset F$, with tr.d. E/F finite, has "very many" F-monomorphisms into an algebraically closed field $C \supset E$. If V is an F-subspace of E, finite dimensional over F, then the cardinality of the set $\{\varphi|_V | \varphi \in \mathrm{Aut}_F\, C\}$ is bounded by $[V: F]$. This bound is attained for every F-subspace V if and only if every F-free subset of E is also F_0-free, where $F_0 = \mathfrak{f}(\mathrm{Aut}_F\, C)$. We shall use the latter condition to define the "separable extensions" of F. First we give

Definition 4.3. Let $C \supset E_i \supset F$, $i = 1, 2$, be field towers. E_1 is *linearly disjoint from* E_2, *over* F, if every subset of E_1 which is free over F is free over E_2. ///

REMARK. The reader may show, by an argument involving linear independence, that if E_1 is linearly disjoint from E_2 over F, then E_2 is linearly disjoint from E_1 over F. The following is an alternative method. Let $E_1[E_2]$ be the subring of C generated by $E_1 \cup E_2$, and consider $E_1[E_2]$ as an F-module. Note that E_1 is linearly disjoint from E_2 over F if and only if the map φ, from the F-module $E_1 \otimes_F E_2$ to $E_1[E_2]$, defined by $\varphi(\sum_i \alpha_i \otimes \beta_i) = \sum_i \alpha_i\beta_i$ is an F-isomorphism ($\alpha_i \in E_1, \beta_i \in E_2$). Since $\sum_i \alpha_i \otimes \beta_i \mapsto \sum_i \beta_i \otimes \alpha_i$ ($\alpha_i \in E_1, \beta_i \in E_2$) defines an F-isomorphism of $E_1 \otimes_F E_2$ onto $E_2 \otimes_F E_1$, and $\sum_i \alpha_i\beta_i = \sum_i \beta_i\alpha_i$, E_1 is linearly disjoint from E_2 over F if and only if E_2 is linearly disjoint from E_1 over F (see Exercise 4.2). For this reason, we shall from now on use the simpler terminology: E_1 and E_2 are linearly disjoint over F.

Definition 4.4. Let $C \supset E \supset F$ be a tower of fields with C algebraically closed, and let F_0 denote the fixed field of $\mathrm{Aut}_F\, C$. Then E is *separable over* F if E and F_0 are linearly disjoint over F. ///

We shall see that the separability of an extension field is independent of the choice of C (Remark following Theorem 4.5).

Corollary 1. *E is separable over F if and only if for every finite subset, S, of E, $F(S)$ is separable over F.* □

Corollary 2. *Let $C \supset E \supset F$ be a field tower, with C algebraically closed, and $[E: F]$ finite. Then E is separable over F if and only if $|\mathrm{Mon}_F(E,C)| = [E: F]$.*

PROOF. Corollary 2 to Theorem 4.4 implies that $|\mathrm{Mon}_F(E,C)| = [E: F]$ if and only if $|E(F_0): F_0| = |E: F|$, where F_0 is the fixed field of $\mathrm{Aut}_F\, C$. But $[E(F_0): F_0] = [E: F]$ if and only if E and F_0 are linearly disjoint over F, whence E is separable over F if and only if $|\mathrm{Mon}_F(E,C)| = [E: F]$. ∎

Corollary 3. *Let $C \supset E \supset F$ be a tower of fields with C algebraically closed. If* Char $F = 0$, *then E is separable over F.*

PROOF. By Theorem 4.2c, $F =$ the fixed field of $\mathrm{Aut}_F\, C = F_0$. But then E and F_0 are linearly disjoint over F, and E is separable over F. ∎

NOTATION. Let F be a subfield of an algebraically closed field C. If Char $F = p > 0$, then, for $k \in \mathbf{Z}$, $k \geq 0$,

$$F^{1/p^k} = \{\alpha \in C \mid \alpha^{p^k} \in F\},$$

$$F^{1/p^\infty} = \{\alpha \in C \mid \text{there exists } n \in \mathbf{Z},\ n \geq 0, \text{ such that } \alpha^{p^n} \in F\}.$$

REMARKS.

1. F^{1/p^k} and F^{1/p^∞} are subfields of C.

2. From Theorem 4.2c it follows that $\mathfrak{f}(\mathrm{Aut}_F\, C)$ (the fixed field of $\mathrm{Aut}_F\, C$) is equal to F^{1/p^∞}.

Theorem 4.5. *Let $C \supset E \supset F$ be a tower of fields, where C is algebraically closed and* Char $F = p > 0$. *Then the following statements are equivalent:*

a. *E is separable over F.*

b. *E and F^{1/p^∞} are linearly disjoint over F.*

c. *E and $F^{1/p}$ are linearly disjoint over F.*

PROOF. Since F^{1/p^∞} is the fixed field of $\mathrm{Aut}_F\, C$, a and b are, by definition, equivalent.

$F^{1/p}$ is a subfield of F^{1/p^∞}. Therefore, if E and F^{1/p^∞} are linearly disjoint over F, then E and $F^{1/p}$ are linearly disjoint over F. Hence b $\Rightarrow$ c.

Assume c and let $\{\alpha_i\}$ be a subset of E which is free over F. Since E and $F^{1/p}$ are linearly disjoint over F, $\{\alpha_i\}$ is free over $F^{1/p}$. It follows that $\{\alpha_i^p\}$ is free over F. (For, if $\sum a_i\alpha_i^p = 0$ with $a_i \in F$, then $0 = \sum a_i\alpha_i^p = (\sum b_i\alpha_i)^p$ with $b_i \in F^{1/p}$, $b_i^p = a_i$, $\sum b_i\alpha_i = 0$, and $b_i = 0 = a_i$.) By induction, $\{\alpha_i^{p^n}\}$ is free over F for each $n \in \mathbf{Z}$, $n \geq 0$. But then $\{\alpha_i\}$ is free over F^{1/p^∞}. For, if there exist $a_i \in F^{1/p^\infty}$, not all zero, and all but finitely many a_i equal to 0, such that $\sum a_i\alpha_i = 0$, then there exists $n \geq 0$ such that $\sum a_i^{p^n}\alpha_i^{p^n} = (\sum a_i\alpha_i)^{p^n} = 0$ with $a_i^{p^n} \in F$, and $\{\alpha_i^{p^n}\}$ is not free over F. Hence c $\Rightarrow$ b. ∎

REMARK. We are now in a position to observe that our definition of the separability of an extension field E of a field F is independent of the choice of the algebraically closed field C in which E and F are embedded. If F has characteristic 0, this follows immediately from Definition 4.4, Corollary 3. If F has characteristic $p > 0$, then, by Theorem 4.5, the separability of E over F is equivalent to the linear disjointness of E and $F^{1/p}$ over F, where $F \subset E \subset C$, $F^{1/p} \subset C$, C algebraically closed. Let $\bar{C}$ be an algebraic closure of E, with $E \subset \bar{C} \subset C$. Note that $F^{1/p} \subset \bar{C}$. Similarly, for C' another algebraically closed field with $F \subset E \subset C'$, let $(F^{1/p})' = \{\alpha \in C' \mid \alpha^p \in F\}$, and let $\bar{C}'$ be an algebraic closure of E, with $E \subset \bar{C}' \subset C'$. Note that $(F^{1/p})' \subset \bar{C}'$. Since $\bar{C}$ and $\bar{C}'$ are both algebraic closures of E, there is an E-isomorphism $\rho\colon \bar{C} \to \bar{C}'$. Since ρ is certainly an F-isomorphism, it maps $F^{1/p}$ onto $(F^{1/p})'$, hence induces an E-isomorphism of $E(F^{1/p})$ onto $E(F^{1/p})'$. But then an F-free subset of E is $F^{1/p}$-free if and only if it is $(F^{1/p})'$-free; i.e., E and $F^{1/p}$ are linearly disjoint in C, over F, if and only if E and $(F^{1/p})'$ are linearly disjoint in C', over F. Put another way: E is separable over F, in C, if and only if E is separable over F, in C'.

Corollary 1. *Let C be an algebraically closed field containing F, with* Char $F = p > 0$, *and let $\alpha \in C$ be algebraic over F. Then the following statements are equivalent:*

a. *$m_{\alpha/F}$ has no repeated roots.*
b. *$F(\alpha)$ is separable over F.*
c. *$F(\alpha) = F(\alpha^p)$.*
d. *$m_{\alpha/F} \notin F[x^p]$.*

PROOF.

a $\Rightarrow$ b. If $m_{\alpha/F}$ has no repeated roots, then (by Theorem 3.5), $|\text{Mon}_F(E,C)| = \deg m_{\alpha/F} = [F(\alpha): F]$, hence (by Definition 4.4, Corollary 2), $F(\alpha)$ is separable over F.

b $\Rightarrow$ c. Obviously, $F(\alpha^p) \subset F(\alpha)$. Suppose $[F(\alpha): F] = n$. Then $\{\alpha^i\}_{i=0}^{n-1}$ is a basis for $F(\alpha)$ over F. Since $F(\alpha)$ is separable over F, $\{\alpha^i\}_{i=0}^{n-1}$ is free over $F^{1/p}$ (by Theorem 4.5). Hence $\{\alpha^{ip}\}_{i=0}^{n-1}$ is an F-free subset of $F(\alpha^p)$. But then $[F(\alpha^p): F] \geq [F(\alpha): F]$. It follows that $F(\alpha^p) = F(\alpha)$.

c $\Rightarrow$ d. Suppose $m_{\alpha/F} \in F[x^p]$. If $m_{\alpha/F} = a_0 + a_p x^p + \cdots + a_{pk}x^{pk}$, then α^p is a root of the polynomial

$$p(x) = a_0 + a_p x + \cdots + a_{pk}x^k$$

where $k < \deg m_{\alpha/F}$. But then $[F(\alpha^p): F] < [F(\alpha): F]$, contrary to the hypothesis that $F(\alpha) = F(\alpha^p)$.

d $\Rightarrow$ a. Suppose $m_{\alpha/F} = a_0 + a_1 x + \cdots + a_n x^n$ has a repeated root, θ, in C. Then 0 is a repeated root of the polynomial $h(x) = m_{\alpha/F}(x + \theta)$. If $h(x) = b_0 + b_1 x + \cdots + b_n x^n$, then $b_0 = b_1 = 0$. But

$$b_1 = a_1 + 2a_2\theta + 3a_3\theta^2 + \cdots + (n-1)a_{n-1}\theta^{n-2} + n\theta^{n-1}.$$

Since the minimal polynomial of θ is $m_{\alpha/F}$, of degree n, we conclude that $1 \cdot a_1 = 2a_2 = 3a_3 = \cdots = (n-1)a_{n-1} = n \cdot a_n = 0$ in F, where $a_n = 1$. But then $p|ka_k$ for each $k = 1,\ldots, n$. Hence, for each $k = 1,\ldots, n$, either $a_k = 0$ or $p|k$. It follows that $m_{\alpha/F} \in F[x^p]$, contrary to hypothesis. ∎

Corollary 2. *If a field E is pure transcendental over a field F, then E is separable over F.*

PROOF. If Char $F = 0$, E is separable over F (Definition 4.4, Corollary 3). Suppose Char $F = p > 0$. Since E is purely transcendental over F, there exists a transcendence base B over F such that $E = F(B)$. Let $\mathscr{M}$ be the set of all monomials based on B; i.e., the set of all finite products of elements of B. Then $\mathcal{M}$ is free over F and $E = F(\mathcal{M})$. It is sufficient (Exercise 4.6) to prove that $\mathcal{M}$ is free over $F^{1/p}$. Since $\mathcal{M}^p = \{M^p | M \in \mathcal{M}\}$ is free over F, $\mathcal{M}$ is free over $F^{1/p}$. ▮

We have seen (Definition 4.4, Corollary 3) that every field containing a field F, of characteristic 0, is separable over F. We shall now characterize those fields F with the property that every extension of F is separable over F.

Definition 4.5. A field F is *perfect* if every field containing F as a subfield is separable over F. ///

Theorem 4.6. *Let F be a field. The following statements are equivalent.*

a. *F is perfect.*

b. *Every algebraic extension E of F, $E \supset F$, is separable over F.*

c. *If C is an algebraic closure of F, $C \supset F$, then $F = \mathfrak{f}(\mathrm{Aut}_F(C))$ (the fixed field of* $\mathrm{Aut}_F C$).

d. Char $F = 0$, *or* Char $F = p > 0$ *and $F = F^p$, where*

$$F^p = \{\alpha^p | \alpha \in F\}.$$

PROOF. Clearly, a $\Rightarrow$ b. Assume b. Then, if $C \supset F$ is an algebraic closure of F, C is separable over F. By definition of separability, C and $\mathfrak{f}(\mathrm{Aut}_F C)$ are linearly disjoint over F. But then, applying the linear disjointness condition to the F-subspace $\mathfrak{f}(\mathrm{Aut}_F C)$ of C, $[\mathfrak{f}(\mathrm{Aut}_F C): F] = [\mathfrak{f}(\mathrm{Aut}_F C): \mathfrak{f}(\mathrm{Aut}_F C)] = 1$, and $\mathfrak{f}(\mathrm{Aut}_F C) = F$. Hence b $\Rightarrow$ c.

Assume c. If Char $F = p > 0$, then from $\mathfrak{f}(\mathrm{Aut}_F C) = F^{1/p^\infty} = F$, it follows that every element of F is the pth power of an element in F. But then $F^p = F$, and c $\Rightarrow$ d.

Assume d. Suppose that $C \supset E \supset F$ is a field tower with C algebraically closed. If Char $F = 0$, then F is perfect. Suppose Char $F = p > 0$. Assumption d implies that $F^{1/p} = F$. Since E and F are linearly disjoint over F, it follows, by Theorem 4.5, that E is separable over F. Thus d $\Rightarrow$ a. ▮

Corollary. *Fields of characteristic* 0, *algebraically closed fields, and finite fields are perfect.*

PROOF. We note only that, if F is a finite field of characteristic $p \neq 0$, then $F = F^p$. For: the map $\alpha \mapsto \alpha^p$ $(\alpha \in F)$ is a one-to-one map, hence a bijection, of F onto F. ▮

We shall see later (Theorem 4.8, Corollary), that algebraic extensions of perfect fields are perfect.

Unlike normal extensions, separable extensions do have the "transitivity" property: A separable extension of a separable extension of F is separable over F. To prove this, we first prove the following lemma concerning linear disjointness.

Lemma. *Let $C \supset E \supset K \supset F$ and $C \supset F_0 \supset F$ be field towers. Then E and F_0 are linearly disjoint over F if and only if*

a. *K and F_0 are linearly disjoint over F.*

b. *E and $K(F_0)$ are linearly disjoint over K.*

PROOF. Assume that E and F_0 are linearly disjoint over F. Then K and F_0 are linearly disjoint over F. Let $\{\alpha_i\}$, $\{\beta_j\}$, and $\{\gamma_k\}$ be bases, respectively, for E over K, K over F, and F_0 over F. Then, since E and F_0 are linearly disjoint over F, $\{\alpha_i\beta_j\gamma_k\}$ is a basis for $E(F_0)$ over F. Suppose $\sum a_i\alpha_i = 0$, where $a_i \in K(F_0)$. There exists $d = \sum b_{jk}\beta_j\gamma_k$, $b_{jk} \in F$, such that $a_i = c_i/d$, where $c_i = \sum e_{ijk}\beta_j\gamma_k$, $e_{ijk} \in F$. But then, $\sum a_i\alpha_i = 0$ implies $\sum c_i\alpha_i = 0$, $\sum e_{ijk}\alpha_i\beta_j\gamma_k = 0$, $e_{ijk} = 0$, $c_i = 0$, and $a_i = 0$. Thus $\{\alpha_i\}$ is free over $K(F_0)$, whence E and $K(F_0)$ are linearly disjoint over K. This proves the lemma in one direction.

Assume that a and b hold. Let $\{\gamma_k\}$ be a free set of F_0 over F. From a it follows that $\{\gamma_k\}$ is free over K. Thus, $\{\gamma_k\}$ is a subset of $K(F_0)$ which is free over K. By b $\{\gamma_k\}$ is free over E. But then E and F_0 are linearly disjoint over F. ▮

The lemma may be proved somewhat more simply by making use of tensor products. This is left as an exercise (Exercise 4.7).

Theorem 4.7.

a. *If E is separable over F, then every subfield of E containing F is separable over F.*

b. *If E is separable over K, and K is separable over F, then E is separable over F.*

PROOF. Let C be an algebraically closed field containing E and let $F_0 = \mathfrak{f}(\text{Aut}_F\, C)$, the fixed field of the group of F-automorphisms of C.

Assertion a follows directly from the definition of separability: If E is separable over F, then E and F_0 are linearly disjoint over F; but then K and F_0 are linearly disjoint over F, where K is any subfield of E which contains F and K is separable over F.

To prove b we consider the towers $C \supset E \supset K \supset F$ and $C \supset F_0 \supset F$, and use the lemma: If E is separable over K, then, since $K(F_0) \subset \mathfrak{f}(\text{Aut}_K\, C)$, E and $K(F_0)$ are linearly disjoint over K. If K is separable over F, then K and F_0 are linearly disjoint over F. Hence, by the lemma, if E is separable over K, and K is separable over F, then E and F_0 are linearly disjoint over F. But then, E is separable over F. ∎

We have seen that, if $E \supset K \supset F$ and E is normal over F, then E is normal over K. However, if $E \supset K \supset F$ and E is separable over F, then E need not be separable over K. For example, if $E = (\mathbf{Z}/(p))(x)$, $K = (\mathbf{Z}/(p))(x^p)$, and $F = \mathbf{Z}/(p)$, where x is transcendental over F, then E is separable over F but not separable over K. However, we shall see that if E is separable over F, then E is separable over every field lying between E and F which is algebraic over F.

Theorem 4.8. *Let $E \supset K \supset F$ be a tower of fields where E is separable over F. If K is algebraic over F, then E is separable over K.*

PROOF. We may assume without loss of generality that Char $F = p > 0$. Under the given hypotheses, if $\{\alpha_i\}_{i\in I}$ is a basis for K over F, then $\{\alpha_i^p\}_{i\in I}$ is also a basis for K over F. For, by Theorem 4.7a, K is separable over F, and hence K and $F^{1/p}$ are linearly disjoint over F. Therefore, $\{\alpha_i\}_{i\in I}$ is free over $F^{1/p}$, and it follows that $\{\alpha_i^p\}_{i\in I}$ is free over F. It remains to show that $K = F(\{\alpha_i^p\}_{i\in I})$. Clearly, $F(\{\alpha_i^p\}_{i\in I}) \subset K = F(\{\alpha_i\}_{i\in I})$. By Definition 4.4, Corollary 1, $F(\alpha_i)$ is separable over F for each $i \in I$. By Theorem 4.5, Corollary 1, $F(\alpha_i) = F(\alpha_i^p)$, whence $F(\{\alpha_i\}_{i\in I}) \subset F(\{\alpha_i^p\}_{i\in I})$. But then, $K = F(\{\alpha_i^p\}_{i\in I})$, and $\{\alpha_i^p\}_{i\in I}$ is a basis for K over F.

We prove that E is separable over K by showing that E and $K^{1/p}$ are linearly disjoint over K. It suffices to prove that every basis for E over K is a $K^{1/p}$-free set. Let $\{\beta_j\}_{j\in J}$ be a basis for E over K and $\{\alpha_i\}_{i\in I}$ a basis for K over F. Then $\{\alpha_i\beta_j\}_{i\in I, j\in J}$ is a basis for E over F (Theorem 1.3). Since E is separable over F, $\{\alpha_i\beta_j\}_{i\in I, j\in J}$ is free over $F^{1/p}$, whence $\{\alpha_i^p\beta_j^p\}_{i\in I, j\in J}$ is free over F. Furthermore, $\{\alpha_i^p\}_{i\in I}$ is a basis for K over F. If $\sum_j b_j\beta_j = 0$ with $b_j \in K^{1/p}$, then $\sum_j c_j\beta_j^p = 0$ with $c_j = b_j^p \in K$, $c_j = \sum_i a_{ij}\alpha_i^p$ with $a_{ij} \in F$, $\sum_{i,j} a_{ij}\alpha_i^p\beta_j^p = 0$, $a_{ij} = 0$, for all $i \in I$, $j \in J$, and $c_j = b_j = 0$ for all $j \in J$. Thus $\{\beta_j\}_{j\in J}$ is free over $K^{1/p}$, and E is separable over K. ∎

Corollary. *Algebraic extensions of perfect fields are perfect.* □

We now turn our attention to a more detailed study of separability in the case of algebraic extensions.

Theorem 4.9. *Let $C \supset E \supset F$ be a tower of fields where C is algebraically closed and E is algebraic over F. The following statements are equivalent.*

a. *E is separable over F.*
b. *If $\alpha \in E$, then $F(\alpha)$ is separable over F.*

PROOF. That a $\Rightarrow$ b follows immediately from Definition 4.4, Corollary 1.

b $\Rightarrow$ a. By Definition 4.4, Corollary 1, it is sufficient to show that if b holds, then for every finite subset, S, of E, $F(S)$ is separable over F. The proof is by induction on the number of elements in S. If $|S| = 0$, then $F(S) = F$ is separable over F. Assume that if $|S| < n - 1$, then $F(S)$ is separable over F. If $S = \{\alpha_1,\alpha_2,\ldots,\alpha_{n-1},\alpha_n\} \subset E$, then $K = F(\alpha_1,\alpha_2,\ldots,\alpha_{n-1})$ is separable over F. Since $m_{\alpha/K}(x)|m_{\alpha/F}(x)$, $m_{\alpha/K}(x)$ factors into a product of distinct linear factors over C, whence $K(\alpha)$ is separable over K. But then, by Theorem 4.7b, $F(S) = K(\alpha)$ is separable over F. ▮

The following theorem now follows easily. Its proof is left to the reader (Exercise 4.8).

Theorem 4.10. *For $i \in J$, let $C \supset E_i \supset F$ be a tower of fields with E_i algebraic and separable over F and C algebraically closed, and let K be a subfield of C containing F. Then*

a. *$F(\bigcup_{i\in J} E_i)$ is separable over F.*
b. *$F(\bigcap_{i\in J} E_i)$ is separable over F.*
c. *For every $i \in J$, $E_i(K)$ is separable over K.* □

Definition 4.5. Let C be an algebraically closed field containing a field F. An element $\alpha \in C$ is *separable over F* if α is algebraic over F and $F(\alpha)$ is separable over F. An element $\alpha \in C$, algebraic over F, is *inseparable over F* if $F(\alpha)$ is not separable over F, or if $\alpha \in F$. A polynomial $f(x) \in F[x]$ is *(inseparable over F) separable over F* if (not) every root of $f(x)$ in C is separable over F. ///

REMARKS. An irreducible polynomial $f \in F[x]$ is separable over F if and only if it has no multiple roots.

The elements of F (and only the elements of F) are both separable and inseparable over F.

Theorem 4.11. *Let E be an algebraic extension of a field F, and let $E_s = \{\alpha \in E | \alpha$ separable over $F\}$. Then*

a. *$E_s = F\left(\bigcup_{\substack{E \supset K \supset F \\ K \text{ separable over } F}} K\right)$, E_s is separable over F, and E is purely inseparable over E_s.*
b. *If $[E_s: F]$ is finite, then $[E_s: F] = |\mathrm{Mon}_F(E,C)|$ where C is an algebraically closed field containing E.*
c. *If $[E: E_s]$ is finite, then $[E: E_s] = p^n$ $(n \geq 0)$ if* Char $F = p$, *and $[E: E_s] = 1$ if* Char $F = 0$.

PROOF. If Char $F = 0$, then $E_s = E$ and all the assertions of the theorem are trivial. We assume, therefore, that Char $F = p > 0$.

Theorems 4.9 and 4.10a imply that

$$E_s = F\left(\bigcup_{\substack{E \supset K \supset F \\ K \text{ separable over } F}} K\right),$$

and E_s is separable over F.

Suppose $\beta \in E$ is separable over E_s. Then $E_s(\beta)$ is separable over E_s, $E_s(\beta)$ is separable over F (since E_s is separable over F, and a separable extension of a separable extension is separable), and $\beta \in E_s$ (Theorem 4.9). Hence, if $\alpha \in E$ and $\alpha \notin E_s$, then α is inseparable over E_s. By Theorem 4.5, Corollary 1, $E_s(\alpha) \neq E_s(\alpha^p)$, whence $[E_s(\alpha^p): E_s] < [E_s(\alpha): E_s]$. If $\alpha^p \notin E_s$, then $[E_s(\alpha^{p^2}): E_s] < [E_s(\alpha^p): E_s] < [E_s(\alpha): E_s]$. Since α is algebraic over E_s, $[E_s(\alpha): E_s]$ is finite. Therefore, if $\alpha \in E$ and $\alpha \notin E_s$, there exists a positive integer m such that $\alpha^{p^m} \in E_s$. But then, by Theorem 4.1, α is purely inseparable over E_s. We have shown that every element of E not in E_s is purely inseparable over E_s, whence E is purely inseparable over E_s. In Theorem 4.1 we saw that if α is purely inseparable over E_s, then $[\alpha: E_s]$ is a power of p. It follows easily (Exercise 4.9) that if $[E: E_s]$ is finite, then $[E: E_s] = p^n$ for some nonnegative integer n. We have proved assertions a and c of the theorem.

We now prove assertion b. If $\varphi,\psi \in \text{Aut}_F(C)$ are such that $\varphi|_{E_s} = \psi|_{E_s}$. Then $\varphi\psi^{-1}$ acts as the identity on E_s; since E is a purely inseparable extension of E_s, $\varphi\psi^{-1}$ fixes every element of E, whence $\varphi|_E = \psi|_E$. Conversely, if $\varphi,\psi \in \text{Aut}_F\, C$ are such that $\varphi|_E = \psi|_E$, then, a fortiori, $\varphi|_{E_s} = \psi|_{E_s}$. It follows that $|\text{Mon}_F(E_s,C)| = |\text{Aut}_F\, C|_{E_s}| = |\text{Aut}_F\, C|_E| = |\text{Mon}_F(E,C)|$. Since E_s is a separable extension of F, $|\text{Aut}_F\, C|_{E_s}| = [E_s: F]$ (Definition 4.4, Corollary 2). ∎

Definition 4.7. Let the notation be as in Theorem 4.11. The *separability degree of E over F*, denoted by $[E: F]_s$, is equal to $[E_s: F]$. The *inseparability degree of E over F*, denoted by $[E: F]_i$, is equal to $[E: E_s]$. ///

We restate part of Theorem 4.11 in terms of the new notation.

Corollary. *Let E be an algebraic extension of F. Then*

a. $[E: F] = [E: F]_i[E: F]_s$.
b. *If* $[E: F]_i$ *is finite, then it is a power of the characteristic of F.*
c. *If* $[E: F]_s$ *is finite, then it is equal to the number of F-monomorphisms of E into an algebraically closed extension of E.* □

The separability and inseparability degrees are "multiplicative" in the sense that if $E \supset K \supset F$ is a tower of fields, with E finite over F, then $[E: F]_s = [E: K]_s[K: F]_s$ and $[E: F]_i = [E: K]_i[K: F]_i$. We leave the proof as an exercise (Exercise 4.10).

The next theorem indicates what conclusions can be drawn if we assume that E is not only algebraic but also normal over F.

Theorem 4.12. *Let $E \supset F$ with E normal over F, let $K = \mathfrak{f}(\text{Aut}_F E)$, the subfield of E fixed by the group of F-automorphisms of E, and let $E_s = \{\alpha \in E \mid \alpha$ separable over $F\}$. Then*

a. *K is purely inseparable over F.*
b. *E is separable over K.*
c. *E_s is normal over F, $E_s \cap K = F$, $E_s(K) = E$.*
d. *$\text{Aut}_K E = \text{Aut}_F E \cong \text{Aut}_F E_s$.*

PROOF. In view of the normality of E over F, assertion a follows easily from the definition of a purely inseparable extension (Definition 4.1).

Suppose $\alpha \in E$. Then α is algebraic over F and hence has only finitely many, say n, distinct F-conjugates in any algebraic closure of E. Since E is normal over F, these conjugates are in E, and there exist $\varphi_i \in \text{Aut}_F(E)$, $i = 1, 2, \ldots, n$, such that $\{\varphi_i(\alpha)\}_{i=1}^n$ is a complete set of distinct F-conjugates of α in E. If $\varphi \in \text{Aut}_F E$, then $\{\varphi\varphi_i(\alpha)\}_{i=1}^n = \{\varphi_i(\alpha)\}_{i=1}^n$. If $f(x) = \prod_{i=1}^n (x - \varphi_i(\alpha))$, then, since every element φ of $\text{Aut}_F E$ permutes the roots of $f(x)$, the coefficients of $f(x)$ are fixed by every element of $\text{Aut}_F E$, and $f(x) \in K[x]$. Since $f(x)$ has distinct roots, and the minimum polynomial, $m_{\alpha/K}(x)$, divides $f(x)$, $m_{\alpha/K}(x)$ has distinct roots, and α is separable over K (Theorem 4.9). Hence, every element of E is separable over K, and E is a separable extension of K. This proves b.

Let σ be an F-monomorphism of E_s into an algebraically closed field containing E. Since E is normal, σ extends to an F-automorphism of E. Hence, $\sigma(E_s) \subset E$. Furthermore, $\sigma(E_s)$ is separable over F. But then $E_s \supset \sigma(E_s)$. Since E_s is algebraic over F, $E_s = \sigma(E_s)$, and E_s is normal over F.

If $\alpha \in E_s \cap K$, then α is separable over F and is an element of the purely inseparable extension K of F. But then $\alpha \in F$, whence $E_s \cap K = F$.

By Theorem 4.11, E is purely inseparable over E_s, whence E is purely inseparable over $E_s(K)$. E is separable over K, whence E is separable over $E_s(K)$. But then, E is both separable and purely inseparable over $E_s(K)$, and $E = E_s(K)$.

The mappings $\text{Aut}_K E \to \text{Aut}_F E$ and $\text{Aut}_F E \to \text{Aut}_F E_s$ defined by $\varphi \mapsto \varphi$ and $\varphi \mapsto \varphi|_{E_s}$, respectively, are isomorphisms. We leave the details to the reader. ▮

Corollary. *Let $E \supset F$ with E normal and separable over F. Then $\mathfrak{f}(\mathrm{Aut}_F E) = F$. If, in addition, $[E: F]$ is finite, then $|\mathrm{Aut}_F E| = [E: F]$.*

PROOF. In this case, $E_s = E$, and $\mathfrak{f}(\mathrm{Aut}_F E) = E_s \cap \mathfrak{f}(\mathrm{Aut}_F E) = F$. Since E is normal over F, $|\mathrm{Mon}_F(E,C)| = |\mathrm{Aut}_F E|$, where C is an algebraically closed field containing E as a subfield. But then, by Definition 4.4, Corollary 2, $|\mathrm{Aut}_F E| = [E: F]$. ∎

In Theorem 4.11 we saw that every algebraic extension can be realized as a separable extension followed by a purely inseparable extension. Theorem 4.12 indicates that in the case of normal extensions this sequencing can be reversed.

We conclude our discussion of separable algebraic extensions by showing that every finite separable extension of F is a simple extension of F. First we prove two lemmas which we shall use in the proof.

Lemma 1. *Let V be a vector space over a field F and let $\{W_i\}_{i=1}^k$ be a set of proper F-subspaces of V. If $|F| \geq k$, then the set union of the W_i is not all of V: i.e., $\bigcup_{i=1}^k W_i \neq V$.*

PROOF. Suppose that $\bigcup_{i=1}^k W_i = V$. We may assume that there is no redundancy in the relation $\bigcup_{i=1}^k W_i = V$, i.e., that no set union of subspaces in a proper subset of $\{W_i\}_{i=1}^k$ equals V. Then $W_k \not\subset \bigcup_{i=1}^{k-1} W_i$ and $\bigcup_{i=1}^{k-1} W_i \not\subset W_k$. It follows that there exists an $\alpha \in W_k$, $\alpha \notin \bigcup_{i=1}^{k-1} W_i$, and there exists a $\beta \in \bigcup_{i=1}^{k-1} W_i$, $\beta \notin W_k$. Since $|F| \geq k$, there exist distinct $a_i \in F$, $i = 1, 2, \ldots, k$. Consider the set $\{a_i\alpha + \beta\}_{i=1}^k$. Since $\beta \notin W_k$ and $\alpha \in W_k$, $a_i\alpha + \beta \notin W_k$ for $i = 1, 2, \ldots, k$. We have supposed that $V = \bigcup_{i=1}^k W_i$, and hence each of the k elements of $\{a_i\alpha + \beta\}_{i=1}^k$ must belong to at least one of the $(k - 1)$ subspaces W_i $(i = 1, \ldots, k - 1)$. It follows that there exist i_0, i_1, i_2, with $i_0 \neq k$ and $i_1 \neq i_2$, such that $a_{i_1}\alpha + \beta$ and $a_{i_2}\alpha + \beta$ are both elements of W_{i_0}. But then

$$\alpha = \frac{1}{a_{i_1} - a_{i_2}} [(a_{i_1}\alpha + \beta) - (a_{i_2}\alpha + \beta)] \in W_{i_0} \subset \bigcup_{i=1}^{k-1} W_i,$$

and we have arrived at a contradiction. ∎

Lemma 2. *If E is a field and if G is a finite subgroup of E^*, the multiplicative group of the nonzero elements of E, then G is cyclic. In particular, the multiplicative group of nonzero elements of a finite field is cyclic.*

PROOF. Let $|G| = n$. Let α be an element of maximal order m in G. If $m = n$, then G is cyclic with generator α. We show that $m < n$ is impossible.

Suppose $m < n$. Since E is a field, the number of elements in G which are roots of $x^m - 1$ does not exceed m. Hence, there exists a $\beta \in G$ whose order, k, does not divide m. But then there are integers r and s such that $\alpha^r\beta^s$ is an element of G of order $m[k/(k,m)] > m = \text{ord } \alpha$. This is impossible, since, by the choice of α, every element of G has order not exceeding ord α. ▮

Theorem 4.13. *If E is separable over a field F, with $[E\colon F]$ finite, then there exists $\alpha \in E$ such that $E = F(\alpha)$.*

PROOF. We consider two cases: (1) F has infinitely many elements, and (2) F (and hence also E) has only finitely many elements.

CASE 1. Let $\varphi_1, \varphi_2, \ldots, \varphi_n$ be the distinct F-monomorphisms of E into an algebraically closed field $C \supset E$, and let $W_{ij} = \{\alpha \in E \mid \varphi_i(\alpha) = \varphi_j(\alpha)\}$, $i, j = 1, 2, \ldots, n$. Since the φ_i are distinct, W_{ij} is a proper F-subspace of E for $i \neq j$. By Lemma 1, $\bigcup_{i,j=1}^{n} W_{ij} \neq E$, whence there exists an $\alpha \in E$ such that no two of $\varphi_1(\alpha), \varphi_2(\alpha), \ldots, \varphi_n(\alpha)$ are equal. Thus α has at least n distinct F-conjugates, and $[F(\alpha)\colon F] = [\alpha\colon F] \geq n$. But E is separable and of finite degree over F, whence (Definition 4.4, Corollary 2) $n = [E\colon F]$. Since $F(\alpha)$ is a subfield of E, $n = [E\colon F] \geq [F(\alpha)\colon F] \geq n$. But then $[F(\alpha)\colon F] = n$, $E = F(\alpha)$, and we have proved the theorem in case 1.

CASE 2. By Lemma 2, E^* is cyclic with generator, say, α. But then $E = F(\alpha)$, and the theorem holds in case 2. ▮

We have seen in Section 1 that an arbitrary extension E of F can be realized as a pure transcendental extension K of F followed by an algebraic extension of K. It is not true, in general, that a separable (and transcendental) extension of F can be realized as a separable algebraic extension of a pure transcendental extension of F, as the example given in Exercise 4.11 shows. We close this section by showing that fields which are separable and finitely generated over the base field can be structured in this way.

Definition 4.8. Let F be a subfield of a field E. A subset B of E is a *separating transcendence base for E over F* if B is a transcendence base for E over F and E is a separable algebraic extension of $F(B)$. ///

Theorem 4.14. *Let F be a subfield of a field E.*

a. *If every subfield of E which is finitely generated over F has a separating transcendence base over F, then E is separable over F.*
b. *If E is separable over F, then every finite set $S \subset E$ has a subset B which is a separating transcendence base for $F(S)$ over F.*

PROOF.

a. Assume that every subfield of E, finitely generated over F, has a separating transcendence base over F. Let S be a finite subset of E, and let B be a separating transcendence base for $F(S)$ over F. Then $F(S)$ is separable over $F(B)$, and $F(B)$ is separable over F (Theorem 4.5, Corollary 2), whence $F(S)$ is separable over F (Theorem 4.7c). But then E is separable over F (Definition 4.4, Corollary 1).

b. Assume that E is separable over F. We show, by induction on $|S|$, that every finite subset S of E has a subset B which is a separating transcendence base for $F(S)$ over F. Suppose $S = \{\alpha\}$. If α is transcendental over F, then $B = S$ is a separating transcendence base for $F(S)$ over F; if α is algebraic over F, then α is separable over F and $B = \varnothing$ has the desired property. Hence b is true for $|S| = 1$. Assume that b holds for $|S| < n$. Suppose $|S| = n$, $S = \{\alpha_1,\alpha_2,\ldots,\alpha_n\}$. Let T be a maximal algebraically independent (Definition 1.5) subset of S. Then T is a transcendence base for $F(S)$. If $T = S$, then T is a separating transcendence base for $F(S)$ over F. Assume, therefore, that $T = \{\alpha_1,\alpha_2,\ldots,\alpha_k\} \neq S$. Then α_n is algebraic but not necessarily separable—there is the rub—over $F(T)$. If α_n is separable over $F(T)$, then α_n is separable over $F(\alpha_1,\alpha_2,\ldots,\alpha_{n-1})$, and by our induction assumption there is a subset, B, of $\{\alpha_1,\alpha_2,\ldots,\alpha_{n-1}\}$ which is a separating transcendence base for $F(\alpha_1,\ldots,\alpha_{n-1})$. B is a subset of S and is easily seen to be a separating transcendence base for $F(S)$ over F. We are left to consider the case where α_n is inseparable (but algebraic) over $F(T)$.

In this case, the primitive polynomial of least degree in $F[\alpha_1,\alpha_2,\ldots,\alpha_k][x]$ which has α_n as a root is of the form $f(\alpha_1,\ldots,\alpha_k, x) = \sum_{i=0}^{r} f_i(\alpha_1,\alpha_2,\ldots,\alpha_k)x^{pi}$ (Theorem 4.5, Corollary 1), where $p = \operatorname{Char} F$ and $f_r \neq 0$. There exists an α_j such that $f(\alpha_1,\ldots,\alpha_k, x)$ is not a polynomial in α_j^p. Suppose otherwise. Then

$$0 = \sum_{i=0}^{r} f_i(\alpha_1,\alpha_2,\ldots,\alpha_k)\alpha_n^{pi} = \left(\sum_{i=0}^{r} g_i(\alpha_1,\alpha_2,\ldots,\alpha_k)\alpha_n^{i}\right)^p = \left(\sum_{j=1}^{t} a_j M_j\right)^p,$$

where $g_i(\alpha_1,\alpha_2,\ldots,\alpha_k) \in F^{1/p}[\alpha_1,\alpha_2,\ldots,\alpha_k]$, $a_j \in F^{1/p}$, and the M_j are monomials based on $\{\alpha_1,\alpha_2,\ldots,\alpha_k,\alpha_n\}$. The set $\{M_j\}_{j=1}^t$ is dependent over $F^{1/p}$. Since E is separable over F, E and $F^{1/p}$ are linearly disjoint, and $\{M_j\}_{j=1}^t$ is dependent over F. Since the degree in α_n of each M_j is less than or equal to $r < rp$, the dependence of $\{M_j\}_{j=1}^t$ over F implies that α_n is a root of a polynomial over $F[\alpha_1,\alpha_2,\ldots,\alpha_k]$ of degree less than rp. This is impossible. Hence at least one of the α_j, say α_1, occurs in $f(\alpha_1,\ldots,\alpha_k, x)$ raised to a power which is relatively prime to p. $f(z,\alpha_2,\ldots,\alpha_k,\alpha_n) = \sum_{i=0}^{r} f_i(z,\alpha_2,\ldots,\alpha_k)\alpha_n^{pi}$ is a polynomial in $F[\alpha_2,\ldots,\alpha_k,\alpha_n][z]$ of least degree which has α_1 as a root. Since $f(z,\alpha_2,\ldots,\alpha_k,\alpha_n)$ is not a polynomial in z^p, the minimal polynomial, $m(z)$, of α_1 over

$F(\alpha_2,\ldots,\alpha_k,\alpha_n)$ is not a polynomial in z^p, and α_1 is separable over $F(\alpha_2,\ldots,\alpha_k,\alpha_n)$. But then α_1 is separable over $F(S - \{\alpha_1\})$. Our induction assumption enables us to extract a subset B from $S - \{\alpha_1\}$ which is a separating transcendence base for $F(S - \{\alpha_1\})$ over F. In the tower, $F(S) \supset F(S - \{\alpha_1\}) \supset F(B) \supset F$, each field is separable over the field following it in the tower, whence $F(S)$ is separable over F. $F(S)$ is algebraic over $F(S - \{\alpha_1\})$, and $F(S - \{\alpha_1\})$ is algebraic over $F(B)$. Hence, $F(S)$ is algebraic over $F(B)$, and B is a separating transcendence base for $F(S)$ over F. Statement b of the theorem follows by induction. ▮

REMARK. Let E be separable over F, with the transcendence degree of E over F finite. If B is a transcendence base for E over F, then B is not necessarily a separating transcendence base. For example, let $F = \mathbf{Z}/(p)$ and let $E = \mathbf{Z}/(p)(x)$, with x transcendental over $\mathbf{Z}/(p)$. Then $B = \{x^p\}$ is a transcendence base for E over F but E is inseparable over $F(B)$.

5. Galois Theory of Finite Extensions

If E is a normal extension of a field F, $E \supset F$, then every F-monomorphism of E into an algebraically closed field $C \supset E$ is an F-automorphism of E. We shall see that if E is normal and separable over F, then there is an intimate connection between the set of subgroups of the group of F-automorphisms of E and the set of subfields of E which contain F. In this section we concern ourselves primarily with finite extensions and in Section 6 we deal with infinite extensions.

Definition 5.1. If $F \subset E$, and E is normal and separable over F, then E is a *Galois extension* of F (or *E is Galois over F*). If E is a Galois extension of F, then the group $\mathrm{Aut}_F\, E$ is the *Galois group*, $\mathcal{G}(E/F)$, of E over F. ///

In the next theorem we see that an isomorphism $\sigma: E \to \sigma(E)$ of a Galois extension E of F induces an isomorphism of the Galois group of E over F onto the Galois group of $\sigma(E)$ over $\sigma(F)$.

Theorem 5.1. *Let E be Galois over F and let $\sigma: E \to \sigma(E)$ be an isomorphism. Then*

a. *$\sigma(E)$ is Galois over $\sigma(F)$.*
b. *The mapping $\hat{\sigma}: \mathcal{G}(E/F) \to \mathcal{G}(\sigma(E)/\sigma(F))$ defined by $\hat{\sigma}(\varphi) = \sigma\varphi\sigma^{-1}$ is an isomorphism.*

PROOF. The proof of a is left to the reader. To prove b we note that $\sigma\mathcal{G}(E/F)\sigma^{-1} \subset \mathcal{G}(\sigma(E)/\sigma(F))$ and that $\sigma^{-1}\mathcal{G}(\sigma(E)/\sigma(F))\sigma \subset \mathcal{G}(E/F)$. But then, $\mathcal{G}(\sigma(E)/\sigma(F)) \subset \sigma\mathcal{G}(E/F)\sigma^{-1}$, and therefore $\mathcal{G}(\sigma(E)/\sigma(F)) = \sigma\mathcal{G}(E/F)\sigma^{-1}$. It follows that the map defined by $\varphi \mapsto \sigma\varphi\sigma^{-1}$ is an isomorphism of $\mathcal{G}(E/F)$ onto $\mathcal{G}(\sigma(E)/\sigma(F))$. ∎

REMARKS. If $F \subset K \subset E$ is a field tower, and E is a Galois extension of F, then (by Theorem 3.4 and Theorem 4.8) E is a Galois extension of K, and $\mathcal{G}(E/K)$ is a subgroup of $\mathcal{G}(E/F)$.

If $[E: F]$ is finite, then (by Theorem 4.12, Corollary), $|\mathcal{G}(E/F)| = [E: F]$, and for each intermediate field K, $F \subset K \subset E$, $|\mathcal{G}(E/K)|$ is finite, equal to $[E: K]$.

If $F \subset K_2 \subset K_1 \subset E$, and E is Galois over F, then K_1 is separable over K_2 (by Theorems 4.7 and 4.8), but K_1 need not be normal over K_2. Thus, $\mathcal{G}(K_1/K_2)$ is defined if and only if K_1 is normal over K_2. In particular, for $F \subset K \subset E$, $\mathcal{G}(K/F)$ is defined if and only if K is normal over F.

We continue to write $\mathfrak{f}(H)$ for the fixed field, in E, of any subset H of $\mathcal{G}(E/F)$. Note that $F \subset \mathfrak{f}(H) \subset E$.

NOTATION. Let E be a Galois extension of F. We write

$$\mathcal{S}_{E/F} = \{K \mid F \subset K \subset E\},$$

$$\mathcal{S}_{\mathcal{G}} = \{H \mid H \text{ is a subgroup of } \mathcal{G}\}.$$

In the following theorem, we study the maps $\mathfrak{f}: \mathcal{S}_{E/F} \to \mathcal{S}_{\mathcal{G}}$ and $\mathfrak{g}: \mathcal{S}_{\mathcal{G}} \to \mathcal{S}_{E/F}$ defined by

$$\mathfrak{f}(H) = \text{fixed field of } H, \text{ for each } H \in \mathcal{S}_{\mathcal{G}},$$

$$\mathfrak{g}(K) = \mathcal{G}(E/K), \text{ for each } K \in \mathcal{S}_{E/F}.$$

We prove first

Theorem 5.2. *Let E be Galois over F, and let $\varphi \in \mathcal{G}(E/F)$.*

a. *If $K \in \mathcal{S}_{E/F}$, then*

$$\mathfrak{g}(\varphi K) = \varphi\mathfrak{g}(K)\varphi^{-1}.$$

b. *If $H \in \mathcal{S}_{\mathcal{G}}$, then*

$$\mathfrak{f}(\varphi H\varphi^{-1}) = \varphi\mathfrak{f}H.$$

PROOF.

a. Is an immediate consequence of Theorem 5.1.

b. If $\alpha \in \mathfrak{f}H$, $\psi \in H$, then $(\varphi\psi\varphi^{-1})\varphi\alpha = \varphi\psi\alpha = \varphi\alpha$, whence $\varphi\alpha \in \mathfrak{f}(\varphi H\varphi^{-1})$.

Thus $\varphi\mathfrak{f}H \subset \mathfrak{f}(\varphi H\varphi^{-1})$. On the other hand, if $\beta \in \mathfrak{f}(\varphi H\varphi^{-1})$, then $\psi\varphi^{-1}\beta = \varphi^{-1}\varphi\psi\varphi^{-1}\beta = \varphi^{-1}\beta$, hence $\varphi^{-1}\beta \in \mathfrak{f}H$ and $\beta \in \varphi\mathfrak{f}H$. Thus $\mathfrak{f}(\varphi H\varphi^{-1}) \subset \varphi\mathfrak{f}H$, and the equality follows. ▮

Theorem 5.3. (Fundamental Theorem of Galois Theory.) *Let E be a Galois extension of F, and let $\mathscr{S}_{E/F}$, $\mathscr{S}_G$, $\mathfrak{f}$, $\mathfrak{g}$ be defined as above. Then:*

a. *$\mathfrak{f}\mathfrak{g} = \iota_{\mathscr{S}_{E/F}}$, hence $\mathfrak{f}$ is surjective and $\mathfrak{g}$ is injective.*

a′. *If $[E: F]$ is finite, then $\mathfrak{g}\mathfrak{f} = \iota_{\mathscr{S}_{\mathscr{G}}}$, hence $\mathfrak{g}$ is surjective and $\mathfrak{f}$ is injective. (Thus, if $[E: F]$ is finite, then $\mathfrak{f}$ and $\mathfrak{g}$ are inverse bijections.)*

b. *Let $K_1, K_2 \in \mathscr{S}_{E/F}$. Then K_1 is normal over K_2 if and only if $\mathfrak{g}(K_1) \lhd \mathfrak{g}(K_2)$.*

In this case, $\mathscr{G}(K_1/K_2) \cong \mathfrak{g}(K_2)/\mathfrak{g}(K_1)$.

b′. *Suppose $[E: F]$ is finite. Let $H_1, H_2 \in \mathscr{S}_{\mathscr{G}}$. Then $H_1 \lhd H_2$ if and only if $\mathfrak{f}(H_1)$ is normal over $\mathfrak{f}(H_2)$.*

In this case, $H_2/H_1 \cong \mathscr{G}(\mathfrak{f}(H_1)/\mathfrak{f}(H_2))$.

PROOF.

a. Suppose $K \in \mathscr{S}_{E/F}$. Since E is a Galois extension of K, we have $\mathfrak{f}\mathfrak{g}(K) = K$, by the Corollary of Theorem 4.12. Thus, $\mathfrak{f}\mathfrak{g} = \iota_{\mathscr{S}_{E/F}}$, $\mathfrak{f}$ is surjective and $\mathfrak{g}$ is injective.

a′. Suppose $[E: F]$ is finite. If $H \in \mathscr{S}_{\mathscr{G}}$, then $|H|$ is finite since $|H| \leq |\mathfrak{g}(F)| = [E: F]$. Clearly, $\mathfrak{g}(\mathfrak{f}H) \supset H$. To prove that $\mathfrak{g}(\mathfrak{f}H) = H$, it is sufficient to show that $|\mathfrak{g}(\mathfrak{f}H)| \leq |H|$.

By Theorem 4.13, since E is finite separable over F, there is an element $\alpha \in E$ such that $E = F(\alpha)$. Since $\mathfrak{f}H \supset F$, we have $E = \mathfrak{f}H(\alpha)$.

Suppose $H = \{\varphi_1, \ldots, \varphi_h\}$, where $h = |H|$. Since α generates E over F, and the φ_i are distinct F-automorphisms of E, the $\varphi_i\alpha$ $(i = 1, \ldots, h)$ are distinct elements of E. Form $p(x) = \prod_{i=1}^{h} (x - \varphi_i\alpha)$. Then $p(\alpha) = 0$ since $\iota_E \in H$. For each $\varphi \in H$, $p^{\varphi}(x) = \prod_{i=1}^{h} (x - \varphi\varphi_i\alpha) = p(x)$; hence the coefficients of $p(x)$ are in $\mathfrak{f}H$. But then

$$|\mathfrak{g}\mathfrak{f}H| = [E: \mathfrak{f}H] = [\mathfrak{f}H(\alpha): \mathfrak{f}H] = \deg m_{\alpha/\mathfrak{f}H} \leq \deg p(x) = |H|.$$

We conclude that $\mathfrak{g}\mathfrak{f}H = H$. Thus $\mathfrak{g}\mathfrak{f} = \iota_{\mathscr{G}}$, $\mathfrak{f}$ is injective and $\mathfrak{g}$ is surjective.

b. Suppose $K_1, K_2 \in \mathscr{S}_{E/F}$, with K_1 normal over K_2. Then K_1 is a Galois extension of K_2, and $\mathscr{G}(K_1/K_2)$ is defined. For each $\varphi \in \mathfrak{g}(K_2) = \mathscr{G}(E/K_2)$, $\varphi|_{K_1} \in \mathscr{G}(K_1/K_2)$, by the normality of K_1 over K_2. We define $\Lambda: g(K_2) \to \mathscr{G}(K_1/K_2)$ by $\Lambda(\varphi) = \varphi|_{K_1}$. Clearly, Λ is a homomorphism. By the normality of E over K_2, every K_2-automorphism of K_1 can be extended to a K_2-automorphism of E. Thus, every element of $\mathscr{G}(K_1/K_2)$ is $\varphi|_{K_1} = \Lambda\varphi$ for some $\varphi \in \mathfrak{g}(K_2)$, and Λ is an epimorphism.

Ker $\Lambda = \{\varphi \in \mathfrak{g}(K_2) | \varphi|_{K_1} = \iota_{K_1}\} = \mathcal{G}(E/K_1) = \mathfrak{g}(K_1)$. But then $\mathfrak{g}(K_1) \lhd \mathfrak{g}(K_2)$, and $\mathcal{G}(K_1/K_2) \cong \mathfrak{g}(K_2)/\mathfrak{g}(K_1)$.

Now suppose that $\mathfrak{g}(K_1) \lhd \mathfrak{g}(K_2)$ $(K_1, K_2 \in \mathcal{S}_{E/F})$. We want to prove that K_1 is a normal extension of K_2. We obtain a somewhat stronger result: if $H \lhd \mathfrak{g}(K_2)$ $(H \in \mathcal{S}_{\mathcal{G}})$, then $\mathfrak{f}H$ is a normal extension of K_2. Suppose $\varphi \in \mathfrak{g}(K_2)$. Then $\varphi H \varphi^{-1} = H$, hence $\mathfrak{f}H = \mathfrak{f}\varphi H \varphi^{-1} = \varphi \mathfrak{f} H$ (by Theorem 5.2b). Thus, every K_2-automorphism of E induces a K_2-automorphism of $\mathfrak{f}H$. By the normality of E over K_2, every K_2-monomorphism of $\mathfrak{f}H$ into an algebraically closed field $C \supset E$ can be extended to a K_2-automorphism of E, and is therefore a K_2-automorphism of $\mathfrak{f}H$. But then $\mathfrak{f}H$ is normal over K_2. In particular, if $H = \mathfrak{g}(K_1)$, then $K_1 = \mathfrak{f}\mathfrak{g}K_1 = \mathfrak{f}H$, and so K_1 is normal over K_2.

b′. Suppose $[E: F]$ is finite. If $H_1, H_2 \in \mathcal{S}_{\mathcal{G}}$, with $H_1 \lhd H_2$, then, by a′, we have $H_1 = \mathfrak{g}(\mathfrak{f}H_1)$, $H_2 = \mathfrak{g}(\mathfrak{f}H_2)$. By b, it follows that $\mathfrak{f}H_1$ is normal over $\mathfrak{f}H_2$, and that

$$\mathcal{G}(\mathfrak{f}H_1/\mathfrak{f}H_2) \cong \mathfrak{g}\mathfrak{f}H_2/\mathfrak{g}\mathfrak{f}H_1 = H_2/H_1.$$

If $H_1, H_2 \in \mathcal{S}_{\mathcal{G}}$, with $\mathfrak{f}H_1$ normal over $\mathfrak{f}H_2$, then by b and a′, $H_1 = \mathfrak{g}\mathfrak{f}H_1 \lhd \mathfrak{g}\mathfrak{f}H_2 = H_2$. ▮

$$\begin{array}{ccccccc}
F & \subset & K_2 & \subset & K_1 & \subset & E \\
\mathfrak{g}\downarrow\uparrow\mathfrak{f} & & \mathfrak{g}\downarrow\uparrow\mathfrak{f} & & \mathfrak{g}\downarrow\uparrow\mathfrak{f} & & \mathfrak{g}\downarrow\uparrow\mathfrak{f} \\
\mathcal{G}(E/F) & \supset & \mathcal{G}(E/K_2) & \supset & \mathcal{G}(E/K_1) & \supset & \mathcal{G}(E/E)
\end{array}$$

We note that the maps $\mathfrak{f}$ and $\mathfrak{g}$ reverse inclusion. For $K_1, K_2 \in \mathcal{S}_{E/F}$, let "$K_1 \sqcup K_2$" be the subfield $K_1(K_2)$ of E generated by K_1 and K_2, and for $H_1, H_2 \in \mathcal{S}_{\mathcal{G}}$, let "$H_1 \sqcup H_2$" be the subgroup of $\mathcal{G}(E/F)$ generated by H_1 and H_2. Then $\mathfrak{f}$ and $\mathfrak{g}$ have the additional property of interchanging $\sqcup$ and $\cap$:

Corollary. *Let E be a Galois extension of F. If $K_1, K_2 \in \mathcal{S}_{E/F}$ and $H_1, H_2 \in \mathcal{S}_{\mathcal{G}}$, then:*

1. *$K_1 \subset K_2$ if and only if $\mathfrak{g}(K_1) \supset \mathfrak{g}(K_2)$.*
2. *If $H_1 \subset H_2$, then $\mathfrak{f}(H_1) \supset \mathfrak{f}(H_2)$; if $[E: F]$ is finite and $\mathfrak{f}(H_1) \supset \mathfrak{f}(H_2)$, then $H_1 \subset H_2$.*
3. $\mathfrak{g}(K_1 \sqcup K_2) = \mathfrak{g}(K_1) \cap \mathfrak{g}(K_2)$.
4. $\mathfrak{g}(K_1 \cap K_2) = \mathfrak{g}(K_1) \sqcup \mathfrak{g}(K_2)$.
5. $\mathfrak{f}(H_1 \sqcup H_2) = \mathfrak{f}(H_1) \cap \mathfrak{f}(H_2)$.
6. *If $[E: F]$ is finite, then*

$$\mathfrak{f}(H_1 \cap H_2) = \mathfrak{f}(H_1) \sqcup \mathfrak{f}(H_2). \qquad \square$$

REMARK. If $\langle S,\subset\rangle$ is a partially ordered set, and $\cup$, $\cap$ are binary operations on S such that $a \cup b$ and $a \cap b$ are, respectively, least upper and greatest lower bounds for a and b ($a,b \in S$), then $\langle S,\subset,\cup,\cap\rangle$ is a *lattice*. In this sense, $\langle \mathscr{S}_{E/F},\subset,\sqcup,\cap\rangle$ and $\langle \mathscr{S}_{\mathscr{G}},\subset,\sqcup,\cap\rangle$ are lattices. The Corollary implies that, if $[E: F]$ is finite, then f and g are "dual isomorphisms" between $\mathscr{S}_{E/F}$ and $\mathscr{S}_{\mathscr{G}}$, i.e., bijections which reverse inclusion and interchange $\sqcup$ and $\cap$.

Suppose that $C \supset E \supset F$ is a tower of fields and that $K \supset F$ is a subfield of C. If E is Galois over F, then (Theorems 3.4c and 4.10c) $E(K)$ is Galois over K. In the next theorem we show that $\mathscr{G}(E(K)/K)$ is isomorphic to a subgroup of $\mathscr{G}(E/F)$, in particular to the fixing group of $E \cap K$.

Theorem 5.4. *Let $C \supset E \supset F$ be a tower of fields, with E a finite Galois extension of F, and let $K \supset F$ be a subfield of C. Then $E(K)$ is Galois over K, and $\mathscr{G}(E(K)/K)$ is isomorphic to the subgroup of $\mathscr{G}(E/F)$ which has $E \cap K$ as its fixed field. Thus, $\mathscr{G}(E(K)/K) \cong \mathscr{G}(E/E \cap K)$.*

PROOF. We have already noted that $E(K)$ is Galois over K. If $\varphi \in \mathscr{G}(E(K)/K)$, then $\varphi|_E$ is an automorphism of E which leaves every element of $E \cap K$ fixed. Since $E \cap K \supset F$, $\varphi|_E \in \mathscr{G}(E/F)$. Consider the map Λ: $\mathscr{G}(E(K)/K) \to \mathscr{G}(E/F)$ defined by $\Lambda(\varphi) = \varphi|_E$. Λ is clearly a homomorphism. If $\varphi \in \operatorname{Ker} \Lambda$, then φ acts as the identity on E, and, since φ leaves K fixed, φ also acts as the identity on K, whence φ is the identity map on $E(K)$. Thus, Ker Λ consists of the identity map and Λ is a monomorphism. If $\alpha \in E \cap K$, then, clearly, α is fixed by every element of Im Λ. Conversely, if $\alpha \in E$ is fixed by every element of Im Λ, then $\alpha \in E \cap K$. For, if Im Λ fixes $\alpha \in E$, then $\mathscr{G}(E(K)/K)$ fixes α, whence $\alpha \in K$ and $\alpha \in E \cap K$. Hence, the fixed field of Im $\Lambda = \mathfrak{f}(\text{Im } \Lambda) = E \cap K$. By Theorem 5.3a′, Im $\Lambda = \mathfrak{g}(E \cap K)$. But then $\mathscr{G}(E(K)/K) \cong \mathfrak{g}(E \cap K) = \mathscr{G}(E/E \cap K)$. ∎

Corollary. *If E, K, and F are as in the theorem, then* $[E(K): K] | [E: F]$.

We conclude this section with several examples which illustrate various aspects of Theorem 5.3.

Example 1. Let E be the splitting field in $\mathbf{C}$ of the polynomial $f(x) = x^3 - 2$ over $\mathbf{Q}$. Then E is a Galois extension of $\mathbf{Q}$. Let $\mathscr{G} = \mathscr{G}(E/\mathbf{Q})$.

The roots of $x^3 - 2$ in $\mathbf{C}$ are $\sqrt[3]{2}$, $\omega\sqrt[3]{2}$, and $\omega^2\sqrt[3]{2}$, where ω and ω^2 are the complex cube roots of 1 $[\omega = (-1 + \sqrt{-3})/2]$. Thus, $E = \mathbf{Q}(\omega,\sqrt[3]{2})$. Every $\mathbf{Q}$-automorphism of E permutes the roots of $x^3 - 2$. In fact, the map $\varphi \to \varphi|_R$ where $R = \{\sqrt[3]{2},\omega\sqrt[3]{2},\omega^2\sqrt[3]{2}\}$ is a monomorphism of $\mathscr{G}$ into S_3. We prove that $\mathscr{G} \cong S_3$.

Since ω is a root of $x^2 + x + 1$, irreducible over $\mathbf{Q}(\sqrt[3]{2})$, we have the field tower

$$\mathbf{Q} \subset \mathbf{Q}(\sqrt[3]{2}) \subset \mathbf{Q}(\sqrt[3]{2})(\omega) = E,$$

with $[\mathbf{Q}(\sqrt[3]{2}) : \mathbf{Q}] = 3$ and $[E : \mathbf{Q}(\sqrt[3]{2})] = 2$. Hence $[E : \mathbf{Q}] = 6$. But then $|\mathscr{G}| = 6$ and $\mathscr{G} \cong S_3$.

We find a pair of generators for $\mathscr{G}$. Since ω and ω^2 are conjugates over $\mathbf{Q}(\sqrt[3]{2})$, there is a $\mathbf{Q}(\sqrt[3]{2})$-automorphism σ of E such that $\sigma\omega = \omega^2$. Clearly, $\sigma \in \mathscr{G}$ and $\sigma^2 = \iota_E$.

Another field tower for E is $\mathbf{Q} \subset \mathbf{Q}(\omega) \subset \mathbf{Q}(\omega)(\sqrt[3]{2}) = E$. Since $\sqrt[3]{2}$ and $\omega\sqrt[3]{2}$ are conjugates over $\mathbf{Q}(\omega)$, there is a $\mathbf{Q}(\omega)$-automorphism τ of E such that $\tau\sqrt[3]{2} = \omega\sqrt[3]{2}$. Clearly, $\tau \in \mathscr{G}$ and $\tau^3 = \iota_E$. Since $T = \{\iota,\tau,\tau^2\}$ is a normal subgroup of $\mathscr{G}$, we have

$$\mathscr{G} = T \cup \sigma T = \{\iota,\tau,\tau^2,\sigma,\sigma\tau,\sigma\tau^2\}.$$

The lattice of subroups of $\mathscr{G}$ is

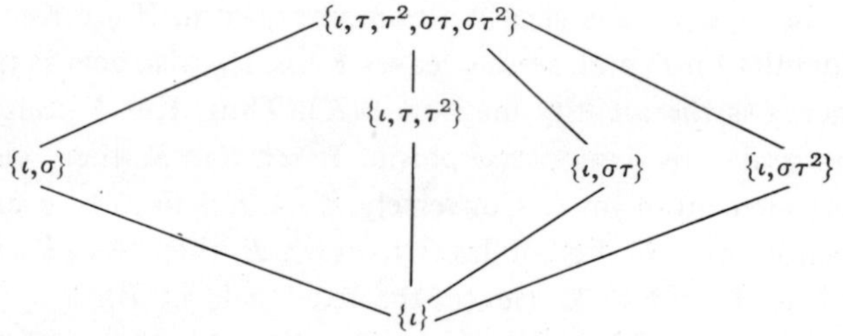

To find the corresponding lattice of intermediate fields, we reason as follows: since $\tau\omega = \omega$, $\mathbf{Q}(\omega)$ is contained in the fixed field of T. Since $[E : \mathbf{Q}(\omega)] = 3$, we conclude that $\mathbf{Q}(\omega)$ *is* the fixed field of T. A similar argument can be applied to each of the subgroups of $\mathscr{G}$. The following lattice results:

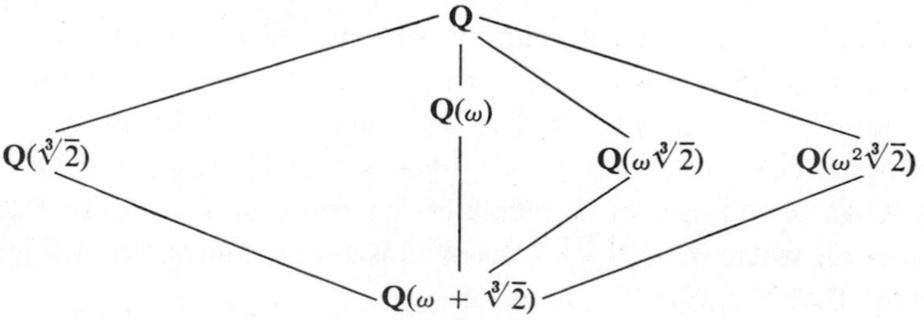

E can be obtained from $\mathbf{Q}$ by adjoining a single primitive element, e.g., $\omega + \sqrt[3]{2}$, or $\sqrt{-3}\sqrt[3]{2}$. The six elements of $\mathscr{G}$ can be obtained directly as the $\mathbf{Q}$-automorphisms which map a primitive element for E to its $\mathbf{Q}$-conjugates. (In the case of $\sqrt{-3}\sqrt[3]{2}$, these are the elements $\pm\sqrt{-3}\sqrt[3]{2}$, $\pm\omega\sqrt{-3}\sqrt[3]{2}$, $\pm\omega^2\sqrt{-3}\sqrt[3]{2}$.)

Example 2. Let E be the subfield of the complex field which is the splitting field over $\mathbf{Q}$ of $f(x) = x^3 - 3x + 1$. If α is one root of $f(x)$, then $\alpha^2 - 2$ and $-\alpha^2 - \alpha + 2$ are the other roots. Hence, $E = \mathbf{Q}(\alpha)$, and $\{1,\alpha,\alpha^2\}$ is a basis for E over $\mathbf{Q}$. Let $\varphi(\alpha) = \alpha^2 - 2$, and $\varphi(\alpha^2) = [\varphi(\alpha)]^2 = (\alpha^2 - 2)^2 = -\alpha^2 - \alpha + 4$. Extend φ to a $\mathbf{Q}$-linear map of E. Then φ is a $\mathbf{Q}$-automorphism of E and $\mathscr{G}(E/\mathbf{Q}) = \{1,\varphi,\varphi^2\}$.

The mappings 1, φ, and φ^2 permute the roots α, $\alpha^2 - 2$, and $\alpha^2 - \alpha + 2$. However, not every permutation of these roots can be extended to an automorphism of E.

For this example, $\mathscr{S}_{\mathscr{G}} = \{\mathscr{G},\{1\}\}$ and $\mathscr{S}_{E/F} = \{\mathbf{Q},E\}$.

Example 3. The details of this example are left to the reader. Let E be the subfield of the complex field which is the splitting field over $\mathbf{Q}$ of $x^4 - 5$. Then $E = \mathbf{Q}(i,\alpha)$, where $i^2 = -1$ and α is the positive real number such that $\alpha^4 = 5$. $\mathscr{G}(E/\mathbf{Q}) = \{1,\sigma,\sigma^2,\sigma^3,\tau,\sigma\tau = \tau\sigma^3,\sigma^2\tau = \tau\sigma^2,\sigma^3\tau = \tau\sigma\}$, where

$$\sigma(\alpha) = i\alpha \quad \text{and} \quad \tau(\alpha) = \alpha,$$
$$\sigma(i) = i \qquad\qquad \tau(i) = -i.$$

The lattice of subgroups of $\mathscr{G}(E/\mathbf{Q})$ may be diagrammed as follows:

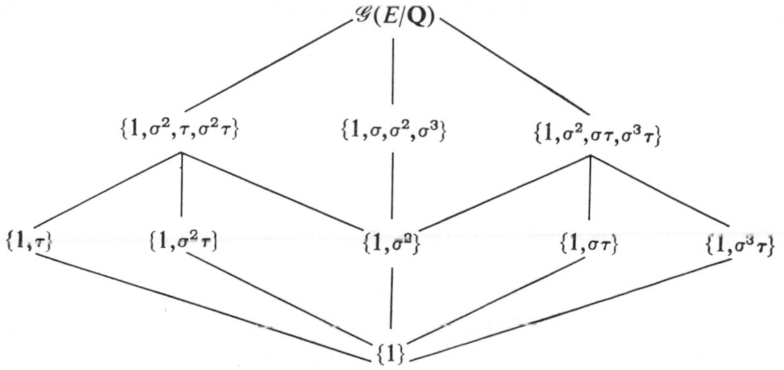

The corresponding diagram of subfields of E is given by

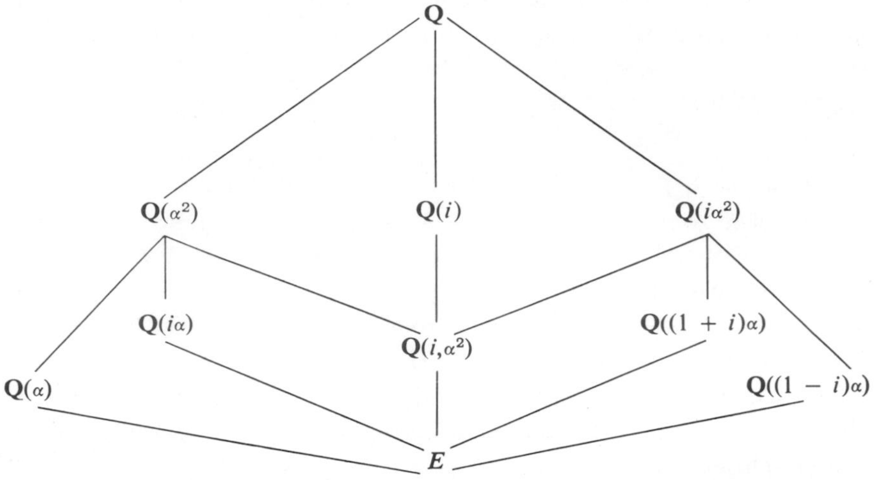

Example 4. In this example we determine the structure of finite fields.

Let F_q be a field with $|F_q| = q$, q finite. Then, by Theorem 1.2, the characteristic of F_q is a prime $p > 0$, and F_q contains a subfield F_p, isomorphic to $\mathbf{Z}/(p)$. Since $|F_q|$ is finite, $[F_q\colon F_p]$ is finite, equal to, say, n. If $\{\alpha_i\}_{i=1}^n$ is a basis for F_q over F_p, then every element of F_q is expressible uniquely in the form $\sum_{i=1}^n a_i\alpha_i$, $a_i \in F_p$. Hence $q = p^n$.

Let $\varphi\colon F_q \to F_q$ be defined by $\varphi(\alpha) = \alpha^p$ for all $\alpha \in F_q$. Then φ is an F_p-automorphism of F_q. By Theorem 4.4, Corollary 2, the order of the group of F_p-automorphisms of F_q is less than or equal to n. We determine the order of φ in this group. Note that for every positive integer k, φ^k is the map defined by $\varphi^k(\alpha) = \alpha^{p^k}$ for all $\alpha \in F_q$. If $\varphi^r = \iota_{F_q}$, then $\alpha^{p^r} = \alpha$ for all $\alpha \in F_q$. Since $x^{p^r} - x$ cannot have more than p^r roots, and $|F_q| = p^n$, $r \geq n$. But then the order of φ is n, every element of F_q is a root of $x^{p^n} - x$, F_q is a splitting field of $x^{p^n} - x$ over F_p, and there are precisely n F_p-automorphisms of F_q, namely, φ^i, $i = 1, 2, \ldots, n$. Hence, by Theorem 3.1, any two fields, each with q elements, are isomorphic. Furthermore; by Theorem 3.3 and Definition 4.4, Corollary 2, F_q is Galois over F_p, and $\mathcal{G}(F_{p^n}/F_p)$ is cyclic of order n. If $F_p \subset E \subset F_{p^n}$, then $[E\colon F_p] | [F_{p^n}\colon F_p]$, hence $E = F_{p^m}$, where $m|n$. By Theorem 5.2, $\mathcal{G}(F_{p^n}/F_{p^m}) = \mathfrak{g}(F_{p^m})$, and the latter group is the cyclic group of order n/m generated by φ^m.

Suppose, on the other hand, that p is a prime and n a positive integer. Then there exists a field with exactly p^n elements. For let C be an algebraic closure of $F_p = \mathbf{Z}/(p)$, and let E be the set of all roots in C of $f(x) = x^{p^n} - x$. It is easy to verify that every F_p-linear combination of roots of $f(x)$ is a root of $f(x)$, and that if $f(\alpha) = 0$, then $f(\alpha^{-1}) = 0$. Hence E is a field containing

F_p. The polynomial $x^{p^n} - x$ has no multiple roots in C. For, $\alpha \in E$ is a multiple root of $x^{p^n} - x$ if and only if $x^2 | [(x + \alpha)^{p^n} - (x + \alpha)]$. But $(x + \alpha)^{p^n} - (x + \alpha) = x^{p^n} - x + \alpha^{p^n} - \alpha$ is not divisible by x^2. It follows that $|E| = p^n$. Thus, for every prime p and every positive integer n there exists a unique field F_{p^n} of p^n elements contained in an algebraic closure, C, of $F_p = \mathbf{Z}/(p)$, namely, the splitting field in C of $x^{p^n} - x$ over F_p.

We combine the results of this example in

Theorem 5.5. *If E is a finite field with q elements, then $q = p^n$, where $p = \text{Char } E$, every element of E is a root of $x^{p^n} - x$, and E is a splitting field of $x^{p^n} - x$ over $\mathbf{Z}/(p)$.*

Let p be a prime and C an algebraic closure of $F_p = \mathbf{Z}/(p)$. For every positive integer n, there exists exactly one subfield, F_{p^n}, of C with p^n elements, namely, the splitting field in C of $x^{p^n} - x$ over F_p. $F_{p^m} \subset F_{p^n}$ if and only if $m | n$. If $m | n$, then F_{p^n} is Galois over F_{p^m}, and $\mathscr{G}(F_{p^n}/F_{p^m})$ is the cyclic group of order $\dfrac{n}{m}$ generated by $\varphi^m|_{F_{p^n}}$, where $\varphi: C \to C$ is defined by $\varphi(\alpha) = \alpha^p$ for all $\alpha \in C$. □

Example 5. In this example we show that if E is Galois but not finite over F, then the map $\mathfrak{f}: \mathscr{S}_{\mathscr{G}} \to \mathscr{S}_{E/F}$ is not necessarily injective.

We use the notation of Theorem 5.5. Let C be an algebraic closure of $F_p = \mathbf{Z}/(p)$, and $\varphi: C \to C$ the map defined by $\varphi(\alpha) = \alpha^p$ for all $\alpha \in C$. C is Galois over F_p (by Theorem 3.3 and the Corollary of Theorem 4.6) and φ is an element of $\mathscr{G}(C/F_p)$ and generates a subgroup $H = [\varphi]$ of $\mathscr{G}(C/F_p)$. We prove that the fixed field of H is F_p and that H is a proper subgroup of $\mathscr{G}(C/F_p)$. But then $\mathfrak{f}(H) = \mathfrak{f}(\mathscr{G}(C/F_p))$ with $H \neq \mathscr{G}(C/F_p)$, and $\mathfrak{f}$ is not injective.

An element $\alpha \in C$ is in the fixed field of H if and only if $\varphi(\alpha) = \alpha^p = \alpha$. Hence, the fixed field of H consists of the roots in C of $x^p - x$, and $\mathfrak{f}(H) = F_p$.

Let $E = \bigcup_{i=1}^{\infty} F_{p^{2^i}}$; i.e., E is the smallest subfield of C which contains every subfield $F_{p^{2^i}}$, $i = 0, 1, 2, \ldots$. If $\alpha \in E$, then $[\alpha: F_p]$ is a power of 2. Hence, as is easily seen, $C \neq E$ and $[C: E] > 1$. C is Galois over E, $\mathscr{G}(C/E)$ is a subgroup of $\mathscr{G}(C/F_p)$, and there exists a $\sigma \in \mathscr{G}(C/E)$ with $\sigma \neq \iota_C$, $\sigma \notin H$. For suppose, to the contrary, that $\sigma = \varphi^k$. Then $\alpha \in C$ is fixed by σ if and only if α is a root of $x^{p^k} - x$. Thus, if $\sigma = \varphi^k$, then the field fixed by σ is F_{p^k}. Since $\sigma \in \mathscr{G}(C/E)$, σ fixes (at least) $E \neq F_{p^k}$, and we have a contradiction. We have shown that $\mathscr{G}(C/F_p)$ contains an element $\sigma \notin H = [\varphi]$, whence H is a proper subgroup of $\mathscr{G}(C/F_p)$ which has the same fixed field as $\mathscr{G}(C/F_p)$.

One can show that $\mathscr{G}(C/F_p)$ is abelian. Let $H_1 = H = [\varphi]$, φ as above, and let $H_2 = \mathscr{G}(C/F_p)$. Then $\{e\} \subset H_1 \lhd H_2 = \mathscr{G}(C/F_p)$, and $\mathscr{G}(\mathfrak{f}(H_1)/\mathfrak{f}(H_2)) = \mathscr{G}(F_p/F_p) = \{e\} \not\cong H_2/H_1$. Hence, part b′ of Theorem 5.3 is not true for infinite Galois extensions.

6. Galois Theory for Infinite Extensions; Projective Limit of Groups

We use the same notation as in Section 5. Let E be Galois over F. We have seen in Section 5 that $\mathfrak{f}\mathfrak{g} = \iota_{\mathscr{S}_{E/F}}$, and that, if $[E: F]$ is finite, then $\mathfrak{g}\mathfrak{f} = \iota_{\mathscr{S}_{\mathscr{G}}}$; however, if $[E: F]$ is infinite, then $\mathfrak{g}\mathfrak{f}$ is not necessarily the identity on $\mathscr{S}_{\mathscr{G}}$. We can restrict $\mathfrak{f}$ to a subset of $\mathscr{S}_{\mathscr{G}}$ so as to obtain a mapping which is bijective, whether $[E: F]$ is finite or infinite. For example, let $\mathscr{S}_c = \{\mathfrak{g}\mathfrak{f}(H) | H$ subgroup of $\mathscr{G}\}$. Then $\mathfrak{g}(K) = \mathfrak{g}\mathfrak{f}\mathfrak{g}(K) \in \mathscr{S}_c$ for $K \in \mathscr{S}_{E/F}$, $\mathfrak{f}|_{\mathscr{S}_c}\mathfrak{g} = \iota_{\mathscr{S}_{E/F}}$, and $\mathfrak{g}\mathfrak{f}|_{\mathscr{S}_c} = \iota_{\mathscr{S}_c}$. Note that the definition of $\mathscr{S}_c$ is not "intrinsic"; i.e., it is not given in terms of the abstract group $\mathscr{G}$ but rather depends on the action of $\mathscr{G}(E/F)$ on E. In this section we shall define (intrinsically) on $\mathscr{G}$ a topology, $\mathscr{T}$, and show that the set of all closed subgroups of $\mathscr{G}$ is precisely the set $\mathscr{S}_c$. (Pertinent topological ideas are assumed known. See [8] or [17] of the Bibliography.) If we limit our attention to the closed subgroups of $\mathscr{G}(E/F)$, then each part of Theorem 5.3 and its corollary is true for infinite Galois extensions E/F. If E/F is finite, then $\mathscr{T}$ is discrete, hence every subgroup of $\mathscr{G}(E/F)$ is closed, and the story of Section 5 remains unaltered.

Let E be Galois over F. We define a topology on the Galois group, $\mathscr{G}(E/F)$, by specifying a set, $\mathscr{N}$, of subsets of $\mathscr{G}(E/F)$ which serves as a basis for the topology on $\mathscr{G}(E/F)$; i.e., the open sets of $\mathscr{G}(E/F)$ are $\varnothing$, $\mathscr{G}(E/F)$, and all unions of sets in $\mathscr{N}$. Let $\mathscr{N} = \{gH | H$ subgroup of $\mathscr{G}(E/F)$, $[\mathscr{G}(E/F): H]$ finite, $g \in \mathscr{G}(E/F)\}$. In order to show that $\mathscr{N}$ can serve as a basis for a topology, it is sufficient to show that for $g_1H_1, g_2H_2 \in \mathscr{N}$ and $g_3 \in g_1H_1 \cap g_2H_2$ there exists a $gH \in \mathscr{N}$ with $g_3 \in gH \subset g_1H_1 \cap g_2H_2$. But if $g_3 \in g_1H_1 \cap g_2H_2$ ($g_1H_1, g_2H_2 \in \mathscr{N}$), then $g_1H_1 = g_3H_1$, $g_2H_2 = g_3H_2$, and $g_3 \in g_3(H_1 \cap H_2) = g_1H_1 \cap g_2H_2$. Furthermore, from $[\mathscr{G}(E/F): H_1 \cap H_2] = [\mathscr{G}(E/F): H_1] \times [H_1: H_1 \cap H_2] \leq [\mathscr{G}(E/F): H_1][\mathscr{G}(E/F): H_2]$, it follows that $g_3(H_1 \cap H_2) \in \mathscr{N}$ and we may choose $\mathscr{N}$ as a basis for a topology on $\mathscr{G}(E/F)$. The reader may verify that, in this topology, $\mathscr{G}(E/F)$ is a topological group; i.e., the map from the Cartesian product $\mathscr{G}(E/F) \times \mathscr{G}(E/F)$ to $\mathscr{G}(E/F)$ defined by $(g_1,g_2) \mapsto g_1g_2^{-1}$ is continuous (Exercise 6.1).

We shall prove that if E is Galois over F, then, for any subgroup H of $\mathscr{G}(E/F)$, the Galois group of E over the fixed field of H is the closure, $\overline{H}$, of H in $\mathscr{G}(E/F)$ (with the topology as described above).

Lemma. *Let E be Galois over F. If M is a subgroup of finite index in $\mathscr{G}(E/F)$, then $[\mathfrak{f}(M): F]$ is finite and $\mathfrak{g}\mathfrak{f}(M) = M$. (The notation is as in Section* 5.)

PROOF. Suppose $[\mathscr{G}(E/F): M]$ is finite. Clearly, $\mathfrak{gf}(M) \supset M$, hence $\mathfrak{gf}(M)$ is of finite index in $\mathscr{G}(E/F)$. Since $[\mathscr{G}(E/F): \mathfrak{g}f(M)]$ is equal to the number of F-monomorphisms of $\mathfrak{f}(M)$ into E, $[\mathfrak{f}(M): F]$ is finite. It follows that there exists a subfield, N, of E containing $\mathfrak{f}(M)$ which is normal and finite over F. By Theorem 5.3b, $\mathscr{G}(N/f(M)) \cong \mathfrak{gf}(M)/\mathfrak{g}(N)$. It is easy to verify that the fixed field of the subgroup of $\mathscr{G}(N/\mathfrak{f}(M))$ corresponding to $M/\mathfrak{g}(N)$ under this isomorphism is $\mathfrak{f}(M)$. Hence, by the finite Galois theory (Theorem 5.3a′), $M/\mathfrak{g}(N) = \mathfrak{gf}(M)/\mathfrak{g}(N)$, and $M = \mathfrak{gf}(M)$. ▮

Theorem 6.1. *Let E be Galois over F, let $\mathscr{G}(E/F)$ be topologized as described above, and let the notation be as in Section 5. For any subgroup H of $\mathscr{G}(E/F)$, $\mathfrak{gf}(H) = \overline{H}$ [$\overline{H}$ the closure of H in $\mathscr{G}(E/F)$].*

PROOF. We show first that $\overline{H} \subset \mathfrak{gf}(H)$. Let $\bar{h} \in \overline{H}$, and $\alpha \in \mathfrak{f}(H)$. Then $\bar{h}\mathfrak{g}(F(\alpha)) \in \mathscr{N}$, and, since $\bar{h}$ is in the closure of H, $\bar{h}\mathfrak{g}(F(\alpha))$ contains an element $h \in H$. But then $\bar{h} \in h\mathfrak{g}(F(\alpha))$. Every element of $\mathfrak{g}(F(\alpha))$ fixes α, and h fixes α, whence $\bar{h}$ fixes α. We have shown that if $\bar{h} \in \overline{H}$, then $\bar{h}$ fixes every $\alpha \in \mathfrak{f}(H)$. We conclude that $\bar{h} \in \mathfrak{gf}(H)$ and $\overline{H} \subset \mathfrak{gf}(H)$.

We show now that $\mathfrak{gf}(H) \subset \overline{H}$. Let $g \in \mathfrak{gf}(H)$. We prove that every neighborhood of g contains an element of H, whence $g \in \overline{H}$. Let $gM \in \mathscr{N}$ be a neighborhood of g. By the lemma, $[\mathfrak{f}(M): F]$ is finite, hence there exists an $\alpha \in E$ such that $\mathfrak{f}(M) = F(\alpha)$. Let N be a subfield of E, containing $\mathfrak{f}(H)(\alpha)$, which is normal and finite over $\mathfrak{f}(H)$.

Consider the map $\varphi: H \to \mathscr{G}(N/\mathfrak{f}(H))$ defined by $h \mapsto h|_N$. Clearly φ is a homomorphism. Since the fixed field of $\operatorname{Im} \varphi$ is $\mathfrak{f}(H)$, $\operatorname{Im} \varphi = \mathscr{G}(N/\mathfrak{f}(H))$ (by finite Galois theory). The element $g \in \mathfrak{gf}(H)$ induces a map $\mathfrak{f}(H)(\alpha) \to \mathfrak{f}(H)(\alpha')$, where $\alpha' = g(\alpha)$. The field N is normal over $\mathfrak{f}(H)$ and contains $\mathfrak{f}(H)(\alpha')$, whence there is an element in $\mathscr{G}(N/\mathfrak{f}(H))$ which induces the same map as g. From $\operatorname{Im} \varphi = \mathscr{G}(N/\mathfrak{f}(H))$, we conclude that there is an element $h \in H$ which induces the same map as g on $\mathfrak{f}(H)(\alpha)$. But then $g^{-1}h(\alpha) = \alpha$, $g^{-1}h \in \mathfrak{g}(F(\alpha)) = \mathfrak{gf}(M)$. By the lemma, $\mathfrak{gf}(M) = M$, whence $g^{-1}h \in M$ and $h \in gM$. Every neighborhood of an element in $\mathfrak{gf}(H)$ contains an element of H, and $\mathfrak{gf}(H) \subset \overline{H}$. ▮

Corollary 1. $\mathfrak{gf}$ *is the identity map on the set of closed subgroups of* $\mathscr{G}(E/F)$.

PROOF. If H is closed, then $\mathfrak{gf}(H) = \overline{H} = H$. ▮

Corollary 2. *All the assertions of Theorem* 5.3 *and its corollary* (*without finiteness assumptions*) *are true for a* (*finite or infinite*) *Galois extension E of F, if the subgroups appearing there are restricted to the set of closed subgroups of $\mathscr{G}(E/F)$.*

PROOF. An examination of the proof of Theorem 5.3 shows that assertions a′ and b′ hold if $\mathfrak{g}\mathfrak{f}$ acts as the identity on the groups under consideration Hence Corollary 2 follows from Corollary 1. ▮

Corollary 3. *If H is a subgroup of finite index in $\mathscr{G}(E/F)$, then H is both open and closed.*

PROOF. Since $H \in \mathscr{N}$, H is open. By the Lemma and Theorem 6.1 $\mathfrak{g}\mathfrak{f}(H) = H = \overline{H}$, whence H is closed. ▮

Galois groups serve as an excellent illustration of a type of structure which is of importance in both algebra and topology: the projective limit of a family of groups. We shall define the projective limit of an "inverse system of groups" and shall show that $\mathscr{G}(E/F)$ is isomorphic to a projective limit of an inverse system of finite groups.

Definition 6.1. Let J be a set, and let $\leq$ be a relation on J. Then J is a *directed set with respect to* $\leq$ if $\leq$ is reflexive (i.e., $i \leq i$ for all $i \in J$) and transitive (i.e., for $i,j,k \in J$, if $i \leq j$ and $j \leq k$, then $i \leq k$), and for each $i,j \in J$ there exists a $k \in J$ such that $i \leq k$ and $j \leq k$. ///

Clearly, if $<$ is a total order on a set S (i.e., $<$ is transitive, and for any two elements $s_1,s_2 \in S$ one and only one of the following holds: $s_1 = s_2$, $s_1 < s_2$, $s_2 < s_1$), then S is a directed set with respect to the order relation $\leq$. A more interesting illustration of a directed set is furnished in

Example 1. Let G be a group and let J be an indexing set for the set S of normal subgroups of G which are of finite index in G. Then $S = \{H \mid H \lhd G, [G\colon H] \text{ finite}\} = \{H_i\}_{i \in J}$. Define a relation, $\leq$, on J as follows: $i \leq j$ if $H_j \subset H_i$. The relation $\leq$ is obviously reflexive and transitive. Furthermore, if H and K are normal subgroups of finite index in G, then $[G\colon H \cap K] = [G\colon H][H\colon H \cap K] = [G\colon H][HK\colon K]$, and $H \cap K$ is a normal subgroup of finite index in G. Hence for every $i,j \in J$ there exists a $k \in J$ such that $H_k = H_i \cap H_j$. But then $i \leq k$, $j \leq k$, and J is a directed set with respect to $\leq$.

Definition 6.2. Let J be a directed set with respect to $\leq$. Then $\langle \{G_i\}_{i \in J}, \{\sigma_i^j\}_{i,j \in J, i \leq j} \rangle$ is *an inverse system of groups over J with connecting maps* σ_i^j if, for each $i \in J$,

a. G_i is a group.
b. σ_i^i is the identity map on G_i.
c. $\sigma_i^j\colon G_j \to G_i$ is a homomorphism of G_j into G_i, for $j \in J$ with $i \leq j$.
d. $\sigma_i^j \sigma_j^k = \sigma_i^k$ for $j,k \in J$ with $i \leq j \leq k$. ///

Example 2. Let J be the set discussed in Example 1. Thus, J is an indexing set for the set of normal subgroups of finite index in a group G, and J is a directed set with respect to $\leq$, where $i \leq j$ if $H_j \subset H_i$. For $i,j \in J$, with $i \leq j$, let $\sigma_i^j: G/H_j \to G/H_i$ be the canonical epimorphism of G/H_j onto G/H_i. Then $\langle \{G/H_i\}_{i \in J}, \{\sigma_i^j\}_{i,j \in J, i \leq j}\rangle$ is an inverse system of groups over J.

Definition 6.3. Let $\langle \{G_i\}_{i \in J}, \{\sigma_i^j\}_{i,j \in J, i \leq j}\rangle$ be an inverse system of groups over J. Then $\langle G, \{\sigma_i\}_{i \in J}\rangle$ is a *projective limit* (or *inverse limit*) of this inverse system (and we write $\varprojlim G_i = G$) if

a. G is a group.
b. For each $i \in J$, $\sigma_i: G \to G_i$ is a homomorphism of G into G_i.
c. For $i,j \in J$ with $i \leq j$, the diagram

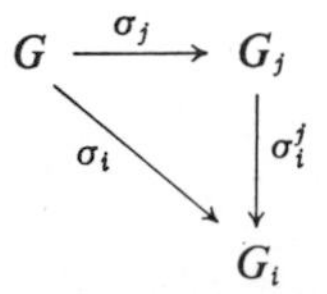

commutes.

d. For each system $\langle G', \{\sigma_i'\}_{i \in J}\rangle$ satisfying a, b, and c, there exists a unique homomorphism $\tau: G' \to G$ such that for $i \in J$, the diagram

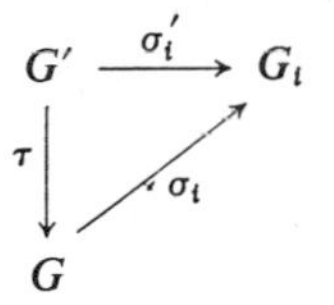

commutes. ///

Inverse systems and projective limits, although defined here only on the category of groups, can be defined on an arbitrary category, e.g., on the category of topological groups or on the category of topological spaces. The projective limit is a universal attracting object in a particular category.

We leave the proof of the following theorem to the reader.

Theorem 6.2. *Let* $\langle \{G_i\}_{i \in J}, \{\sigma_i^j\}_{i,j \in J, i \leq j}\rangle$ *be an inverse system of groups over the directed set* J.

a. *If* $\langle G, \{\sigma_i\}_{i \in J}\rangle$ *and* $\langle G', \{\sigma_i'\}_{i \in J}\rangle$ *are projective limits of the given inverse system, then there exists a unique isomorphism* $\theta: G' \to G$ *such that* $\sigma_i \theta = \sigma_i'$ *for each* $i \in J$.
b. *Let* $\langle \prod_{i \in J} G_i, \{\pi_i\}_{i \in J}\rangle$ *be the product of* $\{G_i\}_{i \in J}$. *Let* $Y = \{g \in \prod_{i \in J} G_i \mid$ *for all* $i,j \in J$, *with* $i \leq j$, $\pi_i(g) = \sigma_i^j \pi_j(g)\}$. *Then* $\langle Y, \{\pi_i|_Y\}_{i \in J}\rangle$ *is a projective limit of the given inverse system.* □

The subgroup, Y, of $\prod_{i \in J} G_i$ defined in part b of the theorem is the subgroup consisting of those elements of $\prod_{i \in J} G_i$ whose "coordinates" match up in the sense that if g_i and g_j are the ith and jth "coordinates," respectively, of $g \in \prod_{i \in J} G_i$, with $i \leq j$, then $g_i = \sigma_i^j(g_j)$.

Let $\mathscr{G}$ be a group, let $\langle \{\mathscr{G}/H_i\}_{i \in J}, \{\sigma_i^j\}_{i,j \in J, i \leq j} \rangle$ be the inverse system of groups discussed in Example 2, and let $\langle \prod_{i \in J} \mathscr{G}/H_i, \{\pi_i\}_{i \in J} \rangle$ be the product of $\{\mathscr{G}/H_i\}_{i \in J}$. We put $\hat{\mathscr{G}} = \{g \in \prod_{i \in J} \mathscr{G}/H_i \mid$ for all $i,j \in J$, with $i \leq j$, $\pi_i(g) = \sigma_i^j \pi_j(g)\}$. Then (by Theorem 6.2b) $\varprojlim \mathscr{G}/H_i = \hat{\mathscr{G}}$, and $\langle \hat{\mathscr{G}}, \{\pi_i|_{\hat{\mathscr{G}}}\}_{i \in J} \rangle$ is a projective limit of finite groups. For each $i \in J$, let $\nu_i : \mathscr{G} \to \mathscr{G}/H_i$ be the natural epimorphism of $\mathscr{G}$ onto $\mathscr{G}/H_i$. Note that for $i,j \in J$ with $i \leq j$ the diagram

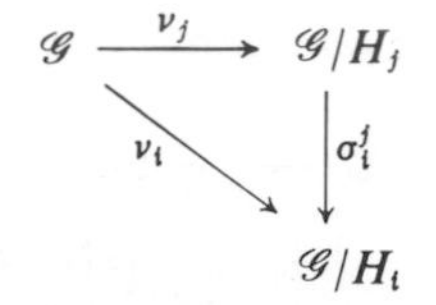

commutes. It follows from the definition of projective limit that there exists a unique homomorphism $\tau : \mathscr{G} \to \hat{\mathscr{G}}$ such that $\pi_i|_{\hat{\mathscr{G}}} \tau = \nu_i$ for each $i \in J$.

If $\mathscr{G}(E/F)$ is the Galois group of a field E Galois over F, then the unique homomorphism $\tau : \mathscr{G}(E/F) \to \widehat{\mathscr{G}(E/F)}$ is an isomorphism. We have

Theorem 6.3. *Let the notation be as in the preceding discussion. If E is Galois over F, then $\mathscr{G}(E/F)$ is isomorphic to $\widehat{\mathscr{G}(E/F)}$. Thus, $\mathscr{G}(E/F)$ is isomorphic to a projective limit of finite groups.*

PROOF. Let $\tau : \mathscr{G}(E/F) \to \widehat{\mathscr{G}(E/F)}$ be the unique homomorphism such that $\pi_i|_{\widehat{\mathscr{G}(E/F)}} \tau = \nu_i$ for all $i \in J$.

We show first that τ is injective. Let $g \in \mathscr{G}(E/F)$, $g \neq e$. Then there exists an $\alpha \in E$ such that $g(\alpha) \neq \alpha$. Let K be the smallest subfield of E which contains $F(\alpha)$ and which is normal over F, and let $H = \mathfrak{g}(K)$ be the subgroup of $\mathscr{G}(E/F)$ which fixes K (elementwise). Then by Theorem 5.3c and d, H is a normal subgroup of $\mathscr{G}(E/F)$ and $\mathscr{G}(E/F)/H \cong \mathscr{G}(K/F)$. Hence H is a normal subgroup of finite index in $\mathscr{G}(E/F)$, and $H = H_i$ for some $i \in J$. Since $g(\alpha) \neq \alpha$, $g \notin H_i$. But, for the canonical epimorphism $\nu_i : \mathscr{G}(E/F) \to \mathscr{G}(E/F)/H_i$, $\nu_i(g)$ is not the identity. From $\nu_i = \pi_i|_{\hat{\mathscr{G}}(E/F)} \tau$, we conclude that $\tau(g)$ is not the identity, whence τ is injective.

We show now that τ is surjective. Let $\hat{g} \in \widehat{\mathscr{G}(E/F)}$. We define a map $g : E \to E$ as follows: For $\alpha \in E$, let K be the smallest subfield of E which contains $F(\alpha)$ and which is normal over F, and let $H = \mathfrak{g}(K)$. Then $H = H_i$

for some $i \in J$, and we may identify $\mathscr{G}(E/F)/H_i$ with $\mathscr{G}(K/F)$. Let $g(\alpha) = [\pi_i(\hat{g})](\alpha)$. It is easy to see that $g \in \mathscr{G}(E/F)$ and that $\tau(g) = \hat{g}$. We leave the details to the reader. Hence τ is surjective. But then τ is an isomorphism of $\mathscr{G}(E/F)$ onto $\widehat{\mathscr{G}(E/F)}$. ▮

We now define a topology on $\hat{\mathscr{G}}$ ($\mathscr{G} = \mathscr{G}(E/F)$): Let $\mathscr{G}/H_i$ be given the discrete topology (i.e., every subset of $\mathscr{G}/H_i$ is open), and let $\prod_{i \in J} \mathscr{G}/H_i$ be given the Cartesian product topology (i.e., the open sets are $\prod_{i \in J} \mathscr{G}/H_i$, $\varnothing$, and all arbitrary unions of finite intersections of sets of the form $\pi_i^{-1}(U_i)$, U_i open in $\mathscr{G}/H_i$, $i \in J$). Finally, we topologize $\hat{\mathscr{G}}$ by giving $\hat{\mathscr{G}}$ the induced (or relative) topology (i.e., the open sets are $U \cap \hat{\mathscr{G}}$, where U is open in $\prod_{i \in J} \mathscr{G}/H_i$). With this topology, $\hat{\mathscr{G}}$ is a topological group. Since $\tau: \mathscr{G} \to \hat{\mathscr{G}}$ is an isomorphism, we can transfer the topology on $\hat{\mathscr{G}}$ to a topology on $\mathscr{G}$: The open sets in $\mathscr{G}$ are $\tau^{-1}(U)$, U open in $\hat{\mathscr{G}}$. The reader may wish to show that this topology is equivalent to the topology on $\mathscr{G}$ introduced in the discussion preceding Theorem 6.1, and that $\mathscr{G}$ is compact and totally disconnected in this topology.

7. Roots of Unity

Definition 7.1. A nonzero element of a field F is a *root of unity* if its order in the multiplicative group F^* is finite. If the order of θ divides n (n a positive integer); i.e., if $\theta^n = 1$, then θ is an nth *root of unity*. If the order of θ equals n, then θ is a *primitive* nth *root of unity*. ///

Theorem 7.1. *Let C be an algebraically closed field.*

a. *C contains a primitive nth root of unity if and only if* Char $C \nmid n$.
b. *If F is a subfield of C and $\zeta \in C$ is a primitive nth root of unity, then $[F(\zeta): F]$ divides $\varphi(n)$ (the number of positive integers less than, and prime to, n), $F(\zeta)$ is Galois over F, and the Galois group of $F(\zeta)$ over F is isomorphic to a subgroup of $(\mathbf{Z}/(n))^*$, the unit group of $\mathbf{Z}/(n)$.*

PROOF.

a. Let S be the set of roots, in C, of the polynomial $x^n - 1$. Then S is a subgroup of C^*, for S is not empty, and $\theta^{-1}\eta \in S$ for each $\theta,\eta \in S$. Since $|S| \leq n$, S is (Theorem 4.13, Lemma 2) a finite cyclic group. But then C contains a primitive nth root of unity if and only if $|S| = n$, that is, if and only if $x^n - 1$ has no multiple roots. An element θ of C is a multiple root of $x^n - 1$ if and only if 0 is a multiple root of $(x + \theta)^n - 1$, i.e., if and only if x^2 divides $(x + \theta)^n - 1 = x^n + n\theta x^{n-1} + \cdots + n\theta^{n-1}x$. Hence C contains a primitive nth root of unity if and only if Char $C \nmid n$.

b. If $\zeta \in C$ is a primitive nth root of unity, then ζ is a generator for the cyclic group, S, formed by the nth roots of unity in C. But then $F(\zeta)$ is a splitting field for the separable polynomial $x^n - 1$ over F, and $F(\zeta)$ is a finite Galois extension of F.

Let $\sigma \in \mathcal{G}(F(\zeta)/F)$, the Galois group of $F(\zeta)$ over F. If $\theta,\eta \in S$, then $\sigma(\theta),\sigma(\eta) \in S$ and $\sigma(\theta\eta) = \sigma(\theta)\sigma(\eta)$. Hence, $\sigma \mapsto \sigma|_S$ defines a map from $\mathcal{G}(F(\zeta)/F)$ to Aut S, the automorphism group of S. This map is clearly a homomorphism. Since ζ generates S, and generates $F(\zeta)$ over F, σ (hence $\sigma|_S$) is completely determined by its effect on ζ. Thus the map defined by $\sigma \mapsto \sigma|_S$ is a monomorphism. We have proved that $\mathcal{G}(F(\zeta)/F)$ is isomorphic to a subgroup of Aut S.

The map $\rho_k: S \to S$ defined by $\rho_k(\theta) = \theta^k$, $\theta \in S$, is an automorphism of S if and only if $(n,k) = 1$. Obviously $\rho_k\rho_l = \rho_{kl}$, and $\rho_r = \rho_s$ if and only if $r \equiv s \bmod n$. For each $\tau \in$ Aut S, there is some $k < n$, with $(n,k) = 1$, such that $\tau = \rho_k$. Hence, Aut S is isomorphic to the multiplicative group, $(\mathbf{Z}/(n))^*$, of integers relatively prime to n, mod n. We have seen (Chapter 2, Exercise 3.15) that $|(\mathbf{Z}/(n))^*| = \varphi(n)$. We conclude that $\mathcal{G}(F[\zeta]/F)$ is isomorphic to a subgroup of $(\mathbf{Z}/(n))^*$ and that $[F(\zeta): F]$ (which is equal to $|\mathcal{G}(F(\zeta)/F)|$) divides $\varphi(n)$. ▮

In general, $[F(\zeta): F] < \varphi(n)$. Thus, for example, if $\mathbf{R}$ is the real field and ζ is a primitive nth root of unity in the complex field, $n \geq 3$, then $[\mathbf{R}(\zeta): \mathbf{R}] = 2$. We show that if the base field is the rational field, $\mathbf{Q}$, then $[\mathbf{Q}(\zeta): \mathbf{Q}] = \varphi(n)$.

Theorem 7.2. *Let ζ be a primitive* nth *root of unity in a field containing the rational field,* $\mathbf{Q}$.

a. $[\mathbf{Q}(\zeta): \mathbf{Q}] = \varphi(n)$.

b. *If $n = 2^e p_1^{e_1} p_2^{e_2} \cdots p_s^{e_s}$ is the factorization of n into a product of powers of distinct primes, then the Galois group of $\mathbf{Q}(\zeta)$ over $\mathbf{Q}$ is a direct product of a cyclic group of order* 2 *(if $e > 1$), a cyclic group of order 2^{e-2} (if $e > 2$), and cyclic groups of orders $p^{e_i - 1}(p_i - 1)$, $i = 1, 2, \ldots, s$.*

PROOF.

a. Let $\Phi_n(x)$ be the minimum polynomial of ζ over $\mathbf{Q}$. Since ζ is a root of $x^n - 1$, there exists a monic polynomial $g(x) \in \mathbf{Q}[x]$ such that $x^n - 1 = g(x)\Phi_n(x)$. From Chapter 2, Section 3, Lemmas 3 and 4, it follows that $g(x)$ and $\Phi_n(x)$ are primitive polynomials in $\mathbf{Z}[x]$.

To prove that $[\mathbf{Q}(\zeta): \mathbf{Q}] = \varphi(n)$, it is sufficient to show that for every root θ of $\Phi_n(x)$ (in an algebraically closed field containing $\mathbf{Q}$) and for every prime p, with $(p,n) = 1$, θ^p is a root of $\Phi_n(x)$. For then θ^k is a root whenever

θ is a root and $(k,n) = 1$, and therefore $[\mathbf{Q}(\zeta): \mathbf{Q}] = \deg \Phi_n(x) \geq \varphi(n)$; but by Theorem 7.1b, $[\mathbf{Q}(\zeta): \mathbf{Q}] \leq \varphi(n)$, whence $[\mathbf{Q}(\zeta): \mathbf{Q}] = \varphi(n)$.

We assume that for some root, θ, of $\Phi_n(x)$, and for some prime p with $(p,n) = 1$, θ^p is not a root of $\Phi_n(x)$ and arrive at a contradiction. Both θ and θ^p are nth roots of unity. Since θ^p is a root of $x^n - 1 = g(x)\Phi_n(x)$ and not a root of $\Phi_n(x)$, it is a root of $g(x)$. But then θ is a root of $g(x^p)$, hence $\Phi_n(x)|g(x^p)$, and there is a polynomial $h(x) \in \mathbf{Q}[x]$ such that $g(x^p) = h(x)\Phi_n(x)$. As above, $h(x) \in \mathbf{Z}[x]$. The canonical homomorphism $\mathbf{Z} \to \mathbf{Z}/(p)$ extends to a homomorphism $\mathbf{Z}[x] \to \mathbf{Z}/(p)[x]$. Let $\bar{f}(x)$ denote the image of $f(x) \in \mathbf{Z}[x]$ under the extended homomorphism. Then $\bar{h}(x)\bar{\Phi}_n(x) = \bar{g}(x^p) = [\bar{g}(x)]^p$. Since $\mathbf{Z}/(p)[x]$ is a unique factorization domain, and $\deg \bar{\Phi}_n(x) \geq 1$, $\bar{\Phi}_n(x)$ and $\bar{g}(x)$ have a common divisor $\bar{d}(x)$ of degree greater than or equal to 1. But then, $x^n - \bar{1} = \bar{g}(x)\bar{\Phi}_n(x) = \bar{t}(x)[\bar{d}(x)]^2$, for some polynomial $\bar{t}(x) \in \mathbf{Z}/(p)[x]$, and $x^n - \bar{1}$ has a multiple root in an extension field of $\mathbf{Z}/(p)$. Since $p \nmid n$, this is impossible in view of Theorem 7.1a. We have proved that $[\mathbf{Q}(\zeta): \mathbf{Q}] = \varphi(n)$.

b. By Theorem 7.1b, $\mathcal{G}(\mathbf{Q}(\zeta)/\mathbf{Q})$ is isomorphic to a subgroup of $(\mathbf{Z}/(n))^*$. Since $|\mathcal{G}(\mathbf{Q}(\zeta)/\mathbf{Q})| = [\mathbf{Q}(\zeta): \mathbf{Q}] = \varphi(n) = |(\mathbf{Z}/(n))^*|$, $\mathcal{G}(\mathbf{Q}(\zeta)/\mathbf{Q}) \cong (\mathbf{Z}/(n))^*$. In Chapter 2, Exercise 3.14, the structure of $(\mathbf{Z}/(n))^*$ was determined to be as stated in the theorem. ▮

Corollary. *If ζ is a primitive* n*th root of unity in the complex field* **C** *and $\Phi_n(x)$ is its minimum polynomial over* **Q**, *then $\Phi_n(x) = \prod_{1 \leq i \leq n, (i,n)=1} (x - \zeta^i)$, the roots of $\Phi_n(x)$ are all primitive* n*th roots of unity, and every primitive* n*th root of unity in* **C** *is a root of $\Phi_n(x)$.* □

***Definition* 7.2.** Let F be a field, and ζ a primitive nth root of unity (lying in an extension $C \supset F$). The nth *cyclotomic polynomial* over F is the polynomial $\Phi_n(x) = \prod_{1 \leq i \leq n, (i,n)=1} (x - \zeta^i)$. An extension field E of F is *cyclotomic over F* if E is a splitting field of a set of cyclotomic polynomials over F. ///

REMARK. Let F be a field and n a positive integer such that Char $F \nmid n$. Then $x^n - 1 = \prod_{1 \leq d, d|n} \Phi_d(x)$, where $\Phi_d(x)$ is the dth cyclotomic polynomial over F. For, every root of $x^n - 1$ is a primitive dth root of unity for one and only one divisor d of n; and conversely, if $d|n$, then every primitive dth root of unity is a root of $x^n - 1$.

It follows easily from the above equality that the coefficients of $\Phi_n(x)$ lie in $\mathbf{Z} \cdot 1_F$ (Exercise 7.3).

8. Norm and Trace

In this section we define two functions which are of great importance in the study of field theory and number theory: the norm and the trace.

Definition 8.1. Let E be a finite extension of a field F, $E \supset F$. For $\alpha \in E$, let $\alpha_L \in \mathrm{Hom}_F(E,E)$ be the F-linear transformation induced on the vector space E over F by the left multiplication by α; i.e., $\alpha_L(\beta) = \alpha\beta$. The *norm from E to F*, $N_{E/F}: E \to F$, is the map from E to F defined by $N_{E/F}(\alpha) = \det \alpha_L$, $\alpha \in E$. The *trace from E to F*, $\mathrm{tr}_{E/F}: E \to F$, is the map from E to F defined by $\mathrm{tr}_{E/F}(\alpha) = \mathrm{tr}(\alpha_L)$, $\alpha \in E$. ///

REMARKS. It follows immediately from the definitions of norm and trace that for $a,b \in F$, $\alpha,\beta \in E$,

$$N_{E/F}(\alpha\beta) = N_{E/F}(\alpha)N_{E/F}(\beta),$$

$$\mathrm{tr}_{E/F}(a\beta + b\beta) = a\,\mathrm{tr}_{E/F}(\alpha) + b\,\mathrm{tr}_{E/F}(\beta).$$

Hence, $N_{E/F}$ induces a homomorphism from the multiplicative group E^*, of E to the multiplicative group, F^*, of F, and $\mathrm{tr}_{E/F}$ induces an F-homomorphism from the additive group of E to that of F.

If $a \in F$, then $N_{E/F}(a) = a^{[E:F]}$ and $\mathrm{tr}_{E/F}(a) = [E: F]a$.

Example. Consider $\mathbf{Q}(i)$, where $\mathbf{Q}$ is the rational field and $i^2 = -1$. The element $(x + iy) \in \mathbf{Q}(i)$, with $x,y \in \mathbf{Q}$, induces, by left multiplication, a $\mathbf{Q}$-linear transformation of $\mathbf{Q}(i)$ whose matrix relative to the basis $\{1,i\}$ of $\mathbf{Q}(i)$ is

$$\begin{bmatrix} x & -y \\ y & x \end{bmatrix}.$$

Hence, $N_{\mathbf{Q}(i)/\mathbf{Q}}(x + iy) = x^2 + y^2$ and $\mathrm{tr}_{\mathbf{Q}(i)/\mathbf{Q}}(x + iy) = 2x$. Note that $N_{\mathbf{Q}(i)/\mathbf{Q}}(x + iy)$ is equal to the product of $x + iy$ and its $\mathbf{Q}$-conjugate, $x - iy$ and that $\mathrm{tr}_{\mathbf{Q}(i)/\mathbf{Q}}(x + iy)$ is equal to the sum of $x + iy$ and its $\mathbf{Q}$-conjugate; this is a particular case of a more general theorem (Theorem 8.2).

Theorem 8.1. *Let E be an extension of a field F, with $E \supset F$ and $[E: F] = n$. Let α be an element of E, with $[F(\alpha): F] = m$ and minimum polynomial $m_{\alpha/F}(x) = x^m + \sum_{i=1}^m a_i x^{m-i}$. Then*

$$N_{E/F}(\alpha) = (-1)^n a_m^{n/m},$$

$$\mathrm{tr}_{E/F}(\alpha) = -\frac{n}{m}\,a_1.$$

PROOF. Let α_L be the F-linear transformation on E induced by left multiplication by α, and let $f(x) = x^n + \sum_{i=1}^{n} b_i x^{n-i}$ be the characteristic polynomial of α_L. Then (Chapter 4, Theorem 4.4 and Theorem 4.5, Corollary 2), $\det \alpha_L = (-1)^n b_n$ and $\operatorname{tr} \alpha_L = -b_1$. The map $\alpha \mapsto \alpha_L$ extends to a homomorphism $\sum c_i\alpha^i \mapsto \sum c_i\alpha_L^i$ (actually an isomorphism) of $F(\alpha)$ to $F(\alpha_L) \subset \operatorname{Hom}_F(E,E)$. Since $m_{\alpha/F}(\alpha_L) = 0$, the minimum polynomial $m_{\alpha_L}(x)$, of α_L divides $m_{\alpha/F}(x)$. But $m_{\alpha/F}(x)$ is irreducible over F, whence $m_{\alpha_L}(x)$ is irreducible and equal to $m_{\alpha/F}(x)$. Every irreducible factor of the characteristic polynomial of a linear transformation is a factor of the minimum polynomial of this transformation (Chapter 4, Theorem 4.4). We conclude that

$$f(x) = x^n + \sum_{i=1}^{n} b_i x^{n-i} = [m_{\alpha/F}(x)]^{n/m} = \left[x^m + \sum_{i=1}^{m} a_i x^{m-i}\right]^{n/m},$$

$$\operatorname{tr}_{E/F}(\alpha) = -b_1 = -\frac{n}{m} a_1,$$

$$N_{E/F}(\alpha) = (-1)^n b_n = (-1)^n a_m^{n/m}. \quad \blacksquare$$

Theorem 8.2. *Let $C \supset E \supset F$ be a tower of fields where C is algebraically closed and $[E: F] = n$. Let $n_s = [E: F]_s$, the separability degree of E over F, $n_i = [E: F]_i$, the inseparability degree of E over F, and let $\tau_1, \tau_2, \ldots, \tau_{n_s}$ be the distinct F-monomorphisms of E into C. Then, for $\alpha \in E$,*

$$N_{E/F}(\alpha) = \left[\prod_{k=1}^{n_s} \tau_k(\alpha)\right]^{n_i},$$

$$\operatorname{tr}_{E/F}(\alpha) = n_i \sum_{k=1}^{n_s} \tau_k(\alpha).$$

PROOF. Let $\alpha \in E$. Consider the tower $C \supset E \supset F(\alpha) \supset F$. There exist exactly $m_s = [F(\alpha): F]_s$ distinct F-monomorphisms $\rho_1, \rho_2, \ldots, \rho_{m_s}$, of $F(\alpha)$ into C. Each ρ_j extends to an F-automorphism of C which we also denote by ρ_j. There exist exactly $r = [E: F(\alpha)]_s$ distinct $F(\alpha)$-monomorphisms, $\sigma_1, \sigma_2, \ldots, \sigma_r$, of E into C. If τ_k is an F-monomorphism of E into C, then, on $F(\alpha)$, τ_k coincides with a unique ρ_j. But then, $\rho_j^{-1}\tau_k$ is an $F(\alpha)$-monomorphism of E into C, and $\rho_j^{-1}\tau_k = \sigma_l$ for a unique l. We conclude that $\{\tau_k\}_{k=1}^{n_s} = \{\rho_j\sigma_l\}_{j=1,2,\ldots,m_s,\, l=1,2,\ldots,r}$ and that $r = n_s/m_s$.

Let $F(\alpha)_s$ denote the maximal separable subfield of $F(\alpha)$ over F. Then $F(\alpha)$ is purely inseparable of degree $[F(\alpha): F(\alpha)_s] = [F(\alpha): F]_i$ over $F(\alpha)_s$ (Theorem 4.11). Let $m_i = [F(\alpha): F]_i$. Since α is purely inseparable over

$F(\alpha)_s$, the minimum polynomial of α over $F(\alpha)_s$ is of the form $x^{m_i} - \beta$ with $\beta = \alpha^{m_i} \in F(\alpha)_s$. For $k \neq l$,

$$\rho_k(\beta) - \rho_l(\beta) = \rho_k(\alpha)^{m_i} - \rho_l(\alpha)^{m_i} = [\rho_k(\alpha) - \rho_l(\alpha)]^{m_i} \neq 0.$$

(We have used the fact that the degree of inseparability is a power of the characteristic of the base field.) Therefore, β has precisely m_s F-conjugates in C, and the minimum polynomial, $m_{\beta/F}(x)$, of β over F is equal to $\prod_{j=1}^{m_s} (x - \rho_j(\beta))$. The monic polynomial $m_{\beta/F}(x^{m_i})$ is of degree $m_s m_i = m = [F(\alpha): F]$ and has α as a root, whence $m_{\alpha/F}(x) = m_{\beta/F}(x^{m_i})$. Since σ_l fixes $F(\alpha)$ and $\beta \in F(\alpha)$, $\sigma_l(\beta) = \beta$ for $l = 1, 2, \ldots, r$. But then,

$$\prod_{k=1}^{n_s} (x - \tau_k(\alpha))^{m_i} = \prod_{k=1}^{n_s} (x^{m_i} - \tau_k(\beta)) = \prod_{j=1}^{m_s} \prod_{l=1}^{r} (x^{m_i} - \rho_j \sigma_l(\beta))$$

$$= \prod_{j=1}^{m_s} (x^{m_i} - \rho_j(\beta))^r = [m_{\beta/F}(x^{m_i})]^r = [m_{\alpha/F}(x)]^r.$$

Hence if $m_{\alpha/F}(x) = x^m + \sum_{t=1}^{m} a_t x^{m-t}$, then $a_m^r = [(-1)^{n_s} \prod_{k=1}^{n_s} \tau_k(\alpha)]^{m_i}$, and $r a_1 = -m_i \sum_{k=1}^{n_s} \tau_k(\alpha)$. Applying Theorem 8.1 and noting that $r \cdot (n_i/m_i) = n/m$, we conclude that

$$N_{E/F}(\alpha) = (-1)^n a_m^{n/m} = \left[\prod_{k=1}^{n_s} \tau_k(\alpha)\right]^{n_i},$$

$$\operatorname{tr}_{E/F}(\alpha) = \frac{-n}{m} a_1 = n_i \sum_{k=1}^{n_s} \tau_k(\alpha). \quad ▮$$

Associated with a tower $K \supset E \supset F$ of finite extensions are the maps $N_{K/E}: K \to E$ and $N_{E/F}: E \to F$. We show that $N_{K/F}: K \to F$ is the composite of these maps. An analogous result holds for the trace.

Corollary 1. *Let $K \supset E \supset F$ be a tower of finite extensions. Then,*

$$N_{K/F} = N_{E/F} N_{K/E},$$

$$\operatorname{tr}_{K/F} = \operatorname{tr}_{E/F} \operatorname{tr}_{K/E}.$$

PROOF. Let $n_s = [K: F]_s$, $n_i = [K: F]_i$, $m_s = [E: F]_s$, $m_i = [E: F]_i$, $r_s = [K: E]_s$, and $r_i = [K: E]_i$. Then $n_i = m_i r_i$. Let $\rho_1, \rho_2, \ldots, \rho_{m_s}$ be the F-monomorphisms of E into an algebraically closed field $C \supset K$, and let $\sigma_1, \sigma_2, \ldots, \sigma_{r_s}$ be the E-monomorphisms of K into C. It follows, precisely as in the proof of the theorem, that $\{\rho_j\sigma_l\}_{j=1,2,\ldots,m_s,l=1,2,\ldots,r_s}$ is the set of F-monomorphisms of K into C. But then, for $\alpha \in K$,

$$N_{K/F}(\alpha) = \left[\prod_{j=1}^{m_s}\prod_{l=1}^{r_s} \rho_j\sigma_l(\alpha)\right]^{n_i} = \left[\prod_{j=1}^{m_s} \rho_j\left(\left[\prod_{l=1}^{r_s} \sigma_l(\alpha)\right]^{r_i}\right)\right]^{m_i}$$
$$= N_{E/F}(N_{K/E}(\alpha)).$$

We leave the computations involving the trace to the reader. ▮

Corollary 2. *Let E, F, and $\{\tau_k\}$ be as in the theorem. If E is separable over F, then*

$$N_{E/F}(\alpha) = \prod_{k=1}^{n} \tau_k(\alpha),$$

$$\mathrm{tr}_{E/F}(\alpha) = \sum_{k=1}^{n} \tau_k(\alpha). \qquad \square$$

Corollary 3. *Let E be a finite extension of F. Then E is separable over F if and only if there exists an $\alpha \in F$ such that $\mathrm{tr}_{E/F}(\alpha) \neq 0$, i.e., if and only if $\mathrm{tr}_{E/F}\colon E \to F$ is not the zero map.*

PROOF. If E is separable of degree n over F, then for each $\alpha \in E$, $\mathrm{tr}_{E/F}(\alpha) = \sum_{k=1}^{n} \tau_k(\alpha)$. By Theorem 4.3, $\{\tau_k\}_{k=1}^{n}$ is free over E. But then there exists an $\alpha \in E$ such that $\mathrm{tr}_{E/F}(\alpha) \neq 0$.

The inseparability degree, n_i, of E over F is a power of the characteristic of F. Hence, if there exists an $\alpha \in E$ such that $\mathrm{tr}_{E/F}(\alpha) = n_i \sum_{k=1}^{n} \tau_k(\alpha) \neq 0$, then $n_i = 1$ and E is separable over F. ▮

The map $N_{E/F}$ induces a homomorphism from the multiplicative group E^* to the multiplicative group F^*. The groups $N_{E/F}(E^*) = \mathrm{Im}\, N_{E/F}$, $\mathrm{Ker}\, N_{E/F}$, and $F^*/N_{E/F}(E^*)$ play an important role in various aspects of number theory. We give a trivial illustration. We have seen that $N_{\mathbf{Q}(i)/\mathbf{Q}}(x + iy) = x^2 + y^2$. Thus, finding $\mathrm{Im}\, N_{\mathbf{Q}(i)/\mathbf{Q}}$ is equivalent to finding those rational numbers which are representable as the sum of two (rational) squares. In our next theorem we shall determine $\mathrm{Ker}\, N_{E/F}$ for a special class of extensions E of F.

Definition 8.2. A Galois extension, E, of a field F is *cyclic* over F if the Galois group of E over F is cyclic. ///

Theorem 8.3. *Let E be a finite cyclic extension of F, and let σ be a generator for $\mathscr{G}(E/F)$. Let $\alpha \in E$.*

a. $N_{E/F}(\alpha) = 1$ *if and only if there exists $\beta \in E$, $\beta \neq 0$, such that $\alpha = \beta/\sigma(\beta)$. β is unique up to a nonzero factor from F.*

b. $\mathrm{tr}_{E/F}(\alpha) = 0$ *if and only if there exists $\beta \in E$ such that $\alpha = \beta - \sigma(\beta)$. β is unique up to a summand from F.*

PROOF.

a. Let $n = [E: F]$. Suppose that $N_{E/F}(\alpha) = 1$. Let f be the map from E to E defined by

$$f(t) = 1 \cdot t + \alpha\sigma(t) + \alpha\sigma(\alpha)\sigma^2(t) + \cdots + \alpha\sigma(\alpha)\cdots\sigma^{n-2}(\alpha)\sigma^{n-1}(t).$$

By Theorem 4.3, the set $\{\sigma^i\}_{i=0}^{n-1}$ is free over E, whence f is not the zero map, and there exists $t_0 \in E$ such that $f(t_0) \neq 0$. Let $\beta = f(t_0)$. Since $N_{E/F}(\alpha) = \alpha\sigma(\alpha)\cdots\sigma^{n-1}(\alpha) = 1$, $\alpha\sigma(\beta) = \beta$, and $\alpha = \beta/\sigma(\beta)$.

If, for $\beta_1 \in E$, $\alpha = \beta/\sigma(\beta) = \beta_1/\sigma(\beta_1)$, then $\beta_1\beta^{-1} = \sigma(\beta_1\beta^{-1})$, $\beta_1\beta^{-1}$ is fixed by the Galois group of E over F, hence $\beta_1\beta^{-1} = a \in F$ and $\beta_1 = a\beta$.

To prove the converse, we note that if E is any finite Galois extension of F (not necessarily cyclic) and if $\sigma \in \mathscr{G}(E/F)$, then $N_{E/F}(\alpha) = N_{E/F}(\sigma(\alpha))$ for all $\alpha \in E$. For, $N_{E/F}(\alpha) = \prod_{\rho \in \mathscr{G}(E/F)} \rho(\alpha) = \prod_{\rho \in \mathscr{G}(E/F)} \rho\sigma(\alpha) = N_{E/F}(\sigma(\alpha))$. Hence, if $\alpha = \beta/\sigma(\beta)$, then $N_{E/F}(\alpha) = 1$.

We may interpret a of the theorem as stating that, in a finite cyclic extension, the elements of norm 1 are precisely those which are trivially of norm 1.

b. Suppose $\mathrm{tr}_{E/F}(\alpha) = 0$. By Theorem 8.2, Corollary 3, there exists $\gamma \in E$ such that $\mathrm{tr}_{E/F}(\gamma) \neq 0$. Let

$$\beta = \frac{1}{\mathrm{tr}_{E/F}(\gamma)} [\alpha\sigma(\gamma) + (\alpha + \sigma(\alpha))\sigma^2(\gamma) + \cdots + (\alpha + \sigma(\alpha) + \cdots + \sigma^{n-2}(\alpha))\sigma^{n-1}(\gamma)].$$

Since $\mathrm{tr}_{E/F}(\alpha) = \alpha + \sigma(\alpha) + \cdots + \sigma^{n-1}(\alpha) = 0$, $\alpha = \beta - \sigma(\beta)$.

If $\alpha = \beta - \sigma(\beta) = \beta_1 - \sigma(\beta_1)$, then $\beta_1 - \beta = \sigma(\beta_1 - \beta)$, $\beta_1 - \beta = a \in F$, and $\beta_1 = \beta + a$.

If E is any finite Galois extension of F and if $\sigma \in \mathscr{G}(E/F)$, then $\mathrm{tr}_{E/F}(\alpha) = \mathrm{tr}_{E/F}(\sigma(\alpha))$ for all $\alpha \in E$. Hence, if $\alpha = \beta - \sigma(\beta)$, then $\mathrm{tr}_{E/F}(\alpha) = 0$. ▮

Example. The field $\mathbf{Q}(\omega)$ is a cyclic extension of degree 2 over $\mathbf{Q}$, where $\mathbf{Q}$ is the rational field and ω is a primitive cube root of unity. $N_{\mathbf{Q}(\omega)/\mathbf{Q}}(x + \omega y) = 1$ if and only if there exist $u,v \in \mathbf{Q}$ such that

$$x + \omega y = \frac{u + \omega v}{u + \omega^2 v} = \frac{(u^2 - v^2) + \omega(2uv - v^2)}{u^2 - uv + v^2}.$$

Since $N_{\mathbf{Q}(\omega)/\mathbf{Q}}(x + y) = x^2 - xy + y^2$, the complete set, $\{(x,y)\}$, of rational solutions of $x^2 - xy + y^2 = 1$ is given by

$$\left\{\left(\frac{u^2 - v^2}{u^2 - uv + v^2}, \frac{2uv - v^2}{u^2 - uv + v^2}\right) \middle| u,v \in \mathbf{Z},\ u \text{ and } v \text{ are not both } 0,\ (u,v) = 1\right\}.$$

9. Cyclic Extensions

Finite cyclic extensions are the building blocks for an important kind of extension, obtainable by a sequence of finite cyclic extensions. In this section we characterize (1) cyclic extensions of degree n over a field F under the assumption that F contains a primitive nth root of unity, and (2) cyclic extensions of degree p over F, where p is the characteristic of F.

Theorem 9.1. *Let F be a field which contains a primitive* nth *root of unity.*

a. *If $E \supset F$ is a cyclic extension of degree n over F, then there exist $a \in F$, $\alpha \in E$ such that the minimum polynomial of α over F is $x^n - a$, and $E = F(\alpha)$.*

b. *If $E = F(\alpha)$, where α is a root of the polynomial $x^n - a$ over F, then E is a cyclic extension of F, $[E: F]|n$, and $[E: F] = \min\{r \in \mathbf{N}' \mid \alpha^r \in F\}$.*

PROOF.

a. Suppose E is a cyclic extension of degree n over F. Let $\zeta \in F$ be a primitive nth root of unity, and let σ be a generator for $\mathscr{G}(E/F)$. Since $\zeta \in F$, $N_{E/F}(\zeta) = \zeta^{[E:F]} = \zeta^n = 1$. By Theorem 8.3a, there exists a nonzero $\alpha \in E$ such that $\zeta = \alpha/\sigma(\alpha)$. Then, $\sigma^i(\alpha) = \zeta^{-i}\alpha$ for $i = 1, 2, \ldots, n$, and α has at least n distinct F-conjugates. Since $n = [E: F] \geq [F(\alpha): F] \geq n$, $E = F(\alpha)$, and $[F(\alpha): F] = n$. From $\zeta = \alpha/\sigma(\alpha)$ it follows that $1 = \zeta^n = \alpha^n/\sigma(\alpha^n)$, and that $\sigma^i(\alpha^n) = \alpha^n$ for $i = 1, 2, \ldots, n$, whence α^n is in the fixed field of $\mathscr{G}(E/F)$, and $\alpha^n = a \in F$. Thus, α is a root of the polynomial $x^n - a$ over F. Since α is of degree n over F, $x^n - a$ is the minimum polynomial of α over F.

b. If α is a root of $x^n - a$ and $\zeta \in F$ is a primitive nth root of unity, then $\{\zeta^i\alpha\}_{i=1}^n$ is a complete set of distinct roots of $x^n - a$. Thus $E = F(\alpha)$ is a splitting field of a separable polynomial over F, hence a finite Galois extension of F with Galois group $\mathscr{G}(E/F)$. If $\sigma \in \mathscr{G}(E/F)$, then $\sigma(\alpha) = \zeta_\sigma\alpha$, where $\zeta_\sigma = \zeta^{k(\sigma)}$ and $k(\sigma)$ is an integer uniquely determined mod n by σ. The mapping of $\mathscr{G}(E/F)$ into the multiplicative group of nth roots of unity defined by $\sigma \mapsto \zeta_\sigma$ is a monomorphism. But then $\mathscr{G}(E/F)$ is isomorphic to a subgroup of a cyclic group of order n, whence $\mathscr{G}(E/F)$ is cyclic and $[E: F] = |\mathscr{G}(E/F)|$ divides n.

Since $N_{E/F}(\alpha) = \prod_{\sigma \in \mathscr{G}(E/F)} (\zeta_\sigma \alpha) = \alpha^{[E:F]} \prod_{\sigma \in \mathscr{G}(E/F)} \zeta_\sigma \in F$ and $\zeta_\sigma \in F$ for each $\sigma \in \mathscr{G}(E/F)$, $\alpha^{[E:F]} \in F$. If $r < [E: F]$, then $\alpha^r \notin F$. For otherwise, $\alpha^r = b \in F$, α is a root of $x^r - b$, and $[E: F] = [\alpha: F] \leq r < [E: F]$, which is impossible. We conclude that $[E: F] = \min\{r \in \mathbf{N}' | \alpha^r \in F\}$. ▮

Corollary. *Let F be as in the theorem, let $a \in F$, and let n be a prime. Then either the polynomial $x^n - a$ is a product of linear factors over F, or it is irreducible over F.* □

We now consider the case of cyclic extensions of $\deg p$ over F, p the characteristic of F.

Theorem 9.2. *Let F be a field of characteristic p.*

a. *If $E \supset F$ is a cyclic extension of $\deg p$ over F, then there exist $a \in F$, $\alpha \in E$ such that the minimum polynomial of α over F is $x^p - x - a$, and $E = F(\alpha)$.*
b. *If $E = F(\alpha)$, where α is a root of the polynomial $x^p - x - a$ over F, then $E = F$ or E is a cyclic extension of $\deg p$ over F.*

PROOF.

a. Suppose E is a cyclic extension of degree p over F. Let σ be a generator for $\mathscr{G}(E/F)$. Then, $\mathrm{tr}_{E/F}(1) = \sum_{i=1}^{p} \sigma^i(1) = p \cdot 1 = 0$. By Theorem 8.3b there exists $\alpha \in E$ such that $\sigma(\alpha) = \alpha - 1$. Then $\sigma^i(\alpha) = \alpha - i$ for $i = 1, 2, \ldots, p$, and α has at least p distinct F-conjugates. Since $p = [E: F] \geq [F(\alpha): F] \geq p$, $E = F(\alpha)$, and $[F(\alpha): F] = p$. From $\sigma(\alpha) = \alpha - 1$ it follows that $\sigma(\alpha^p - \alpha) = (\alpha - 1)^p - (\alpha - 1) = \alpha^p - \alpha$, and that $\sigma^i(\alpha^p - \alpha) = \alpha^p - \alpha$ for $i = 1, 2, \ldots, p$, whence $\alpha^p - \alpha$ is in the fixed field of $\mathscr{G}(E/F)$, and $\alpha^p - \alpha = a \in F$. Thus, α is a root of the polynomial $x^p - x - a$ over F. Since α is of degree p over F, $x^p - x - a$ is the minimum polynomial of α over F.

b. If α is a root of the polynomial $x^p - x - a$, then $\{(\alpha - i)\}_{i=1}^{p}$ is a complete set of distinct roots of $x^p - x - a$. It follows that $E = F(\alpha)$ is a splitting field of a separable polynomial over F, hence a finite Galois extension of F with Galois group $\mathscr{G}(E/F)$. If $\sigma \in \mathscr{G}(E/F)$, then $\sigma(\alpha) = \alpha - i(\sigma)$, where $i(\sigma)$ is an integer uniquely determined $\bmod p$ by σ. The mapping of $\mathscr{G}(E/F)$ into the additive group of integers $\bmod p$ defined by $\sigma \mapsto i(\sigma)$ is a monomorphism. But then $\mathscr{G}(E/F)$ is isomorphic to a subgroup of a cyclic group of order p, whence either $\mathscr{G}(E/F)$ consists of the identity only and $E = F$, or $\mathscr{G}(E/F)$ is cyclic of order p and $[E: F] = p$. ▮

Corollary. *Let F be a field of characteristic p, and let $\alpha \in F$. Then either the polynomial $x^p - x - a$ is a product of linear factors over F, or it is irreducible over F.* □

The case where E is a cyclic extension of degree p^e over F, p the characteristic of F, is discussed in Exercise 9.2.

10. Radical Extensions

Intuitively, E is a radical extension of F if every element of E may be expressed in terms of elements of F by means of operations involving addition, multiplication, and extraction of roots. If such an expression for an element of E were to involve a fourth root of a^2, it would not be apparent whether a root of $x^2 - a$ or a root of $x^2 + a$ is intended. We therefore require that $x^n - a$ be irreducible whenever an nth root of a occurs in such an expression.

Not all ambiguity is removed by this requirement. However, if the polynomial $x^n - a$ is irreducible over F and if ρ_1, ρ_2 are any two of its roots, then there is an F-monomorphism which takes ρ_1 into ρ_2 so that ρ_1 and ρ_2 are "operationally" alike.

We have seen in Theorems 9.1 and 9.2 that extension by a root of $x^p - a$, in the case Char $F \neq p$, has an analog, in the case Char $F = p$, namely, extension by a root of $x^p - x - b$. If the characteristic of F is p, we, therefore, also allow roots of polynomials of thc form $x^p - x - b$ to occur in a representation.

We formalize these remarks in

Definition 10.1. A finite tower of fields

$$F = F_0 \subset F_1 \subset F_2 \subset \cdots \subset F_k$$

is a *radical tower for F_k over F* if, for $i = 0, 1, \ldots, k - 1$, $F_{i+1} = F_i(\alpha_i)$, where α_i is a root of an irreducible polynomial over F_i of the form $x^{n_i} - a_i$, $a_i \in F_i$, or also of the form $x^p - x - b_i$, $b_i \in F_i$, if the characteristic of F is p.

An extension $E \supset F$ is a *radical extension of F* or an *extension of F by radicals* if E is contained in a field which has a radical tower over F.

A polynomial $f(x) \in F[x]$ is *solvable by radicals over F* if a splitting field for $f(x)$ over F is a radical extension of F. ///

Let C be an algebraically closed field containing a field E. In this section we show that E is an extension of F by radicals if and only if the group of F-automorphisms of the smallest subfield of C which contains E and which is normal over F is solvable.

Lemma 1. *Let $C \supset F$, where C is algebraically closed. Let n be a positive integer, and $K_n = F(S)$, where S is the set of all nth roots of unity in C. Then there exists a finite Galois extension, L_n, of F such that*

a. $L_n \supset K_n$.
b. *L_n has a radical tower over F.*
c. *$\mathcal{G}(L_n/F)$ is solvable.*

PROOF. The lemma is true for $n = 1$. Assume the lemma true for all $n < r$, $r > 1$. If p, the characteristic of F, divides r, then $K_r = K_{r/p}$ and the lemma holds with $n = r$. Suppose, therefore, that $p \nmid r$. Then $K_r = F(\zeta)$, where ζ is a primitive rth root of unity in C, and (by Theorem 7.1) K_r is a Galois extension of F, with $\mathcal{G}(K_r/F)$ abelian and of order dividing $\varphi(r)$. Since $r > 1$, $\varphi(r) < r$. By our induction assumption, there exists a finite Galois extension, $L_{\varphi(r)}$, of F with solvable Galois group over F such that $L_{\varphi(r)} \supset K_{\varphi(r)}$ and such that $L_{\varphi(r)}$ has a radical tower over F. Let $L_r = K_r(L_{\varphi(r)})$. We claim that L_r has the desired properties. Clearly, L_r is a finite Galois extension of F which contains K_r as a subfield. We must show that $\mathcal{G}(L_r/F)$ is solvable and that L_r has a radical tower over F.

By Theorem 5.4, $\mathcal{G}(L_r/L_{\varphi(r)})$ is isomorphic to a subgroup of $\mathcal{G}(K_r/F)$, hence is abelian (and a fortiori solvable) with order dividing $\varphi(r)$. Since $\mathcal{G}(L_r/F)/\mathcal{G}(L_r/L_{\varphi(r)}) \cong \mathcal{G}(L_{\varphi(r)}/F)$, $\mathcal{G}(L_r/F)$ is solvable, by Chapter 1, Theorem 6.2.

Let

$$\{e\} = H_0 \subset H_1 \subset \cdots \subset H_k = \mathcal{G}(L_r/L_{\varphi(r)})$$

be a composition series for $\mathcal{G}(L_r/L_{\varphi(r)})$, and let

$$L_r = E_0 \supset E_1 \supset \cdots \supset E_k = L_{\varphi(r)},$$

the tower of fields corresponding to this series under the Galois correspondence. Then for $i = 1, 2, \ldots, k$, E_{i-1} is a cyclic extension of E_i with $[E_{i-1}: E_i]$ a prime dividing $\varphi(r)$. Since $L_{\varphi(r)}$ contains all $\varphi(r)$th roots of unity, E_{i-1} must be an extension of E_i of the type discussed in Theorem 9.1a or Theorem 9.2a. But then this tower of fields is a radical tower for L_r over $L_{\varphi(r)}$. By the induction assumption, $L_{\varphi(r)}$ has a radical tower over F, whence L_r has a radical tower over F. The lemma follows by induction. ∎

Lemma 2. *Let $E \supset F$ be a finite extension of F, and let E_s denote the maximal separable subfield of E over F. Then E is a radical extension of F if and only if E_s is a radical extension of F.*

PROOF. If E is a radical extension of F, then E, and hence also E_s, is contained in a field which has a radical tower over F. But then E_s is a radical extension of F.

Conversely, suppose that E_s is a radical extension of F. Then E_s is contained in a field, K, which has a radical tower over F. By Theorem 4.11, E is a pure inseparable extension of E_s, whence there exist $\beta_i \in E$, $i = 1, 2, \ldots, r$ such that the minimum polynomial of β_i over E_s is of the form $x^{p^{n_i}} - \alpha_i$, n_i a positive integer, $\alpha_i \in E_s$, p the characteristic of F, and $E = E_s(\beta_1, \beta_2, \ldots, \beta_r)$. The tower

$$K = K_1 \subset K_2 = K_1(\beta_1) \subset K_3 = K_2(\beta_2) \subset \cdots \subset K_{r+1} = K_r(\beta_r)$$

is a radical tower for K_{r+1} over K. For, $x^{p^{n_i}} - \alpha_i$ is a power of an irreducible polynomial of the form $x^{p^{m_i}} - \gamma_i$ over K_i. But then K_{r+1} has a radical tower over F, $K_{r+1} \supset E$, and E is an extension of F by radicals. ▮

In the next lemma, we summarize several results which we require. Some of these results were obtained in the sections on separability and normality (Sections 3 and 4, in particular Theorem 4.12), the others follow directly from our considerations there.

Lemma 3. *Let $C \supset N \supset E \supset F$ be a tower of fields, where C is algebraically closed, N is any (the smallest) subfield of C which contains E and which is normal over F. Let N_s and E_s be the maximal separable subfields of N and E over F, respectively. Then, N_s is a (the smallest) Galois extension of F containing E_s, and $\mathcal{G}(N_s/F)$ is isomorphic to the group, G, of F-automorphisms of N. If K is the fixed field of G, then $\mathcal{G}(N/K) \cong \mathcal{G}(N_s/F)$.* □

Theorem 10.1. *Let $C \supset N \supset E \supset F$ be a tower of fields, where C is algebraically closed, N is the smallest subfield of C which contains E and which is normal over F, and $[E: F]$ is finite. Then E is a radical extension of F if and only if the group of F-automorphisms of N is solvable.*

PROOF. It follows from Lemmas 2 and 3 that it is sufficient to prove the theorem for the case where E is a separable extension of F. We assume, therefore, that E is separable over F and let $N \subset C$ be the smallest Galois extension of F containing E.

Suppose that $\mathcal{G}(N/F)$ is solvable. Then there is a composition series for $\mathcal{G}(N/F)$,

$$H_k = \{e\} \subset H_{k-1} \subset \cdots \subset H_1 \subset H_0 = \mathcal{G}(N/F),$$

such that H_{i-1}/H_i is cyclic of prime order, $i = 1, 2, \ldots, k$. Let $N = F_k \supset F_{k-1} \supset \cdots \supset F_1 \supset F_0 = F$ be the tower of fields which corresponds to this series under the Galois correspondence. For $i = 1, 2, \ldots, k$, F_i is a cyclic extension of prime degree over F_{i-1}. Let $n = \prod_{i=1}^{k} [F_i : F_{i-1}]$. By Lemma 1, there exists a field, L, which contains all nth roots of unity and has a radical tower over F. Consider the tower

$$(1) \qquad N(L) = F_k(L) \supset F_{k-1}(L) \supset \cdots \supset F_1(L) \supset F_0(L) = L.$$

By Theorem 5.4, $\mathscr{G}(F_i(L)/F_{i-1}(L))$ is isomorphic to a subgroup of $\mathscr{G}(F_i/F_{i-1})$, whence $\mathscr{G}(F_i(L)/F_{i-1}(L))$ either consists of the identity only, in which case $F_i(L) = F_{i-1}(L)$, or is cyclic with order equal to the prime $[F_i : F_{i-1}]$. In the latter case, $F_i(L)$ is an extension of $F_{i-1}(L)$ of the type discussed in Theorem 9.1a or in Theorem 9.2a. But then, (1) is a radical tower for $N(L)$ over L. Since L has a radical tower over F, so does $N(L)$. But $N(L) \supset E$, hence E is a radical extension of F.

Conversely, suppose that E is a radical extension of F. Then there exists a subfield, F_k, of C which contains E and which has a radical tower over F. (We note that, although E is, by assumption, separable over F, we do not know, at this point, that we may assume F_k separable over F.) For any F-monomorphism, σ, of F_k into C, $\sigma(F_k)$ has a radical tower over F. But then the field composite, M, of all the F-conjugates of F_k in C has a tower

$$(2) \qquad M = M_r \supset M_{r-1} \supset \cdots \supset M_1 \supset M_0 = F$$

such that, for $i = 0, 1, \ldots, r - 1$, $M_{i+1} = M_i(\alpha_i)$, where α_i is a root of a polynomial $x^{n_i} - a_i$, $a_i \in M_i$, or of a polynomial $x^p - x - b_i$, $b_i \in M_i$, p the characteristic of F. [We do not claim that (2) is a radical tower for M over F since the polynomials $x^{n_i} - \alpha_i$ need not be irreducible over the M_i.] Note that M_r is normal over F.

Let $n = \prod_{i=1}^{r} n_i$. (If M_{i+1} is an extension of M_i by a root of a polynomial $x^p - x - b_i$, let $n_i = 1$.) By Lemma 1, there exists a Galois extension, L, of F which contains all nth roots of unity, has a radical tower over F, and is such that $\mathscr{G}(L/F)$ is solvable. Clearly, $M_r(L)$ is normal over F. Let K be the fixed field of the group of F-automorphisms of $M_r(L)$. Then, $M_r(L) \supset K \supset F$, and, by Theorem 4.12, $M_r(L)$ is Galois over K, and hence also over $L(K)$. We "lift" the tower (2) to a tower over the composite field $L(K)$:

$$(3) \quad M_r(L) = M_r(L(K)) \supset M_{r-1}(L(K)) \supset \cdots$$
$$\supset M_1(L(K)) \supset M_0(L(K)) = L(K).$$

In order to simplify our notation we let $M_i' = M_i(L(K))$, $i = 0, 1, \ldots, r$. Let

$$\text{(4)} \qquad \{e\} = H_r \subset H_{r-1} \subset \cdots \subset H_1 \subset H_0 = \mathcal{G}(M_r'/M_0')$$

be the series corresponding to the tower (3) under the Galois correspondence. For $i = 0, 1, \ldots, r-1$, $M_{i+1}' = M_i'(\alpha_i)$, where α_i is a root of $x^{n_i} - a_i$ or of $x^p - x - b_i$. Since M_{i+1}' is separable over M_i', we may (by changing the a_i, if necessary) assume that $p \nmid n_i$. Our choice of the field L ensures that M_0' contains primitive n_ith roots of unity. But then, by Theorems 9.1b and 9.2b, M_{i+1}' is a cyclic extension of M_i' for $i = 0, 1, \ldots, r-1$, whence $H_{i+1} \lhd H_i$, H_i/H_{i+1} is cyclic, and (4) is a solvable series for $\mathcal{G}(M_r'/M_0') = \mathcal{G}(M_r(L)/L(K))$. Since $\mathcal{G}(M_r(L)/K)/\mathcal{G}(L(K)/K) \cong \mathcal{G}(M_r(L)/L(K))$, and $\mathcal{G}(L(K)/K)$ is solvable, $\mathcal{G}(M_r(L)/K)$ is solvable. By Lemma 3, the maximal separable subfield of $M_r(L)$ over F is a Galois extension of F, and its Galois group, G, is isomorphic to $\mathcal{G}(M_r(L)/K)$. But then G is solvable. The Galois group, $\mathcal{G}(N/F)$, of the smallest Galois extension, N, of F containing E is a homomorphic image of G, hence solvable. The theorem is proved. ∎

11. Solvability by Radicals

We recall that $f(x) \in F[x]$ is solvable by radicals over F if any splitting field, K, for $f(x)$ over F is a radical extension of F. Hence, in the separable case, $f(x)$ is solvable by radicals if and only if $\mathcal{G}(K/F)$ is solvable. If $\{t_i\}_{i=1}^n$ is a transcendence set over F, the polynomial $g(x) = x^n - t_1x^{n-1} + \cdots + (-1)^n t_n$ is called "the generic polynomial of degree n over F." In this section we show that the Galois group of a splitting field for a generic polynomial of degree n is S_n, the symmetric group of degree n. It follows that the generic polynomial of degree n is not solvable by radicals if $n \geq 5$.

Theorem 11.1. *Let $\{t_i\}_{i=1}^n$ be a transcendence set over a field F, let $E = F(t_1, t_2, \ldots, t_n)$, and let $K \supset E$ be a splitting field over E of the generic polynomial $g(x) = x^n - t_1x^{n-1} + \cdots + (-1)^n t_n$. Then K is a Galois extension of E, and $\mathcal{G}(K/E) \cong S_n$, the symmetric group of degree n.*

PROOF Let $\{s_i\}_{i=1}^n$ be a transcendence set over F, and let $\{\sigma_i\}_{i=1}^n$ be the set of elementary symmetric functions in the s_i, that is,

$$\sigma_1 = \sum_{1 \leq i \leq n} s_i, \qquad \sigma_2 = \sum_{1 \leq i < j \leq n} s_i s_j,$$

$$\sigma_3 = \sum_{1 \leq i < j < k \leq n} s_i s_j s_k, \ \ldots, \ \sigma_n = s_1 s_2 \cdots s_n.$$

Since $\prod_{i=1}^{n}(x - s_i) = x^n - \sigma_1 x^{n-1} + \cdots + (-1)^n\sigma_n = \bar{g}(x)$, $\bar{g}(x)$ is a separable polynomial over $F(\sigma_1,\sigma_2,\ldots,\sigma_n) = \bar{E}$, $F(s_1,s_2,\ldots,s_n) = \bar{K}$ is a splitting field over $\bar{E}$ of $\bar{g}(x)$, and $\bar{K}$ is a Galois extension of $\bar{E}$. We claim that $\mathscr{G}(\bar{K}/\bar{E}) \cong S_n$, the symmetric group of degree n. For, any permutation of the s_i induces an automorphism of $F[s_1,s_2,\ldots,s_n]$ which fixes $F[\sigma_1,\sigma_2,\ldots,\sigma_n]$, and this automorphism extends to an automorphism of the quotient field $\bar{K}$ which fixes the field $\bar{E}$; conversely, since the s_i are roots of $\bar{g}(x)$, every automorphism of $\bar{K}$ which fixes $\bar{E}$ must induce a permutation of the s_i.

To prove the theorem, it suffices to exhibit an isomorphism, φ, of E onto $\bar{E}$ such that the map $\varphi'\colon E[x] \to \bar{E}[x]$ defined by $\sum_{i=0}^{r} \alpha_i x^i \mapsto \sum_{i=0}^{r} \varphi(\alpha_i)x^i$ takes $g(x)$ into $\bar{g}(x)$. For, if φ is such an isomorphism, then, by Theorem 3.1, φ extends to an isomorphism of K onto $\bar{K}$, and, by Theorem 5.1, $\mathscr{G}(K/E) \cong \mathscr{G}(\bar{K}/\bar{E}) \cong S_n$, as desired.

Define $\varphi\colon F[t_1,t_2,\ldots,t_n) \to F[\sigma_1,\sigma_2,\ldots,\sigma_n]$ by: $h(t_1,t_2,\ldots,t_n) \mapsto h(\sigma_1,\sigma_2,\ldots,\sigma_n)$. Since $\{t_i\}_{i=1}^{n}$ is a transcendence set over F, φ is a map. It is easy to see that φ is an epimorphism and that $\varphi'(g(x)) = \bar{g}(x)$. We show that φ is, in fact, an isomorphism. By Theorem 1.9, tr.d. $\bar{K}/F =$ tr.d. $\bar{K}/\bar{E} +$ tr.d. $\bar{E}/F$. Since $\bar{K}$ is an algebraic extension of $\bar{E}$, tr.d. $\bar{K}/\bar{E} = 0$, tr.d. $F(\sigma_1,\sigma_2,\ldots,\sigma_n)/F =$ tr.d. $\bar{E}/F =$ tr.d. $\bar{K}/F = n$, and $\{\sigma_i\}_{i=1}^{n}$ is a transcendence set over F. But then $h(\sigma_1,\sigma_2,\ldots,\sigma_n) = 0$ if and only if h is the zero polynomial, whence φ is an isomorphism. φ extends to an isomorphism of the quotient field E of $F[t_1,t_2,\ldots,t_n]$ onto the quotient field $\bar{E}$ of $F[\sigma_1,\sigma_2,\ldots,\sigma_n]$. We have produced an isomorphism of the desired type, and the proof of the theorem is complete. ▌

Since S_n is not solvable if $n > 4$ (Chapter 1, Theorem 6.3), and is solvable if $n \leq 4$, we have the

Corollary. *The generic polynomial* $g(x) = x^n - t_1x^{n-1} + \cdots + (-1)^n t_n \in F(t_1,\ldots,t_n)$, $\{t_i\}_{i=1}^{n}$ *a transcendence set over* F, *is solvable by radicals over* $F(t_1,\ldots,t_n)$ *if and only if* $n \leq 4$. ▌

REMARK. This corollary shows that, for any field F, there exists a polynomial with coefficients in $F(t_1,t_2,\ldots,t_n)$, where $\{t_i\}_{i=1}^{n}$ is a transcendence set over F and $n \geq 5$, which is not solvable by radicals over $F(t_1,t_2,\ldots,t_n)$. It is clear, on the other hand, that every polynomial with real (complex) coefficients is solvable by radicals over the real (complex) field. Thus, the assertion "the generic polynomial over $F(t_1,t_2,\ldots,t_n)$ is not solvable by radicals" does not imply the assertion "there exists a polynomial in $F[x]$ which is not solvable by radicals over F." There do exist, however, polynomials with coefficients in the rational field, **Q**, which are not solvable by radicals. It can be shown, for example, that the Galois group of the splitting field of $x^5 - x - 1$ over $\mathbf{Q}$ is S_5. (Exercise 10.2.) Hence, $x^5 - x - 1$ is not solvable by radicals over $\mathbf{Q}$. This polynomial is "solvable" by elliptic functions.

Exercises

Section 1

1.1. (a) Prove Theorem 1.1.

(b) Let F be a commutative ring with identity $1 \neq 0$. Is the following assertion true? If every nonzero endomorphism of F is a monomorphism, then F is a field.

1.2. Prove Theorem 1.2.

1.3. (a) The identity map is the only automorphism of a prime field.

(b) Give an example of a field which is not a prime field, whose only automorphism is the identity map.

1.4. Let F be a field of characteristic $p > 0$, and let x_1, x_2 be algebraically independent over F. Show that $[F(x_1,x_2)\colon F(x_1^p,x_2^p)] = p^2$. Show that there are infinitely many fields E such that $F(x_1,x_2) \supset E \supset F(x_1^p,x_2^p)$.

1.5. Let E be a field which is finitely generated over F; i.e., there exist $\alpha_1,\alpha_2,\ldots,\alpha_n \in E$ such that $E = F(\alpha_1,\alpha_2,\ldots,\alpha_n)$. If K is a field with $E \supset K \supset F$, then K is finitely generated over F.

1.6. Determine the structure of the additive group of a field F:

(a) if F has characteristic 0,

(b) if F has characteristic p.

Section 2

2.1. The complex field $\mathbf{C}$ has infinitely many automorphisms.

2.2. Let F be a subfield of an algebraically closed field C. If tr.d.C/F is finite, then every nonzero F-endomorphism of C is an F-automorphism of C.

Section 3

3.1. Give an example of fields E and F, with $E \supset F$, such that the set of nonzero F-endomorphisms of E is a group (under composition) and such that E is not algebraic over F.

3.2. (a) Find an irreducible polynomial f with coefficients in $\mathbf{Q}$ such that, for any root ρ (in $\mathbf{C}$) of f, $\mathbf{Q}(\rho)$ is not a splitting field for f over $\mathbf{Q}$.

(b) Find an irreducible polynomial f with coefficients in $\mathbf{Q}$ and of degree greater than 2 such that, for any root ρ (in $\mathbf{C}$) of f, $\mathbf{Q}(\rho)$ is a splitting field for $\{f\}$ over $\mathbf{Q}$.

3.3. Let E and F be fields such that $E = F(S)$, where S is a set of elements each of degree 2 over F. Then E is normal over F.

3.4. Consider $i \in \mathbf{C}$ and $\alpha \in \mathbf{R}$, with $i^2 = -1$, $\alpha^4 = 5$, $\alpha > 0$. Show that
(a) $\mathbf{Q}(i\alpha^2)$ is normal over $\mathbf{Q}$.
(b) $\mathbf{Q}((1 + i)\alpha)$ is normal over $\mathbf{Q}(i\alpha^2)$.
(c) $\mathbf{Q}((1 + i)\alpha)$ is not normal over $\mathbf{Q}$.

3.5. Prove Theorem 3.5 and its corollary.

3.6. Prove Theorem 3.6.

Section 4

4.1. Let $\{x_1,x_2\}$ be a transcendence set over a field F of characteristic $p > 2$. Let $E = F(x_1,x_2)$, and let $K = E(\alpha)$, where α is a root of the polynomial $(z^{2p} + x_1z^p + x_2) \in E[z]$. Show that the only elements of K which are purely inseparable over E are the elements of E. Show that K is not separable over E.

4.2. Let $C \supset E_i \supset F$, $i = 1, 2$, be field towers. Let $E_1[E_2]$ be the subring of C generated by E_1 and E_2. Consider $E_1 \otimes_F E_2$ and $E_1[E_2]$ as F-modules, and define the map $\varphi: E_1 \otimes E_2 \to E_1[E_2]$ by $\varphi(\sum_i \alpha_i \otimes \beta_i) = \sum_i \alpha_i\beta_i$ ($\alpha_i \in E_1$, $\beta_i \in E_2$). Then φ is an F-epimorphism. Show that φ is an isomorphism if and only if E_1 is linearly disjoint from E_2 over F.

4.3. Let E and L be fields, each containing a field F as a subfield. Recall (Chapter 3, Exercise 4.7) that $E \otimes_F L$ is a ring. Prove: E is separable over F if and only if for every field $K \supset F$, with $[K: F]$ finite, $E \otimes_F K$ has no nonzero nilpotent elements. (An element r in a ring is nilpotent if $r^n = 0$ for some positive integer n.)

4.4. Let F be a field of characteristic $p > 0$, and let α be an element of an overfield of F. Show that if the polynomial $x^p - \alpha^p$ is reducible over $F(\alpha^p)$, then $\alpha \in F(\alpha^p)$. Conclude that $F(\alpha) \neq F(\alpha^p)$ if and only if $[F(\alpha): F(\alpha^p)] = p$.

4.5. Let E_1 and E_2 be subfields of a field C, and let F be a subfield of E_1 and of E_2. Suppose that E_1 and E_2 are, respectively, quotient fields of domains $D_1 \subset E_1$ and $D_2 \subset E_2$. Show that E_1 and E_2 are linearly disjoint over F if and only if every subset of D_1 which is free over F is free over D_2.

4.6. Let E_1, E_2, and D_1 be as in the preceding exercise. Suppose further that D_1 is a vector space over F. Show that E_1 and E_2 are linearly disjoint over F if and only if every basis for D_1 over F is free over E_2.

4.7. Use Exercise 4.2 and the fact that $(E \otimes_F F_0) \otimes_F K \cong E \otimes_F (F_0 \otimes_F K)$ to prove the lemma preceding Theorem 4.7.

4.8. Prove Theorem 4.10.

4.9. Let $E \supset F$ be an algebraic extension of F, with char $F = p > 0$. Using the fact that E is a purely inseparable extension of E_s, prove that if $[E: E_s]$ is finite, then $[E: E_s]$ is a power of p.

4.10. Let $E \supset K \supset F$ be a tower of fields, with $[E: F]$ finite. Prove that $[E: F]_s = [E: K]_s[K: F]_s$ and that $[E: F]_i = [E: K]_i[K: F]_i$.

4.11. Let F be a field of characteristic $p > 0$, let x be transcendental over F, and let $E = F(x,x^{1/p},x^{1/p^2},\ldots)$. Prove that E is a separable extension of F, but that E does not have a separating transcendence base over F.

4.12. Let $C \supset E \supset F$ be a tower of fields, with C algebraically closed. Let $\bar{F} = \{\alpha \in C \mid \alpha \text{ algebraic over } F\}$. Prove that the following two statements are equivalent:

(a) E is separable over F, and every element of E which is algebraic over F is an element of F.

(b) E and $\bar{F}$ are linearly disjoint over F.

4.13. Let E be a finite extension of a field F, with $E \supset F$. Prove: E is a simple extension of F [i.e., there is an $\alpha \in E$ such that $E = F(\alpha)$] if and only if there are but finitely many fields K such that $E \supset K \supset F$.

Section 5

5.1. Let $E = \mathbf{Q}(\omega\sqrt[3]{2})$ and $K = \mathbf{Q}(\sqrt[3]{2})$. Show that $[E(K){:}\, K]$ does not divide $[E{:}\, \mathbf{Q}]$. Why does this result not contradict the corollary to Theorem 5.4?

5.2. Let E be a splitting field over $\mathbf{Q}$ of the polynomial $(x^3 - 7x + 7) \in \mathbf{Q}[x]$. Find $\mathcal{G}(E/\mathbf{Q})$.

5.3. Prove: E is Galois extension of degree 3 over Q if and only if E is a splitting field of an irreducible polynomial of the form $x^3 - 3(r^2 + 3s^2)x + 2r(r^2 + 3s^2)$ $(r,s \in \mathbf{Q},\ s \neq 0)$.

5.4. Find the Galois group of E over $\mathbf{Q}$, where E is a splitting field over $\mathbf{Q}$ of the polynomial $x^4 - 5x^2 - 10x - 5$.

5.5. Let E be a Galois extension of degree 4 over $\mathbf{Q}$. Then $E = \mathbf{Q}(\alpha)$, where α is a root of a polynomial of the form $x^4 + ax^2 + b$ $(a,b \in \mathbf{Q})$. $\mathcal{G}(E/\mathbf{Q})$ is cyclic if and only if b is not a square in $\mathbf{Q}$.

5.6. (Normal basis theorem.) Let E be a finite Galois extension of F, and let $\mathcal{G}(E/F) = \{\sigma_1,\sigma_2,\ldots,\sigma_n\}$. Then there is an element $\alpha \in E$ such that $\{\sigma_1\alpha,\sigma_2\alpha,\ldots,\sigma_n\alpha\}$ is a basis for E over F.

5.7. Let E be a splitting field over $\mathbf{Q}$ of the polynomial $x^7 - 1$. Show that $\mathbf{Q}(\sqrt{-7})$ is a subfield of E. Find $\mathcal{G}(E/\mathbf{Q}(\sqrt{-7}))$.

5.8. Let F be a finite field, $C \supset F$ an algebraic closure of F, and φ, ψ F-automorphisms of C. Then $\varphi\psi = \psi\varphi$. If $\varphi \neq 1$, then φ has infinite order.

Section 6

6.1. Let E be Galois over F and let $\mathcal{G}(E/F)$ be given the Krull topology (i.e., the topology described in the text). Show that the map $(g_1,g_2) \mapsto g_1g_2^{-1}$ from the Cartesian product $\mathcal{G}(E/F) \times \mathcal{G}(E/F)$ to $\mathcal{G}(E/F)$ is continuous. Show that, in the Krull topology, $\mathcal{G}(E/F)$ is compact and totally disconnected.

6.2. For each prime p, let F_p denote a prime field of characteristic p, and $\bar{F}_p \supset F_p$ an algebraic closure of F_p. Show that for any two primes p_1, p_2, $\mathcal{G}(\bar{F}_{p_1}/F_{p_1}) \cong \mathcal{G}(\bar{F}_{p_2}/F_{p_2})$; in particular, $\mathcal{G}(\bar{F}_{p_1}/F_{p_1})$ is isomorphic to the inverse limit of all finite cyclic groups [i.e., $\mathcal{G}(\bar{F}_{p_1}/F_{p_1}) \cong \varprojlim \mathbf{Z}/(m)$ as (m) ranges over all ideals of $\mathbf{Z}$, ordered by set inclusion].

6.3. Let F be a field and $C \supset F$ an algebraic closure of F. Let H be a cyclic subgroup of $\mathcal{G}(C/F)$ and E the subfield of C fixed by H. Prove: If K is a finite extension of E, then K is Galois over E and $\mathcal{G}(K/E)$ is cyclic.

Section 7

7.1. Let $\zeta \in \mathbf{C}$ be a primitive pth root of unity, p an odd prime. Show that $(\sum_{m=0}^{p-1} \zeta^{m^2})^2 = p^*$, where $p^* = p$ if $p \equiv 1 \bmod 4$ and $p^* = -p$ if $p \equiv 3 \bmod 4$.

7.2. Let $\zeta \in \mathbf{C}$ be a primitive pth root of unity, p a prime of the form $2^k + 1$. Then every element of $\mathbf{Q}(\zeta)$ can be expressed in terms of square roots (i.e., there is a tower of fields $\mathbf{Q} = F_0 \subset F_1 \subset \cdots \subset F_k = \mathbf{Q}(\zeta)$ such that $[F_i : F_{i-1}] = 2$ for $i = 1, 2, \ldots, k$).

7.3. Let n be a positive integer and F a field with Char $F \nmid n$. Show that coefficients of the nth cyclotomic polynomial over F are multiples of the identity of F.

Section 8

8.1. Let F be a finite field, and let $E \supset F$ be a finite extension of F. Show that every element of F is the norm (from E to F) of an element in E; show that every element of F is the trace (from E to F) of an element in E.

8.2. Let E be a separable extension of degree n over a field F. Prove: A set $\{\alpha_1, \alpha_2, \ldots, \alpha_n\}$ of elements of E is a basis for E over F if and only if the determinant of the matrix $(\mathrm{tr}_{E/F}(\alpha_i\alpha_j))$ is not zero.

8.3. Let E and F be as in Exercise 8.2, and let $\sigma_1, \sigma_2, \ldots, \sigma_n$ be the F-monomorphisms of E into an algebraic closure of F. Show that for any set $\alpha_1, \alpha_2, \ldots, \alpha_n$ of elements of E, $\det(\mathrm{tr}_{E/F}(\alpha_i\alpha_j)) = [\det(\sigma_i(\alpha_j))]^2$.

8.4. Find the complete set, $\{(x,y)\}$, of rational solutions of $x^2 + xy + 2y^2 = 11$.

Section 9

9.1. Give an example which shows that, without the assumption that F contains a primitive nth root of unity, the conclusions of Theorem 9.1 do not hold.

9.2. Let F be a field of characteristic $p > 0$, and let $P(F) = \{\gamma^p - \gamma \mid \gamma \in F\}$.

(a) Show that a cyclic extension of F of degree p over F exists if and only if $P(F) \neq F$.

(b) Show that if F admits a cyclic extension of degree p over F, then F admits a cyclic extension of degree p^e over F, $e = 1, 2, 3, \ldots$. [Proceed as follows: Let E be a cyclic extension of degree p^{e-1} over F, and let σ be a generator of $\mathcal{G}(E/F)$. There exist $\alpha, \beta \in E$ such that $\mathrm{tr}_{E/F}(\beta) = 1$, and $\sigma(\alpha) - \alpha = \beta^p - \beta$. The polynomial $x^p - x - \alpha$ is irreducible over E. If ρ is a root of this polynomial, then $F(\rho)$ is a cyclic extension of degree p^e over F.]

9.3. Let C be an algebraically closed field, and let F be a proper subfield of C such that $[C : F]$ is finite. Then $[C : F] = 2$.

Section 10

10.1. (a) A permutation group on p elements, p a prime, which contains an element of order p and a transposition is the full symmetric group S_p.

(b) Let $f \in \mathbf{Q}[x]$ be an irreducible polynomial of prime degree, p. Let E be a splitting field for f over $\mathbf{Q}$. If f has exactly two nonreal roots, then $\mathscr{G}(E/\mathbf{Q}) \simeq S_p$. [Consider $\mathscr{G}(E/\mathbf{Q})$ as a permutation group on the roots of F. Show that $\mathscr{G}(E/\mathbf{Q})$ contains an element of order p, and a transposition.]

(c) Show that $f = 2x^5 - 2x + 1$ is irreducible over $\mathbf{Q}$ and has exactly two nonreal roots. Conclude that the Galois group of a splitting field for f over $\mathbf{Q}$ is isomorphic to S_5.

10.2. (a) Let f be a monic polynomial with integer coefficients, and let $\bar{f}$ be the polynomial obtained by reducing the coefficients of f mod p, p a prime. (Hence $\bar{f} \in \mathbf{Z}/(p)[x]$.) Suppose that $\bar{f}$ has no repeated roots. Let E and $\bar{E}$ be, respectively, splitting fields for f over $\mathbf{Q}$ and f over $\mathbf{Z}/(p)$. Then $\mathscr{G}(E/\mathbf{Z}/(p))$ is isomorphic to a subgroup of $\mathscr{G}(E/\mathbf{Q})$.

(b) The polynomial $f = x^5 - x - 1 \in Z[x]$ is reducible mod 2 $[f \equiv (x^2 + x + 1)(x^5 + x^2 + 1)$ mod 2] and is irreducible mod 3. Conclude that the Galois group, $\mathscr{G}(E/\mathbf{Q})$, of a splitting field for f over $\mathbf{Q}$ (considered as a permutation group on the roots of f) contains an element of order 5 and a transposition. Hence, $\mathscr{G}(E/\mathbf{Q}) \simeq S_5$.

Section 11

11.1. Let G be a finite group. Prove that there exist fields E and F such that E is Galois over F, and $\mathscr{G}(E/F) \simeq G$. (However, it is unknown whether, for every finite group G, there exists a Galois extension of the rational field $\mathbf{Q}$ whose Galois group over $\mathbf{Q}$ is isomorphic to G.)

11.2. Let $\{x_1,x_2,\ldots,x_n,y\}$ be a transcendence set over $\mathbf{Q}$, and let $f(x_1,x_2,\ldots,x_n,y)$ be an irreducible polynomial in $\mathbf{Q}[x_1,x_2,\ldots,x_n,y]$. It is known (Hilbert's irreducibility theorem [21]) that there are infinitely many n-tuples $(a_1,a_2,\ldots,a_n)$ of rational numbers such that $f(a_1,a_2,\ldots,a_n,y)$ is irreducible. It is not known whether the following assertion is true:

(*) Let $E = F(x_1,x_2,\ldots,x_k)$ be a pure transcendental extension of transcendence degree k over F. Let G be a subgroup of the symmetric group S_k, and let K be the subfield of E fixed by G. (Note that each element of S_k, considered as a permutation on the set $\{x_1,x_2,\ldots,x_k\}$, induces an automorphism of E.) Then K is a pure transcendental extension of F.

Use Hilbert's irreducibility theorem to show that if (*) is assumed true, then for every finite group G there exists a Galois extension of $\mathbf{Q}$ whose Galois group over $\mathbf{Q}$ is isomorphic to G.

11.3. Let $E = F(x)$, where x is transcendental over the field. If K is a field with $E \supset K \supset F$, then K is a pure transcendental extension of F.

Chapter 6 / Fields with Real Valuations

1. Real-Valued Valuations; Archimedean and Nonarchimedean Valuations

Mappings of a field to the real field (or more generally to an ordered group), which have properties of the ordinary absolute value on the real field, are of fundamental importance in various aspects of algebraic number theory, the theory of algebraic function fields, and algebraic geometry. We devote this chapter to a study of these mappings and of the fields which admit them. (Some knowledge of the field, **R**, of real numbers and of the exponential and logarithmic functions is presupposed in several of our discussions.)

Definition 1.1. If F is a field, then a (*real-valued*) *valuation of* F is a mapping $|\ |: F \to \mathbf{R}$ from F into the real field $\mathbf{R}$ such that, for all $a,b \in F$,

a. $|a| \geq 0$; $|a| = 0$ if and only if $a = 0$.
b. $|ab| = |a|\,|b|$.
c. $|a + b| \leq |a| + |b|$.

If $|a| = 1$ for each nonzero $a \in F$, then $|\ |$ is the *trivial valuation of* F. ///

Corollary. *If* $|\ |$ *is a valuation of a field F, then*

a. $|-1| = |1| = 1$.
b. $|\zeta| = 1$ *if* ζ *is a root of unity in F.*
c. $|-a| = a$ *for all* $a \in F$.
d. $|1/a| = 1/|a|$ *for all* $a \neq 0 \in F$.

Examples.

1. Let $p > 0$ be a prime in $\mathbf{Z}$. From the Fundamental Theorem of Arithmetic, it follows that each rational number $r \neq 0$ can be expressed uniquely as $p^e r'$, where $e \in \mathbf{Z}$ and $r' = s/t \in \mathbf{Q}$ with $(s,p) = (t,p) = 1$. Define a map $|\ |_p: \mathbf{Q} \to \mathbf{R}$ as follows: $|\ |_p(0) = 0$, and $|\ |_p(r) = 1/p^e$ if $r = p^e r'$. Then $|\ |_p$ is a valuation on $\mathbf{Q}$. For each prime $p > 0$ in $\mathbf{Z}$, the valuation defined in this way is called the p-adic valuation on $\mathbf{Q}$. (Note that, the "more highly" an element of $\mathbf{Z}$ is divisible by a prime p, the "closer" it is to zero in the p-adic valuation.)

In exactly the same way, a p-adic valuation may be defined on the quotient field, F, of an arbitrary principal ideal domain, D, with respect to any prime element $p \in D$.

2. In Chapter 7 we consider a class of integral domains, D, with the property:

(*) Every proper ideal in D may be represented uniquely as a product of prime ideals.

(*Note:* In a commutative ring with identity, the product, HK, of subsets H and K is the set $\{\sum_{i=1}^{m} h_i k_i | h_i \in H, k_i \in K, m \in \mathbf{N}'\}$.) The class of all integral domains with property (*) includes, but is much wider than, the class of all Gaussian domains. Let D be an integral domain satisfying (*) and let $F \supset D$ be a quotient field of D. If $\mathfrak{p}$ is a prime ideal in D, and $r = h/k \neq 0$ in F $(h,k \in D)$, then $(k)Dr = (h)$, where Dr is the D-submodule of F generated by r. Since D satisfies (*), there are integers $e_1,e_2 \geq 0$ and ideals H_1, H_2 in D such that $\mathfrak{p} \nmid H_1$, $\mathfrak{p} \nmid H_2$, and $\mathfrak{p}^{e_1} H_1 Dr = \mathfrak{p}^{e_2} H_2$. Let $e = e_2 - e_1$. Then e is uniquely determined for each $r \neq 0 \in F$. We can now define a map $|\ |_{\mathfrak{p}}: F \to \mathbf{R}$ as follows:

$$|\ |_{\mathfrak{p}}(0) = 0,$$

$$|\ |_{\mathfrak{p}}(r) = 1/c^e \qquad (r \neq 0)$$

where c is a real number greater than 1.

The map $|\ |_p$ is a valuation, called the $\mathfrak{p}$-adic valuation, on F.

3. Let $F[x]$ be a polynomial domain over F. Then $F[x]$ is a principal ideal domain, and its quotient field, $F(x)$, admits valuations of the type

discussed in Example 1. We look at a concrete illustration. Let $a \in F$. Then $x - a$ is irreducible over F (hence prime) and generates a prime ideal in $F[x]$. If $f(x) \in F(x)$, then there exist polynomials $g(x)$, $h(x) \in F[x]$ each relatively prime to $x - a$, and an integer e such that $f(x) = [g(x)/h(x)] \times (x - a)^e$. In the $(x - a)$-adic valuation, $|\ |_a$, of $F(x)$, $|f(x)|_a = 1/c^e$ (c a real number greater than 1). Note that if $|f(x)|_a = 1/c^e < 1$, then $f(x)$ has a zero of order e (i.e., multiplicity e) at a, and if $|f(x)|_a = 1/c^e > 1$, then $f(x)$ has a pole of order e at a. $F(x)$ admits a valuation which can be used to describe the behavior of each $f(x) \in F(x)$ at infinity. In particular, let c be a real number greater than 1. If $0 \neq f(x) \in F(x)$, then $f(x) = g(x)/h(x)$ with $g(x),h(x) \in F[x]$. Define $|f(x)|_\infty = 1/c^{[\deg h - \deg g]}$, and $|0|_\infty = 0$. Then $|\ |_\infty$ is a valuation of $F(x)$. If $|f(x)|_\infty = 1/c^e < 1$, then $f(x)$ has a zero of order e at infinity; if $|f(x)|_\infty = 1/c^e > 1$, then $f(x)$ has a pole of order e at infinity.

REMARK. If $|\ |$ is a valuation of F, then the map $d: F \times F \to R$ defined by $d(a,b) = |a - b|$ is a metric on F, and F is a metric space. Thus every valuation of F induces a topology on F.

Definition 2.1. Two valuations, $|\ |_1$ and $|\ |_2$, of a field F are *equivalent* if they induce the same topology on F, i.e., if every set which is open in the topology defined by $|\ |_1$ is open in the topology defined by $|\ |_2$, and conversely. ///

Theorem 1.1. *Let $|\ |_1$ and $|\ |_2$ be two valuations of a field F. Then the following statements are equivalent.*

a. *The valuations $|\ |_1$ and $|\ |_2$ are equivalent.*
b. *For $a \in F$, $|a|_1 < 1$ if and only if $|a|_2 < 1$.*
c. *There exists a positive real number, t, such that for all $a \in F$, $|a|_2 = |a|_1^t$.*

PROOF.

a $\Rightarrow$ b. We assume that $|\ |_1$ and $|\ |_2$ define the same topology on F. Let a be an element of F such that $|a|_1 < 1$. Let $U = \{x \in F \mid |x|_2 < 1\}$. Clearly U is an open set in the topology induced by $|\ |_2$, hence U is an open set in the topology induced by $|\ |_1$. Since $|a|_1 < 1$ and $|a^n|_1 = |a|_1^n$, $\lim_{n \to +\infty} a^n = 0$ in the topology defined by $|\ |_1$. But $0 \in U$ and U is open, whence there exists a positive integer k such that $a^k \in U$. It follows that $|a^k|_2 < 1$ and $|a|_2 < 1$, as desired. A completely symmetrical argument proves that if $|a|_2 < 1$, then $|a|_1 < 1$.

b $\Rightarrow$ c. We assume that $|a|_1 < 1$ if and only if $|a|_2 < 1$. Then $|a|_1 > 1$ if and only if $|a|_2 > 1$. Hence $|a|_1 = 1$ if and only if $|a|_2 = 1$. If either one of the valuations $|\ |_1$ or $|\ |_2$ is trivial, then so is the other. We may therefore assume that $| \ |_1$ is not trivial. Then there exists $b \in F$ such that $|b|_1 > 1$, and hence also $|b|_2 > 1$. Let $a \in F$. There exists a real number s such that $|a|_1 = |b|_1^s$. Now if $m/n > s$ with $m,n \in \mathbf{Z}$, $n > 0$, then $|a|_1 < |b|_1^{m/n}$, $|a^n/b^m|_1 < 1$, $|a^n/b^m|_2 < 1$, and $|a|_2 < |b|_2^{m/n}$. Similarly, if $m/n < s$ with $m,n \in \mathbf{Z}$, $n > 0$, then $|a|_2 > |b|_2^{m/n}$. We conclude that $|a|_2 = |b|_2^s = |b|_1^{(s \log |b|_2)/\log |b|_1} = |a|_1^{\log |b|_2/\log |b|_1}$. Since $\log|b|_2/\log|b|_1 > 0$, c holds with $t = \log|b|_2/\log|b|_1$.

c $\Rightarrow$ a. If, for some positive real number t and for all $a \in F$, $|a|_2 = |a|_1^t$, then the distance between any two points of F in the metric defined by $| \ |_2$ is a positive power of the distance between these points in the metric defined by $| \ |_1$. It follows that a subset of F is open in the $| \ |_2$-topology if and only if it is open in the $| \ |_1$-topology. But then $| \ |_1$ and $| \ |_2$ define the same topology on F, whence $| \ |_1$ and $| \ |_2$ are equivalent. ∎

Corollary 1. *If a valuation $| \ |$ is equivalent to the trivial valuation, then $| \ |$ is the trivial valuation.* □

Corollary 2. *Let $| \ |_1$ and $| \ |_2$ be equivalent valuations of a field E. Let F be a subfield of E. If $| \ |_1$ is nontrivial on F and if $|a|_1 = |a|_2$ for all $a \in F$, then $|a|_1 = |a|_2$ for all $a \in E$.*

PROOF. Since $| \ |_1$ and $| \ |_2$ are equivalent valuations of E, there exists $t > 0$ such that $|a|_2 = |a|_1^t$ for all $a \in E$. Since $| \ |_1$ is nontrivial on F, there exist $a_0 \in F$ such that $0 < |a_0|_1 < 1$. But then $0 < |a_0|_1^t = |a_0|_2 = |a_0|_1 < 1$, $t = 1$, and $|a|_1 = |a|_2$ for all $a \in E$. ∎

Corollary 3. *Let $| \ |_1$ and $| \ |_2$ be valuations of a field F, with $| \ |_1$ nontrivial. Then $| \ |_1$ and $| \ |_2$ are equivalent if and only if*

$$|a|_1 < 1 \Rightarrow |a|_2 < 1 \qquad (a \in F).$$

PROOF. The necessity of the condition is clear. We prove the condition sufficient. Assume that if $a \in F$ and $|a|_1 < 1$, then $|a|_2 < 1$. We show that if $a \in F$ and $|a|_2 < 1$ then $|a|_1 < 1$. Suppose that, on the contrary, there exists $b \in F$ such that $|b|_2 < 1$ and $|b|_1 \geq 1$. Then $|1/b|_1 \leq 1$. Since $| \ |_1$ is nontrivial on F, there exists $c \in F$ with $0 < |c|_1 < 1$. But then, for every positive integer n, $|c/b^n|_1 < 1$, $|c/b^n|_2 < 1$, and $0 < |c|_2 < |b|_2^n$. Since $\lim_{n \to +\infty} |b|_2^n = 0$, we have a contradiction. The corollary now follows from the theorem. ∎

Definition 1.3. Let $| \ |$ be a valuation of a field F. The valuation $| \ |$ is *archimedean* if for each pair $a,b \in F$, $b \neq 0$, there exists an integer n such that $|a| < |nb|$. The valuation $| \ |$ is *non-archimedean* if it is not archimedean, i.e., if there exists a pair $a,b \in F$, $b \neq 0$ such that $|nb| \leq |a|$ for all $n \in \mathbf{Z}$. ///

Theorem 1.2. *Let* $|\ |$ *be a valuation of a field F. Then the following statements are equivalent:*

a. $|\ |$ *is non-archimedean.*

b. *The set of real numbers* $\{|n1_F|\}_{n\in\mathbf{Z}}$ *is bounded.*

c. *For all* $a,b \in F$, $|a + b| \leq \max\{|a|,|b|\}$.

d. *For all* $n \in \mathbf{Z}$, $|n1_F| \leq 1$.

PROOF.

a $\Rightarrow$ b. If $|\ |$ is non-archimedean, then there exist $a,b \in F$, $b \neq 0$, such that $|nb| \leq |a|$ for all $n \in \mathbf{Z}$. But then $|n1_F| \leq |a/b|$ for all $n \in \mathbf{Z}$.

b $\Rightarrow$ c. Suppose that there exists a positive real number M such that $|n1_F| \leq M$ for all $n \in \mathbf{Z}$. Then for $n \in \mathbf{Z}$, $n > 0$, and for $a,b \in F$,

$$|a + b|^n = |(a + b)^n| = \left|\sum_{i=0}^{n} \binom{n}{i} a^{n-i}b^i\right| \leq \sum_{i=0}^{n} \left|\binom{n}{i} 1_F\right| |a^{n-i}|\ |b^i|$$

$$\leq M\left(\sum_{i=0}^{n} |a|^{n-i}|b|^i\right) \leq M(n + 1)[\max\{|a|,|b|\}]^n.$$

Hence, for all $n \in \mathbf{Z}$, $n > 0$, and for all $a,b \in F$,

$$|a + b| \leq [M(n + 1)]^{1/n} \max\{|a|,|b|\}.$$

Since

$$\lim_{n\to+\infty} [M(n + 1)]^{1/n} = 1, \qquad |a + b| \leq \max\{|a|,|b|\}$$

for all $a,b \in F$.

c $\Rightarrow$ d. If for all $a,b \in F$, $|a + b| \leq \max\{|a|,|b|\}$ then $|2 \cdot 1_F| = |1_F + 1_F| \leq \max\{|1_F|,|1_F|\} = 1$, and an induction argument proves $|n1_F| \leq 1$ for all $n \in \mathbf{Z}$, $n > 0$. Since $|-n1_F| = |n1_F|$, $|n1_F| \leq 1$ for all $n \in \mathbf{Z}$.

d $\Rightarrow$ a. If, for all $n \in \mathbf{Z}$, $|n \cdot 1_F| \leq 1$, then a holds with $a = b = 1_F$. ▌

Corollary 1. *Every valuation of a field of characteristic not equal to* 0 *is non-archimedean.*

PROOF. The prime field, and hence also the set $\{|n1_F|\}_{n\in\mathbf{Z}}$, of a field of characteristic not zero is finite, and every finite set of real numbers is bounded. ▌

Corollary 2. *Let E be a field and F a subfield of E. A valuation* $|\ |$ *of E is (non-)archimedean if and only if the valuation induced by* $|\ |$ *on F is (non-) archimedean.* □

Theorem 1.3. *Let $|\ |$ be a non-archimedean valuation of a field F. If $a_1, a_2, \ldots, a_n$ are elements of F such that $|a_i| < |a_1|$ for $i = 2, 3, \ldots, n$, then $|a_1 + a_2 + \cdots + a_n| = |a_1|$.*

PROOF. We show that if $|a_2| < |a_1|$, then $|a_1 + a_2| = |a_1|$. In fact,

$$|a_1| = |a_1 + a_2 - a_2| \le \max\{|a_1 + a_2|, |a_2|\}.$$

Since $|a_2| < |a_1|$,

$$\max\{|a_1 + a_2|, |a_2|\} = |a_1 + a_2|.$$

Hence

$$|a_1| \le \max\{|a_1 + a_2|, |a_2|\} = |a_1 + a_2| \le \max\{|a_1|, |a_2|\} = |a_1|,$$

and therefore $|a_1| = |a_1 + a_2|$. The proof of the theorem may be completed by an induction argument. ▮

Corollary. *Let F be a subfield of a field E and let $|\ |$ be a valuation of E. If E is algebraic over F and if $|\ |$ induces the trivial valuation on F, then $|\ |$ is trivial on E.*

PROOF. Suppose that E is algebraic over F, that $|\ |$ is trivial on F but nontrivial on E. Then there exists an $\alpha \in E$ such that $|\alpha| > 1$. Since E is algebraic over F, there exist a positive integer n and $a_1, a_2, \ldots, a_n \in F$ such that $\alpha^n + a_1\alpha^{n-1} + \cdots + a_{n-1}\alpha + a_n = 0$. Since $|\ |$ is trivial on F, it is non-archimedean (Theorem 1.2, Corollary 2). But $|a_{n-i}\alpha^i| = |a_{n-i}|\,|\alpha^i| < |\alpha^n|$ for $i = 0, 1, 2, \ldots, n - 1$, whence $0 = |0| = |\alpha^n + a_1\alpha^{n-1} + \cdots + a_n| = |\alpha^n| > 1$. Contradiction! ▮

Examples. If p and q are distinct primes of $\mathbf{Z}$, then the p-adic and q-adic valuations of $\mathbf{Q}$ are not equivalent. In fact, $|p|_p = 1/p < 1$, whereas $|q|_p = 1$.

The p-adic valuation of $\mathbf{Q}$ is non-archimedean. For, if $n \in \mathbf{Z}$, then there exist $e, m \in \mathbf{Z}$ such that $(m,p) = 1$ and $n = p^e m$. But then $|n|_p = 1/p^e \le 1$, hence $|\ |_p$ is bounded on $\mathbf{Z}$, and $|\ |_p$ is non-archimedean.

The ordinary absolute value on $\mathbf{Q}$, defined by $|r|_\infty = r$ if $r \ge 0$ and $|r|_\infty = -r$ if $r < 0$, is archimedean.

Theorem 1.4. *Let $|\ |$ be a valuation of the rational field $\mathbf{Q}$. If $|\ |$ is non-archimedean and nontrivial, then for some prime $p \in \mathbf{Z}$, $|\ |$ is equivalent to the p-adic valuation, $|\ |_p$, of $\mathbf{Q}$. If $|\ |$ is archimedean, then $|\ |$ is equivalent to the ordinary absolute value, $|\ |_\infty$, of $\mathbf{Q}$.*

PROOF. Suppose $| \ |$ is non-archimedean and nontrivial. Then $|m| \leq 1$, $|m + n| \leq \max\{|m|,|n|\}$ for all $m,n \in \mathbf{Z}$ (Theorem 1.2), and $I = \{n \in \mathbf{Z} \mid |n| < 1\}$ is a proper ideal of $\mathbf{Z}$. In fact, I is a prime ideal. For, if $m,n \in \mathbf{Z}$, $m,n \notin I$, then $|m| = 1$, $|n| = 1$, $|mn| = |m|\,|n| = 1$, and $mn \notin I$. Hence, there is a positive prime, p, such that $I = (p)$. If $n \in \mathbf{Z}$ and $n = p^e m$ with $(p,m) = 1$, then $|m| = 1$, and $|n| = |p|^e = [p^{-e}]^{-\log|p|/\log p} = |n|_p^t$ with $t = -\log|p|/\log p > 0$. But then, $| \ |$ is equivalent to the p-adic valuation, $| \ |_p$, of $\mathbf{Q}$.

Before treating the case that $| \ |$ is archimedean, we derive an inequality. Let m, n be integers greater than 1. Then there exist integers $k, a_1, a_2, \ldots, a_k$ with $k \geq 0$, $0 \leq a_i < n$, and $n^k \leq m$ such that $m = \sum_{i=0}^{k} a_i n^i$. Since $|a_i| = |1 + \cdots + 1| \leq a_i < n$, $|m| \leq \sum_{i=0}^{k} |a_i|\,|n|^i \leq \sum_{i=0}^{k} n|n|^i \leq n(k + 1) \times [\max\{1,|n|\}]^k$. Since $n^k \leq m$, $k \leq \log m/\log n$, and hence

$$|m| \leq n((\log m/\log n) + 1)[\max\{1,|n|\}]^{\log m/\log n}.$$

For any positive integer s, we may replace m in the last inequality by m^s and obtain

$$(*) \qquad \left(\frac{|m|}{[\max\{1,|n|\}]^{\log m/\log n}}\right)^s \leq s\,\frac{n \log m}{\log n} + n.$$

Since, for $a > 1$ and any real b, c and sufficiently large s, $a^s > sb + c$, we conclude that the left-hand side of (*) is less than or equal to 1, hence

$$(\dagger) \quad |m| \leq [\max\{1,|n|\}]^{\log m/\log n}, \qquad m,n > 1, \quad m,n \in \mathbf{Z}.$$

Suppose now that $| \ |$ is archimedean. Then there exists a positive integer m such that $|m| > 1$. It follows from the inequality (†) that, for all positive integers n ($n \neq 1$), $|n| > 1$. But then, for all positive integers $m,n > 1$, $|m| \leq |n|^{\log m/\log n}$, $|m|^{1/\log m} \leq |n|^{1/\log n}$, whence $|m|^{1/\log m} = |n|^{1/\log n}$ is a constant, e^{t_0}, independent of m and n, and $|m| = e^{t_0 \log m} = m^{t_0} = |m|_\infty^{t_0}$. Note that $1 < |2| = 2^{t_0} \leq |1| + |1| = 2$, hence $0 < t_0 \leq 1$. Since $| \ |$ is completely determined on $\mathbf{Q}$ by the values it takes on the positive integers, $| \ |$ and $| \ |_\infty^{t_0}$ coincide on $\mathbf{Q}$, whence $| \ |$ is equivalent to the ordinary absolute value. ∎

2. Approximation Theorems

The reader may recall having encountered the following theorem from elementary number theory, the so-called Chinese Remainder Theorem: If $a_i \in \mathbf{Z}$, and $p_i^{e_i}$ are powers of distinct primes, $i = 1, 2, \ldots, n$, then there is an integer x such that $x \equiv a_i \bmod p_i^{e_i}$ for $i = 1, 2, \ldots, n$. Since $p_i^{e_i} | x - a_i$ if and only if $|x - a_i|_{p_i} \leq 1/p_i^{e_i}$, where $| \ |_{p_i}$ is the p_i-adic valuation on $\mathbf{Q}$, the Chinese Remainder Theorem may be restated as follows: If $a_i \in \mathbf{Z}$, and $| \ |_{p_i}$ are nonequivalent nonarchimedean, and nontrivial valuations of $\mathbf{Q}$, $i = 1, 2, \ldots, n$, then for each $\varepsilon > 0$ there is an integer x such that $|x - a_i|_{p_i} < \varepsilon$ for $i = 1, 2, \ldots, n$. In this section we prove similar approximation theorems for valuations of an arbitrary field. We remark that Theorem 2.1, when applied to the rational field $\mathbf{Q}$, is, in one respect, weaker than the Chinese Remainder Theorem, since the approximation is accomplished by an $x \in \mathbf{Q}$ (and not necessarily by $x \in \mathbf{Z}$); in another respect, however, the theorem is stronger, for approximation in the archimedean valuation is allowed. In Theorem 2.2 we restrict ourselves to non-archimedean valuations satisfying certain conditions; when applied to the rational field and the set of its p-adic valuations, the approximation, in this case, is by an element of $\mathbf{Z}$.

We shall use the following

Lemma. *Let $\{| \ |_i\}_{i=1}^n$ be a set of nonequivalent nontrivial valuations of a field F. Then there exists an $a \in F$ such that $|a|_1 > 1$ and $|a|_j < 1$ for $j = 2, \ldots, n$.*

PROOF. Since $| \ |_1$ is nontrivial, the lemma is true for $n = 1$. The lemma is true for $n = 2$: If $| \ |_1$ and $| \ |_2$ are nontrivial and inequivalent, then there is a $b \subset F$ such that $|b|_1 < 1$, $|b|_2 \geq 1$, and there is a $c \in F$ such that $|c|_1 \geq 1$, $|c|_2 < 1$ (Theorem 1.1, Corollary 3). But then $|c/b|_1 > 1$ and $|c/b|_2 < 1$, whence $a = c/b$ satisfies the requirements of the lemma. Suppose the lemma is true for $n < k$, and let $\{| \ |_i\}_{i=1}^k$ be a set of inequivalent nontrivial valuations of F. By the induction assumption, there is a $b \in F$ such that $|b|_1 > 1$ and $|b|_j < 1$ for $j = 2, 3, \ldots, k - 1$. Since the lemma is true for $n = 2$, there is a $c \in F$ such that $|c|_1 > 1$ and $|c|_k < 1$. If $|b|_k \leq 1$, then, for m a sufficiently large positive integer, $|b^m c|_1 > 1$ and $|b^m c|_j < 1$ for $j = 2, 3, \ldots, k$, whence $a = b^m c$ has the desired properties. If $|b|_k > 1$, then

$$\lim_{\substack{m \to +\infty \\ m \in \mathbf{Z}}} \left| \frac{b^m c}{1 + b^m} \right|_i = \begin{cases} |c|_i & \text{for } i = 1, k, \\ 0 & \text{for } i = 2, 3, \ldots, k - 1, \end{cases}$$

whence $a = b^m c/1 + b^m$ with m a sufficiently large integer satisfies the requirements of the lemma. The lemma follows by induction. ∎

Theorem 2.1. (Weak Approximation Theorem.) *Let $\{| \ |_i\}_{i=1}^n$ be a set of nonequivalent and nontrivial valuations of a field F, and let $\{a_i\}_{i=1}^n$ be a family of elements of F. For each real $\varepsilon > 0$ there exists an $a \in F$ such that $|a - a_i|_i < \varepsilon$ for $i = 1, 2, \ldots, n$.*

PROOF. By the lemma, for each $i = 1, 2, \ldots, n$ there exists a $b_i \in F$ such that $|b_i|_i > 1$ and $|b_i|_j < 1$ for $j \neq i$. Note that

$$\lim_{\substack{m \to +\infty \\ m \in \mathbf{Z}}} \left| \frac{a_i b_i^m}{1 + b_i^m} - a_i \right|_i = 0$$

and that for $j \neq i$,

$$\lim_{\substack{m \to +\infty \\ m \in \mathbf{Z}}} \left| \frac{a_i b_i^m}{1 + b_i^m} \right|_j = 0.$$

But then $a = \sum_{i=1}^{n} a_i b_i^m/(1 + b_i^m)$, with m a sufficiently large integer, satisfies the inequalities in the theorem. ▮

Before proceeding to the next theorem we note two properties enjoyed by the p-adic valuations of the rational field. First, if $r \in \mathbf{Q}$, $r \neq 0$, then $|r|_p = 1$ for all but finitely many positive primes p in $\mathbf{Z}$. For, there are primes p_i and integers e_i and k ($k \geq 0$) such that $r = \pm p_1^{e_1} p_2^{e_2} \cdots p_k^{e_k}$. Hence, $|r|_p = 1$ if p is different from p_i for each $i = 1, \ldots, k$. Second, if p_1, p_2 are distinct positive primes in $\mathbf{Z}$, then, for each real $\varepsilon > 0$, there exists an $r \in \mathbf{Q}$ such that $|r - 1|_{p_1} < \varepsilon$, $|r|_{p_2} < \varepsilon$ and $|r|_p \leq 1$ for all primes $p \neq p_1, p_2$. (In fact, let e be a positive integer greater than $-(\log \varepsilon/\log p_i)$, $i = 1, 2$. There exist integers a, b such that $ap_1^e + bp_2^e = 1$. Then $r = 1 - ap_1^e$ satisfies the indicated inequalities.) Since $\mathbf{Z} = \{r \in \mathbf{Q} \mid |r|_p \leq 1 \text{ for all primes } p\}$, and since $|r - 1|_{p_1} < 1$ implies $|r|_{p_1} = 1$ (Theorem 1.3), the second property may be formulated as follows: For any two distinct primes $p_1, p_2 \in \mathbf{Z}$ there is an *integer* which is arbitrarily close to 1 in the p_1-adic topology and arbitrarily close to 0 in the p_2-adic topology.

We use the phrase "for almost all $i \in J$" to mean "for all but finitely many $i \in J$."

Theorem 2.2. (Strong Approximation Theorem.) *Let $\{| \ |_j\}_{j \in J}$ be a nonvoid set of inequivalent, nonarchimedean, and nontrivial valuations of a field F with the following properties:*

a. *For each nonzero $a \in F$, $|a|_j = 1$ for almost all $j \in J$.*
b. *If j_1, j_2 are distinct elements of J, then for each real $\varepsilon > 0$ there exists an $a \in F$ such that $|a - 1|_{j_1} < \varepsilon$, $|a|_{j_2} < \varepsilon$, and $|a|_j \leq 1$ for $j \in J - \{j_1, j_2\}$.*

Let I be a finite subset of J and $\{a_i\}_{i \in I}$ a family of elements of F. Then, for each real $\varepsilon > 0$ there exists an $a \in F$ such that $|a - a_i|_i < \varepsilon$ for all $i \in I$, and $|a|_j \leq 1$ for all $j \in J - I$.

PROOF. We assume, without loss of generality, that $0 < \varepsilon \leq 1$. We may also assume that I contains at least two elements. For, if I is the null set, the conclusion of the theorem holds with $a = 0$. If I consists of one element, say $I = \{i_1\}$, and $I = J$, then the theorem holds with $a = a_i$. If $I = \{i_1\}$, and $I \neq J$, choose $i_2 \in J - I$, let $I_0 = \{i_1, i_2\}$, and let $a_{i_2} = 0$; if the theorem holds for I_0, it obviously holds for I. We therefore assume that I has at least two elements.

Let $I' = \{j \in J - I \mid |a_i|_j > 1$ for at least one $i \in I\}$. Since $\{|\ |_j\}_{j \in J}$ satisfies condition a and I is a finite set, I' is finite. For each $i \in I'$, let $a_i = 0$. Finally, let $I_1 = I \cup I'$. Note that I_1 is finite and contains at least two elements. Clearly, $|a_i|_j \leq 1$ for all $i \in I_1$ and all $j \in J - I_1$. The theorem will follow as soon as we show that, given ε, $1 \geq \varepsilon > 0$, there exists an $a \in F$ such that $|a - a_i|_i < \varepsilon$ for all $i \in I_1$, and $|a|_j \leq 1$ for all $j \in J - I_1$.

Let ε be given, with $0 < \varepsilon \leq 1$. Let $M = \max_{i \in I_1}\{|a_i|_i\}$. We show that, for each $k \in I_1$, there is a $b_k \in F$ which is close to 1 in $|\ |_k$, is close to 0 in $|\ |_{k'}$, for $k' \in I_1 - \{k\}$, and has value less than or equal to 1 in $|\ |_j$ for $j \in J$. In particular, suppose $k \in I_1$. Since $\{|\ |_j\}_{j \in J}$ satisfies conditions b, there exists for each $k' \in I_1 - \{k\}$ a $b_{kk'} \in F$ such that $|b_{kk'} - 1|_k < \varepsilon/(M + 1)$, $|b_{kk'}|_{k'} < \varepsilon/(M + 1)$, and $|b_{kk'}|_j \leq 1$ for $j \in J - \{k,k'\}$. Let $b_k = \prod_{k' \in I_1 - \{k\}} b_{kk'}$. Then $|b_k - 1|_k < \varepsilon/(M + 1)$, $|b_k|_{k'} < \varepsilon/(M + 1)$ for all $k' \in I_1 - \{k\}$, and $|b_k|_j \leq 1$ for all $j \in J$. The element $a = \sum_{k \in I_1} a_k b_k$ satisfies the indicated inequalities. Indeed, for $i \in I_1$,

$$|a - a_i|_i = \left| \sum_{k \in I_1 - \{i\}} a_k b_k + a_i(b_i - 1) \right|_i \leq \max_{k \in I_1 - \{i\}} \{|a_k|_i |b_k|_i, |a_i|_i |b_i - 1|_i\}$$

$$< M \cdot \frac{\varepsilon}{M + 1} < \varepsilon,$$

and, for $j \in J - I_1$,

$$|a|_j = \left| \sum_{k \in I_1} a_k b_k \right|_j \leq \max_{k \in I_1} \{|a_k|_j |b_k|_j\} \leq 1. \quad \blacksquare$$

Corollary 1. *Let $\{|\ |_j\}_{j \in J}$ and I be as in the theorem. Let $\{a_j\}_{j \in J}$ be a family of elements of F such that $|a_j|_j = 1$ for almost all $j \in J$. Then there exists an $a \in F$ such that $|a| = |a_i|_i$ for $i \in I$, and $|a|_j \leq |a_j|_j$ for $j \in J - I$.*

PROOF. Let $I' = \{j \in J - I \mid |a_j|_j \neq 1\}$ and $I_1 = I \cup I'$. Then I_1 is a finite set, and $|a_j|_j - 1$ for all $j \in J - I_1$. Let $\varepsilon = \min_{i \in I_1} \{|a_i|_i\}$. By the theorem, there exists an $a \in F$ such that $|a - a_i|_i < \varepsilon \leq |a_i|_i$ for $i \in I_1$, and $|a|_j \leq 1 = |a_j|_j$ for $j \in J - I_1$. But then (Theorem 1.3) $|a|_i = |a_i|_i$ for $i \in I_1$ and $|a|_j \leq |a_j|_j$ for $j \in J - I_1$. $\blacksquare$

Corollary 2. *Let $\{|\ |_j\}_{j\in J}$ be as in the theorem. Let $\mathcal{O} = \{a \in F \mid |a|_j \leq 1$ for all $j \in J\}$. Then $\mathcal{O}$ is a proper subring of F, and F is a quotient field of $\mathcal{O}$.*

PROOF. Since $|ab|_j = |a|_j|b|_j$ and $|a+b|_j \leq \max\{|a|_j,|b|_j\}$ for $a,b \in F$, $j \in J$, $\mathcal{O}$ is a subring of F. Let j_0 be an element of J. Since $|\ |_{j_0}$ is nontrivial, there is an $a \in F$ such that $|a|_{j_0} > 1$. But then $a \notin \mathcal{O}$, and $\mathcal{O}$ is a proper subring of F.

Let $b \in F$, and $I = \{j \in J \mid |b|_j > 1\}$. Then I is a finite set. By Corollary 1, there is an $a \in F$ such that $|a|_i = |1/b|_i$ for $i \in I$ and $|a|_j \leq |1|_j = 1$ for $j \in J - I$. But then both ab and a are elements of $\mathcal{O}$ and $b = ab/a$, whence F is a quotient field of $\mathcal{O}$. ∎

3. Completion of a Field with a Valuation; Prime Spots

All the topological concepts required in this and the next sections are discussed in [8] or [17] (see the Bibliography). We assume that the reader is familiar with these ideas.

Definition 3.1. Let $|\ |$ be a valuation of a field F. A *completion of F under* $|\ |$ is a triple $\langle \hat{F}, |\ |^\wedge, \varphi\rangle$, where $\hat{F}$ is a field, $|\ |^\wedge$ a valuation of $\hat{F}$, and φ a monomorphism $F \to \hat{F}$, such that

a. In the metric induced by $|\ |^\wedge$ on F, every Cauchy sequence of elements of $\hat{F}$ converges to an element in $\hat{F}$.

b. $|\varphi(a)|^\wedge = |a|$ for each $a \in F$.

c. $\varphi(F)$ is dense in $\hat{F}$ (in the topology induced by $|\ |^\wedge$).

F is *complete under* $|\ |$ if $\langle F, |\ |, \iota_F\rangle$, with ι_F the identity map on F, is a completion of F under $|\ |$. ///

Corollary 1. *If $|\ |$ is the trivial valuation of a field F, then F is complete under $|\ |$.* □

Corollary 2. *If $\langle \hat{F}, |\ |^\wedge, \varphi\rangle$ is a completion of F under $|\ |$, then $\hat{F}$ is complete under $|\ |^\wedge$.* □

Theorem 3.1. *Let $|\ |$ be a valuation of a field F.*

a. *There exists a completion of F under $|\ |$.*

b. *If $\langle \hat{F}, |\ |^\wedge, \varphi\rangle$ and $\langle F', |\ |', \varphi'\rangle$ are completions of F under $|\ |$, then there exists a unique isomorphism $\psi: \hat{F} \to F'$ such that $\psi\varphi = \varphi'$, and $|\psi(\hat{a})|' = |\hat{a}|^\wedge$ for each $\hat{a} \in \hat{F}$. [The map ψ is, then, simultaneously an algebraic isomorphism of the field $\hat{F}$ onto the field F' and a topological isomorphism (homeomorphism) of the topological space $\hat{F}$ onto the topological space F'.]*

c. *Equivalent valuations give rise to (algebraically and topologically) isomorphic completions. Specifically, if* $|\ |$ *and* $|\ |_1$ *are equivalent valuations of F, and if* $\langle \hat{F}, |\ |^{\wedge}, \varphi\rangle$ *and* $\langle \hat{F}_1, |\ |^{\wedge}_1, \varphi_1\rangle$ *are completions of F under* $|\ |$ *and* $|\ |_1$*, respectively, then there exists a unique isomorphism* $\psi: \hat{F} \to \hat{F}_1$ *such that* $\psi\varphi = \varphi_1$*, and such that* $|\ |^{\wedge}$ *is equivalent to the valuation,* $|\ |'$*, of* $\hat{F}$ *defined by* $|\hat{a}|' = |\psi(\hat{a})|^{\wedge}_1$ *for each* $\hat{a} \in F$.

PROOF.

a. We could give a proof of the existence of a completion of F under $|\ |$ by taking the existence of a completion of a metric space as known, and using the fact that the mappings from $F \times F$ to F and from $F^* \times F^*$ to F^* defined by $(a,b) \mapsto a - b$ and $(a,b) \mapsto a \cdot b^{-1}$, respectively, are continuous in both variables. Instead, we give a proof which does not assume the existence of a completion of a metric space and leave most of the details to the reader.

Let $\mathscr{C}$ be the set of all Cauchy sequences of elements of F. Define addition and multiplication in $\mathscr{C}$ componentwise; i.e., $\{a_n\} + \{b_n\} = \{a_n + b_n\}$ and $\{a_n\} \cdot \{b_n\} = \{a_n b_n\}$. Then $\mathscr{C}$ is a commutative ring with identity. The set, $\mathscr{N}$, of all null sequences, i.e., the set of all sequences with limit 0 in F, is a maximal ideal of $\mathscr{C}$. The quotient ring $\mathscr{C}/\mathscr{N}$ is a field $\hat{F}$. Define a map $\varphi: F \to \hat{F}$ by $\varphi(a) = \tau(a,a,a,\ldots)$, where τ is the canonical epimorphism of $\mathscr{C}$ onto $\mathscr{C}/\mathscr{N} = \hat{F}$. Then φ is a monomorphism.

If $\{a_n\} \in \mathscr{C}$, then $\{|a_n|\}$ is a real Cauchy sequence. Hence, if $\{a_n\} \in \mathscr{C}$, then $\lim_{n\to\infty} |a_n|$ exists. If $\tau(\{a_n\}) = \tau(\{b_n\})$, then $\lim_{n\to\infty} |a_n| = \lim_{n\to\infty} |b_n|$. For $\hat{a} \in F$ define $|\hat{a}|^{\wedge} = \lim_{n\to\infty} |a_n|$, where $\tau(\{a_n\}) = \hat{a}$. Then $|\ |^{\wedge}$ is a map of $\hat{F}$ into R, and, in fact, a valuation of $\hat{F}$ such that $|\varphi(a)|^{\wedge} = |a|$ for each $a \in F$.

If $\hat{a} = \tau(\{a_n\}) \in \hat{F}$, then $\lim_{n\to\infty} |\varphi(a_n) - \hat{a}|^{\wedge} = 0$. Hence $\varphi(F)$ is dense in $\hat{F}$. To prove that $\langle \hat{F}, |\ |^{\wedge}, \varphi\rangle$ is a completion of F under $|\ |$, it is sufficient to show that every Cauchy sequence of elements in $\hat{F}$ converges to an element in $\hat{F}$. Let $\{\hat{a}_i\}$ be a Cauchy sequence of $\hat{F}$, where $\hat{a}_i = \tau((a_{i1}, a_{i2}, a_{i3}, \ldots))$. Then there is an increasing sequence, $\{s_n\}$, of integers such that $(a_{1s_1}, a_{2s_2}, a_{3s_3}, \ldots) \in \mathscr{C}$. Let $\hat{a} = \tau((a_{1s_1}, a_{2s_2}, a_{3s_3}, \ldots))$. Then $\lim_{i\to\infty} |\hat{a}_i - \hat{a}|^{\wedge} = 0$, and $\{\hat{a}_i\}$ converges to $\hat{a} \in \hat{F}$.

b. Let $\langle \hat{F}, |\ |^{\wedge}, \varphi\rangle$ and $\langle F', |\ |', \varphi'\rangle$ be completions of F under $|\ |$. Define a map $\psi_1: \varphi(F) \to \varphi'(F)$ as follows: For $\hat{a} = \varphi(a) \in \varphi(F)$, $\psi_1(\hat{a}) = \varphi'(a)$. Clearly $\psi_1\varphi = \varphi'$. Since $|\varphi(a)|^{\wedge} = |a| = |\varphi'(a)|'$ for all $a \in F$, then for $\hat{a}_n \in \varphi(F)$, $\{\psi_1(\hat{a}_n)\}$ is a Cauchy sequence in F' if and only if $\{\hat{a}_n\}$ is a Cauchy sequence in $\hat{F}$. Since $\varphi(F)$ is dense in $\hat{F}$, ψ_1 extends to a map $\psi: \hat{F} \to \hat{F}'$. In particular, if $\hat{a} \in \hat{F}$, then $\hat{a}$ is the limit of a sequence $\{\hat{a}_n\}$ with $\hat{a}_n \in \varphi(F)$; define $\psi(\hat{a})$ to be the limit (in F') of the sequence $\{\psi_1(\hat{a}_n)\}$. We leave it to the reader to show that ψ is a map extending ψ_1; ψ is surjective [since $\varphi'(F)$ is dense in

$F']$; ψ is an algebraic isomorphism of the field $\hat{F}$ onto the field F'; and $|\hat{a}| = |\psi(\hat{a})|'$ for each $\hat{a} \in \hat{F}$.

Suppose that $\rho: \hat{F} \to F'$ is another isomorphism such that $\rho\varphi = \varphi'$, and $|\rho(\hat{a})|' = |\hat{a}|^{\wedge}$ for each $\hat{a} \in F$. If $\hat{a} \in \hat{F}$, then $\hat{a}$ is the limit of a sequence, $\{\hat{a}_n\}$, of elements of $\varphi(F)$. It follows that, in the topology induced on F' by $|\ |'$, $\lim_{n\to\infty} \rho(\hat{a}_n) = \rho(\hat{a})$ and $\lim_{n\to\infty} \psi(\hat{a}_n) = \psi(\hat{a})$. But, for $\hat{a}_n = \varphi(a_n) \in \varphi(F)$, $\rho(\hat{a}_n) = \psi(\hat{a}_n)$, whence $\rho = \psi$ and ψ is unique.

c. Let $|\ |$ and $|\ |_1$ be equivalent valuations of F, and let $\langle \hat{F}, |\ |^{\wedge}, \varphi\rangle$ and $\langle \hat{F}_1, |\ |_{\hat{1}}, \varphi_1\rangle$ be completions of F under $|\ |$ and $|\ |_1$, respectively. By Theorem 1.1, there is a positive real number, t, such that $|a| = |a|_1^t$ for all $a \in F$. Let $|\ |_2$ be the valuation of $\hat{F}_1$ defined by $|\hat{b}|_2 = (|\hat{b}|_{\hat{1}})^t$ for each $\hat{b} \in \hat{F}_1$. It follows easily that $\langle \hat{F}_1, |\ |_2, \varphi_1\rangle$ is a completion of F under $|\ |$. We apply assertion b of this theorem to the completions $\langle \hat{F}, |\ |^{\wedge}, \varphi\rangle$ and $\langle \hat{F}_1, |\ |_2, \varphi_1\rangle$ of F under $|\ |$ and conclude that c holds. ▮

We leave the proof of the following corollary to the reader.

Corollary. *Let F_0, and F be fields, $|\ |_0$ a valuation on F_0, and $\sigma: F \to F_0$ an isomorphism. Let $|\ |_\sigma$ be the valuation on F defined by $|a|_\sigma = |\sigma(a)|_0$, $a \in F$. If $\langle \hat{F}_0, |\ |_{\hat{0}}, \varphi_0\rangle$ and $\langle \hat{F}, |\ |_{\hat{\sigma}}, \varphi\rangle$ are completions of F_0 under $|\ |_0$, and of F under $|\ |_\sigma$, respectively, then there exists a unique (algebraic and topological) isomorphism $\hat{\sigma}: \hat{F} \to \hat{F}_0$ such that $\hat{\sigma}\varphi = \varphi_0\sigma$, and $|\hat{a}|_{\hat{\sigma}} = |\sigma(\hat{a})|_{\hat{0}}$ for each $\hat{a} \in \hat{F}$. If, in particular, φ_0 and φ are embeddings, then $\hat{\sigma}$ is an extension of σ.* □

Informally, the above corollary states that an algebraic and topological isomorphism of fields with valuations extends to an algebraic and topological isomorphism of completions of these fields.

REMARK. Two metrics, d and d', on a set X may induce equivalent topologies on X but the completions of X under d and d' need not be homeomorphic. For example, let d be the ordinary Euclidean metric on the real numbers R, i.e., $d(a,b) = |a - b|_\infty$ for $a,b \in R$, and let d' be the metric on R defined by

$$d'(a,b) = \left| \frac{a}{1 + |a|_\infty} - \frac{b}{1 + |b|_\infty} \right|_\infty \qquad \text{for } a,b \in R.$$

The metrics d and d' define equivalent topologies on R, and R is complete under d. However, R is not complete under d': The sequence 1, 2, 3,... is a Cauchy sequence under the metric d' but does not converge to an element of R. In the case of a field with metrics induced by valuations such a situation, as we see from Theorem 3.1c, cannot arise. A completion of a field F under a valuation $| \ |$ is uniquely determined up to an (algebraic and topological) isomorphism by the equivalence class of valuations to which $| \ |$ belongs. If F is complete under $| \ |$, then F is complete under every valuation equivalent to $| \ |$.

Before giving our next definition, we note that if $| \ |$ and $| \ |'$ are equivalent valuations of a field E, then the restrictions of $| \ |$ and $| \ |'$ to a subfield F of E are equivalent valuations of F.

Definition 3.2. A *prime spot*, $\mathfrak{p}$, on a field F is an equivalence class of equivalent valuations of F. A prime spot $\mathfrak{p}$ on F is an *archimedean prime spot* if there is an archimedean valuation in $\mathfrak{p}$; otherwise, $\mathfrak{p}$ is a *non-archimedean prime spot*. *F is complete at* $\mathfrak{p}$ if there is a valuation $| \ | \in \mathfrak{p}$ such that F is complete under $| \ |$. Let F be a subfield of a field E, and let $\mathfrak{p}$ and $\mathfrak{P}$ be prime spots on F and E, respectively. Then $\mathfrak{P}$ *divides* $\mathfrak{p}$, and we write $\mathfrak{P}|\mathfrak{p}$, if there is a valuation in $\mathfrak{P}$ whose restriction to F is in $\mathfrak{p}$. ///

Corollary 1. *Let F be a subfield of a field E, and let $\mathfrak{P}$ be a prime spot on E. Then there is a unique prime spot $\mathfrak{p}$ on F such that $\mathfrak{P}|\mathfrak{p}$.* □

A simple consequence of the definition and Theorem 3.1 is

Corollary 2. *Let $\mathfrak{p}$ be a prime spot on a field F. Then there is a field $F_\mathfrak{p}$ and a prime spot $\mathfrak{P}$ on $F_\mathfrak{p}$ such that*

a. $F_\mathfrak{p} \supset F$.

b. $\mathfrak{P}|\mathfrak{p}$.

c. *$\langle F_\mathfrak{p}, | \ |^\frown, \iota\rangle$ is a completion of F under $| \ |$, where $| \ |^\frown \in \mathfrak{P}$, $| \ |$ is the restriction of $| \ |^\frown$ to F, and ι is the canonical embedding of F in $F_\mathfrak{p}$.* □

We shall refer to $F_\mathfrak{p}$ (or, at times, to $F_\mathfrak{P}$) with prime spot $\mathfrak{P}$ as a completion of F at $\mathfrak{p}$.

Examples.

1. Every prime ideal (p) in $\mathbf{Z}$ determines a prime spot on the rational field $\mathbf{Q}$, namely, the equivalence class of valuations of $\mathbf{Q}$ which contains the p-adic valuation. There is one other prime spot on $\mathbf{Q}$: the equivalence class of valuations which contains the ordinary absolute value on $\mathbf{Q}$. Theorem 1.4 states that these are the only nontrivial prime spots on $\mathbf{Q}$.

2. Let p_∞ be the prime spot on the rational field $\mathbf{Q}$ which contains the ordinary absolute value of $\mathbf{Q}$. Let $\mathfrak{P}_{\infty_1}$ be the set of valuations of $\mathbf{Q}(\sqrt{2})$

equivalent to the ordinary absolute value of $\mathbf{Q}(\sqrt{2})$, and let $\mathfrak{P}_{\infty_2}$ be the set of valuations of $\mathbf{Q}(\sqrt{2})$ equivalent to the valuation defined by

$$|a + b\sqrt{2}|' = \begin{cases} a - b\sqrt{2} & \text{if } a \geq b\sqrt{2} \\ -(a - b\sqrt{2}) & \text{if } a < b\sqrt{2} \end{cases} \qquad \text{for } a,b \in \mathbf{Q}$$

(i.e., $|a + b\sqrt{2}|' = |a - b\sqrt{2}|_\infty$, where $|\ |_\infty$ is the ordinary absolute value). Then p_∞ is an archimedean prime spot on $\mathbf{Q}$, $\mathfrak{P}_{\infty_1}$ and $\mathfrak{P}_{\infty_2}$ are distinct archimedean prime spots on $\mathbf{Q}(\sqrt{2})$, and $\mathfrak{P}_{\infty_i}|p_\infty$, $i = 1, 2$.

3. The set $\mathcal{O} = \{a + b\sqrt{2} | a,b \in \mathbf{Z}\}$ forms a subring of $\mathbf{Q}(\sqrt{2})$ which satisfies the conditions of Example 2, Section 1. (It is, incidentally, a Euclidean domain, and hence a unique factorization domain.) Hence every prime ideal, $\mathfrak{P}$, of $\mathcal{O}$ gives rise to a $\mathfrak{P}$-adic valuation of $\mathbf{Q}(\sqrt{2})$. Let $\mathfrak{P}$ denote both a prime ideal of $\mathcal{O}$ and the prime spot on $\mathbf{Q}(\sqrt{2})$ which contains the $\mathfrak{P}$-adic valuation of $\mathbf{Q}(\sqrt{2})$. Then $(3 + \sqrt{2})$ and $(3 - \sqrt{2})$ are distinct non-archimedean prime spots on $\mathbf{Q}(\sqrt{2})$. Let (7) denote the prime spot on $\mathbf{Q}$ containing the 7-adic valuation of $\mathbf{Q}$. Then $(3 + \sqrt{2})|(7)$ and $(3 - \sqrt{2})|(7)$.

A prime spot on a field "lies over" a unique prime spot on a given subfield. We have seen in the preceding examples, however, that a prime spot on a subfield may have more than one prime spot lying over it. Uniqueness is recaptured in the case of a finite extension of a field complete at a prime spot. We have

Theorem 3.2. *Let F be a field which is complete at a prime spot $\mathfrak{p}$. Let E be a finite extension of F, with $E \supset F$, and let $\mathfrak{P}$ be a prime spot on E such that $\mathfrak{P}|\mathfrak{p}$. Then E is complete at $\mathfrak{P}$. Furthermore, if $\mathfrak{P}'$ is a prime spot on E such that $\mathfrak{P}'|\mathfrak{p}$, then $\mathfrak{P}' = \mathfrak{P}$.*

PROOF. If F is a field with a valuation $|\ |$ and V a vector space over F, then a norm on V over F is a mapping $\|\ \|: V \to R$ such that $\|v\| \geq 0$ for all $v \in V$, $\|v\| = 0$ if and only if $v = 0$, $\|av\| = |a|\,\|v\|$, and $\|v + w\| \leq \|v\| + \|w\|$ for all $a \in F$, $v,w \in V$. All norms on a finite-dimensional vector space V over a field which is complete under a valuation induce the same topology on V, and V is complete in each of the metrics defined by the norms. (See, for example, [8] and [26] of the Bibliography.)

Suppose $\mathfrak{P}|\mathfrak{p}$ and $\mathfrak{P}'|\mathfrak{p}$. Then there exist $|\ |_{\mathfrak{P}} \in \mathfrak{P}$, $|\ |_{\mathfrak{P}'} \in \mathfrak{P}'$, and $|\ |_{\mathfrak{p}} \in \mathfrak{p}$ such that $|\ |_{\mathfrak{P}}$ and $|\ |_{\mathfrak{P}'}$ both induce $|\ |_{\mathfrak{p}}$ on F. Clearly, $|\ |_{\mathfrak{P}}$ and $|\ |_{\mathfrak{P}'}$ are norms on E considered as a vector space over the field F complete under $|\ |_{\mathfrak{p}}$. But then $|\ |_{\mathfrak{P}}$ and $|\ |_{\mathfrak{P}'}$ induce the same topology on E, and E is complete under $|\ |_{\mathfrak{P}}$ (and under $|\ |_{\mathfrak{P}'}$). We conclude that $\mathfrak{P} = \mathfrak{P}'$ and that E is complete at $\mathfrak{P}$. ∎

Corollary 1. *Let F, E, $\mathfrak{p}$, and $\mathfrak{P}$ be as in the theorem. Let $\mathfrak{Q}$ be a prime spot on a field K. If $\varphi: E \to K$ is an (algebraic) isomorphism of the field E onto the field K such that $\varphi|_F$ is a homeomorphism (topological isomorphism) of F onto $\varphi(F)$, then φ is a homeomorphism of E onto K.*

PROOF. Let $| \,|_{\mathfrak{Q}}$ be a valuation in $\mathfrak{Q}$. Then the mapping $| \,|: E \to R$ defined by $|\alpha| = |\varphi(\alpha)|_{\mathfrak{Q}}$ for $\alpha \in E$ is a valuation of E which determines some prime spot, say $\mathfrak{P}'$, on E. Clearly, φ is a homeomorphism of E, under the topology induced by $\mathfrak{P}'$, onto K, under the topology induced by $\mathfrak{Q}$. Hence $\varphi|_F$ is a homeomorphism of F, under the relative topology induced by $\mathfrak{P}'$, onto $\varphi(F)$, under the relative topology induced by $\mathfrak{Q}$. But we have assumed that $\varphi|_F$ is a homeomorphism of F, under the $\mathfrak{p}$-topology, onto $\varphi(F)$, under the relative $\mathfrak{Q}$-topology, whence $\mathfrak{P}'$ and $\mathfrak{p}$ define the same topology on F and $\mathfrak{P}'|\mathfrak{p}$. Thus, by the theorem, $\mathfrak{P}' = \mathfrak{P}$ and we conclude that φ is a homeomorphism of E onto K. ▮

Informally, our next corollary states that a completion of a finite extension of a field F is a finite extension of a completion of F.

Corollary 2. *Let F be a subfield of a field E, with $[E: F]$ finite. Let $\mathfrak{P}$ be a prime spot on E, and $E_{\mathfrak{P}}$ a completion of E under $\mathfrak{P}$, with $E_{\mathfrak{P}} \supset E$. Let $F_{\mathfrak{P}}$ be the (topological) closure of F in $E_{\mathfrak{P}}$. Then $E_{\mathfrak{P}} = EF_{\mathfrak{P}}$ and $[E_{\mathfrak{P}}: F_{\mathfrak{P}}] \leq [E: F]$.*

PROOF. Let $\mathfrak{p}$ be the restriction of $\mathfrak{P}$ to F. Clearly $F_{\mathfrak{P}}$ is a completion of F at $\mathfrak{p}$. Since a basis for E over F is certainly a spanning set for $EF_{\mathfrak{P}}$ over $F_{\mathfrak{P}}$, $[EF_{\mathfrak{P}}: F_{\mathfrak{P}}]$ is finite and less than or equal to $[E: F]$. By the theorem, $EF_{\mathfrak{P}}$ is complete under the restriction of $\mathfrak{P}$ to $EF_{\mathfrak{P}}$. But E is dense in $E_{\mathfrak{P}}$ in the topology determined by $\mathfrak{P}$, and $EF_{\mathfrak{P}} \supset E$, whence $E_{\mathfrak{P}} = EF_{\mathfrak{P}}$. ▮

4. Complete Archimedean-Valued Fields

Our object in this section is to prove that a field which is complete at an archimedean prime spot is (algebraically and topologically) isomorphic to the real or complex field. We first prove two lemmas.

Lemma 1. *Let F be a field, with characteristic different from 2, which is complete under a valuation $| \,|$. If $a \in F$ and $|a/4| < \frac{1}{4}$, then there exists $c \in F$ such that $c^2 = 1 + a$ (i.e., if the value of $a \in F$ is small enough, then $1 + a$ is a square in F).*

PROOF. It is sufficient to show that F contains a root, ρ, of the polynomial $x^2 + x - (a/4)$. For then $(2\rho + 1)^2 = 1 + a$.

Define a sequence, $\{x_n\}$, of elements of F inductively as follows: $x_0 = 0$, $x_{n+1} = a/[4(x_n + 1)]$. Note that, for all nonnegative integers n, $|x_n + 1| > \frac{1}{2}$. For, the latter inequality holds with $n = 0$, and if the inequality holds with $n = k$, then

$$|x_{k+1} + 1| = \left|1 + \frac{a}{4(x_k + 1)}\right| \geq 1 - \frac{|a/4|}{|x_k + 1|} > \frac{1}{2},$$

and it holds with $n = k + 1$. It now follows that $\{x_n\}$ is a Cauchy sequence. In fact, for $m \geq n \geq 0$ and $r = 4|a/4| < 1$,

$$|x_m - x_n| = \left|\frac{a}{4(x_{m-1} + 1)} - \frac{a}{4(x_{n-1} + 1)}\right| = \left|\frac{a}{4}\right| \frac{|x_{m-1} - x_{n-1}|}{|x_{m-1} + 1|\,|x_{n-1} + 1|}$$
$$< r|x_{m-1} - x_{n-1}|.$$

Hence $|x_m - x_n| < r^n|x_{m-n} - x_0| = r^n|x_{m-n}| < \frac{1}{2}r^n$. But then, for $\varepsilon > 0$, $|x_m - x_n| < \varepsilon$ whenever $m,n > \log \varepsilon/\log r$, and $\{x_n\}$ is a Cauchy sequence. Since F is complete under $|\ |$, there exists $\rho \in F$ such that $\lim_{n\to\infty} x_n = \rho$. From the relation $x_{n+1}x_n + x_{n+1} - (a/4) = 0$, we conclude that ρ is a root of the polynomial $x^2 + x - (a/4)$. ▌

Lemma 2. *Let F be a field which is complete at a prime spot and let $E = F(i)$, where $i^2 = -1$. Then there exists a unique prime spot $\mathfrak{P}$ on E such that $\mathfrak{P}|\mathfrak{p}$.*

PROOF. We may assume that $E \neq F$ and also that Char $F \neq 2$. Let $|\ | \in \mathfrak{p}$. Define a mapping $|\ |_1: E \to R$ by $|\alpha|_1 = \sqrt{|N_{E/F}(\alpha)|}$ for $\alpha \in E$, where $N_{E/F}$ is the norm from E to F. If $\alpha \in F$, then $N_{\alpha/F}(\alpha) = \alpha^2$ and $|\alpha|_1 = |\alpha|$. Hence the restriction of $|\ |_1$ to F is $|\ |$. We show that $|\ |_1$ is a valuation of E and conclude that the set of valuations of E equivalent to $|\ |_1$ is a prime spot $\mathfrak{P}$ on E such that $\mathfrak{P}|\mathfrak{p}$.

It is clear that $|\ |_1$ satisfies the conditions $|\alpha|_1 \geq 0$, $|\alpha|_1 = 0$, if and only if $\alpha = 0$, $|\alpha\beta|_1 = |\alpha|_1|\beta|_1$ for $\alpha,\beta \in E$. To show that $|\ |_1$ satisfies the triangle inequality it is sufficient to prove that, for each $\alpha \in E$, $|1 + \alpha|_1 \leq 1 + |\alpha|_1$. The latter inequality is satisfied for all $\alpha \in F$. Suppose then that $\alpha \in E$, $\alpha \notin F$ and that $m_{\alpha/F}(x) = x^2 + bx + c$. Then the minimum polynomial of $1 + \alpha$ over F is $m_{\alpha/F}(x - 1) = x^2 + (b - 2)x + (1 - b + c)$, $|1 + \alpha|_1 = \sqrt{|1 - b + c|}$, and $|\alpha|_1 = \sqrt{|c|}$. Since $m_{\alpha/F}(x)$ is irreducible over F,

$(b^2 - 4c)/b^2 = 1 - (4c/b^2)$ is not a square in F. Hence, by Lemma 1, $|c/b^2| \geq \frac{1}{4}$ and $|b^2| \leq 4|c|$. But then

$$|1 + \alpha|_1^2 = |1 - b + c| \leq 1 + |b| + |c| \leq 1 + 2\sqrt{|c|} + |c|$$
$$= (1 + \sqrt{|c|})^2 = (1 + |\alpha|_1)^2,$$

whence $|1 + \alpha|_1 \leq 1 + |\alpha|_1$.

That there is at most one prime spot on E which divides $\mathfrak{p}$ follows from Theorem 3.2. ▌

Theorem 4.1. *Let F be a field which is complete at an archimedean prime spot $\mathfrak{p}$. Then there is an algebraic and topological isomorphism of F onto the real field* **R** *or onto the complex field* **C**.

PROOF. Let P be the prime field of F. Then there is an algebraic isomorphism, φ, of P onto the rational field $\mathbf{Q}$ (Theorem 1.2, Corollary 1). φ is also a topological isomorphism. For, the map from P to $\mathbf{R}$ defined by $a \mapsto |\varphi(a)|_\infty$, where $|\ |_\infty$ is the ordinary absolute value, is an archimedean valuation of P. But, by Theorem 1.4, P admits only one archimedean prime spot, whence there is a valuation, $|\ |$, in $\mathfrak{p}$ such that for each $a \in P$, $|a| = |\varphi(a)|_\infty$, and φ is a homeomorphism. (In order to avoid encumbering our notation, we shall also use $|\ |$ to denote the restriction to various subfields of F of the valuation $|\ |$ just determined.) Let $\hat{P}$ be the closure of P in F under the $\mathfrak{p}$-topology. Then $\langle \hat{P}, |\ |, \iota_P \rangle$ is a completion of P. Since $\langle \mathbf{R}, |\ |_\infty, \iota_\mathbf{Q} \rangle$ is a completion of $\mathbf{Q}$, it follows from Theorem 3.1 that there exists an algebraic and topological isomorphism $\hat{\varphi}: \hat{P} \to \mathbf{R}$ such that $\hat{\varphi}|_P = \varphi$. Note that for each $a \in \hat{P}$, $|a| = |\hat{\varphi}(a)|_\infty$. Hence every nonnegative real number is the image, under $|\ |$, of an element in $\hat{P}$.

We consider two cases.

CASE 1. There is a $j \in F$ such that $j^2 = -1$. Then $\hat{\varphi}$ extends to an algebraic isomorphism, ψ, of $\hat{P}[j]$ onto $\mathbf{C} = \mathbf{R}[\sqrt{-1}]$. By the corollary to Theorem 3.2, ψ is also a topological isomorphism. Clearly, $F \supset \hat{P}[j]$. We show that, in fact, $F = \hat{P}[j]$ and conclude that F is algebraically and topologically isomorphic to the complex field **C**.

Suppose, to the contrary, that there is an element $\alpha_0 \in F - \hat{P}[j]$. Let $r = |j - \alpha_0|$ and let $S = \{x \in \hat{P}[j] \mid |x - \alpha_0| \leq r\}$. Then S is a nonvoid, closed, and bounded subset of $\hat{P}[j]$. Since $\hat{P}[j]$ is homeomorphic to **C**, S is compact and every continuous map from S to **R** attains a minimum at a point of S. Let $u_0 \in S$ be a point at which the continuous map from S to **R** defined by $x \mapsto |x - \alpha_0|$ has a minimum. Then, for all $x \in S$, $0 < |u_0 - \alpha_0| \leq |x - \alpha_0|$.

Since $|u_0 - \alpha_0| \leq r < |x - \alpha_0|$ for $x \in \hat{P}[j] - S$, $0 < |u_0 - \alpha_0| \leq |x - \alpha_0|$ for all $x \in \hat{P}[j]$. There is an $a_0 \in \hat{P}$ such that $|a_0| = 2/|u_0 - \alpha_0|$. Let $\beta_0 = a_0(u_0 - \alpha_0)$. Then $\beta_0 \in F - \hat{P}[j]$ and β_0 satisfies

$$(*) \qquad 2 = |\beta| \leq |x - \beta| \qquad \text{for all } x \in \hat{P}[j].$$

We show that if $\beta \in F - \hat{P}[j]$ satisfies (*), then $1 - \beta$ satisfies (*). In fact, for each positive integer n (since $\hat{P}[j]$ is isomorphic to **C**), $\hat{P}[j]$ contains all nth roots of unity, $\zeta_1, \zeta_2, \ldots, \zeta_n$, and

$$2^{n-1}|1 - \beta| \leq \prod_{i=1}^{n} |\zeta_i - \beta| = |1 - \beta^n| \leq 1 + |\beta|^n = 1 + 2^n.$$

Hence $|1 - \beta| \leq 2 + (1/2^{n-1})$ for every positive integer n. Then $|1 - \beta| \leq 2$. But since β satisfies (*), $2 = |\beta| \leq |1 - \beta|$, whence $2 = |1 - \beta| \leq |x - (1 - \beta)|$ for all $x \in \hat{P}[j]$. We conclude that $|n \cdot 1 - \beta_0| = 2$ for all positive integers n. But then $2 = |n \cdot 1 - \beta_0| \geq |n \cdot 1| - |\beta_0| = |n \cdot 1| - 2$, $|n \cdot 1| \leq 4$, and $| \; |$ is bounded on the set $\{n \cdot 1\}$. Since $| \; |$ is an archimedean valuation, we have a contradiction!

CASE 2. There does not exist $j \in F$ with $j^2 = -1$. Let j be an element of an algebraically closed field containing F, with $j^2 = -1$, and let $E = F(j)$. By Lemma 2, there is a prime spot $\mathfrak{P}$ on E such that $\mathfrak{P}|\mathfrak{p}$. Since $\mathfrak{p}$ is archimedean, so is $\mathfrak{P}$. By Theorem 3.2, E is complete at $\mathfrak{P}$. Note that the closure of P in F under the $\mathfrak{p}$-topology coincides with the closure of P in E under the $\mathfrak{P}$-topology. We apply the result of Case 1 to conclude that $E = \hat{P}[j]$, and that there is an algebraic and topological isomorphism, ψ, of E onto **C** with $\psi(\hat{P}) = \mathbf{R}$. But then $\mathbf{R} \subset \psi(F) \subsetneqq \mathbf{C}$, whence $\psi(F) = \mathbf{R}$ and F is algebraically and topologically isomorphic to the real field. ∎

Corollary. *Every archimedean-valued field is isomorphic to a subfield of the field of complex numbers.* □

5. Extension of a Complete Nonarchimedean Prime Spot to an Algebraic Extension

A trivial consequence of the results (Theorem 4.1 and Lemma 2) of the preceding section is that an archimedean prime spot on a complete field F is divisible by one and only one prime spot on an algebraic extension of F. This result may be stated more succinctly as follows: A complete archimedean prime spot extends uniquely to an algebraic extension. In this section we prove the corresponding result for complete nonarchimedean prime spots. We begin by defining certain structures which are of importance in the study of nonarchimedean-valued fields.

Let $\mathfrak{p}$ be a prime spot on a field F. If an element $a \in F$ has value less than (equal to) 1 at one valuation in $\mathfrak{p}$, then a has value less than (equal to) 1 at every valuation in $\mathfrak{p}$. Hence, for $|\ | \in \mathfrak{p}$, the sets $\mathcal{O}(\mathfrak{p}) = \{a \in F|\ |a| \leq 1\}$ and $\mathcal{M}(p) = \{a \in F|\ |a| < 1\}$ are independent of the choice of $|\ | \in \mathfrak{p}$. Assume that $\mathfrak{p}$ is nontrivial and nonarchimedean. Then, by using the strong triangle inequality $|a + b| \leq \max\{|a|,|b|\}$, we see easily that $\mathcal{O}(\mathfrak{p})$ is a subring of F and that $\mathcal{M}(\mathfrak{p})$ is a maximal ideal in $\mathcal{O}(\mathfrak{p})$. In fact, $\mathcal{M}(\mathfrak{p})$ is the only maximal ideal in $\mathcal{O}(\mathfrak{p})$. For, if I is an ideal in $\mathcal{O}(\mathfrak{p})$ not contained in $\mathcal{M}(\mathfrak{p})$, then there is an $a \in I - \mathcal{M}(\mathfrak{p})$, with $|a| = 1$. But then $1/a \in \mathcal{O}(\mathfrak{p})$, $(1/a) \cdot a = 1 \in I$, and $I = \mathcal{O}(\mathfrak{p})$. We leave it to the reader to show that if $\mathfrak{p}_1$, $\mathfrak{p}_2$ are nonarchimedean prime spots on a field F, then $\mathcal{O}(\mathfrak{p}_1) = \mathcal{O}(\mathfrak{p}_2)$ $[\mathcal{M}(\mathfrak{p}_1) = \mathcal{M}(\mathfrak{p}_2)]$ if and only if $\mathfrak{p}_1 = \mathfrak{p}_2$. Note that since $\mathcal{M}(\mathfrak{p})$ is a maximal ideal in $\mathcal{O}(\mathfrak{p})$, $\mathcal{O}(\mathfrak{p})/\mathcal{M}(\mathfrak{p})$ is a field. We now give

Definition 5.1. Let $\mathfrak{p}$ be a nonarchimedean prime spot on a field F, and let $|\ | \in \mathfrak{p}$. Then

$$\mathcal{O}_F(\mathfrak{p}) = \mathcal{O}(\mathfrak{p}) = \{a \in F|\ |a| \leq 1\}$$

is *the ring of (local) integers* of F at $\mathfrak{p}$,

$$\mathcal{M}_F(\mathfrak{p}) = \mathcal{M}(\mathfrak{p}) = \{a \in F|\ |a| < 1\}$$

is *the maximal ideal of F at $\mathfrak{p}$*, and

$$\bar{F} = \mathcal{O}(\mathfrak{p})/\mathcal{M}(\mathfrak{p})$$

is the *residue class field of F at $\mathfrak{p}$*. ///

Example. Let p be the prime spot on $\mathbf{Q}$ which contains the p-adic valuation. Then the ring of local integers of $\mathbf{Q}$ at p is given by

$$\mathcal{O}(p) = \left\{\frac{m}{n}\middle|\ m,n \in \mathbf{Z},\ (n,p) = 1\right\},$$

and the maximal ideal of $\mathbf{Q}$ at p is given by

$$\mathcal{M}(p) = \left\{\frac{m}{n}\middle|\ m,n \in \mathbf{Z},\ (n,p) = 1,\ p|m\right\}.$$

It is easy to verify that $\mathcal{O}(p)/\mathcal{M}(p) \cong \mathbf{Z}/(p)$. Hence the residue class field of $\mathbf{Q}$ at p is a finite field with p elements.

We recall (Definition 3.2, Corollary 2) that a field F with prime spot $\mathfrak{p}$ has a completion $F_{\mathfrak{p}}$ with prime spot $\mathfrak{P}|\mathfrak{p}$. We show that the residue class field of F at (nonarchimedean) $\mathfrak{p}$ is isomorphic to the residue class field of $F_{\mathfrak{p}}$ at $\mathfrak{P}$.

Theorem 5.1. *Let $F_{\mathfrak{p}}$ with prime spot $\mathfrak{P}$ be a completion of the subfield F at the nonarchimedean prime spot $\mathfrak{p}$. Then*

$$\bar{F} = \mathcal{O}_F(\mathfrak{p})/\mathcal{M}_F(\mathfrak{p}) \cong \overline{F_{\mathfrak{p}}} = \mathcal{O}_{F_{\mathfrak{p}}}(\mathfrak{P})/\mathcal{M}_{F_{\mathfrak{p}}}(\mathfrak{P}).$$

PROOF. Note that

$$\mathcal{M}_F(\mathfrak{p}) = \mathcal{O}_F(\mathfrak{p}) \cap \mathcal{M}_{F_{\mathfrak{p}}}(\mathfrak{P}),$$

$$\mathcal{O}_{F_{\mathfrak{p}}}(\mathfrak{P}) = \mathcal{O}_F(\mathfrak{p}) + \mathcal{M}_{F_{\mathfrak{p}}}(\mathfrak{P}).$$

(The first equality is very easy to prove. The second equality follows from the fact that $F_{\mathfrak{p}}$ is a completion of F, and from Theorem 1.3.) But then

$$\begin{aligned}\mathcal{O}_F(\mathfrak{p})/\mathcal{M}_F(\mathfrak{p}) &= \mathcal{O}_F(\mathfrak{p})/[\mathcal{O}_F(\mathfrak{p}) \cap \mathcal{M}_{F_{\mathfrak{p}}}(\mathfrak{P})] \\ &\cong [\mathcal{O}_F(\mathfrak{p}) + \mathcal{M}_{F_{\mathfrak{p}}}(\mathfrak{P})]/\mathcal{M}_{F_{\mathfrak{p}}}(\mathfrak{P}) = \mathcal{O}_{F_{\mathfrak{p}}}(\mathfrak{P})/\mathcal{M}_{F_{\mathfrak{p}}}(\mathfrak{P}). \quad \blacksquare\end{aligned}$$

Let $|\ |$ be a nonarchimedean valuation of a field F. We extend $|\ |$ to a valuation of a simple transcendental extension $F(x)$ of F as follows: For a polynomial $\sum_{i=0}^{n} a_i x^i = f \in F[x]$, we let $|f| = \max_i\{|a_i|\}$, and for $f/g = h \in F(x)$, where $f,g \in F[x]$, we let $|h| = |f|/|g|$. We leave it to the reader to verify that the relation defined in this way is a valuation of $F(x)$, and that equivalent valuations of F define equivalent valuations of $F(x)$.

For $a \in \mathcal{O}(\mathfrak{p})$ ($\mathfrak{p}$ a spot on F with $|\ | \in \mathfrak{p}$), let $\bar{a}$ denote the image of a under the canonical epimorphism of $\mathcal{O}(\mathfrak{p})$ onto the residue class field of F at $\mathfrak{p}$. Then $f = \sum_{i=0}^{n} a_i x^i \mapsto \bar{f} = \sum_{i=0}^{n} \bar{a}_i x^i$ defines an epimorphism of $\mathcal{O}(\mathfrak{p})[x]$ onto $\bar{F}[x]$. If $f \in \mathcal{O}(\mathfrak{p})[x]$, then (with certain exceptions) a factorization of $\bar{f}$ over $\bar{F}$ can be "lifted back" to a factorization of f over $\mathcal{O}(\mathfrak{p})$. In particular, we have

Theorem 5.2. *Let F be a field which is complete at a nonarchimedean prime spot $\mathfrak{p}$, and let $f \in \mathcal{O}(\mathfrak{p})[x]$. If there exist nonzero polynomials $\bar{g}_0,\bar{h}_0 \in \bar{F}[x]$ with $(\bar{g}_0,\bar{h}_0) = 1$ such that $\bar{f} = \bar{g}_0\bar{h}_0$, then there exist $g,h \in \mathcal{O}(\mathfrak{p})[x]$ such that*

a. $f = gh$.
b. $\bar{g} = \bar{g}_0$, $\bar{h} = \bar{h}_0$.
c. $\deg g = \deg \bar{g}_0$.

PROOF. We may assume without losing generality that $\bar{g}_0$ is a monic polynomial. Let g_0 and h_0 be polynomials in $\mathcal{O}(\mathfrak{p})[x]$ (with g_0 monic) whose images (under the canonical map $\mathcal{O}(\mathfrak{p})[x] \to \mathcal{O}(\mathfrak{p})/\mathcal{M}(\mathfrak{p})[x]$) are, respectively, $\bar{g}_0$ and $\bar{h}_0$, and such that $\deg g_0 = \deg \bar{g}_0$, and $\deg h_0 \leq \deg f - \deg g_0$. We fix a valuation $|\ | \in \mathfrak{p}$ and lift it to a valuation on $F(x)$. Since $\bar{f} - \bar{g}_0\bar{h}_0 = 0$, all the coefficients of $f - g_0h_0$ are in $\mathcal{M}(\mathfrak{p})$ and $0 \leq |f - g_0h_0| = \varepsilon_1 < 1$. Since $(\bar{g}_0,\bar{h}_0) = 1$, there exist $\bar{s},\bar{t} \in \bar{F}[x]$ such that $\bar{s}\bar{g}_0 + \bar{t}\bar{h}_0 = 1$. Choose $s,t \in \mathcal{O}(\mathfrak{p})[x]$ whose images are $\bar{s}$ and $\bar{t}$, respectively. Then $sg_0 + th_0 - 1$ has each of its coefficients in $\mathcal{M}(\mathfrak{p})$, and $0 \leq |sg_0 + th_0 - 1| = \varepsilon_2 < 1$ There exists an element $\pi \in \mathcal{M}(\mathfrak{p})$ such that $|\pi| = \max\{\varepsilon_1,\varepsilon_2\}$

We refine the inequality $|f - g_0h_0| \leq |\pi| < 1$ to an equality $|f - gh| = 0$ (i.e., $f = gh$) in the following way: We construct sequences $\{g_i\}_{i=0}^{\infty}$, $\{h_i\}_{i=0}^{\infty}$ of polynomials in $\mathcal{O}(\mathfrak{p})[x]$ such that

(*)
a. $|f - g_ih_i| \leq |\pi|^{i+1}$.
b. $|g_i - g_0| \leq |\pi|$, $|h_i - h_0| \leq |\pi|$.
c. g_i is monic, $\deg g_i = \deg g_0$, $\deg h_i \leq \deg f - \deg g_0$.
d. $|g_{i+1} - g_i| \leq |\pi|^{i+1}$, $|h_{i+1} - h_i| \leq |\pi|^{i+1}$.

Finally, we conclude from the completeness of F that these sequences converge respectively to polynomials g, h in $\mathcal{O}(\mathfrak{p})[x]$ which have the properties stated in the theorem.

Clearly g_0 and h_0 satisfy the conditions listed in (*). Suppose we have constructed polynomials g_i, h_i, $0 \leq i \leq k$ satisfying these conditions. Then there exists a polynomial $w \in \mathcal{O}(\mathfrak{p})[x]$ such that $f = g_kh_k + \pi^{k+1}w$. From $|sg_0 + th_0 - 1| \leq |\pi|$, $|g_k - g_0| \leq \pi$, and $|h_k - h_0| \leq \pi$, it follows that $|sg_k + th_k - 1| \leq |\pi|$. Since $w \in \mathcal{O}(\mathfrak{p})[x]$, $|w| \leq 1$ and $|wsg_k + wth_k - w| \leq |\pi|$. Since g_k is monic, there exist $q,r \in \mathcal{O}(\mathfrak{p})[x]$, with $\deg r < \deg g_k$ or $r = 0$, such that $wt = qg_k + r$. But then

$$|(ws + qh_k)g_k + rh_k - w| \leq |\pi|,$$

and $\bar{v}\bar{g}_k + \bar{h}_k\bar{r} = \bar{w}$, where $\bar{v} = \bar{w}\bar{s} + \bar{q}\bar{h}_k$. Note that $\deg(\bar{w} - \bar{h}_k\bar{r}) \leq \deg(w - h_kr) \leq \deg f$. But then $\deg \bar{v} + \deg \bar{g}_k = \deg(\bar{w} - \bar{h}_k\bar{r}) \leq \deg f$, whence $\deg \bar{v} \leq \deg f - \deg g_0$. Hence there exists a polynomial $v \in \mathcal{O}(\mathfrak{p})[x]$ with $\deg v \leq \deg f - \deg g_0$ such that $|vg_k + rh_k - w| \leq |\pi|$. [For example, if $\deg(ws + qh_k) \leq \deg f - \deg g_o$, let $v = ws + qh_k$; if $\deg(ws + qh_k) > \deg f - \deg g_o$, let v be the polynomial which agrees with $ws + qh_k$ through the $(d + 1)$th term, where $d = \deg f - \deg g_o$.] Let

$$g_{k+1} = g_k + \pi^{k+1}r,$$

$$h_{k+1} = h_k + \pi^{k+1}v.$$

Then

$$f - g_{k+1}h_{k+1} = f - g_k h_k - \pi^{k+1}(vg_k + rh_k) - \pi^{2k+2}rv$$
$$= \pi^{k+1}(w - vg_k - rh_k) - \pi^{2k+2}rv,$$

and $|f - g_{k+1}h_{k+1}| \le |\pi|^{k+2}$. We see easily that g_{k+1} and h_{k+1} satisfy the rest of the conditions in (*). It follows by induction that sequences $\{g_i\}_{i=0}^{\infty}$ and $\{h_i\}_{i=0}^{\infty}$ of the desired type exist.

Each of the sequences $\{g_i\}_{i=0}^{\infty}$, $\{h_i\}_{i=0}^{\infty}$ is a Cauchy sequence of polynomials in $\mathcal{O}(\mathfrak{p})[x]$; furthermore, for each i, $\bar{g}_i = \bar{g}_0$, $\bar{h}_i = \bar{h}_0$, g_i is monic, $\deg g_i = \deg g_0$, and $\deg h_i \le \deg f - \deg g_0$. Since F is complete at $\mathfrak{p}$, there exist polynomials $g,h \in \mathcal{O}(\mathfrak{p})[x]$ such that $\bar{g} = \bar{g}_0$, $\bar{h} = \bar{h}_0$, g is monic, $\deg g = \deg g_0$, $\deg h \le \deg f - \deg g_0$, $\lim g_i = g$, and $\lim h_i = h$. Finally, $|f - gh| = |\lim(f - g_ih_i)| = \lim|f - g_ih_i| = 0$, $f = gh$, and the theorem is proved. ▮

Corollary 1. *Let F and $\mathfrak{p}$ be as in the theorem, and let $|\ |$ be a valuation in $\mathfrak{p}$. If $f = \sum_{i=0}^{n} a_ix^i \in \mathcal{O}(\mathfrak{p})[x]$ is such that $|a_n| < 1$ and $|a_i| = 1$ for some $i > 0$, then f is reducible over $\mathcal{O}(\mathfrak{p})$.*

PROOF. If $|a_n| < 1$ and $|a_i| = 1$ for some $i > 0$, then $1 \le \deg \bar{f} < n = \deg f$. By the theorem, the factorization $\bar{f} = \bar{f}\cdot 1$ lifts to a factorization $f = gh$ with $\bar{g} = \bar{f}$ and $\deg g = \deg \bar{f} < \deg f$. But then f is reducible as desired. ▮

A simple consequence of Corollary 1 is

Corollary 2. *If $f = \sum_{i=0}^{n} a_ix^i \in F[x]$ is irreducible over F, then* $\max_i \{|a_i|\} = \max\{|a_0|,|a_n|\}$. □

Example. Let $\mathbf{Q}_7$ be a completion of $\mathbf{Q}$ under the 7-adic valuation. It follows from Theorem 5.1 and the example preceding it that the residue class field of $\mathbf{Q}_7$ is isomorphic to $\mathbf{Z}/(7)$. The polynomial $x^2 - 2 \in \mathbf{Q}_7[x]$ maps into $x^2 - \bar{2} = (x - \bar{3})(x + \bar{3})$ in the polynomial domain over the residue class field of $\mathbf{Q}_7$. It follows from Theorem 5.2 that $x^2 - 2$ is reducible over $\mathbf{Q}_7$. Thus $\mathbf{Q}_7$ contains a square root of 2. In general, if a is a quadratic residue modulo a prime $p > 2$ (i.e., there is an integer b such that $b^2 \equiv a \bmod p$), then a square root of a is contained in a completion, $\mathbf{Q}_p$, of $\mathbf{Q}$ under the p-adic valuation.

We use Theorem 5.2, Corollary 2, to prove that a complete nonarchimedean prime spot on a field F has a unique extension to an algebraic extension of F.

Theorem 5.3. *Let F be a field, complete at a nonarchimedean prime spot $\mathfrak{p}$, and let E be a finite extension of F, with $E \supset F$. Then there exists a unique prime spot $\mathfrak{P}$ on E such that $\mathfrak{P}|\mathfrak{p}$. E is complete at $\mathfrak{P}$.*

PROOF. All we need prove is that a prime spot $\mathfrak{P}$ on E, with $\mathfrak{P}|\mathfrak{p}$, exists. For, if such a $\mathfrak{P}$ exists, then (Theorem 3.2) $\mathfrak{P} = \mathfrak{P}'$, where $\mathfrak{P}'$ is any prime spot on E with $\mathfrak{P}'|\mathfrak{p}$, and E is complete at $\mathfrak{P}$.

Let $|\ |$ be a valuation in $\mathfrak{p}$, and let $n = [E: F]$. Define a map, $|\ |_E$, from E to the nonnegative reals by $|\alpha|_E = |N_{E/F}\alpha|^{1/n}$, where $N_{E/F}$ is the norm from E to F. Since $N_{E/F}a = a^n$ for $a \in F$, the restriction of $|\ |_E$ to F is $|\ |$. To prove the theorem it suffices to show that $|\ |_E$ is a valuation on E.

Since $N_{E/F}$ is multiplicative, and $N_{E/F}(\alpha) = 0$ if and only if $\alpha = 0$, $|\alpha\beta|_E = |\alpha|_E|\beta|_E$ and $|\alpha|_E = 0$ if and only if $\alpha = 0$ $(\alpha,\beta \in E)$. Now let $\alpha \in E$ and let $m_{\alpha/F}(x) = x^m + \sum_{i=1}^m a_i x^{m-i}$. Then $|\alpha|_E = |N_{E/F}\alpha|^{1/m} = |a_m|^{1/m}$ (Chapter 5, Theorem 8.1). The minimum polynomial of $1 + \alpha$ over F is given by

$$m_{\alpha/F}(x - 1) = x^m + (a_1 - m)x^{m-1} + \cdots \\ + (a_m - a_{m-1} + \cdots + (-1)^{m-1}a_1 + (-1)^m).$$

Again by Chapter 5, Theorem 8.1,

$$|1 + \alpha|_E = |a^m - a_{m-1} + \cdots + (-1)^{m-1}a_1 + (-1)^m|^{1/m}.$$

Since $|\ | \in \mathfrak{p}$, and $\mathfrak{p}$ is nonarchimedean,

$$|a_m - a_{m-1} + \cdots + (-1)^{m-1}a_1 + (-1)^m| \leq [\max_i\{1,|a_i|\}].$$

But $m_{\alpha/F}(x) - x^m + \sum_{i=1}^m a_i x^i$ is irreducible over F, whence (Theorem 5.2, Corollary 2) $\max_i\{|a_i|\} = \max\{1,|a_m|\}$. Hence

$$|1 + \alpha|_E \leq [\max\{1,|a_m|\}]^{1/m} = \max\{1,|a_m|^{1/m}\} = \max\{|1|_E,|\alpha|_E\}.$$

It follows easily that for $\alpha,\beta \in E$, $|\alpha + \beta|_E \leq \max\{|\alpha|_E,|\beta|_E\}$. We conclude that $|\ |_E$ is a valuation, and the theorem is proved. ▌

In the course of proving the theorem we have proved

Corollary 1. *Let F be complete under a nonarchimedean valuation $|\ |$, and let $E \supset F$ with $[E: F] = n$. Then $|\ |$ has a unique extension to a valuation $|\ |_E$ on E. For $\alpha \in E$, $|\alpha|_E = |N_{E/F}\alpha|^{1/n}$.* □

Our next corollary indicates that a complete nonarchimedean prime spot $\mathfrak{p}$ on a field F extends to a unique prime spot $\mathfrak{P}$ on an algebraic extension

$E \supset F$, $[E: F]$ not necessarily finite. However, as we see below, the completeness part of Theorem 5.3 may be lost (i.e., if $[E: F]$ is infinite, then E is not necessarily complete at $\mathfrak{P}$).

Corollary 2. *Let F and $\mathfrak{p}$ be as in Theorem* 5.3, *and let E be an algebraic extension of F, with $E \supset F$. Then there exists a unique prime spot $\mathfrak{P}$ on E such that $\mathfrak{P}|\mathfrak{p}$.*

PROOF. Suppose that $\mathfrak{P}$ and $\mathfrak{P}'$ are prime spots on E such that $\mathfrak{P}|\mathfrak{p}$ and $\mathfrak{P}'|\mathfrak{p}$. Let $|\ |_E$ and $|\ |_E'$ be valuations in $\mathfrak{P}$ and $\mathfrak{P}'$, respectively, and let $|\ |$ and $|\ |'$ be their respective restrictions to F. Then $|\ |$ and $|\ |'$ are equivalent valuations in $\mathfrak{p}$. For each $\alpha \in E$, $F(\alpha)$ is a finite extension of F. By Corollary 1, $|\alpha|_E = |N_{F(\alpha)/F}\alpha|^{1/[F(\alpha):F]}$ and $|\alpha|_E' = |N_{F(\alpha)/F}\alpha|'^{1/[F(\alpha):F]}$. But then $|\ |_E$ and $|\ |_E'$ are equivalent valuations of E, whence $\mathfrak{P} = \mathfrak{P}'$.

On the other hand, let $|\ |$ be a valuation in $\mathfrak{p}$. The reader may readily verify that the map $|\ |_E$ from E to the nonnegative reals defined by $|\alpha|_E = |N_{F(\alpha)/F}\alpha|^{1/[F(\alpha):F]}$ for $\alpha \in E$ is a valuation of E. It follows that there exists a prime spot $\mathfrak{P}$ on E such that $\mathfrak{P}|\mathfrak{p}$. ▮

Corollary 3. *Let F and $\mathfrak{p}$ be as in Theorem* 5.3, *and let $\tilde{F} \supset F$ be an algebraic closure of F. Then there exists a unique prime spot $\mathfrak{P}$ on $\tilde{F}$ such that $\mathfrak{P}|\mathfrak{p}$.* □

Example. We leave the details of this example to the reader (Exercise 5.3). Let $\mathbf{Q}_p$ be a completion of the rational field under the p-adic valuation, and let $\tilde{\mathbf{Q}}_p \supset \mathbf{Q}_p$ be an algebraic closure of $\mathbf{Q}_p$. Let a be an integer which is a quadratic nonresidue mod p (i.e., $x^2 \equiv a \bmod p$ has no integer solution). Then the sequence $\{s_n\}_{n=1}^{\infty}$, with $s_n = \sum_{i=1}^{n} p^i \sqrt[2^i]{a}$, is a Cauchy sequence of elements in $\tilde{\mathbf{Q}}_p$ (with respect to the unique extension of the p-adic valuation on $\mathbf{Q}_p$ to a valuation on $\tilde{\mathbf{Q}}_p$). However, the sequence $\{s_n\}_{n=1}^{\infty}$ does not converge to an element in $\tilde{\mathbf{Q}}_p$. Hence $\tilde{\mathbf{Q}}_p$ is not complete.

REMARK. The preceding example shows that an algebraic closure, C, of a field F complete at a nonarchimedean prime spot need not be complete. If $\hat{C}$ is a completion of C, then $\hat{C}$ is algebraically closed (Exercise 5.4).

6. Extensions of a (Not Necessarily Complete) Prime Spot to a Finite Extension; Local Degree, Local Norm, and Local Trace

We have seen that if $\mathfrak{p}$ is a complete prime spot on a field F, then $\mathfrak{p}$ extends to a unique prime spot on an algebraic extension of F. We now look at the case where $\mathfrak{p}$ is not (necessarily) complete.

Theorem 6.1. *Let $\mathfrak{p}$ be a prime spot on a field F, $F_{\mathfrak{P}_0} \supset F$ a completion of F at $\mathfrak{p}$ (with $\mathfrak{P}_0$ the unique prime spot on $F_{\mathfrak{P}_0}$ such that $\mathfrak{P}_0|\mathfrak{p}$, and $\tilde{F}_{\mathfrak{P}_0} \supset F_{\mathfrak{P}_0}$ an algebraic closure of $F_{\mathfrak{P}_0}$). Let $E \supset F$ be a finite extension of F, $\mathrm{Mon}_F(E,\tilde{F}_{\mathfrak{P}_0})$ the set of F-monomorphisms of E into $\tilde{F}_{\mathfrak{P}_0}$, and let $\mathscr{E} = \{\mathfrak{P} \mid \mathfrak{P}$ a prime spot on E, $\mathfrak{P}|\mathfrak{p}\}$. Then*

a. *$\mathscr{E}$ is nonempty, and there exists a surjection $\Phi\colon \mathrm{Mon}_F(E,\tilde{F}_{\mathfrak{P}_0}) \to \mathscr{E}$.*
b. *For $\sigma,\tau \in \mathrm{Mon}_F(E,\tilde{F}_{\mathfrak{P}_0})$, $\Phi(\sigma) = \Phi(\tau)$ if and only if there exists an $F_{\mathfrak{P}_0}$-automorphism, μ, of $\tilde{F}_{\mathfrak{P}_0}$ such that $\sigma = \mu\tau$.*

PROOF. Since $\tilde{F}_{\mathfrak{P}_0}$ is an algebraically closed field containing F, and E is algebraic over F, $\mathrm{Mon}_F(E,\tilde{F}_{\mathfrak{P}_0})$ is nonempty. Let $|\ |$ be a fixed valuation on $\tilde{F}_{\mathfrak{P}_0}$ which is the unique extension to $\tilde{F}_{\mathfrak{P}_0}$ of a valuation in $\mathfrak{P}_0$. For each $\sigma \in \mathrm{Mon}_F(E,\tilde{F}_{\mathfrak{P}_0})$, define a map, $|\ |_\sigma$, from E to the set of nonnegative reals by $|\alpha|_\sigma = |\sigma(\alpha)|$, $\alpha \in E$. Then $|\ |_\sigma$ is a valuation of E. Let $\sigma^{-1}\mathfrak{P}_0$ be the prime spot on E determined by $|\ |_\sigma$. Clearly $\sigma^{-1}\mathfrak{P}_0|\mathfrak{p}$. Hence $\mathscr{E}$ is nonempty, and $\sigma \mapsto \Phi(\sigma) = \sigma^{-1}\mathfrak{P}_0$ is map from $\mathrm{Mon}_F(E\{\tilde{F}_{\mathfrak{P}_0})$ to $\mathscr{E}$.

We show that Φ is surjective. Let $\mathfrak{P}$ be a prime spot on E such that $\mathfrak{P}|\mathfrak{p}$. Let $E_{\mathfrak{P}} \supset E$ be a completion of E at $\mathfrak{P}$ and $F_{\mathfrak{P}}$ the closure of F in $E_{\mathfrak{P}}$. Then $F_{\mathfrak{P}}$ is a completion of F at $\mathfrak{p}$, and (by the corollary of Theorem 3.1) there exists a unique (topological and algebraic) F-isomorphism, λ, of $F_{\mathfrak{P}}$ onto $F_{\mathfrak{P}_0}$. By Theorem 3.2, Corollary 2, $E_{\mathfrak{P}}$ is algebraic over $F_{\mathfrak{P}}$, and $E_{\mathfrak{P}} = EF_{\mathfrak{P}}$. Let $\tilde{F}_{\mathfrak{P}} \supset E_{\mathfrak{P}}$ be an algebraic closure of $F_{\mathfrak{P}}$. Then there exists an (algebraic) isomorphism $\sigma\colon \tilde{F}_{\mathfrak{P}} \to F_{\mathfrak{P}_0}$ which extends λ. As in the proof of Theorem 3.2, Corollary 1, we see that there is a valuation $|\ |_\sigma \in \mathfrak{P}$ such that, for $\alpha \in E_{\mathfrak{P}}$, $|\alpha|_\sigma = |\sigma(\alpha)|$, where $|\ |$ is the fixed valuation chosen above. Note that $\sigma|_E \in \mathrm{Mon}_F(E,\tilde{F}_{\mathfrak{P}_0})$. But then $\mathfrak{P} = \Phi(\sigma|_E) = (\sigma|_E)^{-1}\mathfrak{P}_0$, and Φ is surjective. This proves part a of the theorem.

Let $\sigma,\tau \in \mathrm{Mon}_F(E,\tilde{F}_{\mathfrak{P}_0})$. Suppose that μ is an $F_{\mathfrak{P}_0}$-automorphism of $\tilde{F}_{\mathfrak{P}_0}$ such that $\sigma = \mu\tau$. Then for $\alpha \in E$, $|\alpha|_\sigma = |\sigma(\alpha)| = |\mu\tau(\alpha)|$. By Theorem 5.3, Corollary 1, $|\mu\tau(\alpha)| = |N_{K/F_{\mathfrak{P}_0}}\mu\tau(\alpha)|^{1/[K:F_{\mathfrak{P}_0}]}$, where $K = F_{\mathfrak{P}_0}(\mu\tau(\alpha))$. Let $L = F_{\mathfrak{P}_0}(\tau(\alpha))$. Since μ is an $F_{\mathfrak{P}_0}$-automorphism of $\tilde{F}_{\mathfrak{P}_0}$, $N_{K/F_{\mathfrak{P}_0}}\mu\tau(\alpha) = N_{L/F_{\mathfrak{P}_0}}\tau(\alpha)$, and $[K: F_{\mathfrak{P}_0}] = [L: F_{\mathfrak{P}_0}]$. But then $|N_{K/F_{\mathfrak{P}_0}}\mu\tau(\alpha)|^{1/[K:F_{\mathfrak{P}_0}]} = |N_{L/F_{\mathfrak{P}_0}}\tau(\alpha)|^{1/[L:F_{\mathfrak{P}_0}]} = |\tau(\alpha)| = |\alpha|_\tau$, whence $|\alpha|_\sigma = |\alpha|_\tau$ and $\Phi(\sigma) = \Phi(\tau)$.

Conversely, suppose $\Phi(\sigma) = \Phi(\tau) = \mathfrak{P}$, for some $\sigma,\tau \in \mathrm{Mon}_F(E,\tilde{F}_{\mathfrak{P}_0})$. Then each of the maps $\sigma\colon E \to \sigma(E)$ and $\tau\colon E \to \tau(E)$ is an algebraic and topological isomorphism of E, with the topology determined by $\mathfrak{P}$, onto a subfield of $\tilde{F}_{\mathfrak{P}_0}$, with the topology determined by $\mathfrak{P}_0$. By Theorem 3.2, Corollary 2, $\sigma(E)F_{\mathfrak{P}_0}$ $(\tau(E)F_{\mathfrak{P}_0})$ is a completion of $\sigma(E)$ $(\tau(E))$ at $\mathfrak{P}_0$. By the corollary of Theorem 3.1, σ (τ) has a unique extension to an algebraic and topological isomorphism $\sigma_{\mathfrak{P}}\colon E_{\mathfrak{P}} \to \sigma(E)F_{\mathfrak{P}_0}$ $(\tau_{\mathfrak{P}}\colon E_{\mathfrak{P}} \to \tau(E)F_{\mathfrak{P}_0})$, where

$E_{\mathfrak{P}} \supset E$ is a completion of E at $\mathfrak{P}$. Since both σ and τ act as the identity on F, $\sigma_{\mathfrak{P}}\tau_{\mathfrak{P}}^{-1}$ acts as the identity in $F_{\mathfrak{P}_0}$. Hence $\sigma_{\mathfrak{P}}\tau_{\mathfrak{P}}^{-1}$ is an $F_{\mathfrak{P}_0}$-monomorphism of $\tau(E)F_{\mathfrak{P}_0}$ into $\tilde{F}_{\mathfrak{P}_0}$. But $\sigma_{\mathfrak{P}}\tau_{\mathfrak{P}}^{-1}$ extends to an $F_{\mathfrak{P}_0}$-automorphism, μ, of $\tilde{F}_{\mathfrak{P}_0}$, whence $\sigma = \mu\tau$, as desired. ▮

Corollary. *Let F be a subfield of a field E, with* $[E\colon F]$ *finite, and let* $\mathfrak{p}$ *be a prime spot on F. Then there are at most* $[E\colon F]$ *prime spots on E which divide* $\mathfrak{p}$. *If, in addition, E is purely inseparable over F, then there is exactly one prime spot on E which divides* $\mathfrak{p}$. □

Examples.

1. We examine the extensions of the 7-adic valuation on $\mathbf{Q}$ to a valuation on $\mathbf{Q}(\sqrt{2})$. There are two $\mathbf{Q}$-monomorphisms, ι and σ, of $\mathbf{Q}(\sqrt{2})$ into an algebraic closure, $\tilde{\mathbf{Q}}_7$, of the 7-adic completion of $\mathbf{Q}$, where (with obvious identifications) $\iota(a + b\sqrt{2}) = a + b\sqrt{2}$ and $\sigma(a + b\sqrt{2}) = a - b\sqrt{2}$, for all $a,b \in \mathbf{Q}$. Let $|\ |_7$ be the extension of the 7-adic valuation on $\mathbf{Q}$ to $\tilde{\mathbf{Q}}_7$. Then $|a + b\sqrt{2}|_\iota = |N_{\mathbf{Q}_7(\sqrt{2})/\mathbf{Q}_7}(a + b\sqrt{2})|_7{}^{1/[\mathbf{Q}_7(\sqrt{2}):\mathbf{Q}]}$. Since α is a quadratic residue mod 7, $\sqrt{2} \in \mathbf{Q}_7$. Hence $|a + b\sqrt{2}|_\iota = |a + b\sqrt{2}|_7$. Similarly, $|a + b\sqrt{2}|_\sigma = |a - b\sqrt{2}|_7$. An application of part b of Theorem 6.1 shows that $|\ |_i$ and $|\ |_\sigma$ are nonequivalent valuations of $\mathbf{Q}(\sqrt{2})$. An alternative way to see that these valuations are nonequivalent on $\mathbf{Q}(\sqrt{2})$ is to note that $1/7 = |7|_7 = |(3 + \sqrt{2})(3 - \sqrt{2})|_7 = |3 + \sqrt{2}|_7|3 - \sqrt{2}|_7$. But then (Exercise 6.1) $3 + \sqrt{2}$ has the value $\frac{1}{7}$ in one of the valuations $|\ |_i$, $|\ |_\sigma$, and has the value 1 in the other valuation, whence these valuations are nonequivalent.

Compare this example with Example 3 of Section 5.

2. Let $\mathbf{Q}(\alpha)$ be a finite extension of $\mathbf{Q}$. We determine the number of distinct archimedean prime spots on $\mathbf{Q}(\alpha)$. Since $\mathbf{Q}$ admits only one archimedean spot p_∞ (Theorem 1.4), each archimedean spot on $\mathbf{Q}(\alpha)$ divides p_∞, and each contains a valuation which extends the ordinary absolute value $|\ |$ on $\mathbf{Q}$.

Consider the tower of fields $\mathbf{C} \supset \mathbf{R} \supset \mathbf{Q}$ where $\mathbf{R}$ is the real field (completion of $\mathbf{Q}$ under $|\ |$) and $\mathbf{C}$ is the complex field (algebraic closure of R). Let $m_{\alpha/\mathbf{Q}}(x)$ be the minimum polynomial of α over $\mathbf{Q}$, and suppose that, over $\mathbf{C}$, $m_{\alpha/\mathbf{Q}}(x) = \prod_{i=1}^{n} (x - \alpha_i)$, with $\alpha_1 = \alpha$. Then there are n $\mathbf{Q}$-monomorphisms, $\sigma_1, \sigma_2, \ldots, \sigma_n$, of $\mathbf{Q}(\alpha)$ into $\mathbf{C}$, where $\sigma_i(\alpha) = \alpha_i$. By Theorem 6.1 (and its proof) each σ_i determines a valuation $|\ |_{\sigma_i}$ of $\mathbf{Q}(x)$ which is given by $|\beta|_{\sigma i} = |\sigma_i(\beta)|$, $\beta \in \mathbf{Q}(\alpha)$; furthermore, σ_i and σ_j determine equivalent valuations if and only if $\sigma_i = \mu\sigma_j$, where μ is an $\mathbf{R}$-automorphism of $\mathbf{C}$. It follows that σ_i and σ_j determine equivalent valuations if and only if $\alpha_i = \bar{\alpha}_j$, where $\bar{\alpha}_j$ is the complex conjugate of α_j. We conclude that the number of nonequivalent valuations arising from the σ_i is equal to the sum of the number of real roots of $m_{\alpha/\mathbf{Q}}(x)$ and one half the number of nonreal roots of $m_{\alpha/\mathbf{Q}}(x)$. Theorems

1.4 and 6.1 imply that every archimedean valuation on $\mathbf{Q}(\alpha)$ is equivalent to one of the valuations $|\ |_{\sigma_i}$.

We incorporate the result of this example in

Theorem 6.2. *Let $\mathbf{Q}(\alpha)$ be a finite extension of the rational field $\mathbf{Q}$. Let r_1 and $2r_2$ be the number of real roots and nonreal roots, respectively, of the minimum polynomial of α over $\mathbf{Q}$. Then $\mathbf{Q}(\alpha)$ admits exactly $r_1 + r_2$ distinct archimedean prime spots.* □

Compare this example with Example 2 of Section 3.

Definition 6.1. Let $\mathfrak{p}$ be a prime spot on a field F and let $F_{\mathfrak{P}_0} \supset F$ be a completion of F at $\mathfrak{p}$ (with $\mathfrak{P}_0$ the unique prime spot on $F_{\mathfrak{P}_0}$ such that $\mathfrak{P}_0|\mathfrak{p}$). Let $E \supset F$ be a finite extension of F, $\mathfrak{P}$ a prime spot on E which divides $\mathfrak{p}$, and $E_{\mathfrak{P}}$, $F_{\mathfrak{P}}$ completions, respectively, of E, F with $E_{\mathfrak{P}} \supset F_{\mathfrak{P}} \supset F$. There is a unique algebraic and topological isomorphism $\lambda\colon F_{\mathfrak{P}} \to F_{\mathfrak{P}_0}$ which is the identity on F. The *local degree of E over F at $\mathfrak{P}$* (or *local degree of $\mathfrak{P}|\mathfrak{p}$*) is $n(\mathfrak{P}|\mathfrak{p}) = [E_{\mathfrak{P}}\colon F_{\mathfrak{P}}]$. The *local norm $N_{\mathfrak{P}|\mathfrak{p}}$, of $\mathfrak{P}|\mathfrak{p}$*, is $\lambda \circ N_{E_{\mathfrak{P}}/F_{\mathfrak{P}}}\colon E_{\mathfrak{P}} \to F_{\mathfrak{P}_0}$. The *local trace* $\mathrm{tr}_{\mathfrak{P}|\mathfrak{p}}$, *of $\mathfrak{P}|\mathfrak{p}$*, is $\lambda \circ \mathrm{tr}_{E_{\mathfrak{P}}/F_{\mathfrak{P}}}\colon E_{\mathfrak{P}} \to F_{\mathfrak{P}_0}$. ///

REMARK. The local degree of $\mathfrak{P}|\mathfrak{p}$ depends only on $\mathfrak{P}$ and not on the particular completions chosen. The local norm and local trace obviously do depend on the completions $E_{\mathfrak{P}}$ and $F_{\mathfrak{P}_0}$.

We now examine how the degree of E over F ($N_{E/F}$;$\mathrm{tr}_{E/F}$) is related to the local degrees (local norms; local traces). In particular, we shall see that if E is a finite separable extension of F, then $[E\colon F]$ ($N_{E/F}$;$\mathrm{tr}_{E/F}$) is the sum of the local degrees (product of local norms; sum of local traces).

Lemma. *Let $\mathfrak{p}$, $\mathfrak{P}_0$, F, $F_{\mathfrak{P}_0}$ be as in Definition* 6.1. *Let $E = F(\alpha)$ be a finite separable extension of F, let $m_{\alpha/F}(x)$ be the minimum polynomial of α over F, and let $m_{\alpha/F}(x) = f_1(x)f_2(x)\cdots f_g(x)$ be a factorization of $m_{\alpha/F}(x)$ into irreducible polynomials over $F_{\mathfrak{P}_0}$. Then*

a. *There are exactly g distinct prime spots $\mathfrak{P}_1, \mathfrak{P}_2, \ldots, \mathfrak{P}_g$ on E which divide $\mathfrak{p}$.*

b. *The local degree of $\mathfrak{P}_i|\mathfrak{p}$ is equal to $\deg f_i(x)$.*

[*Informally, the "factorization" of $\mathfrak{p}$ into prime spots on $F(\alpha)$ parallels the factorization of $m_{\alpha/F}(x)$ over a completion of F at $\mathfrak{p}$.*]

PROOF. First note that since $F(\alpha)$ was assumed separable over F, any two factors $f_i(x)$, $f_j(x)$ $(i \neq j)$ are relatively prime over an algebraic closure

$\tilde{F}_{\mathfrak{P}_0} \supset F_{\mathfrak{P}_0}$ of $F_{\mathfrak{P}_0}$. Any F-monomorphism of $F(\alpha)$ into $\tilde{F}_{\mathfrak{P}_0}$ maps α onto a root of one of the $f_i(x)$ and, conversely, given a root $\rho_i \in \tilde{F}_{\mathfrak{P}_0}$ of $f_i(x)$, there is an F-monomorphism of $F(\alpha)$ into $\tilde{F}_{\mathfrak{P}_0}$ which maps α onto ρ_i. Let $\sigma, \tau \in \mathrm{Mon}_F(F(\alpha), \tilde{F}_{\mathfrak{P}_0})$. Then there is an $F_{\mathfrak{P}_0}$-automorphism, μ, of $\tilde{F}_{\mathfrak{P}_0}$ such that $\sigma = \mu\tau$ if and only if there is an $f_i(x)$ such that σ and τ map α into roots of $f_i(x)$. It follows from Theorem 6.1 that there are precisely g prime spots $\mathfrak{P}_1, \mathfrak{P}_2, \ldots, \mathfrak{P}_g$ on $F(\alpha)$ which divide $\mathfrak{p}$. Furthermore, $\mathfrak{P}_i$ is determined (as in the proof of Theorem 6.1) by a $\sigma_i \in \mathrm{Mon}_F(F(\alpha), \tilde{F}_{\mathfrak{P}_0})$ such that $\sigma_i(\alpha)$ is a root of $f_i(x)$.

Finally, it is easy to see that $n(\mathfrak{P}_i|\mathfrak{p})$, the local degree of $\mathfrak{P}_i|\mathfrak{p}$, is equal to $[F(\sigma_i(\alpha))F_{\mathfrak{P}_0}: F_{\mathfrak{P}_0}]$. But $\sigma_i(\alpha)$ is a root of $f_i(x)$, whence $n(\mathfrak{P}_i|\mathfrak{p}) = \deg f_i(x)$. ▮

Theorem 6.3. *Let E be a finite separable extension of F with $E \supset F$, and let $\mathfrak{p}$ be a prime spot on F. Then*

a. $$[E: F] = \sum_{\substack{\mathfrak{P}|\mathfrak{p} \\ \mathfrak{P} \text{ spot on } E}} n(\mathfrak{P}|\mathfrak{p}).$$

b. *For each $\beta \in E$,* $$N_{E/F}(\beta) = \prod_{\substack{\mathfrak{P}|\mathfrak{p} \\ \mathfrak{P} \text{ spot on } E}} N_{\mathfrak{P}|\mathfrak{p}}(\beta).$$

c. *For each $\beta \in E$,* $$\mathrm{tr}_{E/F}(\beta) = \sum_{\substack{\mathfrak{P}|\mathfrak{p} \\ \mathfrak{P} \text{ spot on } E}} \mathrm{tr}_{\mathfrak{P}|\mathfrak{p}}(\beta).$$

PROOF. Since E is separable over F, there is an $\alpha \in E$ such that $E = F(\alpha)$. With the notation of the lemma, let $m_{\alpha/F}(x) = f_1(x) \cdots f_g(x)$ be a factorization of $m_{\alpha/F}(x)$ into irreducible factors over $F_{\mathfrak{P}_0}$. Then $[E: F] = \deg m_{\alpha/F}(x) = \sum_{i=1}^{g} \deg f_i(x)$. But, by the lemma, $\deg f_i(x) = n(\mathfrak{P}_i|\mathfrak{p})$, and $\{\mathfrak{P}_i\}_{i=1}^{g}$ is a complete set of prime spots on E which divide $\mathfrak{p}$, whence $[E: F] = \sum_{\mathfrak{P}|\mathfrak{p}} n(\mathfrak{P}|\mathfrak{p})$. This proves a.

Implicit in the proof of the lemma is the fact that $\mathrm{Mon}_F(E, \tilde{F}_{\mathfrak{P}_0})$ is a disjoint union of sets $\{\sigma_{i1}, \sigma_{i2}, \ldots, \sigma_{id_i}\}$, where $d_i = \deg f_i(x)$, $i = 1, 2, \ldots, g$, and σ_{ij}, σ_{ik} "induce" the same prime spot $\mathfrak{P}_i$ on E. It is easy to see that, for $\beta \in E$,

$$N_{\mathfrak{P}_i|\mathfrak{p}}(\beta) = \prod_{j=1}^{d_i} \sigma_{ij}(\beta) \quad \text{and} \quad \mathrm{tr}_{\mathfrak{P}_i|\mathfrak{p}}(\beta) = \sum_{j=1}^{d_i} \sigma_{ij}(\beta).$$

But then

$$N_{E/F}(\beta) = \prod_{i=1}^{g} \prod_{j=1}^{d_i} \sigma_{ij}(\beta) = \prod_{i=1}^{g} N_{\mathfrak{P}_i|\mathfrak{p}}(\beta) = \prod_{\mathfrak{P}|\mathfrak{p}} N_{\mathfrak{P}|\mathfrak{p}}(\beta),$$

and, similarly, $\mathrm{tr}_{E/F}(\beta) = \sum_{\mathfrak{P}|\mathfrak{p}} \mathrm{tr}_{\mathfrak{P}|\mathfrak{p}}(\beta)$. ▮

If K is a finite extension of F, with $K \supset F$, then there is a tower $K \supset E \supset F$ where E is separable over F, and K is purely inseparable over E. A prime spot on E is divisible by precisely one prime spot on K (corollary of Theorem 6.1). This and Theorem 6.3a imply that $[K: F] \geq \sum_{\mathfrak{P}|\mathfrak{p},\, \mathfrak{P} \text{ spot on } K} n(\mathfrak{P}|\mathfrak{p})$. We leave the details to the reader.

7. Ramification Index and Residue Class Field Degree

Thus far, our primary concern in our study of fields with valuations has been with the fields and the valuations themselves. We have already met an associated structure: the residue class field $\bar{F}$ (Section 5). In this section we introduce another structure, the value group $\mathscr{V}(F)$, and examine how, for $E \supset F$, the cardinals $[\bar{E}: \bar{F}]$, $[\mathscr{V}(E): \mathscr{V}(F)]$, and $[E: F]$ are related.

Definition 7.1. Let $|\ |$ be a valuation on a field F. Then $\mathscr{V}(F,|\ |) = \{|\alpha| \mid \alpha \in F, \alpha \neq 0\}$ is a multiplicative subgroup of the positive reals, the *value group of F at* $|\ |$. ///

REMARK. If $|\ |$ and $|\ |'$ are equivalent valuations on F, then, in general, $\mathscr{V}(F,|\ |) \neq \mathscr{V}(F,|\ |')$. However, it follows immediately from Theorem 1.1 that $\mathscr{V}(F,|\ |) \cong \mathscr{V}(F,|\ |')$.

The value group of $\mathbf{Q}$ at the ordinary absolute value is the multiplicative group of positive rationals. The value group of a completion of $\mathbf{Q}$ at the extended absolute value is the multiplicative group of positive reals. Such a situation cannot arise in the case of nonarchimedean valuations: The value group remains unaltered when we move up to a completion. Formally, we have

Theorem 7.1. *Let* $|\ |$ *be a nonarchimedean valuation on a field F, and let* $\hat{F}$ *be a completion of F with* $\hat{F} \supset F$ *and* $|\ |^{\wedge}$ *the extension of* $|\ |$ *to a valuation on* $\hat{F}$. *Then* $\mathscr{V}(\hat{F},|\ |^{\wedge}) = \mathscr{V}(F,|\ |)$.

PROOF. Clearly $\mathscr{V}(F,|\ |) \subset \mathscr{V}(\hat{F},|\ |^{\wedge})$. Let $|\alpha|^{\wedge} \in \mathscr{V}(\hat{F},|\ |^{\wedge})$, with $\alpha \in \hat{F} - \{0\}$. There exists a Cauchy sequence $a_1, a_2, \ldots$ ($a_i \in F$) such that $\lim_{i\to\infty} |\alpha_i| = \lim_{i\to\infty} |a_i|^{\wedge} = |\alpha|^{\wedge}$. Choose n large enough so that $|a_i - \alpha|^{\wedge} < |\alpha|^{\wedge}$. Then $|a_i| = |a_i|^{\wedge} = |(a_i - \alpha) + \alpha|^{\wedge} = |\alpha|^{\wedge}$ (Theorem 1.3), whence $|\alpha|^{\wedge} \in \mathscr{V}(F,|\ |)$, and $\mathscr{V}(\hat{F},|\ |^{\wedge}) \subset \mathscr{V}(F,|\ |)$. ∎

Definition 7.2. Let F be a subfield of a field E, $\mathfrak{P}$ a prime spot on E, and $\mathfrak{p}$ a prime spot on F with $\mathfrak{P}|\mathfrak{p}$. Let $|\ |'$ be a valuation in $\mathfrak{P}$ and $|\ |$ the valuation on F which is the restriction of $| \,|'$ to F. Then the *ramification index of* $\mathfrak{P}|\mathfrak{p} = e(\mathfrak{P}|\mathfrak{p}) = [\mathscr{V}(E,| \,|'): \mathscr{V}(F,| \,|)]$. ///

REMARKS.

1. The ramification index $e(\mathfrak{P}|\mathfrak{p})$ is independent of the choice of valuation $| \,|'$ in $\mathfrak{P}$. For if $| \,|_1'$ is another valuation in $\mathfrak{P}$ and $| \,|_1$ is its restriction to F, then (Theorem 1.1) there is a positive real number t such that $x \mapsto x^t$ defines an isomorphism of $\mathscr{V}(E,| \,|')$ onto $\mathscr{V}(E,| \,|_1')$ and this isomorphism carries $\mathscr{V}(F,| \,|)$ onto $\mathscr{V}(F,| \,|_1)$.

2. In view of Theorem 7.1, the ramification index of non-archimedean $\mathfrak{P}$, where $\mathfrak{P}|\mathfrak{p}$ remains unaltered when we move up to completions; i.e., if $\hat{\mathfrak{P}}$, $\hat{\mathfrak{p}}$ are extensions of nonarchimedean $\mathfrak{P}$, $\mathfrak{p}$ to completions $E_{\mathfrak{P}}$, $F_{\mathfrak{p}}$ of E, F, respectively, with $E_{\mathfrak{P}} \supset F_{\mathfrak{p}}$ and $\hat{\mathfrak{P}}|\hat{\mathfrak{p}}$, then $e(\hat{\mathfrak{P}}|\hat{\mathfrak{p}}) = e(\mathfrak{P}|\mathfrak{p})$.

Let $\mathfrak{p}$ be a nonarchimedean prime spot on a field F. We recall (Definition 5.1) that the residue class field $\bar{F}$ of F at $\mathfrak{p}$ is $\mathcal{O}(\mathfrak{p})/\mathcal{M}(\mathfrak{p})$, where $\mathcal{O}(\mathfrak{p})$ is the ring of local integers at $\mathfrak{p}$ and $\mathcal{M}(\mathfrak{p})$ is the maximal ideal at $\mathfrak{p}$. Now let $E \supset F$ be a field and let $\mathfrak{P}$ be a prime spot on E with $\mathfrak{P}|\mathfrak{p}$. Then $\mathcal{O}(\mathfrak{p}) \subset \mathcal{O}(\mathfrak{P})$, $\mathcal{M}(\mathfrak{p}) \subset \mathcal{M}(\mathfrak{P})$, and there exists a unique monomorphism $i^*: \bar{F} \to \bar{E}$ such that the diagram

$$\begin{array}{ccc} \mathcal{O}(\mathfrak{p}) & \xrightarrow{\;i\;} & \mathcal{O}(\mathfrak{P}) \\ \downarrow{\scriptstyle \nu_F} & & \downarrow{\scriptstyle \nu_E} \\ \bar{F} = \mathcal{O}(\mathfrak{p})/\mathcal{M}(\mathfrak{p}) & \xrightarrow[i^*]{} & \mathcal{O}(\mathfrak{P})/\mathcal{M}(\mathfrak{P}) = \bar{E} \end{array}$$

commutes, where ν_F and ν_E are the canonical epimorphisms and i is the canonical embedding. Hence, $\bar{E}$ is an extension of $\bar{F}$, and $[\bar{E}: \bar{F}] = [\bar{E}: i^*(\bar{F})]$.

***Definition** 7.3.* Let E, F, $\mathfrak{P}$, $\mathfrak{p}$, $\bar{E}$, and $\bar{F}$ be as in the preceding discussion. The *residue class field degree of* $\mathfrak{P}|\mathfrak{p} = f(\mathfrak{P}|\mathfrak{p}) = [\bar{E}: \bar{F}]$. ///

As is the case with the ramification index, the residue class field degree remains unchanged when we move up to completions. We have

Theorem 7.2. *Let $\hat{\mathfrak{P}}$, $\hat{\mathfrak{p}}$ be extensions of nonarchimedean prime spots $\mathfrak{P}$, $\mathfrak{p}$ to completions $E_{\mathfrak{P}}$, $F_{\mathfrak{p}}$ of fields E, F, respectively, with $E_{\mathfrak{P}} \supset F_{\mathfrak{p}}$ and $\hat{\mathfrak{P}}|\hat{\mathfrak{p}}$. Then $f(\hat{\mathfrak{P}}|\hat{\mathfrak{p}}) = f(\mathfrak{P}|\mathfrak{p})$.*

PROOF. We have seen above that there is a monomorphism $i^*: \bar{F} \to \bar{E}$ of the residue class field of F into the residue class field of E. By Theorem 5.1 there are isomorphisms $\varphi_{\mathfrak{p}}\colon \bar{F} \to \bar{F}_{\mathfrak{p}}$ and $\varphi_{\mathfrak{P}}\colon \bar{E} \to \bar{E}_{\mathfrak{P}}$. But then there is a monomorphism $i^{**}\colon \bar{F}_{\mathfrak{P}} \to \bar{E}_{\mathfrak{P}}$ such that the diagram

$$\begin{array}{ccc} \bar{F} & \xrightarrow{\ i^*\ } & \bar{E} \\ {\scriptstyle \varphi_{\mathfrak{p}}}\downarrow & & \downarrow{\scriptstyle \varphi_{\mathfrak{P}}} \\ \bar{F}_{\mathfrak{p}} & \xrightarrow[\ i^{**}\ ]{} & \bar{E} \end{array}$$

commutes. We conclude that $f(\hat{\mathfrak{P}}|\hat{\mathfrak{p}}) = [\bar{E}_{\mathfrak{P}}\colon \bar{F}_{\mathfrak{p}}] = [\bar{E}\colon \bar{F}] = f(\mathfrak{P}|\mathfrak{p})$. ∎

The main theorem of this section is

Theorem 7.3. *Let E be a finite extension of a field F, with $E \supset F$, and $[E\colon F] = n$. Let $\mathfrak{P}$ and $\mathfrak{p}$ be nonarchimedean prime spots on E and F, respectively, with $\mathfrak{P}|\mathfrak{p}$. Then*

$$e(\mathfrak{P}|\mathfrak{p})f(\mathfrak{P}|\mathfrak{p}) \le n.$$

PROOF. Let $\bar{E}$ and $\bar{F}$ be the residue class fields of E at $\mathfrak{P}$ and of F at $\mathfrak{p}$, respectively. We identify $\bar{F}$ with a subfield of $\bar{E}$. Let $\{\bar{\beta}_1,\bar{\beta}_2,\ldots,\bar{\beta}_s\}$ be a subset of $\bar{E}$ which is free over $\bar{F}$. There exist $\beta_i \in \mathcal{O}(\mathfrak{P})$, $i = 1, 2,\ldots, s$, such that $\beta_i \mapsto \bar{\beta}_i$ under the canonical epimorphism of $\mathcal{O}(\mathfrak{P})$ onto $\bar{E}$. Let $|\ | \in \mathfrak{P}$. Note that $\beta_i \notin \mathcal{M}(\mathfrak{P})$, whence $|\beta_i| = 1$, $i = 1, 2,\ldots, s$.

Let $\{\pi_1,\pi_2,\ldots,\pi_t\}$ be a subset of E such that $\{|\pi_1|,|\pi_2|,\ldots,|\pi_t|\}$ is a set of representatives of t distinct cosets of $\mathcal{V}(F,|\ |')$ in $\mathcal{V}(E,|\ |)$, where $|\ |'$ is the restriction of $|\ |$ to F. Note that, if $|a_1\pi_i| = |a_2\pi_j|$ for $a_1,a_2 \in F$ and $i \ne j$, then $a_1 = a_2 = 0$. For otherwise $|\pi_i|$ and $|\pi_j|$ belong to the same coset.

We shall show that the set $\{\beta_i\pi_j\}_{i=1,2,\ldots,s,\,j=1,2,\ldots,t}$ of st elements of E is free over F. It will follow that $st \le n$. But then $e(\mathfrak{P}|\mathfrak{p})$ and $f(\mathfrak{P}|\mathfrak{p})$ are both finite (otherwise we could choose s or t to be arbitrarily large), and $e(\mathfrak{P}|\mathfrak{p})f(\mathfrak{P}|\mathfrak{p}) \le n$.

We show first that, for $a_i \in F$, $|\sum_{i=1}^s a_i\beta_i| = \max_i\{|a_i|\}$. Let $\max_i\{|a_i|\} = |a_1|$ (say). If $|a_1| = 0$, there is nothing to prove. Assume, therefore, that $|a_1| \ne 0$. Then

$$\left|\sum_{i=1}^s a_i\beta_i\right| = |a_1|\left|\sum_{i=1}^s \frac{a_i}{a_1}\beta_i\right|.$$

Since $a_i/a_1 \in \mathcal{O}(\mathfrak{p})$, and $\{\bar{\beta}_i\}_{i=1}^s$ is free over $\bar{F}$,

$$\sum_{i=1}^s \frac{a_i}{a_1}\beta_i \in (\mathcal{O}(\mathfrak{P}) - \mathcal{M}(\mathfrak{P})) \quad \text{and} \quad \left|\sum_{i=1}^s \frac{a_i}{a_1}\beta_i\right| = 1.$$

But then $|\sum_{i=1}^{s} a_i\beta_i| = |a_1| = \max_i\{|a_i|\}$.

Suppose that

$$\sum_{i,j} b_{ij}\beta_i\pi_j = \sum_{j=1}^{t}\left(\sum_{i=1}^{s} b_{ij}\beta_i\right)\pi_j = 0, \qquad b_{ij} \in F.$$

Since

$$\left|\sum_{i=1}^{s} b_{ij}\beta_i\pi_j\right| = \left|\sum_{i=1}^{s} b_{ij}\beta_i\right| |\pi_j| = \max_i\{|b_{ij}|\}|\pi_j| = |a_j|\ |\pi_j| = |a_j\pi_j|$$

for some $a_j \in F$,

$$\left|\sum_{i=1}^{s} b_{ij_1}\beta_i\pi_{j_1}\right| \neq \left|\sum_{i=1}^{s} b_{ij_2}\beta_i\pi_{j_2}\right| \quad \text{or} \quad \left|\sum_{i=1}^{s} b_{ij_1}\beta_i\right| = \left|\sum_{i=1}^{s} b_{ij_2}\beta_i\right| = 0$$

for $j_1 \neq j_2$. Hence we may apply Theorem 1.3 to obtain

$$0 = \left|\sum_{j=1}^{t}\left(\sum_{i=1}^{s} b_{ij}\beta_i\right)\pi_j\right| = \max_j\left\{\left|\sum_{i=1}^{s} b_{ij}\beta_i\right| |\pi_j|\right\}.$$

But then, for $j = 1, 2, \ldots, t$,

$$0 = \left|\sum_{i=1}^{s} b_{ij}\beta_i\right| = \max_i\{|b_{ij}|\},$$

whence $b_{ij} = 0$ for $i = 1, 2, \ldots, s$, $j = 1, 2, \ldots, t$, and $\{\beta_i\pi_j\}$ is a free set over F. ∎

The following corollary is a consequence of the theorem and Theorem 6.3.

Corollary. *Let E be a finite separable extension of F, with $E \supset F$, and let $\mathfrak{p}$ be a prime spot on F. Then*

$$\sum_{\substack{\mathfrak{P}|\mathfrak{p} \\ \mathfrak{P} \text{ a spot on } E}} e(\mathfrak{P}|\mathfrak{p})\cdot f(\mathfrak{P}|\mathfrak{p}) \leq [E : F]. \quad \square$$

We have seen that $e(\mathfrak{P}|\mathfrak{p})$ and $f(\mathfrak{P}|\mathfrak{p})$ do not change if we take completions. However, $[E : F]$ may decrease when we move up to completions. Thus, for example, $[\mathbf{Q}(\sqrt{2}) : \mathbf{Q}] = 2$, but $[\mathbf{Q}_7(\sqrt{2}) : \mathbf{Q}_7] = 1$. (See the example following Theorem 5.2). If one were to guess that the inequality in Theorem 7.3 can be replaced by an equality in the case that E and F are complete at their respective prime spots, one would guess wrong (Exercise 7.1). We shall see in Section 8 that $ef = n$ when E and F are complete and the value groups are cyclic.

8. Discrete Valuations

The value group of a field at a valuation is a subgroup of the multiplicative group, P, of the positive reals. In the next theorem we shall see that a subgroup G of P, $G \neq \{1\}$, is either dense in P (i.e., for each $u \in P$, there exists a sequence $\{g_n | g_n \in G\}$ such that $\lim_{n\to\infty} g_n = u$), or G is an infinite cyclic group. (In the latter case, the relative topology on G is, of course, the discrete topology.) This theorem leads naturally to a classification of valuations on a field in terms of the nature of their value groups. Since equivalent valuations on a field F have isomorphic value groups (Theorem 1.1), this classification is, in essence, a classification of the prime spots on F.

Theorem 8.1. *Let P be the multiplicative group of positive real numbers, and let G be a subgroup of P, $G \neq \{1\}$. Let $S = \{s | s \in G, s < 1\}$, and let $l = \text{lub}_{s\in S}\, s$. Then*

a. *G is an infinite cyclic group with generator l if and only if $l < 1$.*

b. *G is dense in P if and only if $l = 1$.*

Hence every subroup of P, not the identity, is either an infinite cyclic group or is dense in P.

PROOF. We shall prove the theorem by showing that if $l = 1$, then G is dense in P, and if $l < 1$, then G is cyclic with generator l.

Suppose that $l = 1$. To prove that G is dense in P, it is sufficient to prove that G is dense in the open interval (0,1). Let $u \in (0,1)$. Then there exists $r \in P$ such that $u = e^{-r}$. Since $l = 1$, and $G \neq \{1\}$, there exist real numbers t_i, $i = 1, 2, \ldots$, such that $t_i < t_{i+1}$, $1 > 1 - (r/t_i) \in G$, and $\lim_{i\to\infty} (1 - (r/t_i)) = 1$. Let [ ] denote the greatest integer function (i.e., [ ]: $R \to \mathbf{Z}$ such that, for any real number x, $[x] \in \mathbf{Z}$ and $[x] \leq x < [x] + 1$). Then

$$\left(1 - \frac{r}{t_i}\right)^{[t_i]} \geq \left(1 - \frac{r}{t_i}\right)^{t_i} > \left(1 - \frac{r}{t_i}\right)^{[t_i]}\left(1 - \frac{r}{t_i}\right).$$

Taking limits we see that

$$\lim_{i\to\infty} \left(1 - \frac{r}{t_i}\right)^{[t_i]} = e^{-r} = u.$$

But $(1 - (r/t_i))^{[t_i]} \in G$, whence G is dense in (0,1).

Suppose now that $l < 1$. First note that, if $l \in G$, then every element of G is an integral power of l. For, assume that $l \in G$ and that there exists $g \in G$, with g not a power of l. Then there is an integer n such that $l^n < g < l^{n-1}$. But then $l < g/l^{n-1} < 1$, with $g/l^{n-1} \in G$. This contradicts the definition of l!

We now prove that $l \in G$. Suppose $l \notin G$. Clearly, there exists a sequence $\{h_i\}_{i=1}^{\infty}$ of elements of S such that $h_i < h_{i+1}$ $(i = 1,2,\ldots)$, and $\lim_{i\to\infty} h_i = l$. Since $l < 1$, $l^2 < l$. Hence for some positive integer n, $l^2 < h_n < h_{n+1} < l$. But then $l < h_n/h_{n+1} < 1$, with $h_n/h_{n+1} \in S$. Contradiction! We conclude that $l \in G$, and the theorem is proved. ▮

Definition 8.1. Let $|\ |$ be a valuation on a field F, and let $\mathfrak{p}$ be a prime spot on F. Then $|\ |$ is a *discrete valuation* on F if the value group $\mathscr{V}(F,|\ |)$ is an infinite cyclic group; $\mathfrak{p}$ is a *discrete prime spot* on F if $\mathfrak{p}$ contains a discrete valuation. ///

REMARKS.

1 If one valuation in a prime spot $\mathfrak{p}$ is discrete, then every valuation in $\mathfrak{p}$ is discrete.

2. If $|\ |$ is a discrete valuation on a field F, then $\mathscr{V}(F,|\ |)$ has the discrete topology. However, the topology induced on F by $|\ |$ is *not* discrete. Only the trivial valuation induces the discrete topology on F.

Example. The p-adic valuations on $\mathbf{Q}$ are all discrete.

We recall that if $\mathfrak{p}$ is a nonarchimedean prime spot on a field F and $|\ |$ is a valuation in $\mathfrak{p}$, then the ring of local integers of F at $\mathfrak{p}$ is $\mathscr{O}(\mathfrak{p}) = \{a \in F \mid |a| \leq 1\}$, and the maximal ideal of F at $\mathfrak{p}$ is $\mathscr{M}(\mathfrak{p}) = \{a \in F \mid |a| < 1\}$. Let $\mathscr{U}(\mathfrak{p})$ be the group of units of $\mathscr{O}(\mathfrak{p})$. It is easy to see that $\mathscr{U}(\mathfrak{p}) = \{a \in F \mid |a| = 1\}$. $\mathscr{O}(\mathfrak{p})$, $\mathscr{M}(\mathfrak{p})$, and $\mathscr{U}(\mathfrak{p})$ depend on $\mathfrak{p}$, and not on the choice of the valuation $|\ | \in \mathfrak{p}$.

Theorem 8.2. *Let $\mathfrak{p}$ be a discrete prime spot on a field F. Then*

a. *$\mathfrak{p}$ is nonarchimedean.*
b. *There is a prime $\pi \in \mathscr{O}(\mathfrak{p})$ such that $\mathscr{M}(\mathfrak{p})$ is the principal ideal generated by π; i.e., $\mathscr{M}(\mathfrak{p}) = (\pi)$.*
c. *Every nonzero ideal of $\mathscr{O}(\mathfrak{p})$ is a power of $\mathscr{M}(\mathfrak{p})$; i.e., if I is a nonzero ideal of $\mathscr{O}(\mathfrak{p})$, then there is a nonnegative integer k such that $I = [\mathscr{M}(\mathfrak{p})]^k = (\pi^k)$.*
d. *$\mathscr{O}(\mathfrak{p})$ is a principal ideal domain.*

PROOF. Let $|\ |$ be a valuation in $\mathfrak{p}$.

a. Suppose $|\ |$ is archimedean. Then $|\ |$ is unbounded on the set $\{n \cdot 1 | n \in \mathbf{Z}, 1 \text{ the identity of } F\}$. For $i = 1, 2, 3, \ldots$, let n_i be the smallest positive integer such that $|n_i \cdot 1| > i$. Then

$$1 - \frac{1}{i} < |1| - \left|\frac{1}{n_i \cdot 1}\right| \leq \left|1 - \frac{1}{n_i \cdot 1}\right| = \frac{|n_i \cdot 1 - 1|}{|n_i \cdot 1|} < 1,$$

and $\text{lub}_{a \in \mathscr{M}(\mathfrak{p})}|a| = 1$. Since $\mathfrak{p}$ was assumed to be discrete, this is impossible. But then $|\ |$ and $\mathfrak{p}$ are nonarchimedean.

b. Let $l = \text{lub}_{a \in \mathscr{M}(\mathfrak{p})}|a|$. By Theorem 8.1, $l \in \mathscr{V}(F,|\ |)$ and $\mathscr{V}(F,|\ |)$ consists of integral powers of l. There is a $\pi \in \mathscr{M}(\mathfrak{p})$ such that $|\pi| = l$. Clearly, $(\pi) \subset \mathscr{M}(\mathfrak{p})$. If $a \in \mathscr{M}(\mathfrak{p})$, then $|a| = l^m = |\pi^m|$, for some integer m, and $|a/\pi^m| = 1$. But then $a/\pi^m = u \in \mathscr{U}(\mathfrak{p})$, whence $a = u\pi^m \in (\pi)$. We conclude that $\mathscr{M}(\mathfrak{p}) = (\pi)$.

Suppose that $\pi = \mu\lambda$ with $\mu,\lambda \in \mathscr{O}(\mathfrak{p})$. Since $|\pi| = \text{lub}_{a \in \mathscr{M}(\mathfrak{p})}|a|$, $|\mu| = 1$ or $|\lambda| = 1$. But then μ or λ is a unit, and π is a prime in $\mathscr{O}(\mathfrak{p})$.

c. Let I be a proper ideal of $\mathscr{O}(\mathfrak{p})$. Then there is a positive integer k such that $\text{lub}_{a \in I}|a| = l^k$, where $l = \text{lub}_{a \in \mathscr{M}(\mathfrak{p})}|a|$. We leave it to the reader to show that $I = [\mathscr{M}(\mathfrak{p})]^k$.

d. Follows directly from assertions b and c. ▮

REMARKS. Let F, $\mathfrak{p}$, and π be as in the theorem. Then $\mathscr{M}(\mathfrak{p})$ is the unique maximal ideal of $\mathscr{O}(\mathfrak{p})$, and π and its associates are the only primes in $\mathscr{O}(\mathfrak{p})$. If π' is any prime in $\mathscr{O}(\mathfrak{p})$, then $\mathscr{M}(\mathfrak{p}) = (\pi')$. If $|\ | \in \mathfrak{p}$, then $|\pi|$ is a generator for $\mathscr{V}(F,|\ |)$.

Theorem 8.3. *Let E be a finite extension of a field F, with $E \supset F$. Let $\mathfrak{P}$ and $\mathfrak{p}$ be prime spots on E and F, respectively, with $\mathfrak{P}|\mathfrak{p}$, and let $e = e(\mathfrak{P}|\mathfrak{p})$ be the ramification index of $\mathfrak{P}$ over $\mathfrak{p}$. Then*

a. *$\mathfrak{P}$ is discrete if and only if $\mathfrak{p}$ is discrete.*

b. *If $\mathfrak{p}$ is discrete, then $\mathscr{O}(\mathfrak{P})\mathscr{M}(\mathfrak{p}) = [\mathscr{M}(\mathfrak{P})]^e$, and $\mathscr{M}(\mathfrak{p}) = [\mathscr{M}(\mathfrak{P})]^e \cap \mathscr{O}(\mathfrak{p})$.*

PROOF.

a. Let $|\ | \in \mathfrak{P}$ and let $|\ |'$ be the restriction of $|\ |$ to F. If $\mathfrak{P}$ is discrete, then $\mathscr{V}(E,|\ |)$ is an infinite cyclic group, and $\mathscr{V}(F,|\ |')$ is a subgroup of $\mathscr{V}(E,|\ |)$ with $\mathscr{V}(F,|\ |') \neq \{1\}$ (corollary to Theorem 1.3). But then, if $\mathfrak{P}$ is discrete, so is $\mathfrak{p}$.

We recall (Theorem 7.3) that $e = e(\mathfrak{P}|\mathfrak{p})$ is finite. The eth power of any element in $\mathscr{V}(E,|\ |)$ is in $\mathscr{V}(F,|\ |')$. If $\mathfrak{p}$ is discrete, then $\mathscr{V}(F,|\ |')$, and hence also $\mathscr{V}(E,|\ |)$, is nowhere dense. But then $\mathfrak{P}$ is discrete.

b. The proof is easy and is left to the reader. ▮

In the next theorem we see that every element in a field with a discrete prime spot may be represented as an infinite series of a special type.

Theorem 8.4. *Let $\mathfrak{p}$ be a discrete prime spot on a field F, let $\mathscr{M}(\mathfrak{p}) = (\pi)$, and let $\mathscr{C}$ be a complete set of distinct representatives in $\mathscr{O}(\mathfrak{p})$ of the residue class field $\bar{F} = \mathscr{O}(\mathfrak{p})/\mathscr{M}(\mathfrak{p})$. Let $|\ | \in \mathfrak{p}$, and let $\{\pi_i\}_{i\in\mathbf{Z}}$ be a subset of F such that $|\pi_i| = |\pi^i|$ for each $i \in \mathbf{Z}$. Finally, let $a \in F$, $a \neq 0$.*

a. *There exists $c_i \in \mathscr{C}$ such that $a = \sum_{i=n}^{\infty} c_i\pi_i$, where n is the integer such that $|a| = |\pi^n|$, and $c_n \neq 0$.*

b. *If $a = \sum_{i=n}^{\infty} c_i\pi_i = \sum_{i=n}^{\infty} c_i'\pi_i$, with $c_i, c_i' \in \mathscr{C}$, then $c_i = c_i'$ for $i = n, n+1, \ldots$.*

c. *If F is complete at $\mathfrak{p}$, then every series*

$$\sum_{i=m}^{\infty} d_i\pi_i \in F \qquad (d_i \in \mathscr{C},\ m \in \mathbf{Z}).$$

PROOF.

a. Since $|a/\pi_n| = 1$, a/π_n is a unit, and there exists a nonzero $c_n \in \mathscr{C}$ such that $\overline{(a/\pi_n)} = \bar{c}_n$, where $\bar{x}$ denotes the image of $x \in \mathscr{O}(\mathfrak{p})$ under the canonical epimorphism of $\mathscr{O}(\mathfrak{p})$ onto $\bar{F}$. Then $|(a/\pi_n) - c_n| < 1$, and $|a - c_n\pi_n| = |a^{(1)}| < |\pi_n|$, where $a^{(1)} = a - c_n\pi_n$. We repeat the procedure with $a^{(1)}$ to obtain $a^{(2)}$. By induction, $a - \sum_{i=n}^{m+n} c_i\pi_i = a^{(m+1)}$ with $|a^{(m+1)}| < |\pi_{m+n}|$. But then $\lim_{m\to\infty} \sum_{i=n}^{m+n} c_i\pi_i = a$, and $a = \sum_{i=n}^{\infty} c_i\pi_i$.

b. Suppose $a = \sum_{i=n}^{\infty} c_i\pi_i = \sum_{i=n}^{\infty} c_i'\pi_i$ with $c_i, c_i' \in \mathscr{C}$. Assume that there is an integer $i \geq n$ such that $c_i \neq c_i'$. Let k be the smallest integer greater than or equal to n such that $c_k \neq c_k'$. Since $\bar{c}_k \neq \bar{c}_k'$, $|c_k - c_k'| = 1$. But then $0 = |0| = |\sum_{i=k}^{\infty} (c_i - c_i')\pi_i| = |\pi_k| \neq 0$. Contradiction! Hence $c_i = c_i'$ for all $i \geq n$.

c. To prove c note that the sequence of partial sums of the series $\sum_{i=m}^{\infty} d_i\pi_i$ is a Cauchy sequence of elements of F. If F is complete at $\mathfrak{p}$, this sequence converges to an element $b \in F$, and $\sum_{i=m}^{\infty} d_i\pi_i = b$. ∎

Examples.

1. Consider the rational field $\mathbf{Q}$ under a p-adic valuation. Then $\mathscr{M}(p) = (p)$ and $\bar{\mathbf{Q}} \cong \mathbf{Z}/(p)$. The set of integers $\{0, 1, \ldots, p-1\}$ is a complete set of distinct representatives in $\mathscr{O}(p)$ of $\bar{\mathbf{Q}}$. Every element of $\mathbf{Q}$ has a unique representation as $\sum_{i=n}^{\infty} a_i p^i$, where the a_i are integers with $0 \leq a_i \leq p-1$, and convergence is in the p-adic topology. Since $\mathbf{Q}$ is not complete at the p-adic valuation, not every series of the above form converges to an element of $\mathbf{Q}$.

2. In $\mathbf{Q}$, under the 7-adic valuation, $-5/6 = \sum_{i=0}^{\infty} 5 \cdot 7^i$. In $\mathbf{Q}_7$, a completion of $\mathbf{Q}$ at the 7-adic valuation, $\sqrt{2}$ has a representation as a series which begins $3 + 1 \cdot 7 + 2 \cdot 7^2 + 6 \cdot 7^3 + \cdots$.

We are now ready to prove that for complete discrete-valued fields the inequality of Theorem 7.3 is an equality.

Theorem 8.5. *Let F be complete at a discrete prime spot $\mathfrak{p}$, and let $\mathfrak{P}$ be the extension of $\mathfrak{p}$ to a field $E \supset F$ with $[E: F] = n$. Let e, f be the ramification index and residue class field degree, respectively, of $\mathfrak{P}|\mathfrak{p}$. Then $ef = n$.*

PROOF. As before, we identify $\bar{F}$ with a subfield of $\bar{E}$. Let $\bar{\beta}_1, \bar{\beta}_2, \ldots, \bar{\beta}_f$ be a basis for $\bar{E}$ over $\bar{F}$. We choose $\beta_1, \beta_2, \ldots, \beta_f \in \mathcal{O}(\mathfrak{P})$ such that $\beta_i \mapsto \bar{\beta}_i$ under the canonical epimorphism of $\mathcal{O}(\mathfrak{P})$ onto $\bar{E}$. We now choose a complete system $\mathscr{C}$ of distinct representatives in $\mathcal{O}(\mathfrak{P})$ for $\bar{E}$ such that each representative is of the form $\sum_{i=1}^{f} b_i\beta_i$ with $b_i \in \mathcal{O}(\mathfrak{p})$.

Since $\mathfrak{P}$ and $\mathfrak{p}$ are discrete, there exist $\Pi \in E$ and $\pi \in F$ such that $\mathscr{M}(\mathfrak{P}) = (\Pi)$ and $\mathscr{M}(\mathfrak{p}) = (\pi)$. Let $|\ | \in \mathfrak{P}$. Since the ramification index is e, $|\pi| = |\Pi^e|$, $|\pi^r\Pi^s| = |\Pi^{re+s}|$, and $\mathscr{V}(E,|\ |) = \{|\pi^r\Pi^s|\}_{-\infty<r<\infty, 0\le s\le e-1}$.

By Theorem 8.4, each element $\alpha \in E$ has a representation $\alpha = \sum_{s=0}^{e-1}\sum_{r=r_0}^{\infty} c_{r,s}\pi^r\Pi^s$, with $c_{r,s} \in \mathscr{C}$. There exist $b_{krs} \in \mathcal{O}(\mathfrak{p})$ such that $c_{r,s} = \sum_{k=1}^{f} b_{krs}\beta_k$. Hence

$$\alpha = \sum_{s=0}^{e-1}\sum_{r=r_0}^{\infty}\left(\sum_{k=1}^{f} b_{krs}\beta_k\right)\pi^r\Pi^s = \sum_{s=0}^{e-1}\sum_{k=1}^{f}\left(\sum_{r=r_0}^{\infty} b_{krs}\pi^r\right)\beta_k\Pi^s.$$

But since F is complete, $\sum_{r=r_0}^{\infty} b_{krs}\pi^r \in F$, whence $\{\beta_k\Pi^s\}_{k=1,2,\ldots,f,\, s=0,1,\ldots,e-1}$ spans E over F, and $n = [E: F] \le ef$. We have seen that $ef \le n$ (Theorem 7.3). We conclude that $ef = n$. ▌

Corollary 1. *Let $\mathfrak{p}$ be a discrete prime spot on a field F, and let E be separable over F, with $E \supset F$ and $[E: F] = n$. Then*

$$\sum_{\substack{\mathfrak{P}|\mathfrak{p} \\ \mathfrak{P} \text{ prime spot on } E}} e(\mathfrak{P}|\mathfrak{p})f(\mathfrak{P}|\mathfrak{p}) = n.$$

PROOF. Let $\mathfrak{P}$ be a prime spot on E dividing $\mathfrak{p}$. Let $E_{\mathfrak{P}}$ and $F_{\mathfrak{P}}$ be completions of E and F, respectively, at $\mathfrak{P}$. We recall that $e(\mathfrak{P}|\mathfrak{p})$, $f(\mathfrak{P}|\mathfrak{p})$, and $n(\mathfrak{P}|\mathfrak{p})$ are, respectively, the ramification index, the residue class field degree, and the local degree of $E_{\mathfrak{P}}$ over $F_{\mathfrak{P}}$. By Theorem 6.3a

$$\sum_{\substack{\mathfrak{P}|\mathfrak{p} \\ \mathfrak{P} \text{ prime spot on } E}} n(\mathfrak{P}|\mathfrak{p}) = n.$$

But by Theorem 8.5, $n(\mathfrak{P}|\mathfrak{p}) = e(\mathfrak{P}|\mathfrak{p})f(\mathfrak{P}|\mathfrak{p})$, whence

$$\sum_{\substack{\mathfrak{P}|\mathfrak{p} \\ \mathfrak{P} \text{ prime spot on } E}} e(\mathfrak{P}|\mathfrak{p})f(\mathfrak{P}|\mathfrak{p}) = n. \quad ▌$$

Corollary 2. *Let $\mathfrak{p}$ be a discrete prime spot on a field F, and let E be a Galois extension of F with $E \supset F$ and $[E: F] = n$. Let $\{\mathfrak{P}_i\}_{i=1}^{g}$ be the complete set of those prime spots on E which divide $\mathfrak{p}$. Then*

a. $e(\mathfrak{P}_1|\mathfrak{p}) = e(\mathfrak{P}_2|\mathfrak{p}) = \cdots = e(\mathfrak{P}_g|\mathfrak{p}) = e.$
b. $f(\mathfrak{P}_1|\mathfrak{p}) = f(\mathfrak{P}_2|\mathfrak{p}) = \cdots = f(\mathfrak{P}_g|\mathfrak{p}) = f.$
c. $efg = n.$

PROOF. We use the same notation as in the proof of Theorem 6.1. Let $\sigma_1, \sigma_2, \ldots, \sigma_g$ be F-monomorphisms of E into $\tilde{F}_{\mathfrak{P}_0}$ which give rise, respectively, to $\mathfrak{P}_1, \mathfrak{P}_2, \ldots, \mathfrak{P}_g$. Then $e(\mathfrak{P}_i|\mathfrak{p}) = [\mathscr{V}(\sigma_i E, |\ |) : \mathscr{V}(F, |\ |)]$ and $f(\mathfrak{P}_i|\mathfrak{p}) = [\overline{\sigma_i E} : \bar{F}]$, $i = 1, 2, \ldots, g$. Since E is Galois over F, there exists for each pair (i,j) an F-automorphism λ_{ij} of E such that $\sigma_i = \sigma_j \lambda_{ij}$ $(i,j = 1, 2, \ldots, g)$. But then the ramification indices are equal to e (say), and the residue class field degrees are all equal to f (say). We conclude from Corollary 1 that $efg = n$. ▮

9. Integers at a Set of Nonarchimedean Prime Spots

Let B be a commutative ring with identity, and let A be a subring of B having the same identity as B. An element $\beta \in B$ is, by definition, integral over A if β is a root of a monic polynomial with coefficients in A. (We shall discuss integrality more fully in Chapter 7.) In this section we take $A = \bigcap_{\mathfrak{p} \in S} \mathcal{O}(\mathfrak{p})$. where S is a set of nonarchimedean prime spots on a field F, take $B = E$ to be a finite extension of F, with $E \supset F$, and address ourselves to the question of what elements in E are integral over A. We shall prove that $\beta \in E$ is integral over A if and only if $\beta \in \bigcap_{\mathfrak{P} \in T} \mathcal{O}(\mathfrak{P})$, where T is the set of all prime spots on E which induce on F a prime spot in S; i.e , $T = \{\mathfrak{P} | \mathfrak{P}$ prime spot on E, and there exists $\mathfrak{p} \in S$ such that $\mathfrak{P}|\mathfrak{p}\}$ An illustration of this result is the following: Let S be the set of all nonarchimedean prime spots on the rational field $\mathbf{Q}$, and let $E \supset \mathbf{Q}$ be a finite extension of $\mathbf{Q}$. Then $\bigcap_{p \in S} \mathcal{O}(p) = \mathbf{Z}$, and an element $\beta \in E$ is integral over $\mathbf{Z}$ (or is an algebraic integer) if and only if β is a local integer at every nonarchimedean valuation of E; stated with more flair: An element of E is a global integer if and only if it is everywhere a local integer.

Theorem 9.1. *Let S be a set of nonarchimedean valuations on a field F. Let $E \supset F$ be a finite extension of F, and let $T = \{\mathfrak{P} | \mathfrak{P}$ prime spot on E, and there exists $\mathfrak{p} \in S$ such that $\mathfrak{P}|\mathfrak{p}\}$. Let $\beta \in E$. Then the following statements are equivalent.*

a. *The coefficients of $m_{\beta/F}(x)$, the minimum polynomial of β over F, are in $\bigcap_{\mathfrak{p} \in S} \mathcal{O}(\mathfrak{p})$.*

b. *β is a root of a monic polynomial with coefficients in $\bigcap_{\mathfrak{p}\in S} \mathcal{O}(\mathfrak{p})$.*
c. $\beta \in \bigcap_{\mathfrak{P}\in T} \mathcal{O}(\mathfrak{P})$.

PROOF. Clearly assertion a implies assertion b.

Assume that β is a root of $x^n + \sum_{i=1}^n a_i x^{n-i}$ with $a_i \in \bigcap_{\mathfrak{p}\in S} \mathcal{O}(\mathfrak{p})$. Let $\mathfrak{P} \in T$, and $|\ | \in \mathfrak{P}$. We claim that $|\beta| \le 1$. For if $|\beta| > 1$, then $|\beta^n| > |\beta^{n-i}| \ge |a_i\beta^{n-i}|$ and $0 = |0| = |\beta^n + \sum_{i=1}^n a_i\beta^{n-i}| = |\beta^n|$. Contradiction! But then $\beta \in \mathcal{O}(\mathfrak{P})$, for every $\mathfrak{P} \in T$, and $\beta \in \bigcap_{\mathfrak{P}\in T} \mathcal{O}(\mathfrak{P})$. Hence statement b implies statement c.

Assume that $\beta \in \bigcap_{\mathfrak{P}\in T} \mathcal{O}(\mathfrak{P})$. Let $m_{\beta/F}(x) = x^r + \sum_{i=1}^r b_i x^{r-i}$, and let $\mathfrak{p} \in S$. We show that $b_i \in \mathcal{O}(\mathfrak{p})$, $i = 1, 2, \ldots, r$. We use the notation of the proof of Theorem 6.1. Let $\sigma_1, \sigma_2, \ldots, \sigma_t$ be F-monomorphisms of E into $\tilde{F}_{\mathfrak{P}_0}$ which give rise to the prime spots $\mathfrak{P}_1, \mathfrak{P}_2, \ldots, \mathfrak{P}_t$ which divide $\mathfrak{p}$. Over $\tilde{F}_{\mathfrak{P}_0}$, $m_{\beta/F}(x) = \prod_{i=1}^r (x - \beta_i)$. Each β_i, $i = 1, 2, \ldots, r$, is the image of β under at least one of the maps $\sigma_1, \sigma_2, \ldots, \sigma_t$. Since $\beta \in \bigcap_{\mathfrak{P}\in T} \mathcal{O}(\mathfrak{P})$, $\beta_i \in \mathcal{O}(\mathfrak{P}_0)$ for $i = 1, 2, \ldots, r$. But then every coefficient, b_i, of $m_{\beta/F}(x)$ is in $\mathcal{O}(\mathfrak{P}_0) \cap F$, whence $b_i \in \mathcal{O}(\mathfrak{p})$, $i = 1, 2, \ldots, r$. We conclude that $b_i \in \bigcap_{\mathfrak{p}\in S} \mathcal{O}(\mathfrak{p})$, $i = 1, 2, \ldots, r$. Thus assertion c implies assertion a. ∎

Exercises

Section 1

1.1. Are the valuations on $F(x)$, discussed in Example 3, archimedean or nonarchimedean?

1.2. Let $|\ |$ be a nontrivial nonarchimedean valuation on a field F, let $\mathcal{O} = \{a \in F \mid |a| \le 1\}$, and let $\mathcal{M} = \{a \in F \mid |a| < 1\}$. Show that $\mathcal{O}$ is a subring of F and that $\mathcal{M}$ is a maximal ideal of $\mathcal{O}$.

1.3. Let $|\ |$ be a nonarchimedean valuation on a field F. If $\sum_{i=1}^n a_i = 0$ $(a_1, a_2, \ldots, a_n \in F)$, then $|a_r| = |a_s|$ for some r, s, $1 \le r < s \le n$.

1.4. Let $|\ |$ be a nonarchimedean valuation on a field F. Prove: The infinite series $\sum_{i=1}^\infty a_i$ $(a_i \in F)$ converges (in the topology induced by $|\ |$) if and only if $\lim_{n\to\infty} a_n = 0$.

Section 2

2.1. Let $\{|\ |_j\}_{j\in J}$ be as in Theorem 2.2. For $j \in J$, let $\mathcal{O}(|\ |_j) = \{a \in F \mid |a|_j \le 1\}$. Let $\mathcal{O} = \bigcap_{j\in J} \mathcal{O}(|\ |_j)$. Prove: For each $j \in J$, the closure of $\mathcal{O}$ in F in the topology induced by $|\ |_j$ is $\mathcal{O}(|\ |_j)$.

2.2. Let $|\ |$ be a nonarchimedean valuation on a field F. If $|a - 1| < \varepsilon$ and $|b - 1| < \varepsilon$ ($a,b \in F$, ε a real number with $0 < \varepsilon < 1$), then $|ab - 1| < \varepsilon$. (This fact is used in the latter part of the proof of Theorem 2.2.)

Section 3

3.1. Let $\mathbf{Q}_p$ be a completion of the rational field $\mathbf{Q}$ at the p-adic prime spot on $\mathbf{Q}$. Show that every element of $\mathbf{Q}_p$ can be represented as an infinite series $\sum_{i=-n}^{\infty} a_i p^i$ (a_i integers with $0 \leq a_i < p$, n an integer).

3.2. Let $\mathbf{Q}_p$ be a completion of the rational field $\mathbf{Q}$ at the p-adic prime spot on $\mathbf{Q}$, and let f be a polynomial with integer coefficients. Prove: There exists $\alpha \in \mathbf{Q}_p$ such that $f(\alpha) = 0$ if and only if for each positive integer n there is an integer a_n such that $f(a_n) \equiv 0 \bmod p^n$.

3.3. Let p and q be distinct positive primes in $\mathbf{Z}$. Let $\mathbf{Q}_p$ and $\mathbf{Q}_q$ be, respectively, completions of the rational field $\mathbf{Q}$ at the p-adic and q-adic prime spots on $\mathbf{Q}$. Prove: $\mathbf{Q}_p$ and $\mathbf{Q}_q$ are not isomorphic.

Section 4

4.1. Show that the complex field $\mathbf{C}$ has infinitely many automorphisms, but has only two automorphisms which are continuous in the topology induced by the ordinary absolute value.

Section 5

5.1. Let the notation be as in Theorem 5.2. Show by example that, if $(\bar{g}_0,\bar{h}_0) \neq 1$, then the conclusions of Theorem 5.2 do not necessarily hold.

5.2. Let F be a field, complete at a nonarchimedean prime spot $\mathfrak{p}$, and let $f(x) = x^n + \sum_{i=1}^{n} a_i x^{n-i}$ be a polynomial in $\mathcal{O}(\mathfrak{p})[x]$. If $a_i \in \mathcal{M}(\mathfrak{p})$ ($i = 1,2,\ldots,n$) and if $a_n \notin [\mathcal{M}(\mathfrak{p})]^2$, then $f(x)$ is irreducible over $\mathcal{O}(\mathfrak{p})$.

5.3. Supply the details for the example following Theorem 5.3, Corollary 3.

5.4. Let F be a field, complete at a nonarchimedean prime spot $\mathfrak{p}$, let $C \supset F$ be an algebraic closure of F, and let $\hat{C}$ be a completion of C (at the unique extension of $\mathfrak{p}$ to a spot on C). Show that $\hat{C}$ is algebraically closed.

5.5. Let $\mathbf{Q}_p$ be a p-adic completion of the rational field. Show that $\mathbf{Q}_p$ contains all $(p - 1)$th roots of unity.

Section 6

6.1. Let $\mathbf{Q}_7$ be a 7-adic completion of the rational field $\mathbf{Q}$, and let $|\ |$ be the extension of the 7-adic valuation on $\mathbf{Q}$ to a valuation on $\mathbf{Q}_7$. Let $\mathscr{V}(|\ |) = \{r \mid r = |a| \text{ for some nonzero } a \in \mathbf{Q}_7\}$. Show that $\mathscr{V}(|\ |) = \{1/7^n \mid n \in \mathbf{Z}\}$.

6.2. Let E and K be fields, each containing the field F as a subfield, and let $C \supset K$ be an algebraic closure of K. Suppose that E is separable and of finite degree n over F. Define an equivalence relation $\sim$ on the set, $\text{Mon}_F(E,C)$, of F-monomorphisms of E into C as follows: $\tau_i \sim \tau_j$

$(\tau_i,\tau_j \in \mathrm{Mon}_F(E,C))$ if there exists $\mu \in \mathrm{Aut}_K(C)$ such that $\tau_i = \mu\tau_j$. Let $\{\sigma_1,\sigma_2,\ldots,\sigma_r\}$ be a complete set of representatives of the $\sim$-equivalence classes of $\mathrm{Mon}_F(E,C)$, and let $E_i = K(\sigma_i(E))$, $i = 1, 2,\ldots, r$. Prove: There is a ring isomorphism $\Lambda: K \otimes_F E \to \bigoplus_{i=1}^r E_i$ such that $\Lambda(1 \otimes \alpha) = \sum_{i=1}^r \sigma_i(\alpha)$ $(\alpha \in E)$.

6.3. The notation and assumptions are as in the preceding exercise. For $\alpha \in E$, let $C_{\alpha/F}$ and $C_{\alpha_i/K}$ be, respectively, the characteristic polynomials of α over F and of $\sigma_i(\alpha)$ over K. [The characteristic polynomial of α over F is the characteristic polynomial of the F-linear transformation on E induced by left multiplication by α. The characteristic polynomial of $\sigma_i(\alpha)$ over K is defined similarly.] Prove: $C_{\alpha/F} = \prod_{i=1}^r C_{\alpha_i/K}$.

6.4. Use Exercise 6.3 to prove Theorem 6.3 in a way different from the proof given in the text.

Section 7

7.1. Let $\mathbf{Q}_2$ be a 2-adic completion of the rational field, let F be a completion of $\mathbf{Q}_2(\{2^{1/2^i}\}_1^\infty)$, and let $E = F(\sqrt{-1})$. Show that $[E: F] = 2$, and the corresponding e and f are both 1.

7.2. For any prime $p > 0$, let (p) be the prime spot on the rational field $\mathbf{Q}$ which contains the p-adic valuation, and let $\mathfrak{P}$ be a prime spot on $Q(\sqrt{m})$ which divides (p), where m is a squarefree integer. Show that if $p \nmid 4m$, then $e(\mathfrak{P}|(p)) = 1$.

Section 8

8.1. Let ζ be a primitive qth root of unity, q a prime. For any prime $p > 0$, let (p) be the prime spot on the rational field $\mathbf{Q}$ which contains the p-adic valuation, and let $\mathfrak{P}$ be a prime spot on $\mathbf{Q}(\zeta)$ which divides (p). Find $e(\mathfrak{P}|(p))$ and $f(\mathfrak{P}|(p))$.

Section 9

9.1. Let E be a finite extension of the rational field $\mathbf{Q}$. Show that the set, I, of algebraic integers in E (i.e., the set of elements in E which are integral over $\mathbf{Z}$) is an integral domain (relative to the addition and multiplication inherited from E). Prove that I is a free $\mathbf{Z}$-module of dimension $[E: \mathbf{Q}]$ over $\mathbf{Z}$.

Chapter 7 / Noetherian and Dedekind Domains

1. Noetherian Rings

Commutative rings which satisfy the ascending chain condition for ideals are of fundamental importance in classical algebraic geometry and algebraic number theory. In this chapter we derive several basic results concerning such rings. (Some of these results hold for noncommutative rings and for modules; a few of the exercises indicate the nature of the generalizations.)

Definition 1.1. A ring A with identity is a *left* (*right*) *Noetherian ring* if for every ascending sequence of left (right) ideals of A,

$$\mathfrak{a}_1 \subset \mathfrak{a}_2 \subset \mathfrak{a}_3 \subset \cdots,$$

there is an integer n such that $\mathfrak{a}_n = \mathfrak{a}_{n+1} = \mathfrak{a}_{n+2} = \cdots$. A commutative Noetherian ring which is an integral domain is a *Noetherian domain*.

A ring A with identity is a *left* (*right*) *Artinian ring* if for every descending sequence of left (right) ideals of A,

$$\mathfrak{a}_1 \supset \mathfrak{a}_2 \supset \mathfrak{a}_3 \supset \cdots$$

there is an integer n such that $\mathfrak{a}_n = \mathfrak{a}_{n+1} = \mathfrak{a}_{n+2} = \cdots$. ///

Henceforth, throughout this chapter, we use the term "ring" to mean "commutative ring with identity" and the term "subring" to mean "subring with identity equal to the identity of the whole ring."

We shall see in Chapter 8 (Theorem 5.4) that a left (right) Artinian ring is a left (right) Noetherian ring. Our concern here will be with commutative Noetherian rings.

Theorem 1.1. *The following statements on a ring A are equivalent.*

a. *A is a Noetherian ring.*

b. *Every nonempty set, S, of ideals of A has a maximal element: i.e., there exists an ideal $\mathfrak{a}_0 \in S$ such that, if $\mathfrak{a} \in S$ and $\mathfrak{a}_0 \subset \mathfrak{a}$, then $\mathfrak{a}_0 = \mathfrak{a}$.*

c. *Every ideal of A is finitely generated: i.e., if $\mathfrak{a}$ is an ideal in A, then there are elements $b_1, b_2, \ldots, b_n$ in $\mathfrak{a}$ such that $\mathfrak{a} = (b_1,b_2,\ldots,b_n) = \{\sum_{i=1}^{n} a_ib_i | a_i \in A, n \in \mathbf{N}'\}$.*

PROOF.

a $\Rightarrow$ b. Let S be a nonempty set of ideals in a Noetherian ring A, and let $\mathfrak{a}_1 \in S$. If $\mathfrak{a}_1$ is not maximal in S, there is an ideal $\mathfrak{a}_2 \in S$ such that $\mathfrak{a}_1 \subsetneqq \mathfrak{a}_2$. Again, if $\mathfrak{a}_2$ is not maximal in S, there is an ideal $\mathfrak{a}_3$ in S such that $\mathfrak{a}_2 \subsetneqq \mathfrak{a}_3$. Proceeding in this way, we may build up an ascending chain of ideals

$$\mathfrak{a}_1 \subsetneqq \mathfrak{a}_2 \subsetneqq \cdots.$$

Since A is Noetherian, this chain must terminate. Hence there is an ideal $\mathfrak{a}_n$ in A which is maximal in S.

b $\Rightarrow$ c. Let $\mathfrak{a}$ be an ideal in A, and let $S = \{\mathfrak{b} | \mathfrak{b} \subset \mathfrak{a}, \mathfrak{b}$ ideal in A, $\mathfrak{b}$ finitely generated$\}$. Then S is nonempty ($(0) \in S$) and hence S contains a maximal element, say $\mathfrak{b}_0$. If $b \in \mathfrak{a}$, then $\mathfrak{b}_0 + (b)$ is a finitely generated ideal, contained in $\mathfrak{a}$ and containing $\mathfrak{b}_0$. It follows that $\mathfrak{b}_0 + (b) = \mathfrak{b}_0$, and $b \in \mathfrak{b}_0$. But then $\mathfrak{a} \subset \mathfrak{b}_0$, whence $\mathfrak{b}_0 = \mathfrak{a}$. We conclude that $\mathfrak{a}$ is finitely generated.

c $\Rightarrow$ a. Let $\mathfrak{a}_1 \subset \mathfrak{a}_2 \subset \mathfrak{a}_3 \subset \cdots$ be an ascending sequence of ideals in A. Then $\mathfrak{a} = \bigcup \mathfrak{a}_k$ is an ideal in A. Hence $\mathfrak{a}$ is finitely generated, say $\mathfrak{a} = (b_1,b_2,\ldots,b_n)$. But then there is an integer m such that $b_i \in \mathfrak{a}_m$ for $i = 1,2,\ldots, n$, and $\mathfrak{a} \subset \mathfrak{a}_m$. From $\mathfrak{a} \subset \mathfrak{a}_m \subset \mathfrak{a} = \bigcup \mathfrak{a}_k$ we conclude that $\mathfrak{a} = \mathfrak{a}_m = \mathfrak{a}_{m+1} = \mathfrak{a}_{m+2} = \cdots$. Thus A is a Noetherian ring, and c $\Rightarrow$ a. ∎

In the next two theorems we see that, in some cases, the Noetherian property of a ring A is inherited by, or extends to, certain rings related to A.

Theorem 1.2. *Let A be a ring.*

a. *If A is Noetherian, then any homomorphic image of A is Noetherian.*

b. *If A is Noetherian, and S is a multiplicative system in A such that $AS^{-1} \neq 0$, then AS^{-1} is Noetherian.*

c. *Let $\mathfrak{a}$ be an ideal of A such that every ascending sequence of ideals of A contained in $\mathfrak{a}$ terminates. If $A/\mathfrak{a}$ is Noetherian, then so is A.*

PROOF.

a. Let $\varphi: A \to B$ be an epimorphism of a Noetherian ring A onto a ring B. If $\bar{\mathfrak{a}}$ is an ideal of B, then $\varphi^{-1}(\bar{\mathfrak{a}})$ is an ideal of A and is finitely generated, say $\varphi^{-1}(\bar{\mathfrak{a}}) = (b_1,b_2,\ldots,b_n)$. But then $\bar{\mathfrak{a}} = (\varphi(b_1),\varphi(b_2),\ldots,\varphi(b_n))$ is finitely generated. Hence every ideal of B is finitely generated, and B is Noetherian.

b. We recall (Chapter 2, Section 2) that, if S is a multiplicative system in a ring A, then there is a homomorphism $\alpha_S: A \to AS^{-1}$ such that the elements of $\alpha_S(S)$ are units in AS^{-1} and such that every element of AS^{-1} may be written in the form $\alpha_S(a)/\alpha_S(s)$ with $a \in A$, $s \in S$.

Let $\bar{\mathfrak{a}}$ be an ideal in AS^{-1}, and let $\mathfrak{a} = \{a \in A \mid \alpha_S a \in \bar{\mathfrak{a}}\}$. Clearly, $\mathfrak{a}$ is an ideal in A, and the ideal $(\alpha_S(\mathfrak{a}))$ generated by $\alpha_S(\mathfrak{a})$ in AS^{-1} is contained in $\mathfrak{a}$. If $\bar{a} \in \bar{\mathfrak{a}}$, then $\bar{a} = \alpha_S(a)/\alpha_S(s)$ for some $a \in A$, $s \in S$. Since $\bar{\mathfrak{a}}$ is an ideal in AS^{-1}, $\alpha_S(a) \in \bar{\mathfrak{a}}$, hence $a \in \mathfrak{a}$, and $\bar{a} \in (\alpha_S(\mathfrak{a}))$. It follows that $\bar{\mathfrak{a}} = (\alpha_S(\mathfrak{a}))$. If A is Noetherian, then $\mathfrak{a}$ is finitely generated; but then $\bar{\mathfrak{a}}$ is finitely generated, and so AS^{-1} is Noetherian.

c. Let $\mathfrak{a}$ be an ideal in A with the property: Every ascending chain of ideals of A, contained in $\mathfrak{a}$, terminates. Suppose $A/\mathfrak{a}$ is Noetherian. Let $\mathfrak{b}_1 \subset \mathfrak{b}_2 \subset \cdots$ be an ascending chain of ideals of A. Then

$$\mathfrak{b}_1 \cap \mathfrak{a} \subset \mathfrak{b}_2 \cap \mathfrak{a} \subset \cdots \tag{1}$$

is an ascending chain of ideals of A, contained in $\mathfrak{a}$, and

$$(\mathfrak{b}_1 + \mathfrak{a})/\mathfrak{a} \subset (\mathfrak{b}_2 + \mathfrak{a})/\mathfrak{a} \subset \cdots \tag{2}$$

is an ascending chain of ideals of $A/\mathfrak{a}$. By our hypotheses, both chains terminate; hence there is an integer n such that

$$\mathfrak{b}_n \cap \mathfrak{a} = \mathfrak{b}_{n+h} \cap \mathfrak{a} \qquad \text{for each } h = 1, 2, \ldots,$$

$$(\mathfrak{b}_n + \mathfrak{a})/\mathfrak{a} = (\mathfrak{b}_{n+h} + \mathfrak{a})/\mathfrak{a} \qquad \text{for each } h = 1, 2, \ldots.$$

Suppose $b_h \in \mathfrak{b}_{n+h}$ $(h \in \mathbf{N}')$. Since $(\mathfrak{b}_n + \mathfrak{a})/\mathfrak{a} = (\mathfrak{b}_{n+h} + \mathfrak{a})/\mathfrak{a}$, there are elements $a \in \mathfrak{a}$, $b \in \mathfrak{b}_n$ such that $b_h - b = a$. But then $b_h - b \in \mathfrak{b}_{n+h} \cap \mathfrak{a} = \mathfrak{b}_n \cap \mathfrak{a}$, and therefore $b_h \in \mathfrak{b}_n$. Thus, $\mathfrak{b}_n = \mathfrak{b}_{n+h}$ for each $h = 1, 2, \ldots$; i.e., the chain $\mathfrak{b}_1 \subset \mathfrak{b}_2 \subset \cdots$ terminates. It follows that A is Noetherian. ∎

Theorem 1.3. (Hilbert Basis Theorem) *If A is a Noetherian ring, then so is the polynomial ring $A[x]$.*

PROOF. We show that every ideal of $A[x]$ is finitely generated. Let $\bar{\mathfrak{a}}$ be an ideal in $A[x]$. For each integer $k \geq 0$, let $\mathfrak{a}_k$ be the set of elements consisting of 0 and the leading coefficients of those polynomials in $\bar{\mathfrak{a}}$ which are of degree k. Then $\mathfrak{a}_0 \subset \mathfrak{a}_1 \subset \mathfrak{a}_2 \subset \cdots$ is an ascending sequence of ideals in A. Since A is Noetherian, there is an integer m such that $\mathfrak{a}_m = \mathfrak{a}_{m+1} = \cdots$. The ideals $\mathfrak{a}_0, \mathfrak{a}_1, \ldots, \mathfrak{a}_m$ are finitely generated. For each $i = 0, 1, \ldots, m$, let $\{a_{i1}, a_{i2}, \ldots, a_{in_i}\}$ be a set of generators for $\mathfrak{a}_i$, and let f_{ij} be a polynomial in $\bar{\mathfrak{a}}$ of degree i, with leading coefficient a_{ij} ($j = 1, 2, \ldots, n_i$). We proceed to show that the set of polynomials $\{f_{ij}\}_{i=0,1,\ldots,m, j=1,2,\ldots,n_i}$ generates $\mathfrak{a}$.

Since $\mathfrak{a}_m = \mathfrak{a}_d$ for any integer $d \geq m$, the leading coefficients of $x^{d-m}f_{m1}, x^{d-m}f_{m2}, \ldots, x^{d-m}f_{mn_m}$ generate $\mathfrak{a}_d$. Hence, if f is a polynomial in $\bar{\mathfrak{a}}$ of degree $d \geq m$, then there are elements $b_1, b_2, \ldots, b_{n_m}$ in A such that $f - \sum_{j=1}^{n_m} b_j f_{mnj}$ is a polynomial in $\bar{\mathfrak{a}}$ of degree less than d. If f is a polynomial in $\bar{\mathfrak{a}}$ of degree $d < m$, then there are elements $c_1, c_2, \ldots, c_{n_d}$ in A such that $f - \sum_{j=1}^{n_d} c_j f_{dj}$ is a polynomial in $\bar{\mathfrak{a}}$ of degree less than d. An induction argument shows that, if $f \in \bar{\mathfrak{a}}$, then f is an A-linear combination of the f_{ij}. But then $\bar{\mathfrak{a}}$ is finitely generated, and the theorem is proved. ▮

Corollary 1. *If A is a Noetherian ring, then so is any polynomial ring in a finite number of indeterminates over A.* □

Corollary 2. *Let B be a commutative ring with identity which is finitely generated over a subring A of B. If A is Noetherian, then so is B.*

PROOF. B is a homomorphic image of a polynomial ring in a finite number of indeterminates over A. Corollary 2 follows from Corollary 1 and Theorem 1.2a. ▮

2. Primary Ideals; Radical of an Ideal; Decomposition Theorem

In a Noetherian ring A, every ideal *contains* a product of prime ideals. For, let S be the set consisting of those ideals of A which are not prime and do not contain any products of prime ideals, and suppose $S \neq \varnothing$. Since A is Noetherian, S contains a maximal element, $\mathfrak{a}$. Since $\mathfrak{a} \in S$, $\mathfrak{a}$ is not a prime ideal, and there exist $a,b \in A$, $a,b \notin \mathfrak{a}$ such that $ab \in \mathfrak{a}$. Let $\mathfrak{a}_1 = (a) + \mathfrak{a}$, and $\mathfrak{a}_2 = (b) + \mathfrak{a}$. Then $\mathfrak{a} \subsetneq \mathfrak{a}_1$, $\mathfrak{a} \subsetneq \mathfrak{a}_1$, and $\mathfrak{a}_1\mathfrak{a}_2 \subset \mathfrak{a}$. Since $\mathfrak{a}$ is a maximal element in S, $\mathfrak{a}_1$ and $\mathfrak{a}_2$ contain products of prime ideals. But then so does $\mathfrak{a}$. Contradiction! Hence S is empty, and the assertion is proved. In general not every ideal in a Noetherian ring is *equal to* a product of prime ideals. In this section we shall prove that in a Noetherian ring, every ideal is a finite intersection of "primary" ideals. In Section 5 we shall consider domains in which every proper ideal is equal to a product of prime ideals.

Definition 2.1. An ideal $\mathfrak{q}$ in a ring A is *primary* if it satisfies the following condition: If $ab \in \mathfrak{q}$, $a,b \in A$, $a \notin \mathfrak{q}$, then there is a positive integer n such that $b^n \in \mathfrak{q}$.

The *radical*, $\sqrt{\mathfrak{a}}$, of an ideal $\mathfrak{a}$ in A is the intersection of all the prime ideals in A which contain $\mathfrak{a}$. ///

Examples.

1. For each prime $p \in \mathbf{Z}$, and each positive integer n, (p^n) is a primary ideal with radical $\sqrt{(p^n)} = (p)$.
2. The ideal (x^m, y^n) in $\mathbf{Z}[x,y]$ (x, y transcendental over $\mathbf{Z}$, m and n positive integers) has radical $\sqrt{(x^m, y^n)} = (x,y)$.

REMARK. An ideal $\mathfrak{q}$ in a ring A is primary if and only if every zero divisor in $A/\mathfrak{q}$ is nilpotent. (An element b of a ring is nilpotent if $b^n = 0$ for some positive integer n.)

Theorem 2.1. *Let $\mathfrak{a}$ be an ideal in a ring A. Then $\sqrt{\mathfrak{a}} = \{a \in A \mid a^n \in \mathfrak{a}$ for some positive integer $n\}$.*

PROOF. Suppose $a \in A$ and $a^n \in \mathfrak{a}$ for some positive integer n. If $\mathfrak{p}$ is a prime ideal containing $\mathfrak{a}$, then $a^n \in \mathfrak{p}$, whence $a \in \mathfrak{p}$. But then $a \in \sqrt{\mathfrak{a}}$. On the other hand, suppose $a \in A$ and, for every positive integer n, $a^n \notin \mathfrak{a}$. The theorem will be proved as soon as we show that there is a prime ideal, $\mathfrak{p}$, in A such that $\mathfrak{a} \subset \mathfrak{p}$, and $a \notin \mathfrak{p}$.

Let $\mathscr{S} = \{\mathfrak{b} \mid \mathfrak{b}$ ideal in A, $\mathfrak{a} \subset \mathfrak{b}$, $\mathfrak{b} \cap \{a,a^2,a^3,\ldots\} = \varnothing\}$. Then $\mathscr{S}$ is partially ordered by set inclusion and satisfies the conditions of Zorn's Lemma, hence has a maximal element, $\mathfrak{p}_0$. Clearly $\mathfrak{a} \subset \mathfrak{p}_0$, and $a \notin \mathfrak{p}_0$. We show that $\mathfrak{p}_0$ is a prime ideal. Suppose b, c are elements in A which do not belong to $\mathfrak{p}_0$. Since $\mathfrak{p}_0$ is maximal in $\mathscr{S}$, each of the ideals $(b) + \mathfrak{p}_0$, $(c) + \mathfrak{p}_0$ has a nonempty intersection with $\{a,a^2,a^3,\ldots\}$. But then $(bc) + \mathfrak{p}_0 = [(b) + \mathfrak{p}_0] \cdot [(c) + \mathfrak{p}_0]$ meets $\{a,a^2,a^3,\ldots\}$, $bc \notin \mathfrak{p}_0$, and $\mathfrak{p}_0$ is prime as desired. (Note that we did not use the commutativity of A in proving the theorem.) ▮

Corollary 1. *The radical of a primary ideal is a prime ideal.*

PROOF. Let $\mathfrak{q}$ be a primary ideal. If $ab \in \sqrt{\mathfrak{q}}$ with $a \notin \sqrt{\mathfrak{q}}$ ($a,b \in A$), then there is a positive integer n such that $a^n b^n \in \mathfrak{q}$, $a^n \notin \mathfrak{q}$. But then, for some positive integer m, $(b^n)^m = b^{nm} \in \mathfrak{q}$, and $b \in \sqrt{\mathfrak{q}}$. We conclude that $\sqrt{\mathfrak{q}}$ is a prime ideal. ▮

Corollary 2. *Let* $\mathfrak{q}_1, \mathfrak{q}_2, \ldots, \mathfrak{q}_n$ *be primary ideals in a ring. If* $\sqrt{\mathfrak{q}_1} = \sqrt{\mathfrak{q}_2} = \cdots = \sqrt{\mathfrak{q}_n} = \mathfrak{p}$, *then* $\mathfrak{q}_1 \cap \mathfrak{q}_2 \cap \cdots \cap \mathfrak{q}_n$ *is a primary ideal having* $\mathfrak{p}$ *as its radical.*

PROOF. Let $\mathfrak{a} = \mathfrak{q}_1 \cap \mathfrak{q}_2 \cap \cdots \cap \mathfrak{q}_n$. If $a \in \mathfrak{p}$, then there are positive integers m_i such that $a^{m_i} \in \mathfrak{q}_i$, $i = 1, 2, \ldots, n$. But then $a^{\max_i\{m_i\}} \in \mathfrak{a}$, $a \in \sqrt{\mathfrak{a}}$, and $\mathfrak{p} \subset \sqrt{\mathfrak{a}}$. If $b \in \sqrt{\mathfrak{a}}$, then $b^m \in \mathfrak{a}$ for some positive integer m. But then $b^m \in \mathfrak{q}_1$, $b \in \mathfrak{p}$, and $\sqrt{\mathfrak{a}} \subset \mathfrak{p}$. We conclude that $\mathfrak{p} = \sqrt{\mathfrak{a}}$.

If $ab \in \mathfrak{a}$, $a \notin \mathfrak{a}$, then there is an integer k such that $a \notin \mathfrak{q}_k$. Since $\mathfrak{q}_k$ is primary, $b^r \in \mathfrak{q}_k$ for some positive integer r. But then $b \in \mathfrak{p}$, and since $\mathfrak{p} = \sqrt{\mathfrak{a}}$, $b^s \in \mathfrak{a}$ for some positive integer s. It follows that $\mathfrak{a}$ is a primary ideal. ▌

NOTATION. Let $\mathfrak{a}$, $\mathfrak{b}$ be ideals in a ring A. Then $\mathfrak{a} : \mathfrak{b} = \{a \in A \mid ab \in \mathfrak{a}$ for all $b \in \mathfrak{b}\}$. (Note that $\mathfrak{a} : \mathfrak{b}$ is an ideal in A which contains $\mathfrak{a}$.)

We shall need the following lemma to prove that in a Noetherian ring every ideal is a finite intersection of primary ideals.

Lemma. *Let* A *be a Noetherian ring and* $\mathfrak{a}$ *an ideal in* A *which is not primary. Then there are ideals* $\mathfrak{b}$, $\mathfrak{c}$ *in* A *such that* $\mathfrak{a} \subsetneqq \mathfrak{b}$, $\mathfrak{a} \subsetneqq \mathfrak{c}$, *and* $\mathfrak{a} = \mathfrak{b} \cap \mathfrak{c}$.

PROOF. Since $\mathfrak{a}$ is not primary, there are elements $b, c \subset A$ such that $bc \in \mathfrak{a}$, $b \notin \mathfrak{a}$, and $c^k \notin \mathfrak{a}$ for any positive integer k. Let $\mathfrak{b} = (b) + \mathfrak{a}$. Then $\mathfrak{b}$ is an ideal in A which contains $\mathfrak{a}$ properly. Now consider the ascending sequence $\mathfrak{a} : (c) \subset \mathfrak{a} : (c^2) \subset \mathfrak{a} : (c^3) \subset \cdots$. Since A is Noetherian, there is a positive integer n such that $\mathfrak{a} : (c^n) = \mathfrak{a} : (c^{n+1}) = \mathfrak{a} : (c^{n+2}) = \cdots$. Let $\mathfrak{c} = (c^n) + \mathfrak{a}$. Then $\mathfrak{c}$ is an ideal in A which contains $\mathfrak{a}$ properly. We claim that $\mathfrak{a} = \mathfrak{b} \cap \mathfrak{c}$. It is sufficient to prove that $\mathfrak{b} \cap \mathfrak{c} \subset \mathfrak{a}$. Let $d \in \mathfrak{b} \cap \mathfrak{c}$. Then there are $a_1, a_2 \subset A$ and $e_1, e_2 \in \mathfrak{a}$ such that $d = a_1 b + e_1 = a_2 c^n + e_2$. Clearly, $dc = a_1 bc + e_1 c \in \mathfrak{a}$. Hence $dc = a_2 c^{n+1} + e_2 c \in \mathfrak{a}$, and $a_2 c^{n+1} \in \mathfrak{a}$. But then $a_2 \in \mathfrak{a} : (c^{n+1}) = \mathfrak{a} : (c^n)$, $a_2 c^n \in \mathfrak{a}$, and $d = a_2 c^n + e_2 \in \mathfrak{a}$. We conclude that $\mathfrak{b} \cap \mathfrak{c} \subset \mathfrak{a}$. ▌

Theorem 2.2. *Every ideal in a Noetherian ring* A *has a primary decomposition: i.e., every ideal in* A *is the intersection of a finite number of primary ideals in* A.

PROOF. Assume that the set, S, of ideals in A which are not intersections of finitely many primary ideals is nonempty. Since A is Noetherian, S has a maximal element, $\mathfrak{a}$. Since $\mathfrak{a} \in S$, $\mathfrak{a}$ is not primary. But then, by the lemma, there are ideals $\mathfrak{b}$, $\mathfrak{c}$, properly containing $\mathfrak{a}$, such that $\mathfrak{a} = \mathfrak{b} \cap \mathfrak{c}$. Since $\mathfrak{a}$ is maximal in S, $\mathfrak{b}, \mathfrak{c} \notin S$. But then $\mathfrak{b}$ and $\mathfrak{c}$ are finite intersections of primary ideals, and so is $\mathfrak{a} = \mathfrak{b} \cap \mathfrak{c}$. Since $\mathfrak{a} \in S$, this is impossible. Hence $S = \varnothing$, and the theorem is proved. ▮

In general, the decomposition of an ideal into an intersection of primary ideals is not unique. For example, we have seen (Theorem 2.2, Corollary 2), that if $\mathfrak{q}_1$, $\mathfrak{q}_2$ are primary ideals with $\sqrt{\mathfrak{q}_1} = \sqrt{\mathfrak{q}_2}$, then $\mathfrak{q}_3 = \mathfrak{q}_1 \cap \mathfrak{q}_2$ is primary. Thus $\mathfrak{a} = \mathfrak{q}_3$ and $\mathfrak{a} = \mathfrak{q}_1 \cap \mathfrak{q}_2$ are two distinct primary decompositions of $\mathfrak{a}$.

In a primary decomposition of an ideal, the intersection of all those primary ideals which have the same radical may be replaced by a single primary ideal (Theorem 2.1, Corollary 2). If this is done, some measure of uniqueness is recovered.

Definition 2.2. A primary decomposition, $\mathfrak{a} = \bigcap_{i=1}^{n} \mathfrak{q}_i$, is *reduced* if $\bigcap_{i \neq j} \mathfrak{q}_i \neq \bigcap_i \mathfrak{q}_i$ for each $j = 1, 2, \ldots, n$, and $\sqrt{\mathfrak{q}_r} \neq \sqrt{\mathfrak{q}_s}$ for $r \neq s$, $r, s = 1, 2, \ldots, n$.

If $\mathfrak{a} = \bigcap_{i=1}^{n} \mathfrak{q}_i$ is a reduced primary decomposition of $\mathfrak{a}$, then $\{\sqrt{\mathfrak{q}_i}\}_{i=1}^{n}$ is a set of *associated prime ideals* of $\mathfrak{a}$.

Let $\{\sqrt{\mathfrak{q}_i}\}_{i=1}^{n}$ be a set of associated prime ideals of an ideal $\mathfrak{a}$. Then $\sqrt{\mathfrak{q}_r}$ $(1 \leq r \leq n)$ is an *isolated prime ideal* of $\mathfrak{a}$ if $\sqrt{\mathfrak{q}_r} \not\supset \sqrt{\mathfrak{q}_i}$ for $i = 1, \ldots, r-1, r+1, \ldots, n$. ///

Theorem 2.3. *Let A be a Noetherian ring, $\mathfrak{a}$ an ideal in A. Let $\mathfrak{a} = \bigcap_{i=1}^{m} \mathfrak{q}_i$ and $\mathfrak{a} = \bigcap_{j=1}^{n} \mathfrak{q}'_j$ be two reduced primary decompositions of $\mathfrak{a}$. Then $m = n$, and $\{\sqrt{\mathfrak{q}_i}\}_{i=1}^{m} = \{\sqrt{\mathfrak{q}'_j}\}_{j=1}^{n}$.*

PROOF. We first prove the following: If $\mathfrak{a} \subset \bigcup_{i=1}^{m} \mathfrak{p}_i$, where $\mathfrak{a}$ is an ideal in A, and the $\mathfrak{p}_i$ are prime ideals in A $(i = 1,2,\ldots,m)$, then $\mathfrak{a} \subset \mathfrak{p}_k$ for some k. We may assume without loss of generality that, for $i \neq j$, $\mathfrak{p}_i \not\supset \mathfrak{p}_j$. (Otherwise, delete $\mathfrak{p}_j$.) Suppose that $\mathfrak{a}$ is not contained in any of the $\mathfrak{p}_i$. Then $\mathfrak{a} \cap \mathfrak{p}_1 \cap \mathfrak{p}_2 \cap \cdots \cap \mathfrak{p}_{i-1} \cap \mathfrak{p}_{i+1} \cap \cdots \cap \mathfrak{p}_m$ is not contained in $\mathfrak{p}_i$, $i = 1, 2, \ldots, m$. For each $i = 1, 2, \ldots, m$, let a_i be an element of A such that $a_i \in \mathfrak{a} \cap \bigcap_{j \neq i} \mathfrak{p}_j$ and $a_i \notin \mathfrak{p}_i$. Then $\sum_{j=1}^{m} a_j \in \mathfrak{a}$, and $\sum_{j=1}^{m} a_j \notin \mathfrak{p}_i$, $i = 1, 2, \ldots, m$. Contradiction!

Let $\mathfrak{a} = \bigcap_{i=1}^{m} \mathfrak{q}_i = \bigcap_{j=1}^{n} \mathfrak{q}'_j$ be reduced primary decompositions of $\mathfrak{a}$, and let $\mathfrak{p}_i = \sqrt{\mathfrak{q}_i}$, $\mathfrak{p}'_j = \sqrt{\mathfrak{q}'_j}$ $(i = 1,2,\ldots,m; j = 1,2,\ldots,n)$. In the set $\{\mathfrak{p}_i\}_{i=1}^{m} \cup \{\mathfrak{p}'_j\}_{j=1}^{n}$ there is an ideal which is not properly contained in any of the other ideals in this set. We may assume without loss that $\mathfrak{p}_1$ is such an ideal. We prove that $\mathfrak{p}_1 = \mathfrak{p}'_j$ for some j. Suppose, to the contrary, that $\mathfrak{p}_1 \neq \mathfrak{p}'_j$ for $j = 1, 2, \ldots, n$. By the remark in the preceding paragraph, $\mathfrak{p}_1 \not\subset \bigcup_{i=2}^{m} \mathfrak{p}_i \cup \bigcup_{j=1}^{n} \mathfrak{p}'_j$. Hence there is an element $a \in \mathfrak{p}_1$ with $a \notin \bigcup_{i=2}^{m} \mathfrak{p}_i \cup \bigcup_{j=1}^{n} \mathfrak{p}'_j$. Since $\mathfrak{p}_1 = \sqrt{\mathfrak{q}_1}$, there is an integer $k \geq 1$ such that $a^k \in \mathfrak{q}_1$. Now

$\mathfrak{a}:(a^k) = \mathfrak{q}_2 \cap \mathfrak{q}_3 \cap \cdots \cap \mathfrak{q}_m$. For, clearly, $\mathfrak{q}_2 \cap \mathfrak{q}_3 \cap \cdots \cap \mathfrak{q}_m \subset \mathfrak{a}:(a^k)$; and, if $b \in A$ and $b \notin \mathfrak{q}_i$ for some $i \geq 2$, then (since $a \notin \mathfrak{p}_i$), $a^k b \notin \mathfrak{q}_i$, and $b \notin \mathfrak{a}:(a^k)$. A similar argument proves that $\mathfrak{a}:(a^k) = \mathfrak{q}'_1 \cap \mathfrak{q}'_2 \cap \cdots \cap \mathfrak{q}'_n$. But then $\mathfrak{q}_2 \cap \mathfrak{q}_3 \cap \cdots \cap \mathfrak{q}_m = \mathfrak{q}'_1 \cap \mathfrak{q}'_2 \cap \cdots \cap \mathfrak{q}'_n = \mathfrak{a}$. This contradicts the assumption that the primary decomposition $\bigcap_{i=1}^m \mathfrak{q}_i$ is reduced. We conclude that $\mathfrak{p}_1 \in \{\mathfrak{p}'_j\}_{j=1}^n$, say $\mathfrak{p}_1 = \mathfrak{p}'_1$.

Since $\mathfrak{p}_1 = \mathfrak{p}'_1$ is maximal in the set $\{\mathfrak{p}_i\}_{i=1}^m \cup \{\mathfrak{p}'_j\}_{j=1}^n$, there is some $a \in \mathfrak{p}_1$ with $a \notin \bigcup_{i=2}^m \mathfrak{p}_i \cup \bigcup_{j=2}^n \mathfrak{p}'_j$. There is an integer $k \geq 1$ such that $a^k \in \mathfrak{q}_1$ and $a^k \in \mathfrak{q}'_1$. An argument similar to the one given above proves that $\mathfrak{a}:(a^k) = \mathfrak{q}_2 \cap \mathfrak{q}_3 \cap \cdots \cap \mathfrak{q}_m = \mathfrak{q}'_2 \cap \mathfrak{q}'_3 \cap \cdots \cap \mathfrak{q}'_n$. The theorem now follows by induction. ▮

Theorem 2.3 tells us that the associated prime ideals of an ideal $\mathfrak{a}$ in an Noetherian ring are uniquely determined. In general, the primary ideals in a primary decomposition of $\mathfrak{a}$ are not unique. However, if $\mathfrak{q}$ is a primary ideal in a primary decomposition of $\mathfrak{a}$ such that $\sqrt{\mathfrak{q}}$ is an isolated prime of $\mathfrak{a}$, then $\mathfrak{q}$ is uniquely determined. We have

Theorem 2.4. *Let $\mathfrak{a}$ be an ideal in a Noetherian ring A, and let $\mathfrak{a} = \mathfrak{q}_1 \cap \mathfrak{q}_2 \cap \cdots \cap \mathfrak{q}_n = \mathfrak{q}'_1 \cap \mathfrak{q}'_2 \cap \cdots \cap \mathfrak{q}'_n$ be reduced primary decompositions of $\mathfrak{a}$ such that $\sqrt{\mathfrak{q}_1} = \sqrt{\mathfrak{q}'_1} = \mathfrak{p}_1$. If $\mathfrak{p}_1$ is an isolated prime of $\mathfrak{a}$, then $\mathfrak{q}_1 = \mathfrak{q}'_1$.*

PROOF. Since $\mathfrak{p}_1$ is an isolated prime of $\mathfrak{a}$, there exists, for each $i = 2, 3, \ldots, n$, some element $a_i \in \sqrt{\mathfrak{q}_i}$ with $a_i \notin \mathfrak{p}_1$. Let $a = \prod_{i=2}^n a_i$. Then $a \in \sqrt{\mathfrak{q}_i}$ for $i = 2, 3, \ldots, n$, and $a \notin \mathfrak{p}_1$. By Theorem 2.3, $\{\sqrt{\mathfrak{q}_i}\}_{i=1}^n = \{\sqrt{\mathfrak{q}'_j}\}_{j=1}^n$. It follows that there exists a positive integer k such that $a^k \in \mathfrak{q}_i$ and $a^k \in \mathfrak{q}'_j$, $i, j = 2, 3, \ldots, n$. We show that, for any such k, $\mathfrak{a}:(a^k) = \mathfrak{q}_1$ and $\mathfrak{a}:(a^k) = \mathfrak{q}'_1$. If $b \in \mathfrak{q}_1$ $(b \in \mathfrak{q}'_1)$, then $a^k b \in \mathfrak{q}_1 \cap \mathfrak{q}_2 \cap \cdots \cap \mathfrak{q}_n$ $(a^k b \in \mathfrak{q}'_1 \cap \mathfrak{q}'_1 \cap \cdots \cap \mathfrak{q}'_n)$. Hence $b \in \mathfrak{a}:(a^k)$, and $\mathfrak{q}_1 \subset \mathfrak{a}:(a^k)$ $(\mathfrak{q}'_1 \subset \mathfrak{a}:(a^k))$. If $c \in \mathfrak{a}:(a^k)$, then $a^k c \in \mathfrak{a}$, and $a^k c \in \mathfrak{q}_1$ $(a^k c \in \mathfrak{q}'_1)$. It follows that $c \in \mathfrak{q}_1$ $(c \in \mathfrak{q}'_1)$. For, if $c \notin \mathfrak{q}_1$ $(c \notin \mathfrak{q}'_1)$, then $a \in \mathfrak{p}_1$; but by the choice of a, we have $a \notin \mathfrak{p}_1$. We conclude that $\mathfrak{a}:(a^k) \subset \mathfrak{q}_1$ $(\mathfrak{a}:(a^k) \subset \mathfrak{q}'_1)$. But then $\mathfrak{a}:(a^k) = \mathfrak{q}_1 = \mathfrak{q}'_1$, and the theorem is proved. ▮

We close this section with a short informal discussion of the connection between polynomial domains over a field and classical algebraic geometry. (Note that, by Theorem 1.3, Corollary 1, a polynomial domain in a finite number of indeterminates over a field is a Noetherian domain.)

Let E be a field, $F \subset E$ a subfield of E; let $\{x_i\}_{i=1}^n$ be a transcendence set over F; and let $\mathfrak{a}$ be an ideal in $F[x_1,x_2,\ldots,x_n]$. Then $V_{E^{(n)}/F}(\mathfrak{a}) = \{(c_1,c_2,\ldots,c_n) \in E^{(n)} \mid f(c_1,c_2,\ldots,c_n) = 0 \text{ for all } f \in \mathfrak{a}\}$ is an *algebraic set* in $E^{(n)}$ (over F), where $E^{(n)} = E \times E \times \cdots \times E$ is the n-fold Cartesian product. For example, the real unit sphere in Euclidean 3-space is an algebraic set $V_{\mathbf{R}^{(3)}/\mathbf{R}}(\mathfrak{a})$, where $\mathfrak{a}$ is the ideal generated by $x_1^2 + x_2^2 + x_3^2 - 1$ in $\mathbf{R}[x_1,x_2,x_3]$. It is easy to prove that $V_{E^{(n)}/F}(\mathfrak{a}_1 \cap \mathfrak{a}_2 \cap \cdots \cap \mathfrak{a}_k) = V_{E^{(n)}/F}(\mathfrak{a}_1) \cup V_{E^{(n)}/F}(\mathfrak{a}_2) \cup \cdots \cup V_{E^{(n)}/F}(\mathfrak{a}_k)$, and $V_{E^{(n)}/F}((\mathfrak{a}_1,\mathfrak{a}_2,\ldots,\mathfrak{a}_k)) = V_{E^{(n)}/F}(\mathfrak{a}_1) \cap V_{E^{(n)}/F}(\mathfrak{a}_2) \cap \cdots \cap V_{E^{(n)}/F}(\mathfrak{a}_k)$ (k a positive integer, $\mathfrak{a}_1,\mathfrak{a}_2,\ldots,\mathfrak{a}_k$ ideals in $F[x_1,x_2,\ldots,x_n]$, and $(\mathfrak{a}_1,\mathfrak{a}_2,\ldots,\mathfrak{a}_k)$ the ideal generated by $\mathfrak{a}_1,\mathfrak{a}_2,\ldots,\mathfrak{a}_k$. An algebraic set V is *irreducible* (*over* F) if it is not the union of two algebraic sets each distinct from V. It is not difficult to show that an algebraic set V has a unique representation (up to order) as a finite union of irreducible algebraic sets V_i, $i = 1, 2,\ldots, k$, with $V_i \not\subset V_j$ for $i \neq j$.

We have associated with every ideal $\mathfrak{a}$ in $F[x_1,x_2,\ldots,x_n]$ a geometric object—the algebraic set $V_{E^{(n)}/F}(\mathfrak{a})$. With every algebraic set in $E^{(n)}$ we now associate an "algebraic" object in $F[x_1,x_2,\ldots,x_n]$: Let $V_{E^{(n)}/F}(\mathfrak{a})$ be an algebraic set in $E^{(n)}$; then $\mathscr{I}_F(V_{E^{(n)}/F}(\mathfrak{a})) = \{f \in F[x_1,x_2,\ldots,x_n] \mid f(c_1,c_2,\ldots,c_n) = 0 \text{ for all } (c_1,c_2,\ldots,c_n) \in V_{E^{(n)}/F}(\mathfrak{a})\}$ is an ideal, *the ideal belonging to* $V_{E^{(n)}/F}(\mathfrak{a})$. The following assertion is easy to prove: V is an irreducible algebraic set if and only if $\mathscr{I}_F(V)$ is a prime ideal.

In general, $\mathscr{I}_F(V_{E^{(n)}/F}(\mathfrak{a})) \neq \mathfrak{a}$. For example, if, in $\mathbf{R}[x_1,x_2,x_3]$, $\mathfrak{a} = ((x_1^2 + x_2^2 - 1)^3, x_3^4)$, then $\mathscr{I}_R(V_{\mathbf{R}^{(3)}/\mathbf{R}}(\mathfrak{a})) = (x_1^2 + x_2^2 - 1, x_3)$. We shall see in Section 4 that, if E is an algebraically closed field, then $\mathscr{I}_F(V_{E^{(n)}/F}(\mathfrak{a})) = \sqrt{\mathfrak{a}}$. Hence, if E is algebraically closed, there is a bijection between the set of algebraic sets in $E^{(n)}$ over F and the set of ideals $\mathfrak{a}$ in $F[x_1,x_2,\ldots,x_n]$ such that $\mathfrak{a} = \sqrt{\mathfrak{a}}$; in particular, there is a bijection between the set of irreducible algebraic sets $E^{(n)}$ over F and the set of prime ideals in $F[x_1,x_2,\ldots,x_n]$.

Let $\mathfrak{p}$ be a prime ideal in $F[x_1,x_2,\ldots,x_n]$, and let $V = V_{E^{(n)}/F}(\mathfrak{p})$ be the associated irreducible algebraic set (E not necessarily algebraically closed). Then $D = F[x_1,x_2,\ldots,x_n]/\mathfrak{p}$ is an integral domain which contains a field, F_1, isomorphic to F. Let L be a quotient field of D with $L \supset D$. Then the transcendence degree, tr.d. L/F_1, is called the *dimension* (dim V) *of* V. As an example, let $\mathfrak{p} = (x_1^2 + x_2^2 + x_3^2 - 1)$ in $\mathbf{R}[x_1,x_2,x_3]$. Then $V = V_{\mathbf{R}^{(3)}/\mathbf{R}}(\mathfrak{p})$ is the unit sphere in $\mathbf{R}^{(3)}$. It is easy to verify that the transcendence degree of the quotient field of $\mathbf{R}[x_1,x_2,x_3]/\mathfrak{p}$ over $\mathbf{R}$ is 2. Thus, dim $V = 2$.

3. Integral Elements; "Lying Over" and "Going Up"; Normalization

In Sections 1 and 2 we have been concerned with rings in which every ideal is finitely generated. In this section we study those elements, α, of a ring B for which the subring, $A[\alpha]$, of B generated by α and a fixed subring A of B is a finitely generated A-module.

Definition 3.1. Let B be a ring, A a subring of B. An element $\alpha \in B$ is *integral over* A if α is a root of a monic polynomial with coefficients in A; i.e., there is a set $\{a_i\}_{i=1}^n$ of elements of A such that $\alpha^n + \sum_{i=1}^n a_i\alpha^{n-i} = 0$. ///

REMARK. Let A be a subring of B. Every element of A is integral over A. If A is an integral domain and F is a quotient field of A ($A \subset F \subset B$), then every element of B which is integral over A is algebraic over F. However, not every element of B which is algebraic over F is integral over A. (For, if an element is algebraic over F, it need not be a root of a *monic* polynomial with coefficients in A.)

Theorem 3.1. *Let $B \neq 0$ be a ring, A a subring of B, and $\alpha \in B$. The following statements are equivalent.*

a. *α is integral over A.*

b. *The subring $A[\alpha]$ of B generated by A and α is a finitely generated A-module.*

c. *$A[\alpha]$ is contained in a subring C of B, where C is a finitely generated A-module.*

d. *B contains a finitely generated A-module, M, such that some element of M is not a zero divisor in B and such that $\alpha M \subset M$.*

PROOF.

a $\Rightarrow$ b. Assume that α is integral over A. Then there are elements $a_1, a_2, \ldots, a_n$ in A such that $\alpha^n = \sum_{i=1}^n a_i\alpha^{n-i}$. Hence α^n is in the A-module generated by $1, \alpha, \alpha^2, \ldots, \alpha^{n-1}$. An induction shows that, for every positive integer k, $\alpha^{n+k} \in A + A\alpha + \cdots + A\alpha^{n-1}$. Since every element in $A[\alpha]$ is representable in the form $\sum_{i=0}^m a_i\alpha^i$ ($a_i \in A$, m a nonnegative integer), we conclude that $A[\alpha]$ is an A-module which is generated by $1, \alpha, \ldots, \alpha^{n-1}$ over A. Thus a $\Rightarrow$ b.

b $\Rightarrow$ c. Let $C = A[\alpha]$.

c $\Rightarrow$ d. Assume c. Then $M = C$ satisfies the conditions stated in d. For, $1 \in C$ and 1 is not a zero divisor; since C is a subring containing α, $\alpha C \subset C$.

d $\Rightarrow$ a. Let M be a finitely generated A-module contained in B such that M contains an element which is not a zero divisor, and $\alpha M \subset M$. Let M be spanned over A by $\beta_1, \beta_2, \ldots, \beta_n$, where β_1 is not a zero divisor. Since $\alpha M \subset M$, there are elements $a_{ij} \in A$ such that $\alpha\beta_i = \sum_{j=1}^n a_{ij}\beta_j$, $i = 1, 2, \ldots, n$. We leave it to the reader to show that $\det[\alpha I - (a_{ij})]\beta_k = 0$ ($k = 1,2,\ldots,n$), where I is the $n \times n$ identity matrix. Since β_1 is not a zero divisor, $\det[\alpha I - (a_{ij})] = 0$. But then α is a root of the polynomial $\det[xI - (a_{ij})]$, a monic polynomial with coefficients in A. Thus d $\Rightarrow$ a. ∎

Corollary 1. *Let A be a subring of a ring B. Let $\alpha_i \in B$ $(i = 1,2,\ldots,n)$ be integral over A. Then $A[\alpha_1,\alpha_2,\ldots,\alpha_n]$ (the subring generated by A, α_1, $\alpha_2,\ldots,\alpha_n$) is a finitely generated A module, and every element of $A[\alpha_1,\alpha_2,\ldots,\alpha_n]$ is integral over A.*

PROOF. By the theorem, the assertion of the corollary holds for $n = 1$. For $n > 1$, suppose the assertion holds if $n < k$. Let $\alpha_1, \alpha_2,\ldots, \alpha_k$ be elements of B which are integral over A. Clearly, α_k is integral over $A[\alpha_1,\alpha_2,\ldots,\alpha_{k-1}]$. Hence $A[\alpha_1,\alpha_2,\ldots,\alpha_{k-1}][\alpha_k] = A[\alpha_1,\alpha_2,\ldots,\alpha_k]$ is a finitely generated $A[\alpha_1,\alpha_2,\ldots,\alpha_{k-1}]$-module. By our induction assumption, $A[\alpha_1,\alpha_2,\ldots,\alpha_{k-1}]$ is a finitely generated A-module. But then $A[\alpha_1,\alpha_2,\ldots,\alpha_k]$ is a finitely generated A-module. For if $\{\beta_i\}_{i=1}^r$ and $\{\alpha_j\}_{j=1}^s$ are sets which span, respectively, $A[\alpha_1,\alpha_2,\ldots,\alpha_k]$ over $A[\alpha_1,\alpha_2,\ldots,\alpha_{k-1}]$ and $A[\alpha_1,\alpha_2,\ldots,\alpha_{k-1}]$ over A, then $\{\beta_i\alpha_j\}_{i=1,2,\ldots,r,\,j=1,2,\ldots,s}$ is a spanning set for $A[\alpha_1,\alpha_2,\ldots,\alpha_k]$ over A. From part c of the theorem we conclude that every element of $A[\alpha_1,\ldots,\alpha_k]$ is integral over A. ▮

An immediate consequence of Corollary 1 is

Corollary 2. *Let A be a subring of a ring B. Then the elements of B which are integral over A form a subring of B containing A.* □

Definition 3.2. Let A be a subring of a ring B. A subring C of B containing A is *integral over A* if every element of C is integral over A. The subring of B consisting of the elements of B which are integral over A is the *integral closure of A in B*. An integral domain A is *integrally closed* if the integral closure of A in its quotient field is A. ///

Corollary 3. *Let A be a subring of a ring B, and let B be a subring of a ring C. If B is integral over A, and C is integral over B, then C is integral over A.*

PROOF. Let $\gamma \in C$. Then there are elements $\beta_1,\beta_2,\ldots,\beta_n \in B$ such that $\gamma^n + \sum_{i=1}^n \beta_i\gamma^{n-i} = 0$. Since $\beta_1, \beta_2,\ldots, \beta_n$ are integral over A, $A[\beta_1,\beta_2,\ldots,\beta_n]$ is a finitely generated A-module (Corollary 1). But $A[\beta_1,\beta_2,\ldots,\beta_n,\gamma]$ is a finitely generated $A[\beta_1,\beta_2,\ldots,\beta_n]$-module, hence a finitely generated A-module. It follows (by the theorem, part c) that γ is integral over A. We conclude that C is integral over A. ▮

Examples.

1. If D is a Gaussian domain, then D is integrally closed. For, let $F \supset D$ be a quotient field of D. Suppose $a/b \in F$ $(a,b \in D)$ is integral over D. Let

$f \in D[x]$ be a monic polynomial of least degree which has a/b as a root. In $F[x]$, $(x - a/b)|f$. But then, (Chapter 2, Section 3, Lemma 3) $f = x - a/b$ and $a/b \in D$.

2. Let $d \neq 0, \neq 1$ be a square free integer (i.e., $p^2 \nmid d$ for any prime p). Consider the field $\mathbf{Q}(\sqrt{d})$. We determine the integral closure of $\mathbf{Z}$ in $\mathbf{Q}(\sqrt{d})$. Suppose that $a + b\sqrt{d} \in \mathbf{Q}(\sqrt{d})$ is integral over $\mathbf{Z}$. From Lemma 3 of (Chapter 2, Section 3, it follows easily that, if $a + b\sqrt{d}$ is a root of a monic polynomial in $\mathbf{Z}[x]$, then its minimum polynomial over $\mathbf{Q}$ is in $\mathbf{Z}[x]$. But then $a + b\sqrt{d}$ is integral over $\mathbf{Z}$ if and only if $2a \in \mathbf{Z}$ and $a^2 - db^2 \in \mathbf{Z}$. Simple computations show that for $d \equiv 2$ or $3 \bmod 4$, $a + b\sqrt{d}$ is integral over $\mathbf{Z}$ if and only if $a,b \in \mathbf{Z}$; for $d \equiv 1 \bmod 4$, $a + b\sqrt{d}$ is integral over $\mathbf{Z}$ if and only if $a,b \in \mathbf{Z}$, or a and b are both halves of odd integers. Hence the integral closure of $\mathbf{Z}$ in $\mathbf{Q}(\sqrt{d})$ is the set $\{a + b\theta | a,b \in \mathbf{Z})$, where $\theta = \sqrt{d}$ if $d \equiv 2$ or $3 \bmod 4$; and $\theta = (1 + \sqrt{d})/2$ if $d \equiv 1 \bmod 4$.

3. Let $D = \{a + b\sqrt{-3} | a,b \in \mathbf{Z}\}$. Then $\mathbf{Q}(\sqrt{-3})$ is the quotient field of D, and $(1 + \sqrt{-3})/2$ is integral over D but is not in D. Hence D is not integrally closed. By Example 1, D is not a Gaussian domain. It can be shown that the domain $\{a + b(1 + \sqrt{-3})/2 | a,b \in \mathbf{Z}\}$ is Gaussian.

4. Let A be a subring of a ring B, and let $\sigma: B \to C$ be a homomorphism of B into a ring C. If B is integral over A, then $\sigma(B)$ is integral over $\sigma(A)$. We leave the details to the reader.

Theorem 3.2. *Let A be a subring of a ring B, and let S be a multiplicative system in A, with $0 \notin S$.*

a. *If B is integral over A, then BS^{-1} is integral over AS^{-1}.*

b. *If A is an integral domain which is integrally closed, then so is AS^{-1}.*

PROOF.

a. There is a homomorphism $\alpha_S: B \to BS^{-1}$ such that every element of BS^{-1} is of the form $\alpha_S(\beta)/\alpha_S(s)$ ($\beta \in B$, $s \in S$), and, for each $s \in S$, $\alpha_S(S)$ is a unit in BS^{-1} (Chapter 2, Theorem 2.7). We identify AS^{-1} with the subring of BS^{-1} consisting of all elements of the form $\alpha_S(a)/\alpha_S(s)$ ($a \in A$, $s \in S$). Consider an element $\alpha_S(\beta)/\alpha_S(s) \in BS^{-1}$ ($\beta \in B$, $s \in S$). Since B is integral over A, there are elements $a_1, a_2, \ldots, a_n \in A$ such that $\beta^n + \sum_{i=1}^n a_i\beta^{n-i} = 0$. But then

$$\left(\frac{\alpha_S(\beta)}{\alpha_S(s)}\right)^n + \sum_{i=1}^{n} \frac{\alpha_S(a_i)}{\alpha_S(s^i)} \left(\frac{\alpha_S(\beta)}{\alpha_S(s)}\right)^{n-i} = 0$$

and $\alpha_S(\beta)/\alpha_S(s)$ is integral over AS^{-1}. We conclude that BS^{-1} is integral over AS^{-1}.

b. Let $\alpha_S: A \to AS^{-1}$ be the homomorphism described in Chapter 2, Theorem 2.7. Since A is an integral domain, α_S is a monomorphism, and α_S extends to a monomorphism of the quotient field of A into the quotient field of AS^{-1}. (For simplicity of notation we use α_S to denote the extended monomorphism.) Let γ be an element of the quotient field of AS^{-1} which is integral over AS^{-1}. Then there exist $a,b,a_1,a_2,\ldots,a_n \in A$ and $s_1,s_2,\ldots,s_n \in S$ such that $\gamma = \alpha_S(a/b)$ and

$$\left[\alpha_S\left(\frac{a}{b}\right)\right]^n + \sum_{i=1}^{n} \frac{\alpha_S(a_i)}{\alpha_S(s_i)}\left[\alpha_S\left(\frac{a}{b}\right)\right]^{n-i} = 0.$$

But then

$$\left[\alpha_S\left(s\frac{a}{b}\right)\right]^n + \sum_{i=1}^{n} \alpha_S\left(\frac{s^i}{s_i}a_i\right)\left[\alpha_S\left(s\frac{a}{b}\right)\right]^{n-i} = 0, \qquad \text{where } s = \prod_{i=1}^{n} s_i.$$

Since α_S is a monomorphism,

$$\left(s\frac{a}{b}\right)^n + \sum_{i=1}^{n} \frac{s^i}{s_i}a_i\left(s\frac{a}{b}\right)^{n-i} = 0,$$

and $s(a/b)$ is integral over A. Since A is integrally closed, $s(a/b) = c \in A$. We conclude that $\gamma = \alpha_S(a/b) = \alpha_S(c)/\alpha_S(s) \in AS^{-1}$, and AS^{-1} is integrally closed, as desired. ▮

We now consider the following problem: If A is a subring of a ring B and $\mathfrak{p}$ is a prime ideal in A, does there exist a prime ideal $\mathfrak{P}$ in B such that $\mathfrak{P} \cap A = \mathfrak{p}$? In general the answer is no. For example, let A be an integral domain, B the quotient field of A. We shall see that, if B is integral over A, then the answer is yes. We also consider the following question: If $\mathfrak{p}_0 \subset \mathfrak{p}_1 \subset \cdots \subset \mathfrak{p}_n$ is an ascending sequence of prime ideals in A, and $\mathfrak{P}_0$ is a prime ideal in B such that $\mathfrak{P}_0 \cap A = \mathfrak{p}_0$, does there exist an ascending sequence of prime ideals in B, $\mathfrak{P}_0 \subset \mathfrak{P}_1 \subset \cdots \subset \mathfrak{P}_n$, such that $\mathfrak{P}_i \cap A = \mathfrak{p}_i$ $(i = 0,1,\ldots,n)$? Again, if B is integral over A, the answer is yes. We can ask a similar question for a descending sequence of prime ideals in A. If A is integrally closed, B integral over A, and if no nonzero element of A is a zero divisor in B, then the answer is yes. (We shall not prove the last assertion.) We shall say that an ideal $\mathfrak{b}$ in B *lies over* an ideal $\mathfrak{a}$ in A if $\mathfrak{b} \cap A = \mathfrak{a}$.

Lemma *Let B be a ring which is integral over a subring A. Let $\mathfrak{p}$ be a prime ideal in A, and let $S = A - \mathfrak{p}$. Let $\mathscr{S} = \{\mathfrak{b} | \mathfrak{b}$ ideal in B, $\mathfrak{b} \cap S = \varnothing\}$.*

a. *$\mathscr{S}$ has a maximal element (relative to the inclusion relation). If $\mathfrak{P}$ is maximal in $\mathscr{S}$, then $\mathfrak{P}$ is prime, and $\mathfrak{P}$ lies over $\mathfrak{p}$ (i.e., $\mathfrak{P} \cap A = \mathfrak{p}$).*

b. *If $\mathfrak{P}$ is a prime ideal in B which lies over $\mathfrak{p}$, then $\mathfrak{P}$ is a maximal element of $\mathscr{S}$.*

PROOF.

a. Since $0 \in \mathscr{S}$, $\mathscr{S}$ is nonempty and Zorn's Lemma obviously applies to $\langle \mathscr{S}, \subset \rangle$. Hence $\mathscr{S}$ has a maximal element, $\mathfrak{P}$, which is a prime ideal in B (see the proof of Theorem 2.1). Since $\mathfrak{P} \cap S = \varnothing$, $\mathfrak{P} \cap A \subset \mathfrak{p}$. Suppose $\mathfrak{P} \cap A \neq \mathfrak{p}$. Then there is an element $a \in \mathfrak{p}$, $a \notin \mathfrak{P}$, hence $(a) + \mathfrak{P} \supsetneqq \mathfrak{P}$. Since $\mathfrak{P}$ is maximal in $\mathscr{S}$, $((a) + \mathfrak{P}) \cap S \neq \varnothing$. Let $s \in ((a) + \mathfrak{P}) \cap S$. Then $s \notin \mathfrak{p}$, and $s = a\beta + \pi$ for some $\beta \in B$, $\pi \in \mathfrak{P}$. Since B is integral over A, $\beta^n + \sum_{i=1}^{n} a_i \beta^{n-i} = 0$ for some $a_1, a_2, \ldots, a_n \in A$. Then $(a\beta)^n + \sum\sum_{i=1}^{n} (a^i a_i) \times (a\beta)^{n-i} = 0$, and $(s - \pi)^n + \sum_{i=1}^{n} a^i a_i (s - \pi)^{n-i} = 0$. It follows that $s^n + \sum_{i=1}^{n} a^i a_i s^{n-i} \in \mathfrak{P} \cap A$, and $s^n + \sum_{i=1}^{n} a^i a_i s^{n-i} \in \mathfrak{p}$. From $a \in \mathfrak{p}$ we conclude that $s^n \in \mathfrak{p}$, whence $s \in \mathfrak{p}$. Contradiction! This contradiction arose from the assumption that $\mathfrak{P} \cap A \neq \mathfrak{p}$. Hence $\mathfrak{P} \cap A = \mathfrak{p}$, as desired.

b. Let $\mathfrak{P}$ be a prime ideal in B such that $\mathfrak{P} \cap A = \mathfrak{p}$. Suppose that $\mathfrak{P}$ is not maximal in $\mathscr{S}$. Then there is an ideal $\mathfrak{b}$ in B such that $\mathfrak{P} \subsetneqq \mathfrak{b}$, and $\mathfrak{b} \cap S = \varnothing$. Choose $\beta \in \mathfrak{b}$ with $\beta \notin \mathfrak{P}$. Since B is integral over A, and $\beta \in B$, the set $\{f | f(\beta) \in \mathfrak{P}\}$, of monic polynomials with coefficients in A such that $f(\beta) \in \mathfrak{P}$ is not empty. Let g be a polynomial of least degree in this set, and suppose that $g(\beta) = \beta^n + a_1\beta^{n-1} + \cdots + a_{n-1}\beta + a_n$. From $\beta \in \mathfrak{b}$, $\beta^n + a_1\beta^{n-1} + \cdots + a_{n-1}\beta + a_n \in \mathfrak{P}$, $\mathfrak{P} \subset \mathfrak{b}$, and $a_n \in A$, we conclude that $a_n \in \mathfrak{b} \cap A$. Since $\mathfrak{b} \cap S = \varnothing$, $\mathfrak{b} \cap A \subset \mathfrak{p}$. But then $\beta(\beta^{n-1} + a_1\beta^{n-2} + \cdots + a_{n-1}) \in \mathfrak{P}$, with $\beta \notin \mathfrak{P}$ and $\beta^{n-1} + a_1\beta^{n-2} + \cdots + a_{n-1} \notin \mathfrak{P}$. Since $\mathfrak{P}$ is a prime ideal we have a contradiction. Hence $\mathfrak{P}$ is maximal in $\mathscr{S}$, as desired. ▌

Theorem 3.3. *Let A be a subring of a ring B, and let B be integral over A.*

a. *("Lying over" theorem.) Let $\mathfrak{p}$ be a prime ideal in A. Then there is a prime ideal $\mathfrak{P}$ in B such that $\mathfrak{P} \cap A = \mathfrak{p}$; $\mathfrak{P}$ is a maximal ideal in B if and only if $\mathfrak{p}$ is a maximal ideal in A. If $\mathfrak{P}_1$ and $\mathfrak{P}_2$ are distinct prime ideals in B lying over $\mathfrak{p}$, then $\mathfrak{P}_1$ and $\mathfrak{P}_2$ are not comparable (i.e., $\mathfrak{P}_1 \not\subset \mathfrak{P}_2$ and $\mathfrak{P}_2 \not\subset \mathfrak{P}_1$).*

b. *("Going up" theorem.) Let $\mathfrak{p}_0 \subset \mathfrak{p}_1 \subset \cdots \subset \mathfrak{p}_n$ be an ascending sequence of prime ideals in A, and let $\mathfrak{P}_0$ be a prime ideal in B lying over $\mathfrak{p}_0$. Then there is an ascending sequence $\mathfrak{P}_0 \subset \mathfrak{P}_1 \subset \cdots \subset \mathfrak{P}_n$ of prime ideals in B such that $\mathfrak{P}_i$ lies over $\mathfrak{p}_i$, $i = 1, 2, \ldots, n$.*

PROOF.

a. An immediate consequence of the first part of the lemma is that every prime ideal in A has a prime ideal in B lying over it. The second part of the lemma assures us that if $\mathfrak{P}_1$ and $\mathfrak{P}_2$ are prime ideals in B lying over the same prime ideal in A, then $\mathfrak{P}_1$ and $\mathfrak{P}_2$ are maximal elements (relative to set inclusion) of some set. But then $\mathfrak{P}_1 \not\subset \mathfrak{P}_2$, and $\mathfrak{P}_2 \not\subset \mathfrak{P}_1$. The following remains to be shown: Let $\mathfrak{P}$ be a prime ideal in B lying over a prime ideal, $\mathfrak{p}$, in A. Then $\mathfrak{P}$ is a maximal ideal in B if and only if $\mathfrak{p}$ is a maximal ideal in A.

If $\mathfrak{P}$ is not a maximal ideal in B, then $\mathfrak{P}$ is contained in a maximal ideal $\mathfrak{P}' \neq \mathfrak{P}$. Since $\mathfrak{P}$ and $\mathfrak{P}'$ are comparable and unequal ($\mathfrak{P} \subsetneqq \mathfrak{P}'$), $\mathfrak{P}$ and $\mathfrak{P}'$ do not lie over the same prime ideal in A. But then $\mathfrak{p}' = \mathfrak{P}' \cap A \supsetneqq \mathfrak{P} \cap A = \mathfrak{p}$ and $\mathfrak{p}$ is not maximal in A. If $\mathfrak{p}$ is not a maximal ideal in A, then $\mathfrak{p}$ is contained in a maximal ideal $\mathfrak{p}' \neq \mathfrak{p}$. Let $\mathfrak{P}''$ be a maximal element of the set $\{\mathfrak{b} | \mathfrak{b}$ ideal in B, $\mathfrak{b} \supset \mathfrak{P}$, $\mathfrak{b} \cap (A - \mathfrak{p}') = \varnothing\}$. By the lemma, part a, $\mathfrak{P}''$ is a prime ideal lying over $\mathfrak{p}'$. But then $\mathfrak{P} \subsetneqq \mathfrak{P}''$, and $\mathfrak{P}$ is not maximal in B.

b. Let $\mathfrak{p}_0$, $\mathfrak{p}_1$ be prime ideals in A with $\mathfrak{p}_0 \subset \mathfrak{p}_1$, and let $\mathfrak{P}_0$ be a prime ideal in B lying over $\mathfrak{p}_0$. Let $\mathfrak{P}_1$ be a maximal element of the set $\{\mathfrak{b} | \mathfrak{b}$ ideal in B, $\mathfrak{b} \supset \mathfrak{P}_0$, $\mathfrak{b} \cap (A - \mathfrak{p}_1) = \varnothing\}$. Then $\mathfrak{P}_1$ is a prime ideal in B lying over $\mathfrak{p}_1$ (by the lemma), and $\mathfrak{P}_1 \supset \mathfrak{P}_0$. Assertion b now follows by induction. ∎

We have seen (Chapter 5, Theorem 4.14) that every field, E, finitely generated and separable over a field F, has a separating transcendence base over F; i.e., if $E = F(S)$ with E separable over F, and S finite, then there is a subset T of S such that T is a transcendence base for E over F and E is separable over $F(T)$. We now consider the following problem. If a ring B is generated (as a ring) over a subring A by a finite subset S, does there exist an algebraically independent set T in B such that B is integral over the subring generated by A and T? If A is a field, the answer is yes. We shall prove a somewhat more general theorem. Before doing so we make a few remarks about terminology and notation.

Let A be a subring of a ring B. A set of elements $\{\beta_1,\beta_2,\ldots,\beta_n\}$ in B is an algebraically independent set over A if there does not exist a relation of the form

$$\sum_{(i_1,i_2,\ldots,i_n)\in J} a_{i_1i_2\ldots i_n}\beta_1^{i_1}\beta_2^{i_2}\cdots\beta_n^{i_n} = 0,$$

where J is a finite set of n-tuples of nonnegative integers, and $a_{i_1,i_2,\ldots,i_n}$ is a nonzero element of A for each $(i_1,i_2,\ldots,i_n) \in J$.

Let B be a ring, A an integral domain which is a subring of B. Let a be an element of A which is not a zero divisor in B and let $B[a^{-1}] = BS^{-1}$, where

S is the multiplicative system $\{1,a,a^2,a^3,\ldots\} \subset B$. [Since a is not a zero divisor in B, $\alpha_S\colon B \to BS^{-1}$ is a monomorphism. We identify B and $\alpha_S(B)$.]

Theorem 3.4. (Normalization Lemma) *Let A be an integral domain, P the subdomain generated by $1 \in A$. Let B be a ring containing A as a subring. Suppose that no nonzero element of A is a zero divisor in B, and that B is generated over A by $\{\beta_1,\beta_2,\ldots,\beta_n\}$. Then there is a set $\gamma_1, \gamma_2, \ldots, \gamma_m \subset P[\beta_1,\beta_2,\ldots,\beta_n]$, $0 \le m \le n$, algebraically independent over A, such that, for some $a \neq 0$ in A, $B[a^{-1}]$ is integral over $A[a^{-1},\gamma_1,\gamma_2,\ldots,\gamma_m]$.*

PROOF. If $\{\beta_1,\beta_2,\ldots,\beta_n\}$ is an algebraically independent set over A, then the theorem holds with $a = 1$ and $\gamma_i = \beta_i$ for $i = 1, 2, \ldots, n$. Suppose that $\{\beta_1,\beta_2,\ldots,\beta_n\}$ is not algebraically independent over A. Then there is a nonempty set J of ordered n-tuples of nonnegative integers, and a set of nonzero elements in A, $\{a_{i_1 i_2 \ldots i_n} | (i_1,i_2,\ldots,i_n) \in J\}$, such that

$$(*) \qquad \sum_{(i_1,i_2,\ldots,i_n)\in J} a_{i_1,i_2,\ldots,i_n}\beta_1^{i_1}\beta_2^{i_2}\cdots\beta_n^{i_n} = 0.$$

We leave it to the reader to show that there is a positive integer w, and an element $(j_1,j_2,\ldots,j_n) \in J$ such that

$$j_1 1 + j_2 w + j_3 w^2 + \cdots + j_n w^{n-1} > i_1 1 + i_2 w + i_3 w^2 + \cdots + i_n w^{n-1}$$

for all $(i_1,i_2,\ldots,i_n) \in J$ with $(i_1,i_2,\ldots,i_n) \neq (j_1,j_2,\ldots,j_n)$.

Let $\delta_2 = \beta_2 - \beta_1^{w}$, $\delta_3 = \beta_3 - \beta_1^{w^2}, \ldots, \delta_n = \beta_n - \beta_1^{w^{n-1}}$. If we substitute $\delta_i + \beta_1^{w^{i-1}}$ for β_i $(i = 2,\ldots,n)$ in (*) and expand, we obtain

$$(**) \qquad a_{j_1 j_2 \ldots j_n}\beta_1^{j_1 + j_2 w + j_3 w^2 + \cdots + j_n w^{n-1}} + f(\beta_1,\delta_2,\ldots,\delta_n) = 0,$$

where f is a polynomial in $\beta_1, \delta_2, \delta_3, \ldots, \delta_n$ with coefficients in A whose degree in β_1 is strictly less than $j_1 + j_2 w + \cdots + j_n w^{n-1}$. Let $a = a_{j_1 j_2 \ldots j_n}$. From (**) it follows that β_1 is integral over $A[a^{-1},\delta_2,\ldots,\delta_n]$. Since $\beta_i = \delta_i + \beta_1^{w^{i-1}}$, β_i is integral over $A[a^{-1},\delta_2,\ldots,\delta_n]$ $(i = 2,3,\ldots,n)$. But then $B[a^{-1}] = A[a^{-1},\beta_1,\beta_2,\ldots,\beta_n]$ is integral over $A[a^{-1},\delta_2,\delta_3,\ldots,\delta_n]$. Note that $\delta_i \in P[\beta_1,\beta_2,\ldots,\beta_n]$ $(i = 1,2,\ldots,n)$. If $\{\delta_2,\delta_3,\ldots,\delta_n\}$ is not algebraically independent over A, we repeat the process: There is an element $b \neq 0$ in A, and there are elements $\eta_i \in P[\beta_1,\beta_2,\ldots,\beta_n]$ $(i = 3,\ldots,n)$ such that $A[a^{-1},\delta_2,\delta_3,\ldots,\delta_n][b^{-1}]$ is integral over $A[a^{-1},b^{-1},\eta_3,\eta_4,\ldots,\eta_n]$. But then, using Theorem 3.1, Corollary 3, we conclude that $B[(ab)^{-1}]$ is integral over $A[(ab)^{-1},\eta_3,\eta_4,\ldots,\eta_n]$. The theorem follows by an induction argument. ∎

Corollary. *Let $B = F[\beta_1,\beta_2,\ldots,\beta_n]$ be an integral domain, finitely generated over a field F, and let m be the transcendence degree over F of the quotient field of B. Then there is a transcendence set $\{\gamma_1,\gamma_2,\ldots,\gamma_m\}$ over F ($\gamma_i \in B$) such that B is integral over $F[\gamma_1,\gamma_2,\ldots,\gamma_m]$.* □

4. Hilbert Nullstellensatz

Let E be an algebraically closed field containing a subfield F. If f is a nonconstant polynomial in $F[x]$, then the set of roots ("zeros") of f in E is not empty. Since $F[x]$ is a principal ideal domain, this assertion may be restated as follows: If $\mathfrak{a}$ is an ideal in $F[x]$, with $\mathfrak{a} \neq F[x]$, then the algebraic set in E determined by the ideal $\mathfrak{a}$ is not empty. (The terminology and notation is that introduced at the end of Section 2.) It is surprising, and nontrivial, that to every proper (or zero) ideal, $\mathfrak{a}$, in a polynomial domain in n indeterminates over F ($n \geq 1$) there corresponds a *nonempty* algebraic set in $E^{(n)}$. We shall prove this result, and we shall also prove that if f is a polynomial which vanishes on the algebraic set determined by $\mathfrak{a}$, the some power of f lies in $\mathfrak{a}$.

Theorem 4.1. Hilbert Nullstellensatz *Let E be an algebraically closed field containing a subfield F. Let $x_1, x_2, \ldots, x_n$ be a transcendence set over F, and let $\mathfrak{a}$ be an ideal in $F[x_1,x_2,\ldots,x_n]$.*

a *If $\mathfrak{a} \neq F[x_1,x_2,\ldots,x_n]$, then $V_{E^{(n)}/F}(\mathfrak{a}) \neq \varnothing$.*

b $\mathscr{I}_F(V_{E^{(n)}/F}(\mathfrak{a})) = \sqrt{\mathfrak{a}}$.

PROOF.

a. In a ring with identity, every proper (or zero) ideal, $\mathfrak{a}$, is contained in a maximal ideal, $\mathfrak{p}$. Since $\mathfrak{a} \subset \mathfrak{p}$ implies $V_{E^{(n)}/F}(\mathfrak{a}) \supset V_{E^{(n)}/F}(\mathfrak{p})$, and since every maximal ideal is a prime ideal, it is sufficient to prove that $V_{E^{(n)}/F}(\mathfrak{p}) \neq \varnothing$ for every prime ideal $\mathfrak{p}$ in $F[x_1,x_2,\ldots,x_n]$.

Let $\mathfrak{p}$ be a prime ideal in $F[x_1,x_2,\ldots,x_n]$, ν the canonical epimorphism of $F[x_1,x_2,\ldots,x_n]$ onto the integral domain $B = F[x_1,x_2,\ldots,x_n]/\mathfrak{p}$, and let $\beta_i = \nu(x_i)$ for each $i = 1, 2,\ldots, n$. Then $B = \nu(F)[\beta_1,\beta_2,\ldots,\beta_n]$. Note that $\nu(F) \cong F$. By the corollary to the normalization lemma (Theorem 3.4), there is a transcendence set $\{\gamma_1,\gamma_2,\ldots,\gamma_m\}$ over $\nu(F)$ in B such that B is integral over $A = \nu(F)[\gamma_1,\gamma_2,\ldots,\gamma_m]$. Let $\mathscr{M}$ be the ideal generated in A by $\{\gamma_1,\gamma_2,\ldots,\gamma_m\}$. Since $A/\mathscr{M} \cong \nu(F) \cong F$, $\mathscr{M}$ is a maximal ideal in A. By the "lying over" theorem (Theorem 3.3a) there is a maximal ideal $\mathscr{M}'$ in B such that $\mathscr{M}' \cap A = \mathscr{M}$. Let η be the canonical epimorphism of B onto $B/\mathscr{M}'$. Note that $\eta(B)$ and $\eta(A) \cong A/(\mathscr{M}' \cap A) \cong A/\mathscr{M} \cong F$ are fields. Since B is integral over A, $\eta(B)$

is an algebraic extension of $\eta(A)$. Since E is algebraically closed, there is (Chapter 5, Theorem 2.5) a monomorphism $\tau\colon \eta(B) \to E$. Let $\varphi = \tau\eta\nu$. Then φ is a homomorphism of $F[x_1,x_2,\ldots,x_n]$ into E and $\varphi(f) = 0$ for each $f \in \mathfrak{p}$. Since $\nu|_F$, $\eta|_{\nu F}$, and $\tau|_{\eta\nu F}$ are monomorphisms, $\varphi|_F$ is a monomorphism. If we identify each element of F with its image in φF, then, for each $f \in \mathfrak{p}$, we have $f(\varphi(x_1),\ldots,\varphi(x_n)) = \varphi(f(x_1,\ldots,x_n)) = 0$. Hence $(\varphi(x_1),\ldots,\varphi(x_n)) \in V_{E^{(n)}/F}(\mathfrak{p})$, and $V_{E^{(n)}/F}(\mathfrak{p}) \neq \varnothing$.

b. We shall prove that a $\Rightarrow$ b. (Actually, a and b are equivalent.) Let $\mathfrak{a}$ be an ideal in $F[x_1,x_2,\ldots,x_n]$. Clearly $\mathscr{I}_F(V_{E^{(n)}/F}(\mathfrak{a})) \supset \sqrt{\mathfrak{a}}$. Suppose that $f \in \mathscr{I}_F(V_{E^{(n)}/F}(\mathfrak{a}))$. If $f = 0$, then $f \in \sqrt{\mathfrak{a}}$. Suppose $f \neq 0$. Let y be an element (in some extension of F) such that $\{x_1,x_2,\ldots,x_n,y\}$ is a transcendence set over F, and let $\mathfrak{b}$ be the ideal generated in $F[x_1,x_2,\ldots,x_n,y]$ by $\mathfrak{a}$ and $yf - 1$. Since f vanishes on $V_{E^{(n)}/F}(\mathfrak{a})$, $yf - 1$ assumes the value -1 at each point $(c_1,c_2,\ldots,c_n,d)$ with $(c_1,c_2,\ldots,c_n) \in V_{E^{(n)}/F}(\mathfrak{a})$. Then $V_{E^{(n)}/F}(\mathfrak{b}) = \varnothing$. By a, $\mathfrak{b} = (1)$. Hence there exist $f_i \in \mathfrak{a}$ and $g_j \in F[x_1,x_2,\ldots,x_n,y]$ $(j = 1,2,\ldots,k)$ such that $1 = \sum_{j=1}^{k-1} g_jf_j + g_k(yf - 1)$. If we apply the substitution map $y \mapsto 1/f$, $x_i \mapsto x_i$ $(i = 1,2,\ldots,n)$ from $F[x_1,x_2,\ldots,x_n,y]$ to $F[x_1,x_2,\ldots,x_n]$, and multiply by a sufficiently high power of f, we obtain $f^r = \sum_{j=1}^{k-1} h_jf_j$, where r is a positive integer, and $h_j \in F[x_1,x_2,\ldots,x_n]$ $(j = 1,2,\ldots,k)$. But then $f \in \sqrt{\mathfrak{a}}$. ▌

5. Dedekind Domains

We have seen (in Section 2) that, in a Noetherian ring, every ideal contains a product of prime ideals. In this section we study several conditions on an integral domain D, each equivalent to the requirement that every ideal of D be *equal* to a finite product of prime ideals of D.

Definition 5.1. Let D be an integral domain, $Q \supset D$ a quotient field of D. A nonzero D-submodule $\mathfrak{a}$ of Q is a *fractional ideal* of D if there is an $a \in D$, $a \neq 0$, such that $a\mathfrak{a} \subset D$. A fractional ideal $\mathfrak{a}$ of D is an *integral ideal* of D if $\mathfrak{a} \subset D$. A fractional ideal $\mathfrak{a}$ of D is *invertible* if there is a fractional ideal $\mathfrak{b}$ of D such that $\mathfrak{a}\mathfrak{b} = D$, where $\mathfrak{a}\mathfrak{b} = \{\sum_{i=1}^{m} a_i b_i \mid a_i \in \mathfrak{a}, b_i \in \mathfrak{b}, m \in \mathbf{N}'\}$ ///

Note that a fractional ideal of D is an integral ideal if and only if it is an ideal of D, in the usual sense.

REMARKS. We leave the details of the following remarks to the reader.

Let D be an integral domain, $Q \supset D$ a quotient field of D.

1. The set of fractional ideals of D is closed under addition, multiplication, and intersection.

2. If $\mathfrak{a}$ is a fractional ideal of D, then so is $\mathfrak{a}^{-1} = \{a \in \mathbf{Q} | a\mathfrak{a} \subset D\}$.
3. For each fractional ideal $\mathfrak{a}$ of D, $\mathfrak{a}\mathfrak{a}^{-1} \subset D$.
4. If $\mathfrak{a}$ and $\mathfrak{b}$ are fractional ideals of D such that $\mathfrak{a}\mathfrak{b} = D$, then $\mathfrak{b} = \mathfrak{a}^{-1}$.
5. A fractional ideal $\mathfrak{a}$ of D is invertible if and only if $\mathfrak{a}\mathfrak{a}^{-1} = D$.
6. The set of fractional ideals of D is a group under multiplication if and only if every fractional ideal of D is invertible.

Examples.

1. Every nonzero principal ideal (a) of an integral domain D is invertible, with inverse $D \cdot 1/a$.

2. Let F be a field, x_1 and x_2 transcendental over F, and $D = F[x_1, x_2]$. Then the ideal $\mathfrak{a} = (x_1, x_2)$ generated by x_1 and x_2 over D is not invertible.

3. Let $D = \mathbf{Z}[\sqrt{-5}]$. The ideal $\mathfrak{a} = (3, 1 + \sqrt{-5})$ generated over D by 3 and $1 + \sqrt{-5}$ is invertible, with $\mathfrak{a}^{-1} = (1, (1 - \sqrt{-5})/3)$.

We prove several lemmas before stating and proving the main theorem of this section.

Lemma 1. *An invertible ideal of an integral domain is finitely generated.*

PROOF. Let $\mathfrak{a}$ be an invertible ideal of an integral domain D. Then $\mathfrak{a}\mathfrak{a}^{-1} = D$. Since $1 \in D$, there exist $b_i \in \mathfrak{a}^{-1}$, $a_i \in \mathfrak{a}$, $i = 1, 2, \ldots, n$, such that $1 = \sum_{i=1}^{n} b_i a_i$. We claim that $\mathfrak{a} = (a_1, a_2, \ldots, a_n)$. In fact, for $a \in \mathfrak{a}$, $a = a \cdot 1 = \sum_{i=1}^{n} (ab_i)a_i$, with $ab_i \in D$. ▌

Lemma 2. *Let $\{\mathfrak{a}_i\}_{i=1}^{n}$ be a finite family of ideals of an integral domain D. If $\prod_{i=1}^{n} \mathfrak{a}_i$ is invertible, then so is $\mathfrak{a}_i$, for each $i = 1, 2, \ldots, n$.*

PROOF. Let $\mathfrak{b}$ be the fractional ideal such that $\mathfrak{b} \prod_{i=1}^{r} \mathfrak{a}_i = D$. Then, for each $i = 1, \ldots, n$, $\mathfrak{a}_i(\mathfrak{b} \prod_{j=1, j \neq i}^{n} \mathfrak{a}_j) = D$, hence $\mathfrak{a}_i$ is invertible. ▌

Lemma 3. *Let $\mathfrak{a}$ be an ideal of an integral domain D, and let $\mathfrak{a} = \prod_{i=1}^{m} \mathfrak{p}_i$ and $\mathfrak{a} = \prod_{j=1}^{n} \mathfrak{q}_j$ be factorizations of $\mathfrak{a}$ into products of prime ideals of D, with $\mathfrak{p}_1, \mathfrak{p}_2, \ldots, \mathfrak{p}_n$ invertible. Then $m = n$ and (with suitable relabeling) $\mathfrak{p}_i = \mathfrak{q}_i$ for $i = 1, 2, \ldots, m$.*

PROOF. The proof is by induction on m. The case $m = 1$ is easy and is left to the reader. Assume the lemma true if $m < r$. Suppose that $\mathfrak{a} = \prod_{i=1}^{r} \mathfrak{p}_i = \prod_{j=1}^{n} \mathfrak{q}_j$. From the family $\{\mathfrak{p}_i\}_{i=1}^{r}$ choose an ideal, say $\mathfrak{p}_1$, which does not properly contain any of the other ideals belonging to the family. Clearly $\prod_{j=1}^{n} \mathfrak{q}_j \subset \mathfrak{p}_1$. Hence some $\mathfrak{q}_j$, say $\mathfrak{q}_1$, is contained in the prime ideal $\mathfrak{p}_1$.

Since $\prod_{i=1}^{r} \mathfrak{p}_i \subset \mathfrak{q}_1$, there is some $\mathfrak{p}_i$, say $\mathfrak{p}_2$, such that $\mathfrak{p}_2 \subset \mathfrak{q}_1$. But then $\mathfrak{p}_2 \subset \mathfrak{q}_1 \subset \mathfrak{p}_1$ and, since $\mathfrak{p}_1$ is minimal, $\mathfrak{q}_1 = \mathfrak{p}_1$. We conclude that

$$\prod_{i=2}^{r} \mathfrak{p}_i = \mathfrak{p}_1^{-1} \prod_{i=1}^{r} \mathfrak{p}_i = \mathfrak{q}_1^{-1} \prod_{j=1}^{n} \mathfrak{q}_j = \prod_{j=2}^{n} \mathfrak{q}_j.$$

The lemma follows by induction. ▮

Lemma 4. *Let D be an integral domain, $\mathfrak{a}$ a fractional ideal of D. Then $\mathfrak{a}$ is invertible if and only if $\mathfrak{a}$ is a projective D-module.*

PROOF. Suppose that $\mathfrak{a}$ is an invertible ideal of D. By Lemma 1, $\mathfrak{a}$ is finitely generated over D, say $\mathfrak{a} = (a_1,a_2,\ldots,a_n)$ $(a_i \in A)$. Let $S = \{x_1,\ldots,x_n\}$ be a set and let $\langle F,\eta\rangle$ be a free D-module on S. The map defined by $\tau x_i \mapsto a_i$ for each $i = 1, 2,\ldots, n$ extends to a D-epimorphism $\varphi\colon F \to \mathfrak{a}$ such that $\varphi\eta = \tau$. Since $\mathfrak{a}$ is invertible, there are elements $b_i \in \mathfrak{a}^{-1}$ $(i = 1,2,\ldots,n)$ such that $\sum_{i=1}^{n} b_i a_i = 1$. Define a D-homomorphism $\psi\colon \mathfrak{a} \to F$ by $\psi(a) = \sum_{i=1}^{n} (ab_i)\eta x_i$ $(a \in \mathfrak{a})$. Note that $\varphi\psi$ is the identity map on $\mathfrak{a}$. But then ψ is a splitting homomorphism for the exact sequence

$$0 \longrightarrow \operatorname{Ker}\varphi \longrightarrow F \longrightarrow \mathfrak{a} \longrightarrow 0,$$

$\mathfrak{a}$ is a direct summand of a free D-module, and $\mathfrak{a}$ is a projective D-module.

Now suppose that $\mathfrak{a}$ is a projective D-module. Let $\{a_i\}_{i\in J}$ be a subset of $\mathfrak{a}$ which generates $\mathfrak{a}$ over D. Let $S = \{x_i\}_{i\in J}$ be a set, $\langle F,\eta\rangle$ a free D-module on S, and $\varphi\colon F \to \mathfrak{a}$ the D-epimorphism defined by $\varphi(\eta x_i) = a_i$. Since $\mathfrak{a}$ is projective, there is a D-homomorphism $\psi\colon \mathfrak{a} \to F$ such that $\varphi\psi = \iota_{\mathfrak{a}}$. For each $i \in J$, let $\pi_i\colon F \to D$ be the projection which takes any element $x = \sum_{i\in J} c_i\eta x_i$ of F to the coefficient, c_i, of ηx_i, and let $\rho_i = \pi_i\psi$. Then $\rho_i\colon \mathfrak{a} \to D$ is a D-homomorphism. Since $\mathfrak{a} \neq 0$, $a_\alpha \neq 0$ for some $\alpha \in J$. Let $\rho_i(a_\alpha) = d_i$. For each $a \in \mathfrak{a}$, $\rho_i(aa_\alpha) = a_\alpha\rho_i(a) = a\rho_i(a_\alpha) = ad_i$. Hence, for each $i \in J, \rho\ (a) = (ad_i)/a_\alpha$, and $d_i/a_\alpha \in \mathfrak{a}^{-1}$. It also follows that, for each $a \in \mathfrak{a}$, $\psi(a) = \sum_i a(d_i/a_\alpha)\eta x_i$. Since $\varphi\psi = \iota_{\mathfrak{a}}$, $\sum_i a(d_i/a_\alpha)a_i = a$. But then $\sum_i (d_i/a_\alpha)a_i = 1$, with $(d_i/a_\alpha) \in \mathfrak{a}^{-1}$, $a_i \in \mathfrak{a}$. Since $1 \in \mathfrak{a}^{-1}\mathfrak{a}$, $\mathfrak{a}$ is invertible. ▮

We have seen (Chapter 6, Theorem 8.2) that the ring of integers of a field with a discrete valuation is a principal ideal domain with exactly one nonzero prime ideal. Conversely, if D is a principal ideal domain with exactly one nonzero prime ideal, then D is the ring of integers of a field with a discrete valuation. For, let (π) be the nonzero prime ideal of D. Let c be a real number, with $0 < c < 1$. Since D is Gaussian, every nonzero element $d \in D$ has a unique representation as $d = u\pi^n$, with u a unit and n a nonnegative integer.

Define a map $|\ |: D \to \mathbf{R}$ by $|d| = c^n$ for $d = u\pi^n \in D$. The map $|\ |$ extends in an obvious way to a map of the quotient field Q of D into $\mathbf{R}$. We leave it to the reader to verify that the extended map is a discrete valuation of Q and that D is the ring of local integers relative to this valuation.

Definition 5.2. An integral domain D is a *discrete valuation ring* if D is a principal ideal domain with exactly one nonzero prime ideal. ///

Lemma 5. *Let D be an integral domain. Then D is a discrete valuation ring if and only if D is Noetherian, is integrally closed, and has exactly one nonzero prime ideal.*

PROOF. Suppose D is a discrete valuation ring. Then clearly D is Noetherian, and D has one and only one nonzero prime ideal. Since D is Gaussian, D is integrally closed (Section 3, Example 1).

Conversely, suppose that D is Noetherian, integrally closed, and has exactly one nonzero prime ideal. Let $\mathfrak{p}$ be the nonzero prime ideal of D. We shall prove that D is a principal ideal domain by showing that every ideal of D is a power of $\mathfrak{p}$ and that $\mathfrak{p}$ is a principal ideal.

We show first that $\mathfrak{p}^{-1} \supsetneqq D$. The set $\mathscr{S} = \{\mathfrak{a} | \mathfrak{a}$ an ideal of D, $\mathfrak{a}^{-1} \supsetneqq D\}$ is not empty, for it contains the ideal (a), where $a \in \mathfrak{p}$, $a \neq 0$. Since D is Noetherian, $\mathscr{S}$ has a maximal element, $\mathscr{M}$. The ideal $\mathscr{M}$ is prime. For, suppose $a,b \in D$, $a \notin \mathscr{M}$, and $ab \in \mathscr{M}$. Choose $c \in \mathscr{M}^{-1}$, $c \notin D$. Then $bc(aD + \mathscr{M}) \subset D$, and, by the maximality of $\mathscr{M}$, $bc \in D$. But then $c(bD + \mathscr{M}) \subset D$, whence $bD + \mathscr{M} = \mathscr{M}$, $b \in \mathscr{M}$, and $\mathscr{M}$ is a prime ideal. Since D contains only one nonzero prime ideal, $\mathscr{M} = \mathfrak{p}$ and $\mathfrak{p}^{-1} \supsetneqq D$.

Let $Q \supset D$ be a quotient field of D. For each fractional ideal $\mathfrak{a}$ of D, define $\bar{\mathfrak{a}} = \{a \in Q | a\mathfrak{a} \subset \mathfrak{a}\}$. It is easy to verify that $\bar{\mathfrak{a}}$ is a subring of Q containing D and that $\bar{\mathfrak{a}}$ is a fractional ideal. Since D is Noetherian, $\bar{\mathfrak{a}}$ is a finitely generated D-module. By Theorem 3.1, every element of $\bar{\mathfrak{a}}$ is integral over D. Since D is integrally closed, we conclude that, for every fractional ideal $\mathfrak{a}$ of D, $\bar{\mathfrak{a}} = D$.

Clearly, $\mathfrak{p} \subset \mathfrak{p}\mathfrak{p}^{-1} \subset D$. Since $\mathfrak{p}$ is a maximal ideal of D, either $\mathfrak{p}\mathfrak{p}^{-1} = \mathfrak{p}$ or $\mathfrak{p}\mathfrak{p}^{-1} = D$. If $\mathfrak{p}\mathfrak{p}^{-1} = \mathfrak{p}$, then $D \subsetneqq \mathfrak{p}^{-1} \subset \bar{\mathfrak{p}} = D$. Contradiction! Hence $\mathfrak{p}\mathfrak{p}^{-1} = D$.

We claim that $\bigcap_{i \in \mathbf{N}'} \mathfrak{p}^i = 0$. For, otherwise, $D \subsetneqq \mathfrak{p}^{-1} \subset \overline{\bigcap_{i \in \mathbf{N}'} \mathfrak{p}^i} = D$, and we have a contradiction.

We now show that $\mathfrak{p}$ is a principal ideal. From $\bigcap_{i \in \mathbf{N}'} \mathfrak{p}^i = 0$ we conclude that there is an element $a \in \mathfrak{p}$ with $aD \not\subset \mathfrak{p}^2$. Then $a\mathfrak{p}^{-1} \subset D$, but (since $\mathfrak{p}^{-1}\mathfrak{p} = D$) $a\mathfrak{p}^{-1} \not\subset \mathfrak{p}$. Since every proper ideal of D is contained in the maximal ideal $\mathfrak{p}$, $a\mathfrak{p}^{-1} = D$ and $\mathfrak{p} = (a)$.

If $\mathfrak{a}$ is an ideal of D, then $\mathfrak{a} \subset \mathfrak{p}$. Since $\bigcap_{i \in \mathbf{N}'} \mathfrak{p}^i = 0$, there is a positive integer k such that $\mathfrak{a} \not\subset \mathfrak{p}^m$ for $m \geq k$. Let n be the largest positive integer such that $\mathfrak{a} \subset \mathfrak{p}^n$. Then $\mathfrak{a}(\mathfrak{p}^{-1})^n \subset D$, but $\mathfrak{a}(\mathfrak{p}^{-1})^n \not\subset \mathfrak{p}$. It follows that $\mathfrak{a}(\mathfrak{p}^{-1})^n = D$, and $\mathfrak{a} = \mathfrak{p}^n$. We have shown that every ideal of D is a power of a principal ideal, whence D is a principal ideal domain, and the lemma is proved. ▌

Definition 5.3. An integral domain D is a *Dedekind domain* if every ideal of D is equal to a finite product of prime ideals of D. ///

Lemma 6. *Let D be a Dedekind domain. Then every proper prime ideal of D is maximal and invertible.*

PROOF. We show first that every invertible proper prime ideal of D is maximal. Let $\mathfrak{p}$ be an invertible proper prime ideal of D, and let $a \in D - \mathfrak{p}$. Denote by $(\mathfrak{p},a)$ and $(\mathfrak{p},a^2)$ the ideals of D generated by $\mathfrak{p}$ and a, and by $\mathfrak{p}$ and a^2, respectively. Since D is a Dedekind domain, there exist prime ideals $\mathfrak{p}_1, \mathfrak{p}_2, \ldots, \mathfrak{p}_m$, and $\mathfrak{q}_1, \mathfrak{q}_2, \ldots, \mathfrak{q}_n$ of D such that $(\mathfrak{p},a) = \prod_{i=1}^m \mathfrak{p}_i$ and $(\mathfrak{p},a^2) = \prod_{j=1}^n \mathfrak{q}_j$. Note that $\mathfrak{p}_i \supset \mathfrak{p}$ and $\mathfrak{q}_j \supset \mathfrak{p}$ $(i = 1,2,\ldots,m; j = 1,2,\ldots,n)$. Let ν be the canonical epimorphism of D onto $D/\mathfrak{p}$. Then $(\nu a) = \prod_{i=1}^m \nu\mathfrak{p}_i$, and $(\nu a^2) = \prod_{j=1}^n \nu\mathfrak{q}_j = (\nu a)^2 = \prod_{i=1}^m [\nu\mathfrak{p}_i]^2$. Since the principal ideals (νa) and (νa^2) are invertible, each of the ideals $\nu\mathfrak{p}_i$ and $\nu\mathfrak{q}_j$ is invertible (Lemma 2). But then (by Lemma 3) $2m = n$ and (with suitable renumbering) $\nu\mathfrak{q}_{2i} = \nu\mathfrak{q}_{2i-1} = \nu\mathfrak{p}_i$ $(i = 1,2,\ldots,m)$. But then $\mathfrak{q}_{2i} = \mathfrak{q}_{2i-1} = \mathfrak{p}_i$, for each $i = 1,\ldots, m$, and $(\mathfrak{p},a^2) = (\mathfrak{p},a)^2$. Hence $\mathfrak{p} \subset (\mathfrak{p},a^2) = (\mathfrak{p},a)^2 \subset (\mathfrak{p}^2,a)$, and every element of $\mathfrak{p}$ is the sum of an element of $\mathfrak{p}^2$ and an element of the form da $(d \in D)$. If $b = c + da \in \mathfrak{p}$ $(c \in \mathfrak{p}^2, d \in D)$, then $da \in \mathfrak{p}$. Since $a \notin \mathfrak{p}$ and $\mathfrak{p}$ is prime, $d \subset \mathfrak{p}$. It follows that $\mathfrak{p} \subset (\mathfrak{p}^2,\mathfrak{p}a) \subset \mathfrak{p}$. But then $\mathfrak{p} = (\mathfrak{p}^2,\mathfrak{p}a) = \mathfrak{p} \cdot (\mathfrak{p},a)$. Since $\mathfrak{p}$ is, by hypothesis, invertible, we conclude that $(\mathfrak{p},a) = \mathfrak{p}^{-1}\mathfrak{p} = D$. Since a was an arbitrary element of D, not in $\mathfrak{p}$, it follows that $\mathfrak{p}$ is a maximal ideal of D.

We now show that every proper prime ideal of D is invertible. Let $\mathfrak{p}$ be a proper prime ideal of D, and let $b \neq 0$ be an element of $\mathfrak{p}$. Then there are prime ideals $\mathfrak{p}_i$ $(i = 1,2,\ldots,m)$ such that $(b) = \prod_{i=1}^m \mathfrak{p}_i \subset \mathfrak{p}$. Note that $\mathfrak{p}$ contains at least one of the $\mathfrak{p}_i$, say $\mathfrak{p}_1$. Since (b) is invertible, so is $\mathfrak{p}_1$ (Lemma 2). Since $\mathfrak{p}_1$ is an invertible prime ideal, $\mathfrak{p}_1$ is maximal. But then $\mathfrak{p} = \mathfrak{p}_1$, and $\mathfrak{p}$ is invertible. ▌

We use the following notation: Let $\mathfrak{p}$ be a prime ideal of an integral domain D. Then $D_\mathfrak{p} = DS^{-1}$, where $S = D - \mathfrak{p}$. We shall identify D with its image $\alpha_S(D) \subset D_\mathfrak{p}$ (Chapter 2, Section 1).

We are now ready to prove the main theorem of this section.

Theorem 5.1. *Let D be an integral domain. The following statements are equivalent.*

a. *D is a Dedekind domain.*

b. *D is a Dedekind domain, and the factorization of each proper ideal of D into a product of proper prime ideals of D is unique* (*or, equivalently, the proper ideals of D form a free abelian group on the set of all proper prime ideals of D*).

c. *Every fractional ideal of D is invertible.*

d. *Every fractional ideal of D is a projective D-module.*

e. *D is Noetherian, integrally closed, and every proper prime ideal of D is maximal.*

f. *D is Noetherian, and for each proper prime ideal of D, $D_{\mathfrak{p}}$ is a discrete valuation ring.*

PROOF.

a $\Rightarrow$ b. By Lemmas 6 and 3.

b $\Rightarrow$ c. By Lemma 6 and the fact that a finite product of invertible ideals is an invertible ideal.

c $\Rightarrow$ d. By Lemma 4.

d $\Rightarrow$ e. In view of Lemma 4, c and d are equivalent, and it is sufficient to prove that c $\Rightarrow$ e. Assume that c holds. By Lemma 1, D is Noetherian. Let $Q \supset D$ be a quotient field of D, and let $\alpha \in Q$ be integral over D. It is easy to see that $\mathfrak{a} = D[\alpha]$ is a subring of Q which is a fractional ideal. But then $\mathfrak{a} = \mathfrak{a} \cdot D = \mathfrak{a} \cdot \mathfrak{a} \cdot \mathfrak{a}^{-1} = \mathfrak{a}\mathfrak{a}^{-1} = D$, $\alpha \in D$, and D is integrally closed.

Let $\mathfrak{p}$ be a proper prime ideal of D, and let $\mathfrak{q}$ be a maximal ideal of D with $\mathfrak{q} \supset \mathfrak{p}$. Then $\mathfrak{q}^{-1}\mathfrak{p}$ is an ideal of D with $\mathfrak{q} \cdot (\mathfrak{q}^{-1}\mathfrak{p}) = \mathfrak{p}$. Since $\mathfrak{p}$ is a prime ideal, either $\mathfrak{q} \subset \mathfrak{p}$ or $\mathfrak{q}^{-1}\mathfrak{p} \subset \mathfrak{p}$. Suppose $\mathfrak{q}^{-1}\mathfrak{p} \subset \mathfrak{p}$. Then $D \subset \mathfrak{q}^{-1} \subset \mathfrak{q}^{-1}\mathfrak{p}\mathfrak{p}^{-1} \subset \mathfrak{p}\mathfrak{p}^{-1} = D$, $\mathfrak{q}^{-1} = D$, and $\mathfrak{q} = D$. Contradiction! Hence $\mathfrak{q} \subset \mathfrak{p} \subset \mathfrak{q}$, and $\mathfrak{p} = \mathfrak{q}$, a maximal ideal. We have shown that d $\Rightarrow$ e.

e $\Rightarrow$ f. Assume that e holds. Let $\mathfrak{p}$ be a proper prime ideal of D. Then $D_{\mathfrak{p}}$ is Noetherian and integrally closed (Theorems 1.2b and 3.2b). Note that $\mathfrak{p} \cdot D_{\mathfrak{p}}$ is the only maximal ideal of $D_{\mathfrak{p}}$ and that $\mathfrak{p} \cdot D_{\mathfrak{p}} \cap D = \mathfrak{p}$. Now let $\mathfrak{a}$ be a proper prime ideal of $D_{\mathfrak{p}}$. Then $\mathfrak{a} \subset \mathfrak{p}D_{\mathfrak{p}}$, and $\mathfrak{a} \cap D \subset \mathfrak{p}D_{\mathfrak{p}} \cap D = \mathfrak{p}$. Since $\mathfrak{a} \cap D$ is a proper prime ideal of D, $\mathfrak{a} \cap D$ is maximal, by e. It follows that $\mathfrak{a} \cap D = \mathfrak{p}$. It is easy to see that $\mathfrak{a} = (\mathfrak{a} \cap D) \cdot D_{\mathfrak{p}}$. We conclude that $\mathfrak{a} = \mathfrak{p} \cdot D_{\mathfrak{p}}$ and that $\mathfrak{p}D_{\mathfrak{p}}$ is the only proper prime ideal of $D_{\mathfrak{p}}$. By Lemma 5, $D_{\mathfrak{p}}$ is a discrete valuation ring. We have shown that e $\Rightarrow$ f.

f $\Rightarrow$ a. Assume that f holds. We show first that every ideal of D is invertible. Let $\mathfrak{a}$ be an ideal of D. To prove that $\mathfrak{a}\mathfrak{a}^{-1} = D$, it is sufficient to show that

$\mathfrak{a}\mathfrak{a}^{-1}$ is not contained in any maximal ideal of D. Since D is Noetherian, $\mathfrak{a}$ is finitely generated, say $\mathfrak{a} = (a_1,\ldots,a_n)$, $a_i \in D$. Let $\mathfrak{p}$ be a maximal ideal of D. Since $D_\mathfrak{p}$ is a discrete valuation ring, $\mathfrak{p}D_\mathfrak{p} = (\alpha)\cdot D_\mathfrak{p}$, where $\alpha \in \mathfrak{p}$, and there are integers e_i and units $u_i \in D_\mathfrak{p}$ $(i = 1,2,\ldots,n)$, such that $a_i = \alpha^{e_i}u_i$. Suppose (without loss of generality) that $e_1 = \min_i\{e_i\}$. Then $a_i/a_1 \in D_\mathfrak{p}$. Hence there are elements $b_i, c_i \in D$, with $c_i \notin \mathfrak{p}$ $(i = 1,2,\ldots,n)$, such that $a_i/a_1 = b_i/c_i$. But then $(\prod_{i=1}^n c_i)/a_1 \in \mathfrak{a}^{-1}$ and $\prod_{i=1}^n c_i = a_1\cdot(\prod_{i=1}^n c_i)/a_1 \in \mathfrak{a}\mathfrak{a}^{-1}$. Since $c_i \notin \mathfrak{p}$ for $i = 1, 2,\ldots, n$, $\prod_{i=1}^n c_i \notin \mathfrak{p}$. We have shown that $\mathfrak{a}\mathfrak{a}^{-1}$ is not contained in any maximal ideal of D, whence $\mathfrak{a}\mathfrak{a}^{-1} = D$, and $\mathfrak{a}$ is invertible.

Now let $\mathfrak{b}$ be any proper ideal of D. Then $\mathfrak{b}$ is contained in some maximal ideal $\mathfrak{p}$ of D. Since $\mathfrak{p}$ is invertible, $\mathfrak{b} = \mathfrak{p}(\mathfrak{b}\mathfrak{p}^{-1})$ with $\mathfrak{b} \subset \mathfrak{b}\mathfrak{p}^{-1} \subset D$. A simple application of the ascending chain condition allows us to conclude that $\mathfrak{b}$ is equal to a product of prime ideals of D. Hence f $\Rightarrow$ a. ∎

Exercises

Section 1

1.1. Show that an Artinian ring has only finitely many prime ideals.

1.2. Show that if D is a domain in which every prime ideal is finitely generated, then D is Noetherian.

1.3. Show that a domain in which every ascending chain of prime ideals terminates is not necessarily Noetherian.

1.4. A subdomain of a Noetherian domain is not necessarily Noetherian.

1.5. Let A be a ring (not necessarily commutative) and let M be an A-module. The module M is called a *Noetherian module* if every submodule of M is finitely generated. State and prove a theorem for A-modules which is the analogue of Theorem 1.1.

1.6. Let A be a ring, and let M be a Noetherian A-module (see Exercise 1.5). Show that every submodule of M and every A-homomorphic image of M is Noetherian.

1.7. Let A be a ring, M an A-module, and N a submodule of M. Show that if N and M/N are Noetherian, then so is M.

1.8. A (not necessarily commutative) ring A is defined to be Noetherian if it is Noetherian as a left A-module over itself. Show that if A is a Noetherian ring and M is a finitely generated left A-module, then M is a Noetherian A-module.

Section 2

2.1. If a is a nonunit in a ring A with identity, then there is a maximal ideal of A which contains a.

2.2. If $\sqrt{\mathfrak{a}}$ ($\mathfrak{a}$ an ideal in a ring with identity) is a maximal ideal, then $\mathfrak{a}$ is a primary ideal.

2.3. Let A be a ring with identity. The Jacobson radical, J, of A is defined to be the intersection of all the maximal ideals of A. Show that if $a \in J$, then $1 + a$ is a unit in A.

2.4. Let $\{x_1,x_2,x_3\}$ be a transcendence set over the complex field $\mathbf{C}$.

(a) Decompose the algebraic set $V_{\mathbf{Q}^{(3)}/\mathbf{Q}}((x_1^2 + x_2^2 - 1, x_1^2 - x_3^2 - 1))$ into a union of irreducible algebraic sets over the rational field $\mathbf{Q}$.

(b) Decompose the algebraic set $V_{\mathbf{C}^{(3)}/\mathbf{C}}((x_1^2 + x_2^2 - 1, x_1^2 - x_3^2 - 1))$ into a union of irreducible algebraic sets over $\mathbf{C}$.

2.5. Let A be a commutative ring with identity, M an A-module, and N an A-submodule of M with $N \neq M$. (Note that M/N is an A-module under the composition $a\bar{m} = \overline{am}$ where $a \in A$, $m \in M$, and, for $r \in M$, $\bar{r}$ is the image of r under the canonical epimorphism of M onto M/N.) The submodule N is called a *primary submodule* if, for each $a \in A$, the map $a_{M/N}: M/N \to M/N$ defined by $a_{M/N}(\bar{m}) = a\bar{m}$ is injective, or $a_{M/N}^k$ is the zero map for some positive integer k (i.e., $a_{M/N}$ is either injective or nilpotent). Show that a submodule, $\mathfrak{a}$, of the A-module A is a primary submodule of A if and only if $\mathfrak{a}$ is a primary ideal of the ring A.

2.6. The notation is as in Exercise 2.5. Let N be a primary submodule of M. Let $\mathfrak{p} = \{a \in A \mid a_{M/N} \text{ is nilpotent}\}$. Show that $\mathfrak{p}$ is a prime ideal of A; $\mathfrak{p}$ is called the *associated prime ideal* of N. State and prove theorems for A-modules which are analogues of Theorems 2.2, 2.3, and 2.4.

Section 3

3.1. If an integral domain A is integrally closed, then so is the polynomial domain $A[x]$.

3.2. If a field F is integral over an integral domain A, $F \supset A$, then A is a field.

3.3. Let A be an integrally closed domain, $F \supset A$ the quotient field of A, $E \supset F$ a finite Galois extension of F, and B the integral closure of A in E. If $\mathfrak{P}_1$ and $\mathfrak{P}_2$ are prime ideals of B lying over a prime ideal $\mathfrak{p}$ of A, then there is some $\sigma \in \mathcal{G}(E/F)$ such that $\sigma(\mathfrak{P}_1) = \mathfrak{P}_2$.

3.4. The notation is as in Exercise 3.3. Let $\mathfrak{p}$ be a prime ideal of A and $\mathfrak{P}$ a prime ideal of B lying over $\mathfrak{p}$. The subgroup of $\mathcal{G}(E/F)$ consisting of those σ such that $\sigma(\mathfrak{P}) = \mathfrak{P}$ is called the decomposition group $G_{\mathfrak{P}}$. Let K be the fixed field of $G_{\mathfrak{P}}$. Then $\mathfrak{P} \cap K$ is a prime ideal in $B \cap K$, and $\mathfrak{P}$ is the only prime ideal of B lying over $\mathfrak{P} \cap K$; if L is a subfield of E containing F such that $\mathfrak{P}$ is the only prime ideal of B lying over the prime ideal $\mathfrak{P} \cap L$ of $B \cap L$, then $L \supset K$.

3.5. The notation is as in Exercises 5.3 and 5.4. Suppose that $\mathfrak{P}$ and $\mathfrak{p}$ are maximal ideals in B and A, respectively. Then $B/\mathfrak{P}$ is a normal extension of $A/\mathfrak{p}$, and there is a homomorphism of $G_{\mathfrak{P}}$ onto the group of $A/\mathfrak{p}$-automorphism of $B/\mathfrak{P}$.

Section 4

4.1. The notation is as in Theorem 4.1. In the course of proving this theorem, we proved that if $f \in \mathscr{I}_F(V_{E^{(n)}/F}(\mathfrak{a}))$, then there is a positive integer r such that $f^r \in \mathfrak{a}$. Show that there is, in fact, a positive integer s such that if $f \in \mathscr{I}_F(V_{E^{(n)}/F}(\mathfrak{a}))$, then $f^s \in \mathfrak{a}$.

Section 5

5.1. Let $\mathfrak{a}$ be a nonzero ideal in a Dedekind domain D. Show that $D/\mathfrak{a}$ satisfies the descending chain condition on ideals.

5.2. Let A be an integrally closed domain with quotient field $F \supset A$. Let E be a finite extension of F, B the integral closure of A in E. Prove: If A is a Dedekind domain, then so is B.

5.3. Let A be a Dedekind domain. Show that every divisible A-module is an injective A-module. [An A-module M is said to be divisible if for each $a \in A$, $a \neq 0$, $aM = M$.]

5.4. Let D be a Dedekind domain and $F \supset D$ its quotient field. Every proper prime ideal $\mathfrak{p}$ of D induces a nonarchimedean prime spot $\bar{\mathfrak{p}}$ on F (Chapter 6, Section 1, Example 2).

(a) Let $\mathfrak{p}$ be a prime ideal in D and $\bar{\mathfrak{p}}$ the prime spot on F induced by $\mathfrak{p}$. Show that $\mathcal{O}_F(\bar{\mathfrak{p}}) = D_{\mathfrak{p}}$.

(b) A nonarchimedean prime spot $\bar{\mathfrak{p}}$ on F is defined to be less than or equal to 1 on D if there is a valuation $|\ | \in \bar{\mathfrak{p}}$ such that $|a| \leq 1$ for all $a \in D$. Let $\bar{\mathfrak{p}}$ be a nontrivial and nonarchimedean prime spot on F which is less than or equal to 1 on D. Show that there is a unique proper prime ideal $\mathfrak{p}$ of D such that $\mathcal{O}_F(\bar{\mathfrak{p}}) = D_{\mathfrak{p}}$.

(c) There is a bijection of the set of proper prime ideals of D onto the set of nontrivial and nonarchimedean prime spots on F which are less than or equal to 1 on D.

5.5. Let D be a Dedekind domain and $F \supset D$ its quotient field. Let $\{\bar{\mathfrak{p}}_i\}_{i \in J}$ be a complete set of nonequivalent nonarchimedean prime spots on F which are less than or equal to 1 on D (see Exercise 5.4). For each $i \in J$, choose $|\ |_i \in \mathfrak{p}$.

(a) Show that $\{|\ |_i\}_{i \in J}$ has properties a and b listed in Chapter 6, Theorem 2.2.

(b) Prove the Chinese Remainder Theorem for Dedekind domains: Let $\mathfrak{p}_1, \mathfrak{p}_2, \ldots, \mathfrak{p}_n$ be distinct prime ideals of D, let $a_1, a_2, \ldots, a_n$ be elements of D, and let $e_1, e_2, \ldots, e_n$ be positive integers. Then there is an element $a \in D$ such that $a \equiv a_i \bmod \mathfrak{p}_i^{e_i}$ for $i = 1, 2, \ldots, n$.

5.6. Let A be an integral domain and $F \supset A$ its quotient field. Prove: A is a Dedekind domain if and only if there is a nonempty set $\{| \ |_i\}_{i \in J}$ of nonequivalent discrete valuations on F such that

(a) $\bigcap_{i \in J} \mathcal{O}_F(| \ |_i) = A$,

(b) $\{| \ |_i\}_{i \in J}$ has properties a and b of Chapter 6, Theorem 2.2.

Chapter 8 / The Structure of Rings

1. Introduction; Representations

In this chapter we introduce some of the basic building blocks of ring theory and prove the main structure theorems for simple and semisimple rings. Since the ideal-theoretic conditions we want to impose on a ring A are equivalent to conditions on submodules of the A-modules A_l, or A_r, we first investigate modules satisfying certain conditions on their submodules.

A basic tool of ring theory is the "representation" of a ring, A, in the ring of endomorphisms of an abelian group, X. Representations of A and A-modules are intimately related. On the one hand, if X is an abelian group and $A = \text{End}(X)$, then X can be made into a left A-module by defining αx to be equal to $\alpha(x)$ for each $\alpha \in A$, $x \in X$. On the other hand, if X is a left A-module, then for each $a \in A$, the mapping $x \mapsto ax$ is an endomorphism, l_a, of the abelian group X. The mapping $\rho(A,X)\colon a \mapsto l_a$ is a homomorphism of the ring A into $\text{End}(X)$. This homomorphism $\rho(A,X)$ is a "representation" of A. If X is a right A-module, the mapping $x \mapsto xa$ is an endomorphism, r_a, of the abelian group X, and the mapping $\bar{\rho}(A,X)\colon a \mapsto r_a$ is an antihomomorphism ("antirepresentation") of A into $\text{End}(X)$.

Definition 1.1. A homomorphism (antihomomorphism) of a ring A into the ring of all endomorphisms of an abelian group X is a *representation* (*antirepresentation*) of A. In particular, if X is a left (right) A-module, the mapping $\rho(A,X)\colon a \mapsto l_a$ ($\bar{\rho}(A,X)\colon a \mapsto r_a$) is *the representation* (*antirepresentation*) *of A associated with X*. A left (right) A-module is *faithful* if the representation (antirepresentation) of A associated with X is injective. The representation (antirepresentation) associated with a faithful left (right) A-module is a *faithful representation* (*antirepresentation*). ///

We shall write $\mathscr{L}_{A,X} = \{l_a | a \in A\} = \operatorname{Im} \rho(A,X)$ if X is a left A-module, and $\mathscr{R}_{A,X} = \{r_a | a \in A\} = \operatorname{Im} \bar{\rho}(A,X)$ if X is a right A-module. In particular, if $X = A_l$ ($X = A_r$), then $\mathscr{L}_{A,X} = \mathscr{L}_A$, the ring of all left multiplications of A ($\mathscr{R}_{A,X} = \mathscr{R}_A$, the ring of all right multiplications of A) (see p. 119).

REMARK. The following conditions on a left (right) A-module X are equivalent:

1. X is faithful.
2. If $a \in A$, $a \neq 0$, then $\operatorname{Ker} l_a \neq X$ ($\operatorname{Ker} r_a \neq X$).
3. $\rho(A,X)$ ($\bar{\rho}(A,X)$) is an isomorphism (antiisomorphism) of A onto $\mathscr{L}_{A,X}$ ($\mathscr{R}_{A,X}$).

In particular, if A is a ring with identity, then both A_l and A_r are faithful, hence $\mathscr{L}_A$ is isomorphic, $\mathscr{R}_A$ antiisomorphic, to the ring A.

2. Simple and Semisimple Modules

Throughout this section and, in fact, throughout the remainder of this chapter, all rings will be rings with identity, and all A-modules will be unitary. Unless otherwise specified, "A-module" means "left A-module."

Definition 2.1. An A-module X is *simple* if it is nonzero and has no submodules other than itself and the zero submodule. ///

The absence of proper submodules imposes severe restrictions on the nature of the homomorphisms of, and into, a given module:

Theorem 2.1. (Schur's Lemma) *Let X be a simple A-module. Then*

a. *Every nonzero homomorphism of X is injective.*
b. *Every nonzero homomorphism of an A-module Y into X is surjective.*
c. $\operatorname{End}_A(X)$ *is a division ring.*

PROOF.

a. If α is a nonzero homomorphism of X, then $\operatorname{Ker} \alpha = 0$, hence α is injective.

b. If α is a nonzero homomorphism of Y into X, then $\operatorname{Im} \alpha = X$, hence α is surjective.

c. If $\alpha \in \operatorname{End}_A(X)$, $\alpha \neq 0$, then α is an automorphism, by a and b. Hence α is a unit in the ring $\operatorname{End}_A(X)$. But then $\operatorname{End}_A(X)$ is a division ring. ∎

We have seen several examples of simple modules. An abelian group $G \neq 0$ is a simple **Z**-module if and only if it is cyclic of prime order. A vector space over a division ring D is a simple D-module if and only if it has dimension 1. If A_l is the left A-module formed by the additive group of a ring A, then a submodule $K \neq 0$ of A_l is simple if and only if it is a minimal left ideal of A. [For example, in the ring $A = \operatorname{End}_D(X)$ of all linear transformations of a left vector space X, the annihilator of a maximal subspace is a minimal left ideal of A, hence a simple submodule of A_l—see Lemma 1, p. 394.] More generally, the structure of any faithful simple A-module is determined by the minimal left ideals of A.

Theorem 2.2. *Let A be a ring and let T be a minimal left ideal of A. If X is a faithful simple left A-module, then X is isomorphic to the left A-module T.*

PROOF. Let $t_0 \in T - 0$. Since X is faithful, there is some $x \in X$ such that $t_0 x \neq 0$, and the map $\alpha_x: T \to X$ defined by $\alpha_x t = tx$ $(t \in T)$ is a nonzero homomorphism. By Schur's Lemma, α_x is a monomorphism since the A-module T is simple, and α_x is an epimorphism since the A-module X is simple. Thus, $\alpha_x: T \to X$ is an isomorphism. ∎

Not all modules have simple submodules. For example, the left **Z**-module $\mathbf{Z}_l$ has no simple submodules since the ring of integers has no minimal ideals. If an A-module has simple submodules, then the sum of a family of simple submodules need not be direct (e.g., the family of subgroups of order 2 in Klein's 4-group). However, the sum of any family of simple submodules can be reduced to a direct sum, as a consequence of the following result:

Lemma 1. *If X is an A-module, $\{X_i\}_{i \in J}$ a family of simple submodules of X such that $X = \sum_{i \in J} X_i$, then for each submodule Y of X there is a subset J' of J such that*

$$X = \bigoplus_{i \in J'} X_i \oplus Y.$$

PROOF. If $Y = X$, take $J' = \varnothing$. If $Y \neq X$, then for some $k \in J$, $X_k \not\subset Y$. Since X_k is simple, $X_k \cap Y = 0$ and $Y + X_k$ is a direct sum. Thus, the set $\mathscr{C}$ of all subfamilies $\{X_i\}_{i \in H}$ $(H \subset J)$ for which the sum $\sum_{i \in H} X_i + Y$ is direct is nonempty. By Zorn's Lemma, $\mathscr{C}$ contains a maximal subfamily, $\{X_i\}_{i \in J'}$. Suppose $\bigoplus_{i \in J'} X_i \oplus Y \neq X$. Then, for some $j \in J$, $X_j \not\subset \bigoplus_{i \in J'} X_i \oplus Y$. Since X_j is simple, $X_j \cap [\bigoplus_{i \in J'} X_i \oplus Y] = 0$, and $X_j + [\bigoplus_{i \in J'} X_i \oplus Y]$ is a direct sum. But then $\{X_i\}_{i \in J' \cup \{j\}}$ belongs to $\mathscr{C}$, contrary to the maximality of $\{X_i\}_{i \in J'}$. It follows that $X = \bigoplus_{i \in J'} X_i \oplus Y$. ∎

Definition 2.2. An A-module X is *semisimple* if it is equal to a direct sum of simple submodules. ///

We shall obtain several equivalent characterizations of semisimple modules.

Lemma 2. *If $X \neq 0$ is a finitely generated A-module, then X has a maximal submodule.*

PROOF. Let $\{x_i\}_{i=1,\ldots,n}$ be a generating set for X, and let Γ be the set of all submodules Y of X, $Y \neq X$, partially ordered by inclusion. Since $X \neq 0$, $\Gamma \neq \varnothing$. Suppose $\{X_j\}_{j \in J}$ is a totally ordered family of submodules in Γ. If $\bigcup_{j \in J} X_j = X$, then there is some integer N such that $x_i \in X_N$ for each $i = 1, \ldots, n$. But then $X_N = X$, contrary to hypothesis. It follows that $\bigcup_{j \in J} X_j \neq X$, and therefore Zorn's Lemma applies to Γ, yielding a maximal submodule for X. ∎

Theorem 2.3. *The following conditions on an A-module X are equivalent:*

a. *X is a sum of simple submodules.*
b. *X is semisimple.*
c. *Every submodule of X is a direct summand of X.*

PROOF.

a ⇒ b. If $X = \sum_{i \in J} X_i$, where $\{X_i\}_{i \in J}$ is a family of simple submodules of X, then, by Lemma 1, with $Y = 0$, there is a subset J' of J such that $X = \bigoplus_{i \in J'} X_i$.

b ⇒ c. Let Y be a submodule of X and let $X = \bigoplus_{i \in J} X_i$, where $\{X_i\}_{i \in J}$ is a family of simple submodules. By Lemma 1, there is a subset J' of J such that $X = \bigoplus_{i \in J'} X_i \oplus Y$.

c ⇒ a. Now suppose X is an A-module with the property: Every submodule of X is a direct summand of X. We prove first that X has simple submodules and that, in fact, every nonzero submodule of X contains a simple submodule. Let $x \in X$, $x \neq 0$, and let $Y = Ax$. By Lemma 2, the (finitely generated) A-module Y has a maximal submodule Z. By Chapter 1, Theorem 4.10, Y/Z is a simple A-module. By our hypothesis, Z has a complementary submodule Z' such that $X = Z \oplus Z'$. But then $Y = Z \oplus (Y \cup Z')$, and therefore $Y \cup Z'$ is a submodule of X, isomorphic to Y/Z, hence simple. Since every nonzero submodule of X contains the cyclic submodule generated by each of its nonzero elements, we conclude that every nonzero submodule contains a simple submodule.

Now let Q be the sum of the simple submodules of X. Then $X = Q \oplus Q'$ for some submodule Q'. If Q' is not zero, then it contains a simple submodule —impossible, since all the simple submodules are contained in Q. It follows that $X = Q$. But then X is a sum of simple submodules. ▮

Corollary 1. *Every submodule, and every homomorphic image, of a semisimple module is semisimple.*

PROOF. Let X be a semisimple A-module. Let Y be a submodule of X and let Z be a submodule of Y. Then there is a submodule Z' of X such that $Z \oplus Z' = X$. But then $Z \oplus (Z' \cap Y) = Y$. Thus, every submodule of Y is a direct summand of Y, and therefore Y is semisimple.

Every homomorphic image of the A-module X is isomorphic to X/Y for some submodule Y of X. But, X/Y is isomorphic to a complementary submodule Y' of Y, hence semisimple. ▮

Corollary 2. *If X is a semisimple A-module, equal to the direct sum of a family $\{X_i\}_{i\in I}$ of simple submodules, then every simple submodule of X is isomorphic to one of the X_i.*

PROOF. If T is a simple submodule of X, then T is a direct summand of X. Hence there is an epimorphism $\beta: X \to T$, and $T = \sum_{i\in J} \beta X_i$. Since T is simple, $T = \beta X_k$ for some $k \in J$. But X_k is simple; hence, by Schur's Lemma, β is an isomorphism. ▮

The following terminology will be helpful in discussing semisimple modules:

Definition 2.3. If an A-module Y is equal to a direct sum of submodules, all isomorphic to a fixed A-module, S, then Y is a *homogeneous A-module* (*of type S*). ///

Theorem 2.4. *Let X be a semisimple A-module. Then there is a unique family of submodules $\{Y_h\}_{h\in H}$ such that for some family of simple modules $\{X_h\}_{h\in H}$, the following conditions are satisfied:*

a. *For each $h \in H$, Y_h is homogeneous of type X_h.*

b. *For $h \neq k$ $(h,k \in H)$, X_h and X_k are nonisomorphic.*
c. *Every simple submodule of X is contained in Y_h for exactly one $h \in H$.*
d. $X = \bigoplus_{h\in H} Y_h$.

PROOF. We partition the set of all simple submodules of X into equivalence classes of isomorphic submodules and let $\{X_h\}_{h\in H}$ be a complete set of representatives of the equivalence classes. For each $h \in H$, we let Y_h be the sum of all simple submodules of X isomorphic to X_h. By our lemma, each Y_h is equal to a direct sum of simple submodules, all isomorphic to X_h. Clearly the X_h and Y_h satisfy a, b, and c. Since X is a sum of simple submodules, and $\sum_{h\in H} Y_h$ is the sum of all simple submodules of X, $X = \sum_{h\in H} Y_h$. It remains to show that the sum of the Y_h is direct. If, for some $k \in H$, the intersection $Y_k \cap \sum_{h\neq k,\, h\in H} Y_h$ is not zero, then it is semi-simple and therefore contains a simple submodule, T. As a submodule of the semi-simple module Y_k, T must be isomorphic to X_k (Corollary 2, Theorem 2.3). On the other hand, $\sum_{h\neq k,\, h\in H} Y_h$ is a semi-simple module, equal to the direct sum of a subfamily of the simple components of the Y_h $(h \neq k)$. Hence T, being a submodule of $\sum_{h\neq k,\, h\in H} Y_h$, is also isomorphic to X_h for some $h \neq k$. (Corollary 2 of Theorem 2.3). But this is impossible since a holds. It follows that the sum of the homogeneous submodules Y_h is direct.

To prove the uniqueness, we note first that, if Z is a homogeneous submodule of X, of simple type, then Z is of type X_h for some $h \in H$, and $Z \subset Y_h$. Thus if X is the direct sum of another family $\{Z_h\}_{h\in I}$ of homogeneous submodules, each of simple type X_h, then $I \subset H$ and $Z_h \subset Y_h$, for each $h \in I$. Now suppose that, for some $h \in H$, $\bar{X}$ is a simple submodule of X contained in Y_h. Since $\{Z_h\}_{h\in I}$ satisfies c, $\bar{X}$ is contained in Z_k for some $k \in I$. But then, by Theorem 2.3, Corollary 2, $\bar{X}$ is isomorphic to X_k. Since X_k is the type of Y_k, $X_k = X_h$, by b. But then $Z_k = Z_h$, and $\bar{X} \subset Z_h$. Hence $Y_h \subset Z_h$. It now follows that $I = H$, and $Z_h = Y_h$ for each $h \in H$. ▌

We shall refer to the submodules Y_h of Theorem 2.4 as the *homogeneous components* of X.

3. Homomorphisms of Simple and Semisimple Modules

We recall that A is a ring with identity.

If X is a left A-module and α is an endomorphism of the abelian group X, then α is an A-endomorphism if and only if $\alpha(ax) = a(\alpha x)$ for each $x \in X$, $a \in A$, i.e., if and only if α commutes with the left multiplication l_a for each

$a \in A$. Thus $\mathrm{End}_A(X) = C(\mathscr{L}_{A,X})$, the centralizer of $\mathscr{L}(A,X)$ in $\mathrm{End}(X)$ (see Chapter 1, Definition 7.1). Let $R = \mathrm{End}_A(X) = C(\mathscr{L}_{A,X})$. We may consider X as a left R-module, with scalar multiplication defined by $\alpha x = \alpha(x)$ for each $x \in X$, $\alpha \in R$. Since, for each $\alpha \in R$, the endomorphism l_α of the group X coincides with α, it follows that $\mathscr{L}_{R,X} = R$, and $\mathrm{End}_R(X) = C(R) = C^2(\mathscr{L}_{A,X})$, the second centralizer of $\mathscr{L}_{A,X}$ in $\mathrm{End}(X)$. Obviously, $\mathscr{L}_{A,X} \subset C^2(\mathscr{L}_{A,X})$, and it is natural to ask under what conditions equality holds. In particular, if X is a *faithful* left A-module such that $\mathscr{L}_{A,X} = C^2(\mathscr{L}_{A,X})$, then $C^2(\mathscr{L}_{A,X})$ is isomorphic to A—or, in other words, $\mathrm{End}_R(X) \cong A$, where $R = \mathrm{End}_A(X)$. We shall see that this is, indeed, the case if X is a faithful semisimple A-module, and the R-module X is finitely generated (corollary of Theorem 3.1).

Lemma 1. *If A is a ring (with identity), then*

a. $\mathrm{End}_A(A_l) = \mathscr{R}_A$, *anti-isomorphic to A.*

b. $\mathrm{End}_{\mathscr{R}_A}(A_l) = \mathrm{End}_A(A_r) = \mathscr{L}_A$, *isomorphic to A.*

PROOF. Let A^+ be the additive group of A.

a. Since $\mathrm{End}_A(A_l) = \mathrm{End}_{\mathscr{L}_A}(A^+)$, $\mathscr{R}_A \subset \mathrm{End}_A(A_l)$. If $\alpha \in \mathrm{End}_A(A_l)$, then $\alpha(x) = \alpha(x \cdot 1) = x \cdot \alpha 1$ for each $x \in A$, hence $\alpha = r_{\alpha 1} \in \mathscr{R}_A$. Thus, $\mathrm{End}_A(A_l) = \mathscr{R}_A$. Since A has an identity, $\mathscr{R}_A$ is anti-isomorphic to A (Remark, p. 384).

b. Obviously, $\mathrm{End}_{\mathscr{R}_A}(A_l) = \mathrm{End}_{\mathscr{R}_A}(A^+) = \mathrm{End}_A(A_r)$. As in a we obtain $\mathrm{End}_A(A_r) = \mathscr{L}_A$. Since A has an identity, $\mathscr{L}_A$ is isomorphic to A (Remark, p. 384). ∎

Note that, if we identify A with $\mathscr{L}_A$, then Lemma 1 asserts that the second centralizer of A in $\mathrm{End}(A^+)$ is isomorphic to A.

Lemma 2. *Let $\bar{X} = \bigoplus_{i \in I} X_i$ be a homogeneous A-module of type X, where $X \subset \{X_i\}_{i \in I}$. For each $i \in I$, let $\varepsilon_i \colon X \to X_i$ be an isomorphism of X onto X_i (ε_i the identity in case $X_i = X$). Let $R = \mathrm{End}_A(X)$ and let $\bar{R} = \mathrm{End}_A(\bar{X})$. Then the restriction map $\varphi \colon \bar{\alpha} \mapsto \bar{\alpha}|_X$ is an isomorphism of $\mathrm{End}_{\bar{R}}(\bar{X})$ onto $\mathrm{End}_R(X)$. For each $\alpha \in \mathrm{End}_R(X)$, there is exactly one $\bar{\alpha} \in \mathrm{End}_{\bar{R}}(X)$ such that $\bar{\alpha}\varepsilon_i = \varepsilon_i\alpha$, for each $i \in I$.*

PROOF. First note that R is isomorphic to a subring of $\bar{R}$ since every A-endomorphism ρ of X can be extended to an A-endomorphism $\bar{\rho}$ of $\bar{X}$ such that $\bar{\rho}|_X = \rho$ and $\bar{\rho}|_{X_i} = 0$ for $X_i \neq X$. The mapping $\rho \mapsto \bar{\rho}$ is a monomorphism of R into $\bar{R}$. We identify R with its image in $\bar{R}$.

Now, if $\bar{\alpha} \in \mathrm{End}_{\bar{R}}(\bar{X})$, then $\bar{\alpha}|_X$ is certainly an R-homomorphism of X into $\bar{X}$. Let π be the projection of the A-module $\bar{X}$ onto the A-module X.

Since $\pi \in \mathrm{End}_A(\bar{X})$, we have $\bar{\alpha}|_X(x) = \bar{\alpha}|_X(\pi x) = \bar{\alpha}\pi(x) = \pi\bar{\alpha}(x) \in X$, for each $x \in X$. But then the restriction map $\varphi: \bar{\alpha} \mapsto \bar{\alpha}|_X$ sends $\mathrm{End}_{\bar{R}}(\bar{X})$ into $\mathrm{End}_R(X)$. Clearly, φ is a ring homomorphism.

We now prove that φ is injective. Suppose $\bar{\alpha}|_X = 0$ for some $\bar{\alpha} \in \mathrm{End}_{\bar{R}}(\bar{X})$. For each $i \in I$, let $\bar{\eta}_i: \bar{X} \to \bar{X}$ be the mapping defined by $\bar{\eta}_i|_{X_i} = \varepsilon_i$, $\bar{\eta}_i|_{X_j} = 0$ for $j \neq i$. Then, for each $i \in I$, $\bar{\eta}_i \in \bar{R}$, and $\bar{\alpha}X_i = \bar{\alpha}\bar{\eta}_i X = \bar{\eta}_i\bar{\alpha}X = 0$. But then $\bar{\alpha} = 0$.

Finally, φ is surjective. For, suppose $\alpha \in \mathrm{End}_R(X)$. For each $i \in I$, the mapping $\alpha_i = \varepsilon_i\alpha\varepsilon_i^{-1}$ is an endomorphism of X_i^+. Let $\bar{\alpha}$ be the (unique) endomorphism of the abelian group $\bar{X}^+$ such that $\bar{\alpha}|_{X_i} = \alpha_i$ for each $i \in I$. We need only prove that $\bar{\alpha}$ is an $\bar{R}$-endomorphism. Thus suppose $\gamma \in \bar{R}$. For each $i \in I$, let $\pi_i \in \mathrm{End}_A(\bar{X})$ be the projection of the A-module $\bar{X}$ onto the A-module X. If $x \in X_k$ $(k \in I)$, then $x = \varepsilon_k y$ for some $y \in X$. With $\eta_k: X_k \to \bar{X}$ the canonical injection, we have

$$\gamma\bar{\alpha}x = \gamma\bar{\alpha}\eta_k\varepsilon_k y = \gamma\alpha_k\eta_k\varepsilon_k y = \gamma\eta_k\varepsilon_k\alpha y,$$

$$\bar{\alpha}\gamma x = \bar{\alpha}\gamma\eta_k\varepsilon_k y = \sum_{i\in I} \alpha_i\pi_i\gamma\eta_k\varepsilon_k y = \sum_{i\in I} \varepsilon_i\alpha\varepsilon_i^{-1}\pi_i\gamma\eta_k\varepsilon_k y.$$

Since $\varepsilon_i^{-1}\pi_i\gamma\eta_k\varepsilon_k$ is clearly an element of R, it commutes with α, and the last expression therefore reduces to $\sum_{i\in I} \pi_i\gamma\eta_k\varepsilon_k\alpha y = \gamma\eta_k\varepsilon_k\alpha y = \gamma\bar{\alpha}x$. It follows that $\gamma\bar{\alpha} = \bar{\alpha}\gamma$, and therefore $\bar{\alpha} \in \mathrm{End}_{\bar{R}}(\bar{X})$. ▮

Lemma 3. *Let X be a semisimple A-module, and let $R = \mathrm{End}_A(X)$. If $x \in X$ and $\alpha \in \mathrm{End}_R(X)$, then there is an element $a \in A$ such that $\alpha x = ax$.*

PROOF. Since A is semisimple, there is a submodule Y of X such that $X = Ax \oplus Y$. For some $a \in A$, $y \in Y$, $\alpha x = ax + y$. If π is the projection of X onto Ax, then

$$\alpha x = \alpha(\pi x) = \pi(\alpha x) = ax. \quad ▮$$

Lemma 3 is a special case of the theorem we are about to prove:

Theorem 3.1. (Jacobson's Density Theorem) *Let X be a semisimple A-module, $R = \mathrm{End}_A(X)$. If $x_1, \ldots, x_n \in X$ and $\alpha \in \mathrm{End}_R(X)$, then there is an element $a \in A$ such that $\alpha x_i = ax_i$ for each $i = 1, \ldots, n$.*

PROOF. Let $\bar{X}$ be a direct sum of n isomorphic copies of X (for convenience including X among them). As in Lemma 2, let ε_i be an A-isomorphism of X onto the ith component of $\bar{X}$ $(i = 1, \ldots, n)$. Let $\bar{R} = \mathrm{End}_A(\bar{X})$. By Lemma 2, there is an $\bar{\alpha} \in \mathrm{End}_{\bar{R}}(\bar{X})$ such that $\bar{\alpha}\varepsilon_i = \varepsilon_i\alpha$ for each $i = 1, \ldots, n$. Let

$\bar{x} = \varepsilon_1 x_1 + \cdots + \varepsilon_n x_n$. Since $\bar{X}$ is a semisimple A-module, Lemma 3 provides an element $a \in A$ such that $a\bar{x} = \bar{\alpha}\bar{x} = \bar{\alpha}(\sum_{i=1}^n \varepsilon_i x_i) = \sum_{i=1}^n \varepsilon_i \alpha x_i$. But then, for each i, the ith component of $a\bar{x}$ is equal to $\varepsilon_i \alpha x_i = a\varepsilon_i x_i = \varepsilon_i a x_i$, whence $\alpha x_i = a x_i$, as required. ∎

Corollary. *Let X be a semisimple A-module, $R = \text{End}_A(X)$. If X is a finitely generated R-module, then $\text{End}_R(X)$ is equal to $\mathscr{L}_{A,X}$. If, in addition, X is a faithful A-module, then $\text{End}_R(X)$ is isomorphic to A.*

PROOF. We need only let $x_1, \ldots, x_n$ be a set of generators for the R-module X. If $\alpha \in \text{End}_R(X)$ and $a \in A$ is such that $ax_i = \alpha x_i$ for each $i = 1, \ldots, n$, then for each $x = \sum_{i=1}^n \rho_i x_i$ ($\rho_i \in R$), we have

$$\alpha x = \alpha\left(\sum_{i=1}^n \rho_i x_i\right) = \sum_{i=1}^n \alpha\rho_i x_i = \sum_{i=1}^n \rho_i \alpha x_i$$

$$= \sum_{i=1}^n \rho_i a x_i = a \sum_{i=1}^n \rho_i x_i = ax.$$

Thus, α is equal to the mapping $l_a: x \mapsto ax$, and we have $\text{End}_R(X) \subset \mathscr{L}_{A,X}$. The opposite inclusion always holds. Hence $\text{End}_R(X) = \mathscr{L}_{A,X}$.

If X is a faithful (left) A-module, then $\mathscr{L}_{A,X}$ is isomorphic to A, hence so is $\text{End}_R(X)$. ∎

This is the result we promised earlier. In Section 4 we obtain a closely related result, the Wedderburn structure theorem for simple rings.

4. Simple and semisimple rings

We continue to let A be a ring with identity.

Definition 4.1. A ring A is *semisimple* if $A \neq 0$ and the left A-module A_l is semisimple.

A ring A is *simple* if it is semisimple and has no proper two-sided ideals. ///

In spite of appearances, our definition of a semisimple ring is, in fact, right–left symmetric; i.e., A_l is a semisimple A-module if and only if A_r is (see Exercise 4.1 and also Theorem 4.2, Corollary 2).

We warn the reader that the term "semisimple ring" is not used consistently in the literature. As we shall see, a ring is semisimple according to

Definition 4.1 if and only if it is left- (right-) Artinian and radical free (Theorem 5.1, Corollary 1). The term "semisimple ring" is sometimes used to designate any radical-free ring.

We recall that an element e of a ring A is *idempotent* if $e^2 = e$. Two idempotents $e, f \in A$ are *orthogonal* if $ef = fe = 0$.

Theorem 4.1. *If A is a semisimple ring, then*

a. *There is a finite set of pairwise orthogonal idempotents such that*
   (1) $1 = \sum_{i=1}^{n} e_i$,
   (2) $A_l = \bigoplus_{i=1}^{n} Ae_i$
   (3) *Ae_i is a minimal left ideal of A, for each $i = 1, \ldots, n$.*

b. *A is left-Artinian and left-Noetherian.*

c. *A subset of A is a minimal two-sided ideal of A if and only if it is equal to one of the homogeneous components of A_l.*

d. *Every minimal two-sided ideal of A is equal to a direct sum of minimal left ideals, all isomorphic as A-modules.*

e. *A has only finitely many minimal two-sided ideals and is equal to their direct sum.*

f. *If $\{A_i\}_{i=1}^{n}$ and $\{B_j\}_{j=1}^{m}$ are sets of minimal left ideals of A such that*

$$A_l = \bigoplus_{i=1}^{n} A_i = \bigoplus_{j=1}^{m} B_j,$$

then $m = n$, and there is a bijection between $\{A_i\}_{i=1}^{n}$ and $\{B_j\}_{j=1}^{m}$ such that corresponding left ideals are isomorphic, as A-modules.

PROOF.

a. The A-module A_l is semisimple. Its simple submodules are the minimal left ideals of A.

If A_l is expressed as a direct sum of simple submodules, then there are finitely many summands, say $A_1, \ldots, A_n$, such that $1 = e_1 + \cdots + e_n$ ($e_i \in A_i$, $i = 1, \ldots, n$). Since $e_j = e_j \cdot 1 = \sum_{i=1}^{n} e_j e_i$, $e_j^2 = e_j$ for each $j = 1, \ldots, n$, and $e_i e_j = e_j e_i = 0$ for $i \neq j$. Since A_i is simple and $Ae_i \subset A_i$, $Ae_i \neq 0$, we have $A_i = Ae_i$ for each $i = 1, \ldots, n$. From $1 = \sum_{i=1}^{n} e_i$ follows $A_l = \bigoplus_{i=1}^{n} Ae_i = \bigoplus_{i=1}^{n} A_i$. The $A_i = Ae_i$, being simple submodules of A_l, are minimal left ideals of A.

b. $A_1 \subset A_1 \oplus A_2 \subset \cdots \subset A_1 \oplus \cdots \oplus A_n$ is, by the simplicity of the A_i, a composition series for the A-module A_l (Chapter 1, Theorem 4.10). But then (Chapter 1, Theorem 5.2), A_l satisfies both chain conditions on submodules, hence A satisfies both chain conditions on left ideals; i.e., A is left-Artinian and left-Noetherian.

c. The two-sided ideals of A are the submodules of A_l which are mapped into themselves by all the right multiplications. Let K be a two-sided ideal, $K \neq 0$. Then K is a submodule of A_l, hence contains a simple submodule, T (see the proof of Theorem 2.3). Let T' be any submodule of A_l isomorphic to T, and let σ be an isomorphism of T onto T'. Since T is a direct summand of A_l, σ can be extended to an endomorphism, $\bar{\sigma}$, of A_l.

By Lemma 1 (p. 389) $\bar{\sigma}$ is a right multiplication of A. Since $T \subset K$ and K is invariant under all right multiplications, it follows that $\bar{\sigma}T = T' \subset K$. Thus, with each minimal left ideal T, the entire homogeneous component of type T belongs to K. Each homogeneous component Y of A_l is, itself, a two-sided ideal of A since every right multiplication of A is an endomorphism of A_l, hence maps the simple components of Y either to 0 or to simple submodules belonging to the same isomorphism class. It follows that a two-sided ideal of A is minimal if and only if it coincides with one of the homogeneous components of A_l.

d. An immediate consequence of c.

e. Since A_l is equal to a sum of finitely many simple submodules, the number of homogeneous components of A_l is certainly finite (Theorem 2.3, Corollary 2) and A_l is equal to their direct sum. Put another way: A has only finitely many minimal two-sided ideals and is equal to their direct sum.

f. Follows from the Jordan–Hölder Theorem, applied to the composition series

$$A_1 \subset (A_1 \oplus A_2) \subset \cdots \subset (A_1 \oplus \cdots \oplus A_n)$$

and

$$B_1 \subset (B_1 \oplus B_2) \subset \cdots \subset (B_1 \oplus \cdots \oplus B_m). \quad \blacksquare$$

Corollary 1. *A ring $A \neq 0$ is simple if and only if it is equal to a direct sum of minimal left ideals, all isomorphic as left A-modules.*

PROOF. If A is simple, the semisimple A-module A_l can have but one homogeneous component, a two-sided ideal of A, equal to a direct sum of minimal left ideals, all isomorphic as A-modules.

If A is a direct sum of minimal left ideals, all isomorphic as A-modules, then clearly A_l is semisimple with but one homogeneous component, whence A has no proper two-sided ideals. $\blacksquare$

Corollary 2. *A ring $A \neq 0$ is simple if and only if it satisfies the descending chain condition on left ideals and has no proper two-sided ideals.*

PROOF. If A is simple, it is semisimple, hence satisfies the descending chain condition on left ideals. By definition, it has no proper two-sided ideals.

Conversely, assume the descending chain condition on left ideals and the absence of proper two-sided ideals. By the descending chain condition, A has minimal left ideals. Let K be the sum of all minimal left ideals. Then K is a left ideal, hence a submodule of A_l which is a sum of simple submodules. Every endomorphism of A_l maps K to a sum of simple submodules, hence maps K into K. By Lemma 1 (p. 389) it follows that K is a two-sided ideal of A. But then $K = A$, and A is semisimple. Since A has no proper two-sided ideals, it is simple. ∎

Corollary 3. *A ring A is semisimple if and only if it is equal to a direct sum of finitely many two-sided ideals, each of which is a simple ring. This decomposition is unique, i.e., if $A = \bigoplus_{i=1}^{n} Y_i = \bigoplus_{j=1}^{m} Z_j$, where Y_i, Z_j are two-sided ideals, each a simple ring, then there is a bijection of $\{Y_i\}_{i=1}^{n}$ onto $\{Z_j\}_{j=1}^{m}$ such that corresponding components are equal.*

PROOF. If A is semisimple, then $A_l = \bigoplus_{i=1}^{n} Y_i$, where the Y_i are minimal two-sided ideals of A. If $1 = \sum_{i=1}^{n} e_i$, $(e_i \in Y_i)$, then each e_i serves as a two-sided identity for the ring Y_i. Since $Y_i Y_j = 0$ for $i \neq j$, each Y_i is a direct summand of the ring A, and every (left) ideal of Y_i is also a (left) ideal of A. But then, for each $i = 1,\ldots, n$, Y_i is a left-Artinian ring with identity, without proper two-sided ideals, and therefore simple, by Corollary 2.

The converse is obvious. The uniqueness follows from Theorem 4.1e since any two-sided ideal of A which is a simple ring must be a minimal two-sided ideal of A. ∎

We are almost ready to prove the theorem of Wedderburn which characterizes simple rings as rings of linear transformations of finite-dimensional vector spaces. We need two lemmas concerning rings of linear transformations.

Lemma 1. *Let X be a left vector space over a division ring D, $A = \mathrm{End}_D(X)$, $\mathscr{P}$ the set of all principal left ideals in A, and Σ the set of all subspaces of X. For each $K \in \mathscr{P}$, let $F(K) = \{x \in X \mid Kx = 0\}$, and for each $Y \in \mathscr{P}$, let $G(Y) = \{\tau \in A \mid \tau Y = 0\}$. Then*

a. *$K \mapsto F(K)$ is an inclusion-reversing bijection of $\mathscr{P}$ onto Σ.*

b. *$Y \mapsto G(Y)$ is an inclusion-reversing bijection of Σ onto $\mathscr{P}$.*

c. *$FG = \iota_\Sigma$ and $GF = \iota_{\mathscr{P}}$.*

PROOF. It is clear that, for each $K \in \mathscr{P}$, $F(K) = \{x \in X \mid Kx = 0\}$ is a subspace of X, and $F(K_1) \supset F(K_2)$ if $K_1 \subset K_2$ $(K_1, K_2 \in \mathscr{P})$. For each $Y \in \Sigma$, $G(Y) = \{\tau \in A \mid \tau Y = 0\}$ is obviously a left ideal in A, and $G(Y_1) \supset G(Y_2)$ if $Y_1 \subset Y_2$ $(Y_1, Y_2 \in \Sigma)$. We show that, if $Y \in \Sigma$, then $G(Y)$ is a principal left ideal in A. Let T be a subspace of X such that $Y \oplus T = X$, and let $\pi\colon X \to X$ be the linear transformation such that $\pi|_Y = 0_Y$ and $\pi|_T = \iota_T$. Since $\pi \in G(Y)$, $A\pi \subset G(Y)$. Suppose $\tau \in G(Y)$ and $x = y + t$ $(y \in Y, t \in T)$. Then $\tau x = \tau t = \tau\pi t = \tau\pi x$, and therefore $\tau = \tau\pi$. But then $G(Y) \subset A\pi$. It follows that $G(Y) = A\pi \in \mathscr{P}$.

Obviously, $F(G(Y)) \supset Y$. On the other hand, if $x = y + t \in F(G(Y)) = F(A\pi)$, then $A\pi x = A\pi y + A\pi t = At = 0$, whence $t = 0$ and $x \in Y$. Thus, $F(G(Y)) = Y$ for all $Y \in \Sigma$; $FG = \iota_\Sigma$; F is surjective, and G is injective.

Now suppose $A\tau \in \mathscr{P}$ $(\tau \in A)$. If $Y = F(A\tau)$, and T and π are as defined above, then $A\pi = G(Y) = G(F(A\tau)) \supset A\tau$. Since $X = Y \oplus T$ and $Y = F(A\tau)) = \text{Ker } \tau$, $\tau|_T$ is injective. Hence there is some $\sigma \in A$ such that $\sigma\tau|_T = \pi|_T$, the identity on T. But then $\pi = \sigma\tau \in A\tau$, and $A\pi \subset A\tau$. Thus, $G(F(A\tau)) = A\tau$ for all $A\tau \in \mathscr{P}$; $GF = \iota_{\mathscr{P}}$; F is injective, and G is surjective.

We have proved that $F: \mathscr{P} \to \Sigma$ and $G: \Sigma \to \mathscr{P}$ are inclusion-reversing inverse bijections. ▮

Lemma 2. *Let $X \neq 0$ be a vector space over a division ring D, and let $A = \text{End}_D(X)$. Then*

a. *X is a simple faithful A-module.*

b. *$\text{End}_A(X)$ is isomorphic to D.*

PROOF.

a. Certainly, X is a faithful A-module, for $\alpha X = 0$ $(\alpha \in A)$ implies $\alpha = 0$. If $x,y \in X$, there is some linear transformation $\tau \in A$ such that $\tau x = y$. Hence, for each $x \in X$ $(x \neq 0)$, $X = Ax$. But then X is a simple A-module.

b. X, as a vector space, is a semisimple, faithful D-module. As an A-module, X is cyclic, hence certainly finitely generated. Thus, by the corollary of the Density Theorem (Theorem 3.1), $\text{End}_A(X)$ is isomorphic to D. ▮

Theorem 4.2. (Wedderburn) *If A is a simple ring, then there is a division ring D, and a positive integer n, such that A is isomorphic to the ring of all endomorphisms of an n-dimensional vector space over D. The integer n is uniquely determined by A, and the division ring D is determined to within isomorphism.*

Conversely, the ring of all endomorphisms of a finite-dimensional vector space is simple.

PROOF. If A is simple, there are minimal left ideals, A_i, of A $(i = 1,\ldots,n)$, all isomorphic as A-modules, such that $A_l = A_1 \oplus \cdots \oplus A_n$. By Schur's Lemma, $\text{End}_A(A_1)$ is a division ring, D, and the left D-module A_1 is a vector space. By Lemma 2 (p. 389) $\text{End}_D(A_1)$ is isomorphic to $\text{End}_{\bar{D}}(A_l)$, where $\bar{D} = \text{End}_A(A_l)$. By Lemma 1 (p. 389) $\bar{D} = \mathscr{R}_A$, hence $\text{End}_{\bar{D}}(A_l) = \text{End}_{\mathscr{R}_A}(A_l)$, isomorphic to A. But then $\text{End}_D(A_1)$ is isomorphic to A.

Since the A_i are minimal left ideals, they are principal left ideals. Hence, by Lemma 1 (p. 394), the composition series $A_1 \subset (A_1 \oplus A_2) \subset \cdots \subset (A_1 \oplus \cdots \oplus A_n)$ for A_l corresponds to a composition series of length n for the vector space A_1. But then A_1 has dimension n over D.

Now suppose A is also isomorphic to $\text{End}_{D'}(X)$, where X is a vector space over a division ring D'. Again by Lemma 1 (p. 394), X has dimension n. By Lemma 2a, X is a simple faithful A-module. Hence, by Theorem 2.2, the A-module X is isomorphic to the minimal left ideal A_1 of A. But then $\text{End}_A(X)$ is isomorphic to $\text{End}_A(A_1)$. By Lemma 2b, $\text{End}_A(A_1)$ is isomorphic to D and $\text{End}_A(X)$ is isomorphic to D'. Thus, D' is isomorphic to D.

Conversely, suppose that X is a finite-dimensional vector space over a division ring D, and let $A = \text{End}_D(X)$. Let $x_1, \ldots, x_n$ be a basis for X. Then $X = \bigoplus_{i=1}^n Dx_i$. By Lemma 1 (p. 394), for each $i = 1, \ldots, n$, the set A_i of all linear transformations mapping the maximal subspace $\bigoplus_{j \neq i} Dx_j$ to 0 is a minimal principal, hence minimal, left ideal of A. It is easy to see that the sum of the A_i is direct. We show that $\bigoplus_{i=1}^n A_i = A$. Suppose $\sigma \in A$. For each $i = 1, \ldots, n$, define $\sigma_i \in A$ by $\sigma_i x_i = \sigma x_i$; $\sigma_i x_j = 0$ if $j \neq i$. Then $\sigma_i \in A_i$ for each i and, for $x = \sum_{i=1}^n c_i x_i$ ($c_i \in D$), we have

$$\sigma x = \sum_{i=1}^n c_i \sigma x_i = \sum_{i=1}^n c_i \sigma_i x_i = \sum_{i=1}^n \sigma_i c_i x_i = \left(\sum_{i=1}^n \sigma_i\right)\left(\sum_{i=1}^n c_i x_i\right) = \left(\sum_{i=1}^n \sigma_i\right) x.$$

Thus, $\sigma = \sum_{i=1}^n \sigma_i$. But then $A = \bigoplus_{i=1}^n A_i$. For each i, j, there is an $\varepsilon_{ij} \in A$ such that $\varepsilon_{ij}|_{Dx_j}$ is a D-isomorphism of Dx_j onto Dx_i, and $\varepsilon_{ij}|_{Dx_k} = 0$ for $k \neq j$. The mapping $\tau \mapsto \tau\varepsilon_{ij}$ is an A-isomorphism of A_i onto A_j. Thus A is simple, by Corollary 1 of Theorem 4.1. ▮

REMARK. Let X be a finite-dimensional left vector space over a division ring D. On the set D, define another operation, $\circ$, by $a \circ b = ba$ for each $a, b \in D$. Then the abelian group D, together with the operation $\circ$, forms a division ring, D°, anti-isomorphic to D under the mapping $a \mapsto a$. The abelian group X forms a right vector space, X°, over D°, with scalar multiplication defined by $xa = ax$ for each $x \in X$, $a \in D$. Since a subset of X is (left) linearly dependent over D if and only if it is (right) linearly dependent over D°, the vector spaces X and X° have the same dimension. If α is an endomorphism of the abelian group X, then, for $a \in D$, $x \in X$, $\alpha(ax) = a(\alpha x)$ in X if and only if $\alpha(xa) = (\alpha x)a$ in X°. Thus, $\text{End}_D(X) = \text{End}_{D^\circ}(X^\circ)$.

From this Remark, and Theorem 4.2, we have

Corollary 1. *A ring A is simple if and only if it is isomorphic to the ring of all linear transformations of a finite-dimensional right vector space.* □

It follows that our definition of "simple ring" is right–left symmetric. But then, by Theorem 4.1, Corollary 3, our definition of "semisimple ring" is right–left symmetric; i.e.,

Corollary 2. *Let A be a ring. Then A_l is semisimple if and only if A_r is semisimple.* □

Corollary 3. *A ring A is simple and commutative if and only if it is a field. A ring A is semisimple and commutative if and only if it is a direct sum of fields.*

PROOF. If A is a field, then A is simple and commutative. Hence, if A is a direct sum of fields, then A is semisimple and commutative.

If A is simple, then A is isomorphic to the endomorphism ring $\text{End}_D(X)$ of a left vector space X of finite dimension n over a division ring D. If $n > 1$, then $\text{End}_D(X)$ is not commutative. (For example, let x_1, x_2 be linearly dependent vectors and let σ, τ be linear transformations such that $\sigma x_1 = x_1$, $\sigma x_2 = x_1$; $\tau x_1 = x_2$, $\tau x_2 = x_1$; then $\sigma\tau x_1 = \sigma x_2 = x_1$, while $\tau\sigma x_1 = \tau x_1 = x_2$.) Thus, if $\text{End}_D(X)$ is commutative, then $n = 1$, and the vector space X over D is isomorphic to the vector space D_l. But then $\text{End}_D(X)$ is isomorphic to the ring $\mathscr{R}_D$ of all right-multiplications of D. It follows that A is anti-isomorphic to D. Since A is commutative, it is a field.

It follows immediately that every commutative semisimple ring is a direct sum of fields. ∎

We now obtain a characterization of the automorphisms of the ring of all linear transformations of a vector space. In view of the Wedderburn Theorem, this characterization applies, in particular, to the automorphisms of any simple ring.

Definition 4.2. Let X be a vector space over a division ring D and let σ be an automorphism of D. If α is an endomorphism of the abelian group X such that, for each $a \in D$, $\alpha(ax) = (\sigma a)\alpha x$, then α is a *semilinear transformation of X relative to σ.* ///

Note that, if α is a bijective semilinear transformation relative to σ, then α^{-1} is semilinear relative to σ^{-1}.

Theorem 4.3. *Let X be a vector space over a division ring D, and let* $A = \text{End}_D(X)$.

a. *If σ is an automorphism of D and α is a bijective semilinear transformation of X, relative to σ, then the mapping $\tau \mapsto \alpha\tau\alpha^{-1}$ is an automorphism of the ring A.*
b. *Every automorphism of A is of the form $\tau \mapsto \alpha\tau\alpha^{-1}$, where α is a semilinear transformation of X relative to some automorphism of D.*

PROOF.

a. The mapping $\varphi: \tau \mapsto \alpha\tau\alpha^{-1}$ is obviously injective and preserves addition and multiplication. For each $\tau \in A$, $\alpha\tau\alpha^{-1}$ is a bijective endomorphism of the abelian group X. If $x \in X$, $a \in D$, then $(\alpha\tau\alpha^{-1})(ax) = \alpha\tau(\sigma^{-1}a\alpha^{-1}x) = \alpha\sigma^{-1}a\tau(\alpha^{-1}x) = a(\alpha\tau\alpha^{-1})x$. Thus, $\alpha\tau\alpha^{-1} \in A$, and therefore φ maps A into A. Since each $\tau \in A$ is equal to $\alpha(\alpha^{-1}\tau\alpha)\alpha^{-1}$, φ is surjective. Hence φ is an automorphism of A.

b. Now let φ be an automorphism of A. By Lemma 2a (p. 395), the abelian group X forms a faithful simple A-module, X, with scalar multiplication defined in the usual way by $\tau x = \tau(x)$ for each $x \in X$, $\tau \in A$. We now make X into an A-module, X_φ, in another way by defining $\tau \circ x$ to be equal to $(\varphi\tau)(x)$ for each $x \in X$, $\tau \in A$. This A-module is, again, faithful and simple. By Lemma 1 (p. 394), since X has maximal subspaces, A has minimal principal, and therefore minimal, left ideals. By Theorem 2.2, the two faithful simple A-modules formed from X are isomorphic to any minimal left ideal of A, hence isomorphic to each other. Let α be an isomorphism of the A-module X onto the A-module X_φ. If $\tau \in A$ and $x = \alpha y$ $(x,y \in X)$, then $(\varphi\tau)(x) = \varphi\tau(\alpha y) = (\tau \circ \alpha)y = \alpha\tau y = \alpha\tau\alpha^{-1}x$. Thus, $\varphi\tau = \alpha\tau\alpha^{-1}$ for each $\tau \in A$.

By the corollary of Theorem 3.2, $\mathrm{End}_A(X) = \mathscr{L}_{A,X}$, and $d \mapsto l_d$ is an isomorphism of D onto $\mathrm{End}_A(X)$. For each $\rho \in \mathrm{End}_A(X)$, $\alpha\rho\alpha^{-1} \in \mathrm{End}_A(X_\varphi)$, and the mapping $\rho \mapsto \alpha\rho\alpha^{-1}$ is an isomorphism of $\mathrm{End}_A(X)$ onto $\mathrm{End}_A(X_\varphi)$. But $\mathrm{End}_A(X_\varphi) = \mathscr{L}_{A,X_\varphi}$. Thus, for each $d \in D$, there is an element $\sigma(d) \in D$ such that $\alpha l_d \alpha^{-1} = l_{\sigma d}$. The mapping $d \mapsto \sigma d$ is the composite of the isomorphisms $d \mapsto l_d$ onto $\mathrm{End}_A(X)$, $l_d \mapsto \alpha l_d \alpha^{-1}$ of $\mathrm{End}_A(X)$ onto $\mathrm{End}_A(X_\varphi)$, and $l_{\sigma d} \mapsto \sigma d$ of $\mathrm{End}_A(X)$ onto D and is therefore an automorphism, σ, of D. For each $x \in X$ and each $d \in D$, $\alpha(dx) = \alpha l_d x = \alpha l_d \alpha^{-1}\alpha x = l_{\sigma(d)}\alpha x = \sigma(d)\alpha x$. Thus α is semilinear with respect to σ, as desired. ∎

Theorem 4.4. *Let X be a finite-dimensional vector space over a division ring D. If D is finite dimensional over its center, then every automorphism of $A = \mathrm{End}_D(X)$ which fixes each element of the center of A is inner; i.e., if φ is an automorphism of A such that $\varphi(\gamma) = \gamma$ for each γ in the center of A, then there exists some $\beta \in A$ such that $\varphi(\tau) = \beta\tau\beta^{-1}$ for all $\tau \in A$.*

PROOF. By the corollary to Theorem 3.1, $\mathrm{End}_A(X) = \mathscr{L}_{D,X}$. It follows that the center of A is equal to $\mathscr{L}_{F,X}$, where F is the center of D. Suppose that φ is an automorphism of A which fixes every element of the center of A. Then (by Theorem 4.3) there exists a semilinear transformation α of X such that $\varphi(\tau) = \alpha\tau\alpha^{-1}$, for all $\tau \in A$. Since φ fixes the center of A, and the center of A is equal to $\mathscr{L}_{F,X}$, $\alpha \in \mathrm{End}_{\mathscr{L}_{F,X}}(X)$.

For $\tau \in A$, $c \in F$, let $\tau c: X \to X$ be the map defined by $\tau c(x) = \tau(cx)$; i.e., $\tau c = \tau \circ l_c$. Then $\tau c \in \text{End}_D(X)$. With this composition, A is an F-module. We form the F-module $A \otimes_F D$. Clearly, A is finite dimensional over its center $\mathscr{L}_{F,X}$, whence A is finite dimensional over F. Let $\{\tau_i\}_{i=1}^m$, $\{\delta_j\}_{j=1}^n$ be bases, respectively, for A and D over F. Then $\{\tau_i \otimes \delta_j\}_{i=1,2,\ldots,m,j=1,2,\ldots,n}$ is a basis for $A \otimes_F D$ over F. Define a multiplication in $A \otimes_F D$ by $(\sum_{i=1,2,\ldots,m,j=1,2,\ldots,n} \tau_i \otimes c_{ij}\delta_j)(\sum_{r=1,2,\ldots,m,s=1,2,\ldots,n} \tau_r \otimes c_{rs}\delta_s) = \sum_{i,j,r,s} \tau_i\tau_r \otimes \sigma_{ij}c_{rs}\delta_j\delta_s$ $(c_{ij}, c_{rs} \in F)$. With this multiplication, $A \otimes_F D$ is a ring. We make X into an $A \otimes_F D$ module by defining $(\sum_{i=1,2,\ldots,m,j=1,2,\ldots,n} \tau_i \otimes c_{ij}\delta_j)x = \sum_{i,j} c_{ij}\delta_j\tau_i(x)$. We leave it to the reader (Exercise 4.4) to show that X is a simple $A \otimes_F D$-module, and that $\mathscr{L}_{F,X} = \text{End}_{A\otimes_F D}(X)$.

Since $\alpha \in \text{End}_{\mathscr{L}_{F,X}}(X)$, and $\mathscr{L}_{F,X} = \text{End}_{A\otimes_F D}(X)$, there exists $\sum_{i,j} \tau_i \otimes c_{ij}\delta_j \in A \otimes_F D$ such that $\alpha x = (\sum_i \tau_i \otimes c_{ij}\delta_j)x$ for all $x \in X$ (Theorem 3.1). For $\delta \in D$, let $\bar{\delta}$ denote the image of δ under the automorphism of D relative to which α is a semilinear transformation. Then, for $\delta \in D$, $\bar{\delta}\alpha x = \alpha\delta x = (\sum_{i,j} \tau_i \otimes c_{ij}\delta_j)(\delta x) = \sum_{i,j} c_{ij}\delta_j\delta\tau_i(x)$. Hence $\alpha x = \sum_{i,j} c_{ij}\bar{\delta}^{-1}\delta_j\delta\tau_i(x) = (\sum_{i,j} \tau_i \otimes c_{ij}\bar{\delta}^{-1}\delta_j\delta)x$. But then, for all $\delta \in D$ and for $i = 1, 2, \ldots, m$, $j = 1, 2, \ldots, n$, $c_{ij}\delta_j = c_{ij}\bar{\delta}^{-1}\delta_j\delta$. At least one of the c_{ij}, say c_{11}, is different from 0. It follows that, for all $\delta \in D$, $c_{ij}\delta_1^{-1}\delta_j = c_{ij}(\delta^{-1}\delta_1^{-1}\bar{\delta})(\bar{\delta}^{-1}\delta_j\delta) = c_{ij}\delta^{-1}\delta_1^{-1}\delta_j\delta$, and $c_{ij}\delta_1^{-1}\delta_j \in F$. Since δ_1 and δ_j $(j \neq 1)$ are independent over F, $c_{ij} = 0$ for $(i,j) \neq (1,1)$. We conclude that, for all $x \in X$, $\tau \in A$, $\alpha x = (\tau_1 c_{11} \otimes \delta_1)x = \delta_1\beta(x)$, where $\beta = \tau_1 c_{11} \in A$, and $\alpha\tau\alpha^{-1}(x) = \alpha\tau\delta_1^{-1}\beta^{-1}(x) = \alpha\delta_1^{-1}\tau\beta^{-1}(x) = \delta_1\beta\delta_1^{-1}\tau\beta^{-1}(x) = \beta\tau\beta^{-1}(x)$. But then $\varphi(\tau) = \alpha\tau\alpha^{-1} = \beta\tau\beta^{-1}$, and φ is an inner automorphism of A. ▌

An immediate consequence of Theorems 4.2 and 4.4 is

Corollary. *If A is a simple ring, finite dimensional over its center, then every automorphism of A which fixes the elements of the center of A is an inner automorphism of A.* □

5. Equivalent Characterizations of Semisimple Rings; the Radical

Definition 5.1. Let A be a ring. An element $a \in A$ is *nilpotent* if $a^n = 0$ for some positive integer n. A (right, left, two-sided) ideal K of A is *nilpotent* if $K^n = 0$ for some positive integer n. A (right, left, two-sided) idcal K of A is *nil* if each of its elements is nilpotent. ///

We note that every nilpotent ideal is nil, but not conversely (Exercise 5.1).

In the next theorem, we summarize some of our conclusions concerning semisimple rings, and give several further characterizations of semisimplicity.

Theorem 5.1. *The following conditions on a ring $A \neq 0$ are equivalent:*

a. *A is semisimple.*
b. *A is a direct sum of finitely many two-sided ideals, each isomorphic to the ring of all linear transformations of a finite-dimensional left vector space.*
c. *Every left ideal of A is a direct summand of A_l.*
d. *Every left ideal of A is the principal left ideal generated by an idempotent.*
e. *A is left-Artinian and, for each $a \in A$, there is some $x \in A$ such that $axa = a$.*
f. *A is left-Artinian and has no nonzero nilpotent left ideals.*
g. *A is left-Artinian and the intersection of all maximal left ideals of A is zero.*
h. *Every left A-module is semisimple.*
i. *Every left A-module is projective.*
j. *Every left A-module is injective.*

NOTE: Since our definition of "semisimple ring" is right–left symmetric the word "left" may be replaced by the word "right" in each of the above assertions.

We prove the equivalence first of a through g, next of a and h, and finally of h, i, and j.

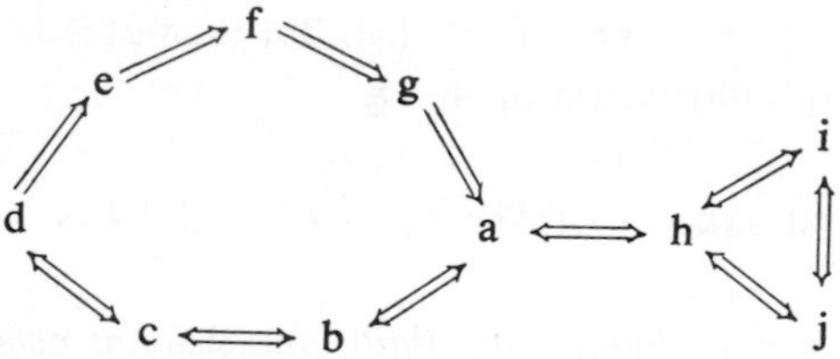

PROOF.

a $\Leftrightarrow$ b follows from Theorem 4.1, Corollary 3, and the Wedderburn Theorem (Theorem 4.2).

b $\Leftrightarrow$ c is now an immediate consequence of Theorem 2.2, since the left ideals of A are the submodules of A.

c $\Leftrightarrow$ d. If T is a left ideal of A such that $T = Ae$ where $e = e^2$ in A, then $T' = A(1 - e)$ is a complementary left ideal for T; i.e., $T \oplus T' = A_l$.

Conversely, if T, T' are left ideals such that $T \oplus T' = A_l$, let e be the component of 1 in T. Then for each $x \in T$, $x = xe + x(1 - e) = xe$. It follows that $e = e^2$, and that $T \subset Ae$. Since $e \in T$, $Ae \subset T$ and so $T = Ae$.

d $\Rightarrow$ e. Since d is equivalent to a, A is Artinian. Given $a \in A$ there is an idempotent $e \in A$ such that $Aa = Ae$. But then $a = ae$ and $e = xa$ for some $x \in A$, whence $a = axa$.

e $\Rightarrow$ f. By hypothesis, A is Artinian. If T is a nilpotent left ideal of A, then $T^k = 0$ for some positive integer k. Suppose $a \neq 0$ in T. Then $a^k = 0$. But there is some $x \in A$ such that $axa = a$, hence $xaxa = xa = e$, an idempotent in T. Since $ae = a(xa) = a$, we have $e \neq 0$. But $e \in T$, hence $e = e^k = 0$. Contradiction! It follows that $T = 0$.

f $\Rightarrow$ g. A is Artinian. Let Q be the intersection of all maximal left ideals of A. If $Q \neq 0$, then Q contains a minimal left ideal T. Since T is not nilpotent, $T^2 = T$. Hence there is some $x \in T$ such that $Tx \neq 0$. Since T is minimal, $Tx = T$. Hence there is an element $e \in T$, $e \neq 0$, such that $ex = x$. But then $(e^2 - e)x = 0$. The mapping $t \mapsto tx$ is a monomorphism of T into A since $\{t \in T \mid tx = 0\}$ is a left ideal contained in T and is therefore equal to zero. Hence $e^2 - e = 0$, and e is idempotent. But $Ae \subset T$, T minimal, implies $Ae = T$. Let $T' = A(1 - e)$. Then $T \oplus T' = A_l$. Since the A-module A_l/T' is isomorphic to the A-module T, and T is a simple A-module, T' is a maximal submodule of A_l (Chapter 1, Theorem 4.10), i.e., a maximal left ideal of A. But T' does not contain T, contrary to hypothesis. It follows that the intersection of all maximal left ideals is zero.

g $\Rightarrow$ a. By hypothesis, A is Artinian and $\bigcap_{m \in \mathscr{M}} M = 0$, where $\mathscr{M}$ is the set of all maximal left ideals. We claim: There are finitely many maximal left ideals, $M_1, \ldots, M_n$, such that $\bigcap_{i=1}^n M_i = 0$. This is clear if $\mathscr{M}$ is finite. Otherwise, there is an ordinal γ such that $\mathscr{M} = \{M_i\}_{i \in J}$, where J is the set of ordinals less than γ. Obviously, the sets $\bigcap_{i < \alpha} M_i$ $(\alpha \in J)$ form a descending chain of left ideals. Since A is Artinian, this chain terminates; i.e., there is an integer n such that $\bigcap_{i<n} M_i = \bigcap_{i<\alpha} M_i$ for $\alpha > n$ $(\alpha \in J)$. But then $\bigcap_{i<n} M_i = \bigcap_{M \in \mathscr{M}} M = 0$. For each $i = 1, \ldots, n$, A/M_i is a simple A-module. Hence $\coprod_{i \in J} A/M_i$ is a semisimple A-module. The map $\sigma\colon A \to \coprod_{i \in J} A/M_i$ defined by $\sigma a = (\nu_1 a, \ldots, \nu_n a)$ $(\nu_i\colon A \to A/M_i$ the canonical epimorphism) is an A-monomorphism of A_l into $\coprod_{i \in J} A/M_i$. Since σA is a submodule of the semisimple A-module $\coprod_{i \in J} A/M_i$, σA is semisimple. But then so is A_l.

We have proved that properties a through g are equivalent. We now consider h, i, and j.

a $\Leftrightarrow$ h. Obviously, h $\Rightarrow$ a. Conversely, let A be a semisimple ring and let X be an A-module. Let $\{A_i\}_{i \in I}$ be the set of all simple submodules of A. Then $A = \sum_{i \in I} A_i$ and, for each $x \in X$, $i \in I$, either $A_i x = 0$ or $A_i x$ is a simple A-module, isomorphic to A_i. Since $X = \sum_{i \in I, x \in X} A_i x$, X is semisimple.

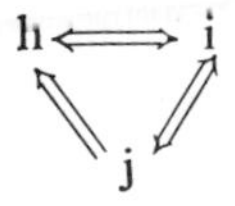

To prove the equivalence of h, i and j, we recall (Chapter 3, Theorem 2.4) that an A-module Z is projective if and only if every exact sequence $X \to Z \to 0$ splits, and (Chapter 3, Theorem 2.7) an A-module Y is injective if and only if every exact sequence $0 \to Y \to X$ splits. By Chapter 3, Theorem 2.3, a short exact sequence $0 \to Y \to X \to Z \to 0$ splits at one end if and only if it splits at the other. From this, it follows that both i and j are equivalent to the condition

(*) Every short exact sequence $0 \to Y \to X \to Z \to 0$ splits (where X, Y, Z are A-modules).

By Chapter 3, Theorem 2.2, an exact sequence $X \xrightarrow{\beta} Z \to 0$ splits if and only if Ker β is a direct summand of X. But then, by Theorem 2.3, it follows that h is also equivalent to (*). Thus h, i, and j are equivalent. ▮

Several of the equivalent properties in Theorem 5.1 bear closer examination. The condition in e: For every $a \in A$ there is some $x \in A$ such that $axa = a$ is the defining property of a class of rings (not necessarily with identity), the "regular rings" introduced by von Neumann. In general, a ring A is a regular ring if and only if every principal left (right) ideal of A is generated by an idempotent (Exercise 5.2). The additional hypothesis that A is left- (or right-) Artinian forces every left (right) ideal to be principal (see d). Every semi-simple ring is a regular ring, but not conversely (Exercise 5.3).

Let us turn now to f and g. In g we require that the intersection of all maximal left ideals of A be zero. This intersection, in any ring, has interesting properties.

Definition 5.2. The intersection, $\mathscr{R}(A)$, of all maximal left ideals of a ring A is called the *radical* of A. A ring A whose radical is zero is *radical free*. ///

[*Note:* Every ring with identity has maximal left ideals (see Lemma 2, p. 386). Hence, for any ring A with identity, $\mathscr{R}(A) \neq A$. In the absence of an identity, one defines $\mathscr{R}(A) = A$ if A has no maximal left ideals.]

Corollary 1. *A left- (right-) Artinian ring $A \neq 0$ is radical free if and only if it is semisimple.*

PROOF. This follows immediately from the equivalence of a and g in Theorem 5.1 (and its right-hand analogue). ▮

In view of Theorem 4.1 (Corollary 3), and Theorem 4.2, Corollary 1 can be restated in the form

Corollary 2. (Artin-Wedderburn Structure Theorem) *A left- (right-) Artinian ring is radical free if and only if it is equal to a direct sum of finitely many subrings, each isomorphic to the ring of all linear transformations of a finite-dimensional vector space.* ▯

As we shall see (p. 404), not every nonzero radical free ring is semisimple (according to our definition).

In the following, if $\rho(A,X)$ is the representation of a ring A associated with a simple A-module X, we shall refer to $\rho(A,X)$ as a *simple* (or *irreducible*) representation of A.

Theorem 5.2. *Let A be a ring with radical $\mathscr{R}(A)$, and let Σ be the set of all ideals K of A which are kernels of simple representations of A. Then*

a. $\mathscr{R}(A) = \bigcap_{K\in\Sigma} K = \{a \in A \mid aX = 0,\ X \text{ any simple left } A\text{-module}\}$.

b. *$\mathscr{R}(A)$ is a two-sided ideal.*

c. *The ring $A/\mathscr{R}(A)$ is radical free.*

d. *If $A \neq 0$ is left-Artinian, then $A/\mathscr{R}(A)$ is semisimple.*

PROOF.

a. If X is a simple left A-module, then $Ax = X$ for each nonzero $x \in X$. Hence, for each $x \neq 0$ in X, the A-homomorphism $\alpha_x\colon a \mapsto ax$ of A_l into X is surjective. Since X is simple, Ker α_x is a maximal left ideal of A. The regular representation $\rho(A,X)$ is simple and Ker $\rho(A,X) = \bigcap_{x\in X} \text{Ker}\ \alpha_x \supset \mathscr{R}(A)$. But then $\bigcap_{K\in\Sigma} K \supset \mathscr{R}(A)$.

The opposite inclusion also holds. If T is any maximal left ideal of A, then the factor module $X = A/T$ is a simple left A-module. Since $T = \text{Ker}\ \alpha_x$ for $x = T + 1$, $T \supset \bigcap_{x\in X} \text{Ker}\ \alpha_x = \text{Ker}\ \rho(A,X) \supset \bigcap_{K\in\Sigma} K$. But then, since $\mathscr{R}(A)$ is the intersection of all maximal left ideals of A, we have $\mathscr{R}(A) \supset \bigcap_{K\in\Sigma} K$. It follows that $\mathscr{R}(A) = \bigcap_{K\in\Sigma} K$. We note that $a \in \mathscr{R}(A)$ if and only if $aX = 0$ for any simple A-module X.

b. Since the representations of A are ring homomorphisms, their kernels are two-sided ideals. Hence $\mathscr{R}(A) = \bigcap_{K\in\Sigma} K$ is a two-sided ideal.

c. Let ν be the natural epimorphism of A onto $A/\mathscr{R}(A)$, and let $\mathscr{M}$ be the set of all maximal left ideals of A. If $M \in \mathscr{M}$, then $M \supset \mathscr{R}(A)$. Hence, by Chapter 1, Theorem 1.10, applied to the left A-module A_l, M is a maximal left ideal of A if and only if νM is a maximal left ideal of $A/\mathscr{R}(A)$. But then

$$\mathscr{R}(\nu A) = \bigcap_{M\in\mathscr{M}} \nu M = \nu\Big(\bigcap_{M\in\mathscr{M}} M\Big) = \nu\mathscr{R}(A) = 0.$$

d. Since A has an identity, $\mathscr{R}(A) \neq A$, and $A/\mathscr{R}(A) \neq 0$. By c, $A/\mathscr{R}(A)$ is radical free. Since A is a left-Artinian ring, A_l and $A_l/\mathscr{R}(A)$ are left-Artinian

A-modules. It is easy to verify that every left ideal of $A/\mathscr{R}(A)$ is a submodule of the A-module $A_l/\mathscr{R}(A)$. But then the $A/\mathscr{R}(A)$-module $(A/\mathscr{R}(A))_l$ is left-Artinian, and the ring $A/\mathscr{R}(A)$ is left-Artinian, hence semisimple (Definition 5.2, Corollary 1). ▮

REMARK. We can now give an example of a radical free ring which is not semisimple, i.e., a non-Artinian ring which is radical free. If X is a vector space over a division ring D, then the ring $A = \text{End}_D(X)$ is radical free. For, if $x,y \in X$, $x \neq 0$, then $y = \tau x$ for some $\tau \in A$. Hence the A-module X has no proper submodules; i.e., X is a simple A-module. If $\alpha \in \mathscr{R}(A)$, then $\alpha X = 0$, hence $\alpha = 0$. Thus $\mathscr{R}(A) = 0$. If X is infinite-dimensional, then A is not Artinian (Lemma 1, p. 394), hence not semisimple according to our definition.

Corollary 1. *If A is a ring with radical $\mathscr{R}(A)$, K a two-sided ideal of A such that A/K is radical free, then $\mathscr{R}(A) \subset K$.*

PROOF. If $a \in \mathscr{R}(A)$, then $aX = 0$ for any simple A-module X. If X is a simple A/K-module, then X is a simple A-module [with scalar multiplication defined by $ax = (K + a)x$ for each $a \in A$, $x \in X$]. Thus, if $a \in \mathscr{R}(A)$, then $(K + a)X = 0$ for any simple A/K-module X. But then, since A/K is radical free, we have $K + a = 0$ in A/K, whence $a \in K$. It follows that $\mathscr{R}(A) \subset K$. ▮

Corollary 2. *Let A be a ring. Then $\mathscr{R}(A)$ is the set of all $t \in A$ such that $1 - at$ has a left inverse in A for each $a \in A$.*

PROOF. Suppose $t \in \mathscr{R}(A)$. If $A(1 - t) \neq A$, then $A(1 - t)$, being a left ideal of A, is contained in a maximal left ideal, T, of A. Since $1 - t \in T$ and $T \neq A$, we have $1 \notin T$ and therefore $t \notin T$. This contradicts the assumption that $t \in \mathscr{R}(A)$. Thus, $A(1 - t) = A$ and there is an element $t' \in A$ such that $t'(1 - t) = 1$. Since $at \in \mathscr{R}(A)$ for each $a \in A$, the same argument provides a left inverse for $1 - at$, for each $a \in A$.

Now suppose $t \in A$ and $1 - at$ has a left inverse for each $a \in A$. If $t \notin \mathscr{R}(A)$, then there is a simple A-module X such that $tX \neq 0$. Hence for some $x \neq 0$ in X, $tx \neq 0$. Since X is simple, $Atx = X$, and there is an element $a \in A$ such that $x = atx$. But then $(1 - at)x = 0$. Since $1 - at$ has a left inverse, t', in A, we have $x = t'(1 - at)x = 0$. Contradiction! Thus, $t \in \mathscr{R}(A)$. ▮

Corollary 3. *The radical $\mathscr{R}(A)$ of a ring A is equal to the sum of all two-sided ideals, K, of A such that $1 - t$ is a unit in A for each $t \in K$.*

PROOF. If K is a two-sided ideal of A such that $1 - t$ is a unit for each $t \in K$, then $K \subset \mathscr{R}(A)$, by Corollary 2. To complete the proof, we need only show that $\mathscr{R}(A)$ itself has this property. Suppose $t \in \mathscr{R}(A)$. By Corollary 2 there is some $y \in A$ such that $y(1 - t) = 1$. Let $u = 1 - y = -yt$. Then $u \in \mathscr{R}(A)$, hence $1 - u$ has a left inverse, z, in A and we have $z(1 - u) = zy = 1$. Thus, y has left inverse z and right inverse $1 - t$. But then $1 - t$ is the two-sided inverse of y, and is, itself, a unit. ▮

We note that Corollary 3 provides a right–left symmetric characterization of the radical. As an immediate consequence, we have

Corollary 4. *The radical $\mathscr{R}(A)$ of a ring A is equal to the intersection of all maximal right ideals of A.* □

Corollary 5. *The radical of a ring A contains every nil left (right) ideal of A.*

PROOF. Let T be a nil left ideal. If $t \in T$, $a \in A$, then $at \in T$ and therefore at is a nilpotent element. There is an integer $n > 1$ such that $(at)^n = 0$, hence

$$[1 + at + (at)^2 + \cdots + (at)^{n-1}](1 - at) = 1 - (at)^n = 1.$$

Thus, $1 - at$ has a left inverse for each $a \in A$. By Corollary 2, $t \in \mathscr{R}(A)$. But then $T \subset \mathscr{R}(A)$. A corresponding argument applies to nil right ideals. ▮

Corollary 6. *Let A be a ring, and let $\mathscr{N}(A)$ be the sum of all nilpotent left ideals of A. Then $\mathscr{R}(A) \supset \mathscr{N}(A)$. (A corresponding assertion holds for nilpotent right ideals.)*

PROOF. Every nilpotent left ideal is nil. ▮

Theorem 5.3. *If A is left-Artinian, then the radical, $\mathscr{R}(A)$, of A is nilpotent, and is equal to the sum, $\mathscr{N}(A)$, of all nilpotent left ideals of A.*

PROOF. It is sufficient to prove that $\mathscr{R}(A)$ is, itself, a nilpotent left ideal of A. Now, $\mathscr{R}(A) \supset [\mathscr{R}(A)]^2 \supset \cdots$ is a descending sequence of left ideals. Since A is left-Artinian, there is some integer N such that $[\mathscr{R}(A)]^N = [\mathscr{R}(A)]^{N+k}$ for all positive integers k. Write $K = [\mathscr{R}(A)]^N$. We want to prove that $K = 0$. Suppose $K \neq 0$. Let S be the set of all left ideals H such that $H \subset K$ and $KH \neq 0$. The set S is not empty since $K \in S$. For, $K \subset K$, and $K^2 = [\mathscr{R}(A)]^{2N} = [\mathscr{R}(A)]^N = K \neq 0$. Since A is left-Artinian, S contains a minimal left ideal H_0. Since $KH_0 \neq 0$, there is an element $h \in H_0$ such that $Kh \neq 0$. Obviously, Kh is a left ideal, and $Kh \subset H_0$. In fact, since K is a two-sided ideal, $Kh \subset K$, and $K(Kh) = K^2h = Kh \neq 0$. Thus, $Kh \in S$, and therefore $Kh = H_0$. Hence there is an element $t \in K$ such that $h = th$; i.e., $(1 - t)h = 0$. By Theorem 5.2, Corollary 2, there is an element t' of A such that $t'(1 - t) = 1$. But then $h = t'(1 - t)h = 0$, contrary to the hypothesis that $Kh \neq 0$.

We conclude that $K = 0$, and therefore $[\mathscr{R}(A)]^N = 0$; i.e., $\mathscr{R}(A)$ is nilpotent. But then $\mathscr{R}(A) = \mathscr{N}(A)$. ∎

The equivalence of f and g in Theorem 5.1 is also a consequence of Theorem 5.3.

In the absence of descending chain conditions, the equality of $\mathscr{R}(A)$ and $\mathscr{N}(A)$ need not hold. For example, if A is a principal ideal domain, p a prime in A and A_p the local ring at p, then $\mathscr{R}(A_p)$ is equal to the (unique) maximal ideal of A_p, but A_p contains no nonzero nilpotent elements, hence no nonzero nilpotent ideals.

For commutative rings which are Artinian, the radical takes a particularly simple form:

Corollary 1. *If A is an Artinian commutative ring, then $\mathscr{R}(A)$ is equal to the set of all nilpotent elements of A.*

PROOF. Since A is Artinian, $\mathscr{R}(A) = \mathscr{N}(A)$, the sum of all nilpotent ideals of A. Let $\mathscr{N}'$ be the set of all nilpotent elements of A. If $x,y \in \mathscr{N}'$, there are positive integers h, k such that $x^k = 0$, $y^h = 0$, hence $(x + y)^{h+k} = 0$, and $x + y \in \mathscr{N}'$. If $x^k = 0$, $a \in A$, then $(ax)^k = 0$. Thus, $\mathscr{N}'$ is an ideal, hence a nil ideal, of A. By Theorem 5.2, Corollary 5, $\mathscr{R}(A) \supset \mathscr{N}'$. Since $\mathscr{R}(A)$ is nilpotent, it is, itself, a nil ideal, contained in $\mathscr{N}'$. Thus, $\mathscr{R}(A) = \mathscr{N}'$. ∎

Corollary 2. *In a left-Artinian ring A, every nil left ideal is nilpotent.*

PROOF. Let K be a nil left ideal of A. By Theorem 5.2, Corollary 5, $K \subset \mathscr{R}(A)$. By Theorem 5.3, $\mathscr{R}(A)$ is nilpotent; i.e., there is some positive integer s such that $[\mathscr{R}(A)]^s = 0$. But then $K^s = 0$, and K is nilpotent. ∎

Theorem 5.4. *Every left-Artinian ring is left-Noetherian.*

PROOF. By Chapter 1, Theorem 5.2, it suffices to prove that A_l has a composition series. Let $\mathscr{R}$ be the radical of A. Since A is left-Artinian, $\mathscr{R}$ is nilpotent, by Theorem 5.3. Let k be the least positive integer such that $\mathscr{R}^k = 0$, and write $A = \mathscr{R}^0$. Then, for each $i = 0, \ldots, k - 1$, the additive group of $\mathscr{R}^i/\mathscr{R}^{i+1}$ may be made into a left $A/\mathscr{R}$-module with scalar multiplication defined by $\nu ax = ax$ in $\mathscr{R}^i/\mathscr{R}^{i+1}$ $(a \in A, x \in \mathscr{R}^i/\mathscr{R}^{i+1}, \nu: A \to A/\mathscr{R}$ the canonical epimorphism). The correspondence $(\nu a, x) \to ax$ does define a map. For suppose $\nu a_1 = \nu a_2$ $(a_1, a_2 \in A)$. Let $x = \mu r^i$ $(r \in \mathscr{R}, \mu: \mathscr{R}^i \to \mathscr{R}^i/\mathscr{R}^{i+1}$ the canonical epimorphism). Then $a_1 - a_2 \in \mathscr{R}$, and $a_1 x - a_2 x = (a_1 - a_2)\mu r^i \in \mu(\mathscr{R}^{i+1}) = 0$, whence $a_1 x = a_2 x$.

By Theorem 5.2d, $A/\mathscr{R}$ is a semisimple ring. By Theorem 5.1h, each of the $A/\mathscr{R}$-modules $\mathscr{R}^i/\mathscr{R}^{i+1}$ is a semisimple $A/\mathscr{R}$-module. Since A is left-Artinian, the A-modules $\mathscr{R}^i$ and $\mathscr{R}^i/\mathscr{R}^{i+1}$ are left-Artinian for each $i = 0, \ldots, k - 1$. But then each $\mathscr{R}^i/\mathscr{R}^{i+1}$ is a direct sum of *finitely many* simple $A/\mathscr{R}$-modules, hence has a composition series, γ_i. Since a subgroup of the additive group of $\mathscr{R}^i/\mathscr{R}^{i+1}$ is an $A/\mathscr{R}$ submodule of the $A/\mathscr{R}$-module $\mathscr{R}^i/\mathscr{R}^{i+1}$ if and only if it is an A-submodule of the A-module $\mathscr{R}^i/\mathscr{R}^{i+1}$, γ_i also serves as a composition series for the A-module $\mathscr{R}^i/\mathscr{R}^{i+1}$ $(i = 0, \ldots, k - 1)$. By Chapter 1, Theorem 4.10, it follows that the sequence of A-modules

$$A_l = \mathscr{R}^0 \supset \mathscr{R}^1 \supset \mathscr{R}^2 \supset \cdots \supset \mathscr{R}^k = 0$$

can be refined to a composition series for A_l. But then, by Chapter 1, Theorem 5.2, A is left-Noetherian. ▮

Similarly, every right-Artinian ring is right-Noetherian.

Exercises

Section 1

1.1. Every A-module is a faithful $(\mathrm{End}_A\, X)$-module.

1.2. If D is a division ring, then every D-module is faithful.

1.3. An abelian group X is a faithful $\mathbf{Z}$-module if and only if X is torsion free, or the set of orders of the nonzero torsion elements of X is infinite.

1.4. (a) If A is a ring with identity, then A_l and A_r are faithful A-modules.

(b) If A has no left (right) zero divisors, then A_l (A_r) is faithful.

(c) If A has no left (right) zero divisors, then every free left (right) A-module is faithful.

1.5. If A is a ring with no proper two-sided ideals and X is a left A-module, then either $AX = 0$ or X is faithful.

Section 2

2.1. There are no faithful simple **Z**-modules.

2.2. Give an example of two nonisomorphic simple A-modules, where
(a) $A = \mathbf{Z}$,
(b) $A = D_n$, the $n \times n$ matrix ring over a division ring D ($n > 1$).

2.3. An A-module $X \neq 0$ is simple if and only if, for each $x \in X$, X is equal to the cyclic submodule generated by x.

2.4. If A is a ring with identity, then an A-module X is simple if and only if X is A-isomorphic to A_l/K, where K is a maximal left ideal of A.

2.5. Let A be a ring with identity. Then
(a) A has a maximal left (right) ideal.
(b) There exists a simple left (right) A-module.

2.6. If A is a commutative ring with identity, then there exists a faithful simple A-module if and only if A is a field.

2.7. The following conditions on a semisimple A-module X are equivalent:
(a) X is finitely generated.
(b) X is a direct sum of finitely many simple submodules.
(c) X (as an A-group) has a composition series.

2.8. The following conditions on an A-module X are equivalent:
(a) X is a finitely generated semisimple module.
(b) X is Noetherian and every maximal submodule of X is a direct summand.
(c) X is Artinian and every simple submodule of X is a direct summand.

Section 3

3.1. Let A be a ring with identity, A_n the ring of all $n \times n$ matrices over A ($n \geq 1$). For each $i, j = 1, \ldots, n$, let E_{ij} be the matrix with 1 in the (i,j)-position, 0 elsewhere. (The E_{ij} are called "matrix units" in A_n.) Prove:
(a) The set $\mathscr{U} = \{E_{ij} | i,j = 1, \ldots, n\}$ is a basis for A_n, considered as an A-module.
(b) The E_{ii} are pairwise orthogonal idempotents such that $\sum_i E_{ii} = I_n$.
(c) $E_{ij}E_{kl} = \delta_{jk}E_{il}$ ($i,j,k,l = 1, \ldots, n$).
(d) The centralizer of $\mathscr{U}$ in A_n is AI_n.
(e) The centralizer of AI_n in A is $\{(t_{ij}) \in A_n | t_{ij} \in C(A)$ for each $i,j = 1, \ldots, n\} = \{\sum t_{ij}E_{ij} | i,j = 1, \ldots, n\}$.

3.2. Let R be a ring with identity containing a subset $\mathscr{U} = \{e_{ij} | i,j = 1, \ldots, n$ ($n \geq 1$)$\}$ such that $\sum_{i=1}^{n} e_{ii} = 1$ and $e_{ij}e_{kl} = \delta_{jk}e_{il}$. Let A be the centralizer of $\mathscr{U}$ in R. Then R is isomorphic to the ring A_n of all $n \times n$ matrices over A, and A is isomorphic to $e_{ii}Re_{ii}$, for each $i = 1, \ldots, n$.

3.3. Let X be a faithful (semi-) simple A-module, $R = \mathrm{End}_A(X)$. Then X is a (semi-) simple R-module.

3.4. Let X be a simple A-module, $R = \mathrm{End}_A(X)$. If $\{x_1,\ldots,x_n\}$ is an R-free set in X and $\{y_1,\ldots,y_n\} \subset X$, then there is an element $a \in A$ such that $ax_i = y_i$ for each $i = 1,\ldots, n$. (*Note:* This statement is equivalent to Theorem 3.2, the Jacobson Density Theorem for simple modules.)

Section 4

4.1. Use Lemma 1 and Exercise 3.3 to prove that, for a ring A with identity, A_l is a (semi-) simple A-module if and only if A_r is a (semi-) simple A-module.

4.2. Let A be a simple ring, and let $e_1,\ldots,e_n$ be a set of pairwise orthogonal idempotents satisfying the conditions of Theorem 4.1a. Prove:

(a) The ring of A-endomorphisms of Ae_i is anti-isomorphic to e_iAe_i for each $i = 1,\ldots, n$.

(b) The rings e_iAe_i are isomorphic division rings.

(c) For each $i = 1,\ldots, n$ there is an A-endomorphism β_{1i} of A_l mapping Ae_i isomorphically onto Ae_1, and there is an element $b_{1i} \in A$ such that $\beta_{1i}x = xb_{1i}$ for each $x \in A$.

4.3. Using the notation of Exercise 4.2, set $e_{1i} = e_{11}b_{1i}e_{ii}$, $e_{i1} = e_{11}b_{1i}^{-1}e_{11}$, and $e_{ij} = e_{i1}e_{1j}$ for $i \neq j, i > 1, j > 1$.

(a) Prove that $\mathscr{U} = \{e_{ij} | i,j = 1,\ldots,n\}$ is a set of matrix units for A; i.e., $\sum_{i=1}^{n} e_{ii} = 1$ and $e_{ij}e_{kl} = \delta_{jk}e_{il}$ $(i,j,k,l = 1,\ldots,n)$.

(b) Prove that the centralizer, D, of $\mathscr{U}$ in A is a division ring.

(c) Using the result of Exercise 3.2, conclude that A is isomorphic to the matrix ring D_n.

(This provides an alternative proof of the Wedderburn Theorem, Theorem 4.2.)

4.4. In the proof of Theorem 4.4, show that X is a simple $A \otimes_F D$-module and that $\mathscr{L}_{F,X} = \mathrm{End}_{A\otimes_F D}(X)$.

4.5. Let X be a left vector space over a division ring D, Σ the set of all subspaces of X, and $\mathscr{P}'$ the set of all principal right ideals of $\mathrm{End}_D\, X$. For each $K \in \mathscr{P}'$, let $F'(K) = \{\tau x | \tau \in K, x \in X\}$, and for each $Y \in \Sigma$, let $G'(Y) = \{\tau \in \mathrm{End}_D X | \tau X \subset Y\}$. Then

(a) $K \mapsto F'(K)$ is an inclusion-preserving bijection of $\mathscr{P}'$ onto Σ.

(b) $Y \mapsto G'(Y)$ is an inclusion-preserving bijection of Σ onto $\mathscr{P}'$.

(c) $F'G' = \iota_\Sigma$ and $G'F' = \iota_{\mathscr{P}'}$.

(Compare this result with Lemma 1 of Section 4.)

Section 5

5.1. In the ring $A = \coprod_{m\in\mathbf{N}'} \mathbf{Z}/(m)$, the nilpotent elements form an ideal which is nil, but not nilpotent.

5.2. A ring A (not necessarily with identity) is a regular ring if and only if every principal left (right) ideal of A is generated by an idempotent.

5.3. The ring of all linear transformations of an infinite-dimensional vector space, X, over a division ring, D, is a regular ring which is not semisimple.

(*Hint:* Prove that, for each $\alpha \in \text{End}_D X$, there are automorphisms $\beta,\gamma \in \text{End}_D X$ such that $\beta\alpha\gamma$ is idempotent.)

5.4. Let A be a ring (not necessarily with identity). On A, define a binary operation $\circ$ ("circle composition") by

$$a \circ b = a + b - ab \qquad (a,b \in A).$$

Prove:

(a) $\langle A,\circ\rangle$ is a monoid with identity 0.

(b) If A has an identity 1, then $a \mapsto 1 - a$ is an isomorphism of the monoid $\langle A,\cdot\rangle$ onto the monoid $\langle A,\circ\rangle$ which maps the unit group of $\langle A,\cdot\rangle$ onto the unit group of $\langle A,\circ\rangle$.

5.5. Let A be a ring and let $\circ$ be the "circle composition" defined in Exercise 5.4. An element $a \in A$ is *left* (*right*) *quasi-regular* if it has a left (right) inverse in $\langle A,\circ\rangle$, and *quasi-regular* if it has a two-sided inverse in $\langle A,\circ\rangle$. A left (right) ideal of A is *quasi-regular* if each of its elements is left (right) quasi-regular. Prove:

(a) Every nilpotent element of A is quasi-regular.

(b) The radical $\mathscr{R}(A)$ is a quasi-regular left ideal which contains every quasi-regular left ideal.

5.6. A ring which is equal to its own radical is called a *radical ring*. Prove: The radical of any ring is a radical ring. (*Hint:* Use Theorem 5.2, Corollary 6.)

5.7. (a) A ring which has a right, left, or two-sided identity is not a radical ring.

(b) A nonzero Noetherian ring is not a radical ring.

(c) A nonzero Artinian ring is not a radical ring.

(d) If a ring has nonzero radical, then the radical is not equal to the right, left, or two-sided ideal generated by an idempotent.

(e) A nonzero radical is neither Artinian nor Noetherian.

(f) If A is a left-Noetherian (or Artinian) ring with radical $\mathscr{R}(A) \neq 0$, then there are infinitely many left ideals of $\mathscr{R}(A)$ which are not left ideals of A.

5.8. (a) Every regular ring is radical free. (*Hint:* Use Exercise 5.7d. Alternatively, use Theorem 5.2, Corollary 2 or 3, for the case where the ring has an identity, or Exercise 5.5b for the general case.)

(b) The ring of integers is radical free but is not a regular ring.

5.9. If X is an infinite-dimensional vector space over a division ring D, then the ring $\text{End}_D X$ has ideals which are not principal. (*Hint:* Consider the set K of all linear transformations on X which are of finite rank.)

5.10. If A is an Artinian commutative ring, then the radical of A is equal to the "radical of the 0-ideal," in the sense of Chapter 7, Definition 2.1.

5.11. A regular ring $A \neq 0$ is a division ring if and only if its only idempotents are 0 and 1.

5.12. If A is a ring with identity such that every A-module is free, then A is a division ring.

5.13. If A is a left-Artinian ring, K a minimal left ideal of A, then either $K^2 = 0$ or $K = Ae$, where $e \in A$ is idempotent. (*Hint:* If $K^2 \neq 0$, there is some $t \in K$ such that $\alpha_t: k \mapsto kt$ is an automorphism. Hence $et = t$ for some $e \in K$.)

5.14. Let A be a left-Artinian ring, K a nonnilpotent left ideal of A.
(a) K contains an indecomposable nonnilpotent left ideal K_0.
(b) For each $t \in K_0$, the map $\sigma: K_0 \to K_0$ defined by $\sigma_t x = xt$ is an A-endomorphism. By Fitting's Lemma (Chapter 1, Exercises 10.2 and 10.3), σ_t is either nilpotent or an automorphism.
(c) There is some $t_0 \in K_0$ for which $\sigma_{t_0} \equiv \sigma$ is an automorphism.
(d) There is some $e \in K_0$ such that $\sigma e = et_0 = t_0$.
(e) e is idempotent.
Thus, a left ideal K of A is either nilpotent or it contains an idempotent.

5.15. Let B be the ring of all 2×2 matrices over the polynomial domain $\mathbf{Z}[x]$, and let

$$\alpha = \begin{pmatrix} x & 0 \\ 0 & 0 \end{pmatrix}, \qquad \beta = \begin{pmatrix} 0 & 1 \\ 0 & 0 \end{pmatrix}.$$

Then $\beta\alpha = 0$ and $\beta^2 = 0$. Let A be the subring of B generated by I, α, and β. Prove:
(a) The subgroup H of $\langle A, + \rangle$ generated by the elements $\alpha^n\beta$ is a right ideal in A which is not finitely generated.
(b) The subring R of A generated by I and α is isomorphic to $\mathbf{Z}[x]$, hence Noetherian.
(c) A is a Noetherian left R-module, hence a Noetherian left A-module.
Thus, A is a left-Noetherian ring which is not right-Noetherian.

5.16. Prove: If a ring A with identity has no nilpotent element, then every idempotent of A is in the center of A. (*Hint:* Consider the elements $ex(1 - e)$, where e is idempotent.)

5.17. Let A be a ring with identity and with $2 = 1 + 1$ a unit. Prove that the centralizer of the set of idempotents of A is equal to the centralizer of the set of involutions of A. Definition: An element u of A is an *involution* if $u^2 = 1$. (*Hint:* e is idempotent if and only if $2e - 1$ is an involution.)

5.18. (a) For n a positive integer, prove that the ring $\mathbf{Z}/(n)$ is semisimple if and only if n is square free.
(b) For n a square free positive integer, find a decomposition of $\mathbf{Z}/(n)$ as a direct sum of simple rings.

Bibliography

[1] Emil Artin. *Algebraic Numbers and Algebraic Functions*. New York: Gordon & Breach, 1967.

[2] Emil Artin. *Galois Theory* (Notre Dame Mathematical Lectures No. 2, 2nd ed.). Notre Dame, Ind.: University of Notre Dame, 1944.

[3] N. Bourbaki. *Algèbre*. Paris: Hermann, 1942–1962.

[4] N. Bourbaki. *Algèbre Commutative*. Paris: Hermann, 1962.

[5] H. Cartan and S. Eilenberg. *Homological Algebra*. Princeton, N.J.: Princeton University Press, 1956.

[6] J. W. S. Cassels and A. Fröhlich (eds.), *Algebraic Number Theory*. New York: Academic Press, 1967.

[7] C. W. Curtis and Irving Reiner. *Representation Theory of Finite Groups and Associative Algebras*. New York: Wiley-Interscience, 1962.

[8] James Dugundji. *Topology*. Boston: Allyn & Bacon, 1966.

[9] L. Fuchs. *Abelian Groups*. Oxford: Pergamon Press, 1960.

[10] Marshall Hall, Jr. *The Theory of Groups*. New York: Macmillan, 1959.

[11] G. H. Hardy and E. M. Wright. *An Introduction to the Theory of Numbers* (3rd ed.). New York: Oxford University Press, 1954.

[12] Nathan Jacobson. *Lectures in Abstract Algebra*. Princeton, N.J.: Van Nostrand, Vol. I, 1951, Vol. II, 1960, Vol. III, 1964.

[13] Nathan Jacobson. *The Structure of Rings*. New York: American Mathematical Society, 1956.

[14] Nathan Jacobson. *The Theory of Rings*. New York: American Mathematical Society, 1943.

[15] J. P. Jans. *Rings and Homology*. New York: Holt, 1964.

[16] Irving Kaplansky. *Infinite Abelian Groups*. Ann Arbor, Mich.: University of Michigan Press, 1954.

[17] J. L. Kelley. *General Topology*. Princeton, N.J.: Van Nostrand, 1955.

[18] A. E. KUROSH. *The Theory of Groups* (translated by K. A. Hirsch, 2nd English ed.). New York: Chelsea, 1960.

[19] SERGE LANG. *Algebra.* Reading, Mass.: Addison-Wesley, 1965.

[20] SERGE LANG. *Algebraic Numbers.* Reading, Mass.: Addison-Wesley, 1964.

[21] SERGE LANG. *Diophantine Geometry.* Reading, Mass.: Addison-Wesley, 1960.

[22] SAUNDERS MACLANE. *Homology.* Berlin: Springer, 1963.

[23] SAUNDERS MACLANE and GARRETT BIRKHOFF. *Algebra.* New York: Macmillan, 1967.

[24] BARRY MITCHELL. *Theory of Categories.* New York: Academic Press, 1965.

[25] D. C. NORTHCOTT. *An Introduction to Homological Algebra.* New York: Cambridge University Press, 1960.

[26] O. T. O'MEARA. *Introduction to Quadratic Forms.* Berlin: Springer, 1963.

[27] W. R. SCOTT. *Group Theory.* Englewood Cliffs, N.J.: Prentice-Hall, 1964.

[28] B. L. VAN DER WAERDEN. *Moderne Algebra* (2 vols.). Berlin: Springer, 1931.

[29] OSCAR ZARISKI and PIERRE SAMUEL. *Commutative Algebra.* Princeton, N.J.: Van Nostrand, Vol. I, 1958, Vol. II, 1960.

Index